A Teaching and Lea[...]
Package as Compreh[...]
as the Book Itself

Family Exploration: Personal Viewpoints from Multiple Perspectives, Fifth Edition

This enriching workbook helps readers consider the role that their family of origin and their current family dynamics play in the development and maintenance of their attitudes, values, and behavior patterns. Readers are encouraged to think about systems theory in general and apply it to their own lives. By working through the in-depth interpersonal family life experience exercises, readers have a powerful subjective experience which can be used as a vehicle for discovering their own strengths and weaknesses as potential family therapists. (ISBN: 0-534-36651-1)

InfoTrac® College Edition

This fully searchable online database gives students access to full-text articles from more than 600 periodicals. *InfoTrac College Edition* offers authoritative sources, updated daily and going back as far as four years. When your students log on, they'll find the latest sources for reading and research and immediately appreciate how easy it is to do searches using the system's superior organization. (Available to North American colleges only.)

Test Items

Written by Herbert Goldenberg, the Test Items manual contains approximately 30 multiple-choice questions for each chapter in the main text. (ISBN: 0-534-36652-X)

Also available electronically in ASCII format (Windows® ISBN: 0-534-36653-8; Macintosh® ISBN: 0-534-36654-6)

Be sure to visit us on the web for more information:
http://helpingprofs.wadsworth.com

5th Edition

FAMILY THERAPY
An OVERVIEW

Irene Goldenberg
University of California, Los Angeles

Herbert Goldenberg
California State University, Los Angeles

Brooks/Cole
Thomson Learning

Australia • Canada • Denmark • Japan • Mexico • New Zealand • Philippines • Puerto Rico
Singapore • South Africa • Spain • United Kingdom • United States

Counseling Editor: *Eileen Murphy*
Assistant Editor: *Julie Martinez*
Marketing Manager: *Jennie Burger*
Marketing Assistant: *Jessica McFadden*
Project Editor: *Tanya Nigh*
Print Buyer: *Karen Hunt*
Permissions Editor: *Susan Walters*

Production Service: *Matrix Productions Inc.*
Test Designer: *Roy R. Nehaus*
Copy Editor: *Jan McDearmon*
Cover Designer: *Yvo Rezebos*
Cover Printer: *Phoenix Color*
Compositor: *Joan Mueller Cochrane*
Printer/Binder: *Quebecor, Crawfordsville*

Printed in the United States of America
1 2 3 4 5 6 7 03 02 01 00 99

Library of Congress
Cataloging-in Publication Data

Goldenberg, Irene.
    Family therapy : an overview / Irene Goldenberg, Herbert
Goldenberg. -- 5th ed.
        p.   cm.
    Includes bibliographical references and index.
    ISBN 0-534-35757-1
    1. Family psychotherapy.   I. Goldenberg, Herbert.   II. Title.
RC488.5.G64   2000
616.89'156--dc21   99-20853

Wadsworth/Thomson Learning
10 Davis Drive
Belmont, CA 94002-3098
USA
www.wadsworth.com

International Headquarters
Thomson Learning
290 Harbor Drive, 2nd Floor
Stamford, CT 06902-7477
USA

UK/Europe/Middle East
Thomson Learning
Berkshire House
168-173 High Holborn
London WC1V 7AA
United Kindom

Asia
Thomson Learning
60 Albert Street #15-01
Albert Complex
Singapore 189969

Canada
Nelson/Thomson Learning
1120 Birchmount Road
Scarborough, Ontario M1K 5G4
Canada

For each other, now more than ever

Contents

Chapter 4

The Family as a Psychosocial System
59

PART II

THE EVOLUTION OF FAMILY THERAPY
81

Chapter 5

Origins and Growth of Family Therapy
83

PART III

THE BASIC MODELS OF FAMILY THERAPY
109

Chapter 6

Psychodynamic Models
111

Chapter 7

Experiential Models
135

Chapter 8

Transgenerational Models
165

Chapter 11

The Milan Model
244

Chapter 12

Cognitive-Behavioral Models
265

PART IV

EVOLVING MODELS OF FAMILY THERAPY
295

Chapter 13

Postmodernism and the Social
Constructionist Family Therapies
297

Chapter 14

Psychoeducational Family Therapy
323

PART V

RESEARCH, TRAINING, AND PROFESSIONAL ISSUES
343

Chapter 15

Family Therapy Research
345

Appendix A

A Comparison of Theoretical Viewpoints in Family Therapy
420

Appendix B

A Comparison of Therapeutic Techniques and Goals in Family Therapy
422

Appendix C

AAMFT Code of Ethics
425

Preface

With this fifth edition of our text, we celebrate the twentieth year of its life, along with heralding the beginning of a new millennium. Anniversaries of this sort deserve observance: they help us look back at what we have been able to achieve and set goals for ourselves for the future. Throughout the five editions, we have tried to live up to our original goal, stated in our first effort, of offering readers a balanced presentation of the major theoretical underpinnings and clinical practices in the field. We set ourselves the task in the first edition of providing an overview of the evolving viewpoints, perspectives, values, intervention techniques, and goals of family therapy. With each subsequent edition, we have tried to keep pace with family therapy's clinical and research developments, while remaining cognizant of its history and theoretical foundations. This present edition represents our best effort to continue to live up to those goals while continuing to improve the final product.

On a more personal level, we've cherished the learning process, broadened our conceptual framework for understanding behavior, and sharpened our clinical skills. It has been an exciting ride, observing, describing, and participating in a field growing from infancy through adolescence and into adulthood, and in the process becoming better integrated. We've tried to make the book reflect our continued enthusiasm for thinking of behavior in the context of family life and planning interventions with families that help them discover workable solutions to their problems.

Reaching a personal milestone commonly evokes thoughts of whether what we have accomplished is developmentally appropriate for the time that has passed. Have we been educated, found a job, established relationships, had children? Family therapy, now close to 50, might ask similar questions of itself. Yes, the field has constructed a set of theories that inform us, found ways and placed to make it work, established professional working relationships with colleagues from related fields, and now has second- and third-generation children to further refine theory, extend research undertakings, and promote more effective clinical interventions. Divergent theories and techniques are less combative than in the past, and the field is moving toward greater integration Family therapy has evolved to a good place: looking for family strengths and resilience rather than pathology, exploring the potentials human beings have for solving problems, and helping them discover appropriate solutions. More problems await resolution, to be sure, but overall it looks as though we are headed for greater maturity and a productive old age.

This current edition has a number of features that reflect the new directions in which family therapy is headed. In addition to updating each chapter, we've added a new chapter on gender, culture, and ethnicity factors in family functioning to reflect a long-neglected area to which family therapists increasingly are turning their attention. In a similar effort, we have elaborated on the developmental sequences in alternative families: single-parent-led families, remarried families, gay and lesbian families, again calling attention to the realities of contemporary family life.

Another new chapter concerns postmodernism and the social constructionist therapies currently at the forefront of family therapy practice. The postmodern revolution has had an important impact on the thinking of many family therapists, leading them to question the "absolute truths" of many dearly held belief systems and opening up possibilities for many theoretical avenues for arriving at useful solutions. Rather than acting as complacent experts prepared to label interactive patterns in troubled families, these therapists have adopted a social constructionist view in which theirs is but one viewpoint about what the family needs, no better or worse than the views of various family members. Conversation and collaboration have democratized the therapeutic process for these therapists, as they and their now-empowered clients together construct new stories allowing new options and possibilities for the future.

In a similar fashion, psychoeducational family therapy has taken center stage for many family therapists, and we have devoted an entire new chapter to its evolvement. Here we address some of the groundbreaking research on family functioning and the major mental disorders such as schizophrenia, but also elaborate on the fast growing area of medical family therapy and the prevalent short-term educational programs aimed at relationship enhancement and marital enrichment in everyday family life.

A number of colleagues have been generous with their time in offering suggestions for improving the text, and they deserve a public acknowledgment of our gratitude. In particular we wish to thank Elyce A. Cron, Oakland University; Joshua M. Gold, University of South Carolina, Columbia; Ingeborg Haug, Fairfield University; and Alice Chornesky, New Mexico State University, Las Cruces.

Finally, we wish to thank our friends at Wadsworth for their faith in our ability to carry out this task, and their prompt response with offers of help whenever needed.

For the two of us, who lived with various editions of this text for more than 20 years, it feels as if we have once again launched a child on a new adventure. Along with our three children and five grandchildren, this book is part of our lives, and as is the case with our growing family, brings us all closer together

Irene Goldenberg
Herbert Goldenberg

I

PERSPECTIVES OF FAMILY THERAPY

1

Adopting a Family Relationship Framework

A family is far more than a collection of individuals sharing a specific physical and psychological space. While families occur in a diversity of forms today, each may be considered a natural social **system**,[1] with properties all its own, one that has evolved a set of rules, is replete with assigned and ascribed roles for its members, has an organized power structure, has developed intricate overt and covert forms of communication, and has elaborated ways of negotiating and problem solving that permit various tasks to be performed effectively. The relationship between members of this microculture is deep and multilayered, and is based largely on a shared history, shared internalized perceptions and assumptions about the world, and a shared sense of purpose. Within such a system, individuals are tied to one another by powerful, durable, reciprocal emotional attachments and loyalties that may fluctuate in intensity over time but nevertheless persist over the lifetime of the family.

Entrance into such an organized system occurs only through birth, adoption, or marriage.[2] As Kaye (1985) observes, families create and indoctrinate new members, and although they ultimately give these members autonomy and no longer expect them to live under the same roof, family membership remains intact for life. He contends that the power of the family is such that despite the possible separation of

[1]Terms in **boldface** are defined in the Glossary at the back of the book.

[2]This issue has, of course, been made far more complex as a result of recent biotechnological advances regarding means of becoming pregnant. A family today may include a couple's biological child, but one conceived in her ovum with his sperm but gestated in the body of a woman who may be biologically unrelated. In other cases, infertile couples, including same-sex female partners, may opt for donor insemination in which sperm from a sperm bank or family planning center is used to fertilize a woman's egg. In some sperm banks, a husband with a low sperm count may have his sperm supplemented by those of other male donors, so that it is not certain whose sperm actually impregnated his wife. In the case of donated eggs used to help infertile couples, eggs from a fertile woman, often anonymous, are surgically removed and implanted in a postmenopausal woman who no longer produces eggs or an infertile woman whose eggs are "old" or damaged, perhaps by chromosomal abnormalities. Thus, while the resulting children may be members of a family, they may have different genetic roots from their parents or siblings.

members by vast distances, sometimes even by death, the family's influence remains. Even when a member experiences a temporary or permanent sense of alienation from one's family, he or she can never truly relinquish family membership.

As Carter and McGoldrick (1988) point out, no other system is subject to similar restraints. A business organization may fire an employee viewed as **dysfunctional**, or conversely, members may resign and permanently sever their relationships with the group if the structure or values of the company are not to their liking. The pressures of retaining family membership allow few such exits even for those who attempt to gain great geographic distance from their **family of origin.**

Further, unlike members of nonfamily systems, who can generally be replaced if they leave, family members are irreplaceable, primarily because the main value in a family is in the network of relationships developed by its members. Should a parent leave or die, for example, and another person be brought in to fill a parenting role, the substitute, regardless of successful effort, can never truly replace the lost parent's personal and emotional ties to the remaining members.

ENABLING AND DISABLING FAMILY SYSTEMS

In the process of growing up, family members develop individual identities but nevertheless remain attached to the family group, which in turn maintains an identity or collective image of its own. These family members do not live in isolation, but rather are interdependent on one another—not merely for money, food, and shelter, but also for love, affection, companionship, socialization, and other nontangible needs. Families maintain a history by telling and retelling their "story" over generations, thus ensuring continuity and shaping the expectations of members regarding the future. To function successfully, members need to adapt to the changing needs and demands of fellow family members as well as the changing expectations of the larger kinship network, the community, and society in general (Rice, 1993).

Apart from its survival as a system, a well-functioning family encourages the realization of the individual potential of its members—allowing them freedom for exploration and self-discovery along with protection and the instillation of a sense of security. Constantine (1986) distinguishes between what he calls "enabled" and "disabled" family systems. The former succeed at balancing system needs as a family unit while simultaneously operating on behalf of the interests of all its members as individuals. Enabling family regimes inevitably invent procedures that attempt to satisfy the sometimes conflicting interests of its members. Constantine maintains that to do less, or to prevail but only at the expense of certain members, reflects family disablement, often manifested in unstable, rigid, or chaotic family patterns.

FAMILY STRUCTURE

Families are organizationally complex emotional systems that may comprise at least three, and increasingly today, as a result of longer life expectancies, four generations.

Whether traditional or innovative, adaptive or maladaptive, efficiently or chaotically organized, a family inevitably attempts, with varying degrees of success, to arrange itself into as functional or enabling a group as possible so that it can meet its collective or jointly defined needs and goals without consistently or systematically preventing particular members from meeting their individual needs and goals (Kantor & Lehr, 1975). In order to facilitate the cohesive process, a family typically develops rules that outline and allocate the roles and functions of its members. Those who live together for any length of time develop preferred patterns for negotiating and arranging their lives to maximize harmony and predictability.

Affection, loyalty, and durability of membership characterize all families and further distinguish them from other social systems (Terkelson, 1980). Even when these qualities are challenged, as in a family crisis situation or where there is severe conflict between members, families are typically resistant to change, and are likely to engage in corrective maneuvers to reestablish familiar interactive patterns. Regardless of format (for example, **nuclear family, stepfamily, single-parent-led family**) or ultimate success, all families must work at promoting positive relationships among members, attend to the personal needs of their constituents, and prepare to cope with developmental or maturational changes (such as children leaving home) as well as unplanned or unexpected crises (divorce, death, a sudden acute illness). In general, all must organize themselves in order to get on with the day-to-day problems of living. More specifically, all must develop their own special styles or strategies for coping with stresses imposed from outside or from within the family itself.

GENDER AND CULTURAL CONSIDERATIONS

Males and females typically are indoctrinated from early in life into different gender-role behavior in the family. As a result of differing socialization experience, members of each sex for the most part develop distinct behavioral expectations, are granted disparate opportunities, and have differing life experiences. However, as society's awareness of the crucial role of gender—as a determinant of personal identity, sociocultural privilege or oppression—has grown in recent decades, largely as a result of the feminist movement, so has recognition of the need to overcome gender stereotypes that limit psychological functioning for both sexes (see Chapter 3) and for men and women to co-construct new interactive patterns (Avis, 1996). As a result, gender-role changes in recent decades have had a powerful impact on family functioning. As the percentage of women in paid employment has risen, at-home responsibilities of men and women have had to be redefined by each couple, and overall, the pattern of gender-linked behaviors, expectations, and attitudes regarding a family's sex-defined roles has begun to change.

Similarly, cultural, ethnic, and social class considerations influence family functioning. Americans live in an increasingly culturally diverse society; early in the twenty-first century, it is estimated that about one-third of the U.S. population will consist of racial and ethnic minority groups (Jones, 1991). The importance of kinship networks, the role of extended family members, expectations of male and female behavioral patterns, levels of acculturation and ethnic identification, and socioeconomic power or lack thereof differ for different groups; all these factors, as well as others, have an impact on how (and how well) families functions.

Social class differences also add to diversity between families. Poor families, for example, often experience interventions by social agencies (departments of welfare, housing authorities, legal agencies, school authorities) that create dislocations in family organizations that such interventions were intended to alleviate (Minuchin, Lee, & Simon, 1996). The variety of subcultures in our complex society also significantly determine such things as incidence of cohabitation, premarital pregnancy, marriage rates, and even family interactive patterns (Saxton, 1996). As noted, we elaborate on the influence of gender, cultural, social class, and ethnic factors on family functioning in Chapter 3.

FAMILY INTERACTIVE PATTERNS

Families typically display stable, collaborative, purposeful, and recurring patterns of interactive sequences. These largely go unnoticed by outsiders, frequently are unstated, and are not always understood by the participants themselves. Nonverbal exchange patterns between family members, in particular, represent subtle, coded transactions that transmit family **rules** and functions governing the range of acceptable behaviors tolerated by the family (for instance, that a son does not speak before his mother speaks; she herself can take her turn only after her husband has spoken). Such patterned interactions are jointly engaged-in, highly predictable transactional patterns generated by all family members on cue, as though each participant feels compelled to play a well-rehearsed part, like it or not.

Minuchin, Lee, and Simon (1996) illustrate this point with the following easily recognizable examples:

> The complementary construction of family members requires long periods of negotiating, compromising, rearranging, and competing. These transactions are usually invisible, not only because context and subject constantly change but also because they are generally the essence of minutiae. Who passes the sugar? Who checks the map for directions, chooses the movie, changes the channel? Who responds to whom, when, and in what manner? This is the cement by which families solidify their relationships. (p. 30)

FAMILY NARRATIVES AND ASSUMPTIONS

A family is a maker of meaning (Constantine, 1986). Throughout the course of its development, a family fashions and helps instill fundamental and enduring assumptions about the world in which it lives. As a result, the meanings and understandings we attribute to events and situations we encounter are embedded in our family's social, cultural, and historical experiences (Anderson, Burney, & Levin, 1999). The narratives or stories a family recounts help explain, and in some cases help justify, their interactive patterns. Despite any differences or disagreements between members, the core of family membership is based on acceptance of, and belief in, a set of abiding suppositions or shared constructs about the family itself and its relationship to its social environment. Some families generally view the world as trustworthy, orderly, predictable, masterable; they are likely to view themselves as competent, to encourage individual input by their members, and to feel comfortable, perhaps enjoyably challenged, as a group coping with life. Other families perceive their environment as mostly menacing, unstable, and thus unpredictable and potentially dangerous; in their view, the outside world appears confusing and at times chaotic, so they band together, insist on agreement from all members on all issues, and in that way protect themselves against intrusion and threat.

Thus, the narrative a family develops about itself, derived largely from its history and passed on from one generation to the next, has a powerful impact on its functioning. The ways in which individuals and their families characteristically deal with their lives are not based on some objective or "true" view of reality, but rather on family *social constructions*—unchallenged views of reality created and perpetuated in conversation with one another, likely to have been carried on over generations. Such views may act as blinders or restraints, limitations a family inevitably places upon itself by its beliefs and values that prevent its members from noticing other aspects of their lives or seeing other behavioral options. Family members typically construct a rationale for why undesirable behavior continues and how they have no alternative but to live their lives in spite of it (Atwood, 1997).

In this **postmodern** outlook, there is no "true" reality but only the family's collectively agreed-upon set of constructions, created through language and knowledge that is relational and generatively based, that the family calls reality. As we will illustrate throughout the book, the postmodern view has had a powerful influence on how many family therapists view family life and how they work collaboratively with families to generate new possibilities and co-construct alternative narratives (Anderson & Goolishian, 1988; White, 1995).

FAMILY RESILIENCY

A family as a whole, or one or more of its members, may manifest dysfunctional behavior during periods of crises or persistent stress, but that is not to say that the system or its component members are necessarily without strengths and resources or lack those interactive processes that strengthen family hardiness. While some families are shattered by crises, others emerge strengthened and resourceful. Rather than view a symptomatic family member as a vulnerable victim (how did the family damage that individual?), thus pathologizing the family, an emerging viewpoint is that while problems may certainly exist within the family, family competencies nevertheless can be harnessed to promote self-corrective changes. Resilience should not be thought of as a static set of strengths or qualities, but more a developmental process unique to each family that enables families to create adaptive responses to stress and, in some cases, to thrive and grow in their response to the stressors (Hawley & deHaan, 1996).

Adopting a resiliency-based approach in working with families calls for identifying and fortifying those key interactional processes that enable families to withstand and rebound from disruptive challenges (Walsh, 1996). Affirming the family's reparative potential, this approach endorses a "challenge model" (as opposed to a "damage model") of family functioning (Wolin & Wolin, 1993). That is, it does not suggest that families are problem-free or that they are not engaging in damaging behavior, but rather that survival, regeneration, and empowerment can occur through collaborative efforts even in the midst of severe personal and family stress and adversity.

All families face challenges during their life cycle; some are expectable strains (brought on by such potential crises as retirement or divorce or remarriage), while others are sudden and untimely (a sudden job loss, the unexpected death of a key family member). How the family organizes itself, how it retains its cohesion, how openly it communicates and problem-solves together to cope with the threat largely forecasts its ability to recover. An affirming belief system aids the process. The support of a network of friends, extended family, clergy, neighbors, employers, and fellow employees and the availability of community resources often contribute to family recovery.

As Karpel (1986) emphasizes, even chaotic, disorganized abusive, and multi-problem families have resources. Here he is referring to the rootedness, intimacy, support, and meaning a family can provide. In poor families, especially, the members need to feel self-worth, dignity, and purpose; resilience is facilitated for them if they experience a sense of control over their lives rather than viewing themselves as helpless victims of an uncaring society (Aponte, 1994a). Walsh (1996) argues that the family's *relational resilience* is the key to recovery. She contends that family resiliency is forged *through* adversity, not *despite* it:

> How a family confronts and manages a disruptive experience, buffers stress, effectively reorganizes, and moves forward with life will influence immediate and long-term adaptation for all family members and for the family unit (p. 267).

We do know that some families, regardless of form, number of problems, ethnic or racial makeup, socioeconomic level, or degree of education, are happier and more stable than others—more competent, showing greater recuperative abilities, more flexible, more collaborative, and more adaptive to changing external conditions. Goldenberg and Goldenberg (1998) suggest the following regarding such well-functioning families:

> Usually organized according to some form of generational hierarchy, such families are able to balance intergenerational continuity and change and to maintain ties among the past, the present, and the future without getting stuck in the past or cut off from it. Clarity and ease of communication also characterize such families; a clear set of expectations about roles and relationships within the family is provided. Whatever their type—whether led by never-married mothers, stepfathers, two working parents, or grandparents—such families respect individual differences and the separate needs of family members. These families have mastered effective problem-solving strategies. (p. 10)

The resiliency construct challenges the family therapist to attend to the family's resources that can be mobilized to deal with a present crisis or adversity (as opposed to focusing on what's wrong with the family). It is intended to have an empowering or enabling effect, as it encourages the family to search for resiliences, including some previously untapped, within its network of relationships. Successfully managing a crisis together deepens the family bond and strengthens its confidence in preventing or managing future adversities.

THE PERSPECTIVE OF FAMILY THERAPY

Scientific models help shape the boundaries of a discipline and set the agenda regarding the subject matter and methodology to be followed in seeking answers. If the individual is the unit of study, clinical theories regarding human behavior, such as **psychoanalysis,** are likely to emphasize internal events, psychic organization, and **intrapsychic** conflict. Methodology in such a situation tends to be retrospective, revisiting the past; explanations of current problems tend to have a historical basis and to search out root causes in early childhood experiences. Symptom formation in an adult individual, for example, is considered a result of unresolved conflict carried over from that person's early formative years. Uncovering significant traumatic childhood events becomes essential if the client is to be helped in alleviating current emotional conflict. Typically, clinicians with this intrapsychic orientation seek answers to the question of *why* symptoms of **psychopathology** have occurred.

Primarily influenced by Freud's psychoanalytic formulations, clinicians traditionally have maintained an intrapsychic outlook; by focusing their attention on uncovering and reconstructing the patient's past, they assumed such knowledge or awareness produced the necessary insights that lead to behavioral changes and the amelioration of symptoms. While Freud acknowledged in theory the sometimes powerful impact of family conflict and alliances (the Oedipus complex in boys is one example) on the development of neurotic behavior in the individual, he assumed that person internalized the problem; thus, Freud chose to direct his treatment toward helping that person resolve intrapsychic conflicts rather than attempting to change or modify the properties of the family system directly.[3] By helping bring about changes in the patient's psychic organization, Freud hoped to evoke behavioral changes, including changes in response to others, that would presumably lead others ultimately to change their response patterns to the patient. Thus, most therapists, following the lead of Freud and others, would treat a distressed individual but refuse to see that person's spouse or other family members, believing that as the patient resolved handicapping problems, a corresponding positive change would occur in his or her relationships with family members. Unfortunately, this was frequently not the case.

---

[3]Karpel (1986) contends that Freud, by limiting himself to uncovering the experiences, fantasies, and mental perceptions of his individual clients, in effect denied the relevance of the family itself as anything other than a locus and source of trauma for that person. In such an essentially negative and pathology-focused view, the potentially positive and enhancing properties of family relationships are likely to be minimized or overlooked entirely.

Without negating the significance of individual internal processes and behavior, today's broader view of human problems focuses on the family context in which individual behavior occurs. While bearing in mind the often complex ways in which individual behavior contributes to that interaction, such an **interpersonal** perspective—as opposed to an intrapsychic one—regards all behavior as part of a sequence of ongoing, interactional, recursive, or recurring events with no obvious beginning or end point. Rather than attempt to discover the single answer to why something occurred by searching the past, the family relational view directs the clinician's attention to transaction patterns taking place currently within the family. People and events are assumed to exist in a context of mutual influence and mutual interaction, as participants share in each other's destiny. Within such a framework, symptoms in a family member, rather than viewed as emanating from his or her past, are seen as having a current stabilizing or adaptive function—detouring a conflict, mobilizing the family's resources, or galvanizing a dysfunctional group into action.

By adopting such a systematic perspective, family psychology—and its clinical application, family therapy—broadens psychology's traditional emphasis on the individual to attend to the nature and role of individuals in primary relationship networks such as marriage and the family (Liddle, 1987). From this perspective, an individual who manifests dysfunctional behavior (for example, substance abuse, an eating disorder, a phobia) is seen as a possible representative of a system that is faulty. Moreover, the causes and nature of that person's problems may not be clear from a study of his or her past alone, but can often be better understood when viewed in the context of an ongoing family relationship system that is in disequilibrium.

Recasting the individual as a unit of a larger system, such as the family,[4] enables us to search for recurring patterns of interaction in which that person might engage. Our conceptualization of what that person does, what his or her motives are for doing so, and how that behavior can be changed therapeutically, takes on new dimensions as we shift our attention to the broader context in which that person functions. From this new wide-angle perspective, psychopathology or dysfunctional behavior can be redefined as more the product of a struggle between persons than simply the result of opposing forces within the individual (Haley, 1963). Put another way, from a relationship perspective, the development of symptomatic behavior in a family member can be understood as a manifestation of flawed transactional processes currently taking place within the family system (Bross & Benjamin, 1982).

A number of therapeutic consequences follow from such a shift of perspective. When the locus of pathology is defined as internal, the property of a single individual or **monad,** the therapist focuses on individual processes and behavior patterns. On the other hand, if the dysfunctional behavior is viewed as the product of a flawed relationship between members of a **dyad** or **triad,** then it is the relationship that becomes

---

[4]The family, in turn, is part of a larger system, and its experiences are often profoundly influenced by involvements with the workplace, the school system, the health care system, the legal system, and so on, in addition to reflecting aspects of the particular family's cultural background, ethnicity, and social class. Imber-Black (1988), employing an **ecosystemic approach,** maintains that if individuals cannot be adequately understood without reference to the family system, families themselves are comprehensible only in this still broader social context. We elaborate on some of these systems-within-systems ideas in Chapter 4.

the center of therapeutic attention and the target of intervention strategies. Collaborating with couples or entire families as they alter their transactional patterns replaces the therapist as "psychological sleuth" seeking ways to uncover and decipher just what goes on within "the mysterious black box"—the mind of the individual.

If successful, family therapy alters the system—perhaps replacing the family's limiting and self-defeating repetitive interactive patterns, or opening up the style and manner of communicating with one another across generations through a consideration of new options, or possibly strengthening the structure of the overall family relationship, or in some cases relieving a family member of symptoms. Within this changed family context, enriched relationship skills, improved communication skills, and enhanced problem-solving skills may lead to more rewarding interpersonal experiences, in most cases extending beyond the family.

A Paradigm Shift

So long as one set of attitudes, philosophy, point of view, procedure, or methodology dominates scientific thinking (known as a **paradigm**), solutions to problems are sought within the perspective of that school of thought. However, should serious problems arise that do not appear to be explained by the prevailing paradigm, scientific efforts occur in an attempt to replace the existing system with a more appropriate rationale. Once the old belief system is replaced, perspectives shift and previous events take on new meaning. The resulting transition to a new paradigm, according to Kuhn (1970), is a scientific revolution. Precisely such a revolution in the thinking of many psychotherapists took place in the 1950s, considered to be the period when family therapy began (Goldenberg & Goldenberg, 1995).

More than simply another treatment method, family therapy represents a "whole new way of conceptualizing human problems, of understanding behavior, the development of symptoms, and their resolution" (Sluzki, 1978, p. 366). Haley (1971) and others have argued that the perspective of family therapy demonstrates a paradigm shift, a break with past ideas, calling for a new set of premises and methods for collecting and interpreting forthcoming data. Beyond a concern with the individual's personality characteristics or repetitive behavior patterns, beyond even a concern with what transpires between people (where individuals remain the unit of study), this conceptual leap focuses attention on the family as subject matter. It is the family as a functioning transactional system, as an entity in itself, that is more than the algebraic sum of the inputs of its participants, that provides the contextual structure for understanding individual functioning.

Sluzki (1978) goes so far as to consider family therapy a major epistemological revolution in the behavioral sciences. Put simply, **epistemology** refers to how one goes about gaining knowledge and drawing conclusions about the world; it is commonly used by family therapists to indicate a conceptual framework or belief system. Epistemology refers to the rules used to make sense of experience, the descriptive language used to interpret incoming information. Such rules, not necessarily consciously stated, determine the underlying assumptions we make in our day-to-day behavior as we attempt to understand what is happening around us and how we can bring about change.

A Cybernetic Epistemology

Family therapy proposes a **cybernetic** epistemology as an alternative to our habitual ways of knowing and thinking. Historically, the science of cybernetics was born during the early 1940s in a series of wartime conferences in New York City under the sponsorship of the Josiah Macy Foundation and attended by a cross section of the leading scientists, engineers, mathematicians, and social scientists of the time. The conferees addressed, among other things, the study of communication in reference to regulation and control (for example, in guided missiles and rockets) through the operation of **feedback** mechanisms. Norbert Wiener (1948), the mathematician who coined the term *cybernetics* and who was to become a principal player in the development of computers, was especially interested in information processing and how feedback mechanisms operate in controlling both simple and complex systems. Wiener chose the term *cybernetics* from the Greek word for steersman, suggestive of an overall governing or regulating system or organization for guiding or piloting a ship by means of feedback cycles. To Wiener, cybernetics represented the science of communication and control in humans as well as in machines.

These Macy conferences made an important breakthrough by providing a new and exciting epistemology—a new paradigm—for conceptualizing how systems retain their stability through self-regulation as a result of reinserting the results of past performance into current functioning. Perhaps even more significant, a way was becoming available to change patterns of future performance by altering feedback information. Researchers from both the physical and social sciences began to explore how these cybernetics notions could be applied to various fields in which both living and nonliving entities could be governed by self-regulating feedback loops that become activated to correct errors or deviations in the system and thus restore stability in the process of reaching its preprogrammed goal.

Thus, what we now think of as simple or **first-order cybernetics** grew out of communication engineering and computer science as a means of understanding the general principles of how systems of all kinds are regulated. Attention became directed at *structure*—patterns of organization—and *control* through feedback cycles; universal laws or codes were sought to explain what governs all systems. It was assumed further that the system being observed was separate from the observer, who could objectively study and carry out changes in the system while remaining outside of the system itself.

It was Gregory Bateson, an English-born anthropologist and ethnologist, who worked for the U.S. Office of Strategic Services in India during the war, who took away from these conferences some of these mathematical and engineering concepts and recognized their application to the social and behavioral sciences. Bateson (1972), increasingly concerned with epistemological issues, understood that cybernetics, with its emphasis on self-correcting feedback mechanisms, pointed to the inseparable relationship between stability and change when he later noted:

> All changes can be understood as the effort to maintain some constancy and all constancy as maintained through change. (p. 381)

Although Wiener himself had begun to reformulate psychological constructs (for example, Freud's idea of an unconscious) in information-processing terms,

Bateson (1972) deserves the major credit for seeing how cybernetic principles apply to human communication processes, including those associated with psychopathology. He introduced the notion that a family might be analogous to a cybernetic system, and while he himself remained outside the realm of family therapy, his cybernetic ideas are credited with providing the field of family therapy with its intellectual foundation (Keeney & Thomas, 1986). Bateson's later contributions to a daring theory of schizophrenia[5] as a relationship phenomenon rather than an intrapsychic disorder were monumental in describing an important psychiatric entity in transactional communication terms, specifically in drawing attention to the family context that gave the symptoms meaning. These contributions were to play a major role in shifting the focus of attention for many clinicians from attempting to gain insight into *why* the troubled individual behaves as she or he does, to examining *what* occurs in the exchange of information and the process of relationships between persons, as in a family.

Reciprocal Determinism

Adopting a relationship outlook inevitably shifts attention from *content* to *process.* That is, rather than dwelling on historical facts as explanations for current problems (Mary: "Our problem began when my husband, Gary, lost his job and our son Greg went to work"), this new perspective focuses on the sequence of linked communication exchanges within a cybernetic family system ("With Gary out of work, our son Greg is contributing more money and seems to be dominating us; I submit to Greg's demands more and more, and I suppose Gary is resentful"). Note how the latter statement shifts attention from the linear sequential actions of individuals to the transactions occurring between them. The "facts" of the case (content) are static and not nearly as clinically illuminating as is the family interactional pattern (process).

Content is the language of **linear causality**—the view that one event causes the next in unidirectional stimulus-response fashion. While such a view may be appropriate for understanding simple mechanical situations (where the machinery does not have too many parts, and the parts do not interact much), it is woefully inadequate for dealing with situations exhibiting organized complexity, such as what transpires within a family (Constantine, 1986). From a cybernetic or systems standpoint, concerned with wholes, a precise part-by-part analysis (such as searching for specific childhood traumatic events as causes of current adult problems) is too reductionistic and inferential to be of much explanatory value. Instead, argue opponents of linear thinking, parts are better understood by the functions they serve in the whole.

In the physical world, the world of Newton, it makes sense to talk of causality in linear terms: A causes B, which acts upon C, causing D. In human relationships, however, this "billiard ball" model, which proposes that a force moves in one direction only and affects objects in its path, rarely, if ever, applies. Consequently, any

---

[5]It needs to be noted here that while this theory of the origin of schizophrenia was groundbreaking in its emphasis on the effects of family transactions on the behavior of individual family members, and thus was useful, its theoretical contribution was incomplete, if not inaccurate. We return to the "double-bind" theory of Bateson and his colleagues in Chapter 5.

Gregory Bateson, Ph.D.

search for the "real" or ultimate cause of any interpersonal event is pointless. A does not cause B, nor does B cause A; both cause each other. Explanations cannot be found in the action of the parts, but in the system as a whole.

If content is the language of linear causality, then process is the language of **circular causality**. The emphasis here is on forces moving in many directions simultaneously, not simply a single event caused by a previous one. Within a family, a change in one member affects all other members and the family as a whole. Such a reverberating effect in turn impacts the first person, and so forth, in a continuous series of circular loops or recurring chains of influence. Problems are not caused by past situations in this view, but rather by ongoing family processes. Parents who ask quarreling children, "Who started the fight?" are almost certain to hear, "He (she) started it, I'm only hitting back." Both children are correct, both are incorrect; it all depends on where in the communication loop the parent begins the investigation. Nor is such mutual participation limited to pairs. Within a large family, for example, a multitude of such chains exist, and who started what is usually impossible to decipher. Reciprocity is the underlying principle in all relationships.

Goldenberg and Goldenberg (1998) offer the following contrasts between statements based on linear and circular causality:

Linear: A bad mother produces sick children.

Implication: Mother's emotional problems cause similar problems in others.

Circular: An unhappy middle-aged woman, struggling with an inattentive husband who feels peripheral to and excluded from the family, attaches herself to her 20-year-old son for male companionship, excluding her adolescent daughter. The daughter, in turn, feeling rejected and unloved, engages in sexually acting out, promiscuous behavior to the considerable distress of her parents. The son, fearful of leaving home and becoming independent, insists he must remain at home because his mother needs his attention. The mother becomes depressed because her children do not seem to be like other "normal" children and blames their dysfunctional behavior on her husband, whom she labels an "absentee father." He in turn becomes angry and defensive, and their sexual relationship suffers. The children respond to the ensuing coldness between the parents in different ways: the son by withdrawing from friends completely and remaining at home with his mother as much as possible, and the daughter by having sexual encounters with one man after another but carefully avoiding intimacy with any of them. Her symptomatic behavior serves not only to draw the family's attention to her, but also leads her parents to draw closer to one another in order to help their distressed daughter.

Implication: Behavior has at least as much to do with the interactional context in which it occurs as with the inner mental processes or emotional problems of any of the players. (p. 22)

What should be clear from this example is that family processes affect individual behavior, and individuals within the family system affect family processes, in a recursive manner. As Bednar, Burlingame, and Masters (1988) point out, family functioning is a classic case of reciprocal determinism

> in which every member of a social system, as well as the system's psychological organization (norms, roles), can be influenced by, and influences, every other member of the system in a never-ending cycle. A psychological event in a family cannot be understood without taking into account the simultaneous psychological influences that shaped it. (p. 408)

The Identified Patient and the Appearance of Symptoms

Within a family frame of reference, problems are recast to take into consideration the fact that an individual family member's behavior cannot be understood without attention to the context in which that behavior occurs. Rather than viewing the source of problems or the appearance of symptoms as emanating from a single "sick" person, family therapists view that individual simply as a symptom bearer—the **identified patient** (IP)—expressing the family's disequilibrium or dysfunction.

Family therapists who adopt such a functionalist viewpoint are likely to look for the meaning or function of a symptom in a family member as a sign that the family has become destabilized and is attempting to adapt or reestablish equilibrium. This view that symptoms have purpose in helping maintain family stability—in effect that dysfunctional families need a "sick" member and are willing to sacrifice that person for the sake of family well-being—has been a mainstay of family therapy theory since its inception. Virginia Satir (1967), a family therapy pioneer, contends that a disturbed person's "symptoms" may in reality be a signal that he or she is reacting to family imbalance and is distorting self-growth as a result of trying to absorb and alleviate "family pain." That is, the IP's symptoms can be seen in this view as stabilizing devices used to help relieve family stress and bring the family back into the normal range of its customary behavior. In this sense, the IP's actions may be based on a desire, although not necessarily a planned or premeditated one, to "help" other family members. For example, Haley (1979) describes disturbed young people who do not leave home as willingly sacrificing themselves in order to protect and maintain family stability. According to Boszormenyi-Nagy and Ulrich (1981), family loyalty may evoke symptomatic behavior when a child "feels obligated to save the parents and their marriage from the threat of destruction" (p. 169). Maintaining symptoms to protect other family members is, of course, not restricted to children and their parents alone, but may occur between marital partners as well (Wachtel & Wachtel, 1986).

Other family therapists, such as Salvador Minuchin (Minuchin & Fishman, 1981), consider the symptomatic behavior as a reaction to a family under stress and unable to accommodate to changing circumstances, and not particularly as a protective solution to retain family balance. In this view, all family members are equally "symptomatic," despite efforts by the family to locate the problem as residing in one family member. Minuchin sees the IP's symptoms as rooted in dysfunctional family transactions; it is the flawed family structure or inflexibility when new behavior is called for that maintains the symptomatic behavior in the identified patient. Change calls for the therapist to understand the family context in which the dysfunctional transactions transpire, and then to attempt with family members as a group to change that existing context in order to permit new interactional possibilities to emerge. As Minuchin and Fishman (1981) argue:

> The therapist, an expander of contexts, creates a context in which exploration of the unfamiliar is possible. She confirms family members and encourages them to experiment with behavior that has previously been constrained by the family system. As new possibilities emerge, the family organism becomes more complex and develops more acceptable alternatives for problem solving. (pp. 15–16)

A less purposeful view of the appearance and maintenance of symptoms in a family member is offered by Watzlawick, Weakland, and Fisch (1974), who contend that symptoms or problems arise from the repeated use of the same flawed solutions rather than being a sign of family system dysfunction. It is their belief that problems (or symptoms) are created and maintained because of the repeated attempt to apply an unworkable solution that only serves to make matters worse, and that ultimately the attempted solution, repeated without variation, becomes the problem. These authors argue that the family therapist must help the family find new solutions to the original problem if the symptomatic behavior is to be alleviated.

The postmodern view of IP symptomatic behavior, increasingly at the forefront of current thinking in family therapy, is offered by Michael White (1989), an Australian social worker, who rejects the notion that a family member's problems reflect underlying family conflict. From White's **constructivist** perspective[6], families tell themselves stories and develop beliefs about themselves; these constructions, in turn, organize their experiences and play a powerful role in shaping their lives. In some cases, such stories come to represent dominant and burdensome discourses

---

[6]*Constructivism* and its related postmodern theory of *social construction* (Gergen 1985) offer new influential epistemological explanations regarding how we know what we know. The former argues that each of our perceptions is not an exact pictorial duplication of the world, but rather a point of view seen through the limiting lens of assumptions about people that we make. The latter agrees that we cannot perceive a true, objective reality, adding that the reality each of us does construct is mediated through language and is socially determined through our relationships with others and the culture's shared set of assumptions.

that lead them to believe they have limited options and are doomed to repeat their self-defeating behavior.

Significantly, in White's view, families feel oppressed rather than protected or stabilized by symptomatic behavior in the family. His therapeutic efforts, especially his posing of deconstructing questions, represent a collaboration with the family directed at helping explore their ongoing stories and, together with them, co-constructing new stories that hold new possibilities, new ways of seeing and being. White gets family members to unite in order to take back control of their lives from the oppressive set of symptoms. In the process, he believes families are freed to view themselves as a healthy unit struggling against a troublesome *external* problem rather than seeing themselves as an inherently flawed and disabled group of people (Doherty, 1991).

We will return to a more detailed discussion of each of the approaches outlined briefly here when we elaborate on contemporary practices of family therapy later in the book.

Second-Order Cybernetics

The clinical thrust of postmodern constructivism, as noted above, calls for creating a therapeutic environment in which therapist and family members together can share their ideas, perceptions, beliefs, and the perspective each participant gives to family experiences. As they explore new information, the family is free to create a new perception of reality, allowing itself to experiment with alternative family narratives. White, along with other postmodern family therapists (Anderson & Goolishian, 1988; Hoffman, 1990; Andersen, 1991; Zimmerman & Dickerson, 1996) are advocates of **second-order cybernetics,** a post-systems reappraisal of cybernetic theorizing that insists that there can be no outside, independent observer of a system, since anyone attempting to observe and change a system is by definition a participant who both influences and in turn is influenced by that system. (By way of contrast, the first-order cybernetic paradigm conceives of two separate systems—the therapist system and the problem-client-family system—in which the therapist remains an external observer, an expert who attempts to effect changes by means of interventions from the outside.)

Second-order cyberneticists retain the cybernetic metaphor but contend that in doing family therapy the therapist must be aware that a number of individuals are present, and each has his or her view of reality and description of the family; in effect, each has his or her sense of family, and each is a separate and legitimate perception (Slovik & Griffith, 1992). Thus, they emphasize that objectivity per se does not exist; so-called objective descriptions of families are merely social constructions that may say more about the describer than about the family. Rather than be discovered through so-called objective means, the family's "reality" is nothing more than the agreed-upon consensus that occurs through the social interaction of its members (Real, 1990).

From this new perspective, a family is composed of multiple perspectives—multiple realities—and the therapist, no longer seen as an outside observer to the problem situation, has a part in constructing the reality being observed. The therapist does not operate as if he or she or any single family member can reveal the "truth" about the family or its problems. Just as with the other participants, what the therapist sees as existing in the family is a product of his or her particular set of assumptions about families and their problems. There are multiple "truths" about every family, not one universal "truth." The therapist, then, can no longer consider any member's viewpoint as a distortion of some presumably correct interpretation of reality that the therapist (or that a particular family member) alone can see.

Since humans are seen in this view as observing systems who describe, distinguish, and delineate through the use of language, none of us sees an objective universe, and each family's interpretation of reality is limited by the "stories" members tell themselves about themselves as individuals or as a family. These "stories" not only reflect but, more important, define and give meaning to the family's experiences, and in that sense are self-perpetuating. Rather than talk of a family's "reality testing," advocates of this view argue that we should speak of "consensus testing." Family therapy in the postmodern era, then, becomes a form of family "conversation" to which the therapist is invited. The therapist and family together generate a new narrative, in effect transforming the pathologizing tale that presumably brought the family to family therapy (Doherty, 1991).

Beginning in the late 1970s, some family therapists sympathetic to the cybernetic ideas of Bateson (1972) began to pay attention to the theories of Chilean biologist Humberto Maturana (1978), cognitive scientist Francisco Varela (1979), cyberneticist Heinz von Foerster (1981), and cognitive psychologist Ernst von Glaserfeld (1987), all of whom urged the abandonment of the simple cybernetic notion that a living system could be observed, studied objectively, and changed from the outside. Instead, they placed the observer in that which was being observed. Family therapists such as Hoffman (1990) and Keeney (1983) applied many of these ideas to their work, adopting a second-order cybernetic model—one in which the observing therapist is an integral and recursive part of the family system being observed, co-constructing with family members the meaning of their lives. Instead of providing answers to the family's problems, the therapist and family members together search for meaning and in the process "reauthor" lives and relationships.

While first-order cybernetics might well remain the primary focus for many therapists who see family systems as analogous to mechanical systems, these second-order cyberneticists argue that living systems should not be seen as objects that can be programmed from the outside, but rather as self-creating, independent entities. Slovik and Griffith (1992) maintain that the latter group's efforts represent a backlash against what critics perceive as the dangers of possible controlling, manipulative, and authoritarian intervention tactics and strategies. As Hoffman (1990, p. 5) illustrates:

> A first-order view in family therapy would assume that it is possible to influence another person or family by using this or that technique: I program you; I teach you; I instruct you. A second-order view would mean that therapists include themselves as part of what must change; they do not stand outside.

Family therapists for the most part continue to practice from a cybernetic approach in some form, although considerable controversy exists over how a troubled and dysfunctional family is best helped to change. Is the family therapist an out-side expert, a powerful, take-charge change agent who enters a family to observe, disrupt its customary interactive patterns, and then design strategies to alter the fam-ily's self-defeating, repetitive patterns? Or is the family therapist a part of the process necessary for change, with his or her own "reality," who creates a context for change through therapeutic conversation and dialogue in the hope of evolving new meaning by changing family premises and assumptions? Should family therapists be action-oriented and push for behavioral change, or focus attention on how language creates a reality for people? Minuchin (1991) questions the extent to which the new approach recognizes the institutions and socioeconomic conditions that influence how people live, pointing out that families of poverty, for example, have been stripped of much of the power to write their own stories.

While second-order cybernetics in no way replaces the validity of first-order cybernetics (Atkinson & Heath, 1990), the issues stirred up by these more recent viewpoints raise many questions about how most effectively to practice family ther-apy. We'll return to these and related issues throughout the book, as we examine the viewpoints and practices of family therapists today.

SUMMARY

A family is a natural social system extending over at least three generations. The way it functions—establishes rules, communicates, and negotiates differences between members—has numerous implications for the development and well-being of its members. Families display a recurring pattern of interactional sequences in which all members participate. Those considered to be enabling families succeed at balancing the needs of their members and the family system as a whole. Gender, cultural back-ground, and social class considerations play decisive roles in behavioral expectations and attitudes. The meanings, understandings, and assumptions a family makes about the world reflect the narratives and stories it has created about itself. Its relational resiliency may enable it to confront and manage disruptive experiences; that resilen-cy is forged through adversity, not despite it.

Adopting a relationship perspective, family therapists do not negate the signifi-cance of individual intrapsychic processes, but take the broader view that individual behavior is better understood as occurring within a family social system. Such a par-adigm shift from traditional ways of understanding a person's behavior calls for a cybernetic epistemology in which feedback mechanisms are seen to operate to pro-duce both stability and change. The circular causality involved in what transpires between people within a family forces the family therapist to focus on understand-ing family processes rather than seeking linear explanations.

Within such a framework, the family symptom bearer or identified patient is viewed as merely a representative of a system in disequilibrium. Some family thera-pists believe the symptom itself acts to stabilize the system and relieve family stress. Others view symptomatic behavior more as a reaction to family stress than as a pro-tective solution to retain family balance. In another view, it is the repeated but unworkable solutions that themselves become the problem. From still another post-modern perspective, symptoms are seen as oppressive, and the family is urged to unite to take back control of their lives from these burdensome symptoms.

While most family therapists adhere to some form of a cybernetic epistemology, there is a developing schism between those who operate from a first-order cybernetic model, in which the therapist remains apart from the system being observed and attempts to change family functioning from the outside, and the second-order cybernetic view in which the therapist is seen as part of the observing system, a participant in constructing the reality being observed. The latter represents the increasingly influential theories of constructivism and social constructionism.

2

Family Development: Continuity and Change

While family life is an ongoing, interactive process and by no means linear, it simultaneously exists in the linear dimension of time. From a multigenerational perspective, such as the one Carter and McGoldrick (1988) offer, generations have an enduring, reciprocal life-shaping impact on each other as families move through **family life cycle** stages. Within the context of the family's current phase of development, a host of intermingled, intergenerational transactions are occurring concurrently. As one generation deals with issues of aging, another is attempting to cope with children leaving home, while still another may be planning careers or beginning to experience intimate adult relationships. Each generation in this system influences and is influenced by the other; development in most families involves multiple simultaneous transitions (Breunlin, 1988).

Thus, a comprehensive view of what is occurring within a large **extended family** calls for looking at the family life cycle in its multi-generational context (Gerson, 1995). Integrating the individual life cycle theories of psychologists such as Erik Erikson (1963), some sociological concepts regarding family development (Duvall, 1977), and the clinical findings of psychiatrists such as Milton Erickson (Haley, 1973) and Salvador Minuchin (1974), many family therapists argue that the life cycle concept can provide a useful framework for studying the predictable stages through which a family passes. Rather than view families from a pathological or deficiency viewpoint, these advocates contend that the family life cycle perspective offers a more positive view of the family's capacity to retain its stability and continuity at the same time that it evolves and changes its structure as new relational processes occur. It is not so much that a competent family passes through a particular stage stress-free or without resisting change, but rather that it has the resilence to use its potential strengths, resources, and effective interpersonal processes to master the necessary transitions. The more resilient the family, the more capably it reorganizes to deal with disruptions, and thus the more buoyant it appears in bouncing back after temporarily being thrown off course as a result of developmental transitions (Hawley & DeHaan, 1996).

Those family therapists who adopt a **structural** (Chapter 9), **strategic** (Chapter 10), or **systemic** (Chapter 11) outlook in particular maintain that general behavior patterns within a family, or perhaps the family's response to a crisis situation, can become more understandable when viewed within the context of the family's current phase of development. From their viewpoint, symptoms that develop within a family may signal the family's inability to negotiate a particular life cycle passage; here the family is thought to have become "stuck" between stages of the life cycle and to "use" a symptomatic member to avoid making the changes the new stage calls for. These therapists view their task as assessing and then actively intervening in order to help families to become "unstuck," enabling them to move successfully on to the next phase of their development.

Different individual as well as family life stages call for the mastery of different **developmental tasks**. For example, contemporary American society expects adolescents to behave differently from younger children or from adults; young adults, economic circumstances permitting, are encouraged to develop some independence. Newly married couples must then develop a process for gaining greater closeness and interdependence; the nature of their involvement with one another inevitably changes once they have a child. Parents must remain involved with young children in a way that would be smothering for adolescents (Minuchin, Lee, & Simon, 1996). Family life cycle advocates argue that the family who has difficulty navigating a particular phase may be temporarily vulnerable—not necessarily dysfunctional—and may need help before feeling empowered to manage the turning point.

Another family therapy pioneer, Murray Bowen (Chapter 8), adopting a wide lens, looked beyond the life cycle of the nuclear family members to include earlier generations and extended family members; his influence is apparent in the work of life cycle theorists Betty Carter and Monica McGoldrick. Bowen's **transgenerational** view pays special attention to family patterns and influences extending over several generations within a family.

Social constructionists, on the other hand, are far less interested in the "stuck" places of family history than the others we have just mentioned, especially the structuralists. Recognizing the varied forms of family life today—single-parent-led families, remarried families, gay couples, cohabiting couples, dual-career families—they challenge traditional concepts of normal family development as well as the assumption that the therapist is an outside expert who can objectively diagnose families. They acknowledge that a family may be influenced by an abusive history, for example, but they emphasize that the family need not be thought of as damaged or without resources and strengths for overcoming earlier adversities.

Far more present- and future-oriented than searching for past deficiencies, the social constructionists help families generate future possibilities, in the process letting them determine for themselves when change is necessary and how best to achieve desired behaviors (Atwood, 1997). If they attend to life cycle issues at all, it is likely to be in helping families search for incidents in the past when they solved problems—what White (1989) calls those "unique outcomes" where their efforts were successful.

A word of caution before proceeding with the life cycle concepts: Any generalizations we are about to make need to be seen within the context of a particular class, culture, and historical period (end of the twentieth century, middle-class America). Cultural, ethnic, and social class variations, to say nothing of the individual variations and coping strategies of different families, need to be considered. With these caveats in place, most family therapists continue to believe that the life course of families evolves through a predictable sequence of stages that are fairly universal (Falicov, 1988a). It is useful to remember that transitions from one stage to the next are rarely as neatly accomplished as stage theory would suggest. Most transitions occur over several years, and life stages often merge into one another, so that a family may be trying to cope with the same issues and challenges over several stages. The key point to remember here, as Gerson (1995) observes, is that

> each transition requires a family to change, to reset priorities, and to organize to meet the challenges of the new life cycle stage. Therapists can learn much about a family and how it is coping and functioning by assessing how that family meets the challenges of each life cycle transition. (p. 91)

THE FAMILY LIFE CYCLE FRAMEWORK

Before we describe the family life cycle concept and evaluate its relevance to family therapy, we need to note that most families, regardless of structure or composition, progress through certain predictable marker events or phases (such as marriage, the birth of a first child, children leaving home, death of grandparents). Each stage is precipitated by a particular life event—what Zilbach (1989) refers to as a *family stage marker* (see Table 2.1)—demanding change and a new adaptation. These passages may occur because of a change in family composition (for example, birth of twins) or perhaps as a result of a major shift in autonomy (starting kindergarten, entering adolescence, retiring from the workforce). The family, as a developmental system, typically must attempt to deal with the developmental tasks or typical problematic patterns that require mastery at each stage.[1] For example, in Zilbach's chart, in which the family life cycle is divided into three primary and seven secondary phases, a stage 1 task as a couple joins together is for each member to forge an individual independence as well as begin to cultivate a couple/dyadic interdependence.

Thus, every family lives in an ever-changing context, according to structuralist Charles Fishman (1988). A key question becomes: Is the family under stress flexible enough to allow new interactive patterns to emerge in order to meet the developmental needs of its members? The answer tells us how easily and how well the family manages conflict and negotiates the transition between stages, and thus has a significant impact on its ability to successfully carry out the tasks of the subsequent stage. Should the family become destabilized as they struggle to accommodate change (for example, the father and mother develop violent disagreements about how late their teenage daughter may stay out on Saturday night), stress will be evident and one or

---

[1]In addition to these predictable developmental challenges, other external factors may also play a part in stressing a family and demanding new adaptations. A move to a new community, a change in career, or a change in economic circumstances can also upset a stable family system (Wachtel & Wachtel, 1986).

Table 2.1   Family Development: Stages of the Family Life Cycle

Gestational: "Going together," courtship, engagement

Early stages: Forming and nesting

Stage 1: Coupling

Family stage marker:	The family begins at the establishment of a common household by two people; this may or may not include marriage.
Family task:	Individual independence to couple/dyadic interdependence.

Stage II: Becoming three

Family stage marker:	The second phase in family life is initiated by the arrival and subsequent inclusion/incorporation of the first child/dependent member.
Family task:	Interdependence to incorporation of dependence.

Middle stages: Family separation processes

Stage III: Entrances

Family stage marker:	The third phase is signaled by the exit of the first child/dependent member from the intrafamilial world to the larger world. This occurs at the point of entrance into school or other extrafamilial environment.
Family task:	Dependence to facilitation of beginning separations—partial independence.

Stage IV: Expansion

Family stage marker:	This phase is marked by the entrance of the last child/dependent member of the family into the community.
Family task:	Support of facilitation of continuing separations—independence.

Stage V: Exits

Family stage marker:	This phase starts with the first complete exit of a dependent member from the family. This is achieved by the establishment of an independent household which may include marriage or another form of independent household entity.
Family task:	Partial separations to first complete independence.

Last stages: Finishing

Stage VI: Becoming smaller/extended

Family stage marker:	Ultimately the moment comes for the exit of the last child/dependent member from the family.
Family task:	Continuing expansion of independence.

Stage VII: Endings

Family stage markers:	The final years start with the death of one spouse/partner and continue up to the death of the other partner.
Family task:	Facilitation of family mourning. Working through final separations.

Source: Zilbach, 1989, p. 65

more family members may become symptomatic (the daughter becomes angry and withdrawn; the mother becomes depressed, the father feels isolated and alone, and their marriage deteriorates). Structuralists argue that the more rigid the family interactive pattern, the less likely the members will be able to negotiate differences, the more the family will struggle against and be stressed by the need to change, and the more likely symptoms will develop within the family system.

As Zilbach (1989) notes, during each stage, family development proceeds through family task accomplishment, and family characteristics of the previous period are carried over into the next stage. If the carrying out of any particular set of tasks is incomplete, impeded, or disturbed, then development is delayed or suspended and these difficulties are carried into the subsequent stage of family development. For example, parents may have fears of separating from a young child and allowing that child to move out of the immediate family to day care, preschool, or kindergarten. That same fear, unresolved, may later cause conflict between parents and the child in adolescence as separation again becomes a family issue when the adolescent seeks greater freedom and self-direction, and still later may delay separation from the family by a young adult.

Both continuity and change characterize the family system as it progresses through time. In some cases, the changes are orderly, gradual, continuous; in others they may be sudden, disruptive, and discontinuous. Both call for transformations in the organization of the system. As an example of the latter, a family may suddenly be confronted by unexpected catastrophic events (serious financial reverses, teenage pregnancy, the birth of a handicapped child). Such crises disrupt the family's normal developmental flow and inevitably produce relationship changes within the family system. As Neugarten (1976) points out, the inappropriate or unanticipated timing of a major event may be particularly traumatic precisely because it upsets the sequence and disturbs the rhythm of the expected course of life. To illustrate the point, Neugarten cites the death of a parent during one's childhood, teenage marriage, a first marriage postponed until late in life, or a child born to parents in midlife.

Certain discontinuous changes are so disruptive and impeding to family life that they suddenly and profoundly shake up and transform a family system so that it never returns to its former way of functioning. Hoffman (1988) notes particularly those events that affect family membership—events representing gains (children acquired through remarriage) or losses (separation of parents, death). Even a natural transition point that requires major shifts in roles (a young mother with a preschool child returns to work outside the home, a husband loses his job or retires from his lifelong work) may produce discontinuous changes and have a similar effect on the family system.

As noted earlier, many family therapists believe that symptoms in a family member are especially likely to appear at these periods of change, signaling the family's difficulty in negotiating a transition. However, not all the difficulties a family experiences coping with change, continuous or discontinuous, need result in symptomatic behavior. The stress on the family system during a transition may actually provide an opportunity for the family to break out of its customary coping patterns and develop more productive, growth-enhancing responses to change. In particular, families who have developed effective collaborative ways of coping with adversity and hardship—what Walsh (1996) calls *relational resilence*—may emerge hardier from crises or persistent stresses or the demands for life cycle transitional changes.

For example, the continuous change of becoming parents for the first time may be feared (and thus postponed) by the childless couple as restricting mobility, increasing responsibility, interrupting sleep, constricting their social life, and so on, or may be welcomed as a move to strengthen the family and invest in its future. (They may, of course, feel a little of both.) The discontinuous changes often brought about as a result of remarriage may result in disequilibrium, role confusion, and heightened conflict in the new family, or may provide a second chance to form a more mature, stable relationship. The family therapist has the responsibility to help the family see its choices, including the possibilities of generating new solutions; together, the therapist's and family's belief in the rebounding adaptability of the family system and its potential for growth and self-healing is crucial in helping families engineer change.

A FAMILY LIFE CYCLE STAGE MODEL

The Developmental Stages

Family sociologists such as Evelyn Duvall and Reuben Hill first proposed a developmental framework for studying families in the late 1940s, in an effort to account for regularities in family life over time (Duvall & Hill, 1948). Their basic premise was that while families change their form and functions over their existence, they do so in an ordered sequence of developmental stages. These sociologists focused on the necessary organizational and adaptational changes a family makes in response to changes in family composition. More specifically, they built their theoretical model on changes in family size due to expansion and later contraction, changes in age composition based on the age of the oldest child, and changes in the work status of the breadwinners.

Duvall, in a text first published in 1957 and now in its sixth edition written with a coauthor (Duvall & Miller, 1985), in particular proposed that the typical development of an intact, middle-class American family proceeds through eight stages,[2] beginning with marriage and ending with the death of both spouses. She portrayed such families in terms of a circle with eight sectors:

1. Married couples without children
2. Childbearing families (oldest child, birth–30 months)
3. Families with preschool children (oldest child 30 months–6 years)

---

[2]The number of stages is, of course, arbitrary, with each theorist emphasizing different aspects of the family life cycle. Duvall (1977) underscores the nodal events in a family's life, related to the comings and goings of family members. Carter and McGoldrick (1980; 1988), who generally are credited with the recent upsurge of interest among many family therapists in life cycle concepts, adds a multigenerational view; their six-stage scheme for intact families begins premaritally, with young single adults leaving home, and realistically considers possible stages of divorce and remarriage (see later section of this chapter). Zilbach's (1989) seven-stage model stresses the accomplishment of specific family tasks. Some family therapists such as Pittman (1987) pay less attention to what transpires within each stage than how successfully families negotiate turning points—the crises that sometimes accompany the transitions between stages.

4. Families with children (oldest child 6–13 years)
5. Families with teenagers (oldest child 13–20 years)
6. Families as launching centers (first to last child leaves home)
7. Middle-aged parents (empty nest to retirement)
8. Aging family members (retirement to death of both spouses)

While no one family is apt to resemble the model in all particulars, the major thrust of Duvall's early (and seemingly uncomplicated) contribution was to plot the stages through which families typically pass, and to predict the approximate time (revised with successive editions of her text) when each stage is reached. Within each stage, each family must perform a series of developmental tasks (for instance, helping adolescents learn to balance freedom with responsibility during stage 5; releasing young adults during stage 6, assisting them as they gain independence while maintaining a supportive family home base) to be better equipped to deal with those tasks requiring mastery at a subsequent stage. Making the appropriate role changes over time may be said to constitute the family's overall developmental task.

Although initially arising out of the National Conference on Family Life held in Washington, D.C., in 1948, where it was proposed as a framework for sociological research on marriage and the family, the life cycle approach was later incorporated by a number of family therapists (especially Carter & McGoldrick, 1980; Haley, 1973) as a framework for conceptualizing what transpires within normal and dysfunctional families. As Carter and McGoldrick (1988) have more recently formulated this position, the life cycle perspective "frames problems within the course the family has moved along in its past, the tasks it is trying to master, and the future toward which it is moving" (p. 4).

Individual life cycles take place within the family life cycle, and the interplay between the two affects what takes place in each. The relationship system within a family expands, contracts, and realigns over the family's life span, and the family must be flexible enough to sustain the entry and exit of members as well as bolster the efforts of members to move on in their own personal development. Families that become derailed in their life cycle (and correspondingly derail individual efforts at independence) need help in getting back on developmental track. Carter and McGoldrick (1988) suggest that a major goal of family therapy in such situations is reestablishing the family's developmental momentum.

One final note: Inevitably today, the relationship between a family's work life (the prevalence of two-paycheck families having long ago exceeded the long-idealized married couple with a single breadwinner father, a homemaker mother, and two children) and family life needs to be factored into any consideration of family development (Carlson, Sperry, & Lewis, 1997). Similarly, divorce, single parenthood, children born out of wedlock to teenagers or older women, and stepfamilies have complicated the probably oversimplified picture of what constitutes normal family development just presented. Nevertheless, the life cycle outlook provides one useful organizing framework for understanding a family's conflicts and negotiations, its flexibility in adapting to changing conditions, and the appearance of problematic or symptomatic behavior at a particularly treacherous crossroad. Perhaps its major value is to "normalize" family difficulties, reveal linkages over generations, and focus on family continuity.

Family Transitions and Symptomatic Behavior

The family life cycle perspective offers a valuable context for understanding individual and family dysfunction, especially for advocates of the structural position, who argue that problems develop within a family with a dysfunctional structure when the family encounters a transition point but lacks the flexibility to adapt to the changing conditions. For example, a young husband and wife who have not achieved sufficient separation from their parents to be able to establish their own independent marital unit may experience considerable distress, conflict, and confusion when they prepare to enter the next phase of their family life—the birth and rearing of their own children.

Strategists too view the appearance of symptoms as a signal that the family is unable to move on to the next stage; as one example, Haley (1979) argues that some families may need therapeutic help in solving problems evoked by a young adult member ready to leave home and embark on a more independent life. In general, Haley views individual symptomatology as arising from an interruption of the family's normal developmental process, and thus he is likely to direct his efforts at helping the family as a whole resolve the impasse that they are experiencing as a group.

Following up on Duvall's classic eight stages of family development, Barnhill and Longo (1978) differentiate specific transition points that require negotiation as families pass through each stage (see Table 2.2). They contend that families, much like individuals, can become fixated or arrested at a particular phase of development, and thus may fail to make the necessary transition at the appropriate time. Under stress, again like individuals, families may regress to an earlier transition point, when a successful life cycle passage had been made. In their conceptualization, symptoms

Table 2.2   Common Transition Points Through the Life Cycle

Duvall Stage	Major Transition to be Achieved
	Commitment to each other
1. Married Couple	
	Developing parent roles
2. Childbearing family	
	Accepting child's personality
3. Preschool children	
	Introducing child to institutions (school, churches, sports groups)
4. School children	
	Accepting adolescence (social and sexual role changes)
5. Teenagers	
	Experimenting with independence of late teens
6. Launching children	
	Accepting child's independent adult role
7. Middle-aged parents	
	Letting go—facing each other again
8. Aging family members	
	Accepting old age

Source: Based on Duvall, 1977, and Barnhill & Longo, 1978

appearing in any family member (for example, adolescent delinquent behavior) is evidence that the immediate family life task has not been mastered.

Carter and McGoldrick (1988) provide a more encompassing, intergenerational view of the impact of multiple stresses on navigating family transitions. They believe the flow of anxiety within a family to be related to both "vertical" and "horizontal" stressors (see Figure 2.1). The former refer to patterns of relating and functioning transmitted down through generations—family attitudes, stories,[3] expectations, taboos, and loaded family issues passed along from grandparents to parents to children. Members of all families receive such legacies growing up, listening to family narratives concerning past family experiences that formed the basis for a "family line" or set of prejudgments in viewing new events and situations.

Horizontal stressors are the anxiety-provoking events experienced by the family as it moves forward through time, coping with changes and transitions of the life cycle—the various predictable developmental stresses as well as unexpected, traumatic ones (such as an untimely death or chronic illness).

With enough stress on the horizontal axis, any family will appear dysfunctional. Any amount of horizontal stress (say, the revelation of a teenage girl's pregnancy or the "outing" of a homosexual adolescent boy) can cause great disruption to a family in which the vertical axis already contains intense stress (excessive family concerns about appearances of moral rectitude).

In general, the greater the anxiety "inherited" from previous generations at any transition point (say, anxieties over being parents and raising children, passed on by a woman's parents), the more anxiety producing and dysfunctional that point will be for that young mother expecting her first child. In this example, when horizontal (or

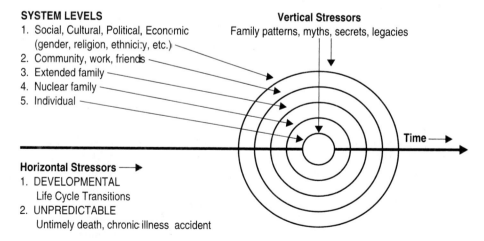

Figure 2.1   Horizontal and vertical stressors

[3]As we noted in Chapter 1, in discussing the constructivist view of the appearance of symptomatic behavior in a family member, each family's self-picture is based, at least in part, on "stories" it has created about itself. These stories often are passed along over generations and may be a source of comfort (how we Joneses always come through adversity whatever the odds) or despair (how we Smiths always end up with the short end of the stick, regardless of our efforts). We'll elaborate on the therapies based upon social constructionism in Chapter 13.

developmental) stresses intersect with vertical (or transgenerational) stresses, there is a quantum leap in anxiety in the system. Concurrent external stresses—death, illness, financial setbacks—as a family progresses through its life cycle add to the stress. The point where the axes converge, then, becomes a key determinant of how well the family will manage the transition point. What we may conclude from Carter and McGoldrick's (1988) work is how imperative it is that family therapists attend not only to current life cycle stresses but also to their connections to family themes handed down over generations.

Critique of the Stage Model

While the stage model of family development just presented offers a valuable context for understanding individual and family dysfunction, its shortcomings too require acknowledgment. The concept is essentially descriptive rather than explanatory. It purports to offer normative data on intact family life at a time in history when a diversity of lifestyles (delayed marriages, cohabitation) and a variety of living arrangements (single-parent-led families, stepfamilies) are prevalent and functional. The approach fails to take individual differences in the timing of nodal events (for example, due to postponed marriages and/or delayed pregnancies) into account, despite the wide array of lifestyles today. To the extent that it suggests that what transpires within the stages is all-important, it does a disservice to the equally important, perhaps more important, transitions between stages, which are key periods of change.

Lee Combrinck-Graham (1988) argues that while family development may be linear, family life is anything but—it does not begin at any one particular point, nor have a clear-cut ending point. Rather, she believes family movement through time is cyclical, or more accurately, proceeds as a spiral. That is, at certain times family members are tightly involved with one another; she considers this pulling together, as when a new child is born or a serious illness in a family member occurs, as *centripetal* periods. At other times (starting school, beginning a career), individual moves take precedent, and *centrifugal* periods occur. In this formulation, there is an oscillation in family life, not the tidy and continuous unidirectional flow suggested by stage theory. At times the family members tend to be oriented inward; at other times they move toward interests outside the family. Combrinck-Graham contends that three-generational families are likely to alternate between centripetal and centrifugal states (keeping members together and pushing them apart, respectively) as events occurring in a particular life cycle period call for greater interdependence or individuation.

Douglas Breunlin (1988) agrees that family development is rarely a discrete and discontinuous shift from one life stage to a subsequent stage separated by arbitrary transitions, but rather occurs as gradual oscillations (or microtransitions) between stages as the family makes its way to the next developmental level. He emphasizes that families are far more complex than the stage model suggests, and that in reality development in most families, as we noted earlier, involves multiple simultaneous transitions as various members are undergoing differing degrees of interlocking life changes.

While these modifications provide a more accurate description of what actually occurs, the life cycle concept nevertheless offers a workable organizing schema for assessing family functioning and planning interventions. Family therapists have attempted to wed a cybernetic epistemology (emphasizing circular causality and feedback loops) to this more sociologically focused developmental framework, going beyond the arbitrary punctuations of stage theory in order to view families as composed of interconnected members engaged in ongoing, interactive processes with one another.

That interconnection may alternate between degrees of closeness and separateness, depending on life circumstances, over the family's life cycle. Family dysfunction may signal that the family is at a developmental impasse. The appearance of symptomatic behavior may thus be seen as a manifestation of the stress the family is experiencing around a transitional event. Or perhaps the family is rigidly organized and cannot change its organizational structure to accommodate new developmental requirements. Finally, the symptom may serve the function of offering the family a "solution" that helps maintain stability in the face of impending change (Falicov, 1988a).

As an example of a family experiencing difficulties in moving on to the next phase of the life cycle, Haley (1973) describes a woman who suffers from postpartum depression following the birth of a child. While she is commonly thought to be experiencing an intense intrapsychic conflict that is producing her symptoms, Haley argues that the entire family may be having difficulty making the transition as it enters this new phase in its development marked by the infant's birth; the mother is simply the identified patient. Haley, offering a strategic outlook, defines the task of the therapist as helping the family resolve the immediate crisis together in order to achieve a new balance and adaptation to the changed family structure. If successful, the family will resume its developmental course.

CHANGING FAMILIES, CHANGING RELATIONSHIPS

We live in a pluralistic society that is itself undergoing dramatic changes in family structure, lifestyles, and inevitably in family life cycle patterns. From a contemporary perspective, it no longer makes sense to refer to what is "typical" when speaking of American family life, since today's families represent diverse organizational patterns and living arrangements. The marked increase in ethnic minorities in recent years has added further to the diversity of value systems, language, family structure, and relationship systems. High divorce rates, the surge of women into the workforce, the greater prevalence of single-parent-led as well as remarried families have all added to that diversity.

In this section we attempt to elaborate on common developmental issues of intact, primarily middle-class families and contrast these with the life cycle disruptions caused families as a result of divorce and remarriage.

Developmental Sequences in Intact Families

Family therapists are apt to depart from the traditional sociological view of the family life cycle commencing at the time of marriage, arguing that single young adults must first complete their primary developmental task: separating from the family of origin without cutting off from them and fleeing to a substitute emotional refuge. Especially in middle-class families, separation from parents is made more difficult today because of longer periods of education leading to prolonged financial dependency, increased housing costs, and so on. Delayed marriages due to career demands, possible fear of sexual experimentation because of sexually transmitted diseases such as AIDS, a general acceptance of later marriages, and apprehension about the longevity of marriage all make commitment to the new relationship more tenuous.

Learning to maintain oneself independently in work and social situations typically occurs at this point. Aylmer (1988) contends that the satisfactory resolution of this task, enabling the young person to leave home and begin to establish an identity in the world of work and intimate relationships, is primarily determined by the quality, tone, and degree of completeness reached in original family relationships, with parents, siblings, and extended family members.

Finding and committing to a partner is, typically, the next developmental task. The pair must move from independence to interdependence in this stage—what Gerson (1995) labels *coupling*. Whether in a heterosexual union involving marriage or cohabitation or a same-sex pairing (hence the generic term *coupling*), the two people must decide to commit to one another. Especially in the case of a legal marriage, more than a union of two people is involved; the mating represents a change in two established family systems and the formation of a subsystem (the new couple) in each. Less formally bound by family traditions than couples in the past, and thus with fewer models to emulate, today's newly married pair must go about differentiating themselves as a couple with primary allegiance to one another and only secondary allegiance to their families of origin. Commitment to the marital partnership is the key to managing the transition of detaching sufficiently from each of their families and forming a new cohesive marital unit (Barnhill & Longo, 1978). Ideally, both partners need to feel they are part of a "we" without sacrificing an "I"—a sense of self as separate and autonomous.

Each partner has acquired from his or her family a set of antecedent patterns, traditions, and expectations for marital interaction and family life. Minuchin, Rosman, and Baker (1978) believe that in marriage both paradigms must be retained so that each person maintains a sense of self; the two paradigms must also be reconciled in order for the couple to have a life in common. In the process of reconciliation, spouses arrive at new transactional patterns—accommodations or tacit agreements to disagree—that then become familiar and ultimately their preferred or habitual way of interacting with each other. For some, such commitment comes easily—they want to be together whenever possible, share private thoughts and intimacies, experience no problem pooling their earnings, call each other at work one or more times a day, and focus on growing closer as a marital couple. For others, such a connection is fraught with hesitations; not unlike the life they led as a single person, they insist on maintaining separate bank accounts, take separate vacations, and prefer weekend activities with friends or separate families of origin over being together. For this latter group, learning to cooperate and compromise differences takes a longer time; in some cases it is never achieved.

In creating a family, the partners must not only provide for their basic physical needs but also continually negotiate such personal issues as when and how to sleep, eat, make love, fight, and make up. They must decide how to celebrate holidays, plan vacations, spend money, do household chores, and what to watch on television or what other forms of entertainment they both enjoy. They are obliged to decide which family traditions and rituals to retain from each of their pasts and which they wish to generate as their own. Together they need to determine the degree of closeness to or distance from each of their families of origin they wish to maintain. Each has to gain admission to the other's family, in some cases as the first person to do so in many years. In the same way, they must meet each other's friends and over time select those who will become the couple's friends. Together they gain new friends and lose touch with some old ones.

In the case of a couple who is married, at first the system tends to be loosely organized and the roles played by the spouses flexible and often interchangeable. The structure of a family without children allows for a wide variety of solutions to immediate problems. For example, either or both of the partners may prepare dinner at home; they may choose to eat out at a restaurant; they may drop in at a friend's or relative's house for a meal; they may eat separately or together. When there are children to be fed, however, a more formal and specific arrangement will have to be formulated in advance of dinnertime. Beyond making room for children in their lives, psychologically as well as physically, the couple must define more clearly the distribution of duties and division of labor: Who will shop, cook, pick up the children at a nursery or child-care center, wash the dishes, put their offspring to bed? The commitment of husband and wife, then, to become mother and father represents a significant transition point in a family's life, changing forever the relatively simple playing out of roles between mates who are childless. As Karpel and Strauss (1983) observe, virtually all patterns of time, schedule, expenditures, leisure, use of space in the home, and especially relationships with in-laws and friends are likely to become reorganized around the child.

The arrival of children—the family *expansion* phase (Gerson, 1995)—thus represents perhaps the most significant milestone in the life cycle of the family. The partners' lives may not have changed nearly as much when the two first married; this is even more likely if they lived together before marriage and/or established a satisfactory premarital sexual relationship. When husband and wife become parents, however, both "move up" a generation and now must provide care for a younger generation. Other members of the family **suprasystem** also move up a notch—parental siblings become uncles and aunts; nieces and nephews now become cousins; the parents of the new mother and father become grandparents. Overall, a vertical realignment occurs for new family and extended family together. A major task here is to integrate their new relationships to the child with their previously existing relationship with one another. A revised sense of individual identity is likely to occur once the partners become parents, and relative commitments to work and family must be reconsidered.

Making this transition, taking and sharing responsibilities, practicing patience, setting limits, tolerating restrictions on free time and mobility, all these tasks must be mastered in the expanding family system. Young parents, particularly if both are employed full-time, each must now juggle schedules and attempt to find an acceptable balance between work and domestic responsibilities. At the same time, husband

and wife need to redefine and redistribute household and child-care chores. Their previously egalitarian role structure may break down and they may resort to more traditional male/female divisions of labor, which may create unexpected conflicts and additional stress. Older parents must learn to accommodate young children in an already established or perhaps fixed pattern of relationships, often without being able to call upon elderly grandparents for support.

Beyond such practical problems, Bradt (1988) observes that a child's arrival may bring a nuclear family **triangle**[4] into play, challenging the stability of the spousal relationship because of one parent's closeness to the child and distancing from a mate. Bradt contends that the failure of either spouse to become a parent and at the same time to continue to grow as a spouse may well threaten the couple's intimacy. He argues that "a marriage that has developed intimacy is a marriage better able to respond to the challenge of parenthood, to integrate the lifelong change that parenthood brings, not only to the new parents but to the entire family" (p. 243).

As noted earlier, Barnhill and Longo (1978) believe that two crucial transition points for the family involve, first, both parents learning to accept the new personality as the child grows up, and second, introducing the child to institutions outside the family, such as school, church, and sports groups. According to Haley (1973), who based many of his life cycle formulations on the clinical work of Milton Erickson, a common crisis period occurs within families when the first child starts school; this represents the family's first step toward the realization that the children will eventually leave home. The symptoms of school refusal or school phobia in young children may reflect family turmoil and restructuring.

When children reach adolescence, the family faces new organizational challenges, particularly around autonomy and independence. Parents may no longer be able to maintain complete authority, but they cannot abdicate authority, either. Here the family is not dealing with entrances and exits into the system but rather with a basic restructuring of the interactive processes between members, all necessary to allow the teenager more independence (Harway & Wexler, 1995).

Rule changing, limit setting, and role renegotiation are all necessary, often disruptively shifting relationships across two or more generations. As Preto (1988) points out, the struggle to meet adolescent demands may reactivate unresolved parent-grandparent conflicts over child rearing, or perhaps bring similar husband-wife conflicts to the surface. Triangles between the teenager and both parents, or perhaps the teenager, parent, and grandparent, are common and often disruptive to the suprasystem.

Adolescents must strike a balance on their own, forging an identity and beginning to establish autonomy from the family. Teenagers who remain too childlike and dependent or who become too isolated and withdrawn from the family put a strain on the family system. Too rapid an exit from family life by adolescents may also impair a family's ability to adapt. Parents, too, need to come to terms with their teenager's rapidly changing social and sexual behavior. Depending on the spacing of

---

[4]Murray Bowen introduced and elaborated the importance of triangles in family relationships, considering them the basic building block of a family's emotional system. We elaborate on these ideas in Chapter 8, which is devoted to Bowen's transgenerational theories.

children, parents may find themselves dealing with issues relevant to differing ages and life cycle stages at the same time.

All of this is likely to occur while simultaneous strains on the system may be taking place: (1) "midlife crises' in which one or both middle-aged parents question not only career choices but also perhaps their earlier marital choices (for some women, this may represent the first opportunity to pursue a career without child-care responsibilities, leading to family dislocations and role changes); (2) the need to care for impaired grandparents, necessitating role reversals between parents and now-dependent grandparents, perhaps calling for changing caretaking arrangements regarding the older generation.

Gerson (1995) refers to the next period as one of *contraction;* Carter and McGoldrick (1988) describe this phase of the intact family's life cycle as "launching children and moving on." Unlike in earlier times, today the low birthrate coupled with longer life expectancy means that this stage now covers a lengthy period; parents frequently launch their families almost 20 years before retirement. They must come to accept their children's independent role and eventual creation of their own families. The development of adult-to-adult relationships with their children is an important developmental task at this stage, as is the expansion of the family to include the spouses, children, and in-laws of their married children.

Parents also need to reassess their relationship with one another now that their children no longer reside at home. Sometimes couples view this change as an opportunity for freedom from child-rearing responsibilities and perhaps, if economically feasible, a chance to travel or explore other activities postponed for financial reasons or time restraints while they cared for their children. Now, in the absence of the care of children, these families see a chance to strengthen their marital bond. In other families, marital strains covered over while they raised children together may resurface with the children gone. Children leaving may in such cases lead to increased marital strife or feelings of depression and loneliness over life becoming empty and meaningless. It is not uncommon for such parents to hold onto their offspring, especially the last child.

Parents now need to cope with moving up a notch to grandparent positions; at the same time, increased caretaking responsibilities for their own needy and dependent parents, especially by women, is likely. In some cases, the renewal of the parent-grandparent relationship provides an opportunity to resolve earlier interpersonal conflicts; in other cases, it may simply exacerbate unresolved conflict from earlier days. A major transition point for the middle-aged adult is apt to revolve around the death of elderly parents.

Another family life cycle stage is reached by the time the children have reached their forties, according to transgenerational theorist Donald Williamson (1991), when another level of intimacy is achieved between generations and when the old hierarchical boundaries, ideally, are replaced by a greater peer relationship. Their parents, now in their retirement years, must cope with a dramatic increase in their daily time together, and, frequently, a reduction in income. Enduring the loss of friends and relatives (and most difficult of all, loss of a spouse), coping with increased dependence on one's children, handling changing relationships with grandchildren, possibly relinquishing power and status, coming to terms with one's own illness, limitations, and ultimate death—these are some of the problems of old age. With the death of one partner, the family must often assume care of the surviving parent at home or in a nursing home, with all family members experiencing a new set of transitional stresses.

Froma Walsh (1988) suggests that changes brought about by retirement, widowhood, grandparenthood, and illness/dependency all represent major adaptational challenges for the entire family system, as it attempts to cope with loss and dysfunction and tries to reorganize itself. The death of a grandparent may be the young child's first encounter with separation and loss and, at the same time, may be a reminder to the parents of their own mortality. How the family deals with the dying process has implications for several generations as all move inevitably toward the aging phase of the life cycle (Brody, 1974).

Developmental Sequences in Alternative Families

The family developmental approach outlined by sociologists in the 1940s, with its predictable life cycle stages and concurrent developmental tasks, could hardly be expected to have anticipated life circumstances a half century later. A relatively rare phenomenon then, divorce today has become a familiar and recognized fact of American life—approximately 1 million divorces occur annually in this country—and thus inevitably touches family members at every generation and throughout the nuclear as well as extended families. The divorce process and its sequelae inevitably have a powerful, disruptive impact on three aspects of the life cycle—individual, marital, and family—all of which must be taken into account in gaining a full measure of the subsequent dislocations to all participants (Sager et al., 1983). In family system terms, divorce adds complexity to whatever developmental tasks the family is currently experiencing. Peck and Manocherian (1988) even suggest that with the shape of the family inevitably altered, each ensuing life phase becomes affected by the divorce and therefore must be viewed within the dual context of that stage itself along with the residual effects of the earlier divorce.

The divorce process itself typically occurs over time and in stages, and more likely than not is marked by a great deal of stress, ambivalence, indecision, self-doubt, and uncertainty, even when both partners agree that the marriage is no longer viable. When children are involved, particularly young children, the decision is all the more deliberate and painful. Kressel (1985) characterizes the divorce process as "one of the more demanding tasks that rational beings are expected to perform" (p. 4).

Starting with an *emotional divorce,* in which both partners are forced to deal with their deteriorating marital relationship, the couple must proceed to physically separate; inevitably each must deal with feelings of failure and question their ability to love or be worthy of love in return. Legal arrangements follow, often filled with acrimony, frequently manifesting itself as conflict over the redistribution of assets, property, child-support payments, and possibly alimony payments. Arrangements for coparenting must be made as child custody and visitation rights are hammered out. Each partner must then redefine his or her separate place in the community as a single, unattached person and begin the often laborious process of seeking and being open to new relationships (Bohannan, 1970).

Single-Parent-Led Families   One-parent families today are likely to be part of one of the following groupings:

- A divorced person (87% women, 13% men) with child custody
- An unmarried teenage biological mother with a planned or unplanned child
- An older unmarried biological mother with a planned or unplanned child
- A single person, male or female, gay or straight, who adopts a child
- A lesbian woman who chooses impregnation through donor insemination

To summarize, then, single-parent-led families, while not a unitary group, typically consist of one parent, who may or may not have been married, and one or more children. As a result of a steady high rate of separation and divorce over several decades, adoptions, widowhood, gay parenting, as well as the increasing number of out-of-wedlock births to both teenage and older women, such families now represent the fastest-growing family type in the United States (Cox, 1996). The number of children living in one-parent households tripled between 1960 and 1994, when it reached between 25 and 30 million youngsters (Saxton, 1996).

The most glaring difference between two-parent families and ones headed by divorced or never-married mothers is the disparity in economic well-being (McLanahan & Booth, 1989); the latter, particularly those with young children, are likely to be worse off financially than any other type of family organization. Mother-headed families especially are characterized by a high rate of poverty, a high percentage of minority representation, relatively low education, and a high rate of mobility (Norton & Glick, 1986).

The divorced mother, with physical custody of her children, usually must deal not only with lowered economic status but also with grief and self-blame, loneliness, lack of an adequate support system, child-care arrangements, custody and visitation problems, and more. Frequently she must carry the entire burden of raising a child alone in what is often an emotionally and physically unstable environment (Miller, 1992). Despite these obstacles, resiliency is often present, and as Seibt (1996) observes:

> The children raised by single parents can be just as healthy and normal as those raised in the traditional two-parent family. In fact, despite the obstacles, children in most single-parent families are provided with the love and nurturing that all children need and deserve. (p. 41)

The single father with custody also experiences financial pressures, although they are likely to be less severe than those with which single mothers, usually with more limited earning potential, must cope. Because commitment to job and career have probably been the highest priority for them, a shift in focus is necessary, and not being able to spend sufficient time with their children is often a major complaint. Those who opt for a close, nurturing relationship with their children must often learn new roles, change their circle of friends, and rebuild their social lives (Seibt, 1996).

The *noncustodial parent*—more likely father than mother—frequently must cope with diminished relationships with his children, disruption of his customary living experiences, loneliness and self-blame for the failed marriage, and custody and visitation conflicts. The *children* may grapple with shame and embarrassment, less contact with the noncustodial parent, conflicting loyalties, adaptation to visitation activities, and perhaps continued fantasies over parental reconciliation (Goldenberg & Goldenberg, 1998). All the family members in this postdivorced arrangement experience problems that affect, and are affected by, problems in the others.

While sole custody still remains the most common situation (65 to 70 percent), joint legal custody, increasingly awarded by the courts, allows both parents equal authority regarding their children's general welfare, education, and so on. The children may reside with one parent, but both have equal access to them. This **binuclear family** (Ahrons & Rodgers, 1987) arrangement, of course, works out best when the former marital partners are each caring and committed parents, are able to cooperate, have relatively equal and consistent parenting skills, and are able to work together without reviving old animosities (Goldenberg & Goldenberg, 1998). The point here is that while the nuclear family no longer lives as one unit, divorce has not ended the family but simply restructured (and frequently expanded) it.

In Carter and McGoldrick's (1988) family life cycle outlook, divorce represents an interruption or dislocation similar to those produced with any shifts, gains, and losses in family membership. As we have noted, relationship changes must be addressed, and a new set of developmental tasks dealt with (see Table 2.3) before the divorcing family can proceed developmentally. As Peck and Manocherian (1988) note, each ensuing life cycle stage will be affected by the divorce and must therefore be viewed within the context of that stage itself as well as the residual effects of the divorce.

Remarried Families   Remarriage today is nearly as common as first marriages; close to half of all new marriages involve a remarriage for at least one partner, and one in four a remarriage for both (Saxton, 1996). Single life is short-lived for most divorced persons: the median interval before remarriage for previously divorced men is 2.3 years, and for women 2.5 years. About 30 percent of all divorced persons remarry within 12 months of becoming divorced (Ganong & Coleman, 1994). Bray (1995) estimates that there are more than 11 million remarried households in the Unites States, and demographer Glick (1989) forecasts that stepfamilies are likely to become the predominant family form as we enter the twenty-first century.

From a family life cycle view, more Americans than ever before are experiencing transitions from nuclear family to single-parent or binuclear family, to remarried family or stepfamily, all within a brief time period. The resulting stepfamilies (far more often than not a stepfather and custodial mother than the reverse) must undergo an entire new stage of the family life cycle before gaining stability (see Table 2.4). One glimpse of the complexity involved comes from McGoldrick and Carter (1988).

> As a first marriage signifies the joining of two families, so a second marriage involves
> the interweaving of three, four, or more families, whose previous life cycle course
> has been disrupted by death or divorce. (p. 399)

Adaptation to remarriage becomes still more complex, McGoldrick and Carter maintain, if spouses come from different individual life cycle phases (for example, an

Table 2.3   Dislocation in the Family Life Cycle Requiring Additional Steps to Restabilize and Proceed Developmentally

Phase	Prerequisite Attitude	Developmental Issues
Divorce		
1. The decision to divorce	Acceptance of inability to resolve marital tensions sufficiently to continue relationship	Acceptance of one's own part in the failure of the marriage
2. Planning the breakup of the system	Supporting viable arrangements for all parts of the system	a. Working cooperatively on problems of custody, visitation and finances b. Dealing with extended family about divorce
3. Separation	a. Willingness to continue cooperative coparental relationship and joint financial support of children b. Work on resolution of attachment to spouse	a. Mourning loss of intact family b. Restructuring marital and parent-child relationships and finances; adaptation to living apart c. Realignment of relationships with extended family; staying connected with spouse's extended family
4. The divorce	More work on emotional divorce: overcoming hurt, anger, guilt, etc.	a. Mourning loss of intact family; giving up fantasies of reunion b. Retrieval of hopes, dreams, expectations from the marriage c. Staying connected with extended families
Postdivorce family Custodial single parent	Willingness to maintain financial responsibilities, continue parental contact with ex-spouse, and support contact of children with ex-spouse and his or her family	a. Making flexible visitation arrangements with ex-spouse and his family b. Rebuilding own financial resources c. Rebuilding own social network
Noncustodial single parent	Willingness to maintain parental contact with ex-spouse and support custodial parent's relationship with children	a. Finding ways to continue effective parenting relationship with children b. Maintaining financial responsibilities to ex-spouse and children c. Rebuilding own social network

Source: Carter & McGoldrick, 1988, p. 22

Table 2.4 Remarried Family Formation: A Developmental Outline

Step	Prerequisite Attitude	Developmental Issues
1. Entering the new relationship	Recovery from loss of first marriage (adequate "emotional divorce")	Recommitment to marriage and to forming a family with readiness to deal with complexity and ambiguity
2. Conceptualizing and planning new marriage and family	Accepting one's own fears and those of new spouse and children about remarriage and forming a stepfamily Accepting need for time and patience for adjustment to complexity and ambiguity of: 1. Multiple new roles 2. Boundaries: space, time, membership, and authority 3. Affective issues: guilt, loyalty conflicts, desire for mutuality, unresolvable past hurts	a. Working on openness in the new relationships to avoid pseudomutuality b. Planning for maintenance of cooperative financial and coparental relationships with ex-spouses c. Planning to help children deal with fears, loyalty conflicts, and membership in two systems d. Realignment of relationships with extended family to include new spouse and children e. Planning maintenance of connections for children with extended family of ex-spouse(s)
3. Remarriage and reconstitution of family	Final resolution of attachment to previous spouse and ideal of "intact" family; acceptance of a different model of family with permeable boundaries	a. Restructuring family boundaries to allow for inclusion of new spouse-stepparent b. Realignment of relationships and financial arrangements throughout subsystems to permit interweaving of several systems c. Making room for relationships of all children with biological (non-custodial) parents, grandparents, and other extended family d. Sharing memories and histories to enhance stepfamily integration

Source: Carter & McGoldrick, 1988, p. 24

older man with adult children marrying a young woman with no children or young children). Moreover, being an effective stepparent to a young child and to an adolescent is likely to be different because of their different developmental needs (Bray, 1995). An additional problem often arises because the nonresident biological father (or mother) looms in the background, may remain a major factor in the family system, and may cause loyalty problems for children.

Adding to their adaptation to a single-parent household, now the entire family must struggle with fears regarding investing in new relationships and forming a new family. Visher and Visher (1988) suggest that the majority of stepfamilies have a number of distinctive problems: They are born out of relationship losses and the abandonment of hopes and dreams in the previous family; they are composed of members with separate family histories and traditions that may be in conflict and that need to be reconciled; children are often members of two households, with differing rules and lifestyles; children often experience loyalty conflicts between parents. Goldenberg and Goldenberg (1998) add that there may be difficulties in assuming parental roles with stepchildren, rivalries and jealousies may develop between stepchildren, and competition between the biological mother and the step-mother may occur.

Visher and Visher (1988) suggest that stepfamily development occurs in stages and that each stage in the process calls for renegotiating and reorganizing a complex and dynamic network of relationships. They conclude from their research that the process is likely to take several years before full stepfamily integration is achieved. Those stepparents who demand "instant love" are likely to end up feeling frustrated and rejected. On the other hand, relationships within stepfamilies that are allowed to blossom slowly in an evolving developmental process often lead to caring and loving bonds that last a lifetime (Visher & Visher, 1993).

Gay and Lesbian Families   Gay and lesbian families are as varied and diverse as heterosexual families: some are formed after unsuccessful heterosexual marriages (in which prolonged and conflictual custody battles may have taken place); they may opt for parenthood by adopting a child; or, in the case of lesbians, they may choose artificial insemination in order to have children. Regardless of family genesis, such families are likely to have life cycle stresses and transitions similar to those of heterosexual families (such as adjusting to new parenthood, sending children off to school) in addition to some unique to their homosexual lifestyle (for example, whether to "come out" or remain "in the closet" to other possibly homophobic parents; how to help their child fit into the mainstream with his or her peers while preserving the parent's homosexual identity) (Carlson, 1996).

It is difficult to determine the exact number of gay or lesbian parents, since many, perhaps the majority, are closeted, preferring to keep their sexual preferences to themselves out of fear of negative attitudes or reprisals from neighbors, employers, or fellow workers. Adoption can be stressful, the nonadoptive parent often remaining hidden (thus back "in" after having "come out") while his or her mate goes through the lengthy adoptive process as a single parent; that adopting applicant may or may not reveal a gay or lesbian lifestyle to the adoption agency. Others, with children, having gone from a heterosexual to a homosexual preference, may find they need to conceal their current behavior from the courts for fear of losing custody or visitation rights. While such factors make exact counts impossible to come by, it is estimated that there are at least 12 to 15 million children residing in homes with gay or lesbian parents in the United States alone (Goldenberg & Goldenberg, 1998).

Contrary to some myths, there is no evidence that gay or lesbian adults are less fit parents than their heterosexual counterparts. Research findings compiled by Patterson (1995) indicate that lesbian women are not markedly different either in their mental health or in their child-rearing practices from heterosexual women. Moreover, the available research suggests that children raised by these mothers (there is less data currently available regarding gay male parenting) develop patterns of gender-role behavior similar to those patterns developed by all other children, with no evidence of elevated levels of homosexuality.

That is not to say, of course, that gay parenting does not present unique problems throughout the family life cycle. Carlson (1996) indicates that these are likely to arise beginning with the preschool and school-age years, when childhood events (scouts, sports, dance classes, and so forth) present an endless series of opportunities to parents to "come out" or remain closeted. Later, during adolescence, when conformity to peer group pressures is likely to be particularly strong, children may attempt to distance themselves from their parents; while this is a developmental task common to all adolescents, as they struggle to find their own identities, in this case the rejection of the alternate lifestyle of their parents may be especially fraught with conflict. Still later, telling a future mate—or probably worse, his or her parents—about one's gay or lesbian parents is often stressful. Navigating these life cycle stages may be hazardous at times, but doing do successfully may help the children grow up with greater tolerance for diversity than might ordinarily be the case. Nevertheless, the negative impact of social disapproval and discrimination by the majority culture should not be underestimated and has many effects similar to those experienced by other minority groups.

SUMMARY

One way of understanding both individuals and their families is to study their development over the family life cycle. Continuity and change characterize family life, as the family system progresses over time. While the progression is generally orderly and sequenced, certain discontinuous changes may be particularly disruptive. The appearance of symptomatic behavior in a family member at transition points in the family life cycle may signal that the family is having difficulty in negotiating change.

The family life cycle perspective, dividing family development into a series of stages through which each family inevitably passes, offers an organizing theme for viewing the family as a system moving through time. Specific developmental tasks are expected to be accomplished at each stage en route. Family therapists, particularly structuralists and strategists, are especially interested in how families navigate transitional periods between stages. Passing expected milestones as well as dealing with unexpected crises may temporarily threaten the family's usual developmental progress, causing realignments in the family's organization.

Intact families typically proceed chronologically through a series of family growth phases—coupling (partners moving from independence to interdependence), expansion (accommodating children), and later, contracting (as children move on). Old hierarchical boundaries between parents and children are likely to be replaced by a greater peer relationship as the children reach middle age.

Alternative families, such as those led by single parents or those where remarriage has created a stepfamily, inevitably experience disruptions in the family life cycle before resuming their orderly development. Gay and lesbian families are likely to experience similar life cycle stresses and transitions as do heterosexual families, in addition to those unique to their usually closeted lifestyle.

3

Gender, Culture, and Ethnicity Factors in Family Functioning

Any comprehensive attempt to understand personal or family functioning must take into account the fundamental influences of **gender, culture,** and **ethnicity** in shaping the lives and experiences of men and women. These issues have assumed center stage for family therapists in recent years, extending their thinking beyond observing internal family interaction processes to include the impact of these outside social, political, and historical forces on the belief systems and everyday functioning of family members.

Largely fueled by postmodern inquiries into the diversity of perspectives with which to view life, such factors as gender, client race or ethnicity, sexual preference, and socioeconomic status are now recognized as powerful influences on personal and family perspectives and behavior patterns (Goldenberg & Goldenberg, 1999). Kliman (1994) stresses the interactive nature of these factors so that one cannot really be considered without the others; for example, the experience of being male or female shapes and is in turn shaped by being working poor or middle class or wealthy and by being Chinese American or African American or a Salvadorian refugee. Gender, culture, ethnicity, and social class must be considered in relationship to one another by a therapist who tries to make sense of a client family's hierarchical arrangement, for example, or perhaps the family's social attitudes, expectations, or feelings of belongingness to the majority culture. To state it succinctly, each of our values, beliefs, and attitudes must be viewed through the prism of our own gender, class position, and cultural experience.

In the case of gender, both the feminist movement and, more recently, the emergence of men's studies, have drawn attention to the limiting, and in some cases, pernicious effects of sexist attitudes and patriarchal behavior on family functioning; gender inequities have begun to be addressed both regarding sex-based role assignments within family groups and regarding the wider culture that defines what relationships are possible within families and who is available to participate in those relationships (McGoldrick, Anderson, & Walsh, 1989). One result has been a self-reassessment by family therapists, many of whom had followed theories produced through men's experiences and value systems, not recognizing that women's experiences might be different. This male perspective permeated their viewpoint regarding what constitutes "healthy" family functioning and as a consequence, in the view of Philpot and Brooks (1995), therapists acted as agents of a society that has been oppressive toward women. Another result of this self-analysis has been the thrust toward developing a **gender-sensitive family therapy** that, regardless of theoretical approach, attempts to overcome confining sex-role stereotyping in any clinical interventions efforts.

One important by-product of the pluralistic outlook of the postmodern movement has been an increased cultural awareness of the varied perspectives and lifestyles of the different groups that increasingly make up our society. Just as family therapy theories in the 1950s broke out of the individually focused restrictions of searching for intrapsychic problems, so these more recent efforts to attend to a larger sociocultural context broaden our understanding of cultural influences on family norms, values, belief systems, and behavior patterns. As in the case of a more gender-sensitive outlook, attention to *multiculturalism* has also challenged any previously entrenched ethnocentric views by family therapists of what constitutes a "healthy" family. As Goldenberg and Goldenberg (1999) contend, a family therapist today must take a client family's cultural background into account in order to avoid pathologizing ethnic minority families whose behavior is unfamiliar, taking care not to misdiagnose or mislabel family behavior in the process.

GENDER ISSUES IN FAMILIES AND FAMILY THERAPY

A full understanding of family functioning must consider that men and women experience family life differently, both in their families of origin and in the families they form through marriage. Typically they are reared with different role expectations, beliefs, values, attitudes, goals, and opportunities. Generally speaking, men and women, beginning early in life, learn different problem-solving techniques, cultivate different communication styles, develop different perspectives on sexuality, and hold different expectations for relationships. Philpot, Brooks, Lusterman, and Nutt (1997) maintain that these gender differences in perception and behavior are the result of a complex interactive process between culture and biological forces.

Men and women typically enter marriage and, later, parenthood with different ideas of what will be expected of them, and, not surprisingly, have different family experiences.[1] While overlap in perceptions certainly exist, this gender dichotomy is likely to lead to men and women assigning differing priorities to different values, personality characteristics, and behavior patterns. Moreover, those differing experiences and expectations may lay the groundwork for future conflict, clashes resulting from their polarizing gender training.

The family therapy field has been relatively slow in recognizing that gender plays a differential role in families. As McGoldrick, Anderson, and Walsh (1989)

---

[1]Bernard (1974) observed over two decades ago that in every marriage there are really two marriages—his and hers.

point out, many early family therapists operated in a gender-free fashion, as if family members were interchangeable units of a system with equal power[2] and control (and thus equal responsibility) over the outcome of interactions occurring within the family. The larger social, historical, economic, and political context of family life in a patriarchal society generally was overlooked; therapists by and large felt comfortable taking a neutral stance regarding a family's gender arrangement, thus running the risk of tacitly approving traditional values oppressive to women. The overall result, typically, was for family therapists to perpetuate a myth of equality between men and women within a family seeking their help, ignoring political (that is, power-related) differences between men and women in most relationships.

However, beginning in the late 1970s, an increasing number of family therapists, primarily women at first, began to challenge the underlying assumptions about gender upon which they claimed the family therapy field (and the culture that created it) is based. A number of pioneering studies (Hare-Mustin, 1978; Gilligan, 1982; Goldner, 1985; Avis, 1985) faulted existing family therapy models for failing to pay sufficient attention to gender and power differences in male-female relationships, in effect ignoring how these gender patterns influence internal family interaction, the social context of family life. Not yet offering an alternative **feminist family therapy** position[3]—that was to come in the late 80s—these critics nevertheless argued that family therapists, reflecting the larger society, often reinforced traditional gender roles (Avis, 1996). Underlying such formulations, they asserted, is an endorsement of traditional male/female roles that depreciate qualities (dependency, nurturing, emotional expressiveness) traditionally associated with women while extolling those qualities (aggressiveness, competitiveness, rationality) held in high regard by men. Attempting to correct this gender bias, these feminist-informed therapists were starting to challenge the social, cultural, historic, economic, and political conditions that shaped not only the unique development and experiences of women but also their relationships with men.

One noteworthy undertaking—The Women's Project in Family Therapy, co-led by Marianne Walters, Betty Carter, Peggy Papp, and Olga Silverstein—begun in 1977 and recently concluded, represents one such ongoing examination of gender patterns in family relationships as well as patriarchal assumptions underlying classic family therapy approaches. Primarily through workshops, these family therapists, despite differences in theoretical outlook and clinical approach, have offered a female-informed clinical perspective that challenged the field's conventional wisdom. They argued that a field devoted to families had, paradoxically, relied on outdated blueprints of male-determined, stereotypic sex roles and gender-defined functions within families. Their text, *The Invisible Web* (Walters, Carter, Papp, & Silverstein, 1989)

[2]Power within a family typically is gained in a variety of ways: by gender, age, earning power, respect, or fear. Within society at large, power is unequally distributed based on such factors as gender, class, race, ethnicity, age, sexual orientation, profession, and degree of physical ability (Forces & Thomas, 1996).

[3]There is no single entity entitled feminist family therapy, since there are therapists practicing from all of the approaches we will consider later in this text who may regard themselves as feminist-informed and thus may take a variety of approaches with families. Rather, as Avis (1996) emphasizes, feminist family therapy is a "*perspective* on gender relations, a lens through which a therapist views his or her clients" (p. 223). Regardless of theoretical outlook, all address gender and power imbalances in their clients' lives.

offers a gender analysis to their clinical work, as they describe their experiences in applying a feminist perspective to their understanding of gender and power-based family issues. Without offering any formal training program, this project has had enormous influence in the field, moving family therapists to think beyond what is occurring within the family to a consideration of broader social and cultural considerations (Simon, 1997). As a result of calling attention to the constraining experiences of women, the foursome have helped to develop a practical, nonsexist set of therapeutic interventions that take gender considerations into account.

Since the field of family therapy was largely defined by men in its earlier years, inevitably male language and attitudes dominated early theories. As McGoldrick, Anderson, and Walsh (1989) observe, one consequence was to consider certain behaviors (for example, emotionality, tenderness) as less mature or less desirable than other behaviors (thinking, objectivity); the result, they noted, was to "unwittingly promote family patterns in which women are devalued, blamed, and made to feel guilty for patterns and lives they have little freedom to change" (p. 10). Hoffman (1990) endorses the notion that a male bias was built into family concepts that take the heterosexual, patriarchal family as the norm, arguing that terms such as "overinvolved mother" or "enmeshed family" are sexist and tend to blame mothers in particular for family problems.

Feminist-informed therapists consider such cybernetic concepts as "circular causality" (to designate a repetitive pattern of mutually reinforcing behavior in a male-female relationship) especially repugnant. They insist that this systems-based concept implies that each participant has equal power and control in a transaction, which they dispute. Particularly in the case of physical abuse (rape, battering, incest) by men against women, they reject the cybernetic notion that both partners are engaging in a mutual causal pattern and that it is the subsequent behavioral sequence, for which they are coresponsible, that results in the violent episode (Goldner, Penn, Sheinberg, & Walker, 1990).

Critical of the implication that no one therefore is to blame—a violation without a violator—thus clearing the aggressor of responsibility, feminists emphasize greater masculine power in human relationships, the superior physical strength of men and the corresponding vulnerability of women. They contend that the cybernetic epistemology tends to blame the victim for colluding in her own victimization either as a coresponsible participant or by remaining in the relationship. Avis (1996) points out that implying that all interactional behavior originates within the interaction itself makes it impossible to search for causes outside the interaction; here she cites such external possible causes as "cultural beliefs about appropriate gender behavior, a preexisting propensity to use violent behavior, or differences in power with which each partner enters the relationship" (p. 225).

Feminists argue further that the field of family therapy has by and large ignored gender issues in conceptualizing family life, except to focus on a woman's role as nurturer, caretaker, and helper to her family (husband, children, parents). A woman, according to Gilligan (1982), tends to define herself within the context of relationships on which she in turn relies (while men are more likely to value autonomy and separation). Gilligan contends that men, in their theories of psychological development, have tended to downplay or devalue that need for affiliation, viewing it as weakness rather than an expression of strength. She believes that such theories, because of their inherent male bias, equate maturity with independence, rationality, and action. Such qualities as caring for the needs of others, warmth, and emotional expressiveness, which our society defines as necessary for feminine behavior, are at the same time given short shrift as expressions of the inferiority of the "weaker sex."

Rachel Hare-Mustin (1987) describes gender as the "basic category on which the world is organized" (p. 15); according to Judith Avis (1996), gender is "a fundamental dimension of personal and social organization—of personal identity, family relationships, therapeutic relationships, sociocultural privilege and oppression" (p. 221). Hare-Mustin, often credited with being the first to raise feminist issues among family therapists, suggests that commonly observed male/female behavioral differences simply reflect established gender arrangements in society, rather than any essential set of differences in the nature of men as opposed to women, as Gilligan proposes. A woman's typically greater concern with relationships, according to Hare-Mustin, can best be understood as a need to please others when one lacks power. In this view, a woman's behavior reflects her less powerful role position vis-à-vis a man's, rather than resulting from an inherent weakness of character. *Where the powerful advocate rules and rationality, the weak espouse relatedness.*

Hare-Mustin (1987) offers the following example:

> Thus, in husband-wife conflicts, husbands use logic, wives call on caring. But, in parent-child conflicts, parents, including mothers, emphasize rules; it is the children who appeal for understanding. Society rewards rationality, not emotions, but which is used is associated with who has the power, and not primarily with being male or female. (p. 22)

The entry of women, whether single, married, or heads of single-parent households, into the world of paid work has had a profound effect on evolving male-female relationships. In recent years, women have been marrying later (or choosing not to marry at all) and are having fewer children. Young couples who do decide to become parents, as noted earlier, must rearrange the family system and renegotiate the roles each plays, particularly if the wife continues to work outside the home, as the overwhelming number do.

Breaking out of stereotypic male/female roles regarding domestic and work responsibilities is essential. However, though to a lesser extent than before, working wives continue to bear the major responsibility for child care and most household chores. In addition, they are likely to take on the obligation of maintaining contact with both their families of origin, as well as sustaining friendships. Traditionally, while women's domain has been the management of the home and the raising of the children, men have taken on the responsibility for financial support and, if necessary, the family's physical protection. According to Weiss's (1985) survey, this traditional family organization is likely to persist even when the woman works, although Silberstein's (1992) more recent survey found that the arrival of children often propels dual-career couples into more egalitarian role sharing. Silberstein's data reveal that the contributions of both parents are now approximately equal on certain school-related tasks and some household chores. However, women still shoulder more of the responsibility for meal-related tasks as well as child-care chores.

With the children out of the house and forming families of their own, men and women may find themselves with differing priorities, according to McGoldrick (1988b). She believes that men may wish to seek greater closeness to their wives, while the latter may begin to feel energized about developing their own lives, perhaps through resumed careers or other activities outside the home. If serious marital tension leads to divorce, as it sometimes does at this stage, McGoldrick contends that women are especially vulnerable. Not only are they less likely than men to remarry, but their embeddedness in relationships, their orientation toward interdependence, their lifelong subordination of achievement to caring for others, and their conflicts over competitive success may make them especially susceptible to despair.

Finally, since women are apt to outlive men, many may find themselves alone and financially impoverished. Very likely they will turn to their daughters (or perhaps daughters-in-law) for support and care, since women in our society shoulder most of the eldercare, with the possible exception of managing finances for the elderly.

Therapy from a Gender-Sensitive Perspective

To be gender-sensitive (or feminist-informed) is to be aware of the differences in behavior, attitudes, and socialization experiences of growing up masculine or feminine, especially differences in power, status, position, and privilege within the family and in society in general. Brooks (1992) observes that past "gender-blindness" on the part of family therapists was first detected by women—not surprising, considering they were most likely, at least overtly, to be harmed by sexist attitudes—and thus focused principally on the woman's perspective. However, he reminds us that men too have been subjected to substantial role constraints and disadvantages as a result of their masculine socialization experiences. They too may have suffered from sexist therapeutic interventions that have condoned restricting men to a narrow range of family roles (such as breadwinner) while robbing them of the experience of participating in roles (say, child rearing) usually assigned to women. Brooks contends that just as the feminist perspective has started to be incorporated into family therapy practices, so should the perspectives of "men's studies" theorists.

Men's studies, a recent addition to the field of gender examination in our society, attempts to extend feminist explorations by attending to role restrictions in men's lives (Brod, 1987; Kimmel, 1987). O'Neil (1982) draws attention to the traditional "masculine mystique" that programs men toward curtailed emotional expressiveness, obsession with achievement and success, restricted affectionate behavior, and concern with power, control, and competition. Homophobia is often a characteristic of such a mystique, resulting in a man's fear that becoming close to another man might cause others to consider him gay. Proof of masculinity from this perspective often derives from the ability to display power and control, most likely at the expense of women.

Doyle (1994) identifies five elements that further define common male gender-role socialization experiences: (1) an *antifeminine* element, in which young boys learn to avoid in their own behavior anything considered feminine; (2) a *success* element that values competition and winning; (3) an *aggressive* element, physically fighting when necessary to defend oneself; (4) a *sexual* element, believing men should be preoccupied with sex; and (5) a *self-reliant* element, calling for men to be independent and self-sufficient and not to seek help from others. In areas ranging from job performance to sexual functioning, athletic skills or mental alertness, men typically compare themselves with other men and concern themselves about how they rank (Philpot, Brooks, Lusterman, & Nutt, 1997).

One interpersonal area where gender, asymmetrical power, and control intersect concerns family violence and sexual abuse. Brooks (1992) is especially concerned that the treatment of violence in men ignores the cultural context—and societal sanction—in which violence in men takes place, since for many men socialization toward violence is part of their upbringing. He argues that to be successful, any antiviolence program must be gender-sensitive and include the preventive antiviolence resocialization of men so that they will not rely on violence as an interpersonal strategy. As he observes (Brooks, 1992):

> Just as young girls deserve the opportunity for socialization into achievement and self-sufficiency, boys deserve to be freed from the extreme emphasis on physical violence and emotional toughness as proof of masculine worth. (p. 31)

Gender-sensitive family therapy is intended to liberate and empower both male and female clients, enabling them to move beyond prescribed roles determined by their biological status to ones in which they can exercise choice. In practice this means overcoming internalized social norms and expectations for every client; gender stereotypes in male as well as female clients require examination (Good, Gilbert, & Scher, 1990). Therapy that is gender-aware is action-oriented, not merely nonsexist in viewpoint (see Table 3.1). Whereas nonsexist counseling attempts to avoid reinforcing stereotypical thinking regarding gender roles, proactive gender-sensitive

Table 3.1   Characteristics of Gender-Sensitive Family Therapy

Nonsexist counseling	Empowerment/feminist/ gender-aware counseling
Does not reinforce stereotyped gender roles.	Helps clients recognize the impact of social, cultural, and political factors on their lives.
Encourages clients to consider a wide range of choices, especially in regard to careers.	Helps clients transcend limitations resulting from gender stereotyping.
Avoids allowing gender stereotypes to affect diagnoses.	Recognizes the degree to which individual behaviors may reflect internalization of harmful social standards.
Avoids use of sexist assessment instruments.	Includes gender-role analysis as a component of assessment.
Treats male and female clients equally.	Helps clients develop and integrate traits that are culturally defined as "masculine" and "feminine."
Avoids misuse of power in the counseling relationship.	Develops collaborative counselor-client relationships.

Source: Reprinted with permission from J. A. Lewis, "Gender Sensitivity and Family Empowerment," *Topics in Family Psychology and Counseling,* 1(4), p. 3, © 1992, Aspen Publishers, Inc.

family therapy goes beyond this goal, deliberately helping clients recognize the limitations on their perceived alternatives imposed by internalizing these stereotypes. As Lewis (1992) observes, clients are better helped when they have an opportunity to perceive and overcome social and political barriers. She maintains that the family as a whole can be more effectively empowered if its members work through its assumptions about what is possible for each of them, freely choosing the life—free of role stereotyping—that makes sense to them. Examples of gender-sensitive therapeutic techniques are offered by Philpot, Brooks, Lusterman, and Nutt (1997), four family therapists with differing theoretical orientations who describe how each goes about bridging the separate gender worlds of men and women.

MULTICULTURAL AND CULTURE-SPECIFIC CONSIDERATIONS

Just as an appreciation of gender is essential in gaining a fuller picture of a family's organization, so too understanding families requires a grasp of the cultural context (race, ethnic group membership, religion, social class) in which that family functions and the subsequent cultural norms by which it lives. Culture—shared, learned behavior transmitted from one generation to the next—impacts families in a variety of ways, some trivial, others central to their functioning. Language, norms, values, ideals, customs, music, and food preferences are all largely determined by cultural factors (Cuellar & Glazer, 1996). As family therapists have attempted in recent years to apply existing therapy models to previously overlooked cultural groups, they have also had to gain greater awareness of their own cultural background and values and to examine the possible impact of these factors in pathologizing ethnic minority families whose values, gender roles, discipline practices, forms of emotional expression, and so forth, are different from theirs or the majority culture (Fontes & Thomas, 1996).

Developing a Multicultural Framework

A multicultural outlook champions a general culturally sensitive approach with families and urges therapists to become more culturally literate and culturally competent, remembering to take client cultural histories into account before undertaking assessments, forming judgments, and initiating intervention procedures. This perspective is intended to alert the family therapist to keep in mind that how he or she assesses, counsels, or in general communicates with families is screened not only through professional knowledge but also through his or her own "cultural filters"—those values, attitudes, customs, religious beliefs and practices, and especially outlooks regarding what constitutes normal behavior that stem from the therapist's particular cultural background (Giordano & Carini-Giordano, 1995).

More than learning about specific cultures, advocates of multiculturalism urge the adoption of an open and flexible attitude about diverse cultures and cultural influences but not one tied to any specific cultural groups. At the same time, they urge therapists to gain greater awareness of their own values, assumptions, and beliefs, understanding that these are not absolutes but arise frcm the therapist's own cultural heritage.

Cultural Specificity and Family Systems

Those family therapists who advocate a cultural-specific approach urge more detailed knowledge of common culturally based family patterns of unfamiliar groups. McGoldrick, Giordano, and Pearce (1996), for example, have brought together several dozen experts to provide detailed knowledge about a wide variety of racial and ethnic groupings. This presentation recognizes that we are increasingly a heterogeneous society, a pluralistic one made up of varying races and ethnic groups, as millions migrate here seeking a better life. One in every four Americans today is a person of color (Homma-True, Greene, Lopez, & Trimble, 19C3). Clearly, with such increased diversity, family therapists need to enlarge their focus from exclusivity on the interior of the family to a broader investigation of family processes that pays attention to the larger sociocultural contexts that influence behavior (Falicov, 1988b).

One way to achieve that goal is to learn as much as possible about a specific culture before assessing a family in order to determine the extent to which its members identify with their ethnic background and to ascertain what part issues relating to their ethnicity play in the presenting problem (Giordano & Carini-Giordano, 1995). Just as it would be a mistake to judge the family behavior of clients from another culture as deviant because it is unfamiliar, so therapists must also be careful not to overlook or minimize deviant behavior, simply attributing it to cultural differences.

Taking gender, social class position, and racial or ethric identification into account, a comprehensive understanding of a family's development and current functioning must assess its cultural group's kinship networks, socialization experiences, communication styles, typical male/female interactive patterns, the role of the extended family, and similar culturally linked attitudinal and behavioral arrangements (Goldenberg & Goldenberg, 1993).

Family therapists must try to distinguish between a client family's patterns that are *universal* (common to a wide variety of families), *culture-specific* (common to a group, such as African Americans or Cuban Americans or perhaps lesbian families), or *idiosyncratic* (unique to this particular family) in their assessment of family functioning. That is, they must discriminate between those family situations where cultural issues are relevant and those where cultural issues are tangential (Falicov, 1988b).

At the same time, they must keep in mind that while it is typically helpful to gain awareness of differences that might be attributable to ethnicity or racial characteristics of a specific group, there is also a risk in assuming a sameness among families sharing a common cultural background. Thus, as Fontes and Thomas (1996) caution, a culture-specific family therapy outlook offers useful guidelines, but these guidelines should not be considered recipe books for working with individual families. Although coming from the same cultural background, different families have differing histories, may come from different social classes, or may show different degrees of acculturation. As an example, these authors observe that members of a

Mexican American family may identify themselves primarily as Catholic, or Californian, or professional, or Democrat; their country of origin or cultural background may actually be peripheral to the way they live their lives. Ultimately the therapist's job is to understand how the client family developed and currently views its own culture.

Family therapists must exercise caution before using norms that stem from the majority cultural matrix in assessing the attitudes, beliefs, and transactional patterns of those whose cultural patterns differ from theirs. Beyond an appreciation of individual cultural influences, the family therapist must pay attention to what is unique about living as an ethnic minority—the language barriers, the cultural shock, the prejudice and discrimination, the feelings of powerlessness, the suspicion of institutions, the hopelessness, the rage. For example, in working with African American families, Thomas and Sillen (1974) point out that for white therapists to be insistently "color blind" to racial differences is no virtue if it means denial of differences in experiences, history, and social existence between themselves and their clients. The myth of sameness in effect denies the importance of color in the lives of African American families, and thus closes off an opportunity for therapist and family members to deal with sensitive race-related issues.

Further, in working with immigrant families, care must be taken to distinguish between recently arrived immigrant families, immigrant-American families (foreign-born parents, American-born or American-educated children), and immigrant-descendent families (Ho, 1987). Each has a special set of adaptational problems—economic, educational, cognitive, affective, emotional. In regard to immigrant groups, their adaptation or acculturation is likely to be a function of four factors: (1) how long ago newcomers arrived; (2) the circumstances of their arrival; (3) the support system they found upon arrival; and (4) the degree of acceptance they found here.

Ethnicity and the Transmission of Culture

Ethnicity refers to "the unique characteristics of a social grouping sharing national origin and linguistic and cultural traditions, with which members may or may not identify" (Kliman, 1994, p. 29). As in the case of racial membership, ethnic background profoundly affects a family's everyday experiences; it surely is a fundamental determinant of how families establish and reinforce acceptable values, attitudes, behavior patterns, and modes of emotional expression. Transmitted over generations by the family, ethnicity patterns may surpass race, religion, or national origin in significance for the family, particularly because they represent the individual's and the family's psychological needs for identity and a sense of historical continuity.

Our ethnic background influences how we think, how we feel, how we work, how we relax, how we celebrate holidays and rituals, how we express our anxieties, and how we feel about illness or life and death. Ethnicity patterns, reinforced by family tradition and perhaps community membership, may operate in subtle ways, frequently outside of our awareness, but their impact may nevertheless be broad, deep, and potent. These patterns are apt to play a significant role throughout the family life cycle, although their impact may vary greatly between groups, as well as within a group itself. In some families who hold on to traditional ways, clinging to cohorts from their religious or cultural background, ethnic values and dentifications may be particularly strong and likely to be retained for generations (Goldenberg & Goldenberg, 1998).

Even the definition of "family" differs in different ethnic groups. The dominant white Anglo Saxon Protestant (WASP) focus is on the intact nuclear family, extending back over generations. Blacks expand their definition to include a wide informal network of kin and community. Italian Americans think in terms of tightly knit three- or four-generational families, often including godfathers and old friends; all may be involved in family decision making, may live in close proximity to one another, and may share life cycle transitions together. The Chinese tend to go even further, including all their ancestors and all their descendants in their definition of family membership (McGoldrick, 1988a).

Native American family systems may be part of extended networks, including several households. A nonkin can become a family member through being a namesake of a child, and consequently assumes family obligations and responsibilities for child rearing and role modeling. Hispanic Americans, the fastest-growing ethnic group in the country, take deep pride in family membership, with a man generally using both his father's and mother's name together with his given name. (The name José García Rivera thus reflects that García is his father's family name and Rivera his mother's. If this person were addressed by a single name, the father's family name, García, would be used, reflecting the Hispanic patriarchal pattern) (Ho, 1987).

Family loyalty, unity, and honor, as well as family commitment, obligation, and responsibility, characterize most Hispanic American families, so much so that sacrifices of family members' own needs or pleasures for the sake of the family are often encouraged, if not expected (McGoldrick, Garcia Preto, Hines, & Lee, 1991). Similarly, the family is typically central in the lives of Asian American families, with members expected to behave with loyalty and devotion to its values. Filial piety— loyalty, respect, and devotion of children to their parents—is of prime importance in traditional Asian families (del Carmen, 1990).

Family life cycle timing is influenced by ethnic considerations. Mexican Americans tend to have longer courtship periods and extended childhoods beyond the dominant American pattern, but shorter adolescent periods and hastened adulthood. Similarly, different groups give different importance to life cycle transition points. The Irish wake is a ritual that represents a view of death as the most important transition, freeing humans so that they can go on to a happier afterlife. Polish American families emphasize weddings, their lengthy celebration reflecting the importance of the family's continuity into the next generation. For Jewish American families, the Bar Mitzvah signifies the transition into adulthood, reflecting the high value placed on continued intellectual development (McGoldrick, 1988a).

Child-rearing practices may also vary greatly. While the dominant American pattern is for the mother to have primary responsibility, African Americans often rely on grandparents and extended family members to care for children, especially if the mother is working outside the home (Manns, 1988). Americans of Greek and Puerto Rican background tend to indulge young infants, but later become strict with children, particularly girls. Adolescent girls from Italian American families may find themselves in intergenerational conflicts with parents and grandparents as they rebel against traditional female roles of waiting on fathers, brothers, and later, husbands and sons.

The danger in these generalizations, of course, is that they run the risk of stereotyping. As we have noted earlier, and as Ho (1987) reminds us, there is not only considerable interethnic group diversity but also marked intraethnic group heterogeneity. It is important to remember that some families are more assimilated than others; some have long histories of intermarriage; some individuals rebel against their cultural mandates; and social class differences play a decisive role, which we elaborate on later in this chapter. The importance of delineating common family patterns is in emphasizing the often-overlooked role of ethnocultural factors in behavior (McGoldrick, Pearce, & Giordano, 1982).

What of families formed by intermarriage between partners from different racial or ethnic groups? While a small group in terms of the percentage of U.S. families, 3 million Americans told the Census Bureau in 1990 that they were living with someone of a different race (Goldenberg & Goldenberg, 1998). Differing experiences with societal rejection or acceptance or being marginalized, differing culturally determined gender-role experiences, and in some cases differing social class upbringings all need to be considered if the cross-cultural couple is to establish a balanced partnership that acknowledges and respects their cultural similarities and differences (Falicov, 1986). A glimpse at the potential set of misunderstandings can be seen in the following:

> An Italian American may interpret her Vermont Yankee husband's and in-laws' (unsolicited) respect for her privacy as cold and unloving; he may respond to his wife's and in-laws' (unsolicited) advice and emotional displays as incursions into his privacy. My WASP husband used to wonder why I phoned my brothers without news to relate; it broke my Jewish heart how rarely he called his sister. Even family members with similar backgrounds may need help in distinguishing assumptions based on culture, class, or family idiosyncracy. They may interpret similar cultural norms differently, or expect partners and in-laws to share beliefs unique to their own families of origin. (Kliman, 1994, p. 31)

Before closing this section, it is necessary to remind ourselves that each therapist's values are inevitably embedded in that person's gender, ethnic, and social class experiences and current circumstances. Since therapists inevitably expose these perspectives (biases?) in their interactions with their clients, they need to be aware of their own values and beliefs as they help client families to sort out theirs. Rather than oversimplified pictures to be taken at face value, the diverse ethnic profiles presented here are intended to call attention to the rich variety of human experiences and behavior—to emphasize the fact that family therapists cannot ignore the influence of cultural idiosyncracies in assessing and treating families they might otherwise label deviant or dysfunctional.

Poverty, Class, and Family Functioning

Every cultural group has social class divisions, and each social class is made up of members from different cultural groups. Men and women in each class experience life differently from one another, differently from their counterparts in other classes, and differently from others of the same class but from another cultural group. No one group is monolithic: not all African Americans are poor; not all whites are middle class. In actuality, most of the nation's poor are white, although African Americans and other people of color are disproportionately represented among the poor. Increasingly it takes two parents—and two paychecks—to maintain a household's grip on middle-class status in the United States today.

Social class differences act as primary dividers within a society. Not only do they largely determine access to many resources (including therapy), but they also are influential in shaping beliefs, values, and behaviors (Fontes & Thomas, 1996). Despite the observation by Kliman (1994) and others that our culture cherishes the myth that we are all middle class (or have equal opportunity to become middle class), the facts are otherwise: over 14 percent of all American families live below the poverty line, and many more live just above it. According to Columbia University's National Center for Children of Poverty, children living with unmarried mothers are five times more likely to be poor than those living with married parents. However, living with both parents offers no guarantee of clearing the poverty hurdle: more than one-third of children living in poverty were living with both parents (Healy, 1998).

Access to power is also largely determined by class membership. As Aponte (1994a) observes:

> The poor are dependent upon and vulnerable to the overreaching power of society. They cannot insulate themselves from society's ills. They canno buy their children private schooling when the public school fails. They cannot buy into an upscale neighborhood when their housing project becomes too dangerous. When society stumbles, its poorest citizens are tossed about and often crushed. (p. 8)

Poor African American families, embedded in a context of chronic unemployment and discrimination, are particularly limited in their abilities to function in ways that permit family members to thrive (Hines, 1988). The decline in marriage rates among African Americans, coupled with the increased number of teenage mothers, has added to their family crises. Edelman (1987), founder of the Children's Defense Fund, argues that the interrelated factors of poverty, male joblessness, and poor, female-headed households operate together to perpetuate generations of membership in America's underclass. In a seemingly endless circle, the loosening of family structure has led to increased out-of-wedlock births and, correspondingly, increased child poverty; joblessness and its resulting poverty have led to a decline in the number of marriageable males and the further weakening of the family structure. Thus, children are poor, according to Edelman's analysis, not only because many live in fatherless homes but also because the single parents with whom they live are likely to be unemployed or, if employed, earn low wages.

Aponte (1987), too, emphasizes the erosion of family structure and the creation of what he terms *underorganized* (rather than disorganized) families. Living in such situations through generations, families of whatever racial background "learn to view as normal their own impotence" (p. 2). They are forced to accept their dependence upon the community's network of social institutions (welfare, public housing, publicly funded health care) without the necessary political or economic power to influence outcomes. Where fatherless homes predominate, roles lose their distinctiveness, and children may grow up too quickly while being at the same time intellectually and emotionally stunted in development.

Life cycle progression among the poor is often accelerated by teenage pregnancy. The stages we have described in Chapter 2 for middle-class, intact families are often fast-forwarded; the "launching" stage for a young mother's children, for example, may occur when she is still at *her* mother's home (Fulmer, 1988). In the same manner, a "single adult" label is not likely to apply to an adolescent mother with children, nor is the parent-child relationship most likely to be the central one around which the family is organized. More probably, grandmother-mother-daughter relationships predominate, and several generations of family are likely to be alive at the same time. The basic family unit in such situations is apt to include extended three- or four-generational networks of kin. Such kinship groups at times function as "multiple-parent families" with reciprocal obligations to one another, sharing meager resources as efficiently as possible (Fulmer, 1988).

The family therapist, likely to be middle class (in viewpoint if not necessarily in origin), must be careful not to regard being poor as synonymous with leading a chaotic, disorganized life, because, for example, long-term planning may not be present. It is essential to distinguish between those families who have been poor for many generations (victims of what Aponte, 1987, calls structural poverty), poor intermittently or temporarily (while divorced but before remarriage), or recently poor because of loss (such as unemployment or the death of the major wage earner). It also helps to be aware that some poor people, including those chronically unemployed, share middle-class values (regarding such things as work and education) while others embrace more survival-based values of the working class as a result of their life experiences. Still others, termed the *underclass* by Incan and Ferran (1990), "make their living illegally or otherwise on the fringes of society" (p. 29). Some lead lives that are a series of crises, and others have forged family and social networks that are resourceful and workable. Above all, any efforts to equate poverty with psychological deviance first must take into account the harsh and confining social conditions usually associated with being poor.

SUMMARY

Gender, culture, and ethnicity are three key interrelated factors in shaping lives. Men and women are reared with different role expectations, experiences, goals, and opportunities, and these differences influence later gender patterns in family relationships. Feminists contend that psychological research and clinical practice have been filled with outdated patriarchal assumptions and offer a male-biased perspective of sex roles and gender-defined functions within a family. They reject certain cybernetic concepts such as circular causality since such concepts fail to take differences in power and control between men and women into account, in effect blaming the victim for her victimization. The entry of women in large numbers into the workforce in recent years has also helped break some long-held stereotypic views regarding domestic and work responsibilities. Gender-sensitive therapy is directed at empowering clients, male and female, to move beyond prescribed sex roles based on biological status to ones in which they can exercise choice.

Cultural diversity is increasingly a part of American life, and family therapists have widened their focus from the family to include larger sociocultural contexts that influence behavior. A multicultural emphasis urges therapists to be more culturally sensitive, while a culturally specific emphasis asserts the importance of learning about culturally based family patterns of specific groups.

Ethnicity and social class considerations also influence family lifestyles. Ethnic heritage may help determine how families establish values, behavior patterns, and modes of emotional expression, and how they progress through the family life cycle. Living in poverty, whether temporarily or as part of poverty patterns extending over generations, may erode family structure and create underorganized families. In poor families, life cycle progression is often accelerated by early pregnancy, frequently of unwed mothers.

4

The Family as a Psychosocial System

We have proposed to this point adopting a relationship frame of reference in studying a family's functioning, paying simultaneous attention to its *structure* (the way it arranges, organizes, and maintains itself at any given cross section of time) and its *processes* (the way it evolves, adapts, and changes over time). At the same time, we have underscored the contextual nature of family functioning: not only are the lives of family members interconnected, but the family's structure and processes are themselves embedded in complex extended family, neighborhood, institutional, class, ethnic, and cultural systems.

Families are living, ongoing entities, organized wholes with members in a continuous, interactive, patterned relationship with one another extending over time and space. A change in any one component inevitably is associated with changes in other components with which it is in relation. Beyond the relationships of its constituent members, the family itself is continuously linked to larger systems in a bidirectional manner; the interplay between families and those social systems tells us a great deal about the level of success of family functioning.

In this chapter we introduce some of the underlying concepts of **general systems theory**, first proposed by biologist Ludwig von Bertalanffy in the late 1920s. The theory, elaborated and refined over decades, represents an ambitious attempt to promulgate a comprehensive theoretical model that would have relevance to all living systems. It offers a set of assumptions regarding the maintenance of any organism or entity as a result of the complex interaction of its elements or parts. Focusing attention on the pattern of relationships within a system, or between systems, instead of studying parts in isolation, Bertalanffy's general systems model was soon seen to have wide applicability to the sciences, social sciences, medicine, and philosophy. Family therapists, seeking a scientific model, were particularly attracted to the notion that they attend more to the transactions taking place between family members than to the separate qualities or characteristics of each family member. For them, systems concepts became a useful *language* for conceptualizing a family's interactive process.

Both general systems theory and the first-order cybernetics concepts described in Chapter 1 catapulted to scientific attention during the 1940s, the former from the biological sciences and the latter from the mechanical concepts of physics and engineering. Arising at a time ripe for a paradigm change, both models are based on many of the same underlying assumptions regarding self-regulating systems. Indeed, both terms—*general systems theory* and *cybernetics*—often are used interchangeably by family therapists who wish to emphasize that a comprehensive view of family patterns requires a look through an interactive prism rather than a study of the movements of the separate family members.

Most family therapists acknowledge a theoretical debt to general systems theory, freely (if somewhat loosely) borrowing such concepts as *homeostasis* (to describe families as seeking balance between stability and change) and *open systems* (to explain how a family sustains itself by exchanging information with its environment). At the same time, they believe that such first-order cybernetic concepts as *recursive sequences* and *circular causality* help clarify the interconnectedness of members as participants in self-corrective feedback loops that help the larger whole, the family system, maintain balance or a steady state.

Systems theory has emerged as an overall concept, encompassing both general systems theory and cybernetics, and focusing on the relationship between elements rather than on the elements themselves. In actuality, according to Constantine (1986), systems terms are not used by therapists with the precision and rigor with which they were originally formulated, but rather simply allude to the idea of a family as a complexly organized, durable, and ongoing causal network of related components.

Indeed, postmodernists have been particularly rejecting of the systems metaphor both as too mechanical and as a modernistic view that erroneously believes it can discover universal truths. They argue that it encourages therapists to deceive themselves into believing they can objectively and impartially diagnose families, looking for flaws in their structure rather than, as White (1995) urges, helping families construct new concepts about themselves. Moreover, postmodernists such as deShazer (1991) criticize systems theorists for reifying concepts—as though families actually possess constructs (rules, feedback, homeostasis) borrowed from cybernetics and general systems theory—rather than simply using the systems metaphor more generally in describing families.

Feminists too have found fault with the systems metaphor for assuming families function according to specific systemic rules divorced from their social, historical, economic, and political contexts. Doing so, as Avis (1996) points out, the systems view, narrowly focused, tends to see family difficulties arising entirely within a family's interpersonal relationships, missing how gender and power relations in society are mirrored in family life.

Nevertheless, although these postmodern and feminist criticisms have merit, and "systems" has become something of a catch word that runs the risk of being taken too literally, the concept should not be undervalued; it has helped bring about a profound shift in thinking, from a reductionistic search for linear cause-and-effect events to "explain" personal disorder to a broader examination of the ongoing context in which current family dysfunctional patterns occur. For most family therapists, systems language continues to provide a basic tool for thinking in interactional terms. Used in a broad sense, systems theory lays the foundation for a comprehensive set of therapeutic interventions

> for treating the family, including individuals, couples, nuclear families, families of origin, medical systems, and other larger contexts (such as schools and work) and the culture and ethnic contexts in which all of these are embedded. At any particular time, a unique feature of systems therapy is that it gives the therapist a paradigm from which to view multiple causes and contexts of behavior. (Mikesell, Lusterman, & McDaniel, 1995, p. xv)

SOME CHARACTERISTICS OF A FAMILY SYSTEM

The concepts of **organization** and **wholeness** are keys to understanding how systems operate. If a system represents a set of units that stand in some consistent relationship to one another, then we can infer that the system is organized around those relationships. Further, we can say that the parts or elements of the system interact with each other in a predictable, "organized" fashion. Similarly, we can assume that the elements, once combined, produce an entity—a whole—that is greater than the sum of its parts. It follows that no system can be adequately understood or fully explained once it has been broken down into its component parts; and that no element within the system can ever be understood in isolation since it never functions independently.

A family represents one such system, in which the member components are organized into a group, forming a whole that transcends the sum of its separate parts. When we speak of the Sanchez family, for example, we are discussing a complex and recognizable entity—not simply the aggregate of Mr. Sanchez plus Mrs. Sanchez plus the Sanchez children. Understanding the dynamic relationships among the components (family members) is far more illuminating than simply summing up those components (Ackerman, 1984). The relationships between the family members are complex, and factions, alliances, coalitions, and tensions exist. Causality within the family system is circular and multidirectional.

According to Nichols and Everett (1986), the way in which the family is organized defines its basic structure—its coherence and fit. As these authors illustrate, a family can be organized around a rigid, dominant male head, his acquiescent wife, and rebellious children. Or perhaps the children are compliant and the wife angry or combative. On the other hand, the family may be more matriarchal—a strong woman, her angrily passive husband, and children who are caught up in the continuous parental struggles. Whatever the arrangement, the family's organization offers important clues as to its consistent or repetitive interactive patterns.

As Leslie (1988) observes, because of the system's wholeness, the movement of each component influences the whole and is explained, in part, by movement in related parts of the system. Focusing on the functioning of one element (member) becomes secondary to understanding the connections or relationships among family members and the overall organization of the system. As an illustration, Leslie notes that a family with two children does not simply add a new member when a baby is born; the family becomes a new entity with accompanying changes in family interactive patterns.

In this family therapy scene, cotherapists work together with a husband and wife who sought help because of their frequent quarrels over disciplining their 6-year-old hyperactive daugther.

Should a 2-year-old start to engage in hostile outbursts, linear explanations often attribute the new behavior to jealousy or infer the toddler is reacting to the loss of his mother's undivided attention, since she now must devote a great deal of attention to the newborn baby. A systems perspective, on the other hand, might look at how the family has reorganized after the new birth. Perhaps in reorganizing around the infant, the mother has assumed primary care of the infant, and the father the major responsibility for the older children, while the older son has been designated a helper to his mother with the newborn. The toddler may have lost his customary role in the family. From this vantage point, his hostile behavior may be signaling the family that their reorganization is inadequate or perhaps incomplete in meeting the needs of all of its members. To examine the motives of the toddler alone, without addressing the system's interactive patterns, would be to miss the point that the system requires alteration (Leslie, 1988). In the same way, it is imperative that the therapist address broader issues—the mother who may be giving up her work to remain at home with the children, the father who may work longer hours away from home in order to compensate for the income loss, the grandparents who may become involved in caring for the children, the availability of adequate child care, and so on. Adopting a systems view calls for more than viewing the family constellation in isolation.

Family Rules

A family is a cybernetically rule-governed system. The interaction of family members typically follows organized, established patterns, based on the family structure; these patterns enable each person to learn what is permitted or expected of him or her as well as others in family transactions. Usually unstated, such rules characterize, regulate, and help stabilize how—and how well—families function as a unit. They form a basis for the development of family traditions, and largely determine expectations of the members vis-à-vis one another. A family's rules, then, reveal its values, help set up family roles consistent with these values, and in the process provide dependability and regularity to relationships within the family system. Rules frequently are carried over from previous generations and often have a powerful cultural component.

The observation that family interactions follow certain persistent patterns—rules—was first made by Don Jackson (1965a), a pioneer in family therapy. He observed that partners in a marriage face multiple challenges as potential collaborators in wage earning, housekeeping, socializing, lovemaking, and parenting. Early in their relationship, they begin to exchange views about one another, as well as express expectations about the nature of their relationship. More or less specifically, according to Jackson (1965a), they define the rights and duties of each spouse: "You can depend on me to be logical, practical, realistic"; "In return, you can depend on me to be a feeling, sensitive, social person." Such determinations often reflect culturally linked sex roles—in this case, traditional male and female roles, respectively—but variations are frequent. If these rules are appropriate for the persons involved, and not too rigid, modifications can be made on the basis of their subsequent experiences together. If carried out while tending to the needs of both, the couple develops a division of labor that is intended to help them pursue the sort of life they wish to lead in the future.

Family rules determine the way people pattern their behavior; thus, for Jackson, as well as many early family therapists, rules become the governing principles of family life, providing guidelines for future interactive patterns. Addressing the marital dyad, Jackson adopted the concept of **marital quid pro quo** to describe a relationship with well-formulated rules in which each partner gives and receives something in return. Departing from his training in psychoanalysis and the search for intrapsychic conflict, Jackson was beginning to develop a language of interaction, a schema for depicting human exchanges. By means of descriptive language, he attempted to account for the stabilizing mechanisms in any ongoing relationship (Greenberg, 1977).

Extending his observations to family communication sequences, Jackson (1965b) hypothesized that a **redundancy principle** operates in family life, according to which a family interacts in repetitive behavioral sequences. That is, instead of using the full range of possible behavior open to them, members settle on a narrow option range or limited redundant patterns when dealing with one another. If you understand their rules—in some cases rigid, in others loose and vaguely defined—you begin to understand how a family defines its internal relationships. Jackson maintained that it is these rules rather than individual needs, drives, or personality traits that determine the interactive sequences between family members.

Rules may be *descriptive* (metaphors describing patterns of interchange) or *prescriptive* (directing what can or cannot occur between members). They are formulas for constructing and maintaining family relationships. For example, within a family group, descriptive rules may be based on individual prerogatives and obligations determined by age, sex, or generation. Some may be negotiable, while others are not; rigid families may have too many rules, chaotic families too few. Whatever the family structure, all members learn the family's **metarules** (literally, the rules about the rules), which typically take the form of unstated family directives offering principles for interpreting rules, enforcing rules, as well as changing rules.

Some prescriptive rules are stated overtly—rules such as: "Children allow parents to speak without interruption"; "Children hang up their clothes"; "Parents decide on bedtime"; "Mother makes decisions regarding the purchase of new clothes"; "Father chooses the television programs on Monday night"; "Heavy lifting is done by the males"; "Sister helps set the table but Brother helps Dad clear the dinner dishes"; "Younger children go to bed earlier than older ones"; "Older children have larger allowances."[1]

Most family rules, however, are covert and unstated. That is, they are inferences that all family members draw from the redundancies or repetitive patterns in the relationships they observe at home—for example, "It's best to ask Mother for money after dinner, when she's in a good mood"; "Show the report card to Mom first because Dad might be tougher"; "Don't be a crybaby"; "If you lose your glasses, avoid mentioning it as long as possible because they'll both be mad"; "Stay away from their room on Sunday morning, they like to be alone." Children learn and perpetuate these rules.

Parents act according to covert rules of their own: "Daughters help in the kitchen, but it isn't right to ask a son"; "Boys have later curfews than girls"; "You kids can fight all you want but don't involve us"; "We can trust our daughter with money, but it seems to burn a hole in our son's pocket." Sometimes a family rule, unstated but understood by all, is that decisions are made by the parents and handed down to the children; in other cases, all family members learn that they may state their own opinions freely. In a well-functioning family, rules help maintain order and stability while at the same time allowing for changes with changing circumstances. The issue for such a family is not that it follows the "correct" rules while other, less successful families do not, but rather that its rules are consistent and clearly communicated to all members.

Virginia Satir (1972), another pioneer in family therapy, and an early associate of Jackson's at the Mental Research Institute in Palo Alto, California, also was interested in aiding a family to clarify its communication patterns. She tried to help a family recognize its unwritten rules, especially those rigidly enforced rules that evoke the exchange of hard feelings or that cause family pain. For example, some families forbid discussion of certain topics (mother's drinking problem, or father's unexplained absence from home certain nights, or brother's inability to read, or sister's sexual promiscuity) and, as a consequence, fail to take realistic steps to alleviate problems. Other families forbid overt expressions of anger or irritation with each other ("Stop! The children will hear us"; "If you can't say something nice to one another, don't say

---

[1]A small child visiting a friend for the first time is apt to be bewildered by observing a family operating under an alien set of rules. Mother and father may greet each other with a kiss, may not get into a quarrel over the dinner table, may include children in the conversation. A visiting child is sometimes startled to learn that, according to the rules in another family, it is not necessary to finish all the food on your plate before you are allowed to have dessert!

anything at all"). Still others foster dependence ("Never trust anyone but your mother or father") or enmeshment ("Keep family business within the family") and thus handicap children as they attempt to deal with the outside world.

Satir argued, simply, that dysfunctional families follow dysfunctional rules. Consistent with that view, she attempted to help such families become aware of those unwritten rules that retard growth and maturity. Once these rules have been identified, she believed it may be possible for the family to revise or discard those that are outmoded, inappropriate, or irrelevant, in order to improve the individual self-esteem of members as well as overall family functioning.

Family Homeostasis

Physiological studies first carried out by Walter Cannon (1932) led to the concept of dynamic equilibrium to explain the body's ability to operate as a self-regulating system, maintaining a steady state despite possibly drastic changes in the outside environment. For example, whatever the change in outside temperature, body temperature varies little from its customary 98.6 degrees Fahrenheit; various body-regulating mechanisms (perspiration, change in water retention, "goose pimples," shivering) are ordinarily called into play to maintain the constancy of body temperature should a sudden change in outside temperature occur. (The same is true for other body mechanisms, such as blood pressure.) The automatic tendency of the body to maintain balance or equilibrium is called **homeostasis**. Restated in cybernetic terms, the body can be seen as a dynamic biosocial system that exchanges information with the outside world and uses feedback processes to maintain internal stability.

Although the end result is a steady state, the process is hardly a static one. On the contrary, a constantly fluctuating interaction of equilibrating and disequilibrating forces is operating, and it is that interaction that generates the bodily pattern we call stability. Just as a tightrope walker is constantly in motion, continuously making body position and weight distribution corrections to maintain balance, so the body strives for dynamic equilibrium (Bloch, 1985).

Early family theorists and researchers, led by Bateson, along with Jackson, recognized the applicability of this cybernetic concept to an upset or threatened family system that initiates homeostatic mechanisms in order to reestablish equilibrium. In their initial formulations, groundbreaking for their time, homeostasis was seen as a way of a family resisting change by returning to its prethreatened steady state. Haley (1963) agreed that families, especially troubled or disturbed families, attempt to deal with disruption by monitoring the family's behavioral sequences and activating its homeostatic mechanisms whenever the status quo is upset. In some cases, the appearance of symptoms in a family member was seen as a homeostatic effort to maintain or restore family balance. In such a situation, it was assumed that family rules helped regulate family interactive patterns and thus helped stabilize family relationships, even if that equilibrium comes at the expense of a symptomatic member becoming the identified patient.

This might be a good place to note that while the family's response to their child's symptomatic behavior (say, an asthmatic attack) may produce a stable, predictable, and thus a restorative homeostatic response, that is not to say that such a response is necessarily constructive or desirable. As we discuss later in this chapter, maintaining homeostasis may sometimes entail maintaining a seriously dysfunctional family behavior pattern. In such cases, the therapist may help the family break out of their repetitive patterns, attaining a homeostatic balance at a new level rather than simply returning to their former ways of achieving balance and equilibrium.

How does a functional family ordinarily seek to maintain equilibrium or homeostasis? In family terms, homeostasis refers to those internal, ongoing, sustaining, dynamically interactional processes that take place within a family and help assure internal balance. That is, family members will attempt to restore a stable environment whenever it becomes disrupted. The family, as an error-activated (or excess-activated) system, usually restricts behavior to a narrow range—for example, a quarrel between two children is not permitted to escalate to the point of physical assault. In such a developing situation, a parent is likely to do one or more of the following: scold one or both; lecture one or both; remind them of their family ties and responsibilities; punish one or both; hug them both and urge them to settle the argument; act as a referee; or send each out of the way of the other, until tempers cool. Whatever the attempted solution, the effort is directed, at least in part, to returning the system to its previous balance or equilibrium.

In a similar manner, couples typically monitor the state of their relationship and—usually without being aware of doing so—provide input to return it to a steady state should certain errors or excesses threaten their previous homeostatic balance. Stimulated by Bateson's application of the biological system's homeostatic principles to family systems, his colleague Jackson (1957; 1965b) noted that during the courting period, most couples' behavior is characterized by wondrously varied amorous advances and flirtatious moves. In the course of a long-term relationship, however, most of these behavioral ploys are dropped from their interactional repertoire. What remains is a narrower range of behavior that may require the couple to restore the balance from time to time. Usually a private code develops, each partner learning to cue the other, homeostatically, perhaps with a glance or gesture that means, for example, "I'm hurt by what you just said (or did) and want you to reassure me that you don't mean it and still love me." Such cues are a signal that disequilibrium has been created and some corrective steps are required in order to return the relationship to its previous balanced state.

The initial mechanical homeostatic analogy Jackson (1965b) offered was to a home heating system with a thermostat set to cause the furnace to respond if the temperature in the house drops below the desired level of warmth. Such a cybernetic system has settings (or what we have called *rules*) that govern the system's operations. Figure 4.1 demonstrates such a situation. Let us say that a temperature of 70 degrees Fahrenheit is desired by the home's occupants. When the temperature in the house dips below that point, that information is fed back into the system, activating the furnace. When the desired temperature is reached again, that new information, once again fed back, alters the ongoing state by deactivating the system until such time as reactivation might be needed to once again warm up the house. Balance is achieved by the system's inclination to maintain a dynamic equilibrium around a set point (called a "bias") and to undertake operations through what cyberneticists call servomechanisms to restore equilibrium whenever it is threatened.

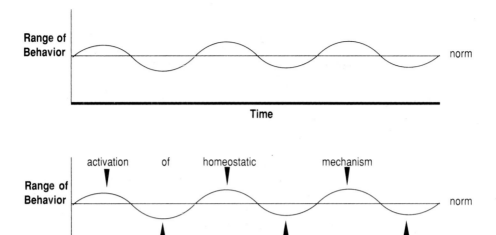

Figure 4.1   The operation of homeostatic mechanisms in the family. In a home heating system, when the temperature deviates from a preset norm, the deviation is registered and counteracted by the homeostatic mechanisms of the thermostat system. Families respond to similar cues to achieve balance and equilibrium.
Source: Jackson, 1965b

Homeostatic mechanisms help to maintain the stability of an ongoing arrangement between family members by activating the rules that define their relationships. What happens, however, when a family must change or modify its rules? How adaptive or flexible are the metarules for changing established or habitual patterns in a particular family? As children grow up, they usually put pressure on the family to redefine its relationships. Many middle-class adolescents expect to be given allowances to spend as they wish, to make their own decisions about a suitable bedtime, to listen to music that may be repellent to their parents' ears. They may wish to borrow the car, sleep over at a friend's, pursue interests other than those traditionally cared about in the family. They may challenge the family's values, customs, and norms; they insist on being treated as equals. All of this causes disequilibrium in the family system, a sense of loss, and perhaps a feeling of strangeness until reorganization restores family balance.

In most cases, a system tends to maintain itself within preferred and familiar ranges. As Minuchin, Rosman, and Baker (1978) point out, a demand for deviation or change that is too great, too sudden, or too far beyond the system's threshold of tolerance is likely to encounter counterdeviation responses. In **pathogenic** families, demands for even the most necessary or modest changes may be met with increased rigidity as the family stubbornly attempts to retain familiar rules. Symptoms in a family member may develop when the family system is not sufficiently flexible to permit change in order to accommodate the changing developmental needs of its members.

While this view of the family operating as a cybernetic system became axiomatic for most family therapists, perhaps the defining metaphor for family therapy in its earlier years, two sets of challenges emerged in the 1980s. One came from feminist family therapists such as Luepnitz (1988), who insisted that one important detail is left out of the simple home heating system analogy: who has greater access to the "bias" and thus is in a stronger position to make changes according to feedback information from the room. As we pointed out in Chapter 3, power within families is typically asymmetrical; within society at large, different people have differing degrees of power in altering an undesirable situation. A landlord in a large building, for example, may control the thermostat for all the apartments; the system may work neatly for him but not from the viewpoint of the freezing tenants. Luepnitz believes that cyberneticists and general systems theorists fail to take power differentials (say, between men and women) into account in their homeostatic formulations. While the less powerful may influence the more powerful, the difference between influence and legitimate power is often substantial.

Another set of critics (Dell, 1982; Hoffman, 1981) also argued that the simple analogy to a home heating system had outlived its usefulness because it is too narrow and too static—returning the system to its former state—and thus fails to deal with *change*. Rather than viewing the family as a homeostatic machine with a governor (for example, a family member develops a symptom when a family breakup is threatened), they contend that this descriptive language is too mechanical—families are not machines that need repair from a detached if skilled observer who remains aloof from the system. What is left out, they assert, is the influence of the outside so-called objective observer on the family's operations, since that observer inevitably has his or her own preconceived notions about how a "healthy" family should work.

The earlier homeostatic position, these new epistemologists assert, incorrectly assumes a dualism between one part of the system and another, when in fact all parts together engage in change. More than seeking to maintain the status quo, homeostasis represents a tendency to seek a steady state when a system is perturbed. That new state is always slightly different from the preceding steady state, since all systems continue to change and evolve. Here the family therapist, as a participant in the system, is called upon to do more than help restabilize a system whose stability has been threatened. Dell (1982) sees the therapist's task in such cases not as helping the family members to return to their former homeostatic balance, but rather as encouraging the family to search for new solutions, in effect pushing the family system out of its old state of equilibrium and into achieving a new level of stability through reorganization and change.

Rather than abandon the cybernetic metaphor, these new epistemologists urge the adoption of a second-order cybernetics (sometimes referred to as the *cybernetics of cybernetics*) in which the therapist is an equal and recursive part of the observing system rather than an outsider looking in, diagnosing and making interventions in order to change what he or she thinks needs fixing in the family. Family therapists who adopt a second-order cybernetic view see family therapy as a cocreation between themselves and family members who together construct potential changes.

Unlike earlier efforts, they do not determine beforehand what needs changing or what changes will come about as a result of their efforts.

Family stability is actually rooted in change. That is, to the degree that a family is functional, it is able to retain sufficient regularity and balance to maintain a sense of adaptability and preserve a sense of order and sameness; at the same time it must subtly promote change and growth within its members and the family as a whole. Well-functioning families are resilient and able to achieve change without forfeiting stability. To use analogies suggested by Keeney (1983), a tightrope walker must continually sway in order to remain balanced. On the other hand, remaining balanced while standing in a canoe calls for making the canoe rock.

Feedback, Information, and Control

Systems are constantly in flux, simultaneously pursuing goals and responding to outside forces. The regulatory mechanism by which a system manages to maintain a steady state, while at the same time monitoring its attempts to achieve certain of its goals, is referred to as *feedback*. As we noted in our earlier discussion of simple cybernetics in Chapter 1, feedback refers to *reinserting into a system the results of its past performance as a method of controlling the system, thereby increasing the system's likelihood of survival*. That is, information about how a system is functioning is looped back from output to input in a circular manner, modifying or self-correcting subsequent input signals. As we noted in the previous section, a thriving system requires both stability and change.

Feedback loops are thus circular mechanisms whose purpose is to introduce information about a system's output back to its input, in order to alter, correct, and ultimately govern the system's functioning and ensure its viability. In any self-regulating system, such servomechanisms (pressure gauges, thermostats) help activate the internal interactional processes that maintain stability within a system and ensure a dynamic but steady state of being. Feedback loops help mitigate against excessive fluctuations, thus serving to maintain and thereby extend the life of the system.

Information thus fed back may be negative or positive. These terms are not value judgments—they do not refer to whether the information is good or bad. Rather, they are of two types: feedback processes that oppose a deviation, thus maintaining the status quo by minimizing or resisting changes (negative), or feedback processes that accept information about a deviation from how the system has been operating and accommodate to a change in the system by modifying its structure (positive). Both are self-corrective mechanisms; both aim to maintain the stability of the system in response to new information. **Negative feedback** information about the performance of the system, fed back through the system, triggers those necessary changes that serve to put the system back "on track" and thus guards the system's steady state, maintaining homeostasis in the face of change. The process of negative feedback[2] is

---

[2]While *negative feedback* and *positive feedback* are commonly used terms in the systems literature, some critics argue that in light of the everyday use of these terms, they may erroneously suggest value judgments to some readers. Constantine (1986) suggests that for *negative feedback* we substitute *attenuating feedback loops* (loops that promote equilibrium) and that for *positive feedback* we use *amplifying loops* (loops that promote change).

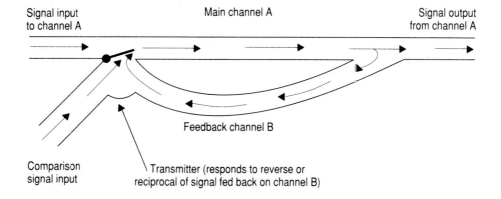

Figure 4.2   In this illustration of negative feedback, part of a system's output is reintroduced into the system as information about the output, thus governing and correcting the process. A negative signal from channel A, fed back to the sender through channel B, alters the signal in A. Feedback loops characterize all interpersonal relationships.

Source: Miller, 1978

illustrated in Figure 4.2. Here we see how attenuating feedback loops operate in a corrective manner, adjusting the input so that the system returns to its preset state.

Positive feedback (amplifying feedback loops) has the opposite effect: it leads to further change by augmenting or accelerating the initial deviation. The room is not yet at the desired temperature and the system continues to respond as it has been programmed to do until it achieves its predetermined goal.

Systems require both positive and negative feedback—the former to accommodate to new information and changing conditions, the latter when appropriate, to maintain the status quo. For example, as children in a family grow into adolescence, they are likely to demand greater independence and self-direction, temporarily destabilizing the family system through their insistence on rule changes. Adaptive or enabling families typically attempt to deal with change by renegotiating teenage privileges and responsibilities and receiving feedback information regarding how easily and appropriately the changes are handled. Positive feedback mechanisms are operating here as the family adapts to change by modifying its structure and the system's stability is regained. Once the system has been modified, negative feedback mechanisms keep it running on a steady course (until further changes become necessary) and the family has dealt effectively with change while maintaining stability.

In a less functional manner, a family whose repertoire is limited to negative feedback may be inflexible and stifling and consequently engage in restrictive behavior detrimental to a system attempting to deal with changing circumstances. For example, parents may continue to treat the teenager as a child, refusing to acknowledge his or her growing maturity. In a similarly dysfunctional manner, positive feedback, helping change or modify a system, may reach runaway proportions without the stability provided by negative feedback, forcing the system beyond its coping limits to the point of exhaustion or self-destruction. The furnace driven beyond its limits explodes; the car oversteered through an oil slick on the road goes out of control; the adolescent does not know how to handle new freedoms and rebelliously defies all family rules.

No family passes through its life cycle transitions unscathed. Periodic imbalance is inevitable, and feedback loops are called into play that restore stability or escalate conflict. Within a marriage, exchange of information through feedback loops helps maintain equilibrium, as disturbing or annoying patterns are adjusted and new, stabilizing patterns evolve. A misunderstanding can be corrected and minimized (attenuating deviation) or escalated (amplifying deviation). In the latter case, an argument may get out of control, becoming increasingly vicious, ugly, or even violent, reaching the point where neither spouse can (or wants to) control the consequences. However, the conflict may also be resolved through positive feedback as the couple strives for a new level of understanding.

Goldenberg and Goldenberg (1998) illustrate the operation of negative and positive feedback loops in the case of a remarried couple. In the former situation, there is attenuation or negative feedback:

Husband: I'm upset at the way you talked to that man at the party tonight, especially the way you seemed to be hanging on every word he said.

Wife: Don't be silly! You're the one I care about. He said he had just come back from a trip you and I had talked about going on and I was interested in what he had to tell me about the place.

Husband: OK. But please don't do it again without telling me. You know I'm touchy on the subject because of what Gina [ex-wife] used to do at parties with other men that drove me crazy.

Wife: Sorry. I hadn't thought about that. I'll try to remember next time. In the meantime, you try to remember that you're married to me now and I don't want you to be jealous.

In a less blissful situation, instead of the previous attenuation, there is amplification or positive feedback:

Husband: I'm upset at the way you talked to that man at the party tonight, especially the way you seemed to be hanging on every word he said.

Wife: One thing I don't appreciate is your spying on me.

Husband: Spying? That's a funny word to use. You must be getting paranoid in your old age. Or maybe you have something to hide.

Wife: As a matter of fact, I was talking to him about a trip he took that we had talked about, but I don't suppose you'd believe that. Talk about paranoid!

Husband: I give up on women! You're no different from Gina, and I suppose all other women.

Wife: With an attitude like that, I'm starting to see why Gina walked out on you.

However, positive feedback, while destabilizing, may also be beneficial if it does not get out of control and helps change the system for the better. Consider a third scenario: the couple expands and deepens their relationship by being nondefensive, willing to share their feelings, and reexamine their rules:

Husband: I'm upset at the way you talked to that man at the party tonight, especially the way you seemed to be hanging on every word he said. Can you help me understand what was going on?

Wife: He said he had just come back from a trip you and I had talked about going on and I was interested in what he had to tell me about the place. Maybe I should have called you over and included you in our conversation.

Husband: No need to invite me. From now on I will come over so I'll know what's happening.

Wife: I'd like that. Keeping in close contact with you at a party always makes me feel good.

Once again, negative and positive feedback loops are in and of themselves neither good nor bad. In the case of families, both are necessary if stability and continuity are to be maintained despite the vagaries of outside pressures. Notwithstanding the potentially escalating impact of the runaway system in the second example, it should be clear from the third example that not all positive feedback should be thought of as damaging or destructive to the system's operations. Homeostatic does not mean static; as a marriage or a family grows, stability calls for acknowledging change, and change often comes about in a family through breakthroughs that push the family beyond its previous homeostatic level. At times it may be advantageous to propel a family with stagnating or otherwise untenable behavior patterns to new levels of functioning. In these cases, the therapist may seize the opportunity of disequilibrium to promote discontinuity and the restoration of family homeostasis at a new, more satisfactory level for all.

How deviant must an outcome be before corrective action is initiated? Broderick and Smith (1979), pointing out the necessity for cybernetic control for stable system operation, offer this example: Parents may respond to their adolescent daughter's return home from a date positively or negatively, depending on whether she has conformed to family rules in the time she arrives home, the condition she is in, and other factors. These authors note that the response will depend on the degree of **calibration** the family has determined—how much deviation it will allow. If the event is calibrated too narrowly, the daughter may not easily achieve a sense of independence and reliance on her own judgment. If it is calibrated too broadly, she may fail to learn limits and a sense of responsibility. Family therapists need to be aware of a family's efforts at calibrating their responses to such events, helping them fine-tune these responses for more effective functioning as a family unit. The appearance of symptoms in a family member may signal the need for recalibration or perhaps that the family lacks the flexibility to restructure in response to changing family circumstances.

Information processing is fundamental to the operation of any system. If faulty, the system is likely to malfunction. The more or less free exchange of information within a family and between the family and the outside world helps reduce uncertainty, thus avoiding disorder. According to Bateson's (1972) elegant definition, information is "a difference that makes a difference." In interpersonal family terms, a word, a gesture, a smile, a scowl—these are differences or changes in the environment comparable to a temperature drop as environmental input. These differences in turn make a difference when the receiver of the new information alters his or her perceptions of the environment and modifies subsequent behavior.

Subsystems

A system, as we have seen, is organized into a more or less stable set of relationships; it functions in certain characteristic ways; it is continuously in the process of evolution as it seeks new steady states. **Subsystems** are those parts of the overall system assigned to carry out particular functions or processes within the system as a whole. Each system exists as part of a larger suprasystem and contains smaller subsystems of which it is the suprasystem.

A family commonly contains a number of coexisting subsystems. The husband-and-wife dyad constitutes a subsystem; so do the mother-child, father-child, and child-child dyads. In a family, subsystems can be formed by generation (mother and father), by sex (mothers and daughters), by interest (intellectual pursuits), or by function (parental caretakers) (Minuchin, 1974). Within each, different levels of power are exercised, different skills learned, and different responsibilities assigned. For example, the oldest child may have power within the sibling subsystem but must cede that power when interacting with his or her parents.

Because each family member belongs to several subsystems simultaneously, he or she enters into different complementary relationships with other members. For example, a woman can be a wife, mother, daughter, younger sister, older sister, niece, granddaughter, and so on, simultaneously. Within each subsystem in which she holds membership, she plays a different role and can be expected to engage in different transactional patterns. Consider this example: While giving her younger sister advice about finding a job, a woman is told by her husband to get off the telephone and hurry up with dinner. She decides how to deal with his demand. Some moments later, she remembers not to be hurt when the children refuse to eat what she has prepared. She even responds diplomatically when her mother, a dinner guest, gives her advice on how to improve the table setting.

The most enduring subsystems are the *spousal, parental,* and *sibling* subsystems (Minuchin, Rosman, & Baker, 1978). The husband-wife dyad is basic; any dysfunction in this subsystem is bound to reverberate throughout the family as children are scapegoated or co-opted into alliances with one parent against the other whenever the parents engage in conflict. The spousal subsystem teaches the children about male-female intimacy and commitment by providing a model of marital interaction. How the marital partners accommodate to one another's needs, negotiate differences, make decisions together, manage conflict, meet each other's sexual and dependency needs, plan the future together, and so on, help influence the effectiveness of relationships between all family members. A viable spousal subsystem, one in which the marital partners have worked out a fulfilling relationship with one another, provides both spouses with the experience of intimacy, support, mutual growth, and an opportunity for personal development.

The parental subsystem (which may include grandparents or older children temporarily assigned parental roles) has the major responsibility for proper child rearing, nurturance, guidance, limit setting, and discipline. Through interaction with parents, children learn to deal with authority, with people of greater power, while strengthening their own capacity for decision making and self-direction. Problems within this subsystem, such as serious intergenerational conflicts involving rebelliousness, symptomatic children, or runaways, often reflect underlying family instability and disorganization.

The sibling set represents a child's first peer group. Through participation in this subsystem, a child develops patterns of negotiation, cooperation, competition, mutual support, and later, attachment to friends. Interpersonal skills honed here influence later school or workplace relationships. The influence of this subsystem on overall family functioning is to a large extent dependent on how viable all family subsystems are. Spousal, parental, and sibling subsystems stand in an overall dynamic relationship, each simultaneously influencing and being influenced by one another. Together, relationships within and between subsystems help define the family's structure.

Other subsystems, most less durable than those just outlined, exist in all families. Father-daughter, mother-son, father–oldest son, and mother–youngest child transitional alliances are common. Their protracted duration, however, especially if the alliance impacts negatively on family functioning, may signal difficulties within the spousal subsystem, alerting the family therapist to the potential instability of the family system.

Boundaries

A **boundary** is an invisible line of demarcation that separates an individual, a subsystem, or a system from outside surroundings. Boundaries help define the individual autonomy of its separate members, as well as help differentiate subsystems from one another. Within a system such as a family, boundaries circumscribe and protect the integrity of the system, determining who is considered an insider and who remains outside. The family boundary may serve a gatekeeper function, controlling information flow into and out of the system ("We don't care if your friend's parents allow her to ————; we don't"; "Whatever you hear at home, you are expected to keep private and not discuss with your friends").

Within a family itself, boundaries distinguish between subsystems, helping define the separate subunits of the overall system and the quality of their interactive processes. Minuchin (1974) contends that such divisions must be sufficiently well defined to allow subsystem members to carry out their tasks without undue interference, while at the same time open enough to permit contact between members of the subsystem and others. Boundaries thus help safeguard each subsystem's autonomy while maintaining the interdependence of all of the family's subsystems.

For example, a mother defines the boundaries of the parental subsystem when she tells her 15-year-old son, the oldest of three children: "Don't you decide whether your sisters are old enough to stay up to watch that TV program. Your father and I will decide that." However, she temporarily redefines that boundary to include the oldest child within the parental subsystem when she announces: "I want all of you children to listen to your older brother while your father and I are away from home tomorrow evening." Or she may invite grandparents to join the parental subsystem for one evening only, asking them to check on how the children are getting along or advise the oldest son on necessary action in case of an emergency.

These examples underscore the idea that the clarity of the subsystem boundaries is far more significant in the effectiveness of family functioning than the composition of the family subsystems. While the parent-child subsystem may be flexible enough to include the oldest child, or grandmother may be pressed into service when both parents are unavailable, the lines of authority and responsibility must remain clear. A grandmother who interferes with her daughter's management of the children in ways that undermine the parent-child subsystem (and perhaps also the spousal subsystem in the process) is overstepping her authority by being intrusive and crossing family boundary lines.[3]

An important issue here involves the permeability of the boundaries, since boundaries vary in how easily they permit information to flow to and from the environment. Not only must boundaries within families be clearly drawn, but also the *rules* must be apparent to all. If boundaries are too blurred or too rigid, they invite confusion or inflexibility, increasing the family's risk of instability and ultimate dysfunction.

In dyadic terms, even a social interaction as brief and tentative as a first date is concerned with boundaries (Broderick & Smith, 1979). A number of rules apply: It is bad form to pay too much attention to someone other than your date, and rude and insulting to abandon your date and return home with someone else. Moreover, others are expected to respect the couple's boundaries and refrain from cutting in on another's partner. It is also understood that the arrangement—the establishment of the unit—is time-limited, and when the date is over, so is the claim, and the rules just described no longer apply. If the two move to a more intimate relationship and see each other more regularly, they—as well as others such as their friends—behave as though the boundary is more clearly drawn and now operates between dates as well.

Open and Closed Systems

A system with a continuous information flow to and from the outside is considered, in systems terms as first outlined by Bertalanffy, to be an **open system**, while one whose boundaries are not easily crossed is considered a **closed system**. The key point here is the degree of interaction with, and accessibility to, the outside environment. Open systems do more than adapt passively to their surroundings; their social transactions are bidirectional. That is, beyond simply adjusting, they also initiate activi-

---

[3]In certain ethnic groups, as we showed in Chapter 3, the lines of authority may deviate from this middle-class American standard. However, if clear and fair, and acceptable to all members, these patterns remain functional.

ties that permit an exchange with the community because their boundaries are permeable. Closed systems, on the other hand, have impermeable boundaries. Thus, they fail to interact with the outside environment, lack feedback corrective mechanisms, become isolated, and resist change. An example of such a closed system is a type of religious cult that closes out the world beyond its borders, specifically to halt the flow of information from the outside world and in that way control the behavior of its members. Similarly, totalitarian countries that do not permit foreign newspapers, radio or television, or access to the Internet or World Wide Web also represent systems deliberately closed to control citizens' behavior.

In family terms, no system is fully open or closed; if totally open, no boundaries would exist between it and the outside world and it would cease to exist as a separate entity; if totally closed, there would be no exchanges with the outside environment, and it would die. Rather, systems exist along a continuum with regard to the flexibility or rigidity of their boundaries. Families that function effectively maintain the system by developing a balance between openness and closeness, tuned to the outside world so that appropriate change and adaptation are accomplished while changes that threaten the survival of the system are resisted.

While all families operate as open systems, some may appear more closed in the sense of being rigid or insular (Kantor & Lehr, 1975). The more open the family system, the more adaptable and accessible to change it is. Such a system tends not only to survive but to thrive, to be open to new experiences and to alter or discard no longer usable interactive patterns; thus it is said to have **negentropy,** or a tendency toward maximum order. Such a family system is able to alter its patterns in response to new information calling for a change in family rules, and discard those established responses that are inappropriate to the new situation. As a result of exchanges beyond its boundaries, open systems, particularly if they have a stable core, increase their chances of becoming more highly organized and developing resources to repair minor or temporary breakdowns in efficiency (Nichols & Everett, 1986).

The lack of such exchanges in relatively closed systems decreases their competence to deal with stress. Limited or perhaps even nonexistent contact with others outside the family unit may lead to fearful, confused, and ineffective responses in times of crisis. Such closed systems run the risk of **entropy;** they gradually regress, decay because of insufficient input, and thus are prone to eventual disorganization and eventual disorder, particularly if faced with prolonged stress.

Closed systems, then, fail to make enabling adaptations. They are apt to seal themselves off from all but necessary exchanges with the outside world; they maintain strict control on who and what should be admitted into the home, screening visitors, certain forms of music, new information, or unwelcomed reading matter or television programs, and thus are destined for eventual dysfunction because of insufficient input. For example, recent immigrants or ethnic groups that live in relative isolation, communicating only among themselves, suspicious of outsiders, and fostering dependence on the family, often tend to hold on to tradition and avoid change thus operating in the manner of a relatively closed system. Parent-child relationships in such families may encounter problems due in part to culture conflict, and these problems, if serious enough, may lead to the development of an entropic family.

FAMILIES AND LARGER SYSTEMS

All families interact with, and are influenced by, one or more of society's larger systems—health care, church, welfare, probation, schools, the legal system. School-family interaction is especially familiar and can illustrate the interlocking nature of systems. Not only is a child a part of a family that has its own unique structure and relationship patterns, but the family itself is embedded in its cultural, ethnic, social class, and social history. The child is at the same time a member of a school classroom with its own structure and interactive processes; that classroom, in turn is located within a matrix of a larger school organization. The two major systems in the child's life, home and school, thus interface and form a new larger system with its own characteristics, objectives, priorities, and regularities; moreover, home and school systems may deal with one another in complementary or antagonistic ways.[4]

The consultant called upon to help with a behavioral problem, for example, needs to adopt an **ecosystemic approach** (Lusterman, 1988), taking into account the interaction of the two systems (home and school) before attempting to sort out whether the child is having difficulties in one or both and how best to proceed. He or she must not only remain aware of the child and the family system but also be familiar with the culture of the school, school law regarding children with special needs, how this school reaches decisions, the role of the school board, and so on (Fine, 1995)

Rotheram (1989) offers the following vignette illustrating one type of problem arising in the interface between family and school:

> An angry parent calls the school, complaining that a seventh-grade teacher has given too much homework and is ruining the family's time together over the weekend, asking too much of a young girl. The teacher is righteously indignant and counters that the parents are encouraging dependence and passivity in their child. She refuses to decrease homework. The next week, the daughter makes a suicide attempt, and the family wants to sue the school. (p. 347)

The liaison-consultant called upon to intervene may be a member of the school system, a therapist brought in by the family, or a social services agency representative. Lusterman (1988) urges "mapping the ecosystem"—evaluating both the school and family before deciding whom to include (child, teachers, school counselors, parents, grandparents, and so on.) in the treatment plan. In his view, it is necessary from the outset to make clear that the task of the therapist is not advocacy but rather creating conditions for change. A systems perspective facilitates the process, since, if carried out successfully, neither party is targeted as causing the presenting problem and the interactive process between participants becomes the focus of the joint meet-

---

[4]Families and school personnel may agree on the child's problem (e.g., a pervasive developmental delay), particularly if their cultural norms are similar. In other cases, they may not agree; the school may perceive a behavioral problem (e.g., hyperactivity) that the family does not agree is problematic, or the family may report a child's behavior as troublesome (stealing from a mother's purse) that the school does not find a particular bother. Ethnic differences often play a part; families and teachers often misperceive each other's intentions and goals because of differences in cultural backgrounds (Rotheram, 1989).

ings (Rotheram, 1989). The family therapist acting as a systems consultant (Wynne, McDaniel, & Weber, 1986) is often able to convene the system, observe interactions, allow differing views of "reality" to emerge, formulate hypotheses, and ultimately facilitate family-school collaboration leading to effective problem solving (Fine, 1995). An ecosystemic approach is by definition a collaborative undertaking.

For most families engagements with larger systems are time-limited and proceed, perhaps with occasional exceptions, in ways that are free of long-term problems. However, a significant portion of families frequently become entangled with these larger systems in unfortunate ways, impeding the growth and development of family members while at the same time contributing to cynicism and burnout among helpers. In such cases, as Elizur and Minuchin (1989) illustrate with examples from families where there is mental illness, it is incumbent upon family therapists to look beyond the dysfunctional family itself to a broader view of social systems that encompasses the entire community. To do otherwise, they insist, in many cases is to arrive at "solutions" for the family that, no matter how therapeutically elegant, are inevitably shortsighted because they fail to take cultural, political, and institutional issues into account. That is, no matter how effective the family therapy intervention, the social context of treatment must be recognized, and the power of organizations in which families are embedded must be understood, lest the frequent inflexibility of agencies such as psychiatric hospitals, isolating patients from their families, undo any therapeutic gain.

Such problems as physical handicaps or chronic illness force some families to spend a significant portion of their lives engaged with larger systems. In the case of long-standing poverty, the relationship with the same public agencies may extend over generations. Problems may develop not only between such families and the agencies in which they often become embedded, but between different public agencies as well. In the case of wife battering that we are about to present, confusion results from conflicting perceptions of various professionals attempting to help.

In the example offered by Imber-Black (1988) illustrated in Figure 4.3, a family initially seeking the aid of a family therapist for their son Billy's aggressive behavior, revealed over the course of therapy that Jim, the father, had been physically abusive to his wife, Cathy. Cathy also disclosed to the therapist that she had been sexually abused, as a child and young adolescent, by her father. The referring family physician knew only of the problems with Billy. By the time they consulted a family therapist, the family had become involved with five larger systems: Jim in a local hospital group for men who batter their wives; Cathy in a program for women who have experienced sexual abuse; Jim and Cathy together in a church counseling program for family violence; Cathy in a women's shelter counseling group; and the entire family in family therapy.

When the family therapist invited the various participants to meet together and coordinate their efforts, differences in approach and fundamental beliefs among the various helpers turned out to be significant. For example, while Jim's group sought the causes of violence within him and from his past experiences, urging a long-term group program, the family therapist took a systemic approach, recommended a short-term approach, and attempted to locate the violence in the context of the cou-

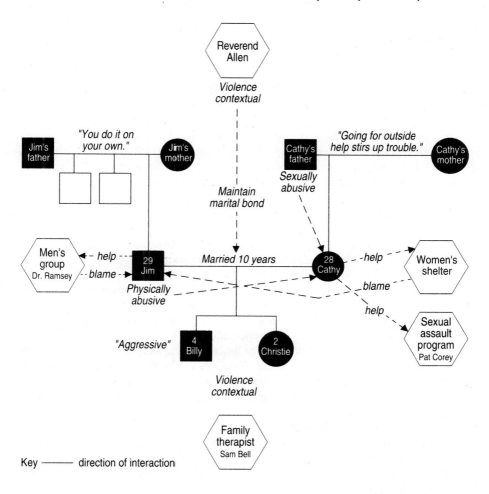

Figure 4.3   Conflicting perceptions and interactions in the Lee family case
Source: Imber-Black, 1988, p 117

ple's ongoing interactions. By contrast, Cathy felt the women's shelter counselors blamed Jim exclusively, and thought it was he who needed treatment.

Because competing definitions of the problem and approaches to a solution surfaced in this macrosystem, a consultant was needed to help untangle the various family member–helper coalitions that had developed. Imber-Black argues that conflict between specialized "helping" systems may, in many cases such as this one, contribute to or enlarge the very problems the helping systems were created to fix or alleviate. In this case, the consultant highlighted their differences to the helpers, pointing out the impact of these differences on how the couple interacted. Stressing the macrosystem level, she designed an intervention that made the boundaries between helpers clearer and less rigid. At the same time, couple-helper boundaries were clarified and thus became less diffuse and confusing. The restructuring allowed the couple themselves to determine the amount and source of help they needed on a weekly basis.

SUMMARY

Systems theory, encompassing the contributions of cybernetics and general systems theory, provides the theoretical underpinnings for much of current family therapy theory and practice. The concepts of organization and wholeness in particular emphasize that a system operates as an organized whole that is greater than the sum of its parts, and that such a system cannot be adequately understood if broken down into component parts.

A family represents a complex relationship system in which causality is circular and multidimensional. Family rules, for the most part unstated but understood by family members, help stabilize and regulate family functioning. Homeostasis is achieved in a family by means of dynamically interacting processes that help restore stability whenever threatened, often by activating the rules that define the relationships. When changes are called for, negative as well as positive feedback loops may help restore equilibrium, in the latter case by promoting discontinuity and necessitating the achievement of homeostasis at a new level. Families need to be able to tolerate change in order to maintain their continuity.

Subsystems carry out specific family functions. Particularly significant are the spousal, parental, and sibling subsystems. Boundaries help separate systems, as well as subsystems within the overall system, from one another. Their clarity and permeability are more germane to family functioning than is their membership composition. Families vary in the extent to which they are open systems; relatively closed systems run the risk of entropy or decay and disorganization.

Family systems interact with larger outside systems, such as the church, schools, or the health care system, and the unbending rules of some institutions may negate any therapeutic gain. Although these systems are often effective in solving problems, in a sizable number of cases confusion may result from competing definitions of the family problem and conflicting solutions offered by different helpers in this macrosystem. In this broader context, boundaries between helpers, as well as boundaries between client families and helpers, may need to be clarified for the macrosystem to operate effectively.

II

THE EVOLUTION
OF FAMILY THERAPY

5

Origins and Growth of Family Therapy

In Part I, we first attempted to establish a family relationship framework for viewing and understanding behavior, before offering a developmental outlook based upon life cycle or multigenerational considerations for both intact and alternative families. We next emphasized that attention needed to be given to gender, culture, and ethnicity factors in any serious effort to fully comprehend family functioning. Finally, to round out this foundation section, we explored some of the fundamental concepts of systems theory as they apply to a family as a psychosocial entity.

In Part II we examine the evolution of family therapy, first reviewing some scientific and clinical developments that coalesced in the 1950s to give birth to that movement, then describing its remarkable growth and change over the ensuing decades. We intend this brief review to serve as a social and historical context for understanding how various theories developed in an attempt to conceptualize family life, and how these ideas helped shape the practice of family therapy.

HISTORICAL ROOTS OF FAMILY THERAPY

It is never easy or entirely accurate to pinpoint the beginning of a scientific endeavor. But most authorities point to the decade following World War II as the period when first researchers, later followed by practitioners, turned their attention to the family's role in creating and maintaining psychological disturbance in one or more family members. The sudden reuniting of families in the aftermath of the war created a number of problems (social, interpersonal, cultural, situational) for which the public sought solutions by turning to mental health specialists. Accustomed to working with individuals, these professionals were now expected to deal effectively with an array of problems within the family. Family members experienced the stress associated with delayed marriages and hasty wartime marriages; the baby boom brought pressures of its own.

Changing sexual mores and increasing acceptance of divorce brought new freedoms—and conflicts. Transitions to new jobs, new educational opportunities, and new homes with mortgages meant new tensions within the family. Adding to all this, the family had entered the nuclear age: the atom bomb had challenged its basic security.

In general, psychological intervention became acceptable to people from a broader range of social and educational backgrounds than had been the case in prewar days. Practitioners from many disciplines—clinical psychologists, psychiatric social workers, marriage counselors, pastoral counselors—began to offer such aid, in addition to psychiatrists, who were the primary prewar providers of psychotherapy. The definition of problems considered amenable to psychotherapy also expanded to include marital discord, separation and divorce, delinquency, problems with in-laws, and various forms of emotional disturbance not requiring hospitalization. Although many clinicians continued to offer individual treatment only, others began to look at family relationships, the transactions between members that needed modification, if individual well-being was to be achieved.

The Macy Foundation Conferences, as described in Chapter 1, begun in wartime, continued in peacetime, and helped provide some of the fundamental postulates of cybernetic theory, later to prove so central to family therapy formulations depicting families as social systems. In addition to the gradual acceptance of a systems theory framework, with its emphasis on exploring relationships between parts that make up an integrated whole, four other seemingly independent scientific and clinical developments during this period help set the stage for the emergence of family therapy:

- The investigation of the family's role in the development of schizophrenia in one of its members
- The evolution of the fields of marital and premarital counseling
- The growth of the child guidance movement
- Advances in group dynamics and group therapy

STUDIES OF SCHIZOPHRENIA AND THE FAMILY

What role does a pathogenic family environment play in the development of **schizophrenia?** Believed at the time to offer an exciting lead in examining whether specific sets of family dynamics might account for different forms of adult psychopathology, postwar researchers began zeroing in on the upbringing and family lives of schizophrenics. Lidz and Lidz (1949), among the first to investigate the family environment of schizophrenic patients, surveyed 50 case histories and found the patients by and large to have come from unstable homes with a frequent absence of one or both parents, whether by death, divorce, or separation. These researchers discovered serious inadequacies and psychological disturbances in both the father-child and the mother-child relationship. Since mothers were typically held accountable for their children's development and behavior, the finding of the father's pernicious influence was especially noteworthy.

Fromm-Reichmann and the Schizophrenogenic Mother

Maternal rejection, on the other hand, was blamed by Frieda Fromm-Reichmann (1948) for the development of male schizophrenia. In a widely quoted paper at the time, this prominent psychoanalyst, known for her work with schizophrenics, introduced the term **schizophrenogenic mother** to denote a domineering, cold, rejecting, possessive, guilt-producing person who, in combination with a passive, detached, and ineffectual father, causes her male offspring to feel confused and inadequate and ultimately to become schizophrenic. Although Fromm-Reichmann emphasized the destructive nature of such parenting, she nevertheless viewed schizophrenia as an intrapsychic disorder, residing within the individual patient; she did not suggest treating the family together, but instead saw the clinician's role as freeing the patient from the parents' noxious influences.

A number of family pathology studies, following Fromm-Reichmann's lead, extended into the late 1950s, narrowly seeking to establish a linear cause-and-effect relationship between pathogenic parents and schizophrenia. These initial efforts to link schizophrenia to family life were ultimately disavowed as too limiting, and later were replaced by a broader, more systemic psychosocial approach to the family as a group of individuals influencing each other and by a sociological perspective in which the family is perceived as a dysfunctional system supporting the disturbed person (Waxler, 1975).

Researchers today no longer look for a culpable parent and a victimized child, but rather search for biological or genetic markers in trying to understand the disorder's origins. Nevertheless, the schizophrenogenic mother concept remains historically important in directing attention to dysfunctional interactions occurring within a family context, and shared by all family members. Family communication difficulties and disturbances in the expression of affect are once again the focus of schizophrenia research today, although precisely how these interactive patterns arise or impact the vulnerable person at risk remains elusive. We'll return to additional discussions of such current research in Chapters 14 and 15.

Bateson and the Double Bind

During the mid-1950s, a major impetus for family research in the area of schizophrenia came from Gregory Bateson in Palo Alto, California; Theodore Lidz at Yale; and Murray Bowen (and later, Lyman Wynne) at the National Institute of Mental Health. Working independently at first, the investigators did not become fully aware of each other's research until later in the decade.

In 1952, Bateson—then affiliated with the Palo Alto Veterans Administration Hospital—received a Rockefeller Foundation grant to study communication patterns and paradoxes. Soon he recruited Jay Haley, then a graduate student studying communication; John Weakland, a former chemical engineer with training in cultural anthropology; and William Fry, a psychiatrist. Calling upon their broad range of interests, the disparate group was given free rein by Bateson; together they examined a variety of communication patterns in humans and animals alike, especially possible contradictions between levels of messages—what is communicated and how it is interpreted or qualified by messages at another level of communication. What ultimately proved most intriguing to this group was the manner and frequency with which schizophrenics sent conflicting and often contradictory messages at one and the same time.

Later, in 1954, with a two-year grant from the Macy Foundation to study schizophrenic communication patterns further, Bateson enlisted Don Jackson, a psychiatrist experienced in working with schizophrenics. Interested in developing a theory around communication patterns that might account for the development of schizophrenia, the research group began to study the possible link between pathological communication patterns within a family and the emergence and maintenance of schizophrenic behavior in a family member. Utilizing some of the then emerging cybernetic concepts, which Bateson, interested in epistemology, brought to the project, they ultimately hypothesized that the family, when upset and thus threatened, seeks a homeostatic state through feedback mechanisms that monitor the family's behavior in an effort to achieve balance and stability. Perhaps, they speculated, the appearance of schizophrenic symptoms in a family member interrupted parental conflict when it occurred, and instead united the adversaries in their parental concerns for their child, returning the system to its former level of equilibrium.

By attending to family communication sequences, these researchers were beginning to redefine *schizophrenia as an interpersonal phenomenon,* challenging the long-held view that schizophrenia was an intrapsychic disorder that subsequently damaged interpersonal relationships. More specifically, they hypothesized that the family might have shaped the strange and irrational behavior of a schizophrenic by means of its contradictory, and thus impossible, communication requirements.

Eager to publish their preliminary results, Bateson, Jackson, Haley, and Weakland (Fry was in the armed services at the time) issued a landmark paper (1956) introducing the **double-bind concept** to account for the development of schizophrenia in a family member. A double-bind situation occurs when an individual (often a child) receives repeated contradictory messages from the same person (say an adult), with whom the child has an important ongoing relationship. That adult forbids comment on the contradiction. The child, perceiving the threat to his or her survival, feels compelled to make some response, but feels doomed to failure whatever response he or she chooses. Their paper reports the following poignant example:

> A young man who had fairly well recovered from an acute schizophrenic episode was visited in the hospital by his mother. He was glad to see her and impulsively put his arm around her shoulders, whereupon she stiffened. He withdrew his arm and she asked, "Don't you love me anymore?" He then blushed, and she said, "Dear, you must not be so easily embarrassed and afraid of your feelings." (p. 259)

Note the sequence of the mother's underlying messages: "Don't touch me" ("Go away"); "Don't trust your feelings in regard to how I respond" ("Come closer"); "Don't challenge the contradictions in my behavior"; "You can't survive without my love"; "You're wrong and at fault no matter how you interpret my messages." The authors report that the distressed patient promptly became violent and assaultive when he returned to the ward.

Confronted by expressions of love and hate, with an invitation to approach and an injunction to stay away issued by the same important figure, Bateson's group hypothesized that a person is forced into an impossible situation of trying to discriminate correctly between the contradictory messages. Unable to form a satisfactory response (and in the case of a child, unable to escape) and unable to comment on the dilemma without being punished further, such a person becomes confused, suspicious that all messages have concealed meanings. Response leads to rejection and failure to respond leads to the loss of potential love, the classic "damned if you do and damned if you don't" situation. If the important figure (a parent, for example) then denies sending simultaneous contradictory messages, this only adds to the confusion. Once the pattern is established, these researchers hypothesized, only a hint of or initial step in the original sequence is enough to set off a panic or rage reaction, and, in the case of schizophrenics, may lead to gradual withdrawal from the world of relationships.

Bateson and his colleagues suggested that the typical result of repeated and prolonged exposure to this kind of impossible situation is that the child learns to escape hurt and punishment by responding with equally incongruent messages. As a means of self-protection, he or she learns to deal with all relationships in this distorted manner and finally loses the ability to understand the true meaning of his or her own or others' communications. At this point the child begins to manifest schizophrenic behavior. Correct or not—it later proved not to be—the historical importance of this landmark research is its focus on *schizophrenia as a prototype of the consequences of failure in a family's communication system.*

A seminal publication in the history of family therapy, the double-bind idea stimulated much controversy. Particularly troublesome was its linear outlook—that double-bind communication from parents, especially mother toward child, caused schizophrenia. Further research made it clear that double binding occurs at one time or another in most families, without any similar pathological consequences such as schizophrenia. More than a simple contradiction between messages—as it is sometimes erroneously thought to be—a true double bind represents a special kind of conflict, often difficult to identify, in which message 1 and message 2 are at different *levels* and thus produce a paradox. (Consider the command "Dominate me!" for a moment and the conflicting levels of what is being commanded should become clearer.) As we demonstrate in Chapter 10, strategic family therapists often deliberately place families in double-bind situations, therapeutically, as an indirect way of forcing a client to abandon a symptom.

Lidz: Marital Schism and Marital Skew

At about the same time that Bateson and his colleagues were doing research on the family and schizophrenia on the West Coast, Theodore Lidz on the East Coast (in Baltimore and later in New Haven, Connecticut) began publishing his findings on the family's role in schizophrenic development of one or more of its children. Refuting Fromm-Reichmann's singling out of rejecting mothers by calling attention to the father's possibly destructive role, Lidz, Cornelison, Fleck, and Terry (1957a) described five patterns of *pathological fathering* (rigid and domineering, hostile, paranoid, nonentities at home, passive and submissive) of schizophrenics. To these researchers, carrying out longitudinal studies of families with hospitalized schizophrenic members, schizophrenia was a "deficiency disease" resulting from the family's failure to provide the essentials for integrated personality development.

Lidz and his associates (1957b) described two patterns of chronic marital discord that are particularly characteristic of families of schizophrenics (although each may exist in "normal" families to a lesser extent). **Marital schism** refers to a disharmonious situation in which each parent, preoccupied with his or her own problems, fails to create a satisfactory role in the family that is compatible with and reciprocal to the other spouse's role. Each parent tends to undermine the worth of the other, especially to the children, and they seem to compete for loyalty, affection, sympathy, and support of the children. Neither valuing nor respecting each other, each parent may fear that a particular child (or children) will grow up behaving like the other parent. Threats of separation or divorce are common; it is usual in such families for the father to become ostracized, a virtual nonentity if he remains in the home.

In the pattern of **marital skew**, which these researchers also observed in families with a schizophrenic offspring, the continuity of the marriage is not threatened, but mutually destructive patterns nevertheless exist. The serious psychological disturbance of one parent (such as psychosis) usually dominates this type of home. The other parent, who is often dependent and weak, accepts the situation and goes so far as to imply to the children that the home situation is normal. Such a denial of what they are actually living through may lead to further denials and distortions of reality by the children. Lidz, Cornelison, Fleck, and Terry (1957b) concluded that male schizophrenics usually come from skewed families in which there is a dominant, emotionally disturbed mother, impervious to the needs of other family members but nevertheless intrusive in her child's life. At the same time, a skewed family usually has a father who can neither counter the mother's child-rearing practices nor provide an adequate male role model.

If marital skew is often an antecedent of schizophrenia in a son, marital schism often precedes schizophrenia in a daughter. Here open marital discord is present and each parent particularly wants the daughter's support. However, the father's disparagement of the mother (or perhaps all women), together with his seductive efforts to gain the daughter's love and support, lead to the daughter's confusion about her identity as a woman, as well as doubt about her eventual ability to carry out an adult role as wife and mother.

Lidz's research, initially focused on individual pathology, developed into an approach that searched for parental—and family—dysfunction as the locus of pathology in schizophrenics. Although his efforts have been criticized by feminist family therapists and others as emphasizing stereotypic sex roles—fathers should be more forceful, mothers more selfless—he nevertheless pointed the way to the detrimental effect of growing up in a strife-torn family in which the child is split in his or her loyalties. (A more contemporary view is interactional—not simply that troubled parents provoke disturbance in a child, but also, in a reciprocal manner, that a disturbed family member with a biological predisposition to schizophrenia may be responded to by parents in a variety of dysfunctional ways.)

Bowen, Wynne, and NIMH Studies

First at the Menninger Foundation in Topeka, Kansas, in the early 1950s, and later at the National Institute of Mental Health (NIMH) near Washington, D.C., Murray Bowen, in a dramatic experiment, arranged for mothers to move into cottages on clinic grounds for several months near their hospitalized schizophrenic children; Bowen was especially interested in identifying unresolved symbiotic mother-child interactions. As he later reported (Bowen, 1960) in a book edited by Don Jackson that brought together for the first time various family theories related to the etiology of schizophrenia, families of schizophrenics often demonstrate interaction patterns resembling Lidz's findings about marital schism.

Bowen termed the striking emotional distance between parents in such a situation *emotional divorce*. He described relationships of this kind as vacillating between periods of overcloseness and overdistance. Eventually the relationship becomes fixed at a point of sufficient emotional distance between the parents to avoid anxiety; they settle for "peace at any price." One area of joint activity—and, commonly, conflicting view—is the rearing of their children, particularly of children who show signs of psychological disturbance. It is as if the parents maintain contact with each other (and therefore a semblance of emotional equilibrium) by keeping the disturbed child helpless and needy. Thus adolescence, the period in which the child usually strives for a measure of autonomy, becomes especially stormy and stressful. This is typically the time when schizophrenic behavior first appears.

Bowen proposed the intriguing notion that schizophrenia is a process that spans at least three generations before it manifests in the behavior of a family member. He suggested that one or both parents of a schizophrenic are troubled, immature individuals who, having experienced serious emotional conflict with their own parents, are now subjecting their offspring to similar conflict situations (for further discussion of Bowen's theories, see Chapter 8).

Succeeding Bowen as head of the Family Studies Section at NIMH, Lyman Wynne, trained both in psychiatry and the social sciences, focused his research on the blurred, ambiguous, and confused communication patterns in families with schizophrenic members. In a series of papers (Wynne, Ryckoff, Day, & Hirsch, 1958; Wynne & Singer, 1963), he and his colleagues addressed the social organization of such families, searching for ways in which their communication patterns could be differentiated from more normal families. For example, observing the families' recurrent fragmented and irrational style of communication, these researchers hypothesized that such a family pattern contributes to the schizophrenic member's tendency to interpret events occurring around him or her in blurred or distorted ways. In turn, such confusion or occasional bafflement increases the schizophrenic's social and interpersonal vulnerability, both within and outside the family.

Wynne offered the term **pseudomutuality**—giving the appearance of a mutual, open, and understanding relationship without really having one—to describe how such families conceal an underlying distance between members. Pseudomutuality is a shared family maneuver designed to defend all of the members against pervasive feelings of meaninglessness and emptiness. One family member typically is designated the "identified patient," permitting the perpetuation of the myth by others that they themselves are normal. A person who grows up in a pseudomutual family setting fails to develop a strong sense of personal identity, since the predominant family theme is fitting together, even at the expense of developing separate identities. Indeed, the effort to cultivate a separate sense of self is viewed as a threat to family unity. This lack of identity handicaps the person from engaging in successful interactions outside the family and makes involvement within his or her own family system all-important. According to Wynne and his associates (1958), the preschizophrenic doubts his or her capacity to accurately derive meaning from a personal experience outside the family, preferring instead to return to the familiar, self-sufficient family system with its enclosed (but safe) boundaries.

Wynne labeled such resistance to outside influences a **rubber fence,** a changeable situation in which the specific boundaries of the family may shift, as though made of rubber, allowing in certain acceptable information, but closing in an unpredictable or arbitrary manner in order to keep unacceptable information out. Here the rules are in a state of continuous flux, as the family attempts to minimize threatening contact with the outside world.

Overview of Early Schizophrenia Family Research

All of the studies described in this section were cross-sectional in design, involving families in which schizophrenia had been diagnosed in a member, usually a young adult, often long before the research was carried out. A common underlying assumption was that disturbances in family relationships are the major cause of mental disorders in general, and that perhaps distinctive patterns of family dynamics can be discovered for each form of psychopathology. Unfortunately, as Goldstein (1988) observes, the major barrier to testing such assumptions is that families were studied long after the major mental disorder such as schizophrenia had affected the family system.

Despite these deficits in research design, however, considerable enthusiasm was aroused by this new field of clinical inquiry into the baffling etiology of schizophrenia. A number of schizophrenia/family researchers met together for the first time at the 1957 national convention of the interdisciplinary American Orthopsychiatric Association. Although no separate organization was formed by this still-small group of researchers, they did learn of each other's work. The subsequent cross-fertilization of ideas culminated in *Intensive Family Therapy* (Boszormenyi-Nagy & Framo, 1965), a report by 15 authorities on their research with schizophrenics and their families. The clinical investigations begun a decade earlier had laid the groundwork for the emerging field of family therapy.

MARRIAGE AND PREMARRIAGE COUNSELING

The fields of marriage and premarriage counseling, precursors of family therapy, are based on the concept that psychological disturbances arise as much from conflicts between persons as from conflict within a person. Focusing on some of the unique problems of this special form of coupling, early marital counselors (gynecologists and sometimes other physicians, lawyers, social workers,[1] college professors who were family-life specialists), viewed as "experts," attempted to provide answers for people with sexual and other marital difficulties (Broderick & Schrader, 1991). Clergy were especially prominent in offering formal premarital counseling, often as part of an optional or mandatory preparation program before a wedding (Stahmann & Hiebert, 1997).

If we assume that people have always been ready to advise or seek advice from others, informal marriage counseling has certainly existed for as long as the institution of marriage. On the other hand, formal counseling by a professional marriage counselor probably began somewhat over 70 years ago in the United States when the physicians Abraham and Hannah Stone opened the Marriage Consultation Center in New York in 1929. A year later, Paul Popenoe (a biologist specializing in human heredity) founded the American Institute of Family Relations in Los Angeles, offering premarital guidance as well as aid in promoting marital adjustment. Family educator Emily Mudd started the Marriage Council of Philadelphia in 1932 and later wrote what is thought to be the first textbook in the field (Mudd, 1951). In 1941, largely through Mudd's prodding, the American Association of Marriage Counselors (AAMC) was formed, bringing together various professionals, primarily physicians, but also others concerned with the new interdisciplinary field of marriage counseling. This organization has led the way in developing standards for training and practice, certifying marriage counseling centers, and establishing a professional code of ethics (Broderick & Schrader, 1991).

Similarly, the first documented premarital intervention program was offered by Ernest Groves (later to be first president of AAMC) in 1924 in a family life preparation course at Boston University. Through the mid-1950s the small batch of pertinent literature available often focused on such individually oriented topics as physical examinations by physicians as part of premarital counseling efforts. Assistance offered by clergy was apt to be educational and informational, and to have an intrapsychic orientation rather than attend to the couple's interpersonal relationship. If relationship problems were addressed at all, they were likely to be seen as a by-product of a problem within one or both the prospective newlyweds (Stahmann & Hiebert, 1997). Rutledge's survey of AAMC members in 1966 found very few performing premarital counseling.

By the mid-1960s, it was still possible to characterize marriage counseling (and premarriage counseling) as a set of practices in search of a theory (Manus, 1966). No breakthrough research was being carried out, no dominant theories had emerged, no

---

[1]Social workers are the unheralded pioneers of what later became the field of family therapy. From the founding of the first citywide charity organization in 1877 in Buffalo, N.Y., social workers have been at the forefront delivering services to needy families. *Family casework* is an integral part of social worker preparation and the Family Service Associations of America, beginning in 1911, have been composed of social work agencies specializing in the treatment of marriage and families. Broderick and Schrader (1991) suggest that a case could be made that both marriage counseling and family therapy had their origins within the broader field of social casework. Beginning with Virginia Satir, and as we illustrate throughout the book, many leading family therapists have come from a social work background.

major figure had gained recognition. The AAMC published no journal of its own. If practitioners published at all, they apparently preferred to submit articles to journals of their own professions. By the 1970s, however, the situation began to change. Among others, Olson (1970) urged an integration of marriage counseling and the emerging field of family therapy, since both focus on the marital relationship and not simply on individuals in the relationship. In 1970, the AAMC, bowing to increased interest by its members in family therapy, changed its name to the American Association of Marriage and Family Counselors (in 1978, it became the present American Association for Marriage and Family Therapy). In 1975, the organization launched the *Journal of Marriage and Family Counseling* (renamed the *Journal of Marital and Family Therapy* in 1979). By then, as Broderick and Schrader (1991) observe, marriage counseling (and by implication premarriage counseling) had "become so merged with the more dynamic family-therapy movement that it had all but lost its separate sense of identity" (p. 15).

The history of sex counseling parallels marriage counseling and had many of the same practitioners. Moving to become a separate specialty, the American Association of Sex Educators and Counselors was formed in 1967, and set up standards and granted certificates for qualified sex therapists. Since 1970, two journals, the *Journal of Sex and Marital Therapy* and the *Journal of Sex Education and Therapy* have disseminated information in this fast growing therapeutic movement.

What exactly is marriage counseling or, as it is called more and more frequently, marital therapy? Not considered to be as deeply probing, intensive, or as prolonged as psychotherapy, marriage counseling, as initially practiced, tended to be short-term, attempted to repair a damaged relationship, and by and large dealt with here-and-now issues rather than reconstructing the past. Unlike psychotherapy, which probed inner meanings, marriage counseling addressed reality issues and offered guidance to troubled couples in order to facilitate their conscious decision-making processes. Early premarital counseling tended to be even less attentive to relationship issues or why this couple chose one another, content to help the pair prepare for marriage by becoming aware of any neurotic individual problems that might cause later hardships.

As the outlook grew during the late 1950s, in conjunction with family research, that problems arise out of a relationship context, a therapy approach offering a systems viewpoint began to replace the earlier counseling orientation. Marital therapy offered a broader perspective, focusing on interlocking problems and neurotic interactions between spouses. Marital therapists today address the affective, cognitive, and behavioral aspects of the husband-wife relationship within the context of marital and family systems (Nichols, 1988).

Couples entering premarital therapy may be doing so as a kind of checkup on the viability of their relationship before marrying, or, more significantly, one or both may fear that some underlying conflict remains unresolved and may lead to a further deterioration of their relationship once married. When one or the other (or both) has been divorced, particularly if there are children from a previous marriage, such caution is especially apparent (Goldenberg & Goldenberg, 1998)

Most people who seek help for their marriage are attempting to cope with a crisis (such as infidelity, threat of divorce, disagreements regarding child rearing, money problems, sexual incompatibilities, ineffective communication patterns, conflicts over power and control) that has caused an imbalance in the family equilibrium. Each partner enters marital therapy with different experiences, expectations, and goals and with different degrees of commitment to the marriage. Both partners are probably somewhat invested in staying married or they would not seek professional help, but the strength of the determination to stay together may vary greatly between them.

As traditionally practiced, marriage counseling was likely to involve a coordinated approach; each spouse was seen by a separate counselor, who could then compare how his or her client saw a conflict situation with how the spouse reported the same situation to the other counselor. Martin and Bird (1963) called it "stereoscopic therapy" to emphasize that each counselor got a double view of each client. While such an approach overcame some of the pitfalls of seeing a single individual about his or her marital problems, firsthand observation of the ongoing relationship is forfeited. No matter how well briefed by the collaborating colleague, each counselor has a necessarily limited view of the marriage and no view whatsoever of the marital interaction (Bodin, 1983).

In concurrent counseling, a less common approach, a counselor worked with both spouses, but saw each one separately. The counselor then had to piece together how the couple functioned by hearing both sides of the same event or marital interaction. Remaining impartial, remembering what information had been learned from whom, and keeping confidential any secrets one spouse requested the counselor not to reveal to the other spouse all became problematic if the counselor was to remain faithful to this concurrent-but-separate rule (Sager, 1966).

As the focus of marital counseling turned more and more to changing the marital relationship as such, it became clear that couples should be seen together in joint therapy sessions. Jackson (1959) introduced the term **conjoint** therapy to describe the situation where a couple (or perhaps the entire family) worked with the same therapist in the same room at the same time. By the end of the 1960s, Olson (1970) was able to declare that marital therapists as a group could be distinguished both by their primary emphasis on understanding and modifying the marital relationship and their preference for conjoint treatment.

THE CHILD GUIDANCE MOVEMENT

Two additional streams of thought and clinical development, frequently overlooked, deserve mention for their influences in the evolution of family therapy. The *child guidance movement*, emerging early in the twentieth century, was based on the assumption that if emotional problems did indeed begin in childhood—as Freud and others were arguing—then early identification and treatment of children could prevent later psychopathology. Alfred Adler, an early associate of Freud's, was especially cognizant of the key role early family experiences played in determining later adult behavior. Adler helped found the child guidance movement in Vienna in the early 1900s, and while he did not work therapeutically with entire families, he did influence one of his disciples, Rudolph Dreikurs, who later emigrated to the United

States, to expand child guidance centers into family counseling centers (Lowe, 1982).

By 1909, William Healy, a psychiatrist, had founded the Juvenile Psychopathic Institute in Chicago, a forerunner among child guidance clinics (now known as the Institute for Juvenile Research). Healy was especially concerned with treating (and, if possible, discovering ways of preventing) juvenile delinquency. Moving to Boston, Healy had, by 1917, established the Judge Baker Guidance Center devoted to the diagnostic evaluation and treatment of delinquent children (Goldenberg, 1983). In 1924, the American Orthopsychiatric Association, largely devoted to the prevention of emotional disorders in children, was organized. Although child guidance clinics remained few in number until after World War II, they now exist in almost every city in the United States.

Early treatment programs were team efforts, organized around a psychiatrist (psychotherapy), a psychologist (educational and remedial programs), and a social worker (casework with parents and outside agencies). It was standard procedure (and still is in traditional clinics) for the parent (almost certainly the more available mother) to visit the clinic regularly for treatment, usually seeing a different therapist from the one working with her child. This collaborative approach has now evolved into joint therapy sessions in most clinics, more than likely involving both parents as well as siblings of the identified patient. Child guidance clinics continue to function on the principle of early intervention in a child's—family's—emotional problems in order to avert the later development of more serious disabilities.

GROUP DYNAMICS AND GROUP THERAPY

Group dynamics and the behavior of small groups served as models of family functioning for some early family therapists such as John Bell (1961). For these therapists, family therapy was a special subset of *group therapy*, except that the participants were not strangers. These practitioners took the position that families are essentially natural groups and that the therapist's task was to promote interaction, facilitate communication, clarify the group process, and interpret interpersonal dynamics—such as any group therapy leader would do. Bell called his approach **family group therapy.**

Group therapy has been practiced in one form or another since the beginning of the twentieth century, but the impetus for its major expansion came from the need for clinical services during and immediately after World War II. The earliest use of the group process in psychotherapy can be credited to the Austrian psychiatrist Jacob Moreno who, around 1910, combined dramatic and therapeutic techniques to create **psychodrama.** Moreno, whose psychodramatic techniques are still used today, believed that it is necessary to recreate in the therapeutic process the various interpersonal situations that may have led to the patient's psychological difficulties. Since this was hard to accomplish in the one-to-one therapist-patient situation, Moreno, in the role of therapist/director, used a stage on which the patient could act out his or her significant life events in front of an audience. In these psychodramas, various people (frequently, but not necessarily, other patients) represented key persons ("auxiliary egos") in the patient's life. At certain junctures, the director might instruct the patient to reverse roles with one of the players so that he or she could gain a greater awareness of how another person saw him or her. The exploration of a family's interpersonal give-and-take and the resolution of its conflicts through psychodramatic means made this model a natural fit for many family therapists.

Stimulated largely by the theories developed by British psychoanalysts Wilfred Bion and Melanie Klein (see Chapter 6), considerable interest in group processes developed during the 1930s at the Tavistock Institute in London. Several therapists began experimenting with group intervention techniques (Bion, 1961). In particular, they emphasized dealing with current problems ("here and now") rather than searching for past causes and explanations or reconstructing possibly traumatic early experiences. Samuel Slavson, an engineer by training, began to do group work at the Jewish Board of Guardians in New York City at about the same time; from this work emerged his activity-group therapy technique, in which a group setting encourages disturbed children or adolescents to interact, thereby acting out their conflicts, impulses, and typical behavior patterns (Slavson, 1964). Slavson's approach was based on concepts derived from psychoanalysis, group work, and progressive education. In 1943 the American Group Psychotherapy Association was formed, largely through Slavson's efforts.

In the 1960s, stimulated by the emergence of various growth centers around the United States, particularly the Esalen Institute in Big Sur, California, the **encounter group** (part of the human potential movement) made a dramatic impact on the therapy scene and seemed to gain the immediate approval of large numbers of people, mostly from the upper-middle class. Today that enthusiasm has waned considerably, although traditional group therapies (Yalom, 1995) and, to a lesser extent, encounter groups, continue to exist side by side (Goldenberg, 1983).

Fundamental to the practice of group therapy is the principle that a small group can act as a carrier of change and strongly influence those who choose to be considered its members. A therapy group is a meaningful and real unit in and of itself, more than a collection of strangers, more than the sum of its parts. Another way of putting it is that the group is a collection of positions and roles and not of individuals (Back, 1974). The Tavistock version of group therapy is a good illustration: The group is treated as if it were a disturbed patient who is hurting because certain functions are not being carried out successfully. In a Tavistock group, the leader helps the group to function in a more balanced, coordinated, and mutually reinforcing way so that the group can accomplish productive work more efficiently. The implications for group therapy with a dysfunctional family are obvious. Table 5.1 summarizes some unique advantages of group therapy.

THE EVOLUTION OF FAMILY THERAPY

The clinical and research endeavors we have described eventuated into the field of family therapy. In this section, we describe that evolvement.

Table 5.1 Some Special Advantages of Group Therapy over Individual Therapy

Principle	Elaboration
Resembles everyday reality more closely	Therapist sees patient interacting with others, rather than hearing about it from the patient and possibly getting a biased or distorted picture; adds another informational dimension regarding his or her customary way of dealing with people.
Reduces social isolation	Patient learns that he or she is not unique by listening to others; thus he or she may be encouraged to give up feelings of isolation and self-consciousness.
Greater feelings of support and caring from others	Group cohesiveness ("we-ness") leads to increased trust; self-acceptance is likely to increase when patient is bolstered by acceptance by strangers.
Imitation of successful coping styles	New group members have the opportunity to observe older members and their successful adaptationa skills.
Greater exchange of feelings through feedback	Group situation demands expression of feelings, both positive and negative, directed at other members who evoke love, frustration, tears, or rage; patient thus gains relief while also learning from responses of others that intense affect does not destroy anyone, as he or she may have feared or fantasized.
Increases self-esteem through helping others	Patient has the opportunity to reciprocate help, to offer others empathy, warmth, acceptance, support, and genuineness, thereby increasing his or her own feelings of self-worth.
Greater insight	Patients become more attuned to understanding human motives and behavior, in themselves and in others.

Source: Goldenberg, 1983

From Family Research to Family Treatment

Most of the surveys of the family therapy movement (Broderick & Schrader, 1991; Goldenberg & Goldenberg, 1983; Guerin, 1976) agree that the 1950s was its founding decade. It was then that the theories and approaches we have been describing seemed to coalesce. Those ideas, to be sure, pertained more to clinical research than to clinical practice. Observation of the family—particularly one with a symptomatic member—could be justified only if it was presented as a research strategy. Observation of a family as a basis for treatment would have been a direct challenge to the prevailing sanction of confidentiality against a therapist's contact with anyone in the family other than her or his own patient.

Family therapy therefore owes its legitimacy to the facts that (1) it was carried out for scientifically defensible research purposes and (2) the "research" was being done on clinical problems such as schizophrenia that did not respond well to the established psychotherapies of that time (Segal & Bavelas, 1983). As Wynne (1983) notes, Bateson's Schizophrenia Communication Research Project in Palo Alto, the work of Lidz and his coresearchers in New Haven, and Bowen's ambitious effort to hospitalize parents of schizophrenics for residential treatment with their disturbed offspring at the Menninger Clinic and later NIMH were all initially research-motivated and research-oriented. Wynne's own work at NIMH with schizophrenics was based on the use of therapy as a source of experimental data. It was the apparent success of the family research that helped give the stamp of approval to the development of therapeutic techniques.

Who actually deserves credit for first adopting a family therapy approach with client families? Certainly no single person, although Nathan Ackerman, a child psychoanalyst in the child guidance movement, is generally credited with having written the first paper dealing specifically with treating an entire family (Ackerman, 1937). In contrast to the coordinated approach practiced by most child guidance clinics, in which parent and child were seen by separate but collaborating therapists, Ackerman began seeing entire families together at least a decade before others joined him.

John Bell, an academic psychologist at Clark University in Worcester, Massachusetts, was another major architect of family therapy. Bell (1975) recalls that a casual remark overheard while he was visiting the Tavistock Clinic in London in 1951—to the effect that Dr. John Bowlby, a prominent psychoanalyst, was experimenting with group therapy with entire families—stimulated his interest in applying the technique to treat behavior problems in children. Bell assumed that Bowlby was treating the entire family, although this later proved to be an erroneous assumption; actually, Bowlby only occasionally held a family conference as an adjunct to working with the problem child. On the basis of this misinformation, Bell began to think through the technical implications of meeting with an entire family on a regular basis. Once back in the United States, a case came to his attention that gave him the opportunity to try out this method as a therapeutic device. Bell's description of his work was not widely disseminated until a decade later (Bell, 1961). That groundbreaking monograph is often thought, along with Ackerman's 1958 text, to represent the founding of family therapy as practiced today. Unlike most of their colleagues in the 1950s, both Bell and Ackerman worked with nonschizophrenic families.

As noted previously, Don Jackson deserves recognition as a family therapy pioneer, introducing an influential set of descriptive constructs for comprehending family communication patterns (family rules, homeostasis, the redundancy principle) and initiating conjoint treatment to help overcome noxious family interactive patterns. Along with other members of the Palo Alto group, particularly seminal thinkers Jay Haley and John Weakland, Jackson helped develop innovative ways to influence a family's relationship context in order to produce change. (Bateson, a founder of the field but himself not a therapist, was less concerned with the application of the clinical ideas his group had generated than he was with the philosophy underlying those ideas. His overriding cybernetic view of circular causality focused instead on the process by which people exchange messages, rather than drawing inferences regarding their motives in doing so.)

A list of family therapy trailblazers must also include Murray Bowen, for his organized set of theoretical proposals (see Chapter 8) as well as his innovative technique of hospitalizing families with a schizophrenic member in order to study mother-child symbiotic influences. Carl Whitaker, too, began working with families at Oak Ridge, Tennessee, the site of the secret government plant taking part in the manufacture of the first atomic bomb during World War II. Pressed into wartime service, he himself had not received the customary psychiatric training, then largely psycho-analytic, and his innovative and often whimsical techniques (Chapter 7) perhaps reflect his less-than-orthodox training: the use of a cotherapist, the inclusion of intergenerational family members in a patient's therapy, a highly active style with patients.

Ackerman, Bell, Jackson, Bowen, Whitaker—working separately at first and unfamiliar with each other's efforts—gave life to the emerging field of family thera-py. During its formative stages, Jay Haley, Virginia Satir, Lyman Wynne, Salvador Minuchin, Ivan Boszormenyi-Nagy, and James Framo played important roles in fur-thering the field's development. However, it was Christian Midelfort, at the 1952 American Psychiatric Association convention, who presented a paper that was prob-ably the first to report on the treatment of psychiatric patients by including their families in the therapeutic sessions. Later expanded into a book (Midelfort, 1957), the paper described Midelfort's experiences and results with family therapy working with relatives and patients in and out of mental hospitals. Unfortunately, Midelfort's pioneering efforts are all but forgotten by most family therapists today since his geo-graphic location (Lutheran Hospital in La Crosse, Wisconsin) and lack of academic or training center affiliation isolated him from the mainstream of activity and the exchange of ideas and techniques then taking place.

Soon after, through organizing a series of family therapy conferences devoted to the treatment of schizophrenia, including a celebrated 1955 event at Sea Island, Georgia, Whitaker was able to bring together many leaders of the emerging family therapy field (for example, John Rosen and Albert Scheflen from Philadelphia as well as Gregory Bateson and Don Jackson from Palo Alto). The conferences, in which schizophrenics and their families were interviewed while being observed behind a one-way mirror,[2] led to the publication of an early text on the psychotherapy of chronic schizophrenic patients (Whitaker, 1958).

By 1957 the family movement had surfaced nationally (Guerin, 1976) as family researchers and clinicians in various parts of the country began to learn of each other's work. Ackerman, having organized and chaired the first meeting on family diagnosis and treatment at the 1955 American Orthopsychiatric Association, had moved to New York and in 1957 established the Family Mental Health Clinic of Jewish Family Services. In that same year, Ivan Boszormenyi-Nagy, having emigrat-ed a decade earlier from Hungary, joined the Eastern Pennsylvania Psychiatric Institute in Philadelphia in order to conduct research on schizophrenia. Boszormenyi-Nagy was able to assemble a distinguished group of researchers and cli-nicians and to help make Philadelphia a major early center for family therapy (Broderick & Schrader, 1991).

By 1959, Don Jackson, remaining a consultant on the Bateson project, had founded the Mental Research Institute (MRI) in Palo Alto; Virginia Satir, Jay Haley, John Weakland, Paul Watzlawick, Arthur Bodin, and Richard Fisch would soon join

---

[2]The use of a one-way mirror lifted the secrecy from the therapeutic process. Introduced into family ther-apy by Charles Fulweiler, its use allowed others to observe families in operation as a group, often pro-ducing insights into their interactive patterns. Slovik and Griffith (1992) consider the introduction of this observational technique as a significant landmark in the history of family therapy, providing, as it did, clincial confirmation of such concepts as circular causality.

the staff. A year later, Ackerman organized the Family Institute in New York (renamed the Ackerman Institute for Family Therapy after the death of its founder in 1971). Representing the East and West coasts, both institutes have played embryonic roles in the evolution of the family therapy field.

The Rush to Practice

Several significant developments in the 1960s indicated the momentum that the field of family therapy was gathering. In 1962, Ackerman and Jackson founded the first—and still the most influential—journal in the field, *Family Process,* with Jay Haley as its editor. From its beginnings, the journal enabled researchers and practitioners alike to exchange ideas and identify with the field. In addition, several important national conferences were organized. A meeting in 1964 dealt with the application of systems theory to understanding dysfunctional families (Zuk & Boszormenyi-Nagy, 1967); in 1967 a conference organized by psychologist James Framo was held to stimulate and maintain an ongoing dialogue between family researchers, theorists, and family therapists (Framo 1972).

Family therapy, gaining professional respectability, was becoming a familiar topic at most psychiatric and psychological meetings. As Bowen (1976) later recalled, dozens of therapists were eager to present their newly minted intervention techniques with whole families. In nearly all cases, this "rush to practice" precluded the development of procedures that were adequately grounded in research or based on sound conceptual formulations. In their clinical zeal—Bowen refers to it as "therapeutic evangelism"—many therapists attempted solutions to family dilemmas using familiar concepts borrowed from individual psychotherapy.

One notable exception to the emphasis on practice over theory and research during this period was Minuchin's Wiltwyck School Project, a pioneering study of urban slum families (Minuchin, Montalvo, Guerney, Rosman, & Schumer, 1967), and his development of appropriate clinical techniques for successful intervention with male juvenile delinquents, many of whom were Puerto Ricans or blacks from New York City. From this landmark study of poor, disadvantaged, unstable families, largely without fathers or stable father figures, Minuchin developed an approach he called *structural family therapy* that was pragmatic and oriented toward problem resolution, always mindful of the social environment or context in which the family problems emerged and were maintained.

By 1965, Minuchin had become director of the Philadelphia Child Guidance Clinic, originally in the heart of the African American ghetto, where he focused on intervention techniques with low-income families. His staff included Braulio Montalvo and Bernice Rosman from Wiltwyck, and in 1967 he invited Jay Haley (who, together with Weakland had joined the MRI in Palo Alto at the close of the Bateson project)[3] to join them. The Philadelphia center was soon transformed from

---

[3]The Bateson research group had officially disbanded in 1962. Bateson, trained in ethnology, and more interested in theoretical ideas regarding communication than in their clinical application to troubled families, moved on to the Oceanic Institute in Hawaii in order to observe patterns of communication among dolphins.

a traditional child guidance clinic into a large family-oriented treatment and training center. By the late 1960s, the Philadelphia group had begun working with psychosomatic families (with particular attention to families of anorexia nervosa patients), applying some of Minuchin's earlier concepts of boundaries and the interplay of a family's subsystems to psychosomatic problems (see Chapter 9).

During this highly productive period, the MRI on the West Coast extended its earlier studies to include families with expressions of dysfunctional behavior other than schizophrenia: delinquency, school underachievement, psychosomatic disorders, marital conflict (Bodin, 1981). The 1964 publication of *Conjoint Family Therapy* by Virginia Satir, then at MRI, did much to popularize the family approach, as did Satir's demonstrations at professional meetings and workshops in many parts of the world. Toward the end of the decade, the character of the work at the MRI changed as the result of Satir's departure to become the director of training at Esalen Institute, a humanistically oriented growth center at Big Sur, California; Haley's move to Philadelphia; and especially Jackson's untimely death in 1968. Although the MRI (Chapter 10) has continued to focus on family interactional patterns (particularly communication), the Brief Therapy Project, begun in 1967, became its major thrust (see Chapter 13).

Behavioral family therapy first appeared in the late 1960s. Initially individually focused, often involving amelioration for discrete problems of young children, the techniques introduced relied heavily on learning theory at first. These interventions with families were likely to be derived from empirical studies, and therapeutic procedures were continuously assessed for effectiveness. Consequently, the development of the behavioral approach with families depended less on charismatic leaders or innovative therapists and more on a clinician-researcher collaboration (Falloon, 1991). Nevertheless, some interdisciplinary leaders did emerge—psychologist Gerald Patterson, psychiatrist Robert Liberman, and social worker Richard Stuart. We discuss behavioral and subsequent cognitive contributions more fully in Chapter 12.

During the 1960s there were corresponding developments in family therapy outside of the United States. At the psychoanalytically oriented Institute of Family Therapy in London, Robin Skynner contributed a brief version of psychodynamic family therapy (Skynner, 1981). The British psychiatrist John Howells (1975) devised a system for family diagnosis as a necessary step in planning therapeutic intervention. In West Germany, Helm Stierlin (1972) called attention to patterns of separation in adolescence and related these patterns to family characteristics.

In Italy, Mara Selvini-Palazzoli (1978), trained in child psychoanalysis but discouraged by her results with anorectic children, was attracted to the new epistemology proposed by Bateson and the Palo Alto group. Shifting to a systems approach that stressed circularity, she was more successful with resistant cases. In 1967 Selvini-Palazzoli, together with colleagues Luigi Boscolo, Guiliana Prata, and Gianfranco Cecchin, formed the Institute for Family Studies in Milan; the Institute would eventually have a worldwide impact on the field of family therapy, particularly with its use of "long" brief therapy in which ten all-day sessions were held at monthly intervals. We will return to the work of the Milan family therapists in Chapter 11.

Innovative Techniques and Self-Examination

For the most part, technique continued to outdistance theory and research in family therapy well into the 1970s. The early part of the decade saw a proliferation of family therapy approaches in various parts of the United States: in Vermont, treating several families with hospitalized schizophrenic members simultaneously, in group therapy fashion, in a procedure called **multiple family therapy** (Laqueur, 1976); in Galveston, Texas, bringing families together for an intensive, crisis-focused two-day period of continuing interaction with a team of mental health professionals, in **multiple impact therapy** (MacGregor, Ritchie, Serrano, & Schuster, 1964); in Philadelphia, working in the home with an extended family group including friends, neighbors, and employers, in **network therapy** (Speck & Attneave, 1973); and in Colorado, treating a family on an outpatient basis in **family crisis therapy** instead of hospitalizing a disturbed, scapegoated family member (Langsley, Pittman, Machotka, & Flomenhaft, 1968).

Behavioral psychologists increasingly began to turn their attention to issues related to family matters, such as teaching parents "behavior management skills" to facilitate effective child rearing (Patterson, 1971), and to propose therapeutic strategies for working with marital discord (Jacobson & Martin, 1976) and family dysfunction (Liberman, 1970). The newly available technology of videotape allowed family therapists to tape ongoing sessions either for immediate playback to the family, for later study by the therapist, or for training purposes (Alger, 1976).

In the 1970s, having come of age, the field of family therapy engaged in its first efforts at self-examination. The so-called GAP report (Group for the Advancement of Psychiatry, 1970) acknowledged clinicians' increasing awareness of the family's role in symptom and conflict formation as well as of the limitations of the traditional psychoanalytic emphasis on intrapsychic processes. The GAP survey of a sample of family therapists found that they belonged largely to three disciplines—psychiatry, psychology, and social work—although practitioners also included marriage counselors, clergy, nonpsychiatric physicians, child psychiatrists, nurses, sociologists, and others. Most family therapists were young, reported dissatisfaction with the results of individual treatment, and were looking for a more efficient method of therapeutic intervention. When asked to select their primary and secondary goals from among eight categories, over 90 percent of the 290 respondents listed improved communication within the family as their primary goal; not a single respondent said it was rarely or never a goal. However, improvement in individual task performance or individual symptomatic improvement was more likely to be a secondary goal. This indicates that these objectives had by no means been abandoned but that change in only part of a family was given less emphasis than a family-wide change such as improved communication.

The 1970 GAP report also presented the results of a survey of practicing family therapists asked to rank the major figures in the field according to their influence at that time. The practitioners placed them in this order: Satir, Ackerman, Jackson, Haley, Bowen, Wynne, Bateson, Bell, Boszormenyi-Nagy.

In another kind of effort to bring order and self-awareness to the developing field, Beels and Ferber (1969) observed a number of leading therapists conducting family sessions and studied videotapes and films of their work with families. Beels and Ferber then distinguished two types of family therapists based on the therapist's relationship to the family group: **conductors** and **reactors.** Conductor therapists are active, aggressive, and colorful leaders who place themselves in the center of the family group. They are likely to initiate rather than respond, to propound ideas vigorously, to make their value systems explicit. Reactors are less theatrical personalities, more subtle and indirect. They observe and clarify the family group process, responding to what the family presents to them, negotiating differences among family members.

Beels and Ferber (1969) contended that each type of therapist is effective in directing and controlling the family sessions and in providing family members with possible new ways of relating to each other; the conductors are more direct in their methods but not necessarily more successful in helping to create a new family experience as the basis for changing its members' interactive behavior patterns.

Further self-examination took the form of outcome research on the effectiveness of family therapy. By the late 1970s the need to take stock was being generally acknowledged. Nevertheless, Wells and Dezen (1978) pointed out after surveying the outcome literature that most family therapy approaches, some of them identified with major figures in the field, "have never submitted their methods to empirical testing and, indeed, seem oblivious to such a need" (p. 266). By the end of the decade there had been some improvement (Gurman & Kniskern, 1981a), but the effectiveness of family therapy still required continuing and systematic evaluation. (For further discussion of this topic, see Chapter 15.)

Perhaps the form of self-analysis that had the most far-reaching impact on the field came from the feminist critique of family therapy. As we noted in Chapter 3, since the mid-1970s a growing number of family therapists, beginning with Hare-Mustin (1978), have argued that family therapy, both as conceptualized and practiced, showed bias in favor of values typically considered masculine—such as autonomy, independence, and control—while devaluing those nurturant and relationship values more customarily associated with females. Moreover, they maintained that developmental schemas typically adopted by family therapists are based on male development, and are assumed to be applicable to women as well. By adopting these schemas, as Slovik and Griffith (1992) point out, therapists tend to devalue qualities such as dependency and caretaking normally linked to women.

The family therapy pioneers, all of whom (with the exception of Satir) were men, have been chastised for failing to pay sufficient attention to the social and political context in which family members live. Even the venerated Bateson came under fire from feminists. In particular, they contended that his disregard of power and control differences between participants in any transaction, in favor of such cybernetic notions as reciprocity and circularity, assumed a lack of unilateral control by any one participant because the system was in a continuous state of flux. While feminists recognize the circular nature of transactions within a family, they argued that Bateson's formulation is oversimplified in its implication of equal responsibility (and equal blame), particularly in failing to acknowledge the crucial role of power differentiation (men and women; adults and children) in any ongoing relationship.

Professionalization and a New Epistemology

In the 1980s, a number of signs documented the phenomenal growth of the family therapy field, now in its "over-thirty" adult years. Whereas barely a decade earlier the field had one professional journal of its own, *Family Process,* there were now approximately two dozen family therapy journals, half of them published in English. Once, family therapy centers could be counted on the fingers of one hand; now more than 300 freestanding family therapy institutes existed in the United States alone.

Several organizations now represented the interests of family therapists. In addition to the interdisciplinary American Orthopsychiatric Association (where Ackerman first brought together practitioners interested in family research and treatment), the major groups are

• The American Association for Marriage and Family Therapy (AAMFT), which grew from fewer than 1000 members in 1970 to over 7500 by 1979, to 16,000 by 1989. The AAMFT has the authority to accredit marriage and family therapy training programs, to develop standards for issuing certificates to qualified persons as Approved Supervisors, to publish a code of ethics for its members, and to actively pursue state licensing and certification for marital and family therapists.

• The American Family Therapy Association (now called the American Family Therapy Academy), founded in 1977, a smaller interest group of approximately 1000 members by the end of the 1980s, concerned exclusively with family therapy issues as distinct from marriage counseling or marital therapy.

• The International Association of Marriage and Family Counselors, a division of the American Counseling Association, which grew from slightly over 100 members in 1986, when it was founded, to close to 8000 members in 1996. The IAMFC conducts educational programs and helps develop training standards for marriage and family counseling programs.

• The Division of Family Psychology of the American Psychological Association was established in 1986. As noted in Chapter 1, family psychology offers a broader perspective than the clinical emphasis of family therapy, paying special attention to relationship networks within marriage and the family. By the close of the 1980s, membership in the Division of Family Psychology was approximately 2000. In a related matter, the American Board of Professional Psychology, authorized by the American Psychological Association to issue diplomas granting competence in the applied areas of psychology, in the late 1980s added family psychology as a certifiable specialty.

• The International Family Therapy Association, made up of therapists, theorists, researchers, trainers, and other professionals working with families, was organized in 1987 and now has more than 500 members from 40 countries around the globe. IFTA conferences, held in various countries, allow for the firsthand exchange of ideas. The organization publishes a semiannual newsletter, the *International Connection,* announcing conferences and offering articles on marriage and family therapy topics.

Family therapy became an international phenomenon in the 1980s, with active training programs and congresses in Canada, England, Israel, Holland, Italy, Australia, West Germany, and elsewhere. The Heidelberg Conference, marking the tenth anniversary of the Department of Basic Psychoanalytic Research and Family Therapy of Heidelberg University in West Germany, took place in 1985, with some 2000 participants from 25 countries attending (Stierlin, Simon, & Schmidt, 1987). Bridging east-west differences in 1987, a family therapy conference attended by over 2500 people from all over the world took place in Prague, Czechoslovakia, followed in 1989 by a similar event in Budapest, Hungary.

Competing models of family therapy, usually associated with one or another of the field's founders, proliferated in the 1980s (Piercy & Sprenkle, 1990). Although each relied heavily on systems theory, differing versions, with differing emphases and perspectives, led to the further evolution, begun a decade or more earlier, of rival "schools" in the field. Nevertheless, the cross-fertilization of ideas continued—helped along by learning from one another through workshops and the videotapes of master family therapists of various persuasions.

One event, destined to have far-reaching consequences for the field for a decade or more, occurred with the publication of a single issue of *Family Process* early in the decade. In it, three sets of family therapists (Dell, 1982; Keeney & Sprenkle, 1982; Allman, 1982) raised important epistemological questions regarding the theoretical foundation, research models, and the clinical practice of family therapy. All were critical of the field's rush to put forth new techniques without first rethinking some of the cybernetic notions taken for granted by most family therapists. Dell, for example, objected to the term *homeostasis* as an "imperfectly defined explanatory notion" because it implied a process that returned a system to its previous state, and as such prevented change.

Arguing for what has become known as the *new epistemology,* Keeney and Sprenkle (1982) challenged the field to look beyond its narrow pragmatic approaches (exemplified by designing and carrying out interventions to overcome a family's specific presenting problem) to a broader consideration of overall family functioning. The pragmatic approach, they maintained, had led the field astray, leading to searching for more and better how-to-do-it methods and packageable techniques, but at the expense of more fully appreciating the context in which families live. In their view, the pragmatic approach's concern with results such as symptom reduction (behavioral and strategic techniques are examples) limits its vision of what really troubles families and how best to help them find solutions. Moreover, pragmatic views, influenced by early cybernetic notions, place the observer outside the phenomenon being observed, in effect equating families with machines, and paying insufficient attention to family interaction and context. Doing so, they argued, erroneously supports a linear notion that such an outsider is in a position unilaterally to manipulate and control a system he or she is observing.

Both Keeney and Sprenkle (1982) and Allman (1982) urged consideration of the *aesthetic*[4] dimensions of family therapy. Allman in particular believes the artistry of

---

[4]The distinction between *pragmatics* and *aesthetics* was first drawn by Bateson (1979), who viewed nature as consisting of interconnected systems. The former term is associated with the mechanics of practical strategies and problem solving. The latter, although a term usually associated with the philosophical study of art and beauty, is used by Bateson to refer to a system's response to patterns that connect the parts to one another. The terms are not antonyms; rather, aesthetics is a more holistic concept and thus underlies pragmatic considerations (Keeney & Thomas, 1986). New epistemologists argue that while "patterns that connect" (a favorite Bateson phrase) within a family can be changed by disrupting them, exactly what the change will be cannot be predicted or designed.

family therapy is revealed in the therapist's ability to grasp the unifying patterns connecting family members and, if stuck in one pattern they wish to change, to help them rearrange the connecting patterns in order to create new meanings in their lives.

To illustrate the difference, Keeney and Sprenkle (1982) offer the case of a woman who complains of severe anxiety attacks. The pragmatically oriented therapist might contract with her to engage in a therapeutic effort aimed specifically at alleviating the anxiety symptom. Success could then be evaluated empirically by quantitatively comparing the occurrence of the symptom before and after treatment. An aesthetically oriented therapist would be more concerned with the larger gestalt of family interactive patterns of which the symptom is but one part. The pragmatic therapist might actually acknowledge that the larger gestalt must change, but would contend that change would follow from symptom removal. The aesthetic therapist, on the other hand, doesn't argue with the pragmatic's technical considerations, but does not consider them to be primary. In the aesthetic view, instead of being an outside change agent, a therapist's presence should help create a new context—in a sense, a new "family"—so that new behavior may emerge.

By drawing attention to the act of observing what is being observed, and by becoming part of the system thus created, the new epistemological challenge led to the idea of second-order cybernetics, a view that was to gain prominence in the subsequent decade.

Integration, Eclecticism, and Postmodernism

While differences in philosophy about the nature of families and how best to intervene continue to exist between family therapists, "schools" as such are becoming less mutually exclusive and a clear trend exists toward integration of family therapy models (for example, psychodynamic, cognitive-behavioral, family systems) into a comprehensive approach (Wachtel, 1997). Therapists continue to view families from different perspectives, but today there is greater overlap and frequent borrowing from one another, as the clinical problem demands, even if such borrowing of technique or concept may not always be theoretically justifiable. Broderick and Schrader (1991) note that the field is moving away from the proliferation of narrowly trained specialists. Instead, most therapists are exposed to an overview of the entire field, developing skills as what these authors call "relational therapists." More than combining models, integrative efforts aim for a more holistic or comprehensive way of assessing and intervening with families. We take up the issues of integration and eclecticism in family therapy practice in Chapter 6.

By the mid-1990s constructionists had forced family therapists to reexamine some cherished systemic theoretical assumptions as well as how most effectively to intervene with troubled families. Constructionists believe objectivity is impossible, and that the therapist, presumably an outside observer of a family, in actuality participates in constructing what is observed. Their view helped move the thinking of many family therapists away from theoretical certainties and toward a greater respect for differences in outlook and viewpoints between themselves and individuals within families and between families with different gender, cultural, ethnic, or experiential backgrounds.

Instead of searching for the "truth" about a family, constructionists argue that each family member has his or her own version of "reality," conditioned by various psychological and biological factors (Maturana, 1978).[5] That is, multiple versions of reality exist within a family, each constructed by individual belief systems each person brings to interpreting a particular problem. The meaning each person derives from an event or situation or relationship is valid for that person; there is no absolute reality, only a set of subjective constructions created by each family member.

In this approach, which stresses a nonpathological approach to the therapeutic process, all therapists can do is help family members understand and reassess the assumptions and meanings each participant has constructed about a common family problem. The therapist does not try to change the family's structure, nor is he or she able to change the social conditions that help determine family functioning. Rather, change occurs as a result of a family reexamining their belief systems.

Therapists can help by introducing information intended to change patterns, but, from this viewpoint, cannot predict or design the exact nature of any subsequent changes. Family therapy, from this new perspective, becomes the collaborative creation of a context in which family members share their constructions of reality with one another, in the hope that the new information thus obtained will facilitate changes in perceptions among the members. As new meaning is co-constructed in conversation, new options and possibilities emerge (Friedman, 1993).

While still controversial, the epistemologies of constructionism and second-order cybernetics have become the cutting edge of family therapy. Instead of attempting to change family members, here efforts are directed at engaging families in "conversations" about their problems (Anderson & Goolishian, 1988) as a result of which they can begin to feel empowered to change themselves by becoming aware of, and accommodating to, each other's needs, wishes, and belief systems.

This clinical effort to make family therapy more focused on creating meanings through language rather than on behavioral sequences or family interactive patterns has been led by Paul Watzlawick (1984), Michael White (1989), and Lynn Hoffman (1990), as well as Harlene Anderson and Harry Goolishian (1988). Tom Andersen (1987), a Norwegian psychiatrist, employs an egalitarian technique he calls a *reflecting team,* in which a clinical team first watches a family and therapist behind a one-way mirror, then reverses roles and holds an open forum regarding what they have just seen while the family observes their discussion behind the one-way mirror. The idea is to offer a variety of new perceptions to the family, and for them to select those that appear to them to be meaningful and useful. The therapist team reflections are meant to stimulate new conversations within the family and ultimately to provoke greater understanding of oneself, one's surroundings, and one's relationships (Andersen, 1993). We'll return to examples of this therapeutic shift to meaning and away from action in Part IV of this text.

---

[5]Maturana, a biologist, believes organisms are *structure determined.* That is, they are limited in their functioning by the repertoire of what their nervous system will allow them to see. Thus, their perceptions are defined by their inner states and past experiences as much as by the process they are perceiving. No one, therefore, perceives an objective universe. Learning is at most an accommodation to a new situation and can occur only within strictly defined limits (Guttman, 1991).

One challenge of the new century calls for integrating the various approaches we are about to consider, developing and matching techniques designed for specific populations.

SUMMARY

Five seemingly independent scientific and clinical developments together set the stage for the emergence of family therapy: *systems theory*, exploring how relationships between parts of a system make up an integrated whole; *schizophrenic research,* helping establish the role of the dysfunctional family in the etiology of schizophrenia and setting the stage for studying interaction patterns in other kinds of families; *marital and premarital counseling*, bringing couples into conjoint treatment to resolve interpersonal conflicts rather than treat the participants separately; the *child guidance movement,* focusing on intervention with entire families; and *group dynamics* and *group therapy,* employing small-group processes for therapeutic gain and providing a model for therapy with whole families.

Stimulated by the research-oriented study of families with schizophrenic members, the family therapy movement gained momentum and national visibility in the 1950s. Technique continued to outpace theory and research well into the 1970s. Innovative therapeutic techniques were introduced, including behavioral approaches to family-related problems. By then, the field was growing at a rapid rate and a number of efforts aimed at self-awareness and self-evaluation were undertaken. Most noteworthy was the feminist critique of family therapy, challenging familiar family therapy tenets that reinforce sexist views and stereotype sex roles.

In the 1980s marital therapy and family therapy became an all-but-unified field. Practitioners from a variety of disciplines made "family therapist" their primary professional identification when joining interdisciplinary organizations. A new epistemology, challenging the early cybernetic notions, gained attention.

The trend, begun in earnest in the 1990s, was away from strict adherence to "schools" of family therapy and toward integration. Today, the postmodern constructionist paradigm concerns itself more with helping families examine their belief systems than in intervening in order to change their underlying structure or behavior patterns.

III

THE BASIC MODELS OF FAMILY THERAPY

6

Psychodynamic Models

All family therapists share a common view of the family as the context for relationships as well as a common therapeutic commitment to address the process of family interaction. Under the umbrella of systems theory, all attempt to examine what lies both within and outside the system—its multiple inputs and possible paths of actions—being careful not to neglect what transpires within the individual participants. Gender and cultural considerations as well as the interface between the family and the broader community in which it is embedded figure more and more prominently in the thinking and clinical approaches of contemporary family therapists.

While noteworthy differences continue to exist in the theoretical assumptions each school of thought makes about the nature and origin of psychological dysfunction, in what precisely they look for in understanding family patterns, and in their strategies for therapeutic intervention, in practice the trend today is toward eclecticism and integration[1] in family therapy (Moultrop, 1986; Mikesell, Lusterman, & McDaniel, 1995; Lebow, 1997). In this postmodern age that emphasizes that all knowledge is inescapably relative and subjective (Held, 1998), there is less and less acceptance of the erstwhile belief in the endless possibilities of a single model. The increasing prevalence of a wide variety of family configurations (single parents, gay couples, remarried families) and culturally diverse groups reinforces the idea that no single theory or set of interventions is likely to fit all equally well. Today's family therapists, including many who identify themselves as disciples of a particular school, are apt to be less doctrinaire than their theoretical differences suggest, incorporating

[1]*Eclecticism* and *integration* are related but not interchangeable notions. The former refers to the selection of concepts or intervention techniques from a variety of theoretical sources, usually based on the experiences of a clinician that a specific approach works with a certain set of presenting problems. Thus, eclecticism is usually unconcerned with theory but rather is pragmatic and case-based. Integration, more controversial, represents a paradigm shift, and calls for an extensive combining of discrete parts of theories and treatment processes into a higher-level theory that crosses theoretical boundaries and uses intervention techniques in a unified fashion. While no one integrative theory has yet emerged as predominant, a number of efforts have appeared, such as Dattilio's (1998) endeavor to combine systemic and cognitive perspectives, Pinsof's (1995) attempt to synthesize family, individual, and biological therapies, and Wachtel's (1997) bid to integrate psychoanalysis, behavior therapy, and the relational world of family therapy.

contributions from "rival" schools in their treatment approaches when appropriate. Greater acceptance of a diversity of ideas within the field allows for a greater range of choices in what specific set of therapeutic interventions to adopt in specific situations or specific kinds of family problems in order to achieve optimal effectiveness. Prochaska and Norcross (1994) contend that the modal orientation of family therapists today is eclecticism/integration.

While the unadulterated practice of a single form of family therapy is becoming less common and therapists today are likely to borrow concepts and techniques from one another that cross theoretical boundaries, there nevertheless are important distinguishing theoretical constructs between the various traditional schools of family therapy. While there may not be slavish devotion in practice, a therapist's theory helps organize what information to seek and how to go about seeking it, how to formulate a therapeutic plan, make interventions, and understand what transpires. (Because of this selectivity factor, each theory is also necessarily limited and one-sided, nor can any single theory explain and predict all the behavior patterns observed or provide a treatment rationale for all behavioral, intrapsychic, or interpersonal problems) (Carlson, Sperry, & Lewis, 1997).

In this and the following six chapters in Part III, we look at the established approaches to family theory and clinical practice, grouping those models that are primarily psychodynamic (concerned with insight, motivation, unconscious conflict, attachments); those that emphasize the experiential/humanistic viewpoint (self-growth, self-determination); those that pay special attention to the family as a system (transaction patterns, alliances, boundaries)—the transgenerational, structural, strategic, and systemic models; and those that are cognitive/behavioral in their approach (emphasizing learning and action therapies).[2]

Later in the text, in Part IV, we present some evolving theories and therapeutic techniques that challenge these entrenched models. Here we offer some fresh outlooks, such as solution-focused and narrative therapy, largely influenced by the postmodern proposition that people invent rather than discover reality. Such considerations have tended to deconstruct the field's complacent notions of objectivity and therapeutic certainty regarding what causes family dysfunction and how best to help families get back on track. We also include psychoeducational approaches to family therapy, which represent another shift in our thinking of what causes problems, symptoms, or disabilities in individual family members; rather than look to the family as the source of the difficulties, therapeutic efforts are directed at maximizing the functioning of families to whom problems, such as schizophrenia in a family member, have occurred.

THE PLACE OF THEORY

The theoretical foundation of the field of family therapy demands to be strengthened lest it become merely a set of clever, even flashy, empirically derived intervention

---

[2]Differences in theoretical outlook as well as therapeutic techniques and goals between models of family therapy appear in chart form at the back of this text. Appendix A compares family therapy theories along several key dimensions, and Appendix B does the same for methods of clinical intervention.

techniques. Important and seemingly effective as some of these techniques may be, they require the kind of rationale or justification that only a coherent, unified theory can provide. Acknowledging the usefulness of employing a variety of therapeutic techniques as called for by the needs of a specific family, Patterson (1997) nevertheless argues that a clear theoretical position provides the structural underpinnings for assessment and treatment planning to occur. He maintains that a therapist must accurately identify the major theoretical orientation from which he or she operates before utilizing congruent intervention methods within it.

While techniques relevant to helping a specific family may be borrowed by an eclectic therapist, there remains considerable controversy over whether an integrated supertheory is ever likely to emerge, since, as Grunebaum (1997) points out, there are too many inherent incompatibilities in the central theoretical constructs of the major theories for such a conceptual integration to occur. As we are about to see, different schools of family therapy make different assumptions about human nature, have different goals, and use different criteria for evaluating what constitutes a successful outcome (Liddle, 1982).

All theories, of course, are inevitably speculations or hypotheses offered in the hope of shedding light or providing fresh perspectives on the causes of family dysfunction. They are never, in and of themselves, true or false; rather, some are more useful than others, particularly in generating research hypotheses that can be verified through testing. All of these theories are tentative; all are expendable in the sense that useful theories lead to new ways of looking at behavior and to the discovery of new relationships that in turn lead to new sets of theoretical proposals.

At this stage in the development of family therapy we need to examine the usefulness of the various contributions that have already been made to our understanding of family development and functioning. Some models have come from the research laboratory, others from the consultation room of a clinician working with seriously disturbed or merely temporarily troubled families. In evaluating each of the models presented in this and subsequent chapters, keep in mind the following criteria of a sound theory:

- Is it *comprehensive?* Does it deal with understanding family functioning and avoid being trivial or oversimplified? Is it generalizable to all families as they behave in all situations (not, for example, only to white middle-class families or only to the ways families behave in special psychotherapeutic situations)?
- Is it *parsimonious?* Does it make as few assumptions as necessary to account for the phenomena under study? If two competing theoretical systems both predict the same behavior, is the theory chosen the one with fewer assumptions and constructs?
- Is it *verifiable?* Does it generate predictions about behavior that can be confirmed when the relevant empirical data have been collected?
- Is it *precise?* Does it define concepts explicitly and relate them to each other and to data (avoiding relying solely on figurative, metaphorical, or analogical language)?
- Is it *empirically valid?* Do systematic empirical tests of the predictions made by the theory confirm the theory?

- Is it *stimulating?* Does it provoke response and further investigation to enhance the theory or even to demonstrate its inadequacies?

SOME HISTORICAL CONSIDERATIONS

Psychoanalysis, both as theory and a form of practice, deserves recognition for playing the central role in establishing and defining the nature of psychotherapy (Sander, 1998). Initially focused on treating neurotic individuals by examining and reconstructing childhood conflicts, generated by the colliding forces of inner drives and external experiences, psychoanalysis became the dominant ideology in American psychiatry after World War II. Shortly before the war, a large number of European clinicians (including Erik Erikson and Erich Fromm), psychoanalytic in their orientation, had come to this country to escape the Nazi regime. The American public had been receptive to Freud's ideas since early in this century. With the arrival of these clinicians, psychoanalysis began to gain greater acceptance among medical specialists, academicians, and clinicians in the psychology community, as well as among sociologists and psychiatric social workers. Indeed, many of family therapy's pioneers—Ackerman, Bowen, Lidz, Jackson, Minuchin, Wynne, Boszormenyi-Nagy—(all men, incidentally), were psychoanalytically trained. Some, such as Jackson and Minuchin, moved far from their psychoanalytic roots in favor of systems thinking, while others (Bowen, Lidz, Wynne) continued to produce theories that reflected some of their earlier allegiances.

Freud, founder of psychoanalysis, had been aware of the impact of family relationships on the individual's character formation, particularly in the development of symptomatic behavior. For example, in his famous case of Little Hans, a 5-year-old boy who refused to go out into the street for fear that a horse might bite him, Freud hypothesized that Hans was displacing anxiety associated with his Oedipus complex. That is, Freud believed Hans unconsciously desired his mother sexually but felt competitive with, and hostile toward, his father, as well as fearful of his father's reaction to his hostility. Hans had witnessed a horse falling down in the street, and Freud speculated that he unconsciously associated the scene with his father, since he wanted his father hurt too. According to Freud, Hans unconsciously changed his intense fear of castration by his father into a phobic symptom about being bitten by the horse, whom Hans had previously seen as innocuous. Having substituted the horse for his father, Hans was able to turn an internal danger into an external one. The fear was displaced onto a substitute object, which is prototypically what takes place in the development of a **phobia.** In this celebrated 1909 case (Freud, 1955), the boy was actually treated by the father, under Freud's guidance.

Historically, the case of Little Hans has conceptual as well as technical significance. Conceptually, it enabled Freud to elaborate on his earlier formulations regarding psychosexual development in children and the use of **defense mechanisms** (such as displacement) as unconscious **ego** devices a person calls on as protection against being overwhelmed by anxiety. Moreover, the case supported Freud's emerging belief that inadequate resolution of a particular phase of psychosexual development can lead to neurotic behavior such as phobias. Technically, as Bloch and LaPerriere (1973) point out, Little Hans represents the first case in the history of both child analysis and family therapy. Note, however, that Freud chose not to work with either the child or the family but encouraged Hans's father, a physician, to treat his own son under Freud's supervision.[3] Thus, the clinical intervention remained individually focused, but transactionally based; ultimately, Hans was relieved of his phobic symptom.

From the case of Little Hans and similar examples from among Freud's published papers, we can appreciate how family relationships came to provide a rich diagnostic aid to Freud's psychoanalytic thinking. He recognized that the family provided the early environment—or context—in which neurotic fears and anxieties developed, although he failed to take matters one step further to identify how current or ongoing family relationships helped maintain the maladaptive or problematic behavior.

Four years earlier, in 1905, he had written that psychoanalysts were "obliged to pay as much attention...to purely human and social circumstances of our patients as to the somatic data and the symptoms of the disorder. Above all, our interest will be directed toward their family circumstances" (Freud, 1959, pp. 25–26). In practice, however, as we have pointed out, Freud preferred working therapeutically with individuals; both his theories and techniques stress the resolution of intrapsychic conflicts rather than restructuring interpersonal or transactional phenomena within a family. So strongly was he opposed to working with more than one family member at a time that his negative assessment became virtually a doctrine among psychoanalysts, who for many years accepted the prohibition against analyzing members of the same family (Broderick & Schrader, 1991).

In fact, as Bowen (1975) notes, one psychoanalytic principle that may have retarded earlier growth of the family therapy movement was the isolation of the therapist-patient relationship and the related concern that contact with the patient's relatives would "contaminate" the therapist. Bowen reports that some hospitals had one therapist deal with the patient's intrapsychic processes while another handled practical matters and administrative procedures, and a third team member, a social worker, talked to relatives. According to Bowen's early experiences, failure to respect these boundaries was considered "inept psychotherapy." It was only in the 1950s that this principle began to be violated—more often for research than for clinical purposes—and that family members began to be seen therapeutically as a group.[4]

Another psychoanalytic influence on family therapy is the work of Alfred Adler, a student of Freud's, who, as we indicated in Chapter 5, helped found the child guidance movement in Vienna in the early 1900s. More cognitive in orientation and less concerned with unconscious motivations than his mentor, Adler challenged Freud's

---

[3]Here, Freud was anticipating a technique used by many of today's family therapists, of using family members, especially parents, as agents of change.

[4]Just how much change has occurred since the 1950s can be gleaned from the fact that today family therapists frequently demonstrate their work with families before large professional audiences, without benefit of one-way mirrors or other devices to shield participants from viewers. Most families report that any initial self-consciousness is quickly overcome.

lack of attention to social elements in personality formation. Instead, he offered a theory rooted in social relationships: All behavior is purposive and interactive and the basic social system is the family (Carlson, Sperry, & Lewis, 1997).

Adler insisted that an individual's conscious personal and social goals as well as subsequent goal-directed behavior could be fully understood only by comprehending the environment or social context, especially the family, in which that behavior originated and was displayed. Adlerian concepts such as sibling rivalry, family constellation, and style of life attest to Adler's awareness of the key role of family experiences in influencing adult behavior. His holistic view of the person as unpartitionable has applicability to the systems outlook of today's family therapists. Adler's direct family therapy connection can be seen today in such psychoeducational efforts as marriage enrichment programs (Dinkmeyer & Carlson, 1984), parent education undertakings aimed at facilitating adult-child understanding and cooperation (Dinkmeyer & McKay, 1976), and in integrating Adlerian concepts with some of the major approaches in family therapy (Sherman & Dinkmeyer, 1987).

Another important theorist, American psychiatrist Harry Stack Sullivan, was psychoanalytically trained but was also influenced by sociology and social psychology. Throughout a career that began in the late 1920s, he stressed the role of interpersonal relationships in personality development. Sullivan (1953) argued that people are essentially products of their social interactions; to understand how people function, he urged the study of their "relatively enduring patterns of recurrent interpersonal situations" (p. 110). Working mostly with schizophrenics, Sullivan noted that the disorder frequently manifested itself during the transitional period of adolescence, leading him to speculate about the possibly critical effects of the patient's ongoing family life in producing the confusion that might lead ultimately to schizophrenia (Perry, 1982).

Don Jackson and Murray Bowen, both of whom were later to become outstanding figures in the emerging field of family therapy, trained under Sullivan and his colleague Frieda Fromm-Reichmann. Jackson's work (see Chapter 4) was clearly influenced by Sullivan's early notion of redundant family interactive patterns. Bowen's theories (see Chapter 8), especially those that pertain to individual pathology emerging from a faulty multigenerational family system, can be traced to Sullivan's influence.

However, it was Nathan Ackerman, a psychoanalyst and child psychiatrist, who is generally credited with deliberately adapting psychoanalytic formulations to the study of the family. In what may have been the first paper to deal specifically with family therapy, published as the first article in the *Bulletin of the Kansas Mental Hygiene Society*, Ackerman (1937) emphasized the role of the family as a dynamic psychosocial unit in and of itself. The constant interaction between the biologically driven person (a psychoanalytic concept) and the social environment (a systems concept) was to preoccupy him for more than three decades, as he attempted to apply an intrapsychic vocabulary to systems phenomena he observed in the family and in society at large. As he summed it up in a paper published shortly after his death (Ackerman, 1972):

Over a period of some thirty-five years, I have extended my orientation to the problems of behavior, step-by-step, from the inner life of the person, to the person within family, to the family within community, and most recently, to the social community itself. (p. 449)

THE PSYCHODYNAMIC OUTLOOK

The **psychodynamic** view of individual behavior, derived from Freud's psychoanalytic model, focuses on the interplay of opposing forces within a person as the basis for understanding that person's motivation, conflicts, and symptomatology. Although Freud emphasized the key role played by the family in individual personality formation—what we have been describing as the family context—he nevertheless was insistent that treatment be individually focused,[5] regarding the presence of family members as an obstacle to psychoanalytic intervention. Freud relied initially on analyzing and resolving the patient's **transference neurosis** as the most effective way to relieve neurotic suffering. However, as Sander (1979), a student of Ackerman's, points out, while psychoanalytic theory appears to be concerned exclusively with the personality development of a single patient, it is deeply grounded in the interaction of the individual and his or her family.

Recent psychoanalytic thinkers have been more receptive to the idea that both intrapsychic and interpersonal forces operate in a reciprocal fashion. As we indicated early in this chapter, most of the family therapy pioneers were psychoanalytically trained, and in their initial zeal, having discovered systems thinking, seemed to dismiss individually focused psychoanalytic ideas as antiquated and, in the linking of adult pathology to childhood developmental conflicts, hopelessly linear. Today, a more integrated view is being advocated by many family therapists, who urge that systems thinkers not neglect the individual family member's personal conflicts and motivation (Wachtel & Wachtel, 1986; Nichols, 1987; Feldman, 1992).

An attempt at specifically integrating psychodynamic and family systems concepts has been offered by Bentovim and Kinston (1991) and by Slipp (1991). The former, British family therapists, present a model called *focal family therapy*. Consistent with the development of family therapy in the United Kingdom, which, unlike the United States, had its origins almost exclusively in child guidance and child psychiatric clinics, this approach is developmentally oriented and looks for family disturbances, especially traumatic events to family members that have led to intrapsychic and interpersonal disturbance within the family.

Slipp (1991), trained in both psychoanalysis and family therapy, sees the two as potentially complementary and both involved in the genesis and maintenance of psychopathology. As a result, he attends to any significant childhood development of the participants while addressing ongoing family interaction using the framework of object

[5]Freud is quoted by Sander (1998) as having questioned how psychoanalytic treatment, which he compared to a surgical procedure, could suceed "in the presence of all the members of the patient's family, who would stick their noses into the field of the operation and exclaim aloud at every incision" (p. 429).

relations theory. Both individual and family diagnoses are part of Slipp's treatment plan in his effort to integrate psychoanalytic and systems concepts and therapeutic methods.

As Nichols (1987) notes, in arguing for the restoration of individual dynamics into psychodynamic family therapy, no matter how much our attention is focused on the entire family system, individual family members remain separate flesh-and-blood persons with unique experiences, private hopes, ambitions, outlooks, expectations, and potentials. At times, people may react out of personal habit and for private reasons. Psychoanalytically oriented therapists who accept Nichols's holistic view—what he calls *interactional psychodynamics*—are urged to remain attentive to the circular nature of personal and family dynamics.

As family therapy has moved beyond early cybernetic formulations as too mechanistic, and as there are renewed efforts to include individual experiences and outlooks in any comprehensive understanding of family functioning, there has been a corresponding revival of interest in psychodynamic postulations. The new look, however, is relationship-based, and seeks to discover how the inner lives and conflicts of family members interlock and how the binding together affects disturbances in family members. Such efforts have been influenced largely by **object relations theory** (see fuller discussion below), a form of psychodynamically oriented therapy that first flourished in Britain in the 1950s, and that emphasizes the fundamental need in people for attachments and relationships. In object relations family therapy (Scharff & Scharff, 1987) the interacting forces both within and between individuals are explored in the process of treatment. In particular, efforts are directed at examining thwarted relationship experiences early in life that become internalized and that impose themselves on current relationship choices and experiences.

As we present various approaches that reflect a psychodynamic perspective, keep in mind that each one simultaneously addresses two levels of understanding and intervention: the motives, fantasies, unconscious conflicts, and repressed memories of each family member and the more complex world of family interaction and family dynamics.

Psychoanalysis and Family Dynamics

As early as the 1930s, Nathan Ackerman, a child psychoanalyst in the child guidance movement, began to attend to the family itself as a social and emotional unit whose impact on the child needed exploration. By the 1940s, he was making clinical assessments of entire families (Green & Framo, 1981) and devising clinical techniques for applying psychoanalytic principles to treating preschool children and their families (Ackerman, 1956). In contrast to the collaborative approach practiced by most child guidance clinics, in which parent (usually mother) and child were seen by separate but collaborating therapists, Ackerman started to experiment with seeing whole families together (Guerin, 1976).

Although he continued to work with both individuals and families for a decade, by the 1950s Ackerman had moved explicitly into family therapy and in 1960 opened the Family Institute in New York City, soon to become the leading family therapy training and treatment center on the East Coast. One of the earliest pioneers in assessing and treating families, Ackerman remained throughout his long career a bold, innovative therapist. He also represents early efforts to integrate a psychoanalytic stance (with its intrapsychic orientation and appreciation of unconscious forces) with the then emerging systems approach (emphasizing family processes and interpersonal relationships).

Ackerman (1970), sometimes thought of as the "grandfather of family therapy," saw the family as a system of interacting personalities; each individual is an important subsystem within the family, just as the family is a subsystem within the community. He grasped early on that fully understanding family functioning calls for acknowledging input from several sources: the unique personality of each member; the dynamics of family role adaptations; the family's commitment to a set of human values; and the behavior of the family as a social unit. At the individual level, the process of symptom formation may be understood in terms of intrapsychic conflict, a defense against anxiety aroused by the conflict, and the resulting development of a neurotic symptom (a classical psychoanalytic explanation); at the family level, the symptom is viewed as part of a recurring, predictable interactional pattern intended to assure equilibrium for the individual, but actually impairing family homeostasis by producing distortions in family role relationships. In family terms, an individual's symptom becomes a unit of interpersonal behavior reflected within a context of shared family conflict, anxiety, and defenses. Conceptualizing behavior in this way, Ackerman was beginning to build a bridge between psychoanalytic and systems theories.

A "failure of **complementarity**," to use Ackerman's terms, characterizes the roles played by various family members in respect to each other. Change and growth within the system become constricted. Roles become rigid, narrowly defined, or stereotyped—or shift rapidly, causing confusion. According to Ackerman (1966), the family in which this occurs must be helped to "accommodate to new experiences, to cultivate new levels of complementarity in family role relationships, to find avenues for the solution of conflict, to build a favorable self-image, to buttress critical forms of defense against anxiety, and to provide support for further creative development" (pp. 90–91). For a family's behavior to be stable, flexibility and adaptability of roles is essential; roles within the family, which change over time, must allow for maturing children to gain an appropriate degree of autonomy.

Conflict may occur at several levels—within an individual family member, between members of the nuclear family, between generations including the extended family, or between the family and the surrounding community. Inevitably, according to Ackerman's observations, conflict at any level reverberates throughout the family system. What begins as a breakdown of role complementarity may lead to interpersonal conflict within the family and ultimately to intrapsychic conflict in one or more individual members; the individual's conflict deepens if the internalized family conflicts are persistent and pathogenic in form. One of Ackerman's therapeutic goals was to interrupt this sequence by extrapolating intrapsychic conflict to the broader area of family interaction.

Should the conflict between members become chronic, the family is at risk of reorganization into competing factions. The process often gets under way when one individual—often noticeably different from the others—becomes the family scapegoat or "whipping post." As that individual is singled out and punished for causing family disunity, various realignments of roles follow within the family. One member

Nathan Ackerman, M.D.

becomes "persecutor," while another may take the role of "healer" or "rescuer" of the "victim" of such "prejudicial scapegoating." Families are thus split into factions and different members may even play different roles at different times, depending upon what Ackerman considers the shared unconscious processes going on within the family at any particular period of time. Typically, observed Ackerman, such family alliances and interpersonal conflicts begin with a failure of complementarity within the marital dyad; the family is precluded from functioning as a cooperative, supportive, integrated whole. In cases such as these, Ackerman's therapeutic mission was to shift a family's concern from the scapegoated person's behavior to the basic disorder of the marital relationship.

In an early paper, Ackerman (1956) presented a conceptual model of **interlocking pathology** in family relationships. Concerned with the impact of the family environment on the development of childhood disorders, Ackerman was one of the first to note the constant interchange of unconscious processes taking place between family members as they are bound together in a particular interpersonal pattern. Accordingly, any single member's behavior can be a symptomatic reflection of confusion and distortion occurring in the entire family. With notions such as "interlocking pathology," Ackerman—by training a Freudian, but personally inclined to attend to social interaction—was able to wed many of the psychoanalytic concepts of intrapsychic dynamics to the psychosocial dynamics of family life.[6]

---

[6]The pattern of interlocking pathology had long been known to therapists, many of whom made the disquieting observation that sometimes when a patient improved, his or her marriage failed (Walrond-Skinner, 1976). This seemed to suggest that prior to treatment the patient had felt locked into a neurotic relationship; after treatment, he or she was no longer willing to take part in the dysfunctional interaction and felt free—and able—to leave the marriage. If in the course of psychoanalytic treatment a spouse became upset in response to the changes occurring in the patient, individual therapy with another therapist was the usual recommendation. It is not surprising that under this approach, a patient's "improvement" was viewed as a threat to other family members who might proceed to subtly undermine the therapeutic progress. It was not until conjoint family therapy began to be practiced that all of the persons involved in a family were treated together.

Ackerman's broadly based therapeutic approach used principles from biology, psychoanalysis, social psychology, and child psychiatry. Unaffected and deceptively casual in manner, Ackerman tried through a series of office interviews and home visits to obtain a firsthand diagnostic impression of the dynamic relationships among family members. Hearty, confident, unafraid to be himself or to disclose his own feelings, he was apt to bring out these same qualities in the family. Soon the family was dealing with sex, aggression. and dependency, the issues it had previously avoided as too threatening and dangerous.

To watch Ackerman on film or videotape is to see an honest, warm, straightforward, provocative, charismatic person at work in the very midst of the family, challenging a prejudice, coming to the aid of a scapegoated child, helping expose a family myth or hypocrisy, vigorously supplying the emotional ingredients necessary to galvanize a previously subdued family. No topic is taboo or off limits, no family rules so sacred they cannot be broken, nothing so shameful as to be unmentionable. Labeled as a "conductor" type of family therapist by Beels and Ferber (1969), Ackerman was said to lend the family "his pleasure in life, jokes, good sex, and limited aggression."

The following brief excerpt is from a therapy session with a family whose crisis was brought on when the 11-year-old daughter threatened to stab her 16-year-old brother and both parents with a kitchen knife. This explosive attack was precipitated by the girl's discovery of a conspiracy among the family members to say that her dog had died when in reality the mother had taken him to the dog pound. Members of the family indulge in many small lies, then cover up and deny their feelings. Note how Ackerman will have none of this charade. He reveals his own feelings in order to cut through the denial and open up the family encounter. The left-hand column is the verbatim account; the right-hand column is Ackerman's analysis of what is taking place.

Transcript	Comments
Dr. A: Bill, you heaved a sigh as you sat down tonight.	Therapist instantly fastens on a piece of nonverbal behavior, the father's sigh.
Father: Just physical, not mental.	
Dr. A: Who are you kidding?	Therapist challenges father's evasive response.
Father: I'm kidding no one.	
Dr. A: Hmmm…	Therapist registers disbelief, a further pressure for a more honest response.
Father: Really not…Really physical. I'm tired because I put in a full day today.	
Dr. A: Well, I'm very tired every day, and when I sigh it's never purely physical.	An example of therapist's use of his own emotions to counter an insincere denial.
Father: Really?	

(continued)

Transcript	Comments
(continued) Dr. A: What's the matter?	
Father: Nothing. Really!	
Dr. A: Well, your own son doesn't believe that.	Therapist now exploits son's gesture, a knowing grin, to penetrate father's denial and evoke a deeper sharing of feelings.
Father: Well, I mean nothing...nothing could cause me to sigh especially today or tonight.	
Dr. A: Well, maybe it isn't so special, but... How about it, John?	Therapist stirs son to unmask father.
Son: I wouldn't know.	Now son wipes grin off his face and turns evasive, like father.
Dr. A: You wouldn't know? How come all of a sudden you put on a poker face? A moment ago you were grinning very knowingly.	Therapist counters by challenging son, who took pot shot from sidelines and then backed away.
Son: I really wouldn't know.	
Dr. A: You...Do you know anything about your pop?	
Son: Yeah.	
Dr. A: What do you know about him?	
Son: Well, I don't know, except that I know some stuff.	
Dr. A: Well, let's hear.	

Source: Ackerman, 1966, pp. 3–4

Trained as a psychoanalyst, Ackerman clearly retained his interest in each family member's personality dynamics. However, influenced by social psychology, he was impressed by how personality is shaped by the particular social roles people are expected to play. In his approach to families, Ackerman was always interested in how people define their own roles ("What does it mean to you to be a father?") and what they expect from other family members ("How would you like your daughter to react to this situation?"). When all members delineate their roles clearly, family interactions proceed more smoothly, he maintained. Members can rework alignments, engage in new family transactions, and cultivate new levels of complementarity in their role relationships.

Ackerman believed the family therapist's principal job is that of a catalyst who, moving into the "living space" of the family, stirs up interaction, helps the family have a meaningful emotional exchange, and at the same time nurtures and encourages the members to understand themselves better through their contact with the therapist. As a catalyst, the therapist must play a wide range of roles from activator, challenger, and confronter to supporter, interpreter, and integrator. Unlike the orthodox psychoanalyst who chooses to remain a neutral, distant, mysterious **blank screen,** Ackerman as family therapist was a vigorous person who engaged a family in the here and now and made his presence felt. He moved directly into the path of family conflict, influenced the interactional process, supported positive forces and counteracted negative ones, and withdrew as the family began to deal more constructively with its problems

Diagnostically, Ackerman attempted to fathom a family's deeper emotional currents—fears and suspicions, feelings of despair, the urge for vengeance. Using his personal emotional responses as well as his psychodynamic insights, he gauged what the family was experiencing, discerned its patterns of role complementarity, and probed the deeper, more pervasive family conflicts. By "tickling the defenses" (gently provoking participants to openly and honestly express what they feel), he caught members off guard and exposed their self-justifying rationalizations. In due course, he was able to trace significant connections between the family dysfunction and the intrapsychic anxieties of various family members. Finally, when the members were more in touch with what they were feeling, thinking, and doing individually, Ackerman helped them expand their awareness of alternate patterns of family relationships through which they might discover new levels of intimacy, sharing, and identification.

Throughout his long career, Ackerman remained staunchly psychodynamic in outlook; his death in 1971 removed one of the major proponents of this viewpoint in family therapy (Nichols & Everett, 1986). A collection of his published papers with commentary by the editors (Bloch & Simon, 1982), called *The Strength of Family Therapy,* attests to his trailblazing efforts as well as his broad range of interests (child psychoanalysis, group therapy, social and cultural issues, marriage, and more). According to these editors, Ackerman practiced what he held dear in theory—namely, not to be bound by professional conventions unless they had some definite theoretical or clinical value for the problem at hand.

Nevertheless, despite his importance in family therapy's early years, there are few therapists today who would call themselves "Ackerman-style" in their approach. The Ackerman Institute, renamed in his memory, while acknowledging his pioneering efforts, does not operate from a psychodynamic perspective today, systems theory (and more recently, strategic and Milan approaches) having by and large replaced psychoanalytic thinking for its staff clinicians. While many therapists continue to be interested in the "psychodynamics of family life," and may from time to time use psychoanalytic concepts, the psychodynamic view is currently best expressed by object relations theory, to which we now turn.

OBJECT RELATIONS THEORY

Classical psychoanalysis is considered to be a drive theory—inborn sexual and aggressive impulses emanate from what Freud termed the *id*. Having created an excitation, these impulses lead to unconscious fantasies as the individual endeavors to achieve gratification through discharge of these drives. However, the drive's behavioral expression may lead to perceived danger or a fear of punishment. The resulting structural conflict—between the *id* impulses and those parts of the personality Freud labeled *ego* and *superego*—is the soil from which psychopathology grows (Slipp, 1988). Acting out an impulse unconsciously becomes associated with the danger of reprisal—physical punishment, loss of love—from parents or other key parent figures in the child's life. Note that while the psychoanalytic emphasis is on the single individual's internal world of fantasies, the resulting anxiety or depression is initially developed in relationship with significant others.

It is precisely this combined attention to individual drives (motives), the development of a sense of self, and unconscious relationship-seeking that object relations theory addresses and that helps explain family therapy's revived interest in psychoanalytic formulations. Object relations theory views the infant's experiences in relationship to the mother as the primary determinant of adult personality formation. According to this theory, the infant's need for *attachment* to the mother is the foundation for the development of the self (the unique psychic organization that creates a person's sense of identity) (Scharff & Scharff, 1992). Bowlby (1969) considers issues of attachment and loss to be central to functioning in humans and all higher mammals; he argues that how people resolve these issues determines personality development and possible psychopathology.

Based on the early work of Melanie Klein, a British psychoanalyst, and developed further by members of the British Middle School[7] (Michael Balint, Ronald Fairbairn, Harry Guntrip, Donald Winnicott), the theory holds that an infant's primary need is for attachment to a caring, nurturing mother (or, in more recent formulations, to any person primarily responsible for the infant's daily care). This is offered in contrast to Freud's intrapsychic, drive-oriented theory, which also focused on the infant's mothering experiences, but which theorized that the infant's basic struggle is to come to terms with sexual and aggressive impulses aimed at acquiring gratification from a parent (J. S. Scharff, 1989).

Fairbairn (1952) maintains that because the child experiences different sets of encounters with a mother—sometimes nurturing, sometimes frustrating—and cannot control the circumstances or leave the relationship, he or she creates a fantasy

---

[7]The British Middle School is so named because it functioned as an independent group, beginning in the 1950s, attempting to maintain a balance between the orthodox or classical psychoanalysts and the followers of Klein, in order for the British Psychoanalytic Society to avoid splitting into rival factions (Slipp, 1988). Klein, as a result of her work dating back to the late 1920s, is usually credited as the first object relations theorist, since she hypothesized that infants were capable of orienting themselves to "objects" from birth, thus earlier than Freud postulated. However, she did not challenge Freud's emphasis on the instinctual basis of development (Sutherland, 1980). It fell to some of her followers, especially Fairbairn, to elaborate on many of the ideas concerning the effects of mother-child interactions on the infant's later intrapsychic and interpersonal functioning. To Fairbairn, the fundamental drive in people is not to gratify an impulse but to develop satisfying human (i.e., object) relationships.

world to help reconcile the discrepant experiences. In this process, called **splitting** by Fairbairn, the child internalizes an image of the mother into a *good object* (the satisfying and loving mother) and a *bad object* (the inaccessible and frustrating mother). The former becomes an idealized object and allows the child to feel loved, the latter a rejecting object that leads to anger, a feeling of being unloved, and a longing to regain that love. Part of her is loved, another part hated; because she is not seen yet as a whole person, one or the other part dominates at different times. The degree to which a person resolves this conflict provides the basis for how well he or she develops satisfying human relationships later in life. If unresolved, the splitting is likely to lead to labile feelings as an adult as a result of viewing people (or the same person at different times) as "all good" or "all bad."

To Fairbairn, these internalized split objects become part of one's personality structure: good-object **introjects** (imprints of parents or other significant figures) remain as pleasing memories, bad-object introjects cause intrapsychic distress. Psychological representations of these introjects unconsciously influence future relationships, since current experiences are interpreted through the filter of one's inner object world of good-bad images. As a result, the person may grow up with distorted expectations of others, unconsciously forcing intimates into fitting the internal role models. As Fairbairn illustrates, the earlier the split (resulting, for example, from an early loss of a parent), the more likely it is that the person will yearn for merger with loved ones so that they become a part of him or her. At the same time, he or she may also yearn for independence and separation, a normal part of growing up, although too much distance may lead to feelings of loneliness and depression.

Dicks (1967) expanded Fairbairn's object relations conceptualizations by proposing that marriages were inevitably influenced by each spouse's infantile experiences. To Dicks, one basis for mate selection was that the potential partner's personality unconsciously matched split-off aspects of oneself. That is, while two people make conscious marital choices based upon many factors, including interpersonal compatibility and sexual attraction, Dicks believed that unconscious motives were also operating; in Jill Scharff's (1995) observation, at the unconscious level, they seek an "extraordinary fit, of which they are unaware" (p. 169). Each one thus hopes for integration of the lost introjects by finding them in the other. He suggested that in a troubled marriage each partner relates to the other in terms of unconscious needs; each partner perceives the other to a degree as an internalized object, and together they function as a *joint personality.* In this way each partner attempts to rediscover, through the other, the lost aspects of his or her primary object relations that had split off earlier in life. This is achieved through the operation of the defense mechanism of **projective identification,** a mental process in which marital partners unconsciously defend against anxiety by projecting or externalizing certain split-off or unwanted parts of themselves onto their partners, who in turn are manipulated to behave in accordance with this projection. As a consequence, each person attempts to reestablish contact with missing or repudiated parts of themselves. As Dicks (1967) states:

> The sense of belonging can be understood on the hypothesis that at deeper levels there are perceptions of the partner and consequent attitudes toward him or her *as if*

the other was part of oneself. The partner is then treated according to how this aspect
of oneself was valued; spoilt and cherished, or denigrated and persecuted. (p. 69)

To put it succinctly, object relations theorists believe we relate to people in the
present partly on the basis of expectations formed by early experiences (Nichols,
1987). That is, the past is alive in people's memories, and unconsciously continues
to influence their lives in powerful ways. People continue to respond to others
largely on the basis of their resemblance to internalized objects from the past, rather
than how these others may truly behave. Thus, a family member may distort the
meaning or implication of another member's statement or action, perhaps misread-
ing or overreacting because of unconscious, emotion-laden, inner images developed
early in life with parents or other important caretaker figures. In order to resolve
current problems with others, it becomes necessary to explore and repair those
faulty unconscious object relationships internalized since infancy.

Family therapists are especially interested in how this plays out in marital relatedness. According to advocates of the object relations view, the two individuals joined
by marriage each bring to the relationship a separate and unique psychological heritage. Each carries a personal history, a unique personality, and a set of hidden, internalized objects into all subsequent transactions with one another. Inevitably, the
dyadic relationship bears resemblances to the parent-child relationships the partners
experienced in their families of origin. As Meissner (1978) observes: "The capacity to
successfully function as a spouse is largely a consequence of the spouse's childhood
relationships to his (or her) own parents" (p. 26). The relative success that marital
partners experience, as well as the manner in which they approach and accomplish
developmental tasks throughout the life cycle, is largely determined by the extent to
which they are free from excessive negative attachments to the past.

Object relations family therapists view troubled marriages as contaminated by
the pathogenic introjects from past relationships with members of the previous generation residing within each partner. Moreover, the partners' unresolved intrapsychic
problems not only prevent them from enjoying a productive and fulfilling marital
experience but are also passed along to their children, who eventually bring psychic
disturbances into their own marriages. Only by gaining insight into, and thus freedom from, such burdensome attachments to the past can individuals—or couples—
learn to develop adult-to-adult relationships in the present with members of their
families of origin.

The object relations focus provides a bridge linking psychoanalytic therapy and
family therapy. Moving beyond drive theory, instinctual loadings of erogenous zones,
or concern exclusively with intrapsychic processes, its two-person (nurturing figure–
infant) emphasis[8] makes it more consistent with the interactional views favored by

---

[8]Traditional psychoanalytic theory is considered *monadic*—explanations of an individual's disturbed
thoughts or behavior are based upon the characteristics of that person. (Arthur experiences frequent guilt
feelings because he has a punishing superego.) Object relations theory moves the focus to a *dyadic* one—
the interaction between two persons. (Arthur experiences frequent guilt feelings because of his early dealings with a critical mother.) Most family therapists operate from a *triadic* viewpoint. (Arthur experiences
frequent guilt feelings because his divorced mother insists he reject his father by refusing to spend time
with him during weekend visitation opportunities.)

systems-oriented family therapists. At the same time, individual intrapsychic issues and past experiences are not overlooked. What is added is the consideration of the development of the self in relation to others—that from birth onward, a person needs to bond, to form attachments, to relate to others. Furthermore, declare the advocates of object relations theory, this powerful relationship-seeking need is so great as to be the fundamental driving force throughout life.

Slipp (1988) suggests that the object relations perspective also supplies an important reminder, sometimes underattended to by family therapists, that individuals may bring serious personal emotional problems into a relationship, and that pathology need not exist mysteriously only in the transactions between people.

OBJECT RELATIONS THERAPY

Object relations therapists are a diverse group, although they share in common the idea that internal images or psychic representations derived from significant relationships in the past may produce faulty or unsatisfying or distorted current dealings with people.

We will elaborate on three such approaches.

Object Relations and Family-of-Origin Therapy

Another first-generation family therapist whose training and early orientation was psychoanalytic, James Framo (1981) stresses the relationship between the intrapsychic and the interpersonal, offering an amalgam of psychodynamic and systems concepts. Framo, one of the few psychologists in the early family therapy movement, was affiliated initially with the Eastern Pennsylvania Psychiatric Institute (EPPI) in Philadelphia, where he began to view family dysfunction as rooted in the extended family system. Ultimately he developed a set of intervention techniques that help couples in marital therapy deal with unresolved issues each partner brings to the marriage from his or her family of origin.

Not wishing to disregard the significant contributions made by psychoanalysis to our understanding of an individual's intrapsychic world, Framo nevertheless believes psychoanalytic theory has not paid sufficient attention to the social context of a person's life, particularly the early crucial role played by family relationships in shaping individual behavior. Framo refuses to polarize the intrapsychic and the interactional, maintaining that both are essential to understanding the dynamic aspects of family life. As he points out in the introduction to a collection of his papers (Framo, 1982), his orientation to marital and family theory and therapy emphasizes "the psychology of intimate relationships, the interlocking of multi-person motivational systems, the relationship between the intrapsychic and the transactional, and the hidden transgenerational and historical forces that exercise their powerful influences on current intimate relationships" (p. IX).

Consistent with the view of object relations theorists, Framo believes that insoluble intrapsychic conflicts derived from one's family of origin continue to be acted

James Framo, Ph.D.

out or replicated with current intimates, such as a spouse or children. Indeed, Framo (1981) contends that efforts at the interpersonal resolution of inner conflict (for example, harshly criticizing a spouse for failing to live up to one's wildly inappropriate expectations) are at the very heart of the kinds of distress found in troubled couples and families.

Extrapolating from Fairbairn's proposals, Framo (1976) theorized that a young child who interprets parental behavior as rejection, desertion, or persecution is in a dilemma; the child cannot give up the sought-after object (the parents), nor can he or she change that object. Typically, the ensuing frustration is dealt with by internalizing aspects of the "loved-hated" parents in order to control the objects in the child's inner world. According to Framo, *the most powerful obstacle to change is people's attachments to their parental introjects.* The more psychologically painful the early life experience, the greater the investment in internal objects, the more an adult will engage in an unconscious effort to make all close relationships fit the internal role models.

Framo's interest in dealing with marital discord reflects in part Fairbairn's emphasis on the impact of splits and introjects on adult relationships and in part the work of Dicks (1967), who argued that marital partners choose one another on the basis of their primary object relations, which they have split off, and which, in interacting with their spouse, they experience once again as a result of projective identification. Framo (1992) insists that *people usually do not select the partner they want; they get the one that they need.* That is, each is drawn to someone who recreates the childhood dream of unconditional love, but also is enough like the bad inner object to allow old hatreds to be projected. According to Framo (1992, p. 115):

> A partner is chosen who, it is hoped, will cancel out, replicate, control, master, live through, or heal, in a dyadic framework, what could not be settled internally. Consequently, one's current intimates, one's spouse and children, are, in part, stand-ins for old images, the embodiments of long-buried introjects.

One major source of marital disharmony results from spouses who project disowned aspects of themselves onto their mates and then fight these characteristics in the mate. Similarly, children may be assigned inappropriate family roles based on parental introjects. Such roles may even be chosen for them before they are born (for example, conceiving a baby in the belief that the offspring will save a shaky marriage).

Framo, who now resides in San Diego, begins by treating the entire family, especially when the presenting problem involves the children. However, symptomatic behavior in a child may simply be a means of deflecting attention from a more basic marital conflict. In such cases, once the child's role as identified patient is made clear and the child is **detriangulated** from the parents, Framo will dismiss the children and proceed to work with the marital dyad.

Framo's unique contribution to family therapy technique is his process of guiding a couple through several treatment stages: conjoint therapy, couples group therapy, and, finally, family-of-origin (intergenerational) conferences. The couples group, in which many couples participate soon after they begin treatment, allows Framo to use many of the positive aspects of group therapy (see discussion in Chapter 5). That is, he takes advantage of the group process, especially the therapeutic feedback from other couples, to assist his efforts as therapist. In many cases it is far more enlightening and potent for a couple to see its own interaction patterns acted out by another couple than to hear a therapist merely comment on the same behavior, with no one else present. The group experience has a secondary function of reducing the individual's resistance to the next stage of treatment, which involves a number of family members meeting together.

In a daring therapeutic maneuver, Framo (1992) involves each individual (without the partner present) in sessions with his or her family of origin (parents, brothers, and sisters). Here, instead of the customary working out of past or current problems with these family members via a relationship with the therapist, Framo's family-of-origin approach provides a direct opportunity for clearing up past misunderstandings or sources of chronic dissatisfaction. In some cases, misinterpretations based upon childhood misperceptions can be straightened out. Clients are encouraged to face their family of origin in order to present their views, perhaps not aired before; the session is not intended to be an opportunity for indictment, blame, recrimination, or condemnation.

Often conducted with a cotherapist, family-of-origin sessions are usually divided into two 2-hour sessions with a break in between (varying from several hours to an overnight interruption). Two major goals are involved—to discover what issues or agendas from the family of origin might be projected onto the current family and to have a corrective experience with parents and siblings. Framo cogently reasons that if adults are able to go back and deal directly with both past and present issues with their original families—in a sense, to come to terms with parents before they die—then they are liberated to make reconstructive changes in their present marriage or family life. Usually held toward the end of therapy, family-of-origin conferences enable individuals to gain insight into the inappropriateness of old attachments, rid themselves of "ghosts," and respond to spouses and children as individuals in their own right—not as figures on whom they project unresolved issues and introjects from the past.

Instead of dealing with introjects with a therapist, family-of-origin sessions take the problems back to their original etiological source. Dealing with family members as real people frequently loosens the hold and intensity of these internalized objects and exposes them to current realities. As Framo (1992) warns, family-of-origin therapy may not change people's lives drastically, nor is it likely to fulfill all fantasies of what clients can get from parents and siblings. However, it often has a restorative function, reconnecting family members to one another, allowing participants to see one another as real people and not simply in their family-assigned roles. Old rifts may be healed by more accurate readings of one another's intentions, or perhaps as past events are reinterpreted from an adult perspective. The intergenerational encounter provides a forum for forgiveness, compromise, acceptance, and resolution. At its best, it helps family members learn techniques for the future betterment of family relationships.

The Open-Systems, Group-Analytic Approach

According to British psychoanalyst A. C. Robin Skynner (1981), trained in the Melanie Klein school of therapy, families evolving over several generations have important developmental milestones similar to the psychosexual stages in Freud's developmental scheme. A mother who lacked adequate mothering or a father who lacked satisfactory fathering is likely to behave inappropriately when called upon to play a role for which he or she has no internal model. When such a family faces stresses that correspond to repeated failures at parenting over several generations, they are likely to break down and decompensate in their functioning. Since poor relationship skills are likely to be passed along to children, developmental failures and deficits will probably occur over generations.

Offering an object relations approach, Skynner, at the Institute of Family Therapy in London, believes that adults with relationship difficulties (due to poor role models or other learning deficits) develop unrealistic attitudes toward others because they still carry expectations—Skynner calls them **projective systems**—left over from childhood deficiencies. When such persons select a spouse, they base the choice at least in part on the mutual "fit" of the potential partner's projective systems. That is, each partner comes equipped with projections corresponding to the stage at which some aspect of his or her development was blocked; each partner unconsciously seeks to create through marriage a situation in which the missing experience can be supplied. The danger, of course, is that since each wants the other to fulfill a parental role (and both wish to play the child), the partners are likely to manipulate, fight for control, and become frustrated. One consequence of this struggle between incompatible projective systems may be the diversion of some aspect of the projections onto the couple's offspring—saving the marriage at the expense of a child. In many cases, says Skynner, the child colludes in the process out of a deep, if unconscious, wish to preserve the marriage or the family.

As Skynner practices it, family therapy requires identification of the projective systems as well as removal of the projections from the symptomatic child, who is likely to be the identified patient. These projections are returned for analysis to the marriage, where more constructive resolutions are sought. Clarifying communication, gaining insight into inappropriate expectations, modifying the family structure, and teaching new parenting skills are all part of Skynner's therapeutic efforts. In many cases, short-term tactics produce sufficient relief of discomfort and distress; in other situations, longer-term psychoanalytically oriented marital and family therapy (Skynner, 1976) is indicated for those families who can manage the conflict, pain, and disruption. In the latter cases, the goal is to facilitate differentiation of the marital partners to the point that they are separate, independent persons enjoying, but no longer simply needing, each other.

Skynner (1981) refers to his therapeutic technique as an "open-systems, group-analytic" approach. He genuinely engages with the family system through a "semi-permeable interface" permitting the exchange of personal information between the family members and himself. To understand the family "from inside," Skynner believes he must open himself up to its projective system, internalize each member separately through identification, and experience personally the suffering and struggles of the family. For Skynner, the key requirement is that the therapist retain a deep awareness of his or her own identity, strong enough to sustain him or her in the face of the overwhelming (if transient) emotional arousal in the family as the result of the therapeutic encounter; arousal is particularly intense in therapy with profoundly disturbed families who seek to externalize their pathology.

To Skynner, the therapeutic encounter is an opportunity for growth for both the family and the therapist. (For more on the idea of the forces and counterforces at work in the interpersonal encounter between families and therapists, see Chapter 7). The therapist, by being receptive and responsive to the presenting problems of the family and its individual members, learns about their transactions and projective systems. In the process, the family is introduced to the family systems viewpoint and begins to look at symptomatic behavior within a family context. As Skynner becomes aware of emotional responses and fantasies in himself, he slowly responds to the family conflict. Gradually he discloses his own emotions; now he is putting his finger on the "real" family problem—what is *not* communicated, what is missing from the content of the session. In some cases, he may act upon his understanding of the family dynamic, even taking the role of scapegoat. In such instances, he consciously personifies the very emotions the family disowns. Although such a maneuver is carried out cautiously—and only after Skynner and the family have established a good therapeutic alliance—the effect may nevertheless be shocking to the family. As Skynner (1981) explains:

> It is as if the family members have been fleeing from a monster and finally find refuge in the safety of the therapist's room only to discover, as they begin to feel secure and to trust him, that he turns into the monster himself! (p. 61)

By expressing the collusively denied or repressed emotions and by absorbing the projective system of a disturbed family, Skynner experiences its dilemma firsthand; by working out for himself a way of escape, he develops a route the family can follow. In his highly responsive approach to therapy, Skynner combines the principles and techniques of object relations theory, group analysis, and social learning (modeling) while retaining an overall view of the family as an ongoing system in need of restructuring.

Object Relations Family Therapy

Unquestionably, the object relations approach most faithful to psychoanalysis comes from the collaboration of David Scharff and Jill Savege Scharff, husband and wife psychiatrists affiliated for many years with the Washington School of Psychiatry, and now directors of their own institute—the International Institute of Object Relations Therapy—in Washington. In their therapeutic approach unconscious themes expressed in dreams and fantasies are evoked and investigated, family histories are explored as they relate to current relationships, interpretations are made to the family, insight is sought, and **transference** and **countertransference** feelings are explored in an effort to arrive at greater understanding and growth. Unlike individual psychoanalysis, however, here the focus is on the family as a system of relationships that function in ways that support or obstruct the progress of the family or any of its separate members as they proceed through the developmental stages of family life (Scharff & Scharff, 1987).

Building upon Freud's classical psychoanalytic formulations, but departing from the instinctual basis of that theory, the Scharffs make use of the object relations contributions of Klein and Fairbairn. For example, they contend that "object relations theory provides the possibility of an analytic family systems approach, because it is an intrapsychic psychoanalytic theory that derives from an interpersonal view of development" (Scharff & Scharff, 1987, p. 16). Historical analysis of current individual as well as relationship difficulties are key components of this technique, since it is assumed that intrapsychic and interpersonal levels are in continuing interaction. Helping family members gain insight, by becoming conscious of precisely how they internalized objects from the past, and how these objects continue to intrude on current relationships, is an indispensable part of providing understanding and instigating change.

Confirming their object relations credentials, the Scharffs emphasize the fundamental human need for attachment, to be in a relationship, and the possible destructive effects of early separation from caring figures. Any anxiety resulting from such separation experiences is assumed to lead to repression, permitting less of the ego to relate freely to others. Because the repressed system is by definition out of contact with the outside world, thus operating as a closed system, new experiences do not provide an opportunity for growth, and the repressed object relationships continue to seek outlets as adults through repetition of their unsatisfying infantile experiences. Responding to introjects from the past, family members cannot respond to one another as they are in reality, but rather respond to an internal object, as though reacting to powerful forces—psychic representations—from the past. Thus unconscious, but also conscious, systems of relationships within individuals as well as families become the subject matter of analysis (J. S. Scharff, 1989).

As do other family therapists, the Scharffs view the family as an interpersonal, cybernetic system that has run into difficulties adjusting to a developmental transition. They also agree that a family member's problems represent manifestations of a family system disturbance. However, they part company with those contemporaries (for example, strategic family therapists) who believe individual change must wait for family changes; they argue that lasting change in the individual sometimes induces changes in the family.

A key therapeutic difference is the object relations view that interpretation by the therapist, in an effort to provide insight, is essential. While they oppose the blank screen stance of classical psychoanalysts, they do adopt a neutral stance of involved impartiality, allowing each family member to project onto the therapist his or her own unfinished problems from the past. In contrast to the second-order cybernetic views of many current family therapists—that they inevitably become an inseparable part of the family system—the Scharffs believe they are able to move outside the family system, and thus are in a position to offer comments on what is happening to *them* as well as what they observe taking place within the family.

That is, they make use of the transference, which they view broadly as occurring between family members, between each family member and the therapist, and particularly between the family as a group and the therapist. This is an essential part of treatment, since it evokes in the therapeutic sessions, in response to the therapist's neutrality, an "object hunger"—a replay of infantile relating with caretakers in the family of origin. At the same time, the therapist experiences countertransference responding to the family struggles, unconsciously evoking his or her own internal struggles from the past. If sufficiently worked through in previous personal analysis and training, and with supervision, this shared venture of object relations may provide greater empathy on the part of the therapist with family vulnerabilities and struggles. As David Scharff (1989) points out, in this way, object relations therapists allow themselves to "be the substrate for a newly emerging understanding, which they then feed back to the family in the form of interpretation" (p. 424).

In forming a therapeutic alliance with a family, the object relations family therapist creates a nurturing climate in which family members can rediscover lost parts of the family as well as their individual selves. The family's shared object relations are assessed, as is the family's stage of psychosexual development, and its use of various mechanisms of defense against anxiety. Observing family interaction, encouraging members to express their separate viewpoints as well as observe the view of one another, obtaining a history of internalized objects from each member, feeding back therapist observations and interpretations—these are all ways of joining the family. Later, helping them work through chronic interaction patterns and defensive projective identifications is necessary if they are to change patterns and learn to deal with one another in a here-and-now fashion attuned to current realities rather than unconscious object relations from the past (David Scharff, 1989).

Successful treatment is measured not by symptom relief in the identified patient but rather by the family's increased insight or self-understanding and its improved capacity to master developmental stress. A fundamental goal for object relations family therapists is for the family to support one another's needs for attachments, individuation, and growth.

SUMMARY

Current trends favor eclecticism and integration in family therapy, as therapists borrow concepts and techniques that cross theoretical boundaries. However, distinguishing theoretical constructs remain between traditional schools, and controversy remains regarding the possibility of ever creating an integrated supertheory of family therapy.

The psychodynamic viewpoint, based initially on a psychoanalytic model, focuses on the interplay of opposing forces within an individual. While treatment based on this model appears to be exclusively concerned with the personality of the single individual patient, the role of family context in personality formation is an essential element of the theory.

Nathan Ackerman, a family therapy pioneer, attempted to integrate psychoanalytic theory (with its intrapsychic orientation) and systems theory (emphasizing interpersonal relationships). He viewed family dysfunction as a failure in role complementarity between members and as the product of persistent unresolved conflict (within and between individuals in a family) and prejudicial scapegoating. His therapeutic efforts were aimed at disentangling such interlocking pathologies.

The psychodynamic position today is largely based on object relations theory. In contrast to Freud's intrapsychic, instinctual theory, here the emphasis is on the infant's primary need for attachment to a caring person, and the analysis of those internalized psychic representations—objects—that continue to seek satisfaction in adult relationships.

Three examples of object relations therapeutic approaches are provided by Framo, Skynner, and Scharff and Scharff. Framo believes that insoluble intrapsychic conflict, derived from the family of origin, is perpetuated in the form of projections onto current intimates such as a spouse or children. He concerns himself with working through and ultimately removing these introjects; in the process he sees couples alone, then in a couples' group, and finally holds separate sessions with each partner and the members of his or her family of origin.

Robin Skynner contends that adults with relationship difficulties have developed unrealistic expectations of others in the form of projective systems related to childhood deficiencies. Marital partners, often with incompatible projective systems, attempt to create in the marriage a situation where the missing experience can be supplied, the deficiency remediated by the other partner. Inevitably frustrated, the couple may direct or transmit these projections onto a child, who becomes symptomatic. Skynner's therapeutic efforts, particularly the extended version, attempt to facilitate differentiation between marital partners so that each may become more separate and independent.

Scharff and Scharff utilize a therapeutic approach that is heavily psychoanalytic, evoking unconscious material, making interpretations, providing insight, relying on transference and countertransference feelings in helping families learn how past internalized objects intrude on current family relationships. A fundamental goal is for family members to support one another's needs for attachments, individuation, and personal growth.

7

Experiential Models

Experience, encounter, confrontation, intuition, process, growth, existence, spontaneity, action, the here-and-now moment—this is the vocabulary used by those family therapists who, in general, minimize theory (and especially theorizing) as a therapeutic hindrance, an artificial academic effort to make the unknowable knowable. They argue that change resides in a *nonrational therapeutic experience,* one that establishes the conditions for personal growth and unblocks family interaction, rather than merely offering intellectual reflection or insight into the origins of problems. It is the immediacy of the relationship between the family and an involved therapist and the process in which they engage together that catalyzes the growth of the individual family members as well as the family system as a whole.

Experiential family therapy is an outgrowth of the **phenomenological** techniques (Gestalt therapy, psychodrama, Rogerian client-centered therapy, the encounter group movement), so popular in the individual therapy approaches of the free-wheeling 1960s, applied to family problems. Developing greater sensitivity, gaining greater access to one's self, learning to recognize and express emotions, achieving intimacy with a partner—these are some of the **humanistic** goals for champions of this viewpoint. Less systemic in their thinking than were most other early family therapists, and out of step with the more currently popular cognitively based and social constructionist approaches such as narrative therapy and solution-focused therapy (Chapter 13), the experiential family therapists focus attention on current ("in the moment") emotionality. That view suffered a serious setback (although not a deathblow) with the passing in the last decade of two of its illustrious leaders, Carl Whitaker and Virginia Satir. Today, despite fewer advocates, the family therapists most identified with this approach include Walter Kempler (1981; 1982), David Keith (1989; 1998), August Napier (1987a; 1987b), Laura Roberto (1991), and William Bumberry (Whitaker & Bumberry, 1988). In addition, a new experiential wave is represented by Leslie Greenberg and Susan Johnson, whose **emotionally focused couple therapy** emphasizes emotional engagement, identifying feelings underlying interactions, and strengthening emotional bonds. In a research endeavor particularly conspicuous because of its rarity among experiential therapists, they

(Greenberg & Johnson, 1988; Johnson & Greenberg, 1995) have spelled out replicable procedures and developed outcome studies to measure the effectiveness of their therapeutic undertakings.

Rather than endorsing a single technique, experiential interventions are, by definition, uniquely fitted to the individual client or family. Each of the approaches we will consider in this chapter engages families in different ways, although they share certain philosophical tenets. All emphasize choice, free will, and especially the human capacity for self-determination and self-fulfillment, thus accentuating the client's goals over any outcomes predetermined by the therapist. Disordered or dysfunctional behavior is viewed as the result of a failure in the growth process, a deficiency in actualizing one's capabilities and possibilities. Because each person (and by extension, each family) is unique, each must be helped to become aware of and reach his, her, or their potential, discovering in the process the solutions to current problems. Psychotherapy, then, with individuals or with families, must be an interpersonal encounter in which therapist and client(s) strive to be real and authentic. Acquiring sensitivity, gaining access to feelings and their expression, and learning to be more spontaneous and creative (by engaging in nonrational experiencing) are typical avenues clients take for arriving at their goals. If the therapeutic intervention succeeds, the results should facilitate growth for all participants, clients and therapists alike.

The primacy of experience over rational thought and especially intellectualization is underscored in each of the approaches we are about to discuss. Consequently, therapists in each are active, often self-disclosing, and likely to make use of a variety of evocative procedures to help clients get closer to their feelings, sensations, fantasies, and inner experiences. Sensitivity to one's here-and-now, ongoing life experiences is encouraged throughout therapy; denying impulses and suppressing affect is viewed as dysfunctional and growth-retarding.

Experiential family therapists strive to behave as real, authentic people (rather than acting as blank screens or wearing therapeutic masks). By having direct encounters with clients, they attempt to expand their own experiences, often having to deal with their own vulnerabilities in the process (which they are likely to share with clients). Their therapeutic interventions attempt to be spontaneous, challenging, and, since personalized, often idiosyncratic, as they attempt to help clients gain self-awareness (of their thoughts, feelings, body messages), self-responsibility, and personal growth. The experiential family therapist takes on the task of enriching a family's experiences and enlarging the possibilities for each family member to realize his or her unique and extraordinary potential.

THE EXPERIENTIAL MODEL

As noted, experiential family practitioners tailor their approach to the unique conflicts and behavior patterns of each family with whom they work. There are probably as many ways to provide an experience for accelerating growth as there are variations in family dysfunction. The work of some experiential therapists such as Carl

Whitaker (1976b) clearly reflects the psychodynamic orientation of their training,[1] though they are careful, as far as possible, not to impose any preconceived theoretical suppositions or techniques upon families. Others such as Kempler (1981) show evidence of their training in Gestalt therapy.

David Kantor, along with Fred Duhl and Bunny Duhl, represent other early influential experiential family therapists. All three cofounded the Boston Family Institute in 1969, and together (Duhl, Kantor, & Duhl, 1973) were instrumental in developing some useful expressive techniques, such as **family sculpting,** a nonverbal communication method whereby a family member can physically place other members in a spatial relationship with one another, symbolizing, among other things, his or her perception of the family members' differences in power or degrees of intimacy with one another. Duhl and Duhl (1981) proposed an integrative approach to family therapy in which they employ an assortment of techniques, including home visits, synergistically aimed at promoting growth in individual family members as well as overall family functioning.

Experiential therapists deal with the present rather than uncovering the past. Their emphasis is on the here and now, the situation as it unfolds from moment to moment between an active and caring therapist and a family. The interactions among family members and with the therapist are confronted in an effort to help everyone involved in the encounter develop more growth-enhancing behavior. Rather than offer insight or interpretation, as psychoanalysts espouse, the therapist provides an experience—an opportunity for family members to open themselves to spontaneity, freedom of expression, and personal growth. The interpersonal experience rather than the reliance on technique, is, in itself, the primary stimulus to growth in this here-and-now approach to psychotherapy.

Symbolic-Experiential Family Therapy

Symbolic-experiential family therapy (S-EFT), pioneered by Carl Whitaker, is a multigenerational approach that addresses both individual and family relational patterns in the process of therapy. Oriented toward personal growth (rather than stability) and family connectedness, the therapist assumes a pivotal role in helping family members dislodge rigid and repetitive ways of interacting by substituting more spontaneous and flexible ways of accepting and dealing with their impulses. Several generations of a family are typically included in the therapeutic process, since practitioners of S-EFT consider the influence of extended families, past and present, to be omnipresent in the family's unverbalized *symbolic* experiences.

Why symbolic? Keith and Whitaker (1982) explain it this way:

[1]Whitaker's early training in child psychiatry and his original orientation with individual patients was influenced by the work of Otto Rank, an early associate of Freud's who emphasized allying himself with the patient's search for growth and providing a "here and now" therapeutic learning experience. British object relations theorist Melanie Klein's insistence that psychopathology represents the patient's efforts toward self-healing was another important early influence on Whitaker's conceptualizations (Neill & Kniskern, 1982).

We presume it is experience, not education that changes families. The main function of the cerebral cortex is inhibition. Thus, most of our experience goes on outside of our consciousness. We gain best access to it symbolically. For us "symbolic" implies that some thing or some process has more than one meaning. While education can be immensely helpful, the covert process of the family is the one that contains the most power for potential changing. (p. 43)

Symbolic-experiential family therapy has a number of identifying characteristics:

- A pragmatic nontheoretical approach to psychotherapy
- A steadfast effort to depathologize human experience
- The replacement of preplanned therapeutic technique with therapist spontaneous creativity
- An emphasis on emotional experience and affectively engaging families
- A commitment to client self-access, self-fulfillment, expanded experiences, and family cohesiveness
- The use of self by the therapist (drawing upon images, fantasies, and personal metaphors from one's own life)
- The use of symbolic, nonverbal methods or play
- The use of **cotherapy**

To understand how symbolic-experiential family therapy evolved, beginning in the 1940s, we must first trace the career of Carl Whitaker, an unconventional, colorful, and provocative psychiatrist who, right up until his death in 1995, was the epitome of an experiential family therapist. He first made his national influence felt with his innovative (often radical) work in individual psychotherapy, especially his trailblazing efforts to redefine a schizophrenic's symptoms as signs that an individual was "stuck" in the process of growth (rather than suffering from a deteriorative condition) and was attempting to apply "creative" solutions to vexing interpersonal problems. Coauthor of a landmark book, *The Roots of Psychotherapy* (Whitaker & Malone, 1953), Whitaker was an early champion of becoming an active therapist, pushing for growth and integration (maturity) in his patients and not simply offering insight or understanding to facilitate their "adjustment" to society. In this publication, Whitaker and psychologist Malone broke ranks with the then prevalent orthodox psychoanalytic position by advocating an epistemological shift away from the search for internal conflict to experientially dealing with the patient's interactional dysfunction (Roberto, 1991).

In his work with schizophrenics, Whitaker took the audacious position, never before espoused, that each participant in therapy is, to some degree, simultaneously patient and therapist to the other. Both invest emotion in the process, both are vulnerable, both regress, both grow as individuals as a result of the experience. Both expose themselves to the risks of change. Each takes responsibility for his or her own maturing process, but not for one another. The therapist must be committed to his or her own growth, personally as well as professionally, if he or she is to catalyze growth in others.

The Use of Cotherapy with Schizophrenics   Trained originally as an obstetrician/gynecologist in the early 1940s, Whitaker found himself interested in the psychological aspects of that field, and, in an unorthodox move, spent his final year of training at a psychiatric hospital working largely with schizophrenic patients. He received further training at the Louisville Child Guidance Clinic and at the nearby Ormsby Village, a live-in treatment center for delinquent adolescents, where he learned to develop "here and now" techniques for reaching patients ordinarily resistant to more conventional forms of psychiatric intervention (Neill & Kniskern, 1982).

With the outbreak of World War II in 1941, Whitaker, a civilian, was called upon to treat patients in Oak Ridge Hospital in Tennessee, a closed community located where the secret U.S. atomic bomb was being assembled. Perhaps because of the heavy workload (Whitaker is said to have treated 12 patients per day in half-hour back-to-back sessions), or perhaps because he believed he lacked sufficient experience with adult patients, or perhaps because he wished to share his intense personal involvement in the therapeutic process, Whitaker began working with colleagues such as John Warkentin as part of a cotherapy team. In any event, following the war, he was asked to establish and chair the psychiatry department at the medical school at Emory University in Atlanta, Georgia, where, together with associates such as Warkentin (who possessed a doctorate in psychophysiology but with additional training as a child therapist) and, later, Thomas Malone (trained in psychoanalytic work with adults), he continued his earlier unconventional cotherapy treatment of schizophrenics. The technique allowed one therapist to serve as an observer while the other engaged the client more directly.

As Whitaker pursued his unorthodox approach to treating schizophrenics, he became increasingly aware of the key role played by the family in the etiology of the disorder. As he later put it, he became intrigued with the idea that "there is no such thing as a person, that a person is merely the fragment of a family" and, in typical Whitaker provocative style, that "marriage is not really a combination of two persons; rather it is the product of two families who send out a scapegoat to reproduce themselves" (Whitaker & Ryan, 1989, p. 116).

Broadening his earlier perspective, he began to conceptualize schizophrenia as both an intrapsychic and interpersonal dilemma and to treat his schizophrenic patients along with their families. The multiple-therapist team—an extension of Whitaker's earlier reliance on cotherapy—was an innovation that helped to prevent a single therapist from becoming entangled in what Whitaker found to be a powerful, enmeshing family system. Two or more therapists working together afforded this protection and at the same time provided a model for desirable interpersonal behavior for the entire family (for example, disagreeing in front of the family, but in a constructive manner).

The Symbolic Aspects of Family Therapy   By the mid-1960s Whitaker had resigned from Emory University, where he had been under political pressure because of his unorthodox administrative and educational procedures. Joined by colleagues

Carl Whitaker, M.D.

Warkentin, Malone, and Richard Felder, a psychiatrist, Whitaker formed the Atlanta Psychiatric Clinic, a private practice group, to pursue working with individuals, including chronic schizophrenics, and their families. By 1965, now defining himself as a family therapist, Whitaker moved to the University of Wisconsin School of Medicine in Madison and began, first with August Napier, a psychologist, and later, David Keith, a child psychiatrist, to elaborate his ideas about affectively engaging a variety of families, not simply those with psychotic members (Napier & Whitaker, 1978; Keith & Whitaker, 1982). Moreover, he was starting to pay closer attention to what he personally was experiencing in the treatment process; he saw the potential for using that awareness to press for changes in his patients at the same time that he himself continued to benefit by investing in the therapeutic encounter.

Symbolic-experiential family therapists insist that both real and symbolic curative factors operate in therapy. They liken the symbolic aspect of therapy to the infrastructure of a city; while not apparent on the surface, what runs underneath the streets and buildings is what permits life on the surface to go on (Whitaker & Bumberry, 1988). Reflecting a psychodynamic influence, they believe our personal subterranean worlds are dominated by the flow of impulses and evolving symbols, even if not always conscious; indeed, they believe it is these "emotional infrastructures" that ensure the flow of our impulse life. Since they contend that the meaning we give to external reality is determined by this internal reality, helping expand the symbolic inner worlds of families can aid in their leading fuller, richer lives.

The Therapist Use of Self   Symbolic-experiential family therapists attempt to understand a family's complex world of impulses and symbols by looking for and giving voice to similar underlying impulses and symbols within themselves. Not willing to settle for material from the surface world of thinking and reasoning, they probe into the covert world beneath the surface words, trying to sense the far more important symbolic meanings of what transpires between themselves and the client family. By showing ease with accepting and voicing their own impulses and fantasies, they help family members become more comfortable in recognizing, expressing, and accepting theirs. The growth and development of individual members, according to S-EFT, is stimulated when members feel themselves to be a part of an integrated family. Once they experience this sense of security and belongingness, they can later feel free ("unstuck") enough to psychologically separate from the family and develop autonomy as unique individuals.

Normalizing Human Behavior   Throughout therapy, advocates of S-EFT listen, observe, stay in immediate touch with what they are experiencing, and actively intervene to repair damage, without being concerned over *why* the breakdown occurred. They make an effort to depathologize human experience, as suggested earlier by Whitaker's view of schizophrenia. Dysfunction is viewed in both its structural and process aspects. Structurally, perhaps disorganized or impermeable family boundaries have resulted in nonfunctional subsystem operations, destructive coalitions, role rigidity, and separation between generations. Process difficulties may have led to a breakdown in negotiation between family members to resolve conflict, perhaps to the loss of intimacy or attachment or trust, as individual relationship needs remain unmet. In general, these therapists assume that symptoms develop when dysfunctional structures and processes persist over a period of time and interfere with the family's ability to carry out its life tasks (Roberto, 1991).

In their view, "psychopathology" arises from the same mechanisms that produce "normal" behavior. Consequently, following Whitaker's lead, they are not afraid to encourage "craziness" (unconventional, childlike, socially unacceptable behavior) in family members or, for that matter, in themselves, believing that new outlooks and creative solutions typically follow, as the family is freed to stretch and grow. Through his sometimes quirky-appearing and irrepressible "right brain" style, Whitaker was often able to help sensitize the family to its own unconscious or symbolic life.

For practitioners of S-EFT, the focus of therapy is the process—what occurs during the family session—and how each participant (therapist included) experiences feelings, exposes vulnerabilities, and shares uncensored thoughts. Whenever an individual or family system seeks to grow, the therapist (or cotherapists) can take advantage of this inherent drive toward fulfillment and maturity to engage that person or group in an existential encounter free from the usual social restraints and the role playing that customarily characterize doctor-patient or therapist-client relationships. The encounter is intended to shake up old ways of feeling and behaving and thus to provide an unsettling experience to reactivate the seemingly dormant but innate process of growth.

Establishing Therapeutic Goals   The family therapist's mission, as S-EFT sees it, is to help the three-generational family (family-of-origin members as well as adults and children in the current family) to simultaneously maintain a sense of togetherness along with a sense of healthy separation and autonomy. Family roles, while largely determined by generation, should remain flexible, and members should be encouraged to explore, and on occasion even exchange, family roles. Healthy families, according to Whitaker and Keith (1981), develop an "as if" structure that permits latitude in role playing, often allowing each family member to try on new roles and gain new perspectives:

> For example, the 6-year-old son says to daddy, "Can I serve the meat tonight?" and daddy says, "Sure, you sit over on this chair and serve the meat and potatoes and I'll sit over in your place and complain." (p. 190)

For practitioners of S-EFT, this exchange is an opportunity to develop a healthy, straight-talking communication, in which all family members are able to look at themselves and grow both as individuals and as a family. Consistent with this experiential perspective, Whitaker viewed family health as an ongoing process of *becoming*, in which each member is encouraged to explore a full range of family roles in order to develop maximum autonomy. Growth as a goal takes precedence over achieving stability or specific planned solutions, and symbolic-experiential therapists may terminate therapy still leaving the family uncertain about future direction, but with better tools for finding their own way.

The Therapeutic Process   Symbolic-experiential family therapy sets itself the goal of encouraging individuation and personal integrity of all family members at the same time that it helps the family members evolve a greater sense of family belonging. Rather than attend to symptoms in an identified patient, here the family therapist immediately engages the entire family, forcing all of them as a group to examine the basis of their existence as a family unit.

In Whitaker's colorful description of the therapeutic process, "the journey of family therapy begins with a blind date and ends with an empty nest" (Whitaker & Bumberry, 1988, p. 53). In its initial stages, the therapist must deal with the inevitable *battle for structure,* as the family sizes up the therapist and his or her intentions and attempts to impose its own definition of the upcoming relationship: what's wrong with the family, who's to blame, who requires treatment, how the therapist should proceed. In S-EFT, therapists insist on controlling the ensuing structure, from the first telephone contact onward, so therapy can begin on a productive note and the therapist does not compromise his or her own needs, beliefs, or standards. If the therapist loses this initial struggle, the family will then bring into therapy the identical behavioral patterns that are likely creating their current problems in the first place.

In the process, the therapist is establishing an "I" position with the family, stimulating them, ultimately, to piece together an identifiable "we" position as a family. For example, by insisting on his own autonomy, Whitaker was telling them that he is interested in his own growth as a result of their experience together, and that they need not be concerned about protecting him. Real caring, for Whitaker, requires distance, partially achieved by caring for himself and not only for his client family. Whitaker and Bumberry (1988) emphasize dealing with the family on a symbolic level in a "metaposition"—establishing what each can expect from the other. Whitaker, who frequently used sports analogies, saw himself as a coach, not interested in playing on the team, only in helping them play more effectively. By stepping in to play first base, he argued, he would be indicating he did not think much of the first baseman they already have, a destructive message. Instead, as coach, he encouraged them to develop their own resources.

If the therapist must win the battle for structure, the family must be victorious in the *battle for initiative* (Napier & Whitaker, 1978). Just as the battle for structure defines the integrity of the therapist, so the battle for initiative defines the integrity of the family. It is they who are in charge of their lives and responsible for decisions about the direction they wish, as a group, for their lives to go. That is, any initiative for change must not only come from the family but also be actively supported by its members. These therapists shun responsibility for changing a family, and especially for seeking family leadership.

Practitioners of S-EFT insist the family convene as a group with all members present, underscoring their sense of a family unit as well as acknowledging that the family itself is the client. Together they are encouraged to probe their relationships—in Whitaker's words "to ante up"—despite efforts to identify specific members as the problem. Rather than comfort or reassure, the therapist is apt to be outspoken and risk-taking, shaking up entrenched family patterns. Keith (1998) suggests an initial goal of increasing family anxiety ("It's really much worse than you think") in order to force family members to take more responsibility for the living pattern they have created.

In the following case offered by Whitaker, a mother, father, and 6-year-old girl attend the first session. The daughter is described as school-phobic, the mother obese, the father a hard-driving executive. Mother and father deny relationship struggles, despite his working nearly 75 hours a week and frequently staying out late.

Carl: You mean he's totally lost interest in you?

Mom: Well, no, it's not that. It's just that his way of contributing to the family is to make sure that we have everything we need.

Carl: Except a husband and father.

Mom: No. He's a good father.

Carl: (turning to the daughter) Sarah, do you think that Mommy worries that Daddy might be kissing the secretary? You know, he's gone at work so much. Maybe he gets lonely too.

Sarah: No. Daddies don't get lonely. Just Mommies, but since Mommy has me, she doesn't have to be lonely either.

Carl: Well, I'm sure glad you take such good care of your Mommy but I still worry about Daddies. It's very hard to tell when they're lonely.

Here Whitaker is beginning to get them to think about family relationships, without specifically suggesting that Sarah's dedication to Mom may be related to her refusal to go to school, or that she may be expressing through remaining at home her desire to help Mom hide from her depression. Later in the same session, Mom begins to complain about her inability to play tennis with her high-powered husband because of her weight.

Carl: (turning to Dad) Do you worry about her weight, too, or do you prefer playing with other partners?

Dad: Of course I'd love her to pick up the sport, but it's just not possible. It would be dangerous for her to exert herself with so much excess weight.

Carl: So you don't want to feel like you killed her by pushing tennis. I suppose I can understand that. How is it that you manage to live with the knowledge that she's slowly committing suicide via her obesity? (Whitaker & Bumberry, 1988, pp. 62–64)

Note how the therapist has started them thinking beyond the presenting symptoms of separate individuals, expanding the symptom framework to now include possible extramarital affairs, self-destructive overeating, and a relationship gap between the parents. Each member's participation in the lives of the other members is in the process of becoming clarified under Whitaker's provocative comments. While they may not yet make the necessary connections, they leave the session with new ideas to consider, all within a relationship or interpersonal perspective. In future sessions, having set the therapeutic structure, the therapist must be careful to get the family to take responsibility for facing themselves, winning the battle for initiative, and, through an experiential exchange with him, come alive and cease playacting.

In Whitaker's view (1977), then, family therapy occurs in stages:

1. *A pretreatment or engagement phase* in which the entire nuclear family is expected to participate; the therapist or cotherapists establish that they are in charge during the sessions but that the family must make its own life decisions outside of these office visits (the latter is intended to convey the message that a therapist does not have better ideas for how family members should run their lives than they themselves do).
2. *A middle phase* in which increased involvement between both therapists and the family develops; care is taken by the therapist not to be absorbed by the family system; symptoms are seen and relabeled for the family as efforts toward growth; and the family is incited to change by means of confrontation, exaggeration, anecdote, or absurdity.
3. *A late phase* in which increased flexibility in the family necessitates only minimal intervention from the therapist or therapy team.
4. *A separation phase* in which the therapists and family part, but with the acknowledgment of mutual interdependence and loss. In the final phase, the family uses more and more of its own resources, and assumes increased responsibility for its way of living. With separation—the "empty nest"—there is joy mingled with a sense of loss.[2]

Symbolic-experiential change-producing interventions have a covert, implicit quality. Symptoms are rarely attacked directly. Insight seems to follow changes in feelings and behavior, not precede such changes. History taking is occasionally important but not carried out routinely; in any case, it must not be allowed to

---

[2]Napier and Whitaker (1978) provide an intriguing full account of family therapy with the Brice family (two parents, a suicidal, runaway teenager, an adolescent son, and a 6-year old daughter) in their book *The Family Crucible*.

impede this approach's major therapeutic thrust—forming a close and personal alliance with the family as a whole and providing an experience that is symbolic to the family but does not reinforce its distress (Keith & Whitaker, 1982). What the family therapist has most to offer, Whitaker believed, is his or her personal maturity; the stage of the therapist's personal development has an influence on the kind of support or assistance provided to the family. He maintained that the therapist who does not derive benefit, therapeutically, from his or her work has little to give, therapeutically speaking, to client families. The use of cotherapists adds another dimension; the ability of both therapists to join together, have fun together, disagree, or even fight with each other, and perhaps to go off on different tangents—one acting "crazy" and the other providing stability—is a model for spontaneous and productive interaction.

The Person of the Therapist   Throughout his work with individuals and families, Whitaker stressed his personal need to "stay alive" as a human being and as a therapist. He frequently asserted that "nothing worth knowing can be taught," insisting that the therapist must uncover his or her own belief system and symbolic world, and then use that self (rather than specific therapeutic techniques) to grow and help families do the same. Over two decades ago he offered a loosely formulated set of rules for therapists that still seem applicable today (Whitaker, 1976b, p. 164):

1. Relegate every significant other to second place.
2. Learn how to love. Flirt with any infant available. Unconditional positive regard probably isn't present after the baby is three years old.
3. Develop a reverence for your own impulses, and be suspicious of your behavior sequences.
4. Enjoy your mate more than your kids, and be childish with your mate.
5. Fracture role structures at will and repeatedly.
6. Learn to retreat and advance from every position that you take.
7. Guard your impotence as one of your most valuable weapons.
8. Build long-term relations so you can be free to hate safely.
9. Face the fact that you must grow until you die. Develop a sense of the benign absurdity of life—yours and those around you—and thus learn to transcend the world of experience. If we can abandon our missionary zeal we have less chance of being eaten by cannibals.
10. Develop your primary process living. Evolve a joint craziness with someone you are safe with. Structure a professional cuddle group so you won't abuse your mate with the garbage left over from the day's work.
11. As Plato said, "practice dying."

In effect, these "rules" urge therapists to be sure to take care of their own needs in the process of caring for others. They need to open themselves up to others, allowing themselves to love without insisting on perfection in their love object. They need to trust their own wishes and desires but not necessarily how they play out in behavior. Their mate—more than children, parents, and so on—should represent their primary love object. Whitaker urged therapists to abandon rigid rules because they inhibit growth, and to try to remain flexible and available for new experiences without insisting on always knowing the right answer. Strong relationships, says Whitaker, are worth cultivating, and once developed can endure angry conflict. Let go, you can't fix everything! Learn to play—both at home and at work—and live every day to its fullest measure!

Gestalt Family Therapy

All of the family therapy approaches we are considering in this chapter are, to a greater or lesser extent, *existential* in character. More an orientation to understanding human behavior than a formal school of psychotherapy, existentially influenced therapies are concerned with entering and comprehending the world as it is being experienced by the individual family members as well as the family as a functioning whole. The therapies have in common an emphasis on the meaning the patient gives to existence, to *being*. Because people define themselves through their current choices and decisions, action in the present, not reflection on the past, is the key to understanding for the existentialist. Even the future—what people choose to become—is charged with more influence than the past and the conflicts associated with the past. In existential therapies, clients are urged to examine and take responsibility for their lives. Unconscious material may be brought forth but is not automatically assumed to be any more meaningful than the conscious data of life.

Psychotherapy in this framework is an *encounter* between two or more persons who are constantly developing, evolving, and fulfilling their inner potential. Technique is deemphasized to preclude one person seeing the other as an object to be analyzed. In contrast to the common therapeutic belief that understanding stems from technique, existentialist therapists believe that technique follows understanding. Formal and conventional doctor-patient roles are replaced by a more egalitarian and open arrangement in which each participant opens his or her world to the other as an existential partner. The emphasis is on presence; in a real, immediate, ongoing relationship between two or more persons, each tries to understand and experience as far as possible the being of the other(s).

If existentialism is concerned with how humans experience their immediate existence, Gestalt psychology focuses on how they perceive it. Having accepted the therapeutic implications of existentialism along with much of the rhetoric of Gestalt psychology, Frederick (Fritz) Perls is generally credited with launching the Gestalt therapy movement in the United States. For Perls (1969), who worked with individuals, change was facilitated when the client's thoughts and feelings became congruent. A major treatment goal, then, was for the client to achieve greater self-awareness in order to become more self-directed, more centered, more congruous. By removing blocks and especially entrenched, intellectualized thinking patterns, the client often was aided to break through to his or her emotionally rooted inner experiences. Extrapolating from the individual focus, Gestalt family therapists focus attention on the immediate—"*What people say, how they say it, what happens when it is said, how it corresponds with what they are doing, and what they are attempting to achieve*" (Kempler, 1982, p. 141). Here the goal is to bring discordant elements (within oneself or between family members) into a self-disclosing confrontation and ultimate resolution.

The Therapeutic Encounter Employing a personally interactive way of working with families, **Gestalt family therapy** represents an effort to blend some of the principles and procedures of family and Gestalt therapies in order to help people reach beyond their customary self-deceptive games, defenses, and facades. To do so, the therapist relies on the forthright expression of what he or she is experiencing, in order to assist clients to become aware of and release previously unrecognized or bottled-up feelings.

Kempler (1981) insists that an effective therapeutic encounter meet the following four demands:

1. A clear knowledge of the "who I am" at any given moment. This requires a dynamic awareness of what I need from moment to moment.
2. A sensitive cognition or appraisal of the people I am with and the context of our encounter.
3. The development and utilization of my manipulating skills to extract, as effectively as I am capable, what I need from the encounter.
4. The capability of finishing an encounter. (p. 38)

Kempler's (1981) therapeutic efforts are provocative, highly personal, uncompromisingly honest, and powerful. He presses for self-disclosure by family members, expecting that the wish or need to resolve their problems or improve relationships will give them the courage to expose their vulnerabilities. He actively and directly insists that everyone, himself included, become more intensely aware of what they are doing or saying or feeling. Like the mechanic who would rather listen to a troublesome engine than hear a description of it, Kempler first starts up a family conversation:

Transcript	Comments
Mother: Our 15-year-old son Jim has been making a lot of trouble for us lately.	
	The healthier the family, the more readily they talk to each other. For instance, should Jim respond immediately to his mother's charge with "That's not true!" it would indicate that he has both self-confidence and the hope of being heard. Let's assume Jim doesn't leap in.
Therapist (to Jim evocatively): Do you agree that the number one problem in this family is that you are a troublemaker?	
Jim: Not really.	
Therapist: Tell her what you think is.	
Jim: It's no use.	
Therapist (to Mother): Do you have anything to say to his hopelessness?	*(continued)*

Walter Kempler, M.D.

Transcript	Comments
(continued)	
Mother: I think we've said all there is to say.	Family members are often reluctant to engage one another, particularly initially. The therapist perseveres by offering himself, if necessary.
Therapist (to Jim): I'd like to know what you think is the problem, Jim.	
Jim: They are too rigid.	The battlelines often have both parents on one side. It is better when it is a free-for-
all.	
Therapist: Both of them identical?	
Jim: Mother more than Father.	
Therapist: Then, maybe you can get some help from him.	
Jim: He's too weak. He always gives in to her.	
Therapist (to Father): Do you agree with him?	
Father: Of course not.	
Therapist: You didn't tell him.	

Source: Kempler, 1974, pp. 27–28)

Kempler is interested in what each person wants and from whom, expressed in the most specific terms possible. Participants are forced to talk to each other, in face-to-face, encounter-group-like fashion. If a wife complains to Kempler that her husband lacks understanding or sensitivity, Kempler directs her to tell that to her husband, not the therapist, and to be specific in her complaint. If she argues that it will do no good, Kempler insists she tell *that* to her husband. If she then breaks down, admits her feelings of hopelessness, and begins to cry—all without provoking a response from her husband—Kempler will point out his silence and invite him to answer her. From the initial interview through the subsequent sessions, the focus remains the immediate present. Self-disclosure and open, honest exchanges with others are basic ground rules for family members to follow if they are to untangle a family problem or overcome an impasse.

Viewing the individual within his or her functional context—the family—Gestalt family therapists attempt to help each family member achieve maximum individuation at the same time as they promote more vital relationships among the various members. Thus, the traditional goals of the Gestalt therapist working with an individual client (growth of the individual and the development of a distinct sense of self) are combined with objectives for the family group as a whole. First helping family members to explore how their awareness is blocked, the therapist then channels the increased awareness so that they may engage in more productive and fulfilling processes with one another (Kaplan & Kaplan, 1978).

The Gestalt therapist facilitates self-exploration, risk taking, and spontaneity. Since such undertakings are all but impossible if an individual or family fears that self-discovery could be harmful, it is essential that the therapist provide an unchecked and unequivocal model for self-disclosure. To strike the familiar pose as a benevolent and accepting therapist only plays into the client's fantasies that disapproval is dangerous, according to Kempler (1982). By contrast, Kempler is emotionally intense, assertive, genuine, challenging, sometimes brutally (if refreshingly) frank; in short, he expresses whatever he is feeling at the moment in the hope of making an impact on the family. As the following excerpt from a couple's therapy session begins, Kempler has just completed a moving exchange with the wife, during which the husband remained silent. Kempler now turns to the husband because he wants his participation.

Transcript	Comments
Therapist: Where are you?	
He: I don't know, (pause) I was thinking of something else. (pause) I don't understand what is going on. I guess that's it (pause) partly thinking what I had to do today.	He was always inarticulate, always speaking haltingly and tentatively. His eyes blinked nervously as if he were being buffeted. I had mentioned this before. On past occasions I had confronted him with his inarticulateness and his blinking, but we had made no progress with it. It seemed that I had tried everything I knew to no avail.

(continued)

Transcript	Comments

(continued)

Therapist: Damn, that makes me angry. You're a clod. That's the word I want to buffet you with. Damn you. So insensitive. No wonder you've got problems in your marriage. (Then, cooling down enough to make an "I" statement instead of the "you" accusations, I continued) I want you to hear; I want you to join in; I want you to at least acknowledge our presence some way other than leaving. At best, I'd want you to appreciate us in what happened, at worst, to tell us you don't like us for being inane, but not just to abandon us.

He: (Thoughtful) Earlier I was aware of something like envy (pause) resentment (pause) I don't know.

Therapist: (Still angry) You never know. That's your standard answer. Now I don't know. I don't know what the hell to do with you to get in touch with you.

He: I'm sorry. (pause) I always say I'm sorry. I guess I'm sorry. I was envious. (pause) I felt angry 'cause I was envious.

> He was trying to be with me now, and I wanted to try harder myself. I decided to try clarifying and/or intensifying his statement.

Therapist: Try on: "I long to be close to both of you, but I never learned how."

> I felt my own sadness when I said that and knew I was on target—or else I would not have been so angry with him. His tears were confirmation as he choked up trying to say the sentence.

Therapist: You don't have to, but I wish you could talk to us now.

He: I can't. It's too sad.

Therapist: It?

He: The sentence…

Therapist: Then try to include all the words "I'm so sad when I think of how I long to be close and can't because I never learned."

> I kept wanting to return to this key phrase and yet I did not want my urging to become more central for him than his experiencing his longing. He sat thoughtfully, still tearing and saying nothing. Several minutes passed.   *(continued)*

Transcript	Comments

(*continued*)

Therapist: I'm suddenly aware of my own difficulty in speaking about longing. I could debate with you more easily than I can speak of feeling the longing to be close. I realize I still haven't spoken to mine and can only hesitantly speak about yours.

   This feels better than debating or idly chatting but it sure is sad. I feel closer to you in our sadness.

He: (Finally) I can do it with my car—feeling close by racing people...I'm so safe that way. I can't just be close.

Therapist: (I seemed finished with me for the moment and was free to turn once again to him. I offered the sentence again—modified.) "I long to be close but never learned how, but now I'm learning finally."

Comments column:

I began to cry. He was now trying harder to look at me through his tears. I found myself smiling through my tears.

"It," I thought. How clever. He nodded, still unable to speak.

He began to cry more heavily as he nodded his head and turned inward again, looking down. His wife reached out warmly. "This reminds me of the time that you..." I interrupted her, "Leave him alone now. You can talk to him later." She grasped, or at least readily accepted, my command. I wanted him to be wherever he was with his feelings, not diverted to some other time and place. Her comment sounded like an "aha" announcement and I felt no compunction to honor it. She could keep it to and for herself.

I left them and was visiting my father, fluttering through historical scenes like a hummingbird. His lovingly tousling my hair—the only times he ever touched me that I could recall. His angrily shouting at me. His intellectual lectures to teach me something. I became painfully aware of his absent touch and never being spoken to affectionately by him. He never told me he loved me or even that he liked me. I recalled the surprise I once felt when I overheard him admiring me to one of his friends. I am sad. Of course, I long.

I came back to our session and was aware of this couple once again. They were both looking at me. I shared my thoughts. Then he related clearly, articulately his own longings, recalling, smiling through his fresh tears, his father teaching him to drive, the only closeness he knew with his father. To intensify his experience, I suggested that he envision his father. He couldn't. He just cried. "Tell him," I suggested, "how you longed to be close to him but just didn't know how because you never learned." After a long pause, he replied: "I used to feel angry and frustrated. I realize now he never learned either."

He was integrating and I was pleased. I became vacant, and we all sat silently, alone and close. [Kempler, 1981, pp. 11–13)

Kempler's demand for a complete and honest emotional encounter with and between family members reflects his Gestalt heritage, and, although far less popular today than in the heyday of encounter groups and sensitivity training three decades ago, offers a useful counterweight to the currently fashionable concerns with cognitive analyses and behavior change.[3] No holds are barred, no feelings stifled. As noted earlier, the therapist is a real flesh-and-blood person who knows who he is, what his needs are, and what he is experiencing from moment to moment during the shared therapeutic encounter with the family. At the same time, he expects—nay, insists—that all participants search for, uncover, and express what they are experiencing *now*, since to Gestaltists, *nothing exists except in the now*. He urges clients to stay with the experience as it is happening and until they recognize and "own" what they are feeling from moment to moment. All efforts to avoid this awareness are counteracted by Kempler as soon as they occur; it is in the now, say Gestaltists, that people are or are not growing, are or are not enhancing their coping abilities, are or are not in touch with themselves and with reality.

The Human Validation Process Model

Virginia Satir's central place in the history of the family therapy movement has been noted several times earlier in this book. In the 1950s, among the founding parents of the family therapy movement, Satir was in the unique position of being both a woman and a social worker among predominantly white male psychiatrists. Actually, she probably preceded most of her male counterparts in working with families, reportedly having seen her first family in therapy in 1951 and having offered the first training program ever in family therapy in 1955 at the Illinois State Psychiatric Institute (Satir, 1982). It was several years later that she read of a group engaging in family research efforts in Palo Alto, California (Bateson, Jackson, Haley, & Weakland, 1956); having contacted them, she was invited by Jackson to help him start what became the Mental Research Institute (MRI). More interested in training than in research, Satir soon set about demonstrating her techniques with families, culminating in the first published description of conjoint family therapy (Satir, 1964), truly a groundbreaking text for therapists and students alike.

Over a 30-year span, until her death in 1988, she continued to be a prolific writer and is especially celebrated for her inspiring family therapy demonstrations (said to number between 400 and 500) around the world. Although linked to the communication approach (see Chapter 10) because of her early MRI affiliation, Satir's work at Esalen, a growth center, during the 1960s, encouraged her to add a humanistic framework and emphasize a number of growth-enhancing techniques (sensory awareness, dance, massage, group encounter techniques) to evoke feelings and clarify family communication patterns. In her more recent writing, Satir (1986; Satir & Bitter, 1991) identified her approach as a Human Validation Process Model in which the therapist and family join forces to stimulate an inherent health-promoting process in the family. Open communication and emotional experiencing were the mechanisms that helped achieve that end.

---

[3]Kempler and Whitaker both seek open, honest, uncensored expression. Whitaker's assertions reflect his efforts to be in tune with his unconscious impulses, while Kempler's statements reflect his insistence that he and the clients stay in the moment. For Kempler, "staying in the moment" helps strip away the defense of escaping into talking about the past.

Virginia Satir was a charismatic leader, truly an original; no discussion of experiential family therapy would be complete without paying homage to her vision. She presented herself to families (often in demonstrations and without prior contact with the family) as a warm, nurturing, genuine person, someone with belief in the goodness of people and in the "healing power of love." (Satir & Baldwin, 1983). While the latter made her appear simplistic and pollyannaish to critics, she nevertheless was revered by followers and profoundly touched those families with whom she worked. The "love" she practiced with clients and that she postulated as a necessary condition for actualizing one's capabilities was based on her assumptions about what best facilitates change. Satir assumed people want to be whole, authentic, sensitive, and genuine with one another. Thus, she looked for and found in people signs of their healthy *intentions,* even when these were embedded in unhealthy behavior (Lawrence, 1999). Symptomatic behavior, for Satir, was "adaptive attempts gone awry" rather than fixed characteristics of the person (Waters & Lawrence, 1993) Summaries of her underlying philosophical assumptions and therapeutic techniques can be found in Satir and Baldwin (1983), Woods and Martin (1984), Brothers (1991), and Satir, Banmen, Gerber, and Gomori (1991).

Symptoms and Family Balance   Satir concerned herself with the family as a balanced system. In particular, she wanted to determine the "price" each part of the system "pays" to keep the overall unit balanced. That is, she viewed any symptom in an individual member as signaling a blockage in growth, and as having a homeostatic connection to a family system that requires blockage and distortion of growth in some form in all of its members to keep its balance.

A presenting symptom in a family member gave Satir (1982) the initial clues for "unraveling the net of distorted, ignored, denied, projected, unnourished, and untapped parts of each person so that they can connect with their ability to cope functionally, healthily, and joyously" (p. 41).

Individual Growth and Development   Satir believed that all humans strive toward growth and development, and that each of us possesses all the resources we need for fulfilling our potential, if only we can gain access to these resources and learn to nourish them. More specifically, she pointed to three types of factors influencing human development: (1) unchangeable genetic endowment, determining our physical, emotional, and temperamental potential; (2) longitudinal influences, the result of learning acquired in the process of growth; and (3) the constant mind-body interaction.

Longitudinal influences—the sum of learning since birth—are especially significant. Here Satir emphasized the child's experiences of the *primary survival triad* (father, mother, child) as the essential source of self-identity. Adult self-worth or self-esteem evolves from the relative proportion of constructive to destructive interaction experiences arising from this triad. The child also learns to decipher parental messages; discrepancies between words, tone, touch, and looks help shape future adult communication patterns.

Virginia Satir, M.D.

Another important factor in individual growth is the *m nd, body, feeling triad*. Body parts may often take on metaphoric meaning; each part usually has a positive or negative value attached to it by its owner. Some are liked, others disliked, some need awakening. In what Satir called a therapeutic *parts party,* clients are encouraged to become aware of these parts and learn to use them "in an harmonious and integrated manner" (Satir & Baldwin, 1983, p. 258).

Satir (1986) contended that the self—the core of every person—consists of eight separate but interacting elements or levels, which together exert a constant influence on a person's well-being. Satir searched for the varying degrees of strength in each of these parts of the person. In order to tap an individual's nourishing potentials, she attempted to work at one or more of the following levels:

Physical (the body)
Intellectual (thoughts, logic, processing of facts, left-brain activity)
Emotional (feelings, intuition, right-brain activity)
Sensual (sound, sight, touch, taste, smell)
Interactional (I-Thou communication between oneself and others)
Contextual (colors, sound, light, temperature, movement, space, time)
Nutritional (solids and fluids ingested to furnish energy)
Spiritual (one's relationship to life's meaning, the soul, life force)

As noted, Satir believed all persons possess all the resources they need for positive growth, if she could help them harness their potential to nourish themselves. Building self-esteem, promoting self-worth, expanding awareness, exposing and correcting discrepancies in how the family communicates—these were the issues Satir tackled as she attempted to help each member of the family develop "wellness" and become as "whole" as possible. The extent to which they could identify and practice new possibilities determined their chances to integrate change into their family life.

With success based upon family resiliency, family members would discover new solutions to their problems.

Family Roles and Communication Styles   Satir contended that the way the family communicates reflects the feelings of self-worth of its members. Dysfunctional communication (indirect, unclear, incomplete, unclarified, inaccurate, distorted, inappropriate) characterizes a dysfunctional family system. One of Satir's lasting contributions is her simple, but far from simplistic, classification of styles of communication. She argued that under stress, a person in a relationship with another person communicates in one of five ways (Satir, 1972). These styles are expressed through body position and body language as much as through verbal behavior. The *placater* acts weak, tentative, self-effacing; always agrees, apologizes, tries to please. The *blamer* dominates, invariably finds fault with others, and self-righteously accuses. The *super-reasonable* person adopts a rigid stance, remains detached, calm, cool, maintaining intellectual control while making certain not to become emotionally involved. The *irrelevant* person distracts others and seems unable to relate to anything going on. Only the *congruent communicator* seems real, genuinely expressive, responsible for sending straight (not double-binding or other confusing) messages in their appropriate context.

Various combinations of these styles exist in most families. For example, take the case of a blaming wife, a blaming husband, and a placating child triad: "It's the school, they don't teach anything anymore"; "It's the child down the street, that's where she's learned those bad words"; "It's the way you've raised her, she's just like you"; "I'll try to do better, Daddy, you're absolutely right. I'll stop watching TV tomorrow, go to the library…leave the dishes and I'll do them tomorrow after school." In a blamer/super-reasonable couple, the wife might complain bitterly, "We hardly ever make love anymore; don't you have any feelings for me?" The husband might respond coldly, "Of course I do or I wouldn't be married to you. Perhaps we define the word *love* differently." In the case of a conversation between a super-reasonable parent ("Let's discuss precisely why you seem to be having difficulties with your math problems tonight") and the irrelevant child ("It's time for my shower now"), nothing gets settled or resolved and the tension is maintained if not increased. Table 7.1 illustrates Satir's four-stance model of dysfunctional family communication.

Satir maintained that these roles are essentially poses that keep distressed people from exposing their true feelings because they lack the self-esteem that would allow them to be themselves. Placaters are afraid to risk disapproval if they speak up or disagree or act in any way independent of a parent or spouse. Blamers also feel endangered and react by attacking in order to cover up feeling empty and unloved themselves. Super-reasonable people feel safe only at a distance and rely on their intellect to keep from acknowledging that they too have feelings and are vulnerable. Irrelevant people (often a youngest child in a family or a family pet) gain approval only by acting cute and harmless. Satir, a warm, caring, nurturing person, but also capable of being fearlessly direct, inevitably tried to facilitate straight talk between family members, encouraging them to be congruent in their communications, matching words to feelings to body stance, without qualification.

Table 7.1   Four Dysfunctional Communication Stances Adopted Under Stress (Satir)

Category	Caricature	Typical verbal expression	Body posture	Inner feeling
Placater	Service	"Whatever you want is okay, I'm just here to make you happy."	Grateful, boo-licking, begging, self-flagellating	"I am like a nothing. Without you I am dead. I am worthless."
Blamer	Power	"You never do anything right. What is the matter with you?"	Finger pointing, loud, tyrannical, enraged	"I am lonely and unsuccessful."
Super-reasonable	Intellect	"If one were to observe carefully, one might notice the workworn hands of someone present here."	Monotone voice, stiff, machine-like, computer-like	"I feel vulnerable."
Irrelevant	Spontaneity	Words unrelated to what others are saying. For example, in midst of family dispute: "What are we having for dinner?"	In constant movement, constant chatter, distracting	"Nobody cares. There is no place for me."

Source: Based on Bandler, Grinder, & Satir, 1976

The "Seed" Model   In her workshops, Satir often presented two contrasting views of the world, which she labeled the "Threat and Reward" model and the "Seed" model. Relationships in the former suppose a hierarchy in which some people define rules for others to follow without question. The hierarchy is based on roles that powerful individuals hold on to for life. While those on top are not necessarily malevolent, their behavior helps create individuals who feel weak and have low self-esteem. Conformity is expected in the "Threat and Reward" model, whether based on gender or lower-status positions in society. The cost of nonconformity is guilt, fear, or rejection. Resentment and hostile feelings also are common, and, for some people, feelings of hopelessness may be present.

In the "Seed" model, *personhood* rather than role determines identity, and every person is born with a potential that may be fulfilled. While roles and status differences exist (parent-child, doctor-patient), they define relationships only within certain contexts, and are not based on permanent status or role differences outside of that context. In the "Seed" model, change is viewed as an ongoing life process, and as an opportunity for growth. Satir was a strong advocate of the "Seed" model, insisting that given the proper conditions of nurture, children, like seedlings, can develop into healthy adults.

Family Assessment and Intervention   Satir tried to help people feel good about themselves, often as a result of her own boundless, optimistic approach to life. She tended to work with families in terms of their members' day-to-day functioning and their emotional experiences with each other. She taught people congruent ways of communicating by helping to restore the use of their senses and the ability to get in touch with and accept what they were really feeling. Thus, she helped individuals (and families) build their sense of self-worth; she opened up possibilities for making choices and bringing about changes in relationships (Bandler, Grinder, & Satir, 1976).

Because Satir believed human beings have within them all the resources that they need in order to flourish, she directed her interventions at helping families gain access to their nourishing potentials—and then learn to use them. This is a growth-producing approach in which she encouraged people to take whatever risks were necessary in order to take charge of their own lives. Early in the therapy process, Satir would present herself as a teacher introducing the family to a new language, helping them to understand their communication "discrepancies," blocking the kinds of repetitive sequences that end with members falling into the incongruent family communication styles discussed earlier.

Satir's primary talent was as a therapist and trainer rather than a theory builder or researcher. She aimed at accessibility in her writing style, consistent with her desire for clear and direct communication, although her concepts (self-esteem, family pain, family health) often lacked precision. She was a vigorous, nurturant, compassionate, down-to-earth, massively perceptive person who engaged a family authoritatively from the first session onward. She spoke simply and directly, kept up a running account of what she was doing with the family, tried to pass along her communication skills to family members, then arranged encounters between members according to the rules she had taught them. In the following example from her early, if somewhat dated, work (Satir, 1967), the parents and their children, Johnny (age 10) and Patty (age 7), are being seen together; Johnny, the identified patient, is having behavior problems at school. Satir wants to clarify what ideas each member has about what to expect from therapy and why each is there. Note how she tries to help the family members (1) recognize individual differences among them by having each member speak for himself or herself; (2) accept disagreements and differing perceptions of the same situation; and most important, (3) say what they see, think, and feel in order to bring disagreements out into the open.

Patty: Mother said we were going to talk about family problems.

Therapist: What about Dad? Did he tell you the same thing?

Patty: No.

Therapist: What did Dad say?

Patty: He said we were going for a ride.

Therapist: I see. So you got some information from Mother and some information from Dad. What about you, Johnny. Where did you get your information?

Johnny: I don't remember.

Therapist: You don't remember who told you?

Mother: I don't think I said anything to him, come to think of it. He wasn't around at the time, I guess.

Therapist: How about you, Dad? Did you say anything to Johnny?

Father: No, I thought Mary had told him.

Therapist: (to Johnny) Well, then, how could you remember if nothing was said?

Johnny: Patty said we were going to see a lady about the family.

Therapist: I see. So you got your information from your sister, whereas Patty got a clear message from both Mother and Dad. (Shortly, she asks the parents what they remember saying.)

Therapist: How about that, Mother? Were you and Dad able to work this out together—what you would tell the children?

Mother: Well, you know, I think this is one of our problems. He does things with them and I do another.

Father: I think this is a pretty unimportant thing to worry about.

Therapist: Of course it is, in one sense. But then we can use it, you know, to see how messages get across in the family. One of the things we work on in families is how family members communicate—how clearly they get their messages across. We will have to see how Mother and Dad can get together so that Johnny and Patty can get a clear message. (Later, she explains to the children why the family is there.)

Therapist: Well, then. I'll tell you why Mother and Dad have come here. They have come here because they were unhappy about how things were going in the family and they want to work out ways so that everyone can get more pleasure from family life.

Source: Satir, 1967, pp. 143–145.[4]

In this brief excerpt we also see Satir's effort to build self-esteem in each family member and to emphasize that each person is unique and has the right to express his or her own views without another person (for example, a parent) answering for him or her. She lets the family know where she is going, thus enabling them to know what to expect as they work together. Warm and caring herself, with a strong set of humanistic values, Satir stressed the role of intimacy in family relationships as a vehicle for growth among all family members. A healthy family, to Satir, is a place where members can ask for what they need, a place where needs are met and individuality is allowed to flourish. Dysfunctional families do not permit individuality and mem-

---

[4]A more detailed description and analysis of Satir's work with a family can be found in Satir and Baldwin (1983). The major portion of the book is devoted to a transcript of one of Satir's family therapy demonstrations, including a step-by-step explanation of her techniques and interventions.

bers fail to develop a sense of self-worth. If parental messages to one another or to their children are incongruent or confusing, then family communication across generations tends to be similarly unclear or confounded. Parents with low self-esteem communicate poorly and contribute to feelings of low self-esteem in their children.

In an early technique, Satir initiated a family's treatment by compiling a **family life fact chronology** to understand the history of the family's development by depicting key elements in its evolution, beginning with the birth of the oldest grandparents. Her goal here was to force family members to think about characteristic family patterns, and especially about the relevant concepts that had formed the basis for their developing relationships.

While she shares with Whitaker the idea that the therapist makes use of himself or herself in dealing with a family, his methods were more apt to reflect his psychoanalytic beginnings while hers revealed her debt to Carl Rogers and the humanistic movement's striving for fulfillment and self-actualization. Satir believed the therapist must be a resource person who shows the family how to change, how to get in touch with their own feelings, how to listen to others, how to ask for clarification if they do not understand another person's message, and so on. Through her gentle, caring, matter-of-fact questioning, Satir enabled parents to listen to their children's statements and opinions, perhaps for the first time, and the children to understand their parents' views and behavior. In time, through such a feedback process, congruent communication replaces the blaming, placating, super-reasonable, and irrelevant family communication styles described earlier.

Family Reconstruction   Another therapeutic innovation developed by Satir in the late 1960s, **family reconstruction** attempts to guide clients to unlock dysfunctional patterns stemming from their families of origin. The technique blends elements of Gestalt therapy, guided fantasy, hypnosis, psychodrama, role playing, and family sculpting (as noted earlier, physically molding family members into characteristic poses representing one family member's view of family relationships at a particular moment, say after the death of a grandmother). The idea is to shed outgrown family rules and dislodge early misconceptions. Used with families as well as in group therapy settings (Nerin, 1986), family reconstruction is a process that takes family members through certain fixed stages of their lives. By reenacting their family's multigenerational drama, members have an opportunity to reclaim their roots, and in the process perhaps view old perceptions in a new light, thereby changing entrenched perceptions, feelings, and beliefs (Nerin, 1989).

Generally speaking, family reconstruction has three goals: (1) to reveal to family members the source of their old learning; (2) to enable them to develop a more realistic picture of the personhood of their parents; and (3) to pave the way for members to find their own personhood. The technique was especially useful for dealing with family issues when there was little or no access to the real family of origin.

Within a group setting, usually with enough members so that separate actors can portray each family member, the client (here called the Explorer) elicits the aid of others to play key family roles in the history of the Explorer's extended family across at least three generations. With the therapist acting as the Guide, the Explorer works through lingering family conflicts (for example, "healing" a relationship between him and his mother) in an effort to reconstruct the past mysteries of his or her life, come away with a new understanding of past events, and as a result become free to maximize his or her potential.

The Guide leads the Explorer through the reconstruction, asking questions based on a chronological account of the family history extending over several generations. A trusting relationship between Guide, Explorer, and auxiliary members is essential if the Explorer is to maximize learning from the process.

Satir is quoted (Nerin, 1989) as saying:

> When one views human life as sacred, as I do, family reconstruction becomes a spiritual as well as a cognitive experience to free human energy from the shackles of the past, thus paving the way for the evolvement of being more fully human. (p. 55)

The Avanta Network   For the last decade of her life, Satir's influence waned in the family therapy movement, probably as a result of conflict with other leaders and her interest in changing larger systems. She moved away from the mainstream of the family therapy movement.[5] While continuing to travel around the world as a kind of roving emissary of humanistic family therapy, Satir was persuaded to try to supply a systematic rationale for her interventions. With two colleagues who had analyzed and devised a model of Satir's linguistic style with families (Bandler, Grinder, & Satir, 1976), she began to identify the key elements in her therapeutic approach: challenging the built-in expectations in the family's existing communication patterns; helping the family members work together to understand what they want in terms of change; preparing the family for a new growth experience; helping the members learn a new family process for coping; and providing the tools they will need to continue the change process after therapy. Most important, their linguistic analysis indicated she taught the actual skills necessary to communicate differently as a family. Having learned these skills, family members presumably would be able to cope more creatively and effectively with any new problem or crisis using the strategies they themselves developed during family therapy.

Having developed a worldwide following, Satir turned her attention to larger systems. In 1977, as an outgrowth of her humanistic orientation, she formed the Avanta Network (*avante* is Italian for "moving ahead"; thus, Avanta referred to "going beyond"), a nonprofit organization to train others in her therapeutic outlook and procedures.

Despite Satir's enormous influence on the field—she was judged during her lifetime to be one of the best family therapy teachers in the world (Braverman, 1986)—

[5]One event hastening her departure, according to Pittman (1989) who was present, occured in Venezuela in 1974, at a meeting of board members of the influential journal *Family Process*. In a heated debate with Salvador Minuchin regarding the future direction of family therapy, Minuchin was critical of what he regarded as Satir's evangelical approach, insisting that more than the healing power of love was involved in order to repair dysfunction within a family. Satir argued otherwise, calling on her colleagues to join her crusade for nothing less than the salvation of humankind through family therapy. When it became clear to all assembled that Minuchin's position represented the direction in which the field was headed, Satir, dissatisfied with its limited mission, directed her efforts away from mainstream family and focused her energies on the Avanta Network and similar organizations.

her way of working with families has a dwindling number of followers today. Possibly this is because many perceive her interventions to be more a manifestation of her personality and clinical artistry—and thus hard to copy—than a systematic set of therapeutic procedures that can be learned. What she did contribute—her insistence on the importance of open and direct communication, her effort to help clients build self-esteem, her belief in the resiliency of every family—were essential to family therapy's early development and a needed balance to rival approaches less concerned with emotionality. Beyond that, Cheung (1997) suggests that Satir's emphasis on the prime importance of language, her belief that people have the potential to change and make their own choices, and her view of the therapist as participant-facilitator may represent an early influence consistent with current social construction theories (Chapter 13). In Cheung's view, family reconstruction resembles a narrative approach that affords an opportunity to reexamine beliefs and reconstruct meanings regarding one's past experiences.

Emotionally Focused Couple Therapy

What's new in experiential family therapy—and not wholly carried over from its hey-day in the 1960s—are efforts to integrate its approach with systems outlooks. Viewing couples in both intrapsychic and interactional terms, helping them gain access to what is emotionally significant for each of the partners and what guides their experiences and actions, and assisting their explorations through the ongoing transactions occurring in the close, personal therapist-client(s) relationship, together become the core of the therapeutic change process. Rather than attempt to understand recurring maladaptive patterns or to achieve predetermined behavioral changes, here the emphasis is on helping clients explore their moment-to-moment inner experiences and relationship events, especially the rigid patterns that block emotional engagement. The therapist's role becomes one of a facilitator, knowing how to help clients explore particular kinds of experiences, rather than the expert who knows *what* the client is experiencing (Greenberg, Rice, & Elliott (1996).

This process-facilitative experiential approach is an outgrowth of humanistic therapy, especially the client-centered procedures of Carl Rogers (creating a safe therapeutic environment and offering empathic understanding), and Fritz Perls's Gestalt therapy (directing clients toward greater awareness by engaging in resolution-enhancing affective processes). Add to this mix the contribution of Satir, particularly her emphasis on congruent communication and closeness in the therapist-client relationship. As a result of this amalgam, people are considered to have an inherent tendency to maximize their capabilities, to actualize themselves. They also organize what they see and give it meaning, filtered through their current emotional states and the ways in which they organize their experiences. If a couple can be helped to change their negative interactive cycles, to bond to one another with genuine emotion, and in the process gain a new experience regarding the relationship, then therapeutic changes can occur.

The thrust of emotionally focused therapy becomes first helping couples identify repetitive negative interactive sequences that restrict accessibility to one another, and second, aiding them to redefine their problem in terms of its underlying and compelling emotional blocks. As the therapist helps them reprocess and restructure these rigid patterns, each partner is better able to form a secure sense of attachment and emotional connectedness. Canadian psychologists Leslie Greenberg and Susan Johnson (1986) believe change occurs as partners gain new experiences, on an emotionally meaningful level, of new aspects of themselves and the new interactions. These clinicians/researchers and their associates have been instrumental in resurrecting the central role of emotion in the therapeutic process, and in effect have helped revitalize the experiential approach with couples and families.

Emotionally focused couple therapy (Greenberg & Johnson, 1988; Johnson & Greenberg, 1995; Johnson, 1998) is a brief, empirically validated approach, based upon experiential and systems family therapy, that focuses on helping clients restructure negative interactive patterns (attacking-withdrawing, pursuing-distancing) that have become habitual and have created emotional removal or remoteness or have led to attack-attack engagement. In distressed relationships, these patterns become rigid and laden with affect, and as a consequence act to curtail closeness or trust, precluding the evolution of new patterns or responses. The emotionally focused (EF) therapist tries to modify the inner experience of both partners, the positions they take in this relationship dance, and the relationship events that define the quality of their attachment in order for them to build secure emotional bonds (Johnson & Greenberg, 1995).

Attachment theory[6] (Bowlby, 1969) plays a central role here: each of us needs the accessibility and responsiveness of attachment figures in order to achieve a sense of personal security, to experience a sense of trust and safety. Marital distress signals the failure of an attachment relationship to provide security, protection, or closeness, resulting in anxiety and a sense of vulnerability in one or both partners. Couples may hide their *primary emotions* (their real feelings, say fear of rejection) and in their place display defensive or coercive emotions (*secondary, reactive emotions* such as expressing anger or blaming when afraid), leading to *negative interactions* in which each partner fears revealing his or her primary emotions. Repeated over time, this pattern builds fears of trusting one's partner enough to exhibit honest primary emotions, which in turn become buried even further. EF therapists use the therapeutic relationship to help the couple access and reprocess the primary emotions underlying their interactional positions, enhance their emotional bond, and change their negative interactional sequences toward affiliation and engagement.

Greenberg and Johnson (1986, p. 261) illustrate the change process in this way:

1. An individual perceives himself or herself differently by bringing into focal awareness experiences not previously dominant in this person's view of self. For example, "I see and accept my vulnerability."
2. The spouse, upon witnessing the partner's new affective expressions, perceives the partner in a new way. For example, "I see your need for caring and contact rather than your hostility."

---

[6]The concept of attachment is used differently here than in object relations theory discussed in the previous chapter. Emotionally focused therapists view all humans as needing security and protection; in distressed relationships, these essentially healthy attachment needs are thwarted as a result of the couple's rigid pattern of interaction.

3. The individual's personal reorganization leads to different behavior in the interaction with the spouse. For example, "I now ask you for reassurance from a position of vulnerability."

4. The spouse's new perception of the partner leads to different responses. For example, "I comfort you rather than withdraw."

5. As a function of their partner's new behaviors, individuals come to see themselves in a new way. For example, "Since I can fulfill your needs, I see myself as valuable and necessary to you."

Put simply by Wetchler and Piercy (1996, p. 87)," as Mary begins to see John's withdrawal as a fear of being emotionally hurt and John understands that her anger is due to her fear of being abandoned by him, they will begin to talk differently to each other and develop a more stable bond."

In contrast with the other forms of experiential family therapy described in this chapter—which typically rely heavily on the charisma of the practitioner—here Johnson and Greenberg (1995) offer a step-by-step treatment manual for conducting EFCT so others can replicate the therapy process:

1. Delineating conflict issues in the core struggle
2. Identifying the negative interaction cycle
3. Accessing the unacknowledged feelings underlying interactional positions
4. Reframing the problem in terms of underlying feelings, attachment needs, and negative cycles
5. Promoting identification with disowned needs and aspects of self, and integrating these into relationship interactions
6. Promoting acceptance of partner's experiences and new interaction patterns
7. Facilitating the expression of needs and wants, and creating emotional engagement
8. Establishing the emergence of new solutions
9. Consolidating new positions

In addition to spelling out these clinical procedures, emotionally focused couple therapy has demonstrated clinical effectiveness (Dunn & Schwebel, 1995; Alexander, Holtzworth-Munroe, & Jameson, 1994). These combined efforts—operationalizing intervention procedures and carrying out outcome studies—augur well for the survival of the experiential approach to family therapy.

SUMMARY

Experiential family therapists use the immediacy of the therapeutic encounter with family members to help catalyze the family's natural drive toward growth and the fulfillment of the individual members' potentials. Essentially nontheoretical and nonhistorical, the approach stresses action over insight or interpretation, primarily by providing a growth-enhancing experience through family-therapist interactions. Attention to moment-by-moment emotional experiences is a defining feature of this form of family therapy.

The major practitioners of the experiential approach have been Carl Whitaker, Walter Kempler, and Virginia Satir. Whitaker, who some 40 years ago began redefining a schizophrenic's symptoms as signs of arrested growth, continued in his work with families to stress both intrapsychic and interpersonal barriers to development and maturity. His family therapy approach, often involving a cotherapist, was designed to capitalize on both the real and symbolic experiences that arise from the therapeutic process, and was aimed at bringing enlightenment. Claiming that his interventions were largely controlled by his unconscious, he sought a growth-producing experience for himself, believing that a therapist who does not personally benefit, therapeutically speaking, from the encounter has little to give to client families.

Kempler, a practitioner of Gestalt family therapy, is adamant in dealing only with the *now*—the moment-to-moment immediacy shared by the therapist and the family members. Like most Gestalt therapists, Kempler guides individuals to reach beyond their customary self-deceptive games, defenses, and facades. Uncompromisingly honest himself, he confronts and challenges all family members to explore how their self-awareness is blocked and to channel their increased awareness into more productive and fulfilling relationships with each other.

The most celebrated humanistically oriented family therapist was Virginia Satir. Her demonstrations with families were known around the world. Her approach to families combined her early interest in clarifying communication "discrepancies" between family members with humanistically oriented efforts to build self-esteem and self-worth in all the members. Believing that human beings have within themselves the resources they need in order to flourish, Satir viewed her task as one of helping people gain access to their nourishing potentials and teaching people to use them effectively.

Experiential family therapy today is best represented by emotionally focused couple therapy developed by Leslie Greenberg and Susan Johnson. Systemic in outlook, and based on client-centered and Gestalt therapy principles, this process-facilitative approach aids couples to change negative interactive patterns at the same time that they build secure emotional bonds. Therapeutic procedures are offered in a step-by-step treatment program that is easy to emulate, and outcome studies are carried out to demonstrate clinical effectiveness.

8

Transgenerational Models

Transgenerational approaches offer a time-sensitive, historical perspective to current family living problems by attending specifically to family relational patterns over decades. While other models we consider are insistently ahistorical and cross-sectional, concerned with ongoing, in some cases moment-by-moment family trans-actions ("the here and now"), transgenerationalists believe current family problems reflect unresolved issues in the families of origin. That is not to say that these prob-lems are caused by earlier generations, but rather that they tend to be unsettled and thus persist in ongoing patterns that span generations.

Such patterns are apt to include explicit interactional and behavioral patterns, and implicit, value-laden patterns formed during periods of family upheaval. As Roberto (1998) observes, the family process in the transgenerational view may "feed forward" in a chronological or spiraling fashion from emotionally influential events in the lives of great-grandparents onto children in the present. How today's family members form attachments, manage intimacy, deal with power, resolve conflict, and so on, may mirror to a greater or lesser extent earlier family patterns. Unresolved issues in families of origin may show up in symptomatic behavior patterns in later generations.

A number of pioneering family therapists—Murray Bowen, Ivan Boszormenyi-Nagy, James Framo, Carl Whitaker—incorporated generational issues in their work with families. We have chosen to place the latter two elsewhere—Framo with the object relations therapies and Whitaker with the experiential therapies—because their efforts are also strongly influenced by these other outlooks and procedures. The remainder of this chapter will focus on the theoretical and therapeutic contributions of Murray Bowen and Ivan Boszormenyi-Nagy.

BOWEN'S FAMILY SYSTEM

By turning first to Murray Bowen, one of the foremost original thinkers in the field, we intend to expound on a theory that represents the intellectual scaffolding upon which much of mainstream family therapy has been erected Bowen, the developer of **family systems theory,** conceptualized the family as an emotional unit, a network of interlocking relationships, best understood when analyzed within a multigenerational or historical framework. His theoretical contributions, along with their accompanying therapeutic efforts, represent a bridge between psychodynamically oriented approaches that emphasize self-development, intergenerational issues, and the significance of the past, and the systems approaches that restrict their attention to the family unit as it is presently constituted and currently interacting.

Unlike many of his fellow pioneers in family therapy, who struggled at first to stretch classical psychoanalytic theory to fit family life, Bowen recognized early on that most concepts derived from psychoanalysis were too individually derived and not readily translatable into the language of the family. Rather than attempt to adapt such concepts as unconscious motivations to family interactive patterns, Bowen believed the driving force underlying all human behavior came from the submerged ebb and flow of family life, the simultaneous push and pull between family members for both distance and togetherness (Wylie, 1990b).

A key figure in the development of family therapy, Murray Bowen remained, until his death in 1990, its major theoretician. Since his early clinical work with schizophrenics and their families at the Menninger Clinic, as well as at NIMH, Bowen stressed the importance of theory for research, for teaching purposes, and as a blueprint for guiding a clinician's actions during psychotherapy. He was concerned with what he considered the field's lack of a coherent and comprehensive theory of either family development or therapeutic intervention and its all-too-tenuous connections between theory and practice. In particular, Bowen (1978) decried efforts to dismiss theory in favor of an intuitive "seat of the pants" approach, which he considered to be especially stressful for a novice therapist coping with an intensely emotional, problem-laden family. The contrast between Bowen's cerebral, deliberate, disciplined, theoretically based approach and Satir's or Whitaker's spontaneous, emotional, nontheoretical way of working with families will surely not be lost on the reader.

By educational background and training, Bowen was imbued with the individual focus of psychoanalysis. His professional interest in the family, however, began early in his career, when, trained as a psychiatrist, he worked at the Menninger Clinic in the late 1940s. There, under the leadership of Karl Menninger, innovative psychoanalytic approaches were being tried in treating hospitalized persons suffering from severe psychiatric illnesses. Intrigued, from a research perspective, by the family relationships of inpatients, especially schizophrenics, Bowen became particularly interested in the possible transgenerational impact of a mother-child **symbiosis** in the development and maintenance of schizophrenia. Extrapolating from the psychoanalytic concept that schizophrenia might result from an unresolved symbiotic attachment to the mother, herself immature and in need of the child to fulfil her own emotional needs, Bowen began working with mother and child together. In 1951, in order to view their relationship close up, he organized a research project in which mothers and their schizophrenic children resided together in cottages on the Menninger grounds for several months at a time.

Murray Bowen, M.D.

In 1954, Bowen, eager to put his new ideas regarding family dynamics into clinical practice but stifled by what he saw as the prevailing emphasis on conventional individual psychiatry at the Menninger Clinic, moved his professional research activities to the National Institute of Mental Health in Bethesda, Maryland. Soon, in what surely was a radical idea for its time, he had entire families with schizophrenic members living on the hospital research wards for months at a time, where he and his associates were better able to observe ongoing family interaction. Here Bowen discovered that the emotional intensity of the mother-child interaction was even more powerful than he had suspected. More important, the emotional intensity seemed to characterize relationships throughout the family,[1] not merely those between mother and child. Fathers and siblings too were found to play key roles in fostering and perpetuating family problems, as triangular alliances were continually formed and dissolved among differing sets of family members.

The reciprocal functioning of all the individual members within the family became so apparent that Bowen began to expand his earlier mother-child symbiosis concepts to now viewing the entire family as an emotional unit made up of members unable to separate or successfully differentiate themselves from one another. Although he did not adopt a cybernetic epistemology per se, nor was he interested especially in directly changing a family's ongoing interactive patterns, Bowen had moved from concentrating on the separate parts (the patient with the "disease") to a focus on the whole (the family). Now he began to direct his attention particularly to what he called the *family emotional system*—a kind of family guidance system shaped

---

[1]Bowen's early observations of the emotional intensity of families with schizophrenic members have been confirmed by recent research on the role of expressed emotions such as anger and hostility on the course of the schizophrenic disorder. As we discuss in Chapter 14, studies of schizophrenics following hospital release indicate that lowering expressed emotion in the family is a major way of reducing relapse (Miklowitz, 1995).

by evolution that governs its behavior—for him a workable descriptive framework for understanding human interaction. The conceptual shift was to prove to be a turning point in his thinking, as Bowen increasingly viewed human emotional functioning as part of a natural system, following the same laws that govern other systems in nature, no less valid than the laws of gravity. Bowen, dissatisfied with what he considered the subjectivity of most psychoanalytic conceptualizations, began the process of making the study of human emotional functioning a more rigorous science. In the forefront of his field, Bowen was beginning to formulate nothing less than a new theory of human behavior.

When the NIMH project ended in 1959, Bowen moved to the Department of Psychiatry at Georgetown University in Washington, D.C.; the university was a place more conducive to his theoretical bent. He remained there until the end of his career. Working in an outpatient setting, and with families many of whom had less severe problems than schizophrenia, Bowen continued to formulate a comprehensive family systems theory that could be applied to processes occurring in all families, functional as well as dysfunctional. At the same time, he proposed a method of therapy based on a solid theoretical foundation (in contrast to those techniques that have evolved on an empirical or experiential basis). Developing a training program in family therapy while continually refining the concepts he first developed in the 1960s, he published *Family Therapy in Clinical Practice* in 1978, detailing his theoretical formulations and offering therapeutic techniques consistent with that theory. Several updated explications of Bowen's theoretical ideas as well as their clinical applications have been offered more recently by Michael Kerr (Kerr & Bowen, 1988), Daniel Papero (1990; 1995), and Edwin Friedman (1991), all longtime associates of Bowen.

Family Systems Theory

Family systems theory (sometimes referred to as *natural systems theory* to differentiate it from other cybernetically based family systems theories) is derived from the biological view of the human family as one type of living system. As Friedman (1991) points out, the theory is not fundamentally about families, but about life (or what Bowen referred to as the "human phenomenon"), and attempts to account for humanity's relationship to other natural systems. As Wylie (1990b, p. 26) explains, Bowen "considered family therapy a by-product of the vast theory of human behavior that he believed it was his real mission to develop." According to the theory, the human family is seen as appearing as the result of an evolutionary process in nature. Thus, like all living systems (ant colonies, the tides, the solar system), humans and the human family are guided by processes common in nature. In particular, the theory concerns itself with a special kind of natural system—the family's emotional system (Kerr & Bowen, 1988).

Family systems theory has attracted many currently influential family therapists, and over the years Bowen became a leading trainer of family therapists. Among his students, committed to viewing behavior in transgenerational terms, are Philip Guerin, Elizabeth Carter, Monica McGoldrick, Thomas Fogarty, and Jack Bradt, along with the previously mentioned Michael Kerr, Daniel Papero, and Edwin Friedman. In 1977, Bowen became the first president of the newly formed American

Family Therapy Association, an organization he helped found to pursue interests in research and theory.

EIGHT INTERLOCKING THEORETICAL CONCEPTS

In its present state of refinement, Bowen's theory of the family as an emotional relationship system consists of eight interlocking concepts. Six of the concepts address emotional processes taking place in the nuclear and extended families; two later concepts, emotional cutoff and societal regression, speak to the emotional process across generations in a family and in society (Papero, 1983). All eight constructs are interlocking in the sense that none is fully understandable without some comprehension of the others.

All of the concepts that follow are tied together by the underlying premise that *chronic anxiety* is omnipresent in life. While it may manifest itself differently, and with different degrees of intensity, depending on specific family situations and differing cultural considerations, chronic anxiety is an inevitable part of nature—a biological phenomenon that Bowen believed humans have in common with all forms of life (Friedman, 1991). From this natural systems perspective, chronic anxiety is transmitted from past generations, whose influence remains alive in the present, as families grapple with balancing togetherness and the self-differentiation of its separate members.

Anxiety—arousal in an organism when perceiving a real or imagined threat—stimulates the anxious-prone person's emotional system, overriding the cognitive system, and leading to behavior that is automatic or uncontrolled (Papero, 1990). In family terms, anxiety is inevitably aroused as families struggle with pressures toward togetherness and also toward individuation. If greater togetherness prevails, the family moves in the direction of increased emotional functioning and there is less individual autonomy. As a by-product of decreased individual autonomy, the person experiences increased chronic anxiety. Chronic anxiety, then, represents the underlying basis of all symptomology; its only antidote is resolution through differentiation (see below), the process by which an individual learns to chart his or her own direction rather than perpetually following the guidelines of family and others.

According to family systems theory, the eight forces shaping family functioning are

1. Differentiation of self
2. Triangles
3. Nuclear family emotional system
4. Family projection process
5. Emotional cutoff
6. Multigenerational transmission process
7. Sibling position
8. Societal regression

Differentiation of Self

The cornerstone of this carefully worked out theory is the notion of forces within the family that make for togetherness and the opposing forces that lead to individuality.

Thus, the degree to which a **differentiation of self** occurs in an individual reflects the extent to which that person is able to distinguish between the intellectual process and the feeling process he or she is experiencing.[2] That is, differentiation of self is demonstrated by the degree to which one is able to avoid having his or her behavior automatically driven by emotion. The degree to which one can separate emotionally from parents in growing up is the key: in extreme cases, the attachment is so complete that a symbiosis exists in which parents and child cannot survive without one another. Such unresolved emotional attachment is equivalent to a high degree of undifferentiation in a person and in a family (Papero, 1995).

The ideal here is not to be emotionally detached or fiercely objective or without feelings, but rather to strive for balance, achieving self-definition but not at the expense of losing the capacity for spontaneous emotional expression. The theory does not assume that rational behavior should be pursued at the expense of feelings, nor is it necessary to suppress emotional expression. Rather, individuals should not be driven by feelings they do not understand. A balance of feelings and cognition remained the goal of self-differentiation. As family systems theory uses the term, *differentiation* refers more to a process than to an achievable goal—a direction in life rather than a state of being (Friedman, 1991).

As Papero (1990, p. 48) notes, any individual's level of differentiation can best be observed under anxious family circumstances:

> To the degree that one can thoughtfully guide personal behavior in accordance with well-defined principles in spite of intense anxiety in the family, he or she displays a level or degree of differentiation.

As an example, suppose a college student, living away from home during the academic year, goes home midyear to attend his sister's wedding. Amid the tensions typically occurring around such an event, to what degree is he drawn into family feuds, conflicts, coalitions, or emotional turmoils? His degree of differentiation can be gauged by the degree to which he is able to remain sufficiently involved to partake and enjoy the pleasures of this landmark family event, but also sufficiently separated so as not to be drawn into the family emotional system.

Individuals with the greatest **fusion** between their thoughts and feelings (for example, schizophrenics and their families) function most poorly; they are likely to be at the mercy of automatic or involuntary emotional reactions and tend to become dysfunctional even under low levels of anxiety. Just as they are unable to differentiate thought from feeling, such persons have trouble differentiating themselves from others and thus fuse easily with whatever emotions dominate[3] or sweep through the family. To the extent to which such automatic emotional attachments to one's family remain intact, the individual is handicapped from differentiating from the family and becoming an effectively functioning human being.

---

[2]Some feminists, such as Hare-Mustin (1978) and Lerner (1986), dispute this, arguing that what Bowen seems to value here are qualities—being autonomous, relying on reason above emotion, being goal-directed—for which men are socialized, while simultaneously devaluing those qualities—relatedness, caring for others, nurturing—for which women typically are socialized.

[3]David Schnarch (1995) has offered a family systems approach using the concepts of fusion and differentiation as organizing principles for exploring and treating a couple's sexual problems (see Chapter 12).

Bowen (1966) introduced the concept of **undifferentiated family ego mass,** derived from psychoanalysis, to convey the idea of a family emotionally "stuck together," one where "a conglomerate emotional oneness...exists in all levels of intensity" (p. 171). For example, the classic example of the symbiotic relationship of interdependency between mother and child may represent the most intense version of this concept; a father's detachment may be the least intense. The degree to which any one member is involved in the family from moment to moment depends on that person's basic level of involvement in the family ego mass. Sometimes the emotional closeness can be so intense that family members feel they know each other's feelings, thoughts, fantasies, and dreams. This intimacy may lead to uncomfortable "overcloseness" and ultimately to a phase of mutual rejection between two members.

In other words, within a family system, emotional tensions shift over time (sometimes slowly, sometimes rapidly) in a series of alliances and splits. What Bowen had initially characterized in psychoanalytic terms—*undifferentiated family ego mass*—he later recast in systems language as *fusion-differentiation*. Both sets of terms underscore the theory's transgenerational view that maturity and self-actualization demand that an individual become free of unresolved emotional attachments to his or her family of origin.

For illustrative purposes, Bowen (1966) proposed a theoretical scale (not an actual psychometric instrument) for evaluating an individual's differentiation level. As noted in Figure 8.1, the greater the degree of undifferentiation (no sense of self or a weak or unstable personal identity), the greater the emotional fusion into a common self with others (the undifferentiated family ego mass). A person with a strong sense of self ("These are my opinions...This is who I am...This is what I will do, but not this...") expresses convictions and clearly defined beliefs. Such a person is said

| 0 | 25 | 50 | 75 | 100 |

Fusion   Differentiation
of self

Figure 8.1 The theoretical differentiation-of-self scale, according to Bowen's conception, distinguishes people according to the degree of fusion or differentiation between their emotional and intellectual functioning. Those at the lower level (0–25) are emotionally fused to the family and others and lead lives in which their thinking is submerged and their feelings dominate. The lives of those in the 25–50 range are still guided by their emotional system and the reactions of others; goal-directed behavior is present but carried out in order to seek the approval of others. In the 50–75 range, thinking is sufficiently developed so as not to be dominated by feeling when stress occurs, and there is a reasonably developed sense of self. Those rare people functioning between 75 and 100 routinely separate their thinking from their feelings; they base decisions on the former but are free to lose themselves in the intimacy of a close relationship. Bowen (1978) consider someone at 75 to have a very high level of differentiation and all those over 60 to constitute a small percentage of society.

to be expressing a *solid self.* He or she does not compromise that self for the sake of marital bliss or to please parents or achieve family harmony, or through coercion.

People at the low end of the scale are those whose emotions and intellect are so fused that their lives are dominated by the feelings of those around them. As a consequence, they are easily stressed into dysfunction. Fearful and emotionally needy, they sacrifice their individuality in order to ensure acceptance from others. They are expressing an undifferentiated *pseudo self,* which they may deceive themselves into thinking is real, but which is composed of the opinions and values of others. Those far fewer individuals at the high end are emotionally mature; they can think and feel and take actions on their own. Because their intellectual or rational functioning remains relatively (although not completely) dominant during stressful periods, they are more certain of who they are and what they believe, and thus more free to make judgments and decisions independent of any emotional turmoil around them. In the midrange are persons with relative degrees of fusion or differentiation. Note that *the scale eliminates the need for the concept of normality.* It is entirely possible for people at the low end of the scale to keep their lives in emotional equilibrium and stay free of symptoms, thus appearing to satisfy the popular criteria for being "normal." However, these people not only are more vulnerable to stress than those higher on the scale but also, under stress, are apt to develop symptoms from which they recover far more slowly than those at the high end of the scale.

To summarize:

- Below 50 (low differentiation): tries to please others; supports others and seeks support; dependent; lacks capacity for autonomy; primary need for security; avoids conflict; little ability to independently reach decisions or solve problems.
- 51–75 (midrange differentiation): has definite beliefs and values but tends to be overconcerned with the opinions of others; may make decisions based on emotional reactivity, especially whether decisions will receive disapproval from significant others.
- 76–100 (high differentiation): clear values and beliefs; goal directed; flexible; secure; autonomous; can tolerate conflict and stress; well-defined sense of solid self and less pseudo self. (Roberto, 1992)

Any person's level of differentiation reflects that individual's degree of emotional independence from the family as well as from others outside the family group. A moderate-to-high level of differentiation permits interaction with others without fear of fusion (losing one's sense of self in the relationship). While all relationships ranging from poorly to well-differentiated ones are in a state of dynamic equilibrium, the flexibility in that balance decreases as differentiation decreases. Figure 8.2 illustrates the varying degrees to which a person's functioning can be influenced by the relationship process.

Family systems theory assumes that an instinctively rooted life force in every human propels the developing child to grow up to be an emotionally separate person, able to think, feel, and act as an individual. At the same time, a corresponding life force, also instinctively rooted, propels the child and family to remain emotion-

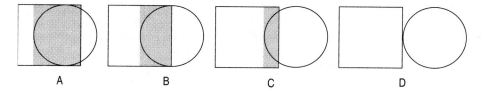

Figure 8.2 Relationship A is one where the functioning of each person is almost completely determined by the relationship process. The degree to which individual functioning is either enhanced or undermined by the relationship is indicated by the shaded area. The clear area indicates the capacity for self-determined functioning while in a relationship. Relationships B and C are progressively better differentiated. Individual functioning, therefore, is less likely to be enhanced or undermined by the relationship process. Relationship D is theoretical for the human. It represents two people who can be actively involved in a relationship yet remain self-determined.
Source: Kerr & Bowen, 1988, p. 71

ally connected. As a result of these counterbalancing forces, no one ever achieves complete emotional separation from the family of origin. However, there are considerable differences in the amount of separation each of us accomplishes, as well as differences in the degree to which children from the same set of parents emotionally separate from the family. The latter is due to characteristics of the different parental relationships established with each child, which we elaborate on later in this section.

Triangles

In addition to its interest in the degree of integration of self, family systems theory also emphasizes emotional tension within the individual or in that person's relationships. Anxiety within either husband or wife or both may arise, for example, as they attempt to balance their needs for closeness with their needs for individuation. The greater their fusion, the more difficult the task of finding a stable balance satisfying to both. One way to defuse such an anxious two-person relationship within a family, according to Bowen (1978), is to triangulate—draw in a significant family member to form a three-person interaction.

The basic building block in a family's emotional or relational system is the *triangle,* according to Bowen. During periods when anxiety is low and external conditions are calm, the dyad or two-person system may engage in a comfortable back-and-forth exchange of feelings. However, the stability of this situation is threatened if one or both participants gets upset or anxious, either because of internal stress or from stress external to the twosome. When a certain moderate anxiety level is reached, one or both partners will involve a vulnerable third person.

According to Bowen (1978), the twosome may "reach out" and pull in the other person, the emotions may "overflow" to the third person, or that person may be emotionally "programmed" to initiate involvement. This triangle dilutes the anxiety; it is both more stable and more flexible than the twosome and has a higher tolerance for dealing with stress. When anxiety in the triangle subsides, the emotional configuration returns to the peaceful twosome plus the lone outsider. However, should anxiety in the triangle increase, one person in the triangle may involve another outsider and so forth until a number of people are involved. Thus, triangles extend and interlock into ever large groups as tension increases (Roberto, 1992). Sometimes such triangulation can reach beyond the family, ultimately encompassing social agencies or the courts.

Generally speaking, the higher the degree of family fusion, the more intense and insistent the triangulating efforts will be; the least well differentiated person in the family is particularly vulnerable to being drawn in to reduce tension. (In this triadic setup, a child making an inadequate attempt to resolve parental tensions may get the label of the identified patient.) The higher a family members degree of differentiation, the better will that person manage anxiety without following the triangulating process (Papero, 1995). Beyond seeking relief of discomfort, the family relies on triangles to help maintain an optimum level of closeness and distance between members while permitting them the greatest freedom from anxiety.

Bowen (1976) refers to the triangle as the smallest stable relationship system. By definition, a two-person system is unstable and forms itself into a three-person system or triad under stress, as each partner attempts to create a triangle in order to reduce the increasing tension of their relationship. When anxiety is so great that the basic three-person triangle can no longer contain the tension, the resulting distress may spread to others. As more people become involved, the system may become a series of *interlocking triangles,* in some cases heightening the very problem the multiple triangulations sought to resolve. For example, a distraught mother's request for help from her husband in dealing with their son is met with withdrawal from the father. As the mother-son conflict escalates, she communicates her distress to another son, who proceeds to get into conflict with his brother for upsetting their mother. What began as a mother-son conflict has now erupted into interlocking conflicts—between mother and son, brother and brother, and mother and father.

Thus, triangulation does not always reduce tension. Kerr and Bowen (1988) point out that triangulation has at least four possible outcomes: (1) a stable twosome can be destabilized by the addition of a third person (for example, the birth of a child brings conflict to a harmonious marriage); (2) a stable twosome can be destabilized by the removal of a third person (a child leaves home and thus is no longer available to be triangulated into parental conflict); (3) an unstable twosome can be stabilized by the addition of a third person (a conflictful marriage becomes more harmonious after the birth of a child); and (4) an unstable twosome can be stabilized by the removal of a third person (conflict is reduced by avoiding a third person who has consistently taken sides).

To give another familiar example, note that conflict between siblings quickly attracts a parent's attention. Let us assume that the parent has positive feelings toward both children who, at the moment, are quarreling with each other. If the parent can control his or her emotional responsiveness and manage not to take sides while staying in contact with both children, the emotional intensity between the siblings will diminish. (A parallel situation exists when parents quarrel and a child is drawn into the triangle in an attempt to dilute and thus reduce the strain between the combatants.) Generally speaking, the probability of triangulation within a family is heightened by poor differentiation of family members; conversely, the reliance on triangulation to solve problems helps maintain the poor differentiation of certain family members.

As we discuss later in this chapter when we describe family systems intervention techniques, a similar situation exists when a couple visits a marital/family therapist. Following from this theory, if the therapist—the third person in the triangle—can remain involved with both spouses without siding with one or the other, the spouses may learn to view themselves as individual, differentiated selves as well as marital partners. However, if the third person loses emotional contact with either of the spouses, the twosome will proceed to triangulate with someone else.

Nuclear Family Emotional System

Bowen (1978) contends that people choose mates with equivalent levels of differentiation to their own. Not surprisingly, then, the relatively undifferentiated person will select a spouse who is equally fused to his or her family of origin. It is probable, moreover, that these poorly differentiated people, now a marital dyad, will themselves become highly fused and will produce a family with the same characteristics. According to Bowen, the resulting **nuclear family emotional system** will be unstable and will seek various ways to reduce tension and maintain stability. The greater the nuclear family's fusion, the greater will be the likelihood of anxiety and potential instability, and the greater will be the family's propensity to seek resolution through fighting, distancing, the impaired or compromised functioning of one partner, or banding together over concern for a child (Kerr, 1981).

More specifically, Kerr and Bowen (1988) regard three possible symptomatic patterns in a nuclear family as the product of the intense fusion between partners (see below). The greater the level of fusion in the marital dyad, the more frequently are these mechanisms likely to occur. Similarly, in a family living with a high level of chronic anxiety, these mechanisms are at work continuously, their intensity or frequency changing in response to acute anxiety being experienced at the moment (Papero, 1990).

Each pattern described below is intensified by anxiety and, when the intensity reaches a sufficient level, results in a particular form of symptom development. The person (or the relationship) who manifests the specific symptom is largely determined by the patterns of emotional functioning that predominate in that family system. The three patterns are as follows:

1. *Physical or emotional dysfunction in a spouse,* sometimes becoming chronic, as an alternative to dealing directly with family conflict; the anxiety generated by the undifferentiated functioning of every family member is being absorbed disproportionately by a symptomatic parent.
2. *Overt, chronic, unresolved marital conflict,* in which cycles of emotional distance and emotional overcloseness occur; both the negative feelings during conflict and the positive feelings for one another during close periods are likely to be equally intense in roller-coaster fashion; the family anxiety is being absorbed by the husband and wife.

3. *Psychological impairment in a child,* enabling the parents to focus attention on the child and ignore or deny their own lack of differentiation; as the child becomes the focal point of the family problem, the intensity of the parental relationship is diminished, thus the family anxiety is being absorbed in the child's impaired functioning; the lower a child's level of differentiation, the greater will be his or her vulnerability to increases in family anxiety and thus to dysfunction.

Furthermore, dysfunction in one spouse may take the form of an *overadequate-underadequate reciprocity,* in which one partner takes on most or even all family responsibilities (earning a living, caring for the children, cooking, shopping, and so on) while the other plays the counterpart role of being underresponsible (can't drive, can't choose clothes, can't have friends to the house). Fused together, the two pseudo selves develop an arrangement in which one partner increasingly underfunctions while the other takes up the slack by assuming responsibility for them both. When the tilt gets too great, according to Singleton (1982), the one giving up more pseudo self for the sake of family harmony becomes vulnerable to physical or emotional dysfunction.

In some cases, this pattern intertwines with marital conflict, the underadequate one complaining of dominance, inconsiderateness, and so forth, from the spouse. The overadequate one is more comfortable with the arrangement until the underadequate one complains or becomes so inadequate as to cause difficulties for the overadequate one. When this occurs, the problem is likely to be seen by the unsophisticated eye as belonging to the unhappy underadequate spouse, rather than as a relationship problem for which both need help.

Almost any family will have one child who is more vulnerable to fusion than the others, and thus likely to be triangulated into parental conflict. Any significant increase in parental anxiety triggers this child's dysfunctional behavior (in school, at home, or both), leading to even greater anxieties in the parent. In turn, the child's behavior becomes increasingly impaired, sometimes turning into a lifelong pattern of poor functioning.

The nuclear family emotional system is a multigenerational concept. Family systems theorists believe individuals tend to repeat in their marital choices and other significant relationships the patterns of relating learned in their families of origin, and to pass along similar patterns to their children. The only effective way to resolve current family problems is to change the individual's interactions with the families of origin. Only then can differentiation proceed and the individuals involved become less overreactive to the emotional forces sweeping through the family.

Family Projection Process

As we have just observed, parents do not respond in the same way to each child in a family, despite their claims to the contrary. That is, they pass on their level of differentiation to the children in an uneven fashion: some emerge with a higher level than their parents, some with a lower level, and others with a more or less identical level (Papero, 1995). In particular, those children more exposed to parental immaturity tend to develop greater fusion to the family than their more fortunate siblings and have greater difficulty separating smoothly from their parents. They remain more vulnerable to emotional stresses within the family and as a consequence live lives more governed by emotions than do their brothers or sisters.

The fusion-prone, focused-on child is the one most sensitive to disturbances and incipient signs of instability within the family. Bowen (1976) believed that poorly differentiated parents, themselves immature, select as the object of their attention the most infantile of all their children, regardless of his or her birth order in the family; Bowen calls this the **family projection process.** This process provides the means by which the parents transmit their own low level of differentiation onto the most susceptible child. In many cases, this child is physically or mentally handicapped or psychologically unprotected in some fashion.

The projection process operates within the mother-father-child triangle; the transmission of undifferentiation occurs through the triangulation of the most vulnerable child into the parental relationship. The sibling positions of the parents in their families of origin offer possible clues as to which child will be chosen in the next generation. As the child most emotionally attached to the parents of all the children within a family, he or she will have the lowest level of differentiation of self and the most difficulty in separating from the family. Moreover, Kerr (1981) believes that the greater the level of undifferentiation of the parents and the more they rely on the projection process to stabilize the system, the more likely it is that several children will be emotionally impaired. This process of projecting or transmitting parental undifferentiation may begin as early as the initial mother-infant bonding.

The intensity of the family projection process is related to two factors: the degree of immaturity or undifferentiation of the parents and the level of stress or anxiety the family experiences. In one triangulating scenario described by Singleton (1982), the child responds anxiously to the mother's anxiety, she being the principal caretaker; the mother becomes alarmed at what she perceives as the child's problem, and becomes overprotective. Thus a cycle is established in which the mother infantilizes the child, who in turn becomes demanding and impaired. The third leg of the triangle is supplied by the father, who is frightened by his wife's anxiety and, by needing to calm her but without dealing with the issues, plays a supportive role in her dealings with the child. As collaborators, the parents have now stabilized their relationship around a "disturbed" child, and in the process perpetuated the family triangle.

Emotional Cutoff

Children less involved in the projection process are apt to emerge with a greater ability to withstand fusion, to separate thinking and feeling. Those who are more involved try various strategies upon reaching adulthood, or even before. They may attempt to insulate themselves from the family by geographic separation (moving to another state), through the use of psychological barriers (cease talking to parents), or by the self-deception that they are free of family ties because actual contact has been broken off. Bowen (1976) considers such supposed freedom an **emotional cutoff,** a flight of extreme emotional distancing in order to break emotional ties, and not true emancipation. In his formulation, cutting oneself off emotionally from one's family of origin often represents a desperate effort to deal with unresolved fusion with one or both parents—a way of managing the unresolved emotional attachment to them. More likely than not, the person attempting the cutoff tends to deny to himself or herself that many unresolved conflicts remain with family-of-origin members. Kerr (1981) contends that emotional cutoff *reflects* a problem (underlying fusion between generations), *solves* a problem (reducing anxiety associated with making contact), and *creates* a problem (isolating people who might benefit from closer contact).

Cutoffs occur most often in families in which there is a high level of anxiety and emotional dependence (Bowen, 1978). As both factors increase and greater family cohesiveness is expected, conflicts between family members may be disguised and hidden. Should the fusion-demanding situation reach an unbearable stage, some members may seek greater distance, emotionally, socially, perhaps physically, for self-preservation. When a family member insists on communication, it is apt to be superficial, inauthentic, and brief (short visits or phone calls where only impersonal topics are discussed). Bowen suggested that when emotional cutoffs exist between parents and their parents, then a cutoff between parents and children of the subsequent generation increases in likelihood.

Bowen insisted that adults must resolve their emotional attachments to their families of origin. In a very revealing paper delivered in 1967 to a national conference of family researchers and therapists ("Towards," 1972),[+] he openly described his personal struggles to achieve a differentiation of self from his own family of origin. Without this differentiation, Bowen argued, family therapists may unknowingly be triangulated into conflicts in their client families (much as they were as children in their own families), perhaps overidentifying with one family member or projecting onto another their own unresolved difficulties. Family therapists need to get in touch with and be free of their own internalized family so that unfinished business from the past does not intrude on current dealings with client families.

Multigenerational Transmission Process

In perhaps his most intriguing formulation, Bowen (1976) proposed the concept of **multigenerational transmission process,** in which severe dysfunction is conceptualized as the result of specific degrees of differentiation transmitted over several generations. Two earlier concepts are crucial here—the selection of a spouse with a similar differentiation level and the family projection process that results in lower levels of self-differentiation for that invested or focused offspring particularly sensitive to parental

[+]The article was published under an anonymous authorship because Bowen was describing real people whose anonymity he wished to protect. Actually, the entire process of achieving greater self-differentiation from his family of origin represents a deliberate effort by Bowen to confront entrenched and complex patterns of family interaction. Given an opportunity to return home for the funeral of a distant relative, Bowen decided to apply his newly formulated ideas about fusion, triangles, and so on, at a time when family members were experiencing anxiety and thus might be more open to change. Purposely provoking a response by raising old family emotional issues, he managed to remain detached, undefensive, to calm his family's anxieties, and in the process differentiate himself once and for all. Wylie (1990b) reports Bowen's exhilaration about successfully carrying out the visit without becoming triangulated or fused into the family's emotional system. Bowen's self-differentiation efforts have sometimes been compared to Freud's self-analysis. Therapists training to practice Bowen's techniques work on differentiating themselves from their families of origin, much as candidates wishing to become psychoanalysts have a training analysis.

emotional patterns. By contrast, children less involved in parental overfocusing can develop a higher level of differentiation than their parents (Roberto, 1992).

Assume for a moment that the least well-differentiated members of two families marry—as Bowen's theory would predict—and that at least one of their children, as the result of the projection process, will have an even lower differentiation level. The eventual marriage of this person—again, to someone with a similarly poor differentiation of self—passes along the increasingly lowered level of differentiation to the members of the next generation, who in turn pass it along to the next, and so forth. As each generation produces individuals with progressively poorer differentiation ("weak links"), those people are increasingly vulnerable to anxiety and fusion.

Although the process may slow down or remain static over a generation or two, ultimately—it may take as many as eight or ten generations—a level of impairment is reached that is consistent with dysfunction—schizophrenia, chronic alcoholism, or other manifestations of psychological impairment (Papero, 1990). If the family encounters severe stress and anxiety, however, serious dysfunction may develop in an earlier generation. In some less stressful cases or under favorable life circumstances, poorly differentiated people may keep their relationship system in relatively symptom-free equilibrium for several generations longer. This process may be reversed, of course, should someone in this lineage marry a person considerably higher on the differentiation-of-self scale. However, as noted earlier, Bowen contended that most persons choose mates at more or less their own level of differentiation.

Sibling Position

Bowen credits Toman's (1961) research on the relationship between birth order and personality with clarifying his own thinking regarding the influence of **sibling position** in the nuclear family emotional process. Toman hypothesized that children develop certain fixed personality characteristics on the basis of their birth order in the family. He offered ten basic personality sibling profiles (such as older brother, younger sister; younger brother, older sister; only child; twins), suggesting that the more closely a marriage duplicates one's sibling place in childhood, the better will be its chance of success. Thus, a firstborn would do well to marry a secondborn, the youngest should marry an older child. He maintained further that, in general, the chances for a successful marriage are increased for persons who grew up with siblings of the opposite sex rather than with same-sex siblings only.

Bowen realized that interactive patterns between marital partners may be related to the position of each partner in his or her family of origin, since birth order frequently predicts certain roles and functions within one's family emotional system. Thus, an oldest child who marries a youngest may expect to take responsibility, make decisions, and so on; this behavior is also expected by the mate on the basis of his or her experiences as the youngest in the family. Two youngest children who marry may both feel overburdened by responsibility and decision making; the marriage of two oldest children may be overly competitive because each spouse is accustomed to being in charge (Kerr, 1981). Note, however, that it is a person's functional position in the family system, not necessarily the actual order of birth, that shapes future expectations and behavior.

Societal Regression

In a final concept, **societal regression,** Bowen extended his thinking to society's emotional functioning. In the least well developed of his theoretical formulations, he argued that society, like the family, contains within it opposing forces toward undifferentiation and toward individuation. Under conditions of chronic stress (population growth, depletion of natural resources) and thus an anxious social climate, there is likely to be a surge of togetherness and a corresponding erosion of the forces intent on achieving individuation. The result, thought Bowen, was likely to be greater discomfort and further anxiety (Papero, 1990).

It was Bowen's (1977) pessimistic view that society's functional level of differentiation had decreased over the last several decades. He called for better differentiation between intellect and emotion in order for society to make more rational decisions rather than act on the basis of feelings and opt for short-term "Band-Aid" solutions.

FAMILY SYSTEMS THERAPY

Family systems therapy occurs in stages. Adopting a neutral and objective role in order to remain untriangled into the family, the therapist first attempts to assess the family's emotional system, past and present, through a series of evaluation interviews and measurement techniques, before intervening therapeutically with the family. Ultimately, therapeutic goals for changing the relational system include decreasing member anxiety, helping members detriangulate from three-person systems, and most important, aiding each family member to increase his or her basic differentiation of self.

The Evaluation Interview

The appraisal of a symptomatic family begins with the initial telephone contact. Kerr and Bowen (1988) caution the therapist against being drawn into the family emotional system by overresponding to the caller's forceful, charming, or theatrical presentation of the family's problem. Throughout the subsequent therapy, they warn, the therapist must guard against becoming incorporated into the family's problem, taking sides in disputes, or becoming overly sympathetic with one member or angry at another. A therapist who thus becomes fused with the family's emotional system, or allows himself or herself to be triangulated into their conflicts, or becomes engulfed by their anxiety, can have a divisive influence on family functioning and fail to promote further differentiation among family members. While the family must become convinced that the therapist cares and remains interested in them, the therapist must resist their efforts to get him or her overinvolved emotionally.

As Friedman (1991, p. 151) advises,

> if you, as a therapist, allow a couple to create a triangle with you, but take care not to get caught up in the emotional process of that triangle either by overfunctioning or being emotionally reactive, *then, by trying to remain a nonanxious presence in that triangle, you can induce a change in the relationship of the other two that would not occur if they said the same things in your absence.* (author's emphasis)

Objectivity, as opposed to emotional reactivity, should characterize the thera-pist's behavior in this system of family therapy. It is important to stay connected to all participants without taking sides or becoming too subjectively involved. Bowen believed that the more a therapist has worked on becoming differentiated from his or her own family of origin, the more the therapist can remain detached, unswayed, and objective. Actually, as Friedman (1991) points out, it is the therapist's pres-ence—engaging without being reactive, stimulating without rescuing, teaching a way of thinking—rather than any specific behavior or therapeutic intervention technique that is the ultimate agent of change.

Family evaluation interviews are carried out with any combination of family members: a parent, husband and wife, the nuclear family, perhaps including extended family members. Since Bowen viewed family therapy as a way of concep-tualizing a problem rather than as a process that requires a certain number of people to attend the sessions, he was content to work with one family member, especially if that person is motivated to work on self-differentiation from his or her family of origin. In fact, according to Kerr and Bowen (1988), while conjoint sessions are generally useful, at times seeing people together may impede the progress of one or the other. Instead, they argue, if one parent can increase his or her basic level of dif-ferentiation, the functioning of the other parent as well as the children will inevitably improve.

Family evaluation interviews begin with a history of the presenting problem, focusing especially on the symptoms (physical, emotional, social) and their impact on the symptomatic person or relationship. If more than one person is present, the therapist is interested in each member's perception of what created and what sustains the problem for which they seek relief, why they seek such help now, and what each hopes to get from the experience. Through a series of such questions,[5] the therapist attempts to assess the pattern of emotional functioning as well as the intensity of the emotional process in the nuclear family of the symp-tomatic person. What is the relationship system like in this family? What are the current stressors? How well differentiated are the family members? What is the family adaptive level? How stable is the family and how (and how successfully) does it handle anxiety? What three-person (or more) triangles exist? Are emo-tional cutoffs operating? The initial interview, which may extend over several ses-sions, seeks information on all of these issues in assessing the degree of family dysfunction associated with the presenting symptoms, which may appear in one or more family members.

Consistent with a transgenerational outlook, Bowenians are particularly inter-ested in the historical pattern of family emotional functioning, the family's anxiety levels at varying stages of its life, and the amount of stress experienced in the past compared with current functioning. Of special interest too is whether one spouse's functioning has improved significantly and the other spouse's has declined signifi-

---

[5]Questioning is a major technique for family systems therapists, since it represents a way of remaining in touch with client problems without directing client behavior or taking responsibility for fixing their dilem-mas. Friedman (1991) believes questioning allows the therapist to maintain objectivity and a differentiation-promoting position with clients. We'll return to the role of questioning as a therapeutic technique in discussing the Milan model (Chapter 11) as well as White's narrative therapy (Chapter 13).

cantly over the course of their relationship. By probing the history of the symptoms in each family member, therapists search for clues as to where the various pressures on the family have been expressed and how effectively the family has adapted to stress since its inception. At this point in the evaluation, the focus has begun to expand beyond the symptomatic person to an examination of the relationship network of the nuclear family.

The final part of the evaluation interview attempts to understand the nuclear family in the context of the maternal and paternal extended family systems. Here the therapists are interested in multigenerational patterns of fusion, the nature of the nuclear family's relationship with the extended families, and the degree of emotional cutoff of each spouse. Parallels in relationship patterns between the husband and wife and his or her parents may offer important clues of poor differentiation from the families of origin. The therapist's goal with this undertaking is to develop a road map of the family's emotional system, since each nuclear family is believed to embody the emotional processes and patterns of preceding generations.

The Genogram

Since Bowen believed multigenerational patterns and influences are crucial determinants of nuclear family functioning, he developed a graphic way of investigating the genesis of the presenting problem by diagramming the family over at least three generations. To aid in the process and to keep the record in pictorial form in front of him, he constructed a family **genogram** in which each partner's family background is laid out. Worked out with the family during early sessions, it provides a useful tool for allowing therapist and family members alike to examine the ebb and flow of the family's emotional processes in their intergenerational context. Each individual's family's biological, kinship, and psychosocial makeup can be gleaned from perusing this visual graph (Roberto, 1992).

Figure 8.3 offers a partial set of commonly used genogram symbols. Together, the symbols provide a visual picture of a family tree: who the members are, what their names are, ages, sibling positions, marital status, divorces, and so on, typically extending back at least three generations for both parents. When relevant, such additional items of information as religious affiliation, occupations, ethnic origins, geographic locations, socioeconomic status, and perhaps significant life events may be included. More than providing a concise pictorial depiction of the nuclear family, the genogram may suggest certain emotional patterns in each partner's family of origin, thus providing data for assessing each spouse's degree of fusion to extended families and to one another. McGoldrick and Gerson (1985), strongly transgenerational in outlook, suggest that family patterns tend to repeat themselves; what happens in one generation will often occur in the next, as the same unresolved emotional issues are replayed from generation to generation.

Genograms often provide families with their first inkling of intergenerational family relationship patterns. Goldenberg and Goldenberg (1998) offer the following example of just such a situation (see Figure 8.4):

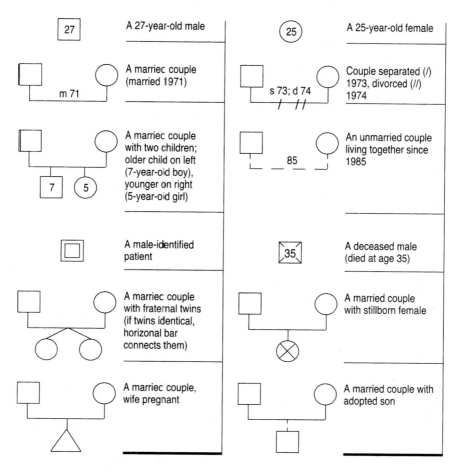

Figure 8.3 A partial set of commonly agreed-upon genogram symbols.
Source: Based on McGoldrick & Gerson, 1985

A family contacted a counselor in 1988 because their son, Ivan, was having school difficulties, disrupting class activity and generally being inattentive. The genogram revealed that his mother, Loretta, was adopted, after her adoptive parents had tried unsuccessfully to have a daughter after three sons. She married early, at 20, soon after the death of her adoptive mother. Steve, a middle child whose parents divorced when he was a preteenager, lived in a single-parent household with his mother and two sisters until he married Loretta. Steve and Loretta started their own family before either was 25, perhaps in an effort to create some stability in contrast to what either had known growing up.

The fact that they now have four children (one died in childbirth) suggests a strong involvement in family life, especially because the children's ages are spread

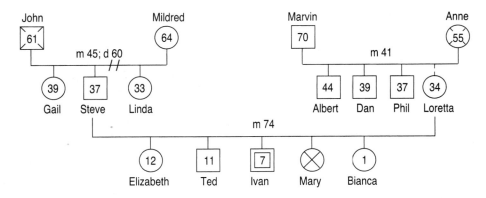

Figure 8.4 Genogram of a three-generation family.
Source: Goldenberg & Goldenberg, 1998, p. 53

over more than ten years. Are the parents being overprotective, perhaps to compensate for what they felt deprived of as youngsters? What has been the effect of Loretta's pregnancies over the last several years on the other children? To what extent does Ivan feel he is being displaced as the youngest child by the birth of Bianca? (pp. 53–54)

Note how many hypotheses spring from the genogram, to be explored with the family subsequently. Fusion-differentiation issues in the family of origin, the nuclear family emotional system, emotional cutoffs by the parents, sibling positions, and many other of Bowen's concepts appear as possibly relevant to Ivan's presenting symptoms. When evaluation interview data are put into schematic form in a family genogram, therapist and family together are better able to comprehend the underlying emotional processes connecting generations. In a sense, the family genogram is never completed, as new information during the course of therapy sheds new light on basic patterns of emotional reactivity in both the nuclear and extended families. Major turning points for the family (such as the unexpected death of a key family member) may mark the start of a series of family problems that may have reverberations across generations (Papero, 1990). Genograms thus provide a relatively emotion-free way of collecting information that makes sense to the family and connects them to the therapeutic exploratory process.

Therapeutic Techniques

Family systems therapy, no matter the nature of the presenting clinical problem, is always governed by two basic goals: (1) reduction of anxiety and relief from symptoms; and (2) an increase in each participant's level of differentiation in order to improve adaptiveness (Kerr & Bowen, 1988). Generally speaking, the family needs to accomplish the former goal first, before the latter can be undertaken. Ultimately, however, overreactive emotional interactions with the extended family must be changed, leading to greater self-differentiation for nuclear family members. In the case of marital conflict, for example, the therapist *tracks* the emotional process between the spouses and then *shifts* the emphasis from the *marital* level to the *self level* as each partner differentiates from the spouse. In the process, equal attention is paid to historical ways in which previous generations have created family patterns as well as current manifestations of those patterns throughout the family system (Aylmer, 1986).

In order to help remove an adult client from a highly charged emotional triangle with parents, solo visits to the family of origin may be arranged. Typically these structured visits are prepared for beforehand by telephone or letter, in which the client makes known those issues causing personal distress. The client is instructed to maintain an "observer" stance as much as possible at first, monitoring distressing emotional and behavioral patterns while retaining a sense of separateness despite surrounding tensions and anxiety. Later, the now more self-directed client can decline getting caught up in old patterns and negotiate for more functional and supportive relationships (Roberto, 1992).

Bowen's standard method of conducting family therapy was to work with a system consisting of two adults and himself. Even when the identified patient was a symptomatic child, Bowen asked the parents to accept the premise that the basic problem is between the two of them—the family's emotional system—and that the identified patient was not the source of the problem. In such a situation, Bowen might never see the child at all. As Kerr (1981) explains, "A theoretical system that thinks in terms of family, with a therapeutic method that works toward improvement of the family system, is 'family' regardless of the number of people in the sessions" (p. 232).

Bowen presented himself as a researcher helping the family members become objective researchers into their own ways of functioning. The term he preferred was *coach* (having moved during his career, in his own words, "from 'couch' to 'coach'") —an active expert who calmly assists family members, through low-key direct questions, in defining and clarifying their emotional responsivity to one another. In the process, family members were encouraged to listen, think about their situation, control their emotional reactivity, and learn to express self-defining "I-positions." When the coach has taught them successfully, often by modeling "I-positions," the individual family members are responsible for the actual work of changing. Their self-differentiation, the basic goal of the therapy, must come from them and not the therapist, on the basis of a rational understanding of the family emotional networks and transmission processes.

Bowen (1976) took the position that the successful addition of a significant other person (a friend, teacher, clergyman) to an anxious or disturbed relationship system can modify all relationships within the family. The family therapist can play this role as long as he or she manages to stay in nonanxious emotional contact with the two most significant family members (usually the parents) but remains uninvested in (or detriangulated from) the family conflict. Bowen's insistence that the therapist not engage with the family system—maintaining what Aylmer (1986) calls a detached-involved position—is dramatically different from the "total immersion" approach of family therapists such as Ackerman, Satir, Kempler, or Whitaker. Here the therapist remains unsusceptible, calm, objective, detriangulated from the emotional entanglements between the spouses. If the therapist can maintain that kind of stance—despite pressures to be triangulated into the conflict—Bowenians believe tension between the couple will subside, the fusion between them will slowly resolve, and other family members will feel the positive repercussions in terms of changes in their own lives—all adding to the likelihood of each member achieving greater self-differentiation.

Family systems therapists may choose one partner, usually the one more mature and better differentiated, and focus on that individual for a period of time. This person is assumed to be the member of the family most capable of breaking through the old emotionally entangling patterns of interaction. When that person succeeds in taking an "I-stand," the others will shortly be forced into changing, subsequently moving off in their own directions. A stormy period may follow before a new equilibrium is reached, but the former pathological ties are broken and each person has achieved a greater sense of individuality.

Family therapy sessions are apt to be controlled and cerebral. Each partner talks to the therapist rather than talking directly to the other. Confrontation between the partners is avoided to minimize emotional reactivity between them. Instead, what each partner is thinking is externalized in the presence of the other. Interpretations are avoided. Calm questioning defuses emotion and forces the partners to think about the issues causing their difficulties. Rather than allowing partners to blame each other or ignore their differences in a rush of intimacy, Bowenians insist that each partner focus on the part he or she plays in the relationship problems.

Because Bowen was particularly concerned that his clients develop the ability to differentiate themselves from their families of origin, the focus of much of his work was on extended families. In this respect Bowen resembled Framo (1981),[6] although Bowen sends clients home for frequent visits (and self-observations) after coaching them in their differentiating efforts, while Framo brings origin family members into the final phases of therapy with his clients (see Chapter 6). Going home again, for Bowen, was directed at greater self-differentiation from one another—not at con-

---

[6]A number of other family therapists, notably Norman Paul and Donald Williamson, endorse the transgenerational viewpoint that certain unfinished issues with one's family of origin must be addressed directly before family therapy is terminated. Paul (1974), a family therapy pioneer, has been particularly concerned that unresolved issues over death, loss, and grief be dealt with therapeutically, arguing that a family's rigid or otherwise dysfunctional behavior patterns are often tied to an earlier denied or inappropriately expressed grief over the death of a loved one. He advocates uncovering the loss and helping family members complete the unresolved mourning process together. Williamson (1991) believes that by the fourth decade of their lives, middle adulthood, grown children should have terminated the earlier hierarchical power structure with their aging parents, and the family should have begun to redistribute power on a more equitable basis between generations. Failure to do so, he hypothesizes, may lead to marital and family behavior in the second generation that becomes dysfunctional and symptomatic, as these adult children fail to take on "personal authority" with their families. Williamson contends that the renegotiation is essential if one is to differentiate from one's parent's, gain a sense of personal authority, and begin an eventual mourning process for the parents. After careful preparation with selected clients (writing an autobiography, taping phone conversations with parents, and so forth), Williamson arranges several office visits extending over three days between the adult child and the parents, aimed at shifting power and achieving peerhood between generations. Williamson's efforts are consistent with the social construction view of rewriting one's family story as a way of creating a more egalitarian and intimate narrative with one's parents.

frontation, the settlements of old scores, or the reconciliation of long-standing differences. Reestablishing emotional connectedness with the family of origin—especially when rigid and previously impenetrable boundaries have been built up—is a critical step in reducing a client's residual anxiety due to emotional cutoff, in detriangulating from members of that family, and in ultimately achieving self-differentiation, free of crippling entanglements from the past or present.

CONTEXTUAL THERAPY

Relational Ethics and the Family Ledger

Another influential family therapy approach that addresses multigenerational patterns of connection within a family comes from the work of Ivan Boszormenyi-Nagy and his associates. His **contextual** therapy, as elaborated in a collection of his papers spanning 30 years (Boszormenyi-Nagy, 1987), is heavily influenced by Fairbairn's (1952) object relations theory, existential philosophy, and Sullivan's interpersonal psychiatry (1953), to which is added an *ethical perspective*—trust, loyalty, transgenerational indebtedness and entitlements, as well as fairness in relationships between family members. Although acknowledging the family as a social system, Boszormenyi-Nagy believes that the burdens for today's families are complex, and a comprehensive picture of their functioning must go beyond a simple appreciation of the interactional sequences occurring between members. What also demands attention, in his view, is the impact of both intrapsychic and intergenerational issues within families, especially each member's subjective sense of claims, rights, and obligations in relation to one another. To function effectively, family members must be held ethically accountable for their behavior with one another and must learn to balance *entitlement* (what one is due or has come to merit)[7] and *indebtedness* (what one owes to whom).

A core concept in contextual theory, **relational ethics** focuses attention on the long-term, oscillating balance of fairness among members within a family, whereby the welfare interests of each participant are taken into account by the others. Relational ethics encompasses both individual psychology (what transpires within the person) and systems characteristics (roles, power alignments, communication sequences within the family). A marital couple, for example, must develop a symmetrical give-and-take, balancing rights and responsibilities toward one another, in order to maintain and continue to build their relationship. At such times, inevitable in any relationship, when the needs of the partners conflict, they must be able, openly and honestly, to negotiate differences that maintain overall fairness. Fairness, decency, consideration of every family member's needs, loyalty, equality, reciprocity, caring, accountability—these together help determine the direction, form, and free-

---

[7]In some cases, "destructive entitlements" exist. As Ulrich (1998) notes, the hurt or deprived child may attempt to wrest from innocent parties what he or she failed to receive from parents, or perhaps to punish innocent parties for his or her own wounds. While such claims may be legitimate, clearly the chosen targets are not.

dom of action within a family (Boszormenyi-Nagy, Grunebaum, & Ulrich, 1991). Symptoms may appear when trustworthiness and caring within a family break down.

To contextual therapists, the patterns of relating within a family that are passed on from generation to generation are keys to understanding individual as well as family functioning. *Trust* is the fundamental property of relationships, and can be depleted or restored, depending on the capacity of family members to act upon a sense of loyalty and indebtedness in their give-and-take with one another. Instead of focusing on symptomatic behavior or family pathology, the contextual therapist attends to relational resources as leverages for change; relationships are viewed as trustworthy to the extent that they permit dialogue among family members regarding issues of valid claims and mutual obligations.

While the reduction of stress is an important goal in this as in all therapies, the fundamental goal of contextual therapy is in the improvement in the family members' capacity for relatedness, rebalancing the give-and-take and emotional ledgers between family members. Well-functioning families are characterized by their ability to negotiate imbalances and especially by their ability to maintain a sense of fairness and accountability in their interactions with one another. Besides Boszormenyi-Nagy, leading exponents of this view include psychologists David Ulrich (1998) and Barbara Krasner (Boszormenyi-Nagy & Krasner, 1986), as well as psychiatrist Catherine Ducommun-Nagy (1999).

Boszormenyi-Nagy, a psychiatrist with psychoanalytic training who emigrated to the United States from Hungary in 1948, founded the Department of Family Psychiatry at the Eastern Pennsylvania Psychiatric Institute in 1957 as a center for studying schizophrenia. (James Framo, along with Geraldine Spark, Gerald Zuk, and David Rubenstein were early associates at the institute.) After a long series of unsuccessful attempts to find biochemical clues to explain the etiology of the disorder, Boszormenyi-Nagy and his colleagues began to focus on the behavioral and psychological aspects of schizophrenia, ultimately turning to transgenerational issues within the family. When the EPPI closed in 1980, due to the loss of state funding, they continued to refine contextual theories at nearby Hahnemann University Medical School in Philadelphia.

Joining initially with Spark, a psychiatric social worker with an extensive psychoanalytic background and experience in child guidance centers, Boszormenyi-Nagy advanced a theory based upon family loyalty, along with a set of therapeutic techniques that pertained to uncovering and resolving family "obligations" and "debts" incurred over time. They introduced such new (nonpsychoanalytic) terms as family *legacy* (expectations handed down from previous generations) and family *loyalty* (allegiances in children based on parental fairness) in order to emphasize that family members inevitably acquire a set of expectations and responsibilities toward each other. Fair and equitable parental behavior engenders loyalty in the children; unfair demands or an exaggerated sense of obligation may produce an *invisible loyalty* in which the child unconsciously continues, endlessly, to pay off a debt to parents, frequently to his or her own detriment as it takes priority over all other concerns.

Figuratively speaking, each person has a sense of unsettled accounts, how much he or she has invested in relationships within the family, and whether there has been a fair balance between what has been given and received. While this is hardly a strict

Ivan Boszormenyi-Nagy, M.D.

bookkeeping system and seldom if ever perfectly balanced, confronting and redressing imbalances is viewed as essential if a family is to stay vital and avoid stagnation. Ulrich (1983) cites a temporary imbalance: a wife works at an unsatisfying job so her husband can finish law school—but with the expectation that what she has invested in the common fund will eventually be replaced, for their mutual enrichment.

Obligations may be rooted in past generations, and need not be consciously recognized or acknowledged to influence the behavior of family members in the present. In a sense, every family maintains a *family ledger*—a multigenerational accounting system of what has been given and who, psychologically speaking, still owes what to whom. Boszormenyi-Nagy and Krasner (1986) argue that traditional interventions, either individually or family focused, consistently ignore family balances due, either owed or deserved, especially intergenerational ones. Yet people, in or out of therapy, constantly raise such questions as: "What do I owe, and to whom?" "What do I deserve, and from whom?" "What relationships do I need and want?" "What relationships am I obliged to retain, whether or not I need or want them?"

Whenever injustices occur, there is the expectation of some later repayment or restitution. Problems in relationships develop when justice comes too slowly or in an amount too small to satisfy the other person. From this perspective, dysfunctional behavior in any individual cannot be fully understood without looking at the history of the problem, the family ledger, and examining unsettled or unredressed accounts. A symptom that develops might represent an accumulation of feelings of injustice that has grown too large.

The family legacy, then, dictates debts and entitlement. One son may be slated to be successful ("We expect you'll be good at anything you try"), another to become a failure ("We don't think you'll ever amount to much"). A son may be entitled to approval, the daughter only to shame. Because of such family imperatives, as Boszormenyi-Nagy and Ulrich (1981) point out, the children are ethically bound to

accommodate their lives somehow to their legacies. Ulrich (_983) gives the following graphic example:

> A son whose familial legacy is one of mistrust among family members, angrily con-
> fronts his wife every time she spends any money without his prior approval. He is
> convinced, and he tries to convince her, that her untrustworthy, spendthrift behav-
> ior is going to bankrupt them. (p. 193)

In fact, the wife, who works full-time as well as tending to their child, may temporarily unbalance the week's budget, but her overall efforts contribute to the family's solvency. If her response to his anger is fear—a legacy she carries from her own
family—she may hide her purchases. His discovery of such concealment reinforces
his mistrust; his subsequent anger strengthens her fears. Together their legacies have
had a corrosive effect on their marriage. In ledger terms, he is still making payment
to his mother's injunction that a wife is not to be trusted. By "overpaying" his mother, he is robbing his wife. She, in turn, may be paying off similar debts. Contextual
therapy would direct them to reassess all their relationships, pay off legitimate filial
debts, and free themselves from oppressive obligations.

The ethical dimension gives contextual therapy its uniqueness. Insisting that they
are not moralizing or taking a judgmental position, practitioners of this approach contend that they offer a realistic strategy for preventing individual and relational imbalance and eventual breakdown. They argue that effective therapeutic intervention must
be grounded in the therapist's conviction that trustworthiness is a necessary condition
for reworking legacy assessments and allowing family members to feel they are entitled
to more satisfying relationships. Practitioners of contextual therapy maintain that families cannot be fully understood without an explicit awareness of family loyalty—who
is bound to whom, what is expected of all family members, how loyalty is expressed,
what happens when loyalty accounts are uneven ("We were there for you when you
were growing up and now we, your aging parents, are entitled to help from you").

Contextual therapy helps rebalance the obligations kept in the invisible family
ledger. Once these imbalances are identified, efforts can be directed at settling old
family accounts (for example, mothers and daughters "stuck" in lifelong conflict),
"exonerating" alleged culprits, or transforming unproductive patterns of relating that
may have existed throughout the family over many past generations. The major therapeutic thrust is to establish or restore trustworthiness and relational integrity in
family relationships. Parental behavior may be reassessed (and forgiven) in light of
its roots in the past.

In the following example, a therapist helps a family split by dissention and conflicting loyalties learn fairer and more ethically responsible ways of dealing with one
another. In the process of overcoming a stagnating relationship with her mother, the
woman gains a more trustworthy level of relating to her husband and daughter.

Overall, each family member is viewed as someone who is a part of a multigenerational pattern. Each is guided to move in the direction of greater trust.
Contextualists believe it is the ethical dimension of trust within a family that is the
invisible thread of both individual freedom and interindividual balance.

Redefining symptomatic behavior as evidence of family loyalty or as the sacrifice
of self-development in the interest of the family led Boszormenyi-Nagy and Spark

Mr. and Mrs. Jones were seeking help for their marriage. The presenting problem had to do with Mrs. Jones's angry outbursts at her husband and mother. An intelligent and compulsively neat person, Mrs. Jones was resentful of the fact that her mother had humiliated and frustrated her. Their relationship, she claimed, was characterized by mistrust and manipulation. She handled her rage through long-distance calls to her parents that inevitably resulted in tortuous arguments with her mother; or else she ignored them for prolonged periods of time.

His wife's hostile outbursts rendered Mr. Jones helpless. A hardworking, meticulously responsible salesman, he was deeply discouraged and never knew what he would face when he came home from work. On occasion, Mrs. Jones would try to ruin the garden equipment that he so highly prized. On other occasions, she would throw out his favorite books. On the other hand, there were times when their marriage seemed to be all right. For example, they could function as a team whenever members of their extended family were in real need. During their brief respite, they could enjoy each other and reported that their sexual relations were good.

However, the couple was often at war over their only child. Sheila, age 12, was chronically caught between them and lived in constant jeopardy of being split in her loyalties to them. Mrs. Jones would greet her husband at the door with complaints about their daughter. He resented being cast into the unfair role of referee and retaliated by forming a subversive alliance with Sheila. In therapy sessions, the couple finally consented to hear each other out. Together, the three of them began to work toward fairer ways of relating.

Mr. and Mrs. Jones and Sheila seemed comforted by the therapist's capacity to elicit the justifications of each of their sides (multidirected partiality). Yet, Mrs. Jones was openly annoyed at any attempts to offer fair consideration to her mother. In the interim, things went better for the family. Until now Mrs. Jones had lacked the security to look for a job commensurate with her intelligence and ability. For a long time she had invested her energies in compulsive housekeeping. Suddenly she found a job that she liked. Immediately, tensions eased as her world widened and opened up. Mr. Jones learned to distance himself from his wife when she regressed into outbursts of anger. And Mrs. Jones began to exchange letters with her mother and managed some pleasant visits with both of her parents.

On occasion, some of the vindictiveness previously channeled toward her parents was now transferred to the therapist. At one point, Mrs. Jones refused to accompany her husband to their therapy session, arguing that the therapist "didn't care" about her. Two weeks later, though, she left an emergency message with the answering service: her mother had died suddenly, unexpectedly! Overcome by the intensity of her emotions, she expressed profound gratitude. What would have happened to her, she wondered, if the therapist had not enabled her to find a way to her mother? What if she had failed to repair their relationship before it was too late? (Boszormenyi-Nagy & Krasner, 1986, pp. 45–46)

(1973) to describe how certain children in dysfunctional families are delegated to play such age-inappropriate, growth-retarding family roles as "parent," pet, scapegoat, or sexual object. Helm Stierlin, a German psychoanalyst and family therapist, has been particularly interested in how the processes of victimization and sacrifice and of exploitation and counterexploitation between generations are evident in the development of schizophrenia in a family member. Stierlin (1977) views all members as participating in a system of "invisible accounts" in which

> massive guilt, an immense though thwarted need for repair work as well as revenge, a deeply felt sense of justice or injustice, and of loyalty confirmed or betrayed—all operating largely outside of awareness—become here formidable dynamic forces, influencing the members' every move. And the stakes in this "morality play" are high. On the one side, we find parents who, exploited and crippled by their own parents, attempt to survive by living through their children, crippling them in turn; and, on the other side, we find children who, as self-sacrificing, lifelong victims, gain the power to devastate their parents by inducing deep guilt. The power of loyalty-bound victims presents perhaps the most difficult single problem in the treatment of schizophrenia. (p. 228)

Stierlin's concept of the schizophrenic as a delegate, ostensibly permitted to move out of the parental orbit but remaining tied and beholden, bound to his or her parents through "invisible loyalties," meshes nicely with the contextual outlook, particularly on the transgenerational influences on individual growth and development. Stierlin has depicted anorectics as struggling with similar stultifying family bonds, their periodic "hunger strikes" representing efforts to withdraw from the family while at the same time remaining bound and united with them (Stierlin & Weber, 1989). Contextual theorists advocate a three-generational therapeutic effort, whenever possible, in which breaking through relationship deadlocks, gaining insight, balancing accounts, and a final reconciliation across generations are the goals.

SUMMARY

Family systems theory, developed primarily by Murray Bowen, has a transgenerational outlook and is based on a natural systems perspective in which human behavior is seen as the result of an evolutionary process and as one type of living system. The major theoretician in the family therapy field, Bowen conceptualized the family as an emotional relationship system and offered eight interlocking concepts to explain the emotional processes taking place in the nuclear and extended families over generations.

These include differentiation of self, triangles, the nuclear family emotional system, the family projection process, emotional cutoff, multigenerational transmission process, sibling position, and societal regression. Chronic anxiety is seen as an inevitable part of nature and as transmitted from previous generations as families attempt to balance togetherness and differentiation.

Family evaluation interviews stress objectivity and neutrality, as therapists make an effort to remain outside, and thus not triangled into, the family's emotional network. Genograms offer helpful pictorial depictions of the family's relationship system over at least three generations. Therapeutically, Bowenians work with marital partners in a calm and carefully detriangulated way, attempting to resolve the fusion between them; their goals are to reduce anxiety and resolve symptoms, and ultimately to maximize each person's self-differentiation within the nuclear family system—and from the family of origin.

Contextual family therapy, developed primarily by Ivan Boszormenyi-Nagy, focuses on relational ethics and transgenerational legacies, and how influences from the past have a bearing on present-day functioning in all members. In this view, families have invisible loyalties—obligations rooted in past generations—and unsettled accounts that must be balanced. Contextual therapy attempts to rebuild responsible, trustworthy behavior, taking into account the entitlements of all concerned. Its goal is to help dysfunctional families rebalance the give-and-take and emotional ledgers between members and develop a sense of fairness and accountability in interactions with one another.

9

The Structural Model

Many of the basic concepts of the structural approach to family therapy are already familiar to the reader: family rules, roles, coalitions, subsystems, boundaries, wholeness, organization. The very fact that these constructs are part of the everyday vocabulary of family therapy—and so readily come to mind in thinking of family relationships and interactional patterns—underscores the prominence of this model. In particular, its clearly articulated theory of family organization, along with its substantiating research, and the specific intervention approaches offered by Salvador Minuchin and his associates (Minuchin, 1974; Minuchin & Fishman, 1981; Minuchin, Rosman, & Baker, 1978; Minuchin & Nichols, 1993) have helped ensure that a legion of systems-oriented family therapists would adopt the structural viewpoint.

Structural family therapy shares with other family systems approaches a preference for a *contextual* rather than an individual focus on problems and solutions. Its uniqueness, however, results from its use of *spatial and organizational metaphors,* both in describing problems and identifying solutions, and its insistence on *active therapist direction* (Colapinto, 1991). The model's major thesis—that an individual's symptoms are best understood as rooted in the context of family transaction patterns, that a change in family organization or structure must take place before the symptoms are relieved, and that the therapist must provide a directive leadership role in changing the structure or context in which the symptom is embedded—has had great impact on the practices of many family therapists for at least three decades. The learning experiences involved in mastering structural techniques has recently been described by Minuchin and nine of his supervisees (Minuchin, Lee. & Simon, 1996).

Structural theorists emphasize (1) the *wholeness* of the family system, (2) the influence of the family's *hierarchical* organization, and (3) the interdependent functioning of its *subsystems* as the major determinants of the well-being of its individual members. It is the family's underlying organizational structure (that is, its enduring and regulating interactional patterns) and its flexibility in responding to changing conditions throughout the family life cycle that help govern the appearance of functional or dysfunctional patterns. Minuchin (1984) views families as going through their life cycles seeking to maintain a delicate balance between stability and change;

the more functional the family, the more open to change during periods of family transitions, and the more willing to modify its structure as changing conditions demand.

Structural therapists actively strive for organizational changes in the dysfunctional family as their primary goal, assuming that individual behavioral changes as well as symptom reduction will follow as the context for the family's transactions changes. They reason that when the family's structure is transformed, the positions of its members are altered, and each person experiences changes as a result. It is the structural therapist's primary role, then, to be an instrument of change—to actively engage the family as a whole. to introduce challenges that force adaptive changes, and to support and coach family members as they attempt to cope with the ensuing consequences (Colapinto, 1991).

Systems-oriented, problem-focused, and concerned with the family's current context, the structural approach is primarily (although not exclusively) associated with Salvador Minuchin and his colleagues (at one time or another including such notable family therapists as Edgar Auerswald, Braulio Montalvo, Harry Aponte, Jay Haley, Lynn Hoffman, Marianne Walters, Charles Fishman, and Jorge Colapinto).

Born in Argentina of European immigrant parents, Minuchin set out to practice pediatrics following his medical training. When Israel declared itself a state in 1948, Minuchin, guided by his sense of social purpose (still present today in his consultative work), volunteered his services to Israel and served as an army doctor for 18 months in the war with the Arab nations. After subsequent training as a child psychiatrist in the United States, a good part of which was under the tutelage of Nathan Ackerman, he returned to Israel in 1952 to work with displaced children from the Holocaust and then with Jewish immigrants from the Arab countries.

Back in the United States once again in 1954, Minuchin began psychoanalytic training at the William Alanson White Institute (where Sullivan's interpersonal psychiatry ideas held sway), eventually becoming the intake psychiatrist at the Wiltwyck School, a residential school for delinquent adolescents outside New York City. Inspired further by an article by Don Jackson in 1959, Minuchin began looking beyond the individual children, primarily African American and Puerto Rican youngsters from New York's inner city, to an examination and analysis of their family predicaments. Because these families often had multiple problems and disconnected family structures, Minuchin started developing a theory and set of special intervention techniques for working with these underorganized poor families. Increasingly, he turned to a sociological analysis of social context—just how the experience of living under poverty conditions impacted on family functioning. To effect change, Minuchin and his coworkers began to search for therapeutic ways of changing family context rather than directing their efforts at individually troubled adolescents with personality or behavioral problems.

Finding long-term, interpretive psychoanalytic techniques with a passive therapist ineffective with this multiproblemed population, Minuchin and his associates proceeded to devise many brief, direct, concrete, action-oriented, and problem-solving intervention procedures to effect context change by restructuring the family. The results of his eight years at Wiltwyck, during which he developed many highly original and action-oriented techniques for working with poor, disadvantaged families,

Salvador Minuchin, M.D.

were described in *Families of the Slums* (Minuchin, Montalvo, Guerney, Rosman, & Schumer, 1967) and earned Minuchin widespread recognition (Simon, 1984). The Wiltwyck experience, especially its revelation of the need for family reorganization and for some effective form of hierarchy among family members, in effect laid the cornerstone for structural family therapy.

Now desirous of testing his techniques with a wider cross section of families, including both working-class and middle-class populations Minuchin took on the directorship of the Philadelphia Child Guidance Center in 1965. To assist with training, he brought along Montalvo from Wiltwyck and also recruited Jay Haley from Palo Alto.[1] Originally a small clinic with a staff of ten located in the heart of the African American ghetto, the Philadelphia Child Guidance Clinic blossomed under Minuchin's boldly imaginative leadership until it grew into the largest facility of its kind ever established. The clinic soon occupied an elaborate modern complex, had close to 300 people on its staff, and became affiliated with Children's Hospital on the campus of the University of Pennsylvania. The clinic has the distinction of being the first clinic in the United States where ghetto families represented a majority of the clients served. In 1974, Minuchin published *Families and Family Therapy,* an elaboration of ideas concerning change in families through structural family therapy.

Minuchin soon turned his attention to the role of family context in psychosomatic conditions; as Colapinto (1982) observes, the urgent problems of a social

---

[1]The cross-fertilization of ideas between these three was extensive and enriching to all concerned, as Minuchin acknowledged in his classic text (Minuchin, 1974). Montalvo, a social worker born and raised in Puerto Rico, is credited by Minuchin as his most influential teacher. He introduced many innovations to the supervisory process (see Chapter 16) and helped train minority paraprofessionals who had no prior educational or therapeutic experience. Haley, also to make an impact on Minuchin's thinking, gave priority to teaching trainees concrete, step-by-step skills rather than emphasizing any underlying theory. Haley's *Problem-Solving Therapy,* a popular 1976 text, began to take form first as a syllabus for training paraprofessionsls (Simon, 1984).

nature Minuchin encountered at Wiltwyck were replaced by urgent medical problems in Philadelphia. More specifically, no medical explanations could be found for the unusually large number of diabetic children who required emergency hospitalization for acidosis (a depletion of alkali in the body), nor would they respond to individual psychotherapy directed at helping them deal with stress. As Minuchin and his coworkers began to accumulate research and clinical data and to redefine the problem in family terms, successful interventions involving the entire family became possible. Later research expanded to include asthmatic children with severe, recurrent attacks as well as anorectic children; the additional data confirmed for Minuchin that the locus of pathology was in the context of the family and not simply in the afflicted individual.

As proposed in *Psychosomatic Families,* written together with research psychologist Bernice Rosman and pediatrician Lester Baker (Minuchin, Rosman, & Baker, 1978), families of children who manifest severe psychosomatic symptoms are characterized by certain transactional problems that encourage somatization. Enmeshment is common, subsystems function poorly, and boundaries between family members are too diffuse to allow for individual autonomy. A *psychosomatic family* was found to be overprotective, inhibiting the child from developing a sense of independence, competence, or interest in activities outside the safety of the family. The physiologically vulnerable child, in turn, feels great responsibility for protecting the family. The manifestation of symptoms typically occurs when stress overloads the family's already dysfunctional coping mechanisms. Thus, the symptoms are regarded as having a regulating effect on the family system, the sick child acting as a family conflict defuser by diverting family attention away from more basic, but less easily resolved, family conflicts.

Unlike the underorganized, often single-parent-led, family population they found at Wiltwyck, here Minuchin and his colleagues were dealing primarily with middle-class, intact families, who, if anything, appeared to be too tightly organized. Therapeutic intervention, while attending to family context, had to be modified to first destructure the family's rigid patterns, and then restructure them in order to permit greater flexibility. In the process, therapeutic efforts were directed at changing the structure of relationships within the family, helping the family develop clearer boundaries, learn to negotiate for desired changes, and deal more directly with hidden, underlying conflicts. According to Colapinto (1991), the Minuchin team's family-focused success in treating anorexia nervosa—which, unlike diabetes or asthma, has no physiological basis—drew many family therapists to the structural model.

After stepping down as director of the Philadelphia Child Guidance Center in 1975, and as director of training there in 1981, Minuchin spent most of his professional time teaching, consulting, supervising, writing, and demonstrating his dramatic techniques in front of professional audiences around the world. In 1981 he founded and, until 1996, led a small group called Family Studies, Inc. (now renamed the Minuchin Center for the Family) in New York City, offering consultative services to community organizations, particularly those dealing with poor families (Minuchin, Colapino, & Minuchin, 1998). Minuchin has now retired to Boston where he continues to act as consultant to the Massachusetts Department of Mental Health.

STRUCTURAL FAMILY THEORY

As Minuchin (1974) describes his viewpoint:

> In essence, the structural approach to families is based on the concept that a family is more than the individual biopsychodynamics of its members. Family members relate according to certain arrangements, which govern their transactions. These arrangements, though usually not explicitly stated or even recognized, form a whole—the structure of the family. The reality of the structure is of a different order from the reality of the individual members. (p. 89)

Like most systems theorists, the structuralists are interested in how the components of a system interact, how balance or homeostasis is achieved, how family feedback mechanisms operate, how dysfunctional communication patterns develop, and so forth. Consistent with Minuchin's background in child psychiatry, he influenced his associates to observe too how families cope with developmental tasks as the family matures, and particularly how families, as complex systems, make adaptational changes during periods of transition. Structuralists pay special attention to family transactional patterns because these offer clues to the family's structure, the permeability of the family's subsystem boundaries, and the existence of alignments or coalitions—all of which ultimately affect the family's ability to achieve a delicate balance between stability and change.

Family Structure

Just as is the case with all adapting organisms, families need some form of internal organization that dictates how, when, and to whom to relate; the subsequent transactional patterns make up the structure of the family (Colapinto, 1991). Put another way, a family's structure is the invisible or covert set of functional demands or codes that organizes the way family members interact with one another (Minuchin, 1974). In essence, the structure represents the sum of the operational rules the family has evolved for carrying out its important functions. It provides a framework for understanding those consistent, repetitive, and enduring patterns that reveal how a particular family organizes itself in order to maintain its stability and, under a changing set of environmental conditions, to seek adaptive alternatives. Typically, once established, such patterns are self-perpetuating and resistant to change. They are unlikely to change until a family's changing circumstances cause tensions and imbalance within the system.

For example, an interactive routine may evolve in a family whereby the young son refuses to comply with his mother's pleading to clean up his room, but will submit to his father's request without hesitation. Repeated over time, and in a variety of situations, a basic family structure may emerge in which the father is seen in the family as the ultimate authority and the mother as possessing insufficient power or clout to be obeyed.

Subsequent transactional patterns between family members are likely to reflect this now-established pattern. These patterns serve to arrange or organize the family's component subunits into more or less constant relationships (Umbarger, 1983) and thus regulate the family's day-to-day functioning. However, structure in and of itself should not necessarily be thought of as static or fixed. On the contrary, certain temporary structures (a mother-son coalition in which the father is kept out, say about erratic school attendance or a bad grade) may occur but not persist beyond a brief arrangement, and thus must be considered to be dynamic.

A family's transactional patterns regulate the behavior of its members, and are maintained by two sets of constraints: *generic* or universal rules, and *idiosyncratic* or individualized rules (Minuchin, 1974). With regard to the former, structuralists contend that all well-functioning families should be hierarchically organized,[2] the parents exercising more authority and power than the children, the older children having more responsibilities as well as more privileges than their younger siblings.

In addition, there must be *complementarity* of functions—the husband and wife, for example, operating as a team and accepting their interdependency. The degree to which the needs and abilities of both spouses dovetail and reciprocal role relations provide satisfaction are key factors in harmonious family functioning. In some cases, family balance is achieved by different family members' being assigned complementary roles or functions (good child–bad child; tender mother–tough father). Thus, complementarity or reciprocity between family roles provides a generic restraint on family structure, allowing the family to carry out its tasks while maintaining family equilibrium. Complementarity takes the form of teamwork in well-functioning families.

Idiosyncratic constraints apply to specific families, and involve the mutual presumptions of particular family members regarding their behavior toward one another. While the origin of certain expectations may no longer be clear to the persons involved, buried in years of implicit and explicit negotiations, their pattern of mutual accommodation, and thus functional effectiveness, is maintained (Minuchin, 1974). The evolved rules and subsequent behavioral patterns of a particular family's game become a part of the family's structure, ensuring that the system will maintain itself.

Thus, a family will try to maintain preferred patterns—its present structure—as long as possible. While alternate patterns may be considered, any deviation from established rules that goes too far too fast will be met with resistance, as the family seeks to reestablish equilibrium. On the other hand, the family must be able to adapt to changing circumstances (a child grows into a young adult; mother goes to work outside the home; grandmother comes to live with them). It must have a sufficient range of patterns (including alternatives to call upon whenever necessary) and must be flexible enough to mobilize these new patterns in the face of impending change,

---

[2]Here some feminists take exception to Minuchin's insistence on family hierarchies, claiming that they run the risk of reinforcing sexual stereotypes. Luepnitz (1988) argues that Minuchin bases many of his ideas regarding family organization on the work of the influential functional sociologist Talcott Parsons (Parsons & Bales, 1955), who saw normal family life neatly organized according to gender roles, family functions, and hierarchical power. Parsons maintained that adaptation to society requires that husbands perform an "instrumental" role (e.g., making managerial decisions) in the family, and that wives perform "expressive" roles (caring for the family's emotional needs). Hare-Mustin, as quoted by Simon (1984), believes Minuchin himself models the male executive functions while working with families, in effect demanding that the father resume control of the family and exert leadership much as Minuchin leads and directs the therapeutic session. Colapinto (1991) contends that the stereotypic division of instrumental vs. expressive roles is not held up as an ideal by Minuchin, but rather that Minuchin believes all families need *some* kind of structure, *some* form of hierarchy, and *some* degree of differentiation between subsystems.

if members are to continue to exist as a family unit. The family must be able to transform itself in ways that meet new circumstances, while at the same time taking care not to lose the continuity that provides a frame of reference for its members.

Family Subsystems

As we pointed out in Chapter 4, families carry out their basic functions in part by organizing themselves into coexisting subsystems, often arranged in hierarchical order. Typically, family subsystem divisions are made according to gender (male/female), generation (parents/children), common interests (intellectual/social), or function (who is responsible for what chores). Beyond these more obvious patterns, various possibilities (older children vs. younger; boys vs. girls; parents vs. teenagers) spring up in most families.

Subsystems, then, are components of a family's structure they exist to carry out various family tasks necessary for the functioning of the overall family system. Each member may belong to several subgroups at the same time, and families are capable of organizing themselves into a limitless number of such units. Each person may have a differing level of power within different subgroups, may play different roles, may exercise different skills, and may engage in different interactions with members of other subsystems within the family. Complementarity of roles is a key here—as Minuchin (1974) points out, a child has to act like a son so his father can act like a father, but he may take on executive powers when he is alone with his younger brother.

Subsystems are defined by interpersonal *boundaries* and rules for membership; in effect, they regulate the amount of contact with other subsystems. Such boundaries determine who participates and what roles those participants will have in dealing with one another and with outsiders who are not included in the subsystem. They may be based on temporary alliances (mother and daughter go shopping together on Saturday afternoon) and may have rules concerning exclusion (fathers and brothers are unwelcome). Or they may be more enduring (based on generational differences in roles and interests between parents and children) with clearly defined boundaries separating the two generations (one watches public television documentaries, the other MTV). Subsystem organization within a family provides valuable training in developing a sense of self, in the process of honing interpersonal skills at different levels.

The spousal, parental, and sibling subsystems are the most prominent and important subsystems in the family. The strength and durability of the *spousal subsystem* in particular offers a key regarding family stability. How husband and wife learn to negotiate differences and eventually accommodate to one another's needs and develop complementary roles tells us a great deal about the likelihood of family stability and flexibility to change as future changing family circumstances demand.

While the arrival of children forces the couple to transform their system to now become a *parental subsystem,* grappling with new responsibilities, complementarity of roles remains essential, as the couple negotiates differences in parenting attitudes and styles. Those accommodations to one another's individual perspectives are apt to continue and get renegotiated as children grow and require different parental responses at different stages of their lives. It is crucial at the start and throughout parenting that, whatever the demands of child rearing and the efforts expended toward the evolvement of an effective parental subsystem, the parents continue to work at maintaining and strengthening their spousal subsystem, which is fundamental to family well-being.

The *sibling subsystem* offers the first experience of being part of a peer group and learning to support, cooperate, and protect (along with compete, fight with, and negotiate differences). Together, the children comprising this subsystem learn to deal with the parental subsystem in order to work out relationship changes commensurate with the developmental changes they are going through.

In a well-functioning family, all three subsystems operate in an integrated way to protect the differentiation, and thus the integrity, of the family system.

Boundary Permeability

The specific composition of any subsystem is not nearly as important as the clarity of its boundaries. Put another way, boundaries within a family vary in their flexibility or **permeability,** and that degree of accessibility helps determine the nature and frequency of contact between family members. *Clearly defined boundaries* between subsystems within a family help maintain separateness and at the same time emphasize belongingness to the overall family system. An ideal arrangement, the clarity enhances the family's overall well-being by providing support and easy access for communication and negotiation between subsystems whenever needed, while simultaneously encouraging independence and the freedom to experiment by the members of the separate subsystems. The autonomy of members is not sacrificed, but at the same time the boundaries remain flexible enough so that care, support, and involvement are available as needed. An important benefit of such clarity becomes apparent whenever the family attempts to make structural changes over time to accommodate to changing life circumstances.

Excessively *rigid or inflexible boundaries* lead to impermeable barriers between subsystems. In this case, the worlds of parents and children—the generational hierarchy—are separate and distinct; the members of neither subsystem are willing or able to enter into the other's world. With parents and children unable to alter or cross subsystem boundaries when necessary, autonomy may be maintained, but nurturance, involvement, and the easy exchange of affection with one another are typically missing. While the child in such a family may gain a sense of independence, it often comes at the price of feeling isolated from others and unsupported during critical times.

Diffuse boundaries are excessively blurred and indistinct, and thus easily intruded upon by other family members. Here, parents are too accessible and contact with their children may take the form of hovering and the invasion of privacy. Children run the risk of becoming too involved with their parents, and in the process failing to develop independent thinking and behaving or to learn the necessary skills for developing relationships outside the family. Because there is no clear generational hierarchy, adults and children may exchange roles easily, and a member's sense of self or personal identity becomes hard to establish for later adulthood. Here children may feel supported and cared for by parents, but it is often at the expense of feeling free to take independent (and possibly disapproved of) actions.

In a well-functioning family, clear boundaries give each member a sense of "I-ness" along with a group sense of "we" or "us." That is, each member retains his or her individuality but not at the expense of losing the feeling of belonging to a family. Most family systems fall somewhere along the continuum between **enmeshment** (diffuse boundaries) and **disengagement** (rigid boundaries) (Minuchin et al., 1967). Most families are neither totally enmeshed nor totally disengaged, although they may contain enmeshed or disengaged subsystems. Minuchin and Nichols (1993) describe a familiar, if troubled, middle-class family pattern in which a disengaged father is preoccupied with work and neglectful of his wife and children, and an enmeshed mother is overinvolved with her children, her closeness to them a substitute for closeness in a marriage.

Enmeshment refers to an extreme form of proximity and intensity in family interactions in which members are overconcerned and overinvolved in each other's lives. In extreme cases, the family's lack of differentiation between subsystems makes separation from the family an act of betrayal. Belonging to the family dominates all experiences at the expense of each member's self-development. Whatever is happening to one family member reverberates throughout the system. A child sneezes, his sister runs for the tissues, his mother reaches for the thermometer, and his father becomes anxious about sickness in the family.

Subsystem boundaries in enmeshed families are poorly differentiated, weak, and easily crossed. Children may act like parents and parental control may be ineffective. Excessive togetherness and sharing leads to a lack of separateness; members, overly alert and responsive to signs of distress, intrude on each other's thoughts and feelings. Members of enmeshed families place too high a value on family cohesiveness, to the extent that they yield autonomy and have little inclination to explore and master problems outside the safety of the family. As we indicated earlier in this chapter, enmeshment is common in psychosomatic families.

At the other extreme, members of disengaged families may function separately and autonomously but with little sense of family loyalty. Interpersonal distance is great, the members frequently lacking the capacity for interdependence or to request support from others when needed. Communication in such families is strained and guarded, and the family's protective functions are limited. When an individual family member is under stress, the enmeshed family responds with excessive speed and intensity while the disengaged family hardly seems to look up, offer emotional support, or even respond at all. As Minuchin (1974) illustrates, the parents in an enmeshed family may become enormously upset if a child does not eat dessert, while in a disengaged family they may feel unconcerned about the child's hatred of school.

Alignments, Power, and Coalitions

While boundaries are defined by how a family is organized, **alignments** are defined by the way family members join together or oppose one another in carrying out a family activity. **Power** within a family has to do with both authority (who is the decision maker) and responsibility (who carries out the decision). Thus, alignments refer to the emotional or psychological connections family members make with one another. Power, on the other hand, speaks to the relative influence of each family member on an operation's outcome.

Aponte and Van Deusin (1981) believe that every stroke of a family transaction makes a statement about boundaries, alignments, and power. As we have noted, the boundaries of a subsystem are the rules defining who participates and what roles they will play in the transactions or operations necessary to carry out a particular function. (For example, should the sex education of young children be carried out by father, mother, older siblings, or be a shared responsibility? Or should the task be left to the schools?) Alignments refer to how supportive or unsupportive of one another the players are in carrying out an operation. (For example, does father agree or disagree with his wife's disciplinary actions with the children?) Power is seldom absolute but is related to the context or situation. (For example, the mother may have considerable influence on her adolescent daughter's behavior at home but minimal influence over the daughter's social contacts outside the home.) Power is also related to the way family members actively or passively combine forces. (For example, the mother's authority depends on her husband's support and backing as well as on the acquiescence of her children.)

Certain alignments are considered by structuralists to be dysfunctional. In what Minuchin (1974) calls **triangulation,** each parent demands the child ally with him or her against the other parent. Whenever the child does side with one parent, however, the other views the alignment as an attack or betrayal and, in such a dysfunctional structure, the child is in a no-win situation. Every movement the child makes causes one or the other parent to feel ganged up on and assailed. Because the problems fail to be worked out between the parents, a third person is brought in (similar to Bowen's concept of triangles) and becomes part of the process taking place.

Coalitions (Minuchin, Rosman, & Baker, 1978) are alliances between specific family members against a third member (see photo). A *stable coalition* is a fixed and inflexible union (such as mother and son) that becomes a dominant part of the family's everyday functioning. A *detouring coalition* is one in which the pair hold a third family member responsible for their difficulties or conflicts with one another, thus decreasing the stress on themselves or their relationship.

Alignments, power, boundaries, and coalitions are interrelated phenomena within a family system. Power often results from alignments between members, and can be an important determinant of functional or dysfunctional living. Structuralists believe that power resulting from a strong parental alignment is often beneficial to child rearing and limit setting. On the other hand, coalitions between a parent and a child against the other parent can have an undermining effect on family functioning. Detouring, while it may give others the impression of family harmony, may often be destructive to maintaining clear boundaries.

Structuralists believe that for parents to achieve a desired outcome in the family, there must be (1) clearly defined *generational boundaries* so that parents together form a subsystem with executive power; (2) *alignments* between the parents on key issues, such as discipline; and (3) *rules* related to power and authority, indicating which of the parents will prevail if they disagree and whether the parents are capable of carrying out their wishes when they do agree. Note that strong generational

According to Minuchin, family coalitions frequently introduce stress into a family system, handicapping the functioning of individual members as well as the family as a whole. In this simulated family scene, the mother and younger daughter sit separately from the father and older daughter, suggesting a division within the family. Mother's whispered secret further strengthens her alliance with one child, while the other members appear to be out of touch with what is going on. Successful structural family therapy may produce role changes, clearer communication patterns, and a restructuring of the family organization.

boundaries also prohibit interference from grandparents as much as they prevent children from taking over parenting functions. Alignments must function properly or individuals will cross generational boundaries—go to Grandmother for permission if Mother says no—to get what they want.

Family Dysfunction

Rosenberg (1983) summarizes the structural position succinctly when he concludes that "when a family runs into difficulty, one can assume that it is operating within a dysfunctional structure" (p. 160). Perhaps the family, proceeding along normal developmental lines, has hit a snag in entering a new developmental stage or in negotiating a particular life cycle crisis such as the birth of another child, children leaving for college, or retirement. Perhaps the family members have become overinvolved or enmeshed with each other (parental behavior that seems supportive and loving to a preadolescent is experienced as suffocating and intrusive by a teenager). Or, at the other end of the continuum, perhaps we are dealing with the dilemma of disengagement (parents' detachment permits growth and encourages children's resourcefulness, but at the same time represents parents' unavailability and lack of support in time of crisis). Dysfunction suggests that the covert rules that govern family transactions have become (perhaps temporarily) inoperative or inappropriate and require renegotiation.

A dysfunctional family by definition has failed to fulfill its function of nurturing the growth of its members (Colapinto, 1991). In the Wiltwyck families (Minuchin et. al., 1967), typically burdened by severe external stressors brought about by poverty, five dysfunctional family structures were differentiated: (1) enmeshed families; (2) disengaged families; (3) families with a peripheral male; (4) families with noninvolved parents; and (5) families with juvenile parents. A sense of feeling overwhelmed and helpless was common to these families, often led by single mothers, who struggled to control or guide their delinquent children.

Just as the social context as stressor was apparent in the Wiltwyck population, so the inadequate internal responses to stress—the other component of the dysfunctional equation—played a key role for the Philadelphia working-class and middle-class families suffering from psychosomatic disorders (Colapinto, 1991). Here the problem stemmed from inflexibility, particularly the family's inability to confront and seek to modify those transactional patterns that had ceased to satisfy the needs of family members. The result was an inadequate and stereotypical family response to stress, as the family persisted in employing obsolete patterns as new situations arose. For example, a couple having negotiated a complementary relationship before the arrival of children, but one not allowing for much open conflict, failed to adapt readily to becoming parents, where a change from their implicit contract was in order due to differing circumstances. To cite another example, parents accustomed to dealing with young children were unable to adapt to growing teenagers who now demanded more autonomy. Fear of oneself or one's partner departing from established patterns often led to rigid repetition of failed patterns. Disengagement or enmeshment—avoiding contact with one another or continuous bickering—were both directed at circumventing change, thus failing to achieve conflict resolution. Overprotection of the sick child by the entire family helped cover up underlying family conflicts and tended to discourage the development of a sense of competence, maturity, or self-reliance on the part of the symptomatic child.

Minuchin (1974) reserves the label of *pathological* for those families who, when faced with a stressful situation, increase the rigidity of their transactional patterns and boundaries, thus preventing any further exploration of alternatives. Normal families, by way of contrast, adapt to life's inevitable stresses by preserving family continuity while remaining flexible enough to permit family restructuring.

STRUCTURAL FAMILY THERAPY

Structural therapeutic efforts are geared to the present and are based on the principle of action preceding understanding. That is, action leads to new experiences, to insight and understanding, to rearranged structures. Their major therapeutic thrust is to challenge the family's patterns of interaction, forcing the members to look beyond the symptoms of the identified patient in order to view all of their behavior within the context of family structures (the covert rules that govern the family's transactional patterns). As Minuchin and Nichols (1998) observe, in a marital relationship, for example, one partner's behavior is yoked to the other's. Their actions are codetermined, subject to reciprocal forces that support or polarize. The structural therapist's task is to disentangle the pair from their automatic yoked reactions, and in the process help each discover his or her individuality, power, and responsibility.

Structuralists offer the family leadership, direction, and encouragement to examine and discard rigid structures that no longer are functional and to make adaptive changes in structure as family circumstances and family developmental stages change. For example, changes in the relative positions of family members may be in order, such as more proximity between husband and wife or more distance between mother and son. Hierarchical relationships in which the parents customarily exercise authority may be redefined and made more flexible in some cases and reinforced in others. Alignments and coalitions may be explored, embedded conflicts acknowledged, alternative rules considered. To use an example offered by Colapinto (1982), a mother may be urged to abstain from intervening automatically whenever the interaction between her husband and son reaches a certain pitch, while father and son may be encouraged not to automatically abort an argument just because it upsets Mom. For structuralists, the most effective way to alter dysfunctional behavior and eliminate symptoms is to change the family's transactional patterns that maintain them.

Although they are not always so neatly separated in practice, structuralists typically organize their therapeutic efforts in the following order:

1. Joining and accommodating
2. Assessing family interactions
3. Monitoring dysfunctional sets
4. Restructuring transactional patterns

Joining and Accommodating

In an attempt to disarm family members who may be suspicious or fearful of being challenged or blamed, structuralists typically begin by adjusting to the family's affective style: in a constricted family to not be too demonstrative, in an expansive family to be open and use expressive movements. Each member is greeted by name and encouraged to participate, but the therapist does not insist on a response or confront silent or resistant members. The therapist shows respect for the family hierarchy by asking first for the parents' observations. (If the children were addressed first, the parents may feel the therapist is blaming them for family problems, and they will likely reject future therapist efforts as biased.) Nonthreatening, friendly, ready to help without being pushy, the structural therapist is at the same time adapting to the family organization, assimilating the family's language patterns, interactive style, and commonly used terms—and gaining a sense of family patterns and structures.

As a therapist, Minuchin (1974) describes himself as acting like a distant relative, **joining** a family system and respectfully **accommodating** to its style. As the therapist links with the family and begins to understand family themes and family myths, to sense a member's pain at being excluded or scapegoated, to distinguish which persons have open communication pathways between them and which closed, he or she is beginning to obtain a picture of the family hierarchical structure, subsystems operations, boundaries, coalitions, and so on.

Mimesis (Greek for "copy") refers to the process of joining the family by imitating the manner, style, affective range, or content of its communications in order to solidify the therapeutic alliance with them. The therapist might tell of personal experiences ("I have an uncle like that") or mimic a family member's behavior (taking off his coat, sitting in a particular position, playing with the baby). These efforts are sometimes spontaneous, sometimes planned; whatever the case, they often have the effect of increasing kinship with the family and building trust as the therapist becomes part of the system.

Joining, then, lets the family know that the therapist, a nonpermanent but concerned member, understands and is working with and for them in a common search for alternate ways of dealing with what has likely become a family impasse. In the process, the structural therapist is encouraging the family to feel secure enough to explore other, more effective, ways of interacting and solving problems together. Acknowledging their areas of pain or stress, the therapist lets them know that he or she will respond to them with sensitivity and thus it is safe for them to confront the distressing—and thus previously avoided—issues.

Affiliating with the family, the therapist might make *confirming statements* regarding what is positive about each member; this technique helps build self-esteem and may also allow other family members to see that person in a new light. Another way of confirming that the therapist is tuned in is to describe an obviously negative characteristic in one family member while at the same time "absolving" that individual of responsibility for the behavior. One effect may be to rebel or begin to seek changes against being controlled by the other person. Minuchin and Fishman (1981) give the following illustrations:

> To a child, the therapist might say: "You seem to be quite childish. How did your parents manage to keep you so young?" To an adult, the therapist could say: "You act very dependent on your spouse. What does she do to keep you incompetent?" (p. 34)

Through this technique, the person feels recognized in a problem area without feeling criticized or guilty or to blame about it. As a result, the dysfunctional behavior is more readily acknowledged by the person, rather than being denied or the individual becoming defensive. By identifying the dysfunction as interpersonal, the family is being prepared to think of their transactions in circular terms (instead of what were probably previous linear explanations) and to attend to the complementarity of family relations. In this simple, nonpathologizing way, the therapist also is subtly suggesting that the participants are capable of (structural) change if they work together to reprogram how they deal with one another—in a word, that they have the power to initiate a structural change in their transaction patterns.

Assessing Family Interactions

Assessment overlaps with joining the family. From the start, structuralists attempt to assess a family by attending primarily to its organizational structure and ongoing transaction patterns, paying special notice to the social context in which any dysfunctional behavior manifested itself. Their ultimate concerns in any family appraisal are the family's hierarchical organization, the ability of its subsystems to carry out their functions, the family's possible alignments and coalitions, the permeability of its current boundaries, and its pliability or rigidity in meeting the needs of individual members as circumstances command. Structuralists are interested in how flexibly the family adapts to developmental changes as well as unexpected situational crises, and how well—and how easily—family members join together to resolve conflict.

Overall, the thrust of the assessment effort, from the initial session onward, is to evaluate the family's ability to change obsolete or no longer workable interactive patterns within the family, helping the family replace these outmoded patterns with ones more consistent with ongoing family development. However the major purpose of the early assessment, for the structuralists, is not so much to diagnose family weaknesses as it is to develop a *road map* for entering the family, adjust to its customary style of dealing with problems, and once inside, plan restructuring interventions.

Assessment is an integral and ongoing part of structural family therapy. Immediately upon joining the family—sometimes before meeting them, based on intake sheet information—the therapist is forming hypotheses about the family's structural arrangement. These early hunches, subject to refinement and revision, help guide early probing into the family's organization. What part of the system appears to be underfunctioning? Why, and how badly, has the system broken down? Why now? Which family interactive patterns seem especially problematic? What latent adaptive structures can the family call upon from their past efforts to cope with crises? These and similar questions are likely to occur to the structural therapist experiencing the family's transactions, as he or she begins to form a tentative diagnosis of family functioning.

Having joined the family, structuralists are likely to want to learn about coalitions, affiliations, the nature of family conflict, and the ways in which this family resolves conflict. One technique is to direct their attention to the family's current organization, which they diagram in graphic form in order to map out relationship patterns within the family. Just as family systems therapists, consistent with a transgenerational theory, utilize genograms to chart family relationships, extending back at least three generations, structuralists use family diagramming to depict a family's current transactional patterns. While the former sought clues regarding the family's intergenerational influences, the latter concern themselves with conveying information, through lines and spatial arrangements, about the family's current organizational structure, boundaries, and behavioral sequences.

Structuralists make use of a simple pictorial device called a *structural map* to formulate hypotheses about those areas where the family functions well and other areas where dysfunction may be occurring. Used as an assessment device, **family mapping** often helps provide an organizing schema for understanding complex family interactive patterns, especially which particular subsystem is involved in perpetuating a problem, and as such may be invaluable in therapeutic planning.

As Minuchin and Fishman (1981) point out:

> The family map indicates the position of family members vis-à-vis one another. It reveals coalitions, affiliations, explicit and implicit conflicts, and the ways family

members group themselves in conflict resolution. It identifies family members who operate as detourers of conflict and family members who function as switchboards. The map charts the nurturers, healers, and scapegoaters. Its delineation of the boundaries between subsystems indicates what movement there is and suggests possible areas of strength or dysfunction. (p. 69)

Figure 9.1 illustrates some common symbols structuralists use to delineate the clarity of family boundaries (clear, diffuse, rigid), subsystem operations, and family transactional styles. Figure 9.2 offers two examples of the use of structural mapping in depicting family conflict. The upper figure exemplifies a familiar detouring coalition within a family in which parents cope with direct conflict with one another by directing the problem they are having onto their child. The lower figure, again familiar, is a simple notation by a structural therapist of an intergenerational coalition in a family with diffuse mother-child boundaries.

Mapping offers an almost endless number of possible combinations for picturing family boundaries, alliances, affiliations, coalitions, detouring strategies, and so on. For example, family enmeshment may be illustrated by the symbol of overinvolvement; a coalition of several members against another can be shown by brackets. Family mapping, although a simple shorthand device, has two especially useful purposes: it graphically describes how the family is organized, and also helps detect the family subunit requiring restructuring (Umbarger, 1983). Figure 9.3 diagrams an overinvolved parent-child bond as well as a family coalition against the other parent. Structural maps are created throughout therapy, and are revised or discarded as new family information becomes available.

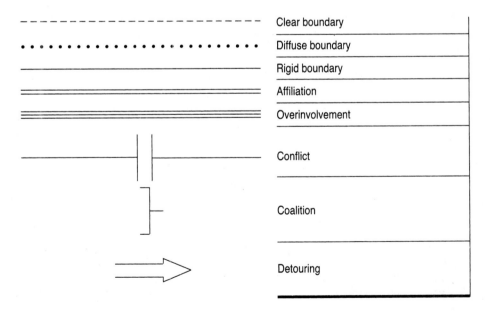

Figure 9.1   Minuchin's symbols for family mapping
Source: Minuchin, 1974, p. 53

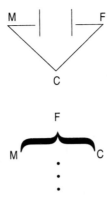

Figure 9.2   The effect of stress on the subsystem boundaries o¯ a family. In the top diagram, a father (F) and mother (M), both stressed at work came home and criticize each other, but then detour their conflict by attacking the child (C). In the lower figure, the husband criticizes the wife, who seeks a coalition with the child against the father. Note the rigid cross-generational subsystem of mother and child; both have the effect of excluding the father. Minuchin refers to this as a cross-generational dysfunctional pattern.

Source: Minuchin, 1974, p. 61

Figure 9.3   This diagram shows a closed-family-unit boundary with an overinvolved mother and son comprising the parental sybsystem. Between them and the other children is a rigid boundary, yet apparently under enough control so that all are in a coalition against the father.

Source: Umbarger, 1983, p. 36.

Monitoring Family Dysfunctional Sets

Monitoring and helping modify troubled or problematic transaction patterns is the crux of the structural intervention process. Once structuralists have gained entrance into the family, they begin to probe the family structure, looking for areas of flexibility and possible change. For example, a family has come for therapy because the teenage daughter is shy, withdrawn, and has difficulties in her social life. The therapist may observe for diagnostic purposes how the family enters the therapy room: The girl sits next to her mother and they move their two chairs close together. When the therapist asks what the problem is, the mother answers, ignoring her daughter's attempts to add her thoughts on the matter. The mother makes comments that suggest she has too intimate a knowledge of her adolescent daughter's personal life, more knowledge than is usual. Within a few minutes after starting, the structural therapist makes the first intervention, asking the mother and father to change chairs. Structural therapy has begun: As the father is brought into the picture, the family flexibility is being tested; with the implication of pathology in the mother-daughter dyad, the family's reason for seeking therapy for the teenager is already being reframed or relabeled as a problem with a larger focus.

Two structural techniques are operating in this example. **Boundary making** represents an effort to create greater psychological distance between the enmeshed mother and daughter, and by bringing the marginalized father closer, to begin to modify the family's customary transactional patterns. The daughter, in turn, gains a greater chance of developing more independence as the diffuse boundary with her mother is starting to be clarified. The strengthened parental subsystem increases the likelihood of increased differentiation between parents and children in the family. At the same time, the therapist is using the technique of **unbalancing**—attempting to change the hierarchical relationship between members of the parental subsystem, as the father takes on an expanded role in the family. By seeming to side with the father, the therapist is upsetting the family homeostasis and making an initial move to change preexisting family patterns by first unbalancing and then realigning the system. In boundary making, then, the therapist tries to change the distance between subsystems; in unbalancing, the goal is to change the hierarchical relationships of the members of a subsystem (Minuchin & Fishman, 1981).

Through **tracking,** the structural therapist adopts symbols of the family's life gathered from members' communication (such as life themes, values, significant family events) and deliberately uses them in conversation with the family. This effort to confirm that the therapist values what family members say, without soliciting the information, is also a way of influencing their later transactional patterns; Minuchin (1974) calls this "leading by following." Tracking a particular family theme may also provide clues as to family structure. For example, in working with an enmeshed family, Minuchin noted the father's statement that he disliked closed doors. Tracking the door issue, Minuchin discovered that the children were not permitted to close the doors of their rooms, that a brother slept in his older sister's room, and that the sex lives of the parents were curtailed because their own bedroom door remained open. Later, Minuchin was able to use the metaphor of the doors to help the family clarify their boundaries. Thus, tracking can be used as a restructuring strategy.

An **enactment** is a staged effort by the therapist to bring an outside family conflict into the session so that the family members can demonstrate how they deal with it and the therapist can observe the sequence and begin to map out a way to modify their interaction and create structural changes. Using this technique, the therapist actively creates a scenario during a session in which the players act out their dysfunctional transactions. To use an example offered by Rosenberg (1983), a mother complained that her 2-year-old daughter had tantrums and embarrassed her in front of grandparents, on buses, and in other situations. The daughter remained well behaved during the early sessions despite (or maybe because of) her mother's insistence that she engaged in this awful behavior away from the therapist. During the third or fourth session, when the child asked for gum, Rosenberg saw his chance: he asked the mother not to give her the gum because lunchtime was approaching.

As the child's whimper turned to crying, to begging, and finally to falling on the floor and undressing herself—and as the mother considered giving in—Rosenberg encouraged the mother to hold firm, despite the by-now deafening noise. More than a half hour later, the child came to a whimpering stop; she seemed fine, although both mother and therapist were exhausted! However, the mother had asserted her control as a result of the enactment, thus learning she could be competent and more resolute than she had previously thought. From a structural viewpoint, the child's problematic behavior was redefined in transactional terms, the generational boundaries were reestablished, effective alternative transactional patterns were introduced, the proper hierarchical order was put into place (mother was again in charge), and the daughter, whose tantrums at home ceased shortly thereafter, was comfortable in knowing that her mother could handle her.

Structuralists deliberately take on a decisive role with families, since they view the therapist, rather than any techniques or interpretations or prescriptions, as the ultimate instrument of change (Colapinto, 1991). Therapeutically, they actively challenge the rigid, repetitive transactional patterns by which some families unsuccessfully attempt to organize themselves and cope with stress, and then, by deliberately "unfreezing" these patterns and unbalancing the system, create an opportunity for the family to structurally reorganize. Generally, this therapeutic effort involves a push for clearer boundaries, increased flexibility in family interactions, particularly at transition points in family life, and most important, modification of the dysfunctional structure.

Here it is important to note that while essentially focused on family transactional patterns, structuralists nevertheless make certain they do not lose track of what is happening to each individual family member; as Minuchin, Rosman, and Baker (1978) caution, therapists would be committing a serious error by "denying the individual while enthroning the family" (p. 9). That is, while they believe problematic or symptomatic behavior typically arises when families, whether enmeshed or disengaged, rigidly resist change, they remain alert to the fact that certain individuals may bring physical, emotional, behavioral, or learning disabilities to the family situation, and that these must be accommodated to in facilitating family restructuring.

Any dysfunctional hierarchical issues within the family typically are explored, since structuralists insist that functional families require parents to be in charge of their children and require differentiation between subsystems. Parents together must form and maintain an executive coalition, a parental subsystem; they have the responsibility to care for and protect and help socialize their children. They also have rights to make decisions (selection of schools, relocation) they believe are best for the survival of the overall family system. However, as the children grow and their needs change, the parental subsystem must change accordingly, sharing opportunities for decision making and self-direction with the children. Disengaged families need to loosen their boundaries and increase family interaction. Enmeshed families need to develop clear yet flexible boundaries to encourage individuation and distinct differentiation between subsystems.

Siblings too must develop a working subsystem of peers; within the sibling system they must learn to negotiate, cooperate, compete, make friends, deal with enemies, and develop a sense of belonging. Spouses, aside from being parents, must also receive support from one another and together develop a subsystem that serves as a model for expressing affection, helping each other deal with stress, and dealing with conflict as equals. If there is a major dysfunction within the spousal subsystem, it will likely reverberate throughout the family (Minuchin & Fishman, 1981).

Minuchin (1974) conceives of family pathology as resulting from the development of *dysfunctional sets*. Dysfunctional sets are the family reactions, developed in response to stress, that are repeated without modification whenever there is family conflict. A husband experiencing stress at work comes home and shouts at his wife. The wife counterattacks, escalating the conflict that continues without change until one partner abandons the field. Both parties experience a sense of nonresolution. In another example, a mother verbally attacks an adolescent son, the father takes his side, and the younger children seize the opportunity to join in and pick on their older brother. All family members become involved and various coalitions develop, but the family organization remains the same and the dysfunctional sets will be repeated in the next trying situation.

Restructuring Transactional Patterns

Structuralists assume that any family seeking treatment is experiencing some stress that has overloaded the system's adaptive and coping mechanisms, handicapping the optimum functioning of its members in the process. Consequently, they set themselves the task of helping families rearrange their organization—restructuring the system that governs its transactions—so that the family will function more effectively and the growth potential of each member will be maximized. Restructuring involves changes in family rules and realignments, changes in the patterns that support certain undesirable behaviors, and changes in the sequences of interaction. We have noted a number of techniques structuralists employ to facilitate structural changes—enactments, boundary making, unbalancing. The therapist may also increase the *intensity* of a remark (by heightening its affective component—"It's essential that you as parents agree about this," by frequently repeating it in different contexts—to a child resisting growing up: "But how *old* are you," or in regard to different transactions) in order to highlight a particular transaction and get the message across to family members.

One particularly useful technique, **reframing,** changes the original meaning of an event or situation, placing it in a new context in which an equally plausible explanation is possible. The idea is to relabel what occurs in order to provide a more constructive perspective, thereby altering the way the event or situation is viewed. As used by structuralists, reframing is directed toward relabeling the problem as a function of the family structure. Typically, within the context of an enactment, the therapist first redefines a presenting problem. For example, in the case of an adolescent daughter's self-starvation, the anorectic girl is labeled as "stubborn" and not "sick," forcing the family members to reconsider their earlier view that she is ill and thus not responsible for what is occurring. Giving new meaning to her behavior creates a new context that can ultimately change their transactional patterns. The fact of the daughter's not eating has not changed, only the meaning attributed to that behavior. Not intended to deliberately deceive, reframing rather is used by structuralists and other family therapists (especially strategic therapists) to change family perspectives and ultimately to change family behavior patterns on the basis of the new options and alternatives.

Structural interventions frequently *increase the stress* (another restructuring technique) on the family system—perhaps even create a family crisis that unbalances family homeostasis—but they also open the way for transformation of the family structure. Now the family has no choice but to face the chronically avoided conflict. In an enmeshed family system, for example, members often believe the family as a whole can neither withstand change nor adapt to it; as a consequence, the system demands that certain members change (develop symptoms) in order to maintain the dysfunctional homeostasis. When the danger level of family stress is approached, the symptom bearer is activated as part of a conflict avoidance maneuver; the family system reinforces the continuance of the symptoms that help maintain the system's balance and status quo. It is the therapist's job to make everyone aware, often through reframing, that the problem belongs and pertains to the family, not an individual; that the implementation of new functional sets must replace the habitual repetition of the dysfunctional ones; and that the family, having located and identified the problem, together can resolve the underlying conflict by making the necessary structural modifications.

The therapeutic tactics employed by Minuchin and his associates are often dramatic and at times theatrical. Like a stage director, he enjoys setting up a situation, creating a scenario for enactment, assigning a task to the family, and requiring the members to function according to the new sets he has imposed. For example, in treating an anorectic adolescent, self-starving and refusing to eat, Minuchin arranges to meet the family at lunch for the first session (Minuchin, Rosman, & Baker, 1978). He creates such an enactment deliberately, to foster a crisis around eating and to experience what the family members are experiencing. He observes the parents pleading, demanding, cajoling, becoming desperate, and feeling defeat. He watches the adolescent girl demonstrate hopelessness and helplessness pathetically asserting through her refusal to eat that she has always given in to her parents at the expense of herself, but will do so no longer. While the daughter has been labeled as the problem, Minuchin, reframing, helps the family see that **anorexia nervosa** is a diagnosis of a family system, not simply the adolescent's symptomatic behavior. All the family members are locked into a futile pattern of interaction that has become the center of their lives; each member has a stake in maintaining the disorder. In turn, the syndrome plays an important role in maintaining family homeostasis. Structural family therapy helps each person in the family to recognize the syndrome and take responsibility for contributing to it. By creating a family crisis, Minuchin forces the family to change the system, substituting more functional interactions.

Typical of Minuchin's directive, unyielding, crisis-provoking approach is his insistence in this case that the parents force the emaciated girl to eat. They coax, cajole, threaten, yell, and finally stuff food down her throat until their daughter collapses in tears. Minuchin believes she will now eat. As he later explains it:

> The anorectic is obsessed with her hopelessness, inadequacy, wickedness, ugliness. I incite an interpersonal conflict that makes her stop thinking about how terrible she is and start thinking about what bastards her parents are. At that demonstration, I said to the parents, "Make her eat," and when they did she had to deal with them as people. Previously, the parents had been saying "We control you because we love you." In the position I put them in, they were finally saying "God damn it, you eat!" That freed her. She could then eat or not eat; she could be angry at them as clearly delineated figures. (Malcolm, 1978, p. 78)

With this approach, Minuchin has been able to show that the anorectic symptom is embedded in the faulty family organization. Changing that organization eliminates the potentially fatal symptom. As the family members begin to experience themselves and each other differently, the stage is set for new transactional patterns to emerge. The emergence of new structures is intended to aid the identified patient along with the family as a whole. From this viewpoint, a symptomatic person's presenting problem is embedded in the family's dysfunctional rules; as inappropriate or constricting rules are replaced, and family members are released from stereotyped positions and functions, there no longer is need for the symptom to maintain family homeostasis, and it becomes unnecessary (Colapinto, 1982). As a result of family reorganization, future symptom development should become less likely as the opportunity is increased for all members, and the family as a whole, to enhance their growth potential.

SUMMARY

The structural approach in family therapy is primarily associated with Salvador Minuchin and his colleagues, first at the Wiltwyck School and later at the Philadelphia Child Guidance Center. Systems-based, structural family theory focuses on the active, organized wholeness of the family unit and the ways in which the family organizes itself through its transactional patterns. In particular, the family's subsystems, boundaries, alignments, and coalitions are studied in an effort to understand its structure. Dysfunctional structures point to the covert rules governing family transactions that have become inoperative or in need of renegotiation.

Structural family therapy is geared to present-day transactions and gives higher priority to action than to insight or understanding. All behavior, including symptoms in the identified patient, is viewed within the context of family structure. Structural interventions are active, carefully calculated, even manipulative efforts to alter rigid, outmoded, or unworkable structures.

By joining the family and accommodating to its style, structuralists gain a foothold to assess the members' way of dealing with problems and with each other, ultimately helping them to change dysfunctional sets and rearrange or realign the family organization. Family mapping provides a simple observational technique for charting the family's transactional patterns.

Enactments (having the family demonstrate typical conflict situations in the therapy session), *boundary making* (realigning inappropriate or outdated boundaries), *unbalancing* (supporting one member to interfere with family homeostasis), and *reframing* (the therapist's relabeling or redefining a problem as a function of the family's structure) are therapeutic techniques frequently used to bring about a transformation of the family structure. The ultimate goal is to restructure the family's transactional rules by developing more appropriate boundaries between subsystems and strengthening the family's hierarchical order.

10

Strategic Models

Strategic and strategic-related therapies derive from the work of the Palo Alto research group projects of 1952–1962 on family communication described earlier in the text. The seminal ideas of Gregory Bateson, Don Jackson, Jay Haley, John Weakland, Paul Watzlawick, and their associates helped shape the family therapy field and are fundamental to how practitioners view family relationships even today. Feedback loops, the redundancy principle, double binds, family rules, marital quid pro quo, family homeostasis—all are such familiar and basic concepts that young family therapists today might assume they were always known. They were not; they are part of **communication theory,** which emerged when Bateson and his colleagues set out to study communication patterns in families with schizophrenic members.

Immeasurably influential in the founding of the family therapy movement, communication theory as it first took form in the late 1950s offered an intriguing alternative to the established linear ways of conceptualizing psychopathology. For example, a psychoanalytic or psychodynamic view of conflict between a mother and adolescent daughter might hold that the mother is unconsciously identifying with her rebellious child and perhaps projecting unresolved problems from her own early childhood or adolescence onto her. The daughter, defiant, conflicted, and with an incompletely formed sense of personal identity, may be introjecting many of her mother's characteristics while simultaneously struggling to forge her own identity. In unidirectional fashion, each player holds the other responsible for her misery.

However, it is entirely possible, argued the communication theorists in the early days of family therapy, to understand this conflict not in terms of the separate issues of two persons, but as a dysfunctional relationship that manifests itself, among other ways, in a faulty communication process. It was that damaged or faulty or poorly developed *process,* and not the *content* of their dispute that required inquiry and ultimate repair.

If we adopt the latter cybernetically based view, notice how the emphasis shifts

- from the past to the present;

217

- from analyzing the inner dynamics of each individual to studying their recursive pattern of interaction and communication;
- from seeing pathology in one or both members of a family to understanding how a dysfunctional relationship pattern becomes established between *any two persons* and, through repetition, represents their characteristic way of relating to each other.

The pair's recurring struggle becomes circular: "I nag because you defy me." "No, Mom, it's the other way around; I defy you because you nag." In this way of conceptualizing their troubled exchange, attention is paid to the question of *what* is occurring rather than *why* it is occurring—to the ongoing process between and among people within a system and the ways in which they interact, define, and redefine their relationships, and not to drawing inferences about each participant's intrapsychic conflicts. Communication patterns—the style or manner in which information is exchanged (that is, coded and encoded) within a family, the precision, clarity, or degree of ambiguity of the transmission, and the behavioral or pragmatic effect of the communication—as much as the content of what is communicated, help determine those relationships.

The major impact of this nonlinear epistemology was to recast human problems as *interactional* and *situational* (specific to a particular time and place). In shifting the locus of pathology from the individual to the social context and the interchange between individuals, these family therapy pioneers were not denying that intrapsychic mechanisms influence individual functioning. Rather, they were giving greater credence to the power of family rules to govern interactive behavior; to them, a breakdown in individual or family functioning follows from a breakdown in rules. This paradigmatic shift in thinking led inevitably to reshaping the appropriate unit of study for the therapist; the observation of exchanges between people became more relevant than the process of drawing difficult-to-validate inferences regarding the character or personality deficits of an individual (Greenberg, 1977). To this day, the strategic therapist's primary way of viewing problems is to attend to the family's *sequence of interactions* and its *hierarchy of interactions* (Keim, 1998).

In the mother-daughter situation just described, according to communication theorists, the attempt to determine cause and effect is pointless, irrelevant, and indeed, incorrect. The mother is not the cause of her daughter's behavior, nor is the daughter causing her mother's behavior. Both are caught up in a reverberating system, a chain reaction that feeds back on itself. Communication theorists argued that this circular interaction continues because each participant imposes her own **punctuation**; each arbitrarily believes that what she says is caused by what the other person says. In a sense, such serial punctuations between family members resemble the dialogue of children quarreling: "You started it!" ("I'm only reacting to what you did.") "No, you started it first!" and so on. As Weakland (1976) contends, it is meaningless to search for a starting point in a conflict between two people because it is a complex, repetitive interaction, not a simple, linear, cause-and-effect situation with a clear beginning and end.

Once considered iconoclastic if not radical, this view of redundant patterns of communication within the family as offering clues to family dysfunction provided a linguistic leap forward for the emerging field. While its early view of the therapist as an authoritative expert manipulating families to change has become largely out of fashion today (replaced by the collaborating therapist without fixed ideas of how the family should change), the communication perspective itself has undergone considerable revision as it has evolved over four decades; current proponents also can be considered to represent the strategic approach. For clarity of presentation, however, we have separated four outlooks: the original Mental Research Institute (MRI) interactional view, the brief therapy principles and therapeutic procedures that characterize current MRI activities, the strategic therapy refinements advanced primarily by Jay Haley and Cloé Madanes, and the strategic-related efforts developed in Milan, Italy, by Mara Selvini-Palazzoli and her associates. The last group's labors, much of which has evolved in the social constructionist direction, are discussed more fully in Chapter 11.

Efficiency and technical parsimony are the hallmark of these models; all are change-oriented, brief in duration, and view families in nonpathological terms. All four approaches involve active therapists who tailor their interventions rather specifically to a family's presenting complaint and terminate therapy as soon as that complaint is resolved. Their specific aim is to help the family resolve its presenting problem; they are less concerned with promoting personal growth or working through any underlying family emotional issues or teaching families specific problem-solving skills (Shoham, Rohrbaugh, & Patterson, 1995).

While there are noteworthy differences in the three approaches, we group them together because all represent, in varying degrees of refinement, elaborations on the theme that therapists are responsible for change and can initiate interventions to change problematic or maladaptive behavior without attending to why that behavior occurred in the first place.

MRI INTERACTIONAL FAMILY THERAPY

Founded by Don Jackson in 1959, and initially with a small staff consisting of social worker Virginia Satir and psychiatrist Jules Riskin, the Mental Research Institute in Palo Alto at first existed side by side with the neighboring Bateson Project. Both had grants underwriting their efforts at studying schizophrenics and their families. When the Bateson team ended its research endeavors in 1962, Haley, Weakland, and for a brief time Bateson himself joined the MRI as research associates, along with psychologists Paul Watzlawick and Arthur Bodin, and psychiatrist Richard Fisch. A number of other prominent family therapists—John Bell, Carlos Sluzki, Cloé Madanes, and Steve deShazer come to mind—have been affiliated with this outstanding training center at one time or another over the years.

Developing a Communication Paradigm

In the decade ending not long after Jackson's death in 1968, the theoretical groundwork for the **interactional approach** of the MRI was laid, based largely on ideas derived from general systems theory, cybernetics, and information theory. Moving beyond schizophrenics and their families, these researchers zeroed in on all family interaction sequences in an effort to understand how faulty communication patterns might lead to family dysfunction. Watzlawick, Beavin, and Jackson's (1967) *Pragmatics of Human Communication* is considered the classic pioneering text in the communication field, drawing the attention of family therapists to the need for the simultaneous study of *semantics* (the clarity of meaning between what is said and received), *syntax* (the pattern as well as manner or style in which information is transmitted), and *pragmatics* (the behavioral effects or consequences of communication). These authors presented a series of axioms regarding the interpersonal nature of communication:

- *All behavior is communication at some level.*

Just as one cannot not behave, so one cannot not communicate. The wife who complains in utter frustration that her husband "refuses to communicate" with her but instead stares at the television set all evening is responding too literally to his failure to talk to her. On a nonverbal level, she is receiving a loud and clear message that he is rejecting her, withdrawing from her, may be angry or bored with her, wants distance from her, and so on.

- *Communication may occur simultaneously at many levels*—gesture, body language, tone of voice, posture, intensity—in addition to the content of what is said.

In some cases, the message at one level contradicts one at another level. People can say one thing and mean another, modifying, reinforcing, or contradicting what they have just said. In other words, they are both communicating ("How are you?") and at another level communicating about their communications ("I do not really expect you to answer, nor do I especially want to know the answer, unless you say you are fine"). All communication takes place at two levels—the surface or content level and a second level called **metacommunication,** which qualifies what is said on the first level. Problems may arise when a message at the first level ("Nice to see you") is contradicted by a facial expression or voice tone that communicates another message ("How can I make a quick getaway from this boring person?") at the second level.

- *Every communication has a content (report) and a relationship (command) aspect.*

Every communication does more than convey information; it also defines the relationship between communicants. For example, the husband who announces "I'm hungry" is offering information but also, more important, is telling his wife that he expects her to do something about it by preparing dinner. He is thus making a statement of his perceived rights in the relationship; he expects his wife to take action based on his statement. The way his wife responds tells him whether she is willing to go along with his *definition of the relationship* or wants to engage in what could be a struggle to redefine it ("It's your turn to make the dinner tonight" or "Let's go out to a restaurant tonight" or "I'm not hungry yet").

- *Relationships are defined by command messages.*

These messages constitute regulating patterns for stabilizing relationships and defining family rules. In operation, the rules preserve family homeostasis. In a family, when a teenager announces she is pregnant, or parents decide to get a divorce, or a handicapped child is born, or a family member becomes schizophrenic, it has an effect similar to flinging open a window when the home heating system has been warmed to the desired temperature. The family goes to work to reestablish its balance.

- *Relationships may be described as symmetrical or complementary.*

If it is a relationship based on equality the interactive pattern is **symmetrical;** if the context of the behavioral exchange is oppositional, the pattern is **complementary.** In the former, participants mirror each other's behavior; if A boasts, B boasts more grandly, causing A to boast still further, and so on in this one-upmanship game. By definition, complementary relationships are based on inequality and the maximization of differences. In this form of reciprocal interaction, one partner (traditionally the male) takes the "one-up" position and the other (traditionally the female) assumes the submissive "one-down" position. However, despite appearances, these positions need not be taken as an indication of their relative strength or weakness or power to influence the relationship.

- *Symmetrical relationships run the risk of becoming competitive.*

In this case, each partner's actions influence the reactions of his or her partner in a spiraling effect called **symmetrical escalation.** Quarrels may get out of hand and become increasingly vicious as a nasty jibe is met with a nastier retort, which prompts the first person to become even more mean and ill-tempered, and so on. Squabbling partners may continually vie for ascendance over one another, neither willing to back down nor to concede a point. (In one Woody Allen movie, an exchange between a bickering couple goes something like this: "The Atlantic is the best ocean"; "You're crazy—the Pacific is a much better ocean"; "You're the one who's crazy and doesn't know what he's talking about"; and so on.) Clearly, in this transaction, the content of the argument is meaningless; it's the escalating conflict that is notable. The process of the exchange rather than its content defines the relationship.

- *Complementary communication inevitably involves one person who assumes a superior position and another who assumes an inferior one (a bossy wife, a submissive husband, or vice versa).*

One partner's behavior complements the other's; if A is assertive, B becomes submissive, encouraging A to greater assertiveness, demanding still more submissiveness from B, and so on.

- *Each person punctuates a sequence of events in which he or she is engaged in different ways.*

Such punctuations organize behavioral events taking place into each participant's view of cause and effect and thus are vital to ongoing interactions.

- *Problems develop and are maintained within the context of redundant interactive patterns and recursive feedback loops.*

Haley, who had been a graduate student in communication when first recruited for the Bateson project, underscored the struggle for power and control in every relationship that is inherent in the messages that sender and receiver exchange.

Who defines the relationship? Will that person attempt to turn it into a symmetrical or complementary one? Who decides who decides? Observe a couple discussing how to allocate expenditures, or what television program to watch, or who will answer the telephone, balance the checkbook, go to the refrigerator to get a snack, or pick up the dirty socks and underwear from the bedroom floor, and in each of these see if you do not learn a great deal about how the partners define their relationship.

Paradoxical Communication

The communication theorists were the first to point out that there is no such thing as a simple message. People continually send and receive a multiplicity of messages by both verbal and nonverbal channels, and every message may be qualified or modified by another message on another level of abstraction (Weakland, 1976). Not infrequently, the receiver can become confused when contradictions appear between what is said and what is expressed in tone or gesture.

A double-bind message is a particularly destructive form of such a **paradoxical injunction.** As we described it in Chapter 5, a double-bind message is communicated when one person, especially someone in a powerful position, issues an injunction to another that simultaneously contains two levels of messages or demands that are logically inconsistent and contradictory, producing a paradoxical situation for the recipient. In addition, the person receiving the paradoxical message is unable to avoid the incongruity or to comment on the impossibility of meeting its requirements, resulting in confusion.

Paradoxical injunctions are forms of communication that must be obeyed but that must be disobeyed to be obeyed! Two conditions typically must exist: (1) the participants must have a close complementary relationship; and (2) the recipient of the injunction cannot sidestep or otherwise avoid responding to the communication or metacommunication. Consider the following injunction from a person in a position of authority:

IGNORE THESE INSTRUCTIONS

To comply with the instructions, one must *not* follow instructions, since one message denies or negates the other ("I order you to disobey me"). Unable to discriminate which order or level of message to respond to, the recipient nevertheless is called upon to make some response. He or she is thus caught in a bind, being called upon to make a response but doomed to failure with whatever response is chosen. Although initially speculated to be the type of paradox that may be responsible for schizophrenia in a child who repeatedly receives such double-bind communications, it is now assumed that double binding, still considered damaging, may exist at times in all families.[1] Admittedly a linear construct, the double-bind concept (Bateson, Jackson, Haley, & Weakland, 1956) nevertheless was truly groundbreaking and heralded a breakthrough in the psychotherapy field by providing a new language and set of assumptions regarding relationships reflected in communication patterns to account for symptomatic behavior.

Therapeutic Assumptions

Led primarily by the innovative thinking of Paul Watzlawick (Watzlawick, 1978; Watzlawick, 1984; Watzlawick, Weakland, & Fisch, 1974), the MRI therapeutic model emphasizes that, ironically, the solutions people use attempting to alleviate a problem often contribute to the problem's maintenance or even its exacerbation. In this view, problems may arise from some ordinary life difficulty, perhaps coping with a transition such as the birth of an infant or an older child going off to school for the first time. Most families handle such transitions with relative ease, although occasionally the difficulty turns into a problem, particularly when mishandled or allowed to remain unresolved while the family persists in applying the same "solution" despite its previous failure to eliminate the difficulty. Ultimately the original difficulty escalates into a problem "whose eventual size and nature may have little apparent similarity to the original difficulty" (Fisch, Weakland, & Segal, 1982, p. 14).

In a pragmatic, therapist-directed approach, the task in such situations is to break into the family's repetitive but negatively self-perpetuating cycle. Confronted with family members engaged in repetitive and often mutually destructive behavior patterns, the therapist wants to know what makes the behavior persist, and what he or she must do to change it (Watzlawick, Weakland, & Fisch, 1974). First, the therapist must carefully delineate the problem in clear and concrete terms. Next, solutions previously attempted by the family must be scrutinized. The therapist is now prepared to define, again as precisely and concretely as necessary, just what change is sought, before implementing a strategy or therapeutic plan for achieving change (Watzlawick, 1978). As a general rule, the interactional therapist is seeking ways to change outmoded family rules, reveal hidden personal agendas, and modify or attempt to extinguish paradoxical communication patterns.

One especially useful set of concepts introduced by Watzlawick, Weakland, and Fisch (1974) concerns the level of change sought by the therapist. **First-order changes** are superficial behavioral changes within a system that do not change the structure of the system itself. These changes are apt to be linear and little more than cosmetic or perhaps simply a reflection of a couple's good intentions—for example, not to raise their voices and argue anymore. These first-order changes are likely to

---

[1]The double-bind situation is no longer believed to be the cause of schizophrenia, although it remains a historically significant formulation in that it drew attention to the possible role of family communication patterns in developing and maintaining family dysfunction. Today it is assumed that many families engage in such flawed communication at times; perhaps this is excessively so in families with severe but unacknowledged interpersonal conflict. Having lost its original pathological referent to schizophrenia, the double-bind concept is currently used loosely to refer to a variety of interactive communication patterns whose messages leave the receiver confused.

be short-lived; even if the symptom is removed—the couple tries to control their quarreling—the underlying systemic rules governing the interaction between them have not changed and the cease-fire is likely to be violated sooner or later.

Second-order changes require a fundamental revision of the system's structure and function. Here the therapist moves beyond merely helping remove the symptom, also striving to help the family alter their systemic interaction pattern—not just calling a halt to fighting, but changing the rules of the family system and as a result reorganizing the system so that it reaches a different level of functioning. If the therapy is successful, the old rules are discarded as obsolete; as a result the family may become temporarily confused, but then attempts to reconstitute itself in a new way.

According to Watzlawick (1978), therapy must accomplish second-order changes (a change in viewpoint, often as the result of a therapist's reframing of a situation) rather than mere first-order changes (a conscious decision by clients to behave differently). He argues that the two cerebral hemispheres have different functions, and each has its own language. The language of change, analogic language, is the language of the right hemisphere; it deals with imagery, symbols, and synthesis. Digital language, corresponding to left-brain activity, is the language of logic, reason, and explanation—to Watzlawick, the language of most psychotherapy. Watzlawick urges gaining access to the right hemisphere, using paradoxes, puns, ambiguities, imagery, and such to facilitate second-order changes. In the process, the left hemisphere—the logical watchdog—must be bypassed, often through reframing techniques (to give an old situation a new social context or new set of rules) or through the use of the **therapeutic double bind.**

The Therapeutic Double Bind

Interactional therapists (and strategic therapists in general) argue that it is their responsibility, as outsiders, to provide the family with an experience that will enable the members to change their rules and metarules concerning their relationships with one another and with the outside world. Couples need to learn how each punctuates an interaction (who each thinks is responsible for what), and how conflict often follows differences in such perceptions. Families must examine their patterns of communication (including report and command functions) and especially the context in which communication occurs. More specifically, faulty but persistent solutions to everyday difficulties must be examined to learn if the family (1) ignores a problem when some action is called for; (2) overreacts, taking more action than is necessary or developing unrealistic expectations from actions taken; or (3) takes action at the wrong level (making cosmetic first-order changes when second-order changes are necessary). As we demonstrate shortly, the MRI Brief Therapy Center approach incorporates this time-limited, highly focused therapeutic effort toward problem resolution.

While focusing on the presenting problem and helping the family develop clear and concise goals, strategists often try to induce change by offering explicit or implicit **directives**—therapeutic tasks aimed at extinguishing undesirable interactional sequences (see examples below). To the therapist, these are clever maneuvers designed to subtly gain control over the presenting symptoms and force families to attempt different solutions; to the family, these often appear to fly in the face of common sense but they nevertheless put themselves in the hands of the expert and follow instructions. The overall purpose of such paradoxical approaches is to jar or interrupt the family's established (if unsuccessful) pattern of interaction by powerful indirect means. Since second-order change is the goal, the therapist is attempting to circumvent family resistance to altering the interactive patterns that maintain the problematic behavior.

One direct outgrowth of research on the pathological double bind has been the notion of the *therapeutic double bind,* a general term that describes a variety of paradoxical techniques used to change entrenched family patterns. Just as a pathological double bind places an individual in a no-win predicament, so a therapeutic double bind is intended to force that person (or couple or family) into a no-lose situation: A symptomatic person is directed by the therapist not to change (for example, a depressed person is told not to be in such a hurry to give up the depression) in a context where the individual has come expecting to be helped to change. In effect, the therapist's directive is to change by remaining the same. The person thus is caught in a trap: If the directive not to do anything is defied and the individual tries to lift the depression, he or she learns to acquire control of the symptom and this constitutes desired therapeutic change; if the person complies and does not attempt to change, he or she acknowledges a voluntary exercise of control over the symptoms. Since symptoms, by definition, are beyond voluntary control, the person can no longer claim to be behaving symptomatically through no fault of his or her own. Either way, the person gains control over the symptom; the symptom no longer controls the person. The symptoms have fallen under therapeutic control.

Technically, Watzlawick, Beavin, and Jackson (1967) outline the structure of the therapeutic double bind as follows:

1. It presupposes an intense relationship, in this case the psychotherapeutic situation, which has a high degree of survival value and of expectation for the patient.
2. In this context, an injunction is given that is so structured that it:
   (a) reinforces the behavior the patient expects to be changed;
   (b) implies that this reinforcement is the vehicle of change; and
   (c) thereby creates paradox because the patient is told to change by remaining unchanged. He is put in an untenable situation with regard to his pathology. If he complies, he no longer "can't help it"; he does "it," and this, as we have tried to show, makes "it" impossible, which is the purpose of therapy. If he resists the injunction, he can do so only by not behaving symptomatically, which is the purpose of therapy. If in a pathogenic double bind the patient is "damned if he does and damned if he doesn't," in a therapeutic double bind he is "changed if he does and changed if he doesn't."
3. The therapeutic situation prevents the patient from withdrawing or otherwise dissolving the paradox by commenting on it. Therefore, even though the injunction is logically absurd, it is a pragmatic reality: The patient cannot not react to it, but neither can he react to it in his usual, symptomatic way. (p. 241)

In a form of therapeutic double bind called **prescribing the symptom,** strategists try to produce a runaway system by urging or even coaching the client to engage in or practice his or her symptoms, at least for the present time. A family is instructed to continue or even to exaggerate what it is already doing (for example, the mother and daughter earlier in this chapter who continually fight might be directed to have a fight on a regular basis, every evening for fifteen minutes immediately after dinner). Since the family has come in desperation for help from the therapist (who seems to have high qualifications) and since the directive not to change appears easy to follow because the symptomatic behavior (the fighting) is occurring anyway, the family attempts to comply.

The therapist, asked to help them change, appears to be asking for no change at all! Such an assignment, however, undermines family members' fearful resistance to anticipated therapist efforts to get them to change by rendering such opposition unnecessary. At the same time, the therapist is challenging the function or purpose of the symptom, suggesting the family behaves that way because it serves to maintain family balance. In our example, confronted with the repugnant task of fighting on a regular basis, thereby exercising voluntary control over a previously uncontrolled situation, the mother and daughter resist the directive and begin to interact in a different manner. The unstated rules by which they operated before may become clearer to them, as does the notion that their previous quarreling did not "just happen" involuntarily but can be brought under voluntary control.[2] Since their interactive pattern no longer serves the family function of providing balance, the entire family must seek new ways of interacting with one another.

Another form of therapeutic double bind, **relabeling** (essentially changing the label attached to a person or problem from negative to positive) attempts to alter the meaning of a situation by altering its conceptual and/or emotional context in such a way that the entire situation is perceived differently. That is, language is used to alter the interpretation of what has occurred, and thus invites the possibility of a new response to the behavior. The situation remains unchanged, but the meaning attributed to it, and thus its consequences, is altered.

The classic example comes from Tom Sawyer, who relabeled as pleasurable the drudgery of whitewashing a fence and thus was in a position to ask other boys to pay for the privilege of helping him. Relabeling typically emphasizes the positive ("Mother's not being overprotective; she merely is trying to be helpful") and helps the family redefine disturbing behavior in more sympathetic or optimistic terms. Relabeling provides a new framework for looking at interaction; as the rules by which the family operates become more explicit, the family members become aware

---

[2]Maurizio Andolfi (179), director of the Family Therapy Institute in Rome, Italy, is particularly adept at unbalancing rigid family systems, often through effective use of "prescribing the symptom." In a family in which an anorectic adolescent girl controls family communication and defines all relations, including the relationship between her parents, Andolfi will forbid the girl to eat during a lunch session when the therapist and family eat together normally. Since her symptom (non-eating) is now involuntary, it no longer serves as a means of controlling family interactions. At the same time, the family can no longer use its typically incongruent message. "Eat, but don't eat." The prescription interrupts the family game based on the daughter's eating problem and helps expose the rules of the anorectic family system.

that old patterns are not necessarily unchangeable. The goal of relabeling, like that of the other therapeutic double-bind techniques, is to change the structure of family relationships and interactions.

MRI BRIEF FAMILY THERAPY

Brief therapy is not just fewer sessions or less of the same. Rather, this approach calls for finding alternative ways of facilitating beneficial changes that are relatively quick and inexpensive, and that are especially suited at symptomatic junctures in the life cycle of individuals and families (Peake, Borduin, & Archer, 1988).

The Brief Therapy Project at the Mental Research Institute in Palo Alto (Weakland & Fisch, 1992) now represents the major application of the earlier MRI theoretical formulations described previously in this chapter. Interactionally based, and with a strategic focus, MRI Brief Therapy advocates have developed a number of systems-based tactics for treating a wide assortment of clinical problems, including anxiety, depression, marital discord, sexual dysfunction, family conflict, psychosomatic illness, and drug and alcohol dependence (Fisch, Weakland, & Segal, 1982; Watzlawick, Weakland, & Fisch, 1974).

The MRI approach offers a generic model of how a problem persists (it is maintained by ongoing interactions) and how it can most efficiently be resolved (by changing or eliminating the problem-maintaining interactions) regardless of the problem's nature, origin, or duration. Relying on the carefully worked out communication/interaction theories and techniques of Bateson, Jackson, Haley, and especially Erickson, the MRI technique is particularly well suited to families with specific symptomatology seeking immediate resolution of problems and relief from symptoms. Segal (1991) credits Heinz von Foerster, a second-order cyberneticist and constructionist, with providing an epistemological basis for the current MRI approach.

Brief family therapy as practiced at the MRI[3] is a time-limited (usually no more than ten sessions), pragmatic, nonhistorical, step-by-step strategic approach based on the notion that most human problems develop through the mishandling of normal difficulties in life. In the MRI view, the attempted "solutions" imposed by families become the problem, as people persist in maintaining self-defeating "more of the same" attempts at problem resolution. Thus, from the MRI perspective, *the client's complaint is the problem, not a symptom of an underlying disorder,* as more psychodynamic approaches might theorize. Furthermore, as we indicated above, the client's problematic behavior is viewed as primarily determined by interaction with significant others; it is this interactive pattern that is said to perpetuate that behavior.

---

[3]A number of brief therapy approaches currently exist side by side, stimulated no doubt in part by the restrictive reimbursement practices by managed care companies. We'll contrast the MRI problem-focused approach with that of the Brief Family Therapy Center in Milwaukee's solution-focused effort in Chapter 13. Later, in Chapter 17, we present a fuller discussion of issues surrounding managed care and insurance reimbursements for clinical services.

Put in more graphic interpersonal terms, the client is like a person caught in quicksand, grabbing onto someone else: The more he or she struggles, the more likely he or she is to sink and pull others in; the more he or she sinks, the more the struggling escalates and the more others are caught in the quicksand. In other words, ineffective attempts persist, and now the "solution" itself only makes matters worse. According to advocates of this approach, it is only by giving up solutions that perpetuate the problem and attempting new solutions that are different *in kind* that changes can occur in the self-perpetuating behavior.

The time limitations of this approach force clients to specifically define their current problem ("We believe our teenage boy is using drugs") rather than speak in generalities ("We're having family problems"). Here the therapist is interested in how, exactly, this problem affects every participant's life, and why they are seeking help just now (rather than earlier or later).

According to Watzlawick, Weakland, and Fisch (1974) the kinds of problems presented in psychotherapy persist because people maintain them through their own behavior and that of others with whom they interact. If, however, the current system of interaction is changed at any point in its sequence, then the problem will be resolved regardless of its history and etiology. Accordingly, the strategically oriented brief therapist tries to obtain a clear picture of the specific problem as well as the current interactive behavior that maintains it, then devises a plan for changing those aspects of the system that perpetuate the problem (Segal, 1987). By restraining people from repeating old unworkable solutions (and by altering the system to promote change) the therapist can help them break out of their destructive or dysfunctional cycle of behavior.

Brief therapy advocates argue that most therapists, in attempting to help a distressed person, encourage that person to do the opposite of what he or she has been doing—an insomniac to fall asleep, a depressed person to cheer up, a withdrawn person to make friends. These approaches, by emphasizing opposites or negative feedback, only lead to internal reshuffling; they do not change the system. Watzlawick and associates (1974) call such moves superficial first-order changes, effecting change within the existing system without changing the structure of the system itself. In the example of feedback loops we used in Chapter 4, such a therapeutic effort is equivalent to the thermostat that regulates room temperature, activating the heating system to cool down when the room gets too hot.

Real change, however, necessitates an alteration of the system itself; it calls for a second-order change to make the system operate in a different manner. To continue the analogy, to obtain relief the thermostat on the wall must be reset; simply allowing the temperature to return to its former position imposes the wrong solution. First-order changes, according to Watzlawick, Beavin, and Jackson (1967), are "games without end"; they are mistaken attempts at changing ordinary difficulties that eventually come to a stalemate by continuing to force a solution despite available evidence that it is precisely what is *not* working (Bodin 1981).

MRI therapists take this position on problem formation—that complaints typically presented to a therapist arise and endure because of the mishandling of those normal, everyday difficulties that occur in all of our lives. Repeatedly employing unsatisfactory solutions only produces new problems, which now may increase in severity and begin to obscure the original difficulty. From the MRI perspective, there are three ways in which a family mishandles solutions so that they lead to bigger problems: (1) some action is necessary but not taken (for example, the family attempts a solution by denying there is a problem—the roof is not leaking, sister is not pregnant, money is no problem even though father has lost his job); (2) an action is taken when it is unnecessary (for example, newlyweds separate soon after the wedding ceremony because their marriage is not as ideal as each partner fantasized it would be); (3) action is taken at the wrong level (for example, marital conflicts or parent-child conflicts are dealt with by "common sense" or first-order changes, such as each party agreeing to try harder next time, when revisions in the family system—second-order changes—are necessary). The third type is probably most common, since people with problems attempt to deal with them in a manner consistent with their existing frame of reference. Repeated failures only lead to bewilderment and intensification of the same responses.

The MRI version of brief therapy focuses on resolving problems that result from prior attempts to solve an ordinary difficulty. Paradoxical interventions, especially reframing, are emphasized in order to redefine the family's frame of reference so that members conceptualize the problem differently and change their efforts to resolve it. As we saw in our earlier discussions of the structural (Chapter 9) approach to therapy, reframing involves a redefining process in which a situation remains unchanged but the meaning attributed to it is revised so as to permit a more constructive outlook. Reframing allows the situation to be viewed differently and thus facilitates new responses to it. As language changes about a problem, feelings are likely to follow.

As practiced at the MRI, brief therapy, presented to the clients as being of short-term duration, sets up a powerful expectation of change. At the same time, the therapists tend to "think small," to be satisfied with minor but progressive changes. They also urge their clients to "go slow" and to be skeptical of dramatic, sudden progress; this restraining paradoxical technique is actually designed to promote rapid change as the family is provoked to prove the therapist wrong in his or her caution and pessimism. In general, the therapists do not struggle with the client's resistance to change, neither confronting the family nor offering interpretations to which the members might react negatively or defensively. Brief therapy aims to avoid power struggles with the family while it reshapes the members' perspectives on current problems and on their previous attempts to overcome difficulties.

MRI brief therapists do not insist that all family members attend sessions, content to deal only with those motivated enough to do so. An important aspect of their work is to first collect data on previously failed solutions so as not to repeat them. They then set up specific goals of treatment, formulating a case plan and implementing interventions whenever there is an opportunity to interrupt earlier repetitive attempted solutions that merely serve to perpetuate the problem (Segal, 1991).

The MRI brief therapy program is a team effort. Although each family is assigned a primary therapist who conducts the interviews, other team members may watch from behind the one-way mirror and telephone the therapist with advice, feedback, and suggestions while treatment is in progress, all directed at speeding up a change in family interactive patterns. In special cases (for example, a therapist-family impasse) one of the team members may enter the room and address the primary therapist or the clients, perhaps siding with the client to increase the likelihood that forthcoming directives from the observer will be implemented. Families are not screened prior to treatment and are taken into the program on a first-come, first-served basis. Team discussions precede and follow each session after the initial family contact. A telephone follow-up, in which each family receiving treatment at the center is asked by a team member other than the primary therapist to evaluate change in the presenting problem, takes place 3 months and 12 months after the last interview.

The cybernetic nature of both problem formation and problem resolution, with its recursive feedback loops and circular causality metaphors, is basic to MRI thinking and therapeutic endeavors. Ineffective solutions to everyday difficulties lead to symptomatic behavior; once a family member manifests a symptom, the family, believing it has the best way to deal with the problem, responds by repeating the interactive behavior that produced the symptom in the first place. The further repetition of poor solutions intensifies the original difficulty, as the family clings to behavior patterns no longer functional or adaptive (Peake, Borcuin, & Archer, 1988). Therapists, then, must direct their efforts at helping families substitute new behavior patterns (new solutions) to replace the old ones.

The following example (Segal, 1982) illustrates the effectiveness of the MRI brief therapy approach. The therapy team helps a concerned wife to revise her earlier self-defeating solutions to a problem and thus to institute second-order changes in her interactions with a resistant husband.

> The author (Segal) and Dr. Fritz Hoebel studied and treated 10 families in which the husbands had suffered a major heart attack but were still continuing to engage in high-risk behaviors: poor diet, smoking, lack of exercise, and excessive consumption of alcohol. All of these families were referred by cardiologists, or by the staff of a cardiac rehabilitation program, who had given up on these individuals, fearing they were on a suicide course. In all 10 cases the identified heart patient would have nothing to do with any further treatment or rehabilitation efforts.
>
> Rather than wasting a lot of time and energy trying to convince the patient to come for treatment, we worked with their spouses. Using a five-session limit, we focused our attention on the way the wives had attempted to reduce their husbands' high-risk behavior—our aim was to change the system, that is, the husband's behavior, by getting the wives to change their attempted solutions. In most cases the wives struggled, argued, and nagged their men to change, so our primary effort was getting the wives to back off from this position. In one case that worked particularly well, on our instructions the wife returned home and told her husband that she had been doing a lot of thinking about him. She said she had decided that he had a right to live out the rest of his life in his own style, no matter how short that might be. Her primary concern now was herself and the children and how they would be provided for when he died. She then insisted that her husband go over all the life insurance and estate planning, instructing her how to handle things after his death. She also called life insurance agencies and asked whether there was any way her husband's life insurance could be increased. As instructed, she told them to call back at times she knew she would not be home but her husband would be there to take the calls. Within 2 weeks after she had begun to deal

with him this way, the husband had resumed his participation in the cardiac rehabilitation exercise program and was watching his diet. (pp. 286–287)

STRATEGIC FAMILY THERAPY

If the original MRI communication/interaction approach drew the greatest attention from family therapy professionals in the 1960s, and Minuchin's structural model was the most consistently studied and emulated in the 1970s, then it is fair to say that the strategic approach took center stage in the 1980s. As its leading advocates Madanes and Haley (1977) contend, the main characteristic of this approach, which evolved from communication theory and interactionist interventions, is that the therapist takes responsibility for devising a strategy for solving the client's presenting problem. Typically their interventions involve creating novel ways of disrupting those entrenched family interactive sequences that help produce and maintain the problem the family comes to therapy to alleviate.

The strategic therapist defines a presenting problem in such a way that it can be solved; goals eliminating the specific problem are clearly set; therapy is carefully planned, in stages, to achieve these goals; problems are defined as involving at least two and most likely three people, thus allowing for an examination of problematic family structures (hierarchies, coalitions) and dysfunctional behavioral sequences. The thrust of the intervention is to shift the family organization so that the presenting problem or symptom no longer serves its previous function in the family. To the strategic therapist, change occurs not through insight and understanding but through the process of the family carrying out directives issued by the therapist.

The career of Jay Haley plays an important part in the development of the strategic approach to family therapy. Haley was a key member of Bateson's schizophrenia research project in the 1950s, and helped develop the double-bind concept. Bateson himself was interested in the concept's theoretical significance, as a description of interaction, and not in the clinical issues of interpersonal influence within a family. Haley (1963), however, saw its clinical application; he took the position that implicit in every interpersonal transaction is a struggle for control of the *definition* of the relationship. He viewed symptomatic behavior in one partner as a maladaptive control strategy, warning that the therapist must maintain control of the therapy relationship, lest the client gain control and perpetuate his or her difficulties in order to "continue to govern by symptomatic methods" (Haley, 1963, p. 19).

In 1953 Haley, along with John Weakland, became interested in understanding the communication occurring in hypnosis between hypnotist and subject, and with Bateson's encouragement began to attend workshops on that subject led by Milton Erickson. Pursuing that interest further, but now more intrigued by Erickson's metaphoric therapeutic style for issuing indirect suggestions, the two visited Erickson regularly in Phoenix over a period of several years. Erickson's influence on many of the underlying assumptions and subsequent therapeutic techniques of strategic therapy is great; Haley (1973; 1976a) actually credits his mentor as the inventor of the general approach of strategic family therapy.

Milton Erickson, M.D.

Erickson's therapy was brief, directive, and carefully planned. Taking responsibility for change, he tailored a novel approach for each case. His use of hypnotic techniques, typically focused on symptom removal, required the therapist to assume full charge of the treatment and to issue directives (however subtle or indirect) as a way of gaining leverage for eliminating the troublesome symptom. Joining with patients, believing in their inherent wisdom to help themselves once shown how, and gaining their trust, he set about through indirect suggestions to encourage them to break out of their old behavior patterns and, in the process, abandon their presenting symptom. Erickson argued that an effective therapist needs to be a strategist who approaches each new client with a specific therapeutic plan, sometimes a simple directive or a paradox, fitted to that individual and intended to solve his or her problem. Erickson's unorthodox but artful stratagems, extraordinary feats of observation, and seemingly uncanny ability to tap unrecognized and previously untapped resources in his clients (usually individuals rather than families) have been chronicled by Haley (1973) as well as by Zeig (1980).

Noted for a number of creative and unconventional hypnotic techniques, Erickson was particularly skilled at "bypassing client resistance" through the use of *paradoxical directives*. That is, he was able to persuade patients to maintain a symptom (by not fighting it or insisting the client work at giving it up) and then subtly introduce directions to induce change. Thus, he was able to avoid direct confrontation with the symptom, a tactic likely to have been met with resistance, and to use the client's own momentum to force symptom abandonment. This technique, developed so that the hypnotic subject would not experience a loss of control to the hypnotist, became the later basis for many of Haley's strategic interventions in working with families. The family's fear of relinquishing control to the therapist often makes it resistant to change. The therapist's not directly confronting such resistance lessens their fear that they will be required to do things against their will. Once they feel safe, and with the aid of a therapist jump-starting the change process, people can begin to call upon their own resources to attempt new ways of thinking and behaving.

As noted in Chapter 9, Haley was also influenced by his long association (1967–1973) as trainer and theory builder with Salvador Minuchin and Braulio Montalvo at the Philadelphia Child Guidance Center. Hoffman (1981) actually classifies Haley's position as a structural-strategic approach; Minuchin himself points out that there are obvious similarities between the structural and strategic outlooks (Simon, 1984). Haley's concern with family hierarchy and coalitions and other family structure issues places him in the former group, while his interest in paradoxical directives and other unobtrusive ways of managing resistance identifies him with the latter.

By 1975, Haley and Cloé Madanes, who had trained at the MRI before moving on to the Philadelphia Child Guidance Clinic, together formed the Family Therapy Institute of Washington, D.C.. a highly respected training program for family therapists. (He has since retired to La Jolla, California, while she remains director of the center.) Haley, a prolific writer, described his strategies for changing the way a family is organized in *Problem-Solving Therapy* (1976a); the following decade he published *Ordeal Therapy* (1984), an account of treatment based on the premise that if a client is maneuvered into a position where he or she finds it more distressful to maintain a symptom than to give it up, the client will abandon the symptom. Updated versions of Haley's strategic approach can be found in Grove and Haley (1993) as well as Haley (1996). In addition to Haley and Madanes, leading strategic therapists today include James Keim (1998), Jerome Price (1996), and Neil Schiff. Their efforts, as well as those of like-minded therapists, can frequently be found in the *Journal of Strategic and Systemic Therapies* (now renamed the *Journal of Systemic Therapies*).

Madanes has presented her unique perspectives in *Strategic Family Therapy* (1981), *Behind the One-Way Mirror* (1984), and most recently *Sex, Love, and Violence* (1990). In this last book she provides a therapeutic philosophy, derived from strategic family therapy, for dealing with struggles between love and violence, which Madanes considers the root of all problems brought to therapy (see elaboration below). Haley and Madanes, separately and together, have demonstrated their active, directive, highly focused therapeutic techniques around the world.

The Meaning of Symptoms

Although the generally accepted view at the time was that symptoms were by definition involuntary and maladaptive, Haley early on (1963) took the position that a symptom, rather than representing behavior beyond one's control, is a strategy, adaptive to a current social situation, for controlling a relationship when all other strategies have failed. The symptomatic person simply denies any intent to control by claiming the symptom is involuntary. ("It's not that I am rejecting you. It's my headache that keeps me from wanting to be sexually intimate with you tonight.")

Haley cites the case of a woman who insists her husband be home every night because she suffers anxiety attacks if left alone. However, she does not recognize her demand as a means of controlling his behavior, but explains it as a function of her anxiety attacks over which she presumably has no control. The husband faces a dilemma; he cannot acknowledge that she is controlling his behavior (the anxiety attacks are at fault for that), but he cannot refuse to let her control his behavior (after all, she has anxiety attacks).

Symptoms (aside from organic illness) are thus seen as adaptive and under the client's voluntary control. By acting helpless, in the example just described, the wife gains considerable power and control over the relationship. Without offering insight or otherwise sharing the view of voluntary control over symptoms with the clients, the strategist seeks to change the situation—perhaps help the couple redistribute power and responsibilities—so that the symptom is no longer necessary to control the husband.

Jockeying for control occurs in all families and in every relationship between two or more people. ("You can't boss me around anymore; I'm not a baby" is a familiar taunt heard from a teenager trying to change family rules.) Most couples develop suitable up-front means of dealing with issues of control; people who present symptoms are resorting to subtle, indirect methods. It is Haley's contention that control struggles in a relationship are inevitable; one cannot not try to define a relationship or attempt to control an outcome. Haley considers the maneuver pathological only if one or both participants deny trying to control the other's behavior and/or exhibit symptomatic behavior in the process of doing so.

As do the interactionists, strategists contend that communication defines the nature of the relationship between partners. If a husband is willing to discuss only the weather when he and his wife are together in the evening, he may be defining the relationship as one where they talk only about conventional matters. If the wife refuses to comment on tomorrow's forecast but instead expresses the idea that they seem distant from each other this evening, she is attempting to redefine the relationship on more personal and intimate terms. *Their conflict is not a struggle to control another person, but a struggle to control the definition of the relationship.* As we have noted, in some marriages a partner's symptoms (for example, anxiety attacks, phobias, depressions, heavy drinking) control what takes place between the partners— where they go, what they do together, whether one can leave the other's side for any length of time, and so on. Traditionally, such symptoms have been explained as expressions of intrapsychic conflict and therefore as involuntary aspects of one person's "illness." Strategists, strongly opposed to intrapsychic explanations, *define symptoms as interpersonal events,* as tactics used by one person to deal with another. In their view, the therapist's goal is to maneuver the client into developing other ways of defining relationships so that the symptomatic methods will be abandoned.

Developing Therapeutic Strategies

Strategic family therapists direct their interventions at a specific presenting problem, deal with the present ways the problem is maintained, and customize strategies (straightforward or indirect directives) designed to track and ultimately alter problem-related interactive sequences. Rather than offer interpretation or provide insight— the family usually resolves a problem without ever knowing why or how—strategic therapists attempt to change only those aspects of the family system that are maintaining the problematic or symptomatic behavior. The emphasis in strategic therapy, according to Madanes (1981), is not on devising a therapeutic method applicable to

all cases, but rather on designing a unique strategy for each specific presenting problem. The focus throughout is on alleviating the presenting problem, not exploring its
roots or buried meanings. Thus, strategic therapy is likely to be short-term, since it
is limited to specific problems and tailored to solutions.

Haley (1963) points out that therapists and patients continually maneuver with
each other in the process of treatment. Elements of a power struggle exist in psychodynamic therapies, hypnosis, behavior therapy, family therapy, and other forms
of treatment. Family members may try to manipulate, deceive, exclude, or subdue a
therapist in order to maintain the homeostatic balance they have achieved, even if it
is at the expense of symptomatic behavior in one of their members. They do so not
to torment a therapist, but rather because they are frightened of change, clinging to
what they believe is the only solution to their problem. The strategic therapist, therefore, must take an authoritative stance. Haley (1976a) sees his task as taking responsibility for changing the family organization and resolving the problem that brought
the family to see him. He is highly directive, giving the family members precise
instructions or directives and insisting that they be followed. Thus, he may at times
be highly manipulative in his procedures. For example, Haley cites the case (1976a)
of a grandmother siding with her grandchild (age 10) against the mother. He saw the
mother and child together, instructing the child to irritate the grandmother and
instructing the mother to defend her daughter against the grandmother. This task
forced a collaboration between mother and daughter and helped detach the daughter from her grandmother, releasing the family to develop a more appropriate hierarchical structure.

As we can see from this example, strategists are urged to be active, take-charge
family therapists. Haley advocates that they intervene when they see the need to
do so (rather than when the family requests therapist input), comment openly
about the family's efforts to influence or control them, give directions and assign
tasks, and assume temporary leadership of the family group. Strategic therapists
attempt to avoid getting enticed into coalitions within the family; however, they
may develop a coalition with one or more members to overcome an impasse but
quickly disengage before becoming entangled with one or another family faction.

Another strategic tactic is to emphasize the positive, usually by relabeling previously defined dysfunctional behavior as reasonable and understandable. In one
often-quoted example, Haley boldly (and at first glance, outrageously) told a wife
whose husband had chased after her with an ax that the man was simply trying to
get close to her! Here, Haley was simply following a principle of communication
theory described earlier; namely, that all communication occurs at two levels and
that the message at the second level (metacommunication) qualifies what takes
place on the surface level. What Haley was communicating by the relabel, and
what the wife also sensed, was that the husband indeed did want to connect with
her, but his rage got in the way of doing so in any constructive manner. (In everyday exchanges, a remark made by a sender in normal conversation can be taken as
a joke or an attack, as praise or as blame, depending on the context in which the
receiver places it.) By addressing the metamessage—he wanted to get close—Haley
changed the context, freeing the participants to think and therefore behave differently in the new context.

The Initial Interview

Haley (1976a) contends that the first interview, which he insists the whole family attend, sets the stage for the entire course of therapy. Proceeding systematically, through stages, strategists negotiate with the family to decide what specific problem requires attention, then formulate a plan of action to change the family's dysfunctional sequences or faulty hierarchy in order to eliminate the problem. Typically, in the opening *brief social stage,* they create a cooperative and relaxed atmosphere while observing family interaction and trying to get all members to participate, thus indicating all are involved and should have a voice in the therapy.

Next, in this highly structured process, strategic therapists shift to the *problem stage,* getting down to the business of why (for example, to solve what specific presenting problem) the family is there. They pose such questions as "Why do you seek help now?"; "What would each of you like to change?"; "Quickly or slowly?"; "Do you wish to realize what is happening or just to change?"; "Are you willing to make sacrifices to change?" (Haley, 1988). In this information-gathering phase, conversation is directed at the therapist, who displays an interest but does not interpret the thoughts and feelings being expressed.

The *interactional stage,* during which the family discusses the problem aloud with one another in the presence of the therapist, permits the therapist to observe any dysfunctional communication sequences, coalitions, power hierarchies, and such, thereby offering clues about future therapeutic interventions.

The fourth segment of the first interview, the *goal-setting stage,* provides an opportunity for therapist and family together to determine precisely the presenting problem they wish to solve or eliminate. This last phase results in a contract that clearly defines goals, allowing all participants to measure change or gauge the success of their efforts as therapy progresses.

In the final or *task-setting stage,* the strategic therapist ends the initial interview with the first set of assignments or directives for changing the presenting problem. If done successfully, the family members feel comfortable with the therapist and committed to working together for change (Haley, 1976a).

The Use of Directives

Directives, or assignments of tasks to be performed outside of the therapeutic session, play a key role in strategic family therapy, and are given for several reasons: (1) to get people to behave differently so they will have different subjective experiences; (2) to intensify the therapeutic relationship by involving the therapist in the family's actions during the time between sessions; and (3) to gather information, by their reactions, as to how the family members will respond to the suggested changes. Advice, direct suggestions, coaching, homework, even assignments of ordeal-like behavior to be followed if a symptom appears, are examples of straightforward directives by the therapist aimed at achieving problem solution.

As Madanes (1991, p. 397) emphasizes:

> The directive is to strategic therapy what the interpretation is to psychoanalysis. It is the basic tool of the approach.

In some cases, strategists issue a straightforward directive (simultaneously a report and a command) to family members to take specific action (for example, instructing a mother to stop intruding when the father and son try to talk to each other) because they want or expect them to follow it in order for them to change their behavior toward one another. However, asking someone to stop engaging in certain behavior is a difficult directive to enforce; its success depends upon the status of the therapist giving the instruction, the severity or chronicity of the behavior, how often the directive is repeated, and the willingness of family members to cooperate with the therapist in accomplishing the task. This last point regarding motivation is a particularly essential factor determining whether the therapist will succeed in this direct approach.

Frequently, the direct approach is unsuccessful. (If direct suggestion were successful, the chances are great that the family would have followed advice from friends and not come to a therapist's office.) Another kind of task assignment, more indirect, is one by which the therapist attempts to influence clients to take some action without directly asking them to do so. Often couched in paradoxical form (see examples below), the strategic therapist hopes to provoke the family to rebel or resist him or her so that they give up the symptom. Assignment of paradoxical tasks can be directed at individual family members, pairs of people, or at the family system (Weeks & L'Abate, 1982).

To be used with relative infrequence, as when a client is in crisis or especially resistant to change, paradoxical directives commonly take one of two forms—*prescriptive* or *descriptive*. Prescriptive paradoxes ask the client(s) to do something, while descriptive paradoxes relabel something already being done by giving it a positive meaning or connotation. As Wachtel and Wachtel (1986) illustrate the former, a client seeking help for his procrastination is asked not to try to accomplish more in the coming week between sessions, but rather to record the various ways he wastes time each day and how long each takes. The changing set, or perhaps the unpleasant task, often leads to a reduction of procrastination. The client may report that there was little to write down the previous week because he got his work done. Or in the case in which a list is made, the client will often gain greater awareness of his self-defeating behavior or perhaps learn that he is less a procrastinator than overdemanding or expecting too much from himself. We offered an example of a descriptive paradox earlier in this section in Haley's relabeling the ax-wielding husband as performing a loving act.

As used by strategists, and borrowed from Erickson's hypnotic techniques, a paradoxical directive asks clients to *restrain from change,* and is designed to provoke defiance in the recipient. The client is told to continue to do what he or she came to therapy to get over doing (that is, continue having the symptom). The therapist, on the other hand, is trying indirectly to get the client or family to decide that they won't do what they have now been directed to do. Confused, the family members perceive that through the assignment of such a task the therapist is asking them not to change at the same time that the therapist has declared the intention of helping them change.

For example, an intelligent son, failing in school, is told to continue to fail so that his less well educated father can feel good about himself. If he conforms to the directive, he admits control and acknowledges how his behavior contributes to family secondary gain (an advantage or benefit, such as reassuring the father, that arises as a result of an illness or appearance of a symptom). If he rebels against the directive to continue to fail, he gives up the symptom. This paradoxical prescription subtly reveals the secondary gain that the patient's symptomatic behavior (poor grades) provides for the family, covertly suggesting change is both possible and desirable.

Paradoxical interventions[*] represent a particularly ingenous way of maneuvering a person or family into abandoning dysfunctional behavior. Similar to "prescribing the symptom," this technique is particularly appropriate for strategists because they assume that families who come for help are also frightened and therefore resistant to the help being offered. The result may be a standoff, a power struggle with the therapist trying to help family members change but in doing so destabilizing their previous homeostatic balance, and the family trying to get the therapist to fail but to go on trying because they realize something is wrong. Andolfi (1979), also considered a structural-strategic therapist, describes such an encounter as a game into which the therapist is drawn, and in which every effort on the part of the therapist to act as an agent of change is nullified by the family group. If not careful, Andolfi warns, the therapist can easily get entangled in the family's contradictory logic of "help me to change, but without changing anything."

The strategic paradoxical approach, aimed at families who defy compliance-based interventions, encompasses several stages. First, the therapist attempts to set up a relationship with the family in which change is expected. Second, the problem to be corrected is clearly defined; third, the goals are clearly stated. In the fourth stage, the therapist must offer a concrete plan; it is helpful if a rationale can be included that makes the paradoxical task seem reasonable. In the fifth stage, the current authority on the problem (such as a physician or a parent) is disqualified as not handling the situation the right way; in the sixth stage, the therapist issues the directive. In the seventh and last stage, the therapist observes the response and continues to encourage the usual problem behavior in order to maintain the paradox.

It is of utmost importance for the therapist using a paradoxical intervention that prescribes the symptom to carefully encourage the member(s) with the behavior to be changed to continue that behavior unchanged—a domineering wife to continue

---

[*]By now the reader is aware that this approach is employed by many family therapists, especially in dealing with defiant or resistant families. We particularly underline its use in our discussion of those therapeutic approaches that emphasize clear communication, because a paradoxical injunction (for example, "Be spontaneous") is a prototype of a double-bind situation. To command someone to be spontaneous is to demand behavior that cannot be spontaneous because it is commanded! Thus, with seeming innocence, the sender is trapping the receiver into a situation where rule compliance also entails rule violation (Watzlawick, Weakland, & Fisch, 1974). The receiver is faced with two conflicting levels of messages, is bewildered, and cannot make an effective response. As Haley, Watzlawick, Erickson, and others use the paradox therapeutically, the family is directed, in effect, "Disobey me." As in the case of commanding someone to be spontaneous, instructing the person to disobey what you are saying is to create a paradox. Thus, the family told not to change in effect defies the therapist's injunction; the family begins to change to prove the therapist wrong in assuming it could not change. If the therapist allows himself or herself to be put down as wrong and even suggests that the change is very likely to be temporary and a relapse probable, the family will resist relapse and continue to change to prove the therapist wrong again. It is essential that the therapist never claim credit for helping the family—indeed, the therapist remains puzzled by the change—in order to preclude the family's need to be disobedient in the form of a relapse.

to run everything in the family; a daughter refusing to attend school to stay home; an adolescent boy masturbating in public to continue doing so but to keep a chart of how often, what days he enjoyed it most, and so on. Strategists might tell a couple who always fight unproductively to go home and fight for three hours. The issue becomes one of control. The domineering wife no longer runs everything if the therapist is telling her what to do, and if she resists his directive she will become less domineering in relation to her husband. Similarly, strategists assume in the other cases that the symptom presented, originally a way of gaining an advantage, will resolve if the symptom now places the person at a disadvantage. In the case of the couple, strategists expect them to stop fighting; people do not like to make themselves miserable because someone else tells them to do so.

Should the individual or family follow instructions and continue the problematic or symptomatic behavior, the therapist has been given the power and control to make the symptom occur at his direction. Should the individual or family resist the paradoxical intervention, the symptomatic behavior is, in the process, given up (and, again, the therapist retains power and control). Strategic therapists devote a great deal of time to devising *nonharmful,* if sometimes seemingly absurd, paradoxical tasks appropriate to the problem of the person desiring to change or get rid of a disturbing symptom. We catalogue some common paradoxical interventions in Table 10.1.

In another form of prescriptive directive called *ordeal therapy* (Haley, 1984), once again based on the work of Erickson, the strategic therapist will instruct a client to carry out an unpleasant chore (for example, rising in the middle of the night to wax the kitchen floor) whenever the symptom appears during the day, thus making the distress of the consequences a greater hardship than the distress of the original

Table 10.1   Common Examples of Paradoxical Interventions

Reframing	"He checks on your whereabouts several times a day not because he's jealous but because he's thinking about you all the time."
Relabeling	"Your wife is being helpful by reminding you about unfinished tasks around the house because she wants to make a nice home for you."
Prescribing the symptom	"Practice quarreling with each other as soon as you wake up."
Restraining	"Don't do anything about the problem this week so we can see how really bad it is."
Offering prescriptions	"Keep a list of everything that might worry you during the day and set aside an hour every night to go over them and become a competent worrier."
Offering descriptions	"The two of you, as a married couple, are to be commended for avoiding confronting your differences. It would be too risky to change things now."
Predicting a relapse	"The two of you got along better this week but you're probably going to have a major blowup soon."
Declaring hopelessness	"You're probably right. There's nothing you can do. It would be a disservice to you to allow you to continue therapy."

Source: Weeks & L'Abate, 1982; Seltzer, 1986

symptom. By selecting a harmless or mildly noxious task, but one consistent with a client's desires (say, keeping a spotless house) yet like an ordeal in its execution, Haley again tries to make it more difficult for the client to have the problem or symptom than to give it up. Ordeal therapy calls for a clear statement of the problem or symptom to be addressed and a commitment to change on the part of the client even if suffering is required, as well as a promised willingness to follow a therapist's directive regardless of its logic or relevance to the presenting problem.

There are three major steps in designing a paradox, according to Papp (1983): *redefining, prescribing,* and *restraining.* Redefining is intended to change the family's perception of the symptom. Toward this end, behavior that maintains the symptom is defined as benignly motivated, loving gestures the family employs to preserve its stability. Thus, anger may be relabeled as caring, suffering as self-sacrifice, distancing as a way of reinforcing closeness. Instead of trying to change the system directly, the therapist appears to be supporting it, respecting the emotional logic upon which it runs. Next, the wording of the prescription ("Practice being depressed"; "Continue being rebellious against your parents") must be brief, concise, and unacceptable (in order for the family to recoil at the instruction), but the therapist must appear sincere by offering a convincing rationale for the prescription. Later, when the family members press for change, the therapist attempts to regulate the pace of change by urging restraint, pointing out to them what new difficulties might arise. At the same time, the therapist seems to be cautiously allowing the family to change despite these anticipated difficulties.

Restraining strategies ("go slow") are efforts to emphasize that the system's homeostatic balance is in danger if improvement occurs too rapidly. Presented with a creditable rationale ("Change takes time and must proceed step-by-step; otherwise there is danger of relapse if too much change occurs too fast'), the client is likely to go along with the directive. The tactic is intended to prepare clients for change, to acknowledge their reluctance to change, and to solidify change once it begins (Shoham, Rohrbaugh, & Patterson, 1995). "Go slow" messages, according to Fisch, Weakland and Seagal (1982), provide the additional benefit of reducing the client's sense of urgency about finding new solutions. Such messages have the added effect of normalizing relapse should it occur, without the family becoming demoralized or giving up trying.

Haley (1976a) inquired, in a case of a young, middle-class couple concerned that their young child soiled his pants, what the consequences would be if he began to go to the toilet normally. (This move suggested that Haley could help them with the problem but would rather not until he was sure of the positive consequences to the entire family.) When they returned the next week and indicated that they could think of no adverse consequences, the therapist suggested some possibilities: for example, could the mother tolerate being successful with her child? This effort to restrain the mother from changing her overinvolved but exasperated behavior contained messages at several levels: (1) Haley thought she could tolerate success; (2) he was benevolently concerned so he wanted to make sure she could tolerate it; and (3) the mother would find the suggestion of not tolerating success to be unacceptable. No mother is likely to think she cannot be successful with her own child, as Haley well knew. Thus provoked (the father was similarly confronted), both parents became highly motivated to solve their problem to prove they could tolerate being normal; the boy's problematic behavior ceased.

Critics have argued that strategic methods are too manipulative and authoritarian, and that many of their paradoxical efforts are simplistic and transparent. They contend further that strategic techniques represent a form of gamesmanship that families will see through and reject. Overall, they seem dated and to be bucking the trend toward a partnership with families based on mutual trust and respect. Haley dismisses these charges as without basis since he claims all therapies, although most do not acknowledge it, rely to a great extent on therapist influence and expertise to resolve family problems. Possibly the blatant nature of the technique, which does not deny its use of power and provocation, opens it up to more than its share of criticism. In any event, challenges to both the ethics and power tactics of strategists helped set the stage in the late 1980s for many of the collaborative therapeutic efforts we consider in Part IV of this text.

Pretend Techniques and Family Metaphors

Madanes (1981, 1984), originally trained in her native Argentina, has developed a number of **pretend techniques** that are paradoxical in nature but less confrontational than Haley's. As such, they are less apt to invite defiance and rebelliousness, but still are helpful in overcoming family resistance. Based on playfulness, humor, and fantasy, these gentler approaches would have a therapist suggest, for example, that a symptomatic child (say one who is a periodic bed wetter or has recurring stomachaches) "pretend" to have a symptom at this moment and that the parents "pretend" to help. In effect, the therapist, changing the context, is subtly asking the clients to voluntarily control behavior (by turning it on and off) that they presumably regard as involuntary and thus, by definition, uncontrollable. By maneuvering the family through this kind of paradoxical intervention, Madanes manages to work out in make-believe what once produced an actual symptom. In many cases, if the family is pretending, then the actual symptom cannot be real and can be abandoned at will.

Madanes searches for the underlying family conflict or behavioral sequences for which the presenting problem or symptom is the metaphor. Then, by strategically helping families abandon symptomatic metaphors, she helps open up the possibility of attempting more adaptive ones. Madanes is especially interested in a family's interactive sequences that relate to the family hierarchy. Here she typically tries to get parents back in control of the family, all members enjoying and caring for each other directly without resorting to the development of symptoms in order to maintain family balance.

For example, with an eye toward designing a strategy for change, Madanes (1981) might direct a child to pretend to help a parent by assuming a superior position in the family. That is, the child is instructed to make a deliberate overt shift in the family hierarchy (in an effort to change the child's customary efforts to "help" parents through developing symptomatic behavior). By asking the parents to pretend to adopt an inferior position to the child, Madanes is attempting to get all concerned to resist such an inappropriate hierarchical organization, so that the family will reorganize in order for the parents once again to regain their authority and clarify the family hierarchy.

As noted earlier, Madanes (1991) views all human dilemmas as stemming from a struggle between love and violence. From her perspective:

> The main issue for human beings is whether to love, protect, and help each other, or to intrude, dominate, and control, doing harm to and using violence on others. The problem is compounded because love involves intrusion, domination, control, and violence, and because violence can be done in the name of love, protection, and helpfulness. (p. 402)

In the area of sexual abuse, for example, Madanes (1990) has offered a 16-step therapeutic model for simultaneously treating offenders and their victims by a single therapist. In the case of an older brother molesting a younger sister, for example, Madanes gathers the family together and instructs each member to tell exactly what occurred, forcing the abandonment of secrets and denial by the offender. Step-by-step, Madanes insists that all look at the "spiritual pain" caused both the victim and her victimizer, as well as all other family members. The abuser is asked to get on his knees and express repentance, as are the other family members for failing to protect her. The remaining steps involve designing acts of reparation before restoring the victimizer's place in the family. Such a treatment approach, still controversial, is consistent with the strategist's active, direct, take-charge therapeutic approach for solving a thorny presenting problem.

SUMMARY

Communication theories, emerging from the research at the Mental Research Institute in Palo Alto in the 1950s, have had a major impact on the family therapy field by recasting human problems as interactional and situational (tied to a set of circumstances that maintains them). The introduction of his epistemology by Bateson, Jackson, and others laid the foundation for the original interactive therapeutic approach of the MRI, now best considered as strategic family therapy. Particularly characteristic of this approach is the use of therapeutic double binds or paradoxical techniques for changing family rules and relationship patterns.

Paradoxes—contradictions that follow correct deductions from consistent premises—are used therapeutically to direct an individual or family not to change in a context that carries with it the expectation of change. The procedure promotes change no matter which action, compliance or resistance, is undertaken. "Prescribing the symptom," as used by Jackson, Watzlawick, and other strategists is a paradoxical technique for undermining resistance to change by rendering it unnecessary.

Haley and Madanes offer a related version of strategic family therapy. Their approach is characterized by carefully planned tactics and the issuance of directives for solving a family's presenting problems. Haley in particular uses straightforward directives or task assignments as well as indirect paradoxical interventions; the latter force the willing abandonment of dysfunctional behavior by means of the family defying the directive not to change.

Madanes employs paradoxical principles in the form of "pretend" techniques, nonconfrontational interventions directed at achieving change without inviting resistance. She is especially interested in a family's behavioral sequences related to the family hierarchy. Working in the area of sexual abuse, Madanes has developed a 16-step therapeutic model for one therapist to simultaneously treat offenders and their victims.

11

The Milan Model

Theories are, by definition, works in progress, more or less organized sets of constructs put forth to explain existing data and predict subsequent phenomena. Inevitably they are tentative, open to revision, but offer the advantage of providing a context that encourages the adoption of new perspectives and allows new ways of explaining and understanding events.

Nowhere is this provisional nature of theory building more apparent than in the approach we are about to consider. Based initially on the first-order cybernetic ideas of the early Palo Alto Mental Research Institute group, with its emphasis on family rules and homeostasis-seeking interactive patterns, the Milan approach has itself undergone continuous change in its 30-year history. Today it is at the cutting edge of family therapy, and has spawned a number of significant new postmodern developments (see Part IV), sometimes referred to as post-Milan, which attempt to understand the implications of second-order cybernetics and build them into family therapy theory and practice (Campbell, Draper, & Crutchley, 1991).

The notion that the therapist as observer is part of what is being observed—and thus is inescapably a part of the system to which he or she is offering therapy—redefines the therapist as someone who, like the other participants, has a particular perspective but not a truly objective view of the family or what's best for them. One consequence of this thinking is to take "truth" away from the therapist and make goal setting a participatory process that therapist and family members engage in together. Doing so empowers the family to make changes (or not make them) as they see fit. The therapist as a nonhierarchical facilitator (although hopefully a knowledgeable and inventive one), curious, and impartial, allows the family to investigate and decide about their future in their own way and at their own pace. The theoretical and therapeutic implications of this very contemporary viewpoint helped catapult the contribution of members of the original Milan group, especially Luigi Boscolo and Gianfranco Cecchin, to the forefront of 1990s family therapy thinking and practice.

MILAN SYSTEMIC FAMILY THERAPY

Three major related approaches to family therapy were strongly influenced by the theorizing of Gregory Bateson: the MRI interaction model, the strategic model developed by Haley and Madanes (both described in detail in Chapter 10), and the model put forth by a group of family therapists in Milan, Italy, led by Mara Selvini-Palazzoli. While all three view problems as arising from the family's interactional sequences, in practice both the MRI and strategic therapeutic approaches were also inspired by the clinical methods of Milton Erickson, while the Milan group's model is the most consistent, conceptually and methodologically, with Bateson's original ideas concerning circular epistemology (MacKinnon, 1983). The Milan approach, as it has continued to evolve, remains focused on information, much as Bateson (1972) did—as exemplified in his famous definition of information as "a difference that makes a difference." Characterized by a systematic search for differences—in behavior, in relationships, in how different family members perceive and construe an event—and by efforts to uncover the connections that link family members and keep the system in homeostatic balance, the approach has come to be known as **systemic family therapy.**

The Milan approach is anything but static; indeed, its numerous revisions over time represent perhaps its most obvious characteristic. Trained as a child psychoanalyst, Selvini-Palazzoli in the late 1960s set about organizing a team of eight fellow psychiatrists—including Luigi Boscolo, Gianfranco Cecchin, and Guiliana Prata—to treat families of severely disturbed children, many of whom were suffering from anorexia nervosa. However, their initial efforts to apply psychoanalytic concepts to the family proved to be very time-consuming and produced limited results. Turning to the published accounts of the works of the Palo Alto group, particularly the book *Pragmatics of Human Communication* (Watzlawick, Beavin, & Jackson, 1967), the four formed a study group to better understand strategic theories and techniques in the hope that such an outlook increased the prospects of helping intervene in families with entrenched interactive patterns.

By 1971, the four together split off from their more psychoanalytically oriented colleagues and formed the Milan Center for the Study of the Family in order to work more exclusively with family systems. While Watzlawick was their major consultant in these early years, visiting them periodically in Italy, the group gradually developed their own theory and set of strategic intervention techniques over the next decade (Boscolo, Cecchin, Hoffman, & Penn, 1987). They published their first article in English in 1974 (Selvini-Palazzoli, Boscolo, Cecchin, & Prata, 1974), introducing a team approach along with a set of powerful and innovative intervention techniques such as *positive connotation* and *rituals* (both of which we describe in detail later in this chapter) designed to overcome therapeutic impasses and change stalemated family interactive sequences. What is now referred to as the "classic" Milan approach—initially the clinical application of some of the theoretical concepts formulated in *Pragmatics of Human Communication*—quickly captured the imagination of many family therapists around the world. Working with families with a wide range of the most severe emotional problems, they reported particular success in treating anorectic children as well as schizophrenics with their team approach.

The first comprehensive exposition of their work in book form in English can be found in *Paradox and Counterparadox: A New Model in the Therapy of the Family in Schizophrenic Transaction* (Selvini-Palazzoli, Boscolo, Cecchin, & Prata, 1978). Showing the still strong influence of strategic techniques on their thinking, especially the use of paradoxical prescriptions intended to loosen rigid family transactions, the four were beginning to focus on the *rules of the game* in psychotic families—tactics by which family members struggle against one another as, together, they act to perpetuate unacknowledged family "games" in order to control each other's behavior. That is, they conceptualized the family as "a self-regulating system which controls itself according to the rules formed over a period of time through a process of trial and error" (p. 3). The symptoms in a family member, then, were not accidental, but were "skillfully fabricated to achieve particular systemic purposes" (Seltzer, 1986).

The schizophrenic family, trapped by the rules of the game, are powerless to effect change. That is, the rules of the family's game, rather than any individual input, define and sustain their relationships. What remained paradoxical was the fact that all family members, presumably seeking therapy in order to change, nevertheless continued to behave in ways that prevented any change from taking place. As Tomm (1984a) observed, it was as though the family were asking the therapist to change their symptomatic member, at the same time that they were insisting the rest of the family was fine and had no intention of changing.

Assuming that symptomatic behavior in a family member helped maintain the system's homeostatic balance, the team began by prescribing no change in that behavior. In this way, they were adapting the MRI technique of paradoxical intervention to their own systemic formulations that all of the family's attitudinal and behavioral patterns were mere moves designed to perpetuate the family game, and thus could not be confronted or challenged head-on. Through the subsequent use of therapeutic **counterparadoxes**—essentially therapeutic double binds—the family was warned against premature change, allowing them to feel more acceptable and unblamed for how they were, as the team attempted to discover and counter their paradoxical patterns, thus interrupting their repetitive, unproductive games.

To put it in the language of the Milan group, the family's behavior was given a positive connotation—positive motives were ascribed to all family transactions, reframed to appear to be carried out in the name of family cohesion and thus as functioning purposefully to maintain family homeostasis. At the same time, each family member's behavior was connoted as related to the identified patient's symptoms, thereby tacitly getting their acknowledgment of overall implication in the "family game." Subsequent interventions typically prescribing assigned rituals aimed at forcing behavior change in the system. (We'll elaborate on these powerful applications of paradoxically inspired techniques, along with examples, shortly.)

Continuing to flesh out their ideas, by 1980 the four were beginning to deemphasize the use of paradoxes, and in a landmark paper "Hypothesizing-circularity-neutrality: Three guidelines for the conductor of the session" (Selvini-Palazzoli,

Boscolo, Cecchin, & Prata, 1980) revealed their thinking to be moving in a systemic direction and away from strategic techniques. They contended that **hypothesizing,** a continual interactive process of speculating and making assumptions about the family situation, provides a guide for conducting a systemic interview. Such a guide to the family system is not true or false, but rather is useful as a starting point, open to revision or abandonment by the family as well as the therapist as new data accumulate. The technique allows the therapist to search for new information, identify the connecting patterns that sustain family behavior, and speculate on how each participant in the family contributes to systemic functioning. Beginning with the family's first telephone contact, and continuing throughout the therapeutic process, hypothesizing represents therapeutic formulations regarding family functioning.

Neutrality is different from noninvolvement; it means the therapist is interested in, and accepts without challenge, each member's unique *perception* of the problem (if not necessarily accepting the problem itself). No one family member's view is seen as more correct than any other. Thus, each family member may repeatedly experience the therapist as being allied with one or another member as that person's views are elicited, but never as allied with any one participant. Cecchin (1987) has now characterized the notion of neutrality as *curiosity,* as a result of widespread misunderstanding that neutrality demonstrated coldness or aloofness. As currently used, the curious therapist is open to numerous hypotheses about the system, and invites the family to explore those which increase the number of options or possibilities for the changes they seek.

Circular questioning, destined to be of prodigious influence for future therapists, involves asking each family member questions that help address a difference or define a relationship between two other members of the family. These differences are intended to expose recursive family patterns. We will define and illustrate these interviewing techniques later but for now perhaps it will suffice to point out that the therapist is trying to construct a map of the interconnections between family members, and here is assuming that asking questions about differences in perception— and questions derived from the feedback from previous questions about differences —is the most effective way of creating such a map (Campbell, Draper, & Crutchley, 1991). One major gain is that each family member is continually exposed to feedback from the others throughout the therapy.

After a decade of work together, the four separated into two autonomous groups (Selvini-Palazzoli and Prata; Boscolo and Cecchin) in 1980, each set pursuing differing emphases in their thinking and practices although retaining similar (but not identical) systemic outlooks. Selvini-Palazzoli and Prata (separately since 1982) have engaged in family systems research, particularly directed at developing techniques for interrupting the destructive games the believe are played by psychotic individuals and their families. Their intervention techniques, as we shall see, represent a return to some of their earlier strategic and structural ways of working (Simon, 1987).

On the other hand, Boscolo and Cecchin, training family therapists worldwide, have continued to elaborate the systemic ideas first presented in the hypothesis-neutrality-circularity paper. Departing from strategic interviewing techniques, they have developed a post-Milan collaborative therapeutic intervention style based on

Mara Selvini-Palazzoli M.D.

the interviewing process itself, particularly the use of circular questioning. Consistent with those views, their most recent efforts have been directed at fine-tuning such questioning techniques in order to aid family members in hearing and attempting to understand the family's relational context from the perspective of fellow family members. In seeking to advance a new systemic epistemology, they have become central players in advancing the constructivist approaches that now are so popular in the family therapy field.

In the United States, the systemic outlook, especially its more recent modifications by Boscolo and Cecchin, has found a particularly receptive audience among some members of the Ackerman Institute for Family Therapy in New York, particularly Peggy Papp (1983), Peggy Penn (1982), and Joel Bergman (1985). Lynn Hoffman, formerly at Ackerman, has since relocated to Amherst, Massachusetts, and to a more social construction viewpoint (Hoffman, 1985). Elsa Jones (1993), as well as David Campbell and Rosalind Draper (1985) in England, are enthusiastic supporters of the Milan viewpoint. In Canada, Karl Tomm of the University of Calgary is a leading interpreter of the Milan (and post-Milan) systemic approach. An updated description of the work of Boscolo and Cecchin can be found in *Milan Systemic Family Therapy* (Boscolo, Cecchin, Hoffman, & Penn, 1987). Selvini-Palazzoli's newer work, carried out in collaboration with a new group of colleagues, is called *Family Games* (Selvini-Palazzoli, Cirillo, Selvini, & Sorrentino, 1989); in it she proposes a universal intervention said to be particularly applicable to breaking up repetitively resistant patterns in families with severely disturbed members.

Long Brief Therapy

Two distinguishing characteristics of classic Milan systemic family therapy have been its *spacing of therapeutic sessions* and its use of a *team of therapists* who work together with a family. The original Milan team method has been described as "long brief

Luigi Boscolo, M.D.

therapy" (Tomm, 1984a), since relatively few sessions (generally about ten) were held approximately once a month and thus treatment might extend up to a year or so. Initially, this unusual spacing of sessions was instituted because so many of the families seen at the Center in Milan had to travel hundreds of miles by train for treatment. Later, the therapy team realized that their interventions—often in the form of paradoxical prescriptions aimed at changing the way an entire family system functioned—took time to incubate and finally take effect. Once the frequency was determined, the therapists did not grant an extra session or move up a session to shorten the agreed-upon interval. Such requests by families are seen as efforts to disqualify or undo the effects of a previous intervention (Selvini-Palazzoli, 1980). Systemicists are adamant in their determination that the therapist not submit to the family's "game" or become subjugated to its rules for maintaining sameness and controlling the therapeutic relationship. Even under pressure from the family, these therapists would remain unavailable in the belief that a request for an exceptional meeting actually means the family is experiencing rapid change and needs the time to integrate any subsequent changes in family rules.

During most of the 1970s, the Milan group worked in an unconventional but consistent way developed from their strategic-based research. The entire family was seen together by one or sometimes two therapists (typically, a man and a woman), while the remainder of the team watched from behind a one-way mirror in order to gain a different perspective. From time to time during the session, the observers would summon one of the therapists out of the room in order to change therapeutic direction; while conferring with the therapist, they would make suggestions, share opinions, provide their own observations, and often issue directives that the returning therapist could then share with the family.

Following this strategy conference, the therapist rejoined the family group, discussed what had transpired with the other team members, and assigned the family members a task, usually a paradoxical prescription. Sometimes such an intervention took the form of a *paradoxical letter,* a copy of which was given to every family member. In the event that a key member missed a session, a copy of the letter would be sent by mail, frequently with comments (again, often paradoxically stated) regarding his or her absence. Prescriptions took the form of opinions ('We believe Father and Mother, by working hard to be good parents, are nevertheless..."), or requests that certain behavioral changes be attempted by means of rituals carried out between sessions ("The immediate family, without any other relatives or outsiders, should meet weekly for one hour, with each person allowed fifteen minutes to..."). By addressing the behavior of all the members, the therapists underscored the connections in the family patterns. Prescriptions usually were stated in such a way that the family was directed not to change for the time being. Box 11.1 offers a typical paradoxical letter with subsequent analysis keyed to specific statements.

Structured Family Sessions

The classic Milan therapeutic interview format thus was divided into five segments: the presession, the session, the intersession, the intervention, and the postsession discussion. Family therapy began with the initial telephone call from the family. The team member who took the call talked to the caller at length, recording the information on a fact sheet. Who calls? Who referred the family? What is the problem? How disturbed is the caller's communication? What tone of voice is used? What is the caller's attitude regarding the forthcoming treatment? What special conditions, if any, does the caller attempt to impose (specific date or time)? These intake issues were then taken up with the entire team in the presession, prior to the first interview, in a lengthy and detailed way, and tentative *hypotheses* regarding the family's presenting problem were proposed by the various team members. Particularly noteworthy is the fact that the referring person or agency was kept involved throughout treatment, a recognition of their part in the larger system.

In a similar fashion, such team conferences occurred before each session, as the group met to review the previous session, and, together, planned strategies for the upcoming one. All of these tactics affirmed the Milan therapists' belief that the family and therapist(s) are part of one system. During the session itself, a major break in the family interview (the intersession) occurred as the observer team had an active discussion with the therapist outside of the hearing of the family, during which hypotheses were validated or modified; the therapist then returned to offer the team's intervention (usually a prescription or ritual) to the family. The team postsession discussion focused on an analysis of the family's reaction to the intervention as well as providing a chance to plan for the following session (Boscolo, Cecchin, Hoffman, & Penn, 1987).

In this earlier version of the Milan model there is more concern with family processes than family structure. Members of dysfunctional families were seen as engaging in unacknowledged destructive, repetitive sequences of interaction. No one seemed able to extricate himself or herself from the family's self-perpetuating "games" in which members tried to control each other's behavior. The identified problem is

BOX 11.1   A paradoxical letter

Dear Norma, Sara, Ann, and Dave:

I was very impressed with the sadness and hurt in your family in our last session. I am glad the two of you were able to express your sadness.[1] It is important when you are sad and hurt to be able to share your feelings with other family members. Family members who share their hurts really love one another.[2]

However, I have grave misgivings about how much you should share at this time. I think it is much too soon for you to communicate these feelings to each other.[3] Instead each of you should continue to protect the family from its sadness by distracting or keeping each other busy.[4] You might even select one family member on whom you can focus all of your attention, or maybe someone in the family has already decided to take this role. This person could be responsible for starting fights and misbehavings.[5] The person selected should be a very responsible and local member of the family; this should make the choice easy because one of you already is acting in an overtly responsible manner (but enjoying it).[6]

Your family is also in a silent crisis.[7] Someone has changed recently, which has the family confused and uncertain about the future. The confusion and chaos in the family are actually part of the preparation for the family's forthcoming growth and change.[8] *Warning:* The family should be prepared for a big fight on Wednesday night.[9]

1. *Cryptic statement:* Raises the question of who expressed sadness, is designed to unite the family in guessing who it was.
2. *Relabeling:* Sharing hurt is equated to love.
3. *Restraining:* Previous statement tells the family members it is good to share hurt, but now they are warned that it may be risky.
4. *Positive connotation:* Distraction is said to protect the family, which puts them all on the same level.
5. *Prescription:* The fighting is prescribed.
6. *Relabeling:* The most distracting member of the family is relabeled as the one who is responsible and loyal.
7. *Cryptic statement:* What is a "silent crisis"?
8. *Relabeling:* Remember, this is a chaotic family; there is no predictability or certainty; the confusion is relabeled as preparation for growth.
9. *Paradoxical question:* Our next session is scheduled for Thursday; the oldest daughter said she would not return; hence we expect a fight about her attendance on Wednesday night, if not earlier.

Source: Weeks and L'Abate, 1982

seen as serving the system in the best way possible at the moment. Why, then, can the family not find a better way to survive and function, one that does not involve sacrificing one of its (symptomatic) members? Perhaps the rules governing the system are too rigid, tolerating an extremely narrow range of behavior. Since the family members, through their communication patterns, maintain the system's rules and thus perpetuate the transactions in which the symptomatic behavior is embedded, the therapist must try to change the rules in order to change that behavior (Selvini-Palazzoli, Boscolo, Cecchin, & Prata, 1978).

Put more succinctly, systemic therapy tried to discover, interrupt, and thus change the rules of the game before the behavior of the players (the symptomatic member as well as other family members) could change. For example, the therapist working with a family with an anorectic daughter must break the code inherent in the following family game, as each parent both insists upon and denies family leadership (Selvini-Palazzoli, 1978):

> **Mother:** I don't let her wear miniskirts because I know her father doesn't like them.
>
> **Father:** I have always backed my wife up. I feel it would be wrong to contradict her. (p. 208)

Note the trap the therapist is drawn into if he or she tries to change such confusing and disqualifying statements. Direct interventions are likely to bring forth countermoves, as the family members fight off any challenge to their rules. Following Bateson's earlier work, Selvini-Palazzoli and her colleagues in their early formulations contended that a family double-bind message, a paradox, can only be undone by a therapeutic double bind, which they call a counterparadox.

MILAN INTERVIEWING TECHNIQUES

We first consider two early Milan therapeutic interventions: positive connotation and ritualized prescriptions.

Positive connotation is a form of reframing the family's problem-maintaining behavior in which symptoms are seen as positive or good because they help maintain the system's balance and thus facilitate family cohesion and well-being. By suggesting a good motive for behavior previously viewed as negatively motivated ("The reason your child refuses to go to school is that he wants to provide companionship for his lonely mother"), the systemic therapist is indicating to the family that the symptomatic behavior formerly looked upon negatively may actually be desirable. Instead of being considered "bad" or "sick" or "out of control," the symptomatic child is considered to be *well-intentioned* and to be *behaving volitionally*. Note that it is not the symptomatic behavior (school refusal) that is connoted to be positive, but rather the intent behind that behavior (family cohesion or harmony).

All members are considered to be motivated by the same positive desire for family cohesion, and thus all are linked as participants in the family system. Because the positive connotation is presented by the therapist as an approval rather than a reproach, the family does not resist such explicit confirmation and accepts the statement. As a result of reframing, the symptomatic behavior is now viewed by the family as voluntary, greatly enhancing the possibilities for change. However, the positive connotation has implicitly put the family in a paradox: Why must such a good thing as family cohesion require the presence of symptomatic behavior in a member?

One other important function of positive connotation deserves mention: It prepares the family for forthcoming paradoxical prescriptions. That is, when each member's behavior is connoted as positive, all view one another as cooperative and thus are more willing to join in complying with any tasks they may be assigned by the therapist, reducing family resistance to future change. If the therapist adds a no-change prescription ("And because you have decided to help the family in this way, we think that you should continue in this work for the time being") (Tomm, 1984b, p. 266), an additional paradox of "no change in the context of change" further increases the impact of the intervention. The seemingly innocuous phrase "for the time being" implies that the current family pattern need not always occur in the current manner, leaving open the possibility of future spontaneous change. The family is left to resolve the paradoxical absurdities on their own.

Family **rituals,** such as weddings, birthday parties, baptisms, bar mitzvahs, graduations, funerals, and so forth, often play a central role in a family's life. Such transitions are designed to mark and facilitate family developmental transitions and changes. Therapeutically, they may be designed to intervene in established family patterns, promoting new ways of doing things, which in turn may alter thoughts, beliefs, and relationship options (Imber-Black, 1988).[1] As Campbell, Draper, and Crutchley (1991) put it:

> The purpose of a ritual is to address the conflict between the family rules operating at the verbal level and those operating at the analogic level by a prescription to change behavior rather than an interpretation to provide insight. (p. 327)

Rather than offer a direct prescription, which the family may fear or resist or otherwise oppose, ritualizing the prescribed behavior offers a new context, and is thus more likely to be carried out by the family. Rituals usually are assigned in paradoxical prescriptions describing in detail what act is to be done, by whom, when, and in what sequence. Typically, carrying out the ritual calls for the performance of a task that challenges some rigid, covert family rule.

Rituals address aspects of family relationships that the therapist or team hypothesizes as significant for family functioning, based on how the team views the family's current difficulty. Generally, they are ceremonial acts proposed by the therapist in a tentative way as suggestions or family experiments, and are not expected to become

---

[1]Strategic therapists make frequent use of assigned rituals in working with individuals as well as families to help them break out of rigid behavior patterns. Fisch, Weakland, and Segal (1982) of the MRI report the case of a perfectionist who was given the task of making one deliberate mistake a day. In this case, a woman potter who expressed various complaints about her creations was directed to produce imperfect pottery for one hour on an agreed-upon day. Similarly, instructing a rigid or compulsive person to fail purposely (say something inappropriate or stupid, behave in clumsy or gauche ways) often has a liberating effect.

a permanent part of family life. The therapist does not insist the ritual be carried out but only indicates that he or she believes the gesture to be useful.

Generally speaking, the purpose of a ritual is to provide clarity where there might be confusion in family relationships; the clarity is gained by the family's enactment of the directive (Tomm, 1984b). Take the case of parents who are inconsistent or competitive with one another in attempting to maintain behavioral control of a disruptive child. An alternating day ritual might be suggested in which Mother takes full charge of discipline on odd days (with father observing and taking exact notes on the ensuing mother-child interaction) and Father takes charge on even days (with mother playing the counter-role). Each is directed to carry out the assigned roles for a certain number of days, and to behave "spontaneously" for the remaining days of the week. Carrying out the ritual clarifies differences in approach for the parents and provides greater awareness of how their differences can cause confusion in their child. It thus highlights the importance of two-parent consistency as a goal if the child is to achieve the comfort level necessary to abandon the disruptive behavior.

Drawing attention to crucial distinctions is thus an important aspect of a ritual. In some cases the message the therapists wish to convey is sufficiently critical that they prepare a written statement for the family to read before carrying out the task. As Tomm (1984b) observes, rituals often enable the family to clarify chaotic patterns and confront inherent but previously unrecognized contradictions.

The three landmark intervention strategies—hypothesizing, circularity, and neutrality—developed near the end of the original Milan group's collaboration are central to post-Milan technical innovations. Circular questioning in particular has become the cornerstone of Boscolo and Cecchin's later modifications of the original systemic outlook. Further refinements have been offered by Penn (1982; 1985) and Tomm (1987a; 1987b). When systemic therapists speak of circularity they are referring both to interactional sequences within the family and, because the therapist is part of the system, to the therapist's interactional relationship with the family. The therapist's hypotheses lead to questions, and the family's responses lead to refined hypotheses and new questions, all leading to changes in the family's belief system.

Central to the basic Milan approach and thus the first act of this type of therapy is *hypothesizing*. Systemicists believe that unless the therapist comes to the family session prepared with hypotheses to be checked out, there is the risk that the family may impose its own definition of the problem and its resolution, which is likely to be faulty and game-perpetuating of the presenting problem. Hypothesizing refers to the active efforts the team makes during the presession to formulate in advance of the family session what they believe might be responsible for maintaining the family's presenting symptoms. Diagnostically useful in formulating a "map" of the family's "game," hypothesizing also serves to orient the therapist to ask the kinds of questions that will elicit answers that confirm, necessitate revision of, or refute the suppositions.

Consider the following hypothesis about how the symptom of anorexia might provide a clue about the family game:

> A 13-year-old girl whose mother has recently returned to work goes on a diet to lose her "baby fat" and continues food refusal to the point of developing symptoms of

anorexia. These symptoms and the resulting danger to the girl's health require that her mother leave her newly acquired job and become active in monitoring her daughter's eating habits. The father, who is 9 years older than the mother, encourages his wife in this diligent detective-like behavior. When viewed within the context of this family's relationship pattern the child's self-destructive behavior can be seen as an ingenious attempt, covertly supported by the father, to keep her mother dependent and tied into the role of wife and mother. Alternately it can be seen as supporting the mother's ambivalence regarding obtaining employment, and her need to pull the father closer to home with worries. Finally, as Selvini-Palazzoli (1986) recently argued, the child's behavior may represent the culmination of concerted efforts among all family members to prove that competition leads nowhere. (Gelcer, McCabe, & Smith-Resnick, 1990, p.52–53)

Hypotheses formulated by the team typically take the form of systemic or relational statements, linking all family members, and thus offer a circular structure regarding family rules and interactive behaviors. They help the team organize forthcoming information from the family and begin to comprehend why the symptomatic behavior manifested itself in this family at this time. Hypotheses are carefully constructed to elicit a picture of how the family is organized around the symptom or presenting problem. Circularity throughout the family system is stressed. Asked for a description of the problem at the start of the first interview, the family might point to the symptom bearer as the one with the problem. The Milan therapist will ask, "*Who noticed the problem first?*" This redefines the problem as relational—it does not exist without a "noticer," and thus it does not belong to one person alone. Moreover, the problem is depicted as an event between two or more family members, thus involving the wider family system (Boscolo, Cecchin, Hoffman, & Penn, 1987).

Hypothesizing permits the therapist to present a view of the family's behavior that is *different*—not true or false, but simply different from their own established self-picture. The therapist is thus offering a conceptualization—of the family's communication patterns, the meaning of a member's symptoms, the way in which the family organizes itself to deal with problems, the family game, and so forth. In doing so, the therapist identifies himself or herself as an active participant, someone who does not necessarily have all the answers but with his or her unique view of the family's reality, intended to open the family up to considering a new perspective on their lives.

As Burbatti and Formenti (1988) contend, *the goal of therapeutic hypotheses is change, not truth.* In the Batesonian tradition, hypothesizing offers information, allowing the family members to choose or reject the therapeutic message from an active therapeutic partner. If, instead, the therapist were simply a passive observer, the Milan group believes the family would impose its own punctuations, and resume its own games; little if any new information would be forthcoming to initiate change, and the system would tend toward entropy. Hypothesizing, on the other hand, offers a structured viewpoint, organizing data provided by the family, encouraging the family to rethink their lives and together begin to form new hypotheses (for example, regarding previously denied coalitions) about themselves and their "games."

One particularly significant accomplishment of the Milan team was to translate Bateson's earlier view of the key role of circular causality in understanding relationships into an exquisite interviewing technique. As Selvini-Palazzoli, Boscolo, Cecchin, and Prata (1980) define it in their landmark paper:

> By circularity, we mean the capacity of the therapist to conduct his investigation on the basis of feedback from the family in response to the information he solicits about relationships and, therefore, about differences and change. (p. 3)

Underscoring the notion of feedback loops, the team developed guidelines for asking questions that led to the construction of a map of the interconnections between family members. More specifically, rather than rely on a free-form set of therapeutic questions, based loosely on previously formulated hypotheses, they insisted on questions that (1) probed differences in perceptions about relationships ("Who is closer to Father, your daughter or your son?"); (2) investigated degrees of difference ("On a scale of one to ten, how bad do you think the fighting is this week?"); (3) studied now-and-then differences ("Did she start losing weight before or after her sister went off to college?"); and (4) sought views of family members on hypothetical or future differences ("If she had not been born, how would your marriage be different today") (Boscolo, Cecchin, Hoffman, & Penn, 1987, p. 11). The idea was to search for mutually causal feedback chains underlying family interactive patterns, and to incorporate these findings into systemic hypotheses, which in turn would form the basis for asking further circular questions, leading to further refined hypotheses, and so forth. Particularly ingenious about the technique is that it allows very little room for a refusal to answer, since questioners are given choices.

The technique focuses attention on family connections rather than individual symptomatology, by framing every question so that it addresses differences in perception by different family members about events or relationships. Asking a child to compare his mother's and father's reactions to his sister's refusal to eat, or to rate each one's anger on a ten-point scale, or to hypothesize what would happen if they divorced—these are all subtle and relatively benign ways to compel people to focus on differences. By asking several people the same question about their attitude toward the same relationship, the therapist is able to probe more and more deeply without being directly confrontational or interrogating the participants in the relationship (Selvini-Palazzoli, Boscolo, Cecchin, & Prata, 1980).

Family members reveal their connections through the communication of information, expressed in verbal as well as nonverbal fashion. Information about the family lies in differences in meaning each participant gives an event. Such differences in turn reflect views of family relationships. Circular questioning aims at eliciting and clarifying confused ideas about family relationships and introducing information about such differences back to the family in the form of new questions. Table 11.1 provides examples of common types of circular questions.

Such triadic questioning (addressing a third person about the relationship between another two) often produces change in the family in and of itself, as well as providing information to the therapist. Families learn in the process to think in circular rather than linear terms, and to become closer observers of family processes. Another member's perspective may prove enlightening when compared with one's own view of an event or relationship. Circular questioning a Milan trademark, always addresses significant family issues and not trivial or irrelevant differences.

Table 11.1 Circular Questions

Category	Definition/Function	Examples
Differences in relationship	Establishes interpersonal relationships, subsystems, and alliances.	Who are you closest to in the family? Who do you confide in the most?
Differences in degree	If a problem can be more or less, then it also has the potential to cease.	Who worries more about your son? Is the fighting worse or is the running away worse? On a scale of 1 to 5, how much does that worry you?
Differences in time	If a problem has a beginning, then it can have an end.	Does she cry more now that you are separated, or did she cry more when you were together? Who noticed first? Who was cooperative before he became cooperative? Are you closer now than you used to be?
Hypothetical/ future	Establishes a sense of control over actions.	If you were to leave, what would he do? When your daughter leaves for college, how will your husband react?
Observer-perspective	Help individuals to recognize how their own reactions, behaviors, and feelings may serve as links in the family interactions.	Who agrees that this is a problem? How does your father express love? Who is your mother likely to get support from? How would your daughter describe your discipline style?
Normative-comparison	Promote healthy functioning by establishing a healthy frame of reference. Allow individuals identified as the problem to feel less abnormal.	Does your family fight more or less than other families? Is your family more or less tight knit than other families? Is your son more rowdy than the other boys his age? Do you and your husband argue more than other couples you know?
Hypothesis introducing	Help move the family toward new insights or solutions by imbedding a working hypothesis into a question.	If you get angry to cover up your vulnerability, does you family interpret that as your being hostile? Do you see your shyness as a way of not getting close to others or as a way of being selective about who you want to be friends with?
Linear	Noncircular questions used when history or specific information is desired.	Where are you employed? How long have you been married? What other problems do you see? How long has he been gone? How do you punish him when he misbehaves?

Source: Prevatt, 1999, p. 191

Such questions need to be guided by hypotheses, since hypotheses are what give order and coherence to the therapist's pattern of circular questioning (Tomm, 1984b).

Neutrality refers to the therapist's efforts to remain allied with all family members, avoiding getting caught up in family coalitions or alliances. Such a position, typically low-key and nonreactive, gives the therapist maximum leverage in achieving change by not being drawn into family "games" or appearing to side with one family member against another. More concerned with curiosity about how the family system works than with attempting to change it, the neutral therapist assumes that the system the family has constructed makes sense; the family could not be any other way than they are at the moment. By not offering suggestions as to how the family should be, the therapist activates the family's capacity to generate its own solutions (Boscolo, Cecchin, Hoffman, & Penn, 1987).

Being neutral does not imply being inactive or indifferent. Actually, the therapist might display neutrality by listening without prejudice to what is being said, but at the same time asking thought-provoking, relationship-focused, circular questions. A report that the family argues a lot might be accepted by the neutral therapist as interesting information. Without joining the family in assuming arguing is bad, the therapist might inquire, *"Who enjoys fighting the most?"* or *"What would be missing if all the arguing suddenly stopped?"* (Tomm, 1984b). (Note that a hypothesis that the family is getting something out of the fighting is subtly being explored.) Nor should the therapist become too committed to the family's changing. As Selvini-Palazzoli has observed, "If you wish to be a good therapist it is dangerous to have too much of a desire to help other people" (quoted in Simon, 1987, p. 28). Rather, the therapist's goal should be to *help the family achieve change in its ability to change*. They also have the right not to change. Neutrality precludes taking a position for or against any specific behavioral goals from therapy or that the therapist must somehow be the one to effect change.

QUESTIONING FAMILY BELIEF SYSTEMS

Despite the continuing evolvement of the Milan team's ideas, their basic therapeutic mission has remained constant: to help families recognize their choices and to assist members in exercising their prerogatives of choosing. Fundamental to accomplishing these goals is the creation of a therapeutic climate where family members can hear each other's perspectives as each answers therapist questions. If differences in viewpoint continue to exist, at least members listen and learn to accept the other viewpoints or belief systems as viable (Gelcer, McCabe, & Smith-Resnick, 1990). Questioning family members, hypothesizing about the family game, and constantly feeding back information to the family have remained the key methods of achieving those goals.

As we have noted, heavy use of the paradox-counterparadox phenomenon characterized the early Milan team efforts. Dysfunctional families with a symptomatic member, presumably seeking change, themselves seemed to behave in a paradoxical manner—the moves each member of the system made seemed to keep change from occurring. In effect their common message was that they had a problematic member who needed to change, but as a family the rest of the members were fine and did not intend to change. Recognizing from a systems perspective that it is impossible for a part to change without a complementary change in the whole, the Milan group began to design interventions in the form of counterparadoxes directed at breaking up such contradictory patterns, thus freeing up the family to change. One common counterparadox, as we have seen, was to declare that although they were change agents, they did not wish to upset what appeared to be a workable family homeo-static balance and therefore would prescribe no change for now (Selvini-Palazzoli, Boscolo, Cecchin, & Prata, 1978). Thus, the therapist might say, "I think the family should continue to support Selma's behavior for the present."

In a later revision that shifted their thinking away from the MRI version of fam-ilies as self-correcting systems governed through rules, the Milan team began to think of systems as evolving and unfolding rather than seeking a return to a previ-ous homeostatic level. Extrapolating from Bateson's (1972) work, they theorized that dysfunctional families are making an "epistemological error"—they are following an outdated or erroneous set of beliefs or "maps" of their reality; that is why they appear to be "stuck" or in homeostatic balance. Put another way, the family was having problems because they had adopted a set of beliefs that did not fit the reality in which they were living their lives. In effect, they were being guided by an out-of-date map when the signs and streets had changed since the map's publication.

In point of fact, according to this new perspective, the family's beliefs about itself were not the same as the actual behavior patterns of its members, so that they only gave the impression of being "stuck"; in reality their behavior was changing contin-uously. The Milan group decided they needed to help families differentiate between these two levels—meaning and action. Therapeutically, they began to introduce new information, new distinctions in thought and action, carefully introducing a differ-ence into the family's belief system. Relying now on circular questioning to present differences for the family to consider, the team attempted to activate a process in which the family creates new belief patterns and new patterns of behavior consistent with those beliefs (Tomm, 1984a). New information was given the family explicitly through reframing or implicitly through the prescription of family rituals.

By uncovering connecting patterns, by revealing family "games," by introducing new information into the system through opinions or requests that certain family rit-uals be carried out between sessions, Milan therapists were trying to bring about a transformation in family relationship patterns. Note that, unlike Haley, whom we discussed in Chapter 10, they did not issue prescriptions to arouse defiance and resistance. Rather, they offered "information" about family connectedness and the interrelatedness of members' behavior. By deliberately trying not to provoke resist-ance to change, they were offering input in the form of information in order to help the family discover its own solutions (MacKinnon, 1983).

Milan therapeutic procedures also changed over time. The classic method—male and female cotherapists, two team members behind the one-way mirror—was amended so that a single therapist was likely to work with the family while the rest of the team (often students learning the technique) observed. The observers, were free to call the therapist out of the room to share ideas and offer hypotheses. The five-part session division (presession, session, intersession, and so on) has been maintained by and large, although the fixed month-long interval between sessions has become more flexible, depending upon feedback from the family and consultants. Generally speaking, a ten-session limit extended over an indeterminate period of time still qualifies the approach as long brief therapy (Jones, 1993).

In offering a case study in which acting-out children "provide a shield for marital difficulties," Prevatt (1999) outlines the following steps in her work with the family:

1. Constructing a working hypothesis
2. Exhibiting a therapeutic stance of neutrality
3. Using circular questioning as both an assessment and therapeutic technique
4. Working with a team to monitor the process
5. Identifying the labels used by the family
6. Identifying openings or themes to be explored
7. Using positive connotation for problematic behaviors
8. Using an end-of-session intervention

The Invariant Prescription

In their evolving therapeutic approach, Selvini-Palazzoli and Prata have sought to avoid employing hit-or-miss end-of-session prescriptions for each new family by specifically seeking a *universal prescription* that would fit all families. Their research has focused on finding similarities in the games that "crazy" families play, and formulating countermoves so that the therapist can interrupt these games and force a change in family interactive patterns (Pirrotta, 1984).

In a later therapeutic modification, developed from research begun with Prata (1990), Selvini-Palazzoli (1986) focused on the impact of a single sustained intervention to unhinge collusive parent-child patterns. Seeking a way to successfully intervene with chronically psychotic adolescents and adults, she and a new set of associates (Selvini-Palazzoli, Cirillo, Selvini, & Sorrentino, 1989) began to elaborate on her earlier conceptualization of severely dysfunctional behavior as linked to a specific "game" within the family. To break up the game, they now suggested the controversial proposal that therapists offer a solitary prescription or task for the parents. Later, Selvini-Palazzoli proposed that this universal or invariant prescription be applied to all families with schizophrenic or anorectic children. Generally limited to ten sessions, using a team approach, and following the structured sessions format, this method calls for a more directive therapist in control of the sessions. Its underlying paradoxical message is that a family member's (say, a child's) symptoms represent understandable motives but contribute to the damaging family games.

The **invariant prescription** is based on a six-stage model of psychotic family games. Selvini-Palazzoli contends that a single process takes place in all schizophrenic and anorectic families, beginning with a stalemated marriage (stage 1) in which a child attempts to take sides (stage 2). Eventually drawn into the family game, the child erroneously considers the actively provoking parent to be the winner over the passive parent, and sides with the "loser." The subsequent development of disturbed behavior or symptomatology in the child (stage 3), requiring parental attention, represents a demonstration to the passive parent of how to defeat the "winner." Instead of joining the child, however, the passive parent or "loser" sides with the "winner" parent (stage 4) in disapproving of the child's behavior. The child, in this scenario, feels betrayed and abandoned and responds by escalating the disturbed behavior, determined to bring down the "winning" parent and show the "loser" what can be done (stage 5). Ultimately the family system stabilizes around the symptomatic behavior (stage 6), all participants resorting to "psychotic family games" as each tries to turn the situation to his or her advantage (Selvini-Palazzoli, 1986).

A provocative therapeutic strategy in such a situation is to offer the parents an invariant prescription—a fixed sequence of directives they must follow if the therapist is to help them interrupt the family game. After an initial family interview, the therapist sees the parents separately from the child and gives them the following prescription intended to introduce a clear and stable boundary between generations (Selvini-Palazzoli, 1986):

> Keep everything about this session absolutely secret at home. Every now and then, start going out in the evenings before dinner. Nobody must be forewarned. Just leave a written note saying, "We'll not be home tonight." If, when you come back, one of your (daughters) inquires where you have been, just answer calmly, "These things concern only the two of us." Moreover, each of you will keep a notebook, carefully hidden and out of the children's reach. In these notebooks each of you, separately, will register the date and describe the verbal and nonverbal behavior of each child, or other family member, which seemed to be connected with the prescription you have followed. We recommend diligence in keeping these records because it's extremely important that nothing be forgotten or omitted. Next time you will again come alone, with your notebooks, and read aloud what has happened in the meantime. (pp. 341–342)

The parental alliance, reinforced by joint action and by secretiveness, is strengthened by the prescription (Selvini-Palazzoli, Cirillo, Selvini, & Sorrentino, 1989; Prata, 1990) and previously existing alliances and family coalitions are broken. Parental disappearance exposes and blocks family games, over which none of the players had complete control but which nevertheless perpetuated psychotic behavior. The overall therapeutic thrust, then, is to separate the parents from the rest of the family, alter previous family interactive patterns, and then reunite the family in a more stable alliance at the conclusion of the treatment.

Although Selvini-Palazzoli (1986) claims a high success rate for this powerful intervention technique, the therapeutic power of a single prescription for all disturbed families still remains to be established, as does its potential applicability to troubled families with less serious dysfunction. Nevertheless, this description of the psychotic process occurring in certain families is intriguing, and the use of this potent intervention procedure aimed at strengthening parental alliances and dislodging family coalitions is an admirable effort to break up a rigid, destructive family game and force family members to invent more flexible ways of living together.

A Post-Milan Systemic Epistemology

Boscolo and Cecchin, in their training seminars, have turned increasingly to developing ways of introducing new ideas and new patterns of thinking to family members (Pirrotta, 1984). Unlike Selvini-Palazzoli's direct, take-charge therapeutic style, offering parents prescriptions, their efforts emphasize neutrality as a more effective device for quietly challenging an entire family to reexamine its epistemology. In effect, they temporarily join the family, becoming part of a whole system from which they can begin to offer information and perspectives on reality. In essence, the therapists and family members influence one another, producing the opportunity for change as a by-product.

Expanding on earlier cybernetic ideas, Boscolo and Cecchin argue that by becoming part of the observing system, the observer loses all objectivity, and there no longer exists a separate observed (family) system. Having adopted such second-order cybernetic concepts, they observe that

> first-order cybernetics pictured a family system in trouble as a homeostatic machine. Jackson's model based on the concept of family homeostasis is such a case. According to Jackson, a symptom plays an important part in maintaining the homeostasis of the family.
>
> This model was, perhaps, an advance over nineteenth-century models for psychopathology...but still separated the therapist from the client. A second-order model conceptualizes the treatment unit as consisting of both the observer and the observed in one large bundle. This cannot be achieved easily as long as pathology is assumed to be in a container: as in a..."dysfunctional family system." (Boscolo, Cecchin, Hoffman, & Penn, 1987, p. 14)

Boscolo and Cecchin now argue that perhaps it is better to do away with the concept of family systems entirely, and think of the treatment unit as a *meaning system* in which the therapist is as active a contributor as anyone else. Any intervention, then, should not be directed at a particular outcome, but rather should be seen as perturbing the system that then will react in terms of its own structure. Here they are in agreement with biologist Humberta Maturana (1978) as we have noted in Chapter 5. For Boscolo and Cecchin, the system does not create the problem! Rather, the problem creates the system; it does not exist apart from the "observing systems" that reciprocally and collectively define the problem. Thus, therapists

> cannot change families through therapeutic interventions but can merely coexist in a therapeutic domain in which they may perturb the system through interaction but that will only lead to therapeutic change if the structure of the family system allows the perturbations to have an effect on its organization. (p. 335)

Consistent with postmodern ideas, therapists do not have the answers but, together with the family, can co-construct or coevolve new ways of looking at the family system, creating the possibility of new narratives or versions of reality that are less saturated with past problems or past failed solutions.

Karl Tomm, in a series of papers (1987a, 1987b, 1988), has elaborated on these second-order cybernetics ideas, arguing that the presence of the therapist in the enlarged therapist-family system calls for him or her to carry out continuous "interventive interviewing." More than simply seeking workable interventions, Tomm (1987a) urges therapists to attend closely to the interviewing process, especially their own intentionality, adopting an orientation in which everything an interviewer does and says, and does not do and say, is thought of as an intervention that could be therapeutic, nontherapeutic, or countertherapeutic.

Tomm thus adds "strategizing" to the original set of Milan techniques of hypothesizing, circularity, and neutrality. His circular questions are carefully constructed, not simply for information-gathering purposes but also as a change-inducing technique (Slovik & Griffith, 1992). Here Tomm is referring to a therapist's ongoing cognitive activity, evaluating the effects of past therapeutic actions, developing new plans of action, anticipating the consequences of possible interventions, and deciding, moment to moment, how most effectively to achieve maximum therapeutic influence. More specifically, Tomm is interested in the kinds of questions a therapist asks to help families exact new levels of meaning from their behavior, in the service of enabling them to generate new ways of thinking and behaving on their own.

Of greatest relevance are what Tomm (1987b) refers to as *reflexive questions*. Intended to be facilitative, they are designed to move families to reflect on the meaning they extract from their current perceptions and actions, stimulating them to consider alternative options. Tomm differentiates eight groups of reflexive questions:

1. *Future-oriented questions* (designed to open up consideration of alternate behavior in the future) ("If the two of you got along better in the future, what would happen that isn't happening now?")
2. *Observer-perspective questions* (intended to help people become self-observers) ("How do you feel when your wife and teenage son get into a quarrel?")
3. *Unexpected counterchange questions* (opening up possibilities of choices not previously considered by altering the context in which the behavior is viewed) ("What does it feel like when the two of you are not fighting?")
4. *Embedded suggestion questions* (allowing therapist to point to a useful direction) ("What would happen if you told her when you felt hurt or angry instead of withdrawing?")
5. *Normative-comparison questions* (suggesting problem is not abnormal) ("Have any of your friends recently dealt with the last child leaving home, so that they would understand what you are going through now?")
6. *Distinction-clarifying questions* (separating the components of a behavior pattern) ("Which would be more important to you—showing up your boss's ignorance or helping him so that the project can be successfully completed?")
7. *Questions introducing hypotheses* (using tentative therapeutic hypotheses to generalize to outside behavior with others) ("You know how you become silent when you think your husband is angry with you? What would happen if next time you told him how you felt?")
8. *Process-interrupting questions* (creating a sudden shift in the therapeutic session) ("You just seemed to get quiet and upset, and I wonder if you thought I was siding with your wife?")

Tomm's classification of questions represents an attempt to alert therapists to what can and should be asked of families, as well as what impact a series of circular questions is likely to have on families. These questions permit the therapist to plan interventive interviewing, ever mindful of the intention behind the questions they construct. Through a series of such questions, Tomm intends for families to break free of their current fixed ideas and achieve new meaning as they go about reorganizing their behavior.

SUMMARY

The Milan team practices systemic family therapy, an outlook based on Bateson's circular epistemology. The technique has undergone a number of changes over the years as the original four principals—Selvini-Palazzoli, Boscolo, Cecchin, and Prata—presented many innovative interviewing techniques aimed at counteracting sustained and entrenched family games. Initially emphasizing paradoxical therapeutic measures, the four later introduced hypothesizing, circular questioning, and therapist neutrality as guidelines for conducting sessions, helping each family member become exposed to information about the perceptions of the other members and interrupt destructive family interactive patterns. Positive connotations and the use of prescribed rituals are other Milan therapeutic trademarks.

The four separated into two groups in 1980—Selvini-Palazzoli and Prata continued to engage in research directed at interrupting destructive family games, while Boscolo and Cecchin pursued the development of training models, seeking to advance a new systemic epistemology. The interviewing process itself, especially the use of circular questioning, has become the cornerstone of Boscolo and Cecchin's modification of the original Milan systemic method of working with families.

Selvini-Palazzoli and Prata have developed an invariant prescription for forcing change in the interactive patterns of severely disturbed families. Boscolo and Cecchin have been influential in stimulating interest in second-order cybernetic ideas, developing a post–Milan view that has had a great impact on postmodern therapeutic efforts. Tomm has elaborated on their thinking, cataloguing sets of circular questions aimed at encouraging families to reflect on the meaning of their life patterns in an effort to trigger families to consider new cognitive and behavioral options.

12

Cognitive-Behavioral Models

Cognitive-behavioral models of family therapy are relatively recent additions to the field, since it is only within the last 25 years or so that the application of **behavioral** concepts has been extended to the couple or family unit. The use of therapeutic behavioral methods with individuals, however, goes back to the early 1960s when, largely as a reaction against what was perceived as unverifiable psychodynamic theory and technique, a movement began to bring the scientific method to bear upon the psychotherapeutic process.

Behavior therapy involves the application of learning theory and other experimentally based principles to changing undesired client behavior. In its initially presented formulations, family members when considered at all were assumed to be a part of the client's natural environment; as such, the manner in which they stimulated or aroused a client's problematic or maladaptive behavior as well as how they responded to reinforce that behavior was observed, as the therapist sought ways to extinguish the client's undesired behavior. While it was assumed that modifying an individual's deviant behavior necessitated changing the behavior of key family members, therapeutic intervention directed at the family as a whole was rarely attempted. When such efforts first were undertaken (Stuart, 1969; Patterson, 1971), behavior therapists were more apt to address specific behavioral problems in families (poor communication between spouses, acting-out behavior in children and adolescents), identified in a family assessment process, than attempt to gain a comprehensive picture of family dynamics (Sanders & Dadds, 1993).

As Falloon (1991) illustrates, a therapist observing a child's deviant behavioral patterns assumed that the maintenance of the troublesome behavior resulted at least in part from the **reinforcement** (the consequences immediately following and contingent upon that behavior) provided by other family members. While therapeutic efforts remained individually focused, the behavior therapist nevertheless attempted, simultaneously, to instruct key family members on how best to change or modify their behavior so they would not participate in sustaining the client's deviant behavior. Psychologist Gerald Patterson (Patterson & Brodsky, 1966) was a pioneer in this **behavioral parent training** effort (often carried out in the client's home), clinically adapting learning principles from the laboratory in order to modify both the behavior of a multiple-problem child and the reinforcing responses of his parents.

Behavior therapists working with couples or entire families adopted a similar role (teacher, coach, model) as well as a corresponding set of intervention procedures directed at imparting skills (for example, in problem solving or communication) to improve client relationships. Robert Liberman (1970), a psychiatrist, and Richard Stuart (1969), a social worker, were early proponents of **behavioral couples therapy.** Both offered interventions based on **operant conditioning,** relying on the Skinnerian principle that certain voluntarily emitted responses can be strengthened by selectively rewarding or reinforcing those responses, so that in the future they will occur more frequently than other responses not rewarded. Liberman also pioneered what is now considered a **psychoeducational** approach to working with families with mentally disordered members (see Chapter 14). Stuart, working primarily with distressed couples, offered a **contingency contract,** a written schedule describing the terms for the exchange of mutually reinforcing behaviors between individuals. Other early behavioral therapists, such as Joseph Wolpe (1958), a psychiatrist then living in South Africa, advanced a set of desensitization techniques based upon the earlier **classical conditioning** laboratory studies of Ivan Pavlov and John Watson.

Table 12.1 lists the major assumptions of behavior therapy. Note especially the emphasis on a scientifically based methodology, the continuous interplay between assessment of family functioning and treatment planning, the introduction of interventions to diminish specific problematic behavior patterns, and the use of feedback information from the implementation of interventions to measure changes of targeted behaviors.

A GROWING ECLECTICISM: THE COGNITIVE CONNECTION

By the late 1970s, some behaviorists, less determined to keep mental activities out of the equation than in the past, began to acknowledge that **cognitive** factors (attitudes, thoughts, beliefs, attributions, expectations) also influence behavior, and an auxiliary cognitive component was sometimes introduced to supplement the main behavioral treatment. Increasingly, since that breakthrough, mental health theorists, researchers, and practitioners have come to recognize **cognitive behavior therapy** as a major part of mainstream psychotherapy (Dattilio, Epstein, & Baucom, 1998). Particularly significant has been the willingness of these therapists to deal with an individual's imagery, mental activities, and thought patterns as frequently being key factors in the development, maintenance, and modification of dysfunctional behavior in individuals.

Albert Ellis, a psychologist, and Aaron Beck, a psychiatrist, are generally considered to have offered the earliest cognitive slants on intimate couple relationships. According to Ellis's (1979) A-B-C theory of dysfunctional behavior, it is not the activating events (A) of people's lives that have disturbing consequences (C), but the unrealistic interpretation they give to the events, or the irrational beliefs (B) about

Table 12.1   Ten Underlying Assumptions of Behavioral Therapy

1. All behavior, normal and abnormal, is acquired and maintained in identical ways (that is, according to the same principles of learning).

2. Behavior disorders represent learned maladaptive patterns that need not presume some inferred underlying cause or unseen motive.

3. Maladaptive behavior, such as symptoms, is itself the disorder, rather than a manifestation of a more basic underlying disorder or disease process.

4. It is not essential to discover the exact situation or set of circumstances in which the disorder was learned; these circumstances are usually irretrievable anyway. Rather, the focus should be on assessing the current determinants that support and maintain the undesired behavior.

5. Maladaptive behavior, having been learned, can be extinguished (that is, unlearned) and replaced by new learned behavior patterns.

6. Treatment involves the application of the experimental findings of scientific psychology, with an emphasis on developing a methodology that is precisely specified, objectively evaluated, and easily replicated.

7. Assessment is an ongoing part of treatment, as the effectiveness of treatment is continuously evaluated and specific intervention techniques are individually tailored to specific problems.

8. Behavioral therapy concentrates on "here-and-now" problems, rather than uncovering or attempting to reconstruct the past. The therapist is interested in helping the client identify and change current environmental stimuli that reinforce the undesired behavior, in order to alter the client's behavior.

9. Treatment outcomes are evaluated in terms of measurable changes.

10. Research on specific therapeutic techniques is continuously carried out by behavioral therapists.

Source: Goldenberg, 1983, p. 221

what has taken place that cause them trouble. Thus, a partner might have unrealistic expectations about a relationship, "catastrophize" a commonplace disagreement, indoctrinating herself with negative evaluations ("I am worthless, a failure") afterward. Ellis suggests it is not the quarrel per se, but the exaggerated, illogical, or otherwise flawed interpretation that causes havoc and leads to negative views of oneself or the future of the relationship. **Cognitive restructuring** would help the client modify her perceptions and allow her new self-statements ("It's really upsetting that we don't agree, but that doesn't mean I'm a failure as a person or that our marriage is doomed").

Beck, originally trained as a psychoanalyst, began to deviate from that position as a result of his research (Beck, 1967) with depressed patients, in which he concluded that they felt as they did because they committed characteristic *errors of thinking* (negative thoughts about themselves, the world, the future). Beck hypothesized that earlier in life these depressed people had, through various unfortunate personal and interpersonal experiences, acquired negative **schemas** (enduring sets of core beliefs and attitudes about people, relationships, and so on) that are reactivated when a new situation arises that resembles, in their thinking, conditions similar to those under which the schema was learned. Cognitive distortions follow, leading to a misperception of reality. Beck's (1976) therapeutic efforts were then directed at providing patients with experiences, both during therapy sessions and outside the consultation room, that disconfirm negative conclusions (such automatic thoughts as "It's hopeless"; "I'm to blame") and attempt to alter negative schemas. Beyond changing current distorted beliefs, Beck advocated the therapist and client work together to teach the latter methods useful in the future for evaluating other beliefs.

Many of the ideas initially proposed by Ellis's rational-emotive therapy[1] and Beck's cognitive therapy were originally considered too simplistic by family therapists when compared to the more complex systems theory then at the height of its popularity, and consequently they received little attention. By the late 1980s, however, as a result of a great deal more systems-friendly research on the role of the partners' perceptions, thoughts, and expectations regarding each other's actions, cognitive interventions in marital and family therapy had gained a foothold (Dattilio & Padesky, 1990; Epstein, 1992).

Acknowledging that some problematic responses within a family are mediated by distorted or dysfunctional beliefs, attitudes, and expectations, many behaviorists working with couples began to broaden their outlook to include the use of cognitive restructuring procedures. This was done in order to help clients explore dysfunctional interpretations, modify automatic thoughts and assumptions, and alter hampering schemas (for example, about a partner's trustworthiness). It is especially in the area of marital or couples therapy that cognitive theory and research has made its strongest contribution to date (Munson, 1994). Just as behaviorists have integrated cognition into behavior therapy, Dattilio (1998) has recently attempted to use cognitive-behavioral theories and techniques as integrative components with other models of couple and family therapy.

Cognitive-behaviorists view people as neither exclusively driven by inner conflicts (the orthodox psychoanalytic stance) nor helplessly buffeted by outside forces (the orthodox behavioral position). Instead, they understand personal functioning to be the result of continuous, reciprocal interaction between behavior and its controlling social conditions. While once behaviorists sought exclusively to change the environmental conditions that maintain undesired behavior, most now also emphasize the importance of *self-regulation* and *self-direction* in altering behavior. Cognitive behavior therapy attempts to modify thoughts and actions by influencing an individual's conscious patterns of thoughts (Meichenbaum, 1977).

As Bandura (1978) points out, humans can observe and evaluate the effect of their behavior on other people and can adapt or modify their behavior accordingly. He suggested that humans have the capacity for engaging in symbolic thought, allowing them the flexibility to be self-regulating in their actions. As currently practiced, behavior, cognition, and such personal factors as emotion, motivation, physi-

---

[1]Ellis (1995) has recently rechristened his approach Rational Emotive Behavior Therapy (REBT) to acknowledge its affinity to the behavioral outlook. According to Ellis, REBT is a more accurate description of the interaction between thinking/feeling/wanting and behaving. Cognitive therapists believe that how we think determines how we feel and behave.

ology, and physical factors are all recognized as mutually influential and overlapping (Granvold, 1994).

Although attending less exclusively to observable behavior than advocates of **radical behaviorism,** and also trying to modify a client's thinking processes, cognitive-behavioral therapists continue to "place great value on meticulous observation, careful testing of hypotheses, and continual self-correction on the basis of empirically derived data" (Lazarus, 1977, p. 550). Gambrill (1994) actually defines behavioral practice as "an empirical approach to personal and social problems in which the selection of assessment and intervention methods is based whenever possible on related research" (p. 32). The unique contribution of this approach, then, lies not in its conceptualizations of psychopathology or adherence to a particular theory or underlying set of principles, cr even to a unique set of interventions, but in its insistence on a rigorous, data-based set of procedures and a regularly monitored scientific methodology.

As we have pointed out, although the traditional behavioral viewpoint continues to focus on the identified patient as the person having the problem, and in that sense remains largely linear in approach, there are efforts by some behaviorally oriented therapists (for example, Alexander & Parsons, 1982; Jacobson & Christensen, 1996) to accommodate a systems/behavioral/cognitive perspective.[2] Most behavioral family therapists today continue to view family interactions as maintained by environmental events preceding and following each member's behavior. These events or contingencies, together with mediating cognitions, are what determine the form as well as the frequency of each family member's behavior (Epstein, Schlesinger, & Dryden, 1988).

THE KEY ROLE OF ASSESSMENT

Cognitive therapists and behavioral therapists share these features, according to Beck (1995):

> They are empirical, present-centered, problem-oriented, and require explicit identification of problems and the situations in which they occur as well as the consequences resulting from them. (p. 232)

Cognitive-behaviorists strive for precision in identifying a problem, employ quantification to measure change, and conduct further research to validate their results. They design programs that emphasize a careful assessment of the presenting problem (a **behavioral analysis** of the family's difficulties) along with a number of direct and pragmatic treatment techniques to alleviate symptoms and teach the family how to improve its skills in communication and self-management.

A behavioral analysis might include an objective recording of discrete acts exchanged by family members, along with the behaviors of others that serve as

---

[2]A particularly interesting conversion involves Geral Patterson, once a strict behaviorist, who modified many of his views after studying systems theory with Salvador Minuchin.

antecedent stimuli, as well as the interactional consequences of the problematic behavior (Epstein, Schlesinger, & Dryden, 1988). Doing so, the interviewer is attempting to pinpoint exactly which behavior needs to be altered and what events precede and follow manifestation of the behavior. For instance, working with a distraught family in which the presenting problem is a 4-year-old boy's "temper tantrums," the behavioral therapist might want to know exactly what the family means by "tantrums," the frequency and duration of such behavior, the specific responses to the behavior by various family members, and especially the antecedent and consequent events associated with these outbursts. By means of this inquiry, the behavioral therapist attempts to gauge the extent of the problem and the environmental factors (such as the presence of a particular family member, a particular cue such as parents announcing bedtime, a particular time and place such as dinnertime at home) that maintain the problematic behavior. The assessment of environmental circumstances is especially crucial, since the behavioral therapist believes that all behavior (desirable and undesirable) is maintained by its consequences.

Similarly, cognitive-behaviorists use many of the same assessment and treatment techniques as other behavioral therapists, but supplement them with a concern for how the individual organizes, stores, and processes information (Kendall, 1981). As Dattilio and Padesky (1990) point out, cognitive therapists work at three interconnected levels: (1) the most accessible level of *automatic thoughts* (ideas, beliefs, images) people have regarding a specific situation ("My husband is late. He doesn't care about my feelings"); (2) at a deeper level, *underlying assumptions* (rules that are the roots of automatic thoughts) ("You can't count on men to be there for you"); and (3) at the core, basic beliefs or *schemas* (inflexible, unconditional beliefs for organizing information) ("I'll always be alone"). Beginning with the automatic erroneous belief, the woman has jumped to the extreme or inappropriate conclusion of anticipated lifelong loneliness. Such a set of beliefs influences her appraisal of her husband's subsequent behavior, in turn causing an emotional and behavioral response to her. Cognitive-behaviorists are especially interested in identifying the frequency and reciprocal patterns of both positive and negative behaviors that couples exchange in assessing relationship distress before introducing a cognitive restructuring program.

Falloon (1991) suggests that a behavioral assessment of family functioning typically occurs at two levels: (1) a **problem analysis** that seeks to pinpoint the specific behavioral deficits ("Seven-year-old Michael steals from his mother's purse"; "Eleven-year-old Joan can't seem to pay attention in school") that underlie the problem areas, which, if modified, would lead to problem resolution; and (2) a **functional analysis** directed at uncovering the interrelationships between those behavioral deficits and the interpersonal environment in which they are functionally relevant. Functional analyses seek understanding of the immediate antecedents and consequences of the problem behavior ("We've tried to stop Michael from watching television (ground Joan on weekday nights) but then we stop enforcing the rules after a few days").

Here the therapist is interested in increasing positive interaction between family members, altering the environmental conditions that oppose or impede such interaction, and training family members to maintain the improved behavior. No effort is made to infer motives, uncover unconscious conflicts, hypothesize needs or drives, or diagnose inner pathological conditions producing the undesired behavior; the individual or family is not necessarily helped to gain insight into the origin of current problems. Instead, emphasis is placed on the environmental, situational, and social determinants that influence behavior (Kazdin, 1984). Those therapists that are more strictly behavioral attempt to train a person's behavior rather than probe those dimensions of personality that, according to other models, underlie behavior.

Cognitive therapists, on the other hand, include a functional analysis of *inner experiences*—thoughts, attitudes, expectations, beliefs. Less linear in outlook, they see individuals as interactive participants, interpreting, judging, and influencing each other's behaviors.

For all cognitive-behavioral therapists, however, proper assessment plays a vital role, not merely to guide or help them focus their intervention efforts but also to provide feedback regarding the success of their efforts so that further modifications can be introduced (Arrington, Sullaway, & Christensen, 1988). Typically, they gather such data using three methods: self-report questionnaires, clinical interviews, and direct observations of family interaction (Epstein, Schlesinger, & Dryden, 1988). As an example of a family self-report, parents complaining about their child's resistance to a bedtime schedule might be asked to keep logs at home, monitoring and recording specific acts and their specific responses ("For the last four nights, our 8-year-old has gone from one of us to the other until his father finally agrees he can stay up past his bedtime and watch the TV program"). In the case of adult relationship problems, specific tests (for example, Eidelson & Epstein's [1982] Relationship Belief Inventory or Fincham & Bradbury's [1992] Relationship Attribution Measure) might be employed, tapping unrealistic beliefs about close relationships in the first example, or attributions (inferences about the cause of events in their relationship), such as a partner's perceived overcriticalness (Dattilio, Epstein, & Baucom, 1998).

As for interview-based data, the therapist might probe automatic thoughts—*beliefs* ("He avoids talking to me at night"), *expectancies* ("I hate to make plans with friends because he's always late"), or *attributions* ("The reason he acts as he does is because he doesn't care about my feelings") as clients report upsetting experiences with one another. Direct observations of couples, for example, might focus on a couple's communication skills deficits as they are directed to plan a night out away from the children, or perhaps their deficits in negotiation skills as their failure to compromise escalates conflict. On the other hand, asked by the therapist to solve a problem together in the therapist's office, they may discover that they possess heretofore untapped problem-solving skills. Such structured tasks (for example, role playing an adolescent's request for a later curfew) are often used by cognitive-behavioral therapists to check on progress in reaching the desired changes in targeted behaviors (Epstein, Schlesinger, & Dryden, 1988).

FORMS OF COGNITIVE-BEHAVIORAL FAMILY THERAPY

Generally speaking, the work of behavioral family therapists (including cognitive-behaviorists) has a number of characteristics that distinguish it from the approaches taken by the systems-oriented family therapists we have considered:

- A direct focus on observable behavior, such as symptoms, rather than an effort to hypothesize causality interpersonally
- A careful, ongoing assessment of the specific, usually overt, behavior to be altered
- A concern with either increasing (accelerating) or decreasing (decelerating) targeted behavior by directly manipulating external contingencies of reinforcement
- An effort to train families to monitor and modify their own reinforcement contingencies
- A standard of empirically evaluating the effects of therapeutic interventions

The behaviorally oriented family therapist is more likely than most systems-based family therapists to use distinct clinical procedures (such as skills training) and not to be insistent on the participation of the entire family. Sometimes the family is brought in when individual procedures fail or when behavioral observation suggests that family members are helping maintain the individual's symptomatic behavior; they are excused after that phase of therapy is completed, the therapist continuing with individually oriented procedures. Extended family members are far less likely to be involved in behavioral therapy. In general, behavioral family therapists view the family as burdened by the patient, or perhaps as unwittingly responding in ways that support and maintain his or her problem behavior, while most systems-oriented family therapists assume that family involvement is always present and plays an active part in symptom maintenance (Todd, 1988).

Moreover, as noted earlier, behavioral family therapists tend to adopt a linear rather than a circular outlook on causality. For instance, a parent's inappropriate, inconsistent, or otherwise flawed response to a temper tantrum is believed to cause as well as maintain a child's behavioral problem (contrary to the more commonly held systems view among family therapists that the tantrum constitutes an interaction, including a cybernetic exchange of feedback information, occurring within the family system). Predictably, the behavioral family therapist is likely to aim his or her therapeutic efforts at changing dyadic interactions (for example, a mother's way of dealing with her child's having a tantrum) rather than adopting the triadic view more characteristic of systems-oriented family therapists, in which the participants in any exchange are simultaneously reacting to other family transactions (for example, a mother who feels neglected by her husband and who attends too closely to the slightest whims of her child; a father who resents his wife taking so much attention away from him in order to interact with their son).

While some of the leading behavioral family therapists such as Gerald Patterson, Robert Liberman, Richard Stuart, and James Alexander do view the family as a social system (whose members exercise mutual control over one another's social reinforcement schedules), others remain far from convinced. Gordon and Davidson (1981), for example, acknowledge that in some cases a strained marital relationship may contribute to the development and/or maintenance of deviant child behavior (or vice versa), but they argue that systems theorists have exaggerated the prevalence of the phenomenon. Their experiences lead them to conclude that deviant child behavior may occur in families with and without marital discord; they state that "the simple presence of marital discord in these families may or may not be causally related to the child's problems" (p. 522).

Behavioral Couple Therapy

Not long after the behavioral approach in psychology began to be applied to clinical problems in individuals, interest grew in adapting this perspective to problems of marital discord. By the end of the 1960s, Robert Liberman and Richard Stuart separately had published their early efforts in this regard, each offering a straightforward, step-by-step set of intervention procedures in which some basic operant conditioning principles were applied to distressed marital relationships. From its inception, the basic premise of behavioral marital therapy (BMT), according to Holtzworth-Munroe and Jacobson (1991), has been that

> the behavior of both partners in a marital relationship is shaped, strengthened, weakened, and modified by environmental events, especially those events involving the other spouse. (p. 97)

Manipulating the Contingencies of Reinforcement.   Liberman's (1970) approach began with a behavioral analysis ("What behaviors would each like to see changed in themselves or their partners?" "What interpersonal contingencies currently support the problematic behavior?") followed by an effort to restructure the reciprocal exchange of rewards between the partners. That is, after assessing what needed fixing, he attempted to increase certain target behaviors and decrease others by directly manipulating the external contingencies of reinforcement. The couple, in turn, was expected to monitor and modify their own reinforcement contingencies. Liberman's goals were simple and straightforward, and especially in their early form focused strictly on behavior change: to guide couples to increase their pleasing interactions and decrease aversive interactions.

Stuart (1969) developed a set of therapeutic procedures he called **operant interpersonal therapy,** especially the use of contingency contracting, to try to get couples to maximize the exchange of positive behaviors. He argued that successful marriages can be differentiated from unsuccessful ones by the frequency and range of reciprocal positive reinforcements the partners exchange ("I'll be glad to entertain your parents this weekend if you accompany me to the baseball game (or ballet performance) next month"). Although this technique today is considered by most family therapists to be an oversimplified, heavyhanded, and mechanical approach to a complex marital exchange, Stuart was beginning to blend Skinner's operant learning principles with *social exchange theory* (Thibaut & Kelley, 1959). Relationship satisfaction was recast as reward-cost ratios: If missing but potentially rewarding events can be identified and maximized and displeasing events occurring in excess can be identified and minimized, then the reward-cost ratio should increase greatly and each partner should not only feel more satisfied but also be more willing to provide more rewards

Robert Liberman, M.D.

for the other partner. As part of Stuart's approach, he had each partner record the number of instances and the type of caring behavior he or she offers each day. Table 12.2 offers a sample of such "caring days" requests.[3]

The use of contingency contracting and the teaching of behavioral exchange strategies characterized the approach of behavioral marital therapists during the 1970s, particularly Jacobson and Margolin (1979). Contingency contracting remained the focal point of the approach, both to enhance the quality and quantity of mutually pleasing interactions and, by nonreinforcement, to diminish the frequency of arguments, provocations, and generally negative communication sequences (Falloon & Lillie, 1988).

From Reinforcements to Skills Building. Communication/problem-solving training was often introduced in the 1980s with the intent of teaching couples to negotiate resolutions of their conflicts (present and future) in noncoercive ways, thus creating positive relationship changes. In some cases, **therapeutic contracts**—written agreements between spouses stipulating specific behavioral changes—were negotiated. Here, each spouse explicitly states what behavior he or she wants increased, thus avoiding the all-too-familiar marital plea for mind reading, "If you really loved me, you'd know what I want." Note how the agreement developed by Stuart (1980) in Table 12.3 offers each partner a range of constructive choices any one of which can

---

[3]In *Helping Couples Change,* Stuart (1980) spelled out in greater detail his "caring days" technique for building commitment in a faltering marriage. All requests must meet the following criteria: (1) they must be positive ("Please ask how I spent my day" rather than "Don't ignore me so much"); (2) they must be specific ("Come home at 6 p.m. for dinner" rather than "Show some consideration for your family"); (3) they must be small instances of behavior that can be demonstrated at least once daily ("Please line up the children's bikes along the back wall of the garage when you get home" rather than "Please train the children to keep their bikes in the proper place"); and (4) they must not have been the subject of recent intense conflict (since neither spouse is likely to concede major points at this stage of treatment).

Table 12.2   A Sample Request List for Caring Days

Wife's Requests	Husband's Requests
1. Greet me with a kiss and hug in the morning before we get out of bed.	1. Wash my back.
2. Bring me pussywillows (or some such).	2. Smile and say you're glad to see me when you wake up.
3. Ask me what recording I would like to hear and put it on.	3. Fix the orange juice.
4. Reach over and touch me when we're riding in the car.	4. Call me at work.
5. Make breakfast and serve it to me.	5. Acknowledge my affectionate advances.
6. Tell me you love me.	6. Invite me to expose the details of my work.
7. Put things away when you come in.	7. Massage my shoulders and back.
8. If you're going to stop at the store for something, ask me if there is anything that I want or need.	8. Touch me while I drive.
9. Rub my body or some part of me before going to sleep, with full concentration.	9. Hold me when you see that I'm down.
10. Look at me intently sometimes when I'm telling you something.	10. Tell me about your experiences at work everyday.
11. Engage actively in fantasy trips with me—e.g., to Costa Rica, Sunshine Coast.	11. Tell me that you care.
12. Ask my opinion about things you write and let me know which suggestions you follow.	12. Tell me that I'm nice to be around.
13. Tell me when I look attractive.	
14. Ask me what I'd like to do for a weekend or a day with the desire to do what I suggest.	

Source: Stuart, 1976

Table 12.3   A Holistic Therapeutic Marital Contract

It is understood that Jane would like Sam to:	It is also understood that Sam would like Jane to:
wash the dishes;	have dinner ready by 6:30 nightly;
mow the lawn;	weed the rose garden;
initiate lovemaking;	bathe every night and come to bed by 10:30;
take responsibility for balancing their checkbooks;	call him at the office daily;
invite his business partners for dinner once every six or eight weeks;	plan an evening out alone for both of them at least once every two weeks;
meet her at his store for lunch at least once a week.	offer to drive the children to their soccer-practice and swim meets;
	accompany him on occasional fishing trips.

It is expected that Sam and Jane will each do as many of the things requested by the other as is comfortably manageable, ideally at least three or four times weekly.

Source: Stuart, 1980, p. 248

satisfy their reciprocal obligations. By not creating the expectation that reciprocation should be forthcoming immediately ("I'll do this if you do that"), a contract can increase the likelihood of spontaneous reciprocation.

Despite modifications from its earlier exclusive focus on behavior, the basic premises and practices of behavioral marital therapy, as outlined by Liberman and Stuart, remained tied to basic learning principles. However, critics charged that some of its earlier assumptions were too simplistic: that both partners, as rational adults, will not resist change but will follow the therapist's suggestions; that a focus on overt behavior change is sufficient, without attending to underlying perceptual processes and interpersonal conflicts; that marital disharmony derives from the same sources, such as insufficient reciprocity, throughout the marital life cycle; that displeasing behavior, such as anger, should simply be held in check without exploring the covert reasons for conflict; that the couple-therapist relationship can be ignored (Gurman & Knudson, 1978).

Increasingly based on **social learning theory** (learning that occurs as a result of interaction with other people) as well as behavioral-exchange principles, behavioral marital therapy has become less technological and more flexible over time. In addition to encouraging the increased exchange of pleasing behavior (and the diminution of aversive behavior) between partners, behavioral marital therapists such as Jacobson and Margolin (1979) also aim at problem reduction through teaching couples more effective problem-solving skills. Such problem solving is broken down into two separate phases: *problem definition* (learning to state problems in clear, specific, nonblaming ways; learning to acknowledge one's own role in creating or perpetuating the problem; attempting to paraphrase the other's view, even if inconsistent with one's own) and *problem resolution*. Brainstorming solutions together and negotiating compromises (which later may be put in writing) often facilitate problem resolution. Rather than the accusatory "You don't love me anymore," the therapists suggest the more concrete, less provocative, more self-revealing "When you let a week go by without initiating sex, I feel rejected" (Jacobson & Margolin 1979, p. 230). These therapists consider contingency contracting as the last phase of developing viable problem-solving skills, for which the partners share responsibility.

By the end of the 1980s, behavioral couples therapy typically included four basic components: (1) a behavioral analysis of the couple's marital distress based on interviewing, self-report questionnaires, and behavioral observations; (2) the establishment of positive reciprocity through techniques such as "caring days"; (3) communication skills training (using "I" messages to express one's own feelings; sticking to here-and-now problems rather than dwelling on the past; describing the other's specific behavior rather than applying a label such as "lazy" or "cold"; providing positive feedback to the other person in response to similar behavior from that person); and (4) training in problem solving, including specifying, negotiating, and contracting (Hahlweg, Baucom, & Markman, 1988).

Recognizing that behavior changes will lead to greater marital satisfaction, practitioners of behavioral marital therapy attempted to create behavior change in two ways: (1) encouraging partners to define the specific behaviors they wish their partners to exhibit, then instructing them in how to increase the frequency of those behaviors; and (2) teaching couples communication and problem-solving skills so that they can produce those changes (Eldridge, Christensen, & Jacobson, 1999).

Broadening the Outlook: The Cognitive Perspective.   Gaining prominence in the late 1980s, cognitive-behavioral therapists argued that distress and conflict in a relationship are influenced by an interaction of cognitive, behavioral, and affective factors, and that a strictly behavioral approach did not fully address such dynamic interplay (Epstein, Schlesinger, & Dryden, 1988). Consequently, they contended, behavior change alone is insufficient in effecting permanent resolution of conflict between partners, particularly if that conflict is intense and ongoing. In order to resolve the likely escalating antagonistic and provocative behavior between the pair, couples need to acquire skills for recognizing and defining problems clearly, identifying mutually acceptable problem-solving strategies, and implementing these solutions quickly and effectively (Dattilio, Epstein, & Baucom, 1998).

Cognitive restructuring directed at changing dysfunctional interactional patterns is called for; only a change in their belief structures about marriage can ensure a happier and more fulfilling relationship. Working with the marital pair, cognitive therapists try to modify their unrealistic expectations about what they should expect from the relationship, and teach them how to decrease destructive interactions. Distortions in evaluating experiences, derived from negative automatic thoughts that flash through one's mind ("I notice her looking at other men whenever we go out. She must be thinking she'd be better off with someone else.") are labeled as beliefs that in effect are *arbitrary inferences* in the absence of supporting evidence. Sometimes such automatic thoughts, which couples are taught to monitor, may take the form of *overgeneralizations* (the housewife who forgets to pick up her husband's shirts at the laundry is labeled by him as "totally undependable"). In other cases, *selective abstractions* may be operating ("You're good at finding the one thing I forgot to do, but you never seem to notice the things around here that I do"). By identifying and exposing each partner's underlying schema about themselves, their partner, and the marital relation, the therapist helps the couple accept responsibility together for the distress they are experiencing (Epstein & Baucom, 1989). Sometimes "homework" assignments to be carried out away from the session are made by the therapist; these often replace Stuart's (1980) therapeutic contracts, but have the same goal: a written agreement to decrease specific negative behaviors by substituting specific positive behaviors each stipulates as wanting to receive, to be reviewed the next session.

Integrative Couples Therapy.   Neil Jacobson, a leading behavioral researcher/practitioner/innovator for two decades, and Andrew Christensen (Jacobson & Christensen, 1996; Christensen, Jacobson, & Babcock, 1995; Eldridge, Christensen, & Jacobson, 1999) have developed behaviorally based therapeutic strategies for promoting more accommodating and collaborative attitudes—"partner acceptance"—in addition to the more traditional behavioral techniques for helping couples attain behavior change. As Jacobson (1991) describes the therapeutic process directed at helping couples achieve an interactional or contextual change:

> By promoting an intimate conversation about the differences between them that make desired changes impossible, the partners are getting much of what they need from the conversation itself, and thus the original problem becomes less important.

In this eclectic approach, strategic techniques (reframing) and experiential techniques (empathic joining of the couple around the problem, self-care) are added to the more commonplace behavioral methods (use of assessment instruments, therapist modeling, behavioral exchange interventions, communication/problem-solving training) in an effort to promote intimacy and understanding in place of anger and blame (Jacobson & Christensen, 1996). A combination of these techniques are directed at overcoming each participant's tendency to see the problem between them as emanating exclusively from his or her partner, and subsequently attempting (unsuccessfully) to change the other person's behavior where changes are not feasible. Instead, **integrative couples therapy** delineates various procedures designed to help couples see certain differences between them as inevitable, helping foster tolerance of perceived negative behaviors in a partner, and acceptance of those behaviors especially resistant to change. Departing from his earlier approach (Jacobson & Margolin, 1979), Jacobson and his associates developed these procedures to accommodate those couples who failed to benefit from traditional skills training, in some cases because underlying emotions hindered the exchange of positive behaviors (Eldridge, Christensen, & Jacobson, 1999).

In contrast to cognitive-behavioral procedures, integrative couples therapy represents a return to a more traditional behavioral emphasis on the functional analysis and external determinants of behavior (Christensen, Jacobson, & Babcock, 1995). However, its therapeutic interventions represent a departure from traditional behavioral couples therapy. Historically, those approaches have focused on achieving *change,* since excesses or deficits in the behavior of one partner were considered to be the causes of distress in the other. Such change was typically generated by behavioral exchange strategies or communication/problem-solving techniques, directed at helping couples change the *rules* of their behavior (the husband learns to kiss his wife upon arriving home since the therapist instructed him to increase positive behaviors leading to the wife's greater satisfaction).

Unfortunately, the underlying *theme of the problem*—that he still "doesn't get it" about being generally more attentive and caring and that she finds that intolerable— does not get addressed, since it would be impossible to review every one of their interactions where change is desired. In other cases, the rule-governed behavior feels fake or contrived or insincere, and backfires and is abandoned. Rule-governed processes may lead to change, argue these therapists, but additional strategies are needed when the couples are unable or unwilling to make the changes the other desires.

Emotional acceptance refers to situations where behavior change either fails to occur, or else occurs but not to the extent the partner would like. Instead of demanding more of what was deemed insufficient (or less of what was excessive), here the partners are urged to alter their reactions to the behavior previously seen as intolerable or unacceptable in their partner, in effect *balancing change with acceptance* of those behaviors not open to change. Acceptance may be enhanced in two ways: (1) by experiencing the problem in a new way, say as a common enemy (from joint empathic understanding of the problem or perhaps from detachment from the problem so it becomes less offensive); or (2) by reducing the aversiveness of the partner's actions (either through greater tolerance of those actions or through the increased ability to take care of oneself when confronted with the partner's negative behaviors) (Christensen, Jacobson, & Babcock, 1995). They may still not like the behavior, or wish it were different, but nevertheless learn to consider it a part of the package of qualities (many appealing, some bothersome) in their mate. In effect, instead of seeking to change aversive behavior in order to achieve relationship satisfaction, this approach also fosters acceptance of that behavior where change is unattainable, so that it is experienced in a new way, as less aversive (Eldridge, Christensen, & Jacobson, 1999).

Behavioral research in couples therapy.   The behavioral analysis of marital distress has become an area of significant research in recent years. Howard Markman (1992), a psychologist, focusing his longitudinal research with couples on what causes marital distress, concludes that it is not so much the differences between people that matter, but rather how those differences are handled (that is, how couples learn to communicate and manage conflict). In a four- to five-year follow-up of a marital distress prevention program directed at teaching more effective communication and conflict management skills, Markman and colleagues (Markman, Renick, Floyd, Stanley, & Clements, 1993) found that those couples functioning at a higher level had maintained more positive communication patterns while those functioning more poorly exchanged more negative communication and showed greater marital violence.

Markman, a prominent longitudinal researcher, has, along with his colleagues, investigated the impact of couples' exchange of negative affect before parenthood on their later marital and family functioning (Lindahl, Clements, & Markman, 1997). Observing and coding the communication patterns of 25 couples before becoming parents and again five years later, these researchers wanted to know how the couples' earlier ability to handle marital conflict predicted how they would handle the competing needs of children and deal with later marital conflict. Using behavioral observations and videotapes of mother-child and father-child interactions, results indicated that the way in which couples handle negative affect with one another after parenthood is a more salient factor in how they manage and regulate negative affect with their children than would have been predicted from pre-child marital functioning. However, the husband's pre-child angry and conflictual behavior and the couples' negative escalation were predictive of marital conflict and the triangulation of the child into their discord. In general, how couples regulate negative affect early in marriage, while not decisive in itself, appears to set the tone for future parent-child interactions. We'll return to the work of Markman and his associates (Floyd, Markman, Kelly, Blumberg, & Stanley, 1995) on preventive intervention and relationship enhancement when we discuss psychoeducational programs for couples and families (Chapter 14).

John Gottman (1979; 1993), perhaps today's most prolific marriage researcher, has offered a number of studies on those aspects of the marital interactive processes that discriminate between happily married and unhappily married couples. Using video cameras, EKG monitors, galvanometer sensors, and specially designed observational instruments, Gottman and his research team (Gottman & Krokoff, 1989; Gottman, Coan, Carrere, & Swanson, 1998) compared how couples communicate, both verbally and nonverbally, microsecond by microsecord. In their sequential analysis, they studied such indicators as body movements, facial expressions, gestures, even heart rates during conflict with one another, attempting to identify those behavioral and physiological responses essential to a stable marriage as well as those that predict the couple is headed for divorce (Gottman, 1994).

According to his findings, and contrary to popular opinion, it is not the exchange of anger that predicts divorce, but rather four forms of negativity that Gottman calls "The Four Horsemen of the Apocalyse"—*criticism* (attacking a spouse's character), *defensiveness* (denying responsibility for certain behavior), *contempt* (insulting, abusive attitudes toward a spouse), and *stonewaling* (a withdrawal and unwillingness to listen to one's partner). In a typical demand-withdrawal transaction, women were found more likely to criticize while men were likelier than women to stonewall.

According to Gottman (1994), there are three types of stable couples: (1) *volatile couples* (those who are emotionally expressive, may bicker frequently and passionately, but are more romantic and affectionate than most couples); (2) *validating couples* (harmonious but less emotionally expressive, these couples listen to one another and try to understand each other's viewpoint); and (3) *conflict-avoding couples* (those low in emotional expressiveness, who typically resolve problems by minimizing or avoiding them, emphasizing the positive aspects of their relationship and accepting negative aspects as unchangeable).

Gottman's findings indicate a greater climate of agreement in these happily married couples: there were five positive to one negative response exchanged in all three stable couples while the positive to negative ratio in unstable marriages was 0.8:1 (that is, more negativity than positivity). Gottman and Krokoff (1989), in a well-designed longitudinal study, found that while *conflict engagement* (that is, direct, if angry, expressions of dissatisfaction) between partners might cause marital distress in the short run, such confrontation is likely to lead to long-term improvement in marital satisfaction by forcing couples, together, to examine areas of disagreements.

Behavioral Parent Training

Much behavioral work, generally following a social learning model, has been directed at problems of child management within the family. Cognitive-behaviorists in particular have attended to those affective and behavioral responses, mediated by thought processes, that occur in parent-child interactions, in an effort to train parents to modify or change a variety of problematic child behaviors. Such programs have focused on serving parents from different cultural, ethnic, or socioeconomic backgrounds; parents whose children have severe developmental disabilities; and parents in various settings, such as schools, residential treatment centers, and so forth. These intervention efforts, primarily directed at teaching parents behavioral strategies for diminishing or extinguishing problematic behavior in their children, have by and large addressed a grab bag of discrete observable behavioral problems (bed-wetting, temper tantrums, chore completion, compliance with parental requests, hyperactivity, sleep problems, and bedtime fears) rather than more global sets of personal or interpersonal problems of children (Dangel, Yu, Slot, & Fashimpar, 1994).

For example, Gerald Patterson, a pioneer in the field of parent training, argues that while out-of-control children are angry, do fail in school, lack self-esteem, and do have poor relationships with their parents, these factors are secondary by-products of an ongoing process and not the causes of delinquency. Advocating parent training for conduct problems, he (Forgatch & Patterson, 1998) contends:

> Aggression in children and adolescents is a behavioral problem, not a mental health problem. The causes lie in the social environment, not in the minds of the youngsters. (p. 85)

That is, for Patterson, external circumstances support deviant behaviors and diminish effective parental responses. Whether due to social disadvantage, parental psychopathology, transitions within the family, or whatever stressful living conditions, Patterson assumes parenting practices (disciplining, appropriately monitoring the child's whereabouts, encouragement for prosocial development) have become disruptive and ineffectual. Thus, parents require training in becoming more consistent and in offering more appropriate consequences for their child's behavior. Research by Patterson and Forgatch (1995) revealed that such a parent training program with preadolescent youngsters significantly led to fewer arrests and out-of-home placements when the parents improved their monitoring, disciplining, and problem-solving practices.

Learning Family Management Skills   Most behavioral parent training (BPT) advocates have had as their goal the alteration of the undesirable behavior in the child, accepting the parents' view that the child is the problem. By changing parental responses, the behavioral therapist hopes to produce a corresponding change in the child's behavior. Psychologists at the Oregon Social Learning Center, under the direction of Gerald Patterson and John Reid, led the way in developing a series of treatment programs, based on social learning principles, teaching parents how to reduce and control disruptive behavior in children (Patterson, Reid, Jones, & Conger, 1975). Initially focused exclusively on parent training, they later acknowledged that teaching parents to change their child-rearing behavior produces parental resistance. Along with educating parents, they now attempt to resolve parental resistance, recognizing that both factors are prime determinants of successful intervention (Patterson, 1985).

Should parents be trained how to most effectively deal with a specific problem from which they seek relief ("Our daughter argues whenever we ask her to do anything"), presumably generalizing learned skills on their own to subsequent problems? Or should they be instructed in a standardized package of skills using behavioral management practices to increase prosocial behavior and decrease problematic behavior in their children, regardless of the presenting problem? Advocating the latter approach, Dangel, Yu, Slot, and Fashimpar (1994) believe in the efficacy of parents acquiring a set of skills that can be used to address a wide range of problems, applicable to a variety of childhood problems and settings such as home or school. More than resolving a particular problem, the skills-building model increases the likelihood that parents will apply the skills to other existing problems or ones that occur in the future or with other children.

Gerald Patterson, Ph.D.

occur in the future or with other children.

Parent skills training has many practical features to recommend it. It is cost-effective in the sense that less time is needed for assessing and developing a specific intervention procedure because the treatment plan is standardized. Its focus is on family empowerment. It minimizes the family's reliance on qualified professional therapists, who may be in short supply. Skills learned with one child may be applicable with his or her siblings should similar conditions arise. Without diminishing parental authority, the training process, if successful, builds competence and a feeling of confidence in parents. Intervention generally begins early, correcting an established problem; parent training thus has a preventive aspect. Perhaps most important, parents possess the greatest potential for generating behavior change because they have the greatest control over the significant aspects of the child's natural environment (Gordon & Davidson, 1981). The use of parents as trainers makes it easier for children to actually use the new behavior they learn, since they do not have to go through the process of transferring what they have acquired from a therapist to their home situation.

The initial request for treatment rarely if ever comes from the child. It is likely to be the parents who are concerned about their child's disturbed (and disturbing) behavior (see Table 12.4) or failure to behave in ways appropriate to his or her age or sex. According to Patterson and Reid (1970), a faulty parent-child interaction pattern has probably developed and been maintained through *reciprocity* (a child responding negatively to a negative parental input) and *coercion* (parents influencing behavior through the use of punishment). BPT intervention aims to change this mutually destructive pattern of interaction, usually by training parents to observe and measure the child's problematic behavior and then to apply social learning techniques for accelerating desirable behavior, decelerating undesirable behavior, and maintaining the consequent cognitive and behavioral changes.

As is true of all cognitive or behavioral interventions, parent training begins with an extensive assessment procedure. Before teaching parenting skills, the behavioral

Table 12.4 Behavior Problems Described as "Severe" by over 4000 Parents During Ten Years of PBT Workshops

Behavior Problem	Percentage Rating as "Severe"
Disobedience; difficulty in disciplinary control	52
Disruptiveness; tendency to annoy and bother others	49
Fighting	45
Talking back	43
Short attention span	42
Restlessness; inability to sit still	40
Irritability; easily aroused to intense anger	37
Temper tantrums	35
Attention seeking; "show-off" behavior	35
Crying over minor annoyances	33
Lack of self-confidence	33
Hyperactivity; "always on the go"	33
Distractibility	33
Specific fears; phobias	17
Bed wetting	16

Source: Falloon & Liberman, 1983, p. 123

observations of parent-child interactions in order to identify the specific problem behavior along with its antecedent and consequent events. Through such a behavioral analysis, the therapist is able to pinpoint the problem more exactly; evaluate the form, frequency, and extent of its impact on the family; and systematically train parents to use social learning principles to replace the targeted behavior with more positive, mutually reinforcing interaction.

The actual training of parents in skills acquisition and knowledge of behavioral principles may be as direct as instructing them, individually or in parent groups, by written material (books, instructional pamphlets), lectures, computer software programs, videotapes, or role-playing demonstrations (Dangel, Yu, Slot, & Fashimpar, 1994). Such focused education is apt to emphasize how, when, and under what circumstances to enforce rules or act consistent, or how to apply behavioral deceleration procedures such as **time out** from positive reinforcement, or acceleration procedures such as home **token economy** techniques (Gordon & Davidson, 1981).

In *Families,* Patterson (1971) first outlined procedures for parents to acquire "behavior management skills" toward more effective child management. Presumably, many adults come by these skills "naturally," that is, without deliberately following a prescribed program. For less well equipped parents, Patterson spelled out a plan for observing a child's behavior to establish a **baseline,** pinpointing the specific behavior the parents wish to change, observing and graphing their own behavior, negotiating a contract with the child, and so on. Figure 12.1 represents a checklist constructed for a boy who displayed a wide range of out-of-control behavior. The parent-child contract, jointly negotiated, stipulated that the parent would check with the teachers daily to get the necessary information and would regulate the consequences for the child's behavior. These consequences included mild but fair punishment for continued problem behavior in addition to "payoffs" (such as no dishwashing chores,

Dave's Program						
	M	T	W	T	F	S
Gets to school on time (2)	2					
Does not roam around the room (1)	0					
Does what the teacher tells him (5)	3					
Gets along well with other kids (5)	1					
Completes his homework (5)	2					
Does homework accurately (5)	3					
Behaves OK on the schoolbus (2)	2					
Gets along well with brothers and sisters in evening (3)	0					
Total	13					

1. If Dave gets 25 points, he doesn't have to do any chores that night and he gets to pick all the TV shows for the family to watch.
2. If Dave gets only 15 points, he does not get to watch TV that night.
3. If Dave get only 10 points, he gets no TV and he also has to do the dishes.
4. If Dave gets only 5 points or less, then he gets no TV, washes the dishes, and is grounded for the next two days (home from school at 4:00 and stays in yard).

Figure 12.1   A parent-child negotiated contract checklist indicating specific duties to be performed and a point system based on the degree of goal achievement.
Source: Patterson, 1971

permission to watch TV) for adaptive behavior. In establishing the contract, the child helps set the "price" in points for each item, sees the results daily (the program is posted in a conspicuous place at home, such as the refrigerator door), and negotiates the backup reinforcers (for example, TV programs) for the accumulated points. The parents are rehearsed and then supervised in the use of these procedures; additional performance training, such as demonstrations by the therapists, may be provided for those having difficulties in carrying out the program. Gordon and Davidson (1981), surveying the literature on the usefulness of the procedure, concluded that "it is an effective intervention for discrete, well-specified behavior problems. In cases of more complex deviant behavior syndromes, the research is encouraging but not conclusive" (p. 547). A major concern, of course, is how long therapeutic changes are maintained after treatment ceases; longer-range follow-up studies are indicated.

The behavioral therapist may also work through the parents when the target for intervention is an adolescent's behavior. By observing the natural interaction between family members (sometimes in a home visit), the behavioral therapist performs a functional analysis of the problem behavior, determining what elicits it, what reinforces and maintains it, and how the family members' interaction reflects their efforts to deal with it (passive acceptance, resignation, anger, bribes, encouragement, and so forth). Such an analysis calls for systematic observation of family behavior, typically recording concrete instances of which behaviors were displayed by which family members in response to which other bits of behavior. Behavioral intervention strategies chosen by the therapist are apt to be specific and directed at helping to resolve or eliminate the problem.

Constructing Contingency Contracts.   Contingency contracting, based on operant conditioning principles, may be a particularly useful "give to get" technique in reducing parent-adolescent problems. The technique is simple and straightforward, usually involving a formally written agreement or contract spelling out in advance the exchange of positively rewarding behaviors between the teenager and his or her parents. Although initially offered by Stuart (1969) in the treatment of marital discord, this reciprocity concept seems especially applicable to parent-adolescent conflict where the previous excessive use of aversive controls by parents (nagging, demanding, threatening) has been met by equally unpleasant responses from the adolescent. The goal here is to acknowledge the power of both sets of participants to reverse this persistent negative exchange by means of a mutual exchange of positive and cooperative giving of pleasurable behavior (Falloon, 1991).

A contract is negotiated wherein each participant specifies who is to do what for whom, under which circumstances, times, and places. Negotiations are open and free from coercion; the terms of the contract are expressed in clear and explicit statements. For example, a contract negotiated between parents and an adolescent with poor grades specifies that she will "earn a grade of 'C' or better on her weekly quiz" rather than "do better in school." The latter is too vague and open to different interpretations by the participants; by that kind of definition the adolescent may believe she has done better and fulfilled her part of the agreement, while the parents believe the gain is insignificant, and the conflict between them over school performance remains unresolved. By the same token, the rewards must be specific ("We will give you $10 toward the purchase of new clothes for each week your quiz grade is 'C' or better") and not general or ambiguous ("We'll be more generous about buying you clothing if you get good grades"). The point here is that each participant must know exactly what is expected of him or her and what may be gained in return.

A contract (Figure 12.2) is an opportunity for success, accomplishment, and reward. However, the desired behavior, such as a "C" grade, must be realistic and within the grasp of the contractor. In addition, each member must accept the idea that privileges are rewards made contingent on the performance of responsibilities. Behavioral therapists believe that a family member will exchange maladaptive behavior for adaptive behavior in anticipation of a positive consequence, a desired change in the behavior of the other. The teenager's responsibility (that is, better grades) is the parents' reinforcer, and the parents' responsibility (money) is the teenager's reinforcer. BPT helps a family set up a monitoring or record-keeping system that enables the contractors and the therapist to assess the reciprocal fulfillment of the terms of the contract. Bonuses are given for consistent fulfillment of the terms, and penalties imposed for failure to adhere to them. Note that as in all behavioral procedures, the

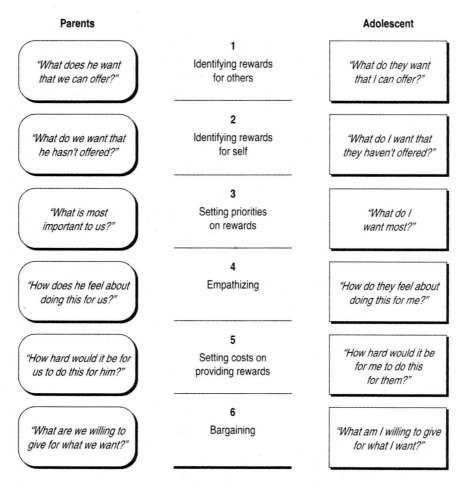

Figure 12.2   Steps in negotiating a contingency contract betwen parents and an adolescent. The family contracting exercise is a structured learning experience conducted by the behaviorally oriented family therapist to help family members, stepwise, to identify their needs and desires (rewards) for themselves and each other, to set priorities for rewards for self, to empathize with the other, to set costs of providing rewards to others, and finally to bargain and compromise.
Source: Weathers & Liberman, 1975

imposed for failure to adhere to them. Note that as in all behavioral procedures, the success of treatment can be measured by the extent to which the contract works for all parties.

Contingency contracting is not an end in itself but merely one motivating and structuring device among a variety of family intervention techniques (for example, modeling, **shaping,** time out, use of tokens, and other operant reinforcement strategies) used in the BPT approach. Contracting may open up communication within a others. In some cases, the contracting process even makes family members aware of wishes or desires they had not previously recognized within themselves. Finally, an important aspect of this approach is its focus on goals and accomplishments. Contingency contracting formalizes the family's natural expectations into concrete actions. By giving recognition for achievement, the family becomes more positive in its interactions. By improving specific interactions between certain family members, the behavioral therapist is teaching a way of negotiating that may serve as a model for conflict resolution in other areas of family life.

FUNCTIONAL FAMILY THERAPY

Based on a clearly stated set of principles, and strongly supported by research findings, **functional family therapy** (Alexander & Parsons, 1982; Barton & Alexander, 1981) is designed to bring about both cognitive and behavioral changes in individuals and their families. The model, which purports to integrate learning theory, systems theory, and cognitive theory, goes beyond most behavioral models by attempting to do more than change overt behavior; it posits that clients need help first in understanding the function the behavior plays in regulating relationships. To accomplish this goal, functional family therapists are apt to employ a mixture of strategic, cognitive, and straight behavioral therapeutic procedures.

Parents in troubled families tend to blame their difficulties on their child's negative traits (laziness, selfishness, irresponsibility), feeling powerless in the process to effect change. As we noted earlier, simply teaching them a parent skills technology, which inevitably includes an examination of their own behavior, may be met with resistance. As developed by Alexander and Parsons (1982), functional family therapy aims at creating a nonblaming relationship focus, providing explanations for the causes of all members' behaviors that do not impute their motives (Morris, Alexander, & Waldron, 1988). By urging adoption of this new perspective, the functional therapist tries to modify the attitudes, assumptions, expectations, labels, and emotions of the entire family.

To the functional family therapist, *all behavior is adaptive*. Rather than being thought of as "good" or "bad," the individual's behavior is viewed as always serving a function, as representing an effort to create a specific outcome in interpersonal relationships. While the interpersonal payoffs or functions for family members may appear to take a variety of forms (a child elicits parental attention by having a tantrum; a teenager creates independence by having himself thrown out of the house; a husband avoids arguments by busying himself at work for long hours into the evening), they are seen, ultimately, as efforts to achieve one of three interpersonal states: contact/closeness (merging), distance/independence (separating), or a combination of the two (midpointing) (Alexander & Parsons, 1982).

Without placing a prior value on the usefulness of the behavior, the functional therapist makes an effort to comprehend why the behavior exists and how and why it is maintained by others within the family. Alexander and Parsons (1982) offer the following illustration of the function of behaviors within the family context:

Mother reports that Debbie, 14 years old, has been receiving increasingly poor grades for 18 months. Within the past 12 months she has begun smoking dope; has been having sexual relations with her 19-year-old boyfriend; has almost stopped going to school; and rarely comes home except late at night. At home she is sullen, argumentative, occasionally hysterical, and rarely truthful. (p. 14)

Looking at the family context, the functional family therapist might speculate on the interpersonal payoffs Debbie's behavior offers each of the family members. One guess is that a function of Debbie's behavior for her is creating justification for running away. What's in it for Debbie's mother that might prompt her to go along with her daughter's behavior, while at the same time protesting that it makes her miserable? The authors infer a number of possible functions for the mother: (1) it enables her to justify coercing her withdrawn husband into becoming more involved with what is happening at home, thus joining her more actively in parenting; (2) it removes her from her overwhelming responsibility because the father is brought in as final authority; (3) it arouses a response from the father, which the mother does not ordinarily receive if she handles the situation herself; and (4) it keeps her in the mothering role, despite her adolescent daughter's becoming more self-sufficient.

Thus, whatever the misery, interpersonal payoffs may exist for the mother (as well as the father), perpetuating Debbie's behavior. The functional family therapist, having attempted to understand what interpersonal functions are served for whom by the problem behavior (for instance, increased closeness between the spouses), might then offer help to the family in finding more effective ways to accomplish the same end result. Note that the *therapist does not try to change the functions but rather the specific behaviors used to maintain these functions.* Table 12.5 illustrates how the same interpersonal functions are retained as a result of intervention, but their behavioral manifestation is altered.

Functional family therapy proceeds in stages. In the initial assessment stage, the therapist is interested in determining the functions served by the behavioral sequences of various family members. Are they creating greater distance, or are they becoming closer through their interpersonal patterns? How do they use merging/separating to enhance or retard or in general to regulate their interactions? The second stage, instituting change in the family system, aims at modifying attitudes, expectations, cognitive sets, and affective reactions. Family members typically enter therapy with a punitive, blaming explanation for their problems ("My mother bugs me; she still thinks I'm a baby"; "My daughter is a chronic liar; she creates all the tension in the house"). The therapist's task during this phase of treatment is to change the focus from an individualistic, blaming outlook to one in which all participants understand that together they form a system and share responsibility for family behavior sequences.

Functional family therapists employ some familiar systems and behavioral principles in their interventions. Relabeling ("Father is uninvolved because he wants to protect the others from the unpleasant emotions he's experiencing") is a primary method used (Morris, Alexander, & Waldron, 1988). By providing reattributions for the causes of family members' behavior, functional family therapists believe they can reduce family members' use of pejorative trait labels for one another, and as a conse-

Table 12.5 Selected Functions in Debbie's Family and Their Behavioral Manifestations Before and During Successful Intervention

Relationship	Interpersonal function	Behavioral manifestations	
		Preintervention	During intervention
Debbie-Mother	Separating	Is truant, is never home, runs away.	Is not truant, has Mother's permission to be away from home, brings reports and calls.
Mother-Debbie	Midpointing	Makes contact via arguing and monitoring, distance via slapping and nagging.	Makes contact via reports and calls, distance via approved absence from home for specified times.
Mother-Father	Merging	Complains about Debbie, coerces Father into responding to her.	Holds daily discussion about family chart.
Father-Mother	Separating	Avoids home, refuses to respond.	Is allowed to fill Father role via family chart rather than direct interaction.
Mother–Good Son	Merging	Elicits and praises information about others' transgressions.	Elicits and praises information about others' accomplishments.
Good Son–Mother	Merging	Snoops and reports to Mother	Reports positive accomplishments of others to Mother.
Debbie-Boyfriend Boyfriend-Debbie	Merging	Avoids school together and have evening contact.	Go to and from school together and have evening contact.
Debbie-Father Father-Debbie	Separating	Have almost no contact except for occasional intense arguing and hitting.	Have almost no contact; information is channeled through Mother

Source: Alexander & Parsons, 1982, p. 28

quence correspondingly lower their resistance to change. Like the strategists and systemicists we considered in the previous two chapters, functionalists contend that giving an event a new and more benign or benevolent meaning will lead to changed perceptions and subsequent behavior change. Recast in behavioral language, relabeling interrupts the automatic eliciting of negative thoughts, emotions, and behavior, which in the past have led to predictable outcomes. Alternate explanations provide an opportunity to activate different and more positive repertoires of thoughts, emotions, or behaviors, in some cases forcing the learning of new repertoires entirely.

Therapy helps people become receptive to learning new skills; however, a third stage, education, is necessary in order to provide a context in which to learn specific skills needed to maintain positive change. In this essential and innovative part of the intervention process, functional family therapists are eclectic, making use of a

variety of conditioning and cognitive techniques (contingency contracting, modeling, communication training) to stamp in new behaviors. This phase is vital if the
family is to learn new skills for future problem resolution. Positive change is more
likely to be produced or reliably maintained if the educational technologies used by
functional family therapists are fitted to the values and functions of the family members (Morris, Alexander, & Waldron, 1988).

CONJOINT SEX THERAPY

Cognitive-behavioral techniques also have been applied to changing behavior in
adults, especially in treating sexual dysfunction. Sexual problems may be a metaphor
for the dynamics of a couple's relationship, in which case the therapist focuses on
helping them repair their interpersonal struggles, or it may be a problem in and of
itself, requiring sex education, cognitive restructuring, or the learning of behavioral
skills (Mason, 1991). More than likely, elements of both are involved. The family
therapist must evaluate the psychological, physical, and interpersonal nature of any
sexual dysfunction, while remaining sensitive to the distress one or both partners
feels as a consequence of the dysfunction. Therapeutic strategy calls for an assessment of the relationship in terms of the commitment of each partner, their sexual histories and expectancies, as well as their ability to communicate their feelings about
sex and other matters openly and to negotiate for what they want or what gives them
pleasure, and their degree of comfort in problem solving together (Walen &
Perlmutter, 1988).

Sex therapists frequently make the assumption that some marriages flounder
primarily because of sexual difficulties or incompatibilities per se, and thus focus
their interventions, likely to be of a cognitive-behavioral nature, specifically on a
couple's sexual problems. These dysfunctions are of several types, grouped according to stages of the sexual response cycle: *desire disorders* (ranging from low sexual
desire to sexual aversion), *arousal disorders* (difficulty achieving sexual excitement),
orgasm disorders (premature, delayed, or nonpleasant orgasms), *sexual pain disorders*
(pain involved in sexual activity), or *problems with sexual frequency* (disparities
between partners regarding desired frequency) (Kaplan, 1979).

Prior to 1970, individuals or couples experiencing any of the sexual dysfunctions just outlined either relied on folk cures or sought psychodynamically oriented
therapies to obtain insight into the early origin of their current problems, usually
with questionable results (Heiman, LoPiccolo, & LoPiccolo, 1981). However, with
the breakthrough publication by Masters and Johnson (1970) of *Human Sexual
Inadequacy,* based on 11 years of clinical research, sex therapy came of age. Seen
within the context of the sexual revolution occurring at the time, this monumental
study not only advanced the open discussion of sexual dysfunction but also pin-
pointed specific learning-based remediation plans for such sexual dysfunctions as
impotence or premature ejaculation in males and nonorgasmic female responses
(heretofore pejoratively labeled frigidity) and dyspareunia (painful intercourse) in
women. In effect, Masters and Johnson demonstrated that sexual problems could

arise from a variety of prior experiences (or lack of experiences), did not necessarily mean that the symptomatic person was struggling with neurotic conflict, and could be treated successfully without much attention to their underlying causes (Burg & Sprenkle, 1996).

A basic assumption in the Masters and Johnson (1970) approach, and what puts it into a systems framework, is that there is no such thing as an uninvolved partner in a relationship in which some form of sexual inadequacy exists. An innovative idea for its time, research-oriented gynecologist William Masters and psychologist Virginia Johnson treated couples conjointly to emphasize that any dysfunction is inevitably in part a relationship problem rather than one that belongs to only one partner.

In their original sex therapy model, they offered a two-week residential program of daily sessions[4] that began with an extensive assessment; a detailed sexual history was taken from each partner, not only in regard to chronological sexual experiences but, more important, in respect to sexually oriented values, attitudes, feelings, and expectations. Next, a medical history was taken and each partner given a thorough physical examination. On the third day, the cotherapists and the marital partners met to review the accrued clinical material and to begin to relate individual and marital histories to current sexual difficulties. During the next several days, the therapists concentrated on giving the couple instructions, to be practiced outside the therapy session.

They taught *sensate focus*—that is, learning to touch and explore each other's bodies and to discover more about each other's sensate areas, but without feeling any pressure for sexual performance or orgasm. Sensate focus exercises are designed to offer both partners pleasure in place of the anxiety previously accompanying a demand for sexual arousal or intercourse; their ultimate value is in eliciting future increased levels of arousal—and progressively increasing degrees of intimacy—without anxiety over sexual performance. This desensitization technique is based on Wolpe's (1958) earlier application of classical conditioning procedures for learning to deal with phobic objects and situations.

According to Masters and Johnson, a primary reason for sexual dysfunction is *performance anxiety*—the participant is critically watching (they refer to it as "spectatoring") his or her own sexual performance instead of abandoning himself or herself to the giving and receiving of erotic pleasure with a partner. Masters and Johnson point out that in order to enjoy fully what is occurring, partners must suspend all such distracting thoughts or anxieties about being evaluated (or evaluating oneself) for sexual performance. Although not cognitive-behaviorists themselves, their treatment efforts involved a number of therapeutic ingredients (sex education, communication training, behavioral exercises, a focus on symptom remission rather than a search for explanations from the past) that fit comfortably with cognitive-behavioral principles and intervention procedures (Heiman & Verhulst, 1990).

---

[4]The Masters and Johnson Institute in St. Louis still recommends daily sessions, away from the participants' everyday routines, but in practice this suggestion is rarely followed elsewhere today because of its impracticality for most couples. According to Heiman, Epps, and Ellis (1995), the majority of sexual desire disorder treatment programs now utilize weekly sessions.

Psychiatrist Helen Singer Kaplan (1974) followed up on the pioneering efforts of Masters and Johnson by distinguishing a variety of personal and interpersonal causes of sexual dysfunction in a couple attempting intercourse (sexual ignorance, fear of failure, demand for performance, excessive need to please one's partner, failure to communicate openly about sexual feelings and experiences). She pointed out that there may be various intrapsychic conflicts (such as early sexual trauma, guilt and shame, repressed sexual thoughts and feelings) within one or both partners that impede satisfying sexual activity. Finally, Kaplan cited a third set of psychological determinants of sexual dysfunction—namely, factors arising from the relationship such as various forms of marital discord, lack of trust, power struggles between partners, and efforts to sabotage any pleasure being derived from the sexual experience. In combination or singly, any of these problems or conflicts can lead to distressing sexual symptoms that threaten a marriage by heightening tensions and that can even lead to its dissolution. Unlike Masters and Johnson, who required participating couples to spend two weeks in residential treatment, Kaplan, as a solo therapist, successfully treated couples on an outpatient basis once or twice a week with an integrated set of procedures based upon miscellaneous behavioral interventions (systematic desensitization, sensate focus, relaxation techniques), cognitive therapy (cognitive restructuring), psychodynamic psychotherapy, antipanic medication, and family systems interventions. Throughout her "psychosexual therapy," she emphasized the relational or interpersonal nature of the treatment. More recently, Kaplan (1995) described her integrated efforts to treat sexual desire disorders (sometimes referred to as inhibited or hypoactive sexual desire), ordinarily the type of sexual problem most resistant to treatment.

Sex therapists today employ a number of familiar techniques—sensate focus, systematic desensitization using a hierarchy of relaxing/sensual images as sexual situations are presented, communication training educating partners in initiating and refusing sexual invitations, and communicating during sexual exchanges, all directed at overcoming disorders of sexual desire. In general, cognitive-behaviorists plan specific exercises for each partner that are aimed at overcoming negative, self-defeating feelings and images regarding sexual experiences (Heiman & Verhulst, 1990).

In addition, as sex therapy has become more "medicalized" (Rosen & Leiblum, 1995) in recent years, drugs (such as Viagra), penile injections of testosterone, or vacuum devices for erectile disorders (failure to achieve or maintain an erection) have gained favor with some men for improving erectile function leading to successful sexual intercourse. Since what is considered "healthy sexuality" is not fixed but varies over time and generations, Heiman, Epps, and Ellis (1995) suggest the adoption of a social constructionist view of sexuality, mediated by the current culture (or subculture) of which the partners are a part.

Finally, as Kaplan (1983) points out, although sex therapy may represent a major advance in our understanding and treatment of a couple's sexual difficulties, it is no panacea for a marriage that has already failed. In this regard, David Schnarch (1991; 1995), deviating from the behavioral viewpoint, attempts to integrate marital and sexual therapy by focusing on a couple's relational context in conceptualizing their sexual problems. In what he calls the *sexual crucible,* he teaches couples how to achieve both greater personal autonomy and sexual intimacy by developing emotionally committed relationships rather than attending exclusively to correcting the presenting symptoms of sexual dysfunction. Based primarily on Bowenian theory regarding fusion and self-differentiation (see Chapter 8), he tries to help couples resolve past individual and interpersonal issues by increasing each partner's sense of self *and* togetherness in the relationship. According to Schnarch, poorly differentiated persons experience an anxiety-driven pressure for togetherness, losing autonomy, and in turn, placing responsibility for adequate functioning in the hands of the other person in the relationship. By contrast, developing a clearly defined sense of oneself allows greater involvement with a partner without the risk of "losing oneself in the process of requiring distancing maneuvers" (Schnarch, 1995, p. 240).

SUMMARY

Behavioral models of family therapy attempt to bring the scientific method to bear upon the therapeutic process by developing regularly monitored, data-based intervention procedures. Drawing on established principles of human learning, these approaches emphasize the environmental, situational, and social determinants of behavior. Increasingly, in recent years, the influence of cognitive factors as events mediating family interactions also has been recognized by most behaviorists. Personal functioning is viewed as the result of continuous, reciprocal interaction between behavior and its controlling social conditions. Cognitive-behavioral therapists attempt to increase positive interaction between family members, alter the environmental conditions that oppose such interactions, and train people to maintain their newly acquired positive behavioral changes.

Currently, cognitive and behavioral approaches are having a significant impact in four distinct areas: behavioral couple therapy, behavioral parent training, functional family therapy, and the conjoint treatment of sexual dysfunction. Proper assessment plays a key role in all of these endeavors, identifying the problem, measuring progress, and validating change. Behavioral couple therapy blends principles of social learning theory and social exchange theory, teaching couples how to achieve positive reciprocity so that their relationship will have more pleasing consequences for both partners. Cognitive interventions view stress in a troubled relationship as influenced by the interaction of cognitive, behavioral, and affective factors; cognitive restructuring is directed at changing dysfunctional interactive patterns and belief systems, as couples acquire skills in problem solving. Partner acceptance is a key factor in integrative couples therapy. While research indicates that stable marriages may take several forms, unstable marriages are characterized by a high ratio of negative to positive exchanges.

Behavioral parent training, largely based on social learning theory, represents an effort to train parents in behavioral principles of child management. Intervention typically attempts to help families develop a new set of reinforcement contingencies in order to begin to learn new behaviors. Skills acquisition, contingency contracting, and the learning of behavioral principles play important roles in parent training.

Functional family therapy attempts to integrate systems, behavioral, and cognitive theories in working with families. Viewing all behavior as serving the interpersonal function of creating specific outcomes in behavior sequences, functional family therapists do not try to change these functions but rather try to change the behaviors used to maintain the functions.

Conjoint sex therapy involves both partners in an effort to alleviate problems of sexual dysfunction. First developed by Masters and Johnson and elaborated by Kaplan, the treatment of sexual dysfunction typically uses a variety of explicitly cognitive and behavioral techniques (sensate focus, systematic desensitization, communication training) aimed specifically at remediation of the sexual problem. Medical interventions are also becoming more popular. While some therapists focus exclusively on the presenting sexual problem, others attempt to integrate marital and sexual therapy by calling attention to the relational context in treating the couple's sexual problems.

IV

EVOLVING MODELS
OF FAMILY THERAPY

13

Postmodernism and the Social Constructionist Family Therapies

The postmodern movement in family therapy continues to gain momentum as we enter the twenty-first century, offering a direct challenge to systems thinking, especially of the first-order cybernetic type. In what Gergen (1993) calls a formidable sea change, therapists with a postmodern outlook show remarkable disinterest in most of those features we traditionally have considered as central to a modernist, problem-focused orientation to human problems—whether they be blocked impulses or unconscious conflicts, flawed family structures, emotional incapacities, distorted cognitions, or dysfunctional personality traits. Nor are they interested in maintaining the conventional barrier between therapist and client—in Gergen's view, "that sacred distance between objectivity, neutrality, and reason on one side, and subjectivity, bias, and passion on the other" (p. ix).

By contrast, therapists with a postmodern outlook argue that preconceived views of what constitutes a functional (or dysfunctional) family are inevitably in the eyes of the beholder. Rather than imposing a single standard for determining a family's functional level, ethnicity, culture, gender, sexual orientation, type of family organization, race, and so on, must also be factored into the assessment. The personal experiences and viewpoints of individual family members need to be attended to, and the family's interaction with larger systems (schools, social agencies) addressed.

A therapist's prejudgments, then, despite his or her expertise, cannot be considered objective or unbiased. Any subsequent interventions to change the way a family operates may run the risk of imposing a conventional or socially sanctioned view of what constitutes a normal or stable or happy family or how a family judged to be dysfunctional must change its behavior. Instead, therapists influenced by postmodern thinking are apt to take a "not knowing" stance (Anderson & Goolishian, 1988), replacing a predetermined view of how a family should change with a collaborative posture in which all participants, family members and therapist equally, examine the belief systems by which the different family members view "reality." Having considered their assumptions about the world that form the basis for the *meanings* they give to events, they are in a position, together, to generate or construct new views of their "reality" and new options they might pursue. Instead of concentrating on the origins of problems, the therapist turns, together with family members, to finding workable solutions.

Postmodernism argues that what we call "reality" is not an exact replica of what is out there, but rather is socially constructed. As Freedman and Combs (1996) observe:

> A central tenet of the postmodern worldview in which we base our approach to therapy is that beliefs, laws, social customs, habits of dress and diet—all the things that make up the psychological fabric of "reality"—arise through social interaction over time. In other words, people, together, construct their realities as they live them. (p. 23)

Postmodern thinkers emphasize that our beliefs about the world—what constitutes reality—are social inventions, not a reflection or map of the world; they evolve from conversations with other people. It is through the interactive process of language (not merely words, but gestures, facial expressions, vocal inflections, silences) that people connect and construct their shared views of reality. The development of knowledge, then, is a social phenomenon, mediated through language, and not an objective representation of reality. The concept of "adolescence," for example, was not considered a specific period of human development until recently, Did that period suddenly appear, or did people begin within this century to sort out their perceptions into types or classes based on chronological ages? Obviously the latter.

Gergen (1985) calls attention to such modern concepts as "romantic love" or "maternal love" as invented **social constructions.** In our times, "co-dependent" or "adult children of alcoholics" or "gay" or "bipolar" or "borderline" are invented terms—social constructions—that we personify, as though they existed. In the postmodern view, each is simply a contrived or invented label clients and therapists alike may bring to therapy. One dangerous consequence, deShazer (1991) maintains, is that as therapists we run the risk of reifying concepts borrowed from first-order cybernetics (such as homeostasis) in describing families as though families really possess those concepts—and those concepts explain their problems!

Postmodern thinkers employ the construct of **constructivism** (see Chapter 1) to emphasize the subjective construction of reality. Our knowledge of the world derives from our own creating, ordering, constructing, and giving meaning to what we experience, not a world as it objectively exists. That is, each of us constructs a sense of the world out there based on our own previously held dominant beliefs, which in turn reflect the dominant beliefs of society. Those beliefs are kept alive and passed along through stories or narratives we share in conversations with one another. Moreover, these narratives play a key role in organizing and maintaining a view of ourselves and our life situations. People organize their experiences and even their memories primarily in the form of self-narratives—personal and family stories, myths about family characteristics or circumstances, reasons for doing or not doing something—in order to gain some sense of order, continuity, and meaning in their lives. Each of us unavoidably views the world, as Parry and Doan (1994, p. 24) put it, "through the lens of a succession of stories—not only a personal story, but gender, community, class, and cultural stories."

A POSTMODERN CLINICAL OUTLOOK

Rather than adopt a systems view—which, according to Lynn Hoffman (1990) runs the risk of seeing family members as objects the therapist can program from the outside—postmodern-oriented therapists (sometimes called social constructionists or second-order cyberneticists) collaborate with family members as self-creating, independent participants. The therapist is no longer a detached, powerful outside observer or expert, but rather a partaker, with his or her own set of prior beliefs, ready to play a role with family members in constructing the reality being observed. No longer in a position to give directives, the therapist works together with the clients to retell and relive stories and to co-construct possible alternative stories or new outcomes. The therapist engages in a dialogue with family members, helping them shake loose from a set or fixed account of their lives (a story from which they often see no escape) so that they might consider alternatives that offer greater promise.

Moving away from exerting power and control over the sessions or establishing authority over clients, these therapists are interested in the shared set of premises of reality a family attaches to a problem that perpetuates its behavior. Together, as part of a unitary therapist-family observer system, therapy becomes a cooperative undertaking in which new meaning and understanding are jointly constructed rather than imposed by the therapist. As a result of new outlooks, the family develops more empowering stories about themselves and how best to actively create new ways of coping with their difficulties.

Instead of the familiar detached and presumably "objective" assessments by an expert, constructivists take the position that what is called for is a collaborative dialogue between therapist and family who respectfully and nonjudgmentally hold "conversations" in which together they examine the meanings each participant has given to the family's problems. The therapist's input is stated openly, but is presented as his or her construction of what is occurring within the family and not as how the family actually exists. There is an assumption that no participant has a monopoly on truth or objectivity; the therapist does not attempt to assume objectivity or impartiality in order to diagnose the client's account of his views of reality, but rather engages in dialogue to examine those views (White, 1995).

Several implications follow from this outlook (Goldenberg & Goldenberg, 1999):

> *The therapist has permission not to be an expert.* He or she does not bring to sessions preconceived ideas of what the family should or should not change. Put another way, the therapists learns to do something *with* the family rather than *to* the family.
>
> *There is greater acceptance of eclecticism.* Moving beyond employing specific intervention techniques, the therapist can more readily combine techniques (cognitve and strategic) or modalities (individual, couple, family).

There is increased likelihood to attend to diversity issues. By avoiding being boxed in by conventional views of normal family life, and not looking for the "truth" of the situation, the therapist can learn about differing views offered by different family members.

Clients and therapists alike are empowered by believing their situation is changeable. If accounts of misery or personal failure that troubled families bring to therapy are redefined not as "truths" but rather as social constructions, the hope for developing alternate accounts of their lives becomes more attainable.

THE POST-MILAN LINK TO THE POSTMODERN VIEW

As we noted in Chapter 11, one of the unique developments of the post-Milan approach, as espoused by Boscolo and Cecchin, has been its move toward a second-order cybernetic viewpoint. In practice, that includes a joint, nonhierarchical relationship with families in order to encourage self-examination and provide an opportunity for change without any prior agenda by the therapists as to specific therapeutic goals. More curious (Cecchin, 1987) than strategically manipulative, Boscolo and Cecchin have taken the position that therapists should invite family members to examine their meaning system, and to explore their options, without intervening with therapist-formulated directives. Together therapists and family members can co-construct new ways of considering their choices, creating the possibility of discovering not heretofore considered ways of looking at their situation and its remediation.

This collaborative post-Milan position provides a link to postmodernism. Through the use of a neutral stance and the technique of circular questioning, the post-Milan therapist allows the family to give meaning to how its members have organized or defined their lives. The initial systemicist efforts to take a neutral stance and employ circular questioning led its creators to understand that the questioning process itself was an intervention, defusing the family's emotional intensity and allowing its members to hear other views of the problem. The therapist's task became adopting a neutral stance, decreasing the emotionality as person-to-person interaction decreased, and knowing what kinds of questions to ask in order to broaden client experiences.

Clinically, the therapist is interested in helping the family to reconsider the meaning of their predicament and, if they choose, to make changes on their own; he or she does not directly try to change the system or determine for it how it should change. This effort to help families explore their choices—and by implication the consequences of those choices—is in sharp contrast with more traditional family approaches in which the therapist more directly tries to undo rigid family structures or what he or she perceives to be faulty family interactive behavior patterns. This post-Milan theoretical perspective, along with its second-order cybernetic therapeutic implications of the therapist being part of the system he or she is observing, is a precursor to the social constructionist approaches in family therapy.

REALITY IS INVENTED, NOT DISCOVERED

Postmodern thinking draws attention to the ways people make assumptions and draw inferences—give meaning—to their problems. This view challenges modern science's assumption that a fixed truth or reality exists and that scientists can objectively discover it. Instead, postmodern thinkers contend that truth is relative and dependent on context, and that our belief systems merely reflect social constructions—points of view, not "true" reality—we make about our world.

To offer some historical context, modern psychology places great emphasis on the development of logical and empirical methods for discovering objective truths. Verifiable through replicated research, valid and generalizable laws regarding human behavior are assumed to emerge that correspond to observable reality. From this perspective, we live in a knowable world in which there are universal truths, expressed in cause-and-effect terms, that can be discovered by a detached observer. That observer, as far as possible, attempts to exclude his or her value biases from the research inquiry. Working from hypotheses stated in propositional form and subject to empirical verification, the researcher strives to control as many variables as possible, narrowing the experimental inquiry to the single independent variable under scrutiny, stripped of any context of which it may be a part.

From a clinical perspective, the modernist outlook, elaborated in previous chapters, would define the therapist's task as helping families (by providing insight, or promoting differentiation, or clarifying boundaries, or prescribing tasks, or restructuring cognitions) deal more effectively with their situations. From this framework, the therapist is viewed as a skilled observer who looks for, diagnoses, and disrupts the family's pathological cycles, enabling the family to move on (Slovik & Griffith, 1992). However, as Doherty (1991) points out, an increasing number of family therapists have become skeptical of modernist preconceptions, claiming that the prevailing theories of family systems are merely a by-product of mid-twentieth-century modernist culture and reflect its biases and underlying assumptions regarding what constitutes truth or reality.

In particular, Doherty argues that a family therapy based on modernism by and large fails to deal with issues such as gender, ethnicity, and the impact of the larger social system such as political and economic forces. Moreover, defining precisely what constitutes normal families becomes harder and harder to do when we live in an era of single-parent-led families, stepfamilies, gay and lesbian couples, dual-career households, and so on. By narrowly focusing on family interaction as the source of family disharmony, the modernist view, as exemplified by the cybernetic outlook in family therapy, fails to consider the underlying assumptions of the broader social context (for example, ingrained, society-reinforced, patriarchal patterns) on therapists' prevailing attitudes. Similarly, ignoring multicultural influences, therapists run the risk of judging ethnically unfamiliar families by their own standards of what "objectively" constitutes a functional family life. The postmodern view rejects such so-called objective knowledge, questioning its certainty and universality.

Philosophically, postmodernism also rejects the modernist notion of an objectively knowable universe and its faith in the ability of a detached, bias-free, neutral, and impartial science mirroring "reality." Instead, advocates of this position argue that there exist multiple, socially constructed realities ungoverned by any universal laws. Differing views of reality held by different individuals are socially and experientially based, dependent for their form and content on the individual who holds them. That is, any person's belief system or version of reality cannot be defined in objective terms, but rather is socially constructed and tied to a particular historical situation and set of personal experiences. Truth, rather than being immutable or absolute, is simply the best-informed understanding for which there exists a high degree of consensus among people. The postmodern researcher, inevitably interlocked with the topic under inquiry, considers his or her findings to be a creation of the inquiry process rather than some extruded fact regarding how things really are or how they really work. As Guba (1990) puts it, reality exists only in the context of each person's set of constructs for thinking about it.

From a **deconstruction** viewpoint of skepticism about absolute truths, challenging the modernist perspective and reexamining its long-taken-for-granted assumptions, the world is anything but simple, nor can it be known with certainty. Each of us has a personally and culturally based "knowledge" of the world—and makes choices based on such "knowledge." However, these life choices are not the only possibilities, but merely reflect our biases regarding how things are and what constitutes our options. In a sense, as Parry (1993) observes, the therapist's job is to assist clients to become agents of their own choices; he urges therapists to first encourage people to tell their stories and then help them deconstruct and later reconstruct these stories in a way that empowers them. Shunning the traditional barriers that often get erected between therapist and clients, Doherty (1991) encourages therapists to engage in a subjective but liberating dialogue with family members. As he describes the outlook of postmodern therapists:

> Their goal is to enable clients to find new meanings in their life situations and to "restory" their problems in ways that free them from the mesmerizing power of the dominant culture. (p. 38)

SOCIAL CONSTRUCTIONIST THERAPIES

While earlier family therapists might have focused on observing family interactive patterns or a dysfunctional family structure, social constructionist therapists concern themselves with the assumptions or premises different family members hold about the problem. These therapists reject the customary therapist-client hierarchy by refusing to place their knowledge regarding clients at a higher plane than client knowledge about themselves. More egalitarian, they focus their efforts instead on engaging families in conversations to solicit everyone's views, and not in imposing "truth," "objectivity," or "the essential insight" based on "established knowledge" on families. By examining the "stories" about themselves that people live by, therapist and clients search together for new empowering ways of viewing and resolving client problems.

As we have noted, social constructionists (Gergen, 1985) subscribe to the notion that the assumptions about reality that each of us makes are not objective mirrors of reality but arise through communication—language and conversation with others—so that any knowledge we have develops out of a social context. More than the mere outward expression of inner thoughts and feelings, language shapes and is shaped by human relationships. If there is no "reality" out there as such, then each of us creates reality by observing, making distinctions about these observations, and sharing our perceptions with others through language. As Campbell, Draper, and Crutchley (1991) contend, "language is a process of consensual agreement between people and is, therefore, the basis of one's view of reality" (p. 336).

In this chapter, we offer five social constructionist therapeutic approaches in which language and meaning given events take precedence for the therapist over attending to behavioral sequences or family interactive patterns. These therapists are intent on engaging families in conversations, calculated to facilitate changes in family members' perceptions of their problems and ultimately in empowering them to restory and actively redirect their lives.

Challenging entrenched and perhaps prematurely sanctified beliefs in the field, these family therapists have urged a shift in attention away from an inspection of the origin or the exact nature of a family's presenting problems to an examination of the stories (interpretations, explanations, theories about relationships) family members have told themselves that account to themselves for how they have lived their lives. People often become convinced that their stories are the truth, the way things really are; in effect, they have confused their personal map of the world with the territory the map is intended to represent.[1] Their fixed belief system, then, influences not only what they see but how they analyze, interpret, and give meaning to those perceptions.

Social constructionist therapists are particularly interested in altering clients' rigid and inflexible views of the world, since such dogmatic convictions, usually negative, make alternative explanations of events or relationships difficult if not impossible for clients to consider. Client views are mirrored in the language they use in constructing their takes on reality. Language—conversation—in turn becomes the therapeutic vehicle for altering old behaviors by considering new explanations leading to new solutions.

Solution-Focused Brief Therapy

Concerned with change, and with little interest in assessing just *why* the family has developed the problems it has, solution-focused therapists insist that families, right from the start of therapy, join them in *therapeutic conversation* as they attempt to

---

[1]This notion that "the map is not territory" was first proposed by philosopher and semanticist Alfred Krozybski (1942) and was a favorite point made by Bateson (1972), who credited Korzybski for its original proposal. What this notion points out, and why it has been resurrected by the social constructionists, is that it emphasizes that the conceptual frame we bring to the analysis or interpretation of a situation is just that—a personal point of reference—and should not be confused with the way the situation really is. The interpretation of reality is only an interpretation and not reality itself. There are numerous, perhaps an infinite number of, possible explanations or interpretations that could be assigned the identical experience.

describe their troublesome situation. Discouraging families from speculating about why a particular dilemma or predicament arose, or ever looking for underlying family pathology, solution-focused therapists listen to the language used as families describe their situations and the conflict resolution they hope to achieve. Led by the therapist, but directed by client goals, they construct possible solutions together to reach those goals. As Berg and deShazer (1993) put it:

> As the client and therapist talk more and more about the solution they want to construct together, they come to believe in the truth or reality of what they are talking about. This is the way language works, naturally. (p. 9)

Instead of "problem talk" (searching for explanations of client problems by piling "facts" upon "facts" about their troubled lives) these therapists urge "solution talk" (therapist and clients discussing solutions they want to construct together). For example, instead of saying to a family in the initial session, "Tell me what problems brought you to see me," the solution-focused therapist might ask, "How can we work together to help you change your situation?" Emphasizing its social construction underpinnings (deShazer, 1991), the therapist thereby sets the stage for dialogue, for expected changes, and for client active and collaborative participation in achieving those changes.

The solution-based therapist's emphasis on language determining meaning, on therapist-clients conversations rather than outside analysis and search for the "truth" from an expert, on multiple perspectives of reality—these are all consistent with the epistemologies of constructivism and second-order cybernetics. If numerous realities exist, each arbitrarily and subjectively based on personal constructions or stories of what's out there, then what we agree to call reality is nothing more than consensus about our perspectives shared through language. As we noted above, the solution-based therapist helps families, by means of solution-talk, to come to believe in the truth or reality of what they are talking about together with the therapist, and to construct solutions consistent with those consensually validated perceptions. Workable solutions result from redescriptions of themselves—in effect the family creates new, empowering stories about themselves. If successful, clients achieve a cognitive change, reconstructing their sense of their own ability to resolve, control, or contain the presenting problem (Shoham, Rohrbaugh, & Patterson, 1995).

This increasingly popular approach, brief, pragmatic, with a nonpathological view of clients, and designed to help them find solutions to current, specified problems, comes from the work of social worker Steve deShazer and his associates (including at one time or another his wife, Insoo Berg; Eve Lipchik; and Michelle Weiner-Davis) at the Brief Family Therapy Center in Milwaukee, founded in 1978. DeShazer (1985) shares with strategists,[2] such as the MRI group (Chapter 10), the

---

[2]Early solution-focused theory was closely identified with the strategic approach to family therapy, incorporating many indirect therapeutic techniques of Milton Erickson. More recently de Shazer (1991; 1994) has turned to the ideas of linguistic philosopher Ludwig Wittgenstein, especially his notions concerning "language games," essentially conversations people engage in with one another to determine reality. Wittgenstein (1968) argued for focusing on descriptions in place of hypotheses or explanations. Today solution-focused therapy is clearly in the social constructionist camp, emphasizing the central role of language in how clients view themselves and their problems. Hence, change comes about as clients learn to shift from "problem-talk" to "solution-talk."

Steve deShazer, M.S.W.

notion that dysfunction essentially arises from faulty attempts at problem solution; the family perceives itself as simply stuck, having run out of ways to deal with the problem. However, they part company with strategists in emphasizing a faulty or negative set of constructions, making family members experience their options as nonexistent or extremely limited (Lipchik, 1993). Rather than focus on why or how the particular presenting problem initially arose, solution-focused therapists attempt to aid the family in discovering their own creative solutions for becoming "unstuck."[3]

The assumption here is that clients already know what they need to do to solve their complaints; the therapist's task is to help them construct a new use for knowledge they already have. The overall aim of this approach, then, is to help clients start the solution process. The solution does not need to be matched to the specific problem to be effective. Actually, solution-focused therapists believe that the *solution process* is more similar from one case to another than the problems each intervention is meant to solve. In describing his approach, deShazer uses a simple metaphor: The complaints clients bring to the therapist are like locks on doors that could open to a more satisfactory life, if only they could find the key. Often time is wasted and frustration heightened in trying to discover why the lock is in the way or why the door won't open, when the family should be looking for the key.

DeShazer's (1985; 1988) overall contribution is to provide the family with "skeleton keys"—interventions that work for a variety of locks. Such keys do not necessarily fit a complex lock perfectly; they only need to fit sufficiently well so that a solution evolves. That is, in constructing a solution, the therapist does not need to know about the history of the problem or what maintains the complaint. Nor is the

[3]The MRI is a problem-focused model while the Milwaukee model is solution-focused. In practice, the former urges clients to *do* things differently while the latter urges *viewing* things differently (Shoham, Rohrbaugh, & Patterson, 1995).

therapist particularly interested in the details of the complaint, preferring to attend instead to developing with the family expectations of change and solution. By limiting the number of sessions[*] (typically five to ten), the therapist helps create the expectation of change, making the achievement of goals appear more attainable.

One theoretical view that particularly sets deShazer and his colleagues at the Brief Family Therapy Center in Milwaukee apart from the MRI Brief Therapy Center (Chapter 10) is the rejection of the idea that clients who come asking for change at the same time resist change. Solution-focused therapists contend that clients really do want to be cooperative and to change; they resist interpretations or other interventions from the therapist only if these do not seem to them to fit. To promote cooperation, they compliment clients on what they are already doing that is useful for problem solving and, once family members become convinced the therapist is on their side, the therapist is in a position to make suggestions that they try something new that might also make them feel better. Typically, therapists offer suggestions for initiating *small changes,* which, once achieved, lead to further changes in the system generated by the clients.

Observe how the therapist sets up an expectation of change in the following situation of a woman trying to be a perfect mother (deShazer, 1985). In the process, he helps create in her a corresponding sense of what to expect after the problem or presenting complaint is gone.

> Mrs. Baker came to therapy complaining about her approach to her children. She thought she should *completely* stop yelling at them because the yelling did not achieve its aim and just left them frustrated. Trying to find a minimal goal, the therapist asked her, "What sort of thing do you think will happen when you start to take a more calm and reasonable approach to your children?" (p. 35)

Several key features are noteworthy in this therapeutic intervention that resembles an Ericksonian directive in hypnosis. The phrasing recasts the goal (a more calm and reasonable approach) as small and thus more reachable than stopping yelling completely. The implied therapist suggestion is not only that Mrs. Baker should take a more calm and reasonable approach, but also that she will (the use of "when" rather than "if"). Moreover, there exists the further expectation that taking a more calm and reasonable approach will make a difference, and that that difference will be sufficient for Mrs. Baker to notice (things will happen).

By turning the goal into a small start, the therapist is encouraging the client to proceed with changes she is likely to view as self-generating, minimizing further therapeutic interference. In fact, as a result of Mrs. Baker's randomizing her approach and permitting herself the solution of yelling or being calm depending on the circumstances, the children no longer found her behavior so predictable (and thus able to be ignored) and therefore the "causes" of her yelling diminished in both frequency and intensity. Soon her occasional yelling took on a new meaning, signaling to the children that she meant business this time. Mrs. Baker did not have to stop yelling

---

[*]Brief therapy has grown in popularity as therapists have had to accommodate to the demands of third-party payers such as managed care organizations, who have pressured therapists to reduce the length of therapy. We discuss managed care and its impact on clinical practice in Chapter 17.

completely in order to be a perfect mother,[5] as she thought she would at the start of therapy, since she now had a solution—she could choose to do so or not according to the situation and the response of others. DeShazer's technique fully accepts her (as a yeller), and does not scold her for yelling nor tell her to change by eliminating the yelling. Any continued yelling, when appropriate, is not seen as a sign of resistance, but rather as cooperation with the therapy.

Again using an Ericksonian ploy, deShazer takes the position with clients that change is inevitable; the only issue is when it will occur. In this way he creates expectations of change as soon as the "key" is found. As just seen in our example, he might wonder aloud what the client expects to be different after the presenting complaint is gone. As this new framework gets established, the therapist and client are then likely to set to work finding a solution to resolve the problem. Just expecting to get somewhere different, somewhere more satisfactory, according to deShazer, creates the expectation of beneficial change in the client, and makes it easier to get there.

Solution-focused therapists have devised a number of therapeutic questions to disrupt problem-maintaining behavioral patterns, change outmoded family beliefs, and amplify **exceptions** to behavior previously thought of by clients as unchangeable. Three kinds of questions, often asked during the initial session, are increasingly central to the solution-focused approach: (1) "miracle questions"; (2) exception-finding questions; and (3) scaling questions (Berg & Miller, 1992).

The *"miracle question"* (deShazer, 1991) states:

> Suppose that one night there is a miracle and while you were sleeping the problem that brought you to therapy is solved: How would you know? What would be different? What would you notice the next morning that will tell you that there has been a miracle? What will your spouse notice? (p. 113)

Future-oriented and designed to illuminate a hypothetical solution, this therapeutic ploy offers each family member an opportunity to speculate on what their lives will be like when the problem the family brought to therapy (say, marital conflict or struggles between parents and adolescents) is solved. Each family member is also encouraged to reveal differences in his or her behavior that the others will notice. Goals are identified in this way and potential solutions revealed. Not only does consideration of a brighter future in which all members change increase its likelihood to occur, but the solution calls for a consideration of how to reach the stated goal offered by the family members themselves. The idea here is for the client to gradually construct an image of a fulfilling, productive, rewarding future when the problem recedes. It is the movement toward a newly constructed life that constitutes a "solution" (Fish, 1995).

---

[5]Solution-focused therapists believe people who focus on problems often give themselves "either/or choices" (in this example, to continue yelling out of control or stop yelling completely). Instead, solutions usually offer constructions of a "both/and choice" (both to continue yelling when appropriate and to contain her yelling when she deems it unnecessary). Couple therapists often see clients each of whom takes an "either/or" position ("I'm right and you're wrong"). Without declaring one the winner, the solution-focused therapist is likely to offer a "both/and" substitute (both have valid positions and their inflexiblity in listening to the other leads to a standoff that is wrong) in order to reexamine their viewpoints (deShazer, 1985).

Exception-finding questions, used as soon as possible in therapy (Shoham, Rohrbaugh, & Patterson, 1995), deconstruct a problem by focusing on exceptions to the rules—times when the adolescent was cooperative, the child did not wet his bed, the dinner did not end in a family free-for-all. Here the solution-focused therapist is encouraging the family to build on times they were able to control the problem. A client who complains of *always* being depressed might be directed to pay attention to an "up day" and later to describe what he did differently that day. Later, when a depressing day is expected, the therapist directs the client to do something normally done on an "up day" in order to find a solution. Clients who report vague complaints might be told to observe and report back next time something happens in their lives that they want to continue to have happen. In the following session, they might be asked what they think they need to do to get those satisfying experiences to continue to happen. As in most solution-focused techniques, the therapist does not teach the client what to do differently or teach her or him new tactics for accomplishing behavioral change. The therapist's interventions tend to be simple and minimal, and in most cases are effective in opening doors.

Scaling questions—asking clients to quantify their own perception of a situation—are intended to build a positive outlook and to encourage its achievement. Consider the following question asked of a client in the first session (Berg & deShazer, 1993, p. 10):

> How confident are you that you can stick with this? Let's say ten means you're confident that you're going to carry this out, that a year from now you'll be back and say, "I did what I set out to do." Okay? And one means you're going to back down from this. How confident are you, between ten and one?

Here the therapist is getting the client to commit to change, and once having done so, publicly, to stick to or even improve the forecast. Used at various times during therapy, scaling questions may help couples gauge each other's perceptions of an event (She to therapist: "I thought the way we dealt with the money issue last night was a seven." He: "Well, at least we didn't end up fighting, but I think we have a long way to go and I would rate it a four"). The therapist then uses these numbers to motivate or encourage: "What might the two of you do to make a small change, say move it up one point?" Or perhaps the therapist points out that previously they rated themselves at two or three, so what exception occurred to bring about the improvement? In this way, change is conveyed as continuous and expected.

Solution-focused therapy is complaint based; it is concluded, usually in a few sessions of "solution-talk," when the presenting complaint is alleviated and the client reconstructs his or her view of the world. Before commencing solution-focused conversation, however, therapists attempt to assess the nature of the therapist-client relationship, categorizing clients as *visitors, complainants,* or *customers* (deShazer, 1988). Visitors may be there at someone else's suggestion or demand, do not describe a clear complaint, do not expect change, and do not really want to engage in therapy. (The therapist may respond politely but offer no task or seek no change.) Complainants are willing to describe the perceived basis for their unhappiness but are not currently willing to work on constructing solutions, perhaps waiting for their partner to change first. (Here the therapist is accepting, sometimes suggesting tasks directed at noticing exceptions to the pattern complained about in the partner.) Customers describe their complaints and are prepared to take action to construct a solution. (The therapist here may be more direct in guiding such clients toward solutions.)

While therapists are complimentary and may attempt to engage in solution-focused conversations with all three, they are more active in helping a client look for exceptions, for example, if he or she is a customer, not just visiting to pacify someone else or complaining without being ready to do something to change an unhappy situation. However, a change in the therapist-client relationship may occur over time, as a complainant, for example, is responsive to an early assignment or set of questions and becomes a customer, willing to participate more fully in seeking solutions.

Solution-focused therapists aim at initiating new behavior patterns without focusing on the details of the presenting complaint. They offer generic *formula tasks* ("Do something different"; "Pay attention to what you do when you overcome the temptation or urge to overeat"), implying that the client can change while simultaneously focusing attention on the future triumphant moment when success is achieved. Rather than argue with the overeater who complains of *never* being able to control herself, the therapist might simply instruct her to watch for the exception— when she does control her urge to eat, thus learning for herself that *never* was a gross overstatement.

The Milwaukee group uses one-way mirrors and intercom systems; it is common for the therapist to take a consultation break for ten minutes or so before the end of the session while the team develops an intervention message. The first part of that message is likely to compliment what the client(s) is doing already that is useful. Subsequent parts might offer clues about possible solutions, give behavioral homework assignments, or issue team-constructed directives that will lead to solutions.

While Fish (1995) applauds the "minimalist elegance" of this approach, critics such as Wylie (1990a) have cautioned that it is too simple, too brief, relies too much on suggestibility, and thus is unlikely to produce the long-term gains claimed. To date, there is little evidence, one way or the other, regarding its effectiveness. Efran and Schenker (1993) find the approach too formulaic and wonder if clients haven't simply learned to go along with their therapist and keep their complaints to themselves. Indeed, there are signs that solution-focused therapists themselves have become less doctrinaire in their insistence on upbeat cognitive discourse, and at times allow client feelings and relationship needs to become a part of the treatment (Lipchik, 1993).

Solution-Oriented Family Therapy

An offshoot of the approach just considered, solution-oriented therapy stresses the importance of keeping open for clients the opportunities for change as they search for solutions that work for them. Therapy is viewed as a brief, joint undertaking to which both clients and therapist bring expertise. The former are experts on their own feelings and perceptions and provide the data from which the therapist can construct a workable problem definition, cast in a solution framework. They, and not therapists, identify the goals they wish to reach in therapy. The therapist, careful not to impose any single "correct" way for a family to live, is the expert at creating a collaborative solution-oriented dialogue. That conversation is guided by two main principles—*acknowledgment* (that clients are being heard, validated, and respected) and *possibility* (keeping alive the prospect for change and solution) (O'Hanlon, 1993).

The solution-oriented approach developed by O'Hanlon and Weiner-Davis (1989) derives its therapeutic rationale from three sources: the ideas advanced earlier by Milton Erickson, the earlier solution-focused brief therapy of deShazer and his colleagues, and the strategic intervention techniques developed at the MRI Brief Therapy Center (see Chapter 10). Bill O'Hanlon had been a student of Milton Erickson's, and later a translator and elaborator of his mentor's ideas. Michelle Weiner-Davis had been affiliated with deShazer at the Milwaukee Brief Therapy Center. O'Hanlon has recently moved from Omaha to Santa Fe, a base from which he conducts numerous workshops around the United States. He is the author of several books emphasizing the application of solution-oriented techniques (O'Hanlon & Martin, 1992; Cade & O'Hanlon, 1993), as well as a popular book based upon these same principles: *Rewriting Love Stories* (Hudson & O'Hanlon, 1992). Weiner-Davis is in private practice in Woodstock, Illinois. She has written a book for the general reader offering solution-oriented prescriptions (exceptions, miracle questions) and recommendations for marital problems: *Divorce-Busting* (Weiner-Davis, 1992).

Solution-oriented therapists concur with the constructivist view that there is no single correct view of reality, not the family members' view, not the therapist's view. Therapists, therefore, rely on the clients to define the goals they wish to reach in treatment. This tactic is based on the assumption that clients have the skills and resources to solve their own problems but somehow have become so focused on the problem and their more-of-the-same unsuccessful solutions that they have lost sight of alternative ways of problem resolution. (The influence of the MRI brief problem-focused approach is clear here.) The therapist's role is to help them use their inherent skills to find solutions[6] not previously considered, or in other cases to remind them of what they have done in the past under similar circumstances that worked. Emphasizing hope, encouragement, client strengths, and possibilities, the solution-oriented therapists believe they empower clients to improve their lives, and in the process help create self-fulfilling prophesies of success (O'Hanlon & Weiner-Davis, 1989).

Selekman (1993) outlines the following seven theoretical assumptions followed by solution-oriented therapists:

1. *Resistance is not a useful concept.* Agreeing with deShazer, they believe clients do want to change and that the therapist should approach the family from a position of cooperation rather than figuring out how to control them to overcome their resistance to help.

---

[6]A frequently told story about Milton Erickson concerns his reported experience of finding a horse without a rider in the meadow. Not knowing to whom the horse belonged, but confident that the horse would know the right direction for returning home, Erickson decided all he had to do was simply follow the horse's lead and keep it on track in order to resolve the problem. Doing so, Erickson rode the horse back to its farm. Durant and Kowalski (1993) see the therapist's job in the same light: helping clients use their resources while the therapist keeps them on track. If therapists follow that strategy, these authors believe clients have the skills that will enable them to find their own way.

2. *Change is inevitable.* Here the therapist emphasizes that it is only a matter of time, employing language that underscores solution possibilities.
3. *Only a small change is necessary.* Once clients are encouraged to value minimal changes, they become more likely to expect and look forward to even greater changes.
4. *Clients have the strengths and resources to change.* The therapist achieves more positive results by supporting family strengths than by focusing on problems or pathology.
5. *Problems are unsuccessful attempts to resolve difficulties.* It is the family's repeated attempts at solutions that maintains the problem. Families need help to get "unstuck" from more-of-the-same attempts at seeking solutions.
6. *You don't need to know a great deal about the problem in order to solve it.* Exceptions when the problem did not occur can be used by the therapist as building blocks for co-constructing solutions with families without determining precisely why the problem surfaced in the first place.
7. *Multiple perspectives.* There is no final or "correct" way of viewing reality, and thus many ways to look at a situation, and more than one way to find a solution.

Hudson and O'Hanlon (1992) illustrate their technique of brief marital therapy by helping couples in conflict "rewrite their love stories." When couples struggle, they develop stories about one another that poison their relationship ("You just want to control me"; "You're exactly like your father"; "You care more about the children than you do about me"). Convincing themselves that their view is the "truth," they mistake their map for the territory and continue to argue over whose view of reality is the correct one. They typically expect the therapist to be the judge of who is right and who is wrong.

Without imposing their own stories as explanations for the couple's problems, Hudson and O'Hanlon try to help couples co-construct new interpretations of each other's behavior that allow new options in behavior to follow. They believe the couple has been looking in the wrong place (their partner's troubling behavior) for the lost key to love and understanding. Instead, these solution-oriented therapists advocate bypassing blame, replacing destructive stories with action language asking the partner to do something new or different in the future. Focusing on specific actions each person requests in the future rather than on what they did not want that occurred in the past, provides hope for change. "Catching your partner doing something right" is another useful exception-seeking therapeutic stratagem in the service of finding new perspectives leading to new solutions. The technique incorporates both solution-focused and MRI problem-focused procedures.

A Collaborative Language Systems Approach

This social construction therapeutic approach, based upon a postmodern philosophy and emphasizing language and communication, reflects the ideas of psychologists Harlene Anderson and the late Harry Goolishian. Anderson, who has written extensively about the underlying rationale for this collaborative conversational approach

(Anderson, 1993; 1995; Anderson, Burney, & Levin, 1999), contends that meaning is created and experienced in dialogue with others and with oneself. She observes:

> This assumes that human action takes place in a reality of understanding that is created through social construction and dialogue and that we live and understand our lives through socially constructed narrative realities, that is, that we give meaning and organization to our experiences and to our self-identity in the course of these transactions. (1993, p. 324)

To advocates of this view, human systems are essentially language and meaning-generating systems. Therapy systems are no exceptions; therapist and client together create meaning with one another as they discuss a "problem."[7] Thus, Anderson and Goolishian do not offer a specific set of intervention procedures; on the contrary, they actually downplay technique, but do outline a viewpoint and underlying philosophy regarding the therapeutic process and the therapy system.

For them, the essence of the therapy process is dialogic conversation in which a client and therapist are *conversational partners who together engage in a shared inquiry* unique to each relationship and each conversation. While the client is the expert on his or her own life, the therapist has expertise in, and responsibility for, facilitating a conversational process, out of which comes the opportunities for change. Conversation, tailored to each family rather than based on preplanned intervention techniques, involves active and responsive listening, immersing oneself in client concerns, and asking conversational questions, all intended to encourage the full telling of the client's current story and what gives it shape. The therapist, who may share opinions or offer tentative ideas, takes care not to operate on preconceived ideas of what the story should be, and is always in need of learning more about the client's views (Anderson, 1993). Together, they engage in a mutual search for altered or new meanings, attitudes, narratives, and behavior. Both must be willing to change as a result of the joint experience.

A pioneer in family therapy as a result of his participation in the Multiple Impact Therapy project in the 1960s (see Chapter 5), Goolishian became a strategic therapist in the 1970s. Later, stimulated by the work of the Milan group, he began to challenge the applicability of early cybernetic theory to human systems. During the 1980s and early 1990s his outlook evolved with social constructionism and postmodern thinking into what he called "language systems." That is, Goolishian maintained that problems are not fixed entities but rather are created through language; if so, he reasoned, they also can be deconstructed through language.

Together with colleague Harlene Anderson, he began to view therapy as a linguistic process of "dissolving" problems in conversation by cocreating stories that open up new possibilities for clients as well as for the thinking of professionals. Goolishian founded the Galveston Family Institute (now the Houston-Galveston Institute) in 1977, an internationally acclaimed training center for family therapy (McDaniel, 1992). The institute's primary orientation is the "language systems approach," based to a large extent on the philosophy of social constructionism.

[7]Anderson (1995) typically places "problem" in quotation marks to underscore her belief that there is no such things as one problem. Rather, there are as many descriptions and explanations of the problem as there are members of the system. Similarly, she does not believe "problems" are solved, but rather that they dissolve.

This approach emphasizes careful dialoguing about a problem with the hope that new meanings will emerge. As Lynn Hoffman (1990), whose ideas have coalesced into a collaborative, conversational viewpoint, puts it, *problems are stories that people have agreed to tell themselves.* This is consistent with the postmodern view that holds that the various accounts of misery or personal failure and so forth that people bring to therapy are not so much approximations of the truth as they are life constructions, made up of narratives, metaphors, and the like (Gergen, 1993). The degree of validity of their claims is less important than the social utility the stories play in explaining one's life. Therapy, then, becomes reconstructive, intended to free the client from a particular self-account in order to open the way for adopting alternative accounts—new linguistic spaces—that offer new options for action.

Building upon Boscolo and Cecchin's idea (Chapter 11) that the problem creates a system of meanings, psychologists Anderson and Goolishian focus on the conversation or meaning system a family organizes around a problem. To their way of thinking, the problem determines the system (which family members are touched by the problem) more than the system determines the problem. Deliberately avoiding the expert's interventionist, change-oriented stance of designing therapeutic outcomes in the modernist tradition, therapists in this postmodern collaborative approach view themselves as "learners" (the clients are the "knowers"), conducting therapy from a position of "not knowing." That is not to say that the therapist lacks knowledge or is without therapeutic skills, but rather that he or she maintains respectful listening, stays in sync with the unfolding story and does not begin with any set ideas about what should or should not change (Anderson, 1997). Ideally, the family and therapist together cocreate a new story—that is, come up with understandings or ideas for actions different from those previously held. As Anderson and Goolishian (1988) put it, "the therapy then takes its shape according to the emergent qualities of the conversation that inspires it" (p. 236).

Believing that people exist in relation to each other, and that language helps negotiate and shape our values, choices, and behavior, Anderson and Goolishian urge therapists to engage family members in "therapeutic conversation" as together they seek understanding and co-constructed meaning, leading to the consideration of new options and new behavioral possibilities. As Anderson and Goolishian (1990) describe their outlook:

> We see therapy as a linguistic event that takes place in what we call a therapeutic conversation. The therapeutic conversation involves a mutual search and exploration through dialogue (a two-way exchange, a crisscrossing of ideas) in which new meanings are continually evolving toward the "dis-solving" of the problems and, thus, the dissolving of the therapy system and what we have called the problem-organizing and problem-dis-solving system. Change is the evolution of new meaning through the narratives and stories created in the therapeutic conversation and dialogue. (p. 161)

The collaborative language systems approach is rooted in the notion that all of our knowledge is based on inventions that arise from social dialogue. Anderson (1993) maintains that language and conversation help us create meaning with each other. Similarly in therapy, all participants are engaged in a language system coalesced around a "problem"—"something or somebody that someone is worried about and wants to change" (p. 324). That system is made up of those people who wish to "talk" about the problem, and may include teachers, members of social agencies, and so forth. Membership in the therapy system is fluid, is determined on a session-to-session basis, and may change as the conversation changes and new units become the focus of therapy (Anderson, Burney, & Levin, 1999).

Family therapy from this perspective involves conversation, dialogue often in minute detail, in which all participants explore the problem together and codevelop new perspectives, leading to new self-narratives, new meanings, new takes on reality aimed at "dis-solving" (rather than solving) the problem The problem, having been created through language, is dissolved (becomes a nonproblem) by the same process, as alternate meanings (new cocreated stories) of the troublesome thoughts or feelings emerge. Greater self-capability occurs as altered understanding leads to no longer viewing or experiencing the previously distressing matter as a problem. Thus, change, whether in understanding or in behavioral action, follows naturally from the "therapeutic conversation" as new solutions arise dissolving the problem.

Narrative Therapy

Michael White, at the Dulwich Center in Adelaide, Australia, and David Epston, at the Family Therapy Center in Auckland, New Zealand, have pioneered an internationally influential and highly focused set of intervention techniques that today epitomize the impact of the postmodern revolution on the practice of family therapy (White & Epston, 1990). Their outlook, presented in workshops around the world, centers on the *narrative metaphor*—that our sense of reality is organized and maintained through stories by which we circulate knowledge about ourselves and the world we inhabit. As people attempt to make sense of their lives, according to these clinicians, they arrange their experiences of events over time to arrive at a coherent account of themselves and their surroundings. Such self-narratives provide each person with a sense of continuity and meaning, and in turn become the basis for interpreting subsequent experiences. Each individual's personal story or self-narrative (how my parents' divorce turned me against marriage; how my mother's alcoholism frightened me about drinking; how my grandmother came to this country penniless and succeeded in business; how my illness as a child made me feel inferior to others) provides the principal framework for structuring those experiences. Put succinctly, it is the stories we develop about our lives that actually shape or constitute our lives.

Cultural stories help influence these personal narratives (White, 1991), providing dominant narratives specifying the customary or preferred ways of behaving within that culture. White in particular has been influenced by Michel Foucault (1965; 1980), a French intellectual and social critic who wrote extensively about the politics of power. Foucault saw language as an instrument of power; he insisted that certain "stories" about life, perpetuated as objective "truths" by the dominant culture, help maintain a society's power structure and eliminate alternate accounts of the same events (for example, regarding what constitutes normal sexuality, or what behavior should be classified as pathological, or how to react to members of a minority community, or what it takes to be a "real" man). Those with dominant or expert knowledge (politicians, clergymen, scientists, doctors, therapists), according to Foucault, hold the most power and determine what knowledge is held to be true, right, or proper in society (Freedman & Combs, 1996). Because oppression is frequently based upon these arbitrary labels, Foucault advocated helping people to get out from under the yoke of the culture's dominant discourses. He urged that certain dominant culture narratives be challenged, because following them unquestioningly eliminates the consideration of alternative knowledge or viewpoints and thus may be anathema to free choice or what's best for a particular individual or family. Issues of power, privilege, oppression, control, ethics, and social justice remain high priorities for White in his therapeutic work.

David Epston (1994; Epston & White, 1992), having introduced narrative metaphor thinking to White, is particularly known for his innovative *therapeutic letters* to families, extensions of conversation aimed at reauthoring lives. (We'll return to these letters later in this chapter.) Cheryl White is a social activist, primarily responsible for overseeing the publications at the Dulwich Center in Adelaide (C. White & Hales, 1997). In the United States, Jill Freedman and Gene Combs (1996) in Evanston, Illinois; Joseph Eron and Thomas Lund (1996) in the Catskills area of New York State; Jeffrey Zimmerman and Victoria Dickerson (1996) in the San Francisco Bay Area; and Jennifer Andrews and David Clark (Andrews, Clark, & Baird, 1998) in Los Angeles are noteworthy advocates of the narrative viewpoint and intervention procedures. In Canada, Stephan Madigan (1994) runs the Vancouver Anti-anorexia/Anti-bulimia League, devoted to helping members shift their thinking about themselves—from being patients to becoming community activists.

Narrative therapy was developed to help people reexamine the stories that formed the basis for the way they have lived their lives. Therapists with a narrative orientation typically view these stories through a political lens, particularly those that oppress people's lives (racism, sexism, gender or class bias, gay bashing). Here they are extending Foucault's analysis of society to the personal or family levels, arguing further that certain internalized narratives (for example, what it means in our society to be successful or worthwhile in life) often become oppressively self-policing and lead to a self-subjugating narrative of failure for falling short of the arbitrary achievement mark. Moreover, internalizing these narrow, culturally based dominant discourses leads to a self-defeating outlook about the future. Policing one's life according to what we have been told by expert knowledge is normal stands in the way of becoming who we truly are.

White (1997) deplores societal repressions that keep us from discovering our true nature. His therapeutic efforts are respectfully directed at liberating the client from the forces of repression, helping that person express his or her authenticity. In place of attempting to play the role of expert and objectively diagnosing someone's motives, needs, drives, ego strengths, or personality characteristics, White is interested in collaborating or consulting with people and helping them construct and realize their true dreams, visions, values, beliefs, spirituality, and commitments. For example, in what he refers to as a nonstructuralist outlook, he wants to explore with a client what a particular belief or act reflects about the client's visions or outlook or dreams (and not the structuralist outlook of what it reflects about the person's need or strength or personality type).

Such a nonstructuralist approach is intended to open up conversation about client values, beliefs, and purposes so that they have the opportunity to consider a wide range of choices, freed from personal or cultural oppressive demands. To White, any interpretations the therapist gives to the client's thoughts or visions is not "privileged" or honored over the meaning the client gives about his or her own views. The narrative therapist is de-centered—still influential but without being at the center of what transpires therapeutically. Here the therapist might ask such questions as "What was that experience like for you?" followed by "What effect did it have on your life?" or "Why was this so important to you?" Asking such questions, the therapist is focusing on the person's expressions of his or her experiences of life, and the interpretative acts the person engages in that give meaning to those experiences and are thus treated as "truths." An important therapeutic twin goal here is the deconstruction of oppressive self-narratives and the reestablishment of freedom, individually and as a family, from the oppressive dominant discourses of the culture.

Narrative therapists engage in *externalizing conversations* to help clients attach new meanings to their experiences. **Externalizations** are designed to help separate the person from the symptoms while helping him or her mobilize to fight the problem's tyrannical influence over his or her life. The client is not the problem and the family is not the problem; *the problem is the problem.* That is, the therapist helps families "externalize" an oppressive problem—in effect, redefining the problem into an objectified external and unwelcome tyrant with a will of its own to dominate their lives that the family is encouraged to unite to combat. Starting with the family's set of beliefs and use of language in describing the problem (an adolescent daughter's anorexia, a mother's depression, a young boy who soils his underpants), the family is encouraged by the therapist's questioning to place the problem as outside the family. To effect this, it helps to personify the problem, making it a separate entity rather than an internal characteristic or attribute of the symptomatic person. Instead of the adolescent identifying herself as "I am anorexic" she might be asked by the therapist: "What do you believe anorexia's purpose might have been in deceiving you by promising you happiness but bringing you despair?" Or perhaps the mother might be challenged to look at her depression not as some internalized, objective truth about herself, but rather as an external burden: "How long has it been now that depression has been controlling your life?" The encopretic young boy might be assisted in externalizing the problem by giving it a name (say, "Mr. Mischief"); it was he who caused the boy to soil his underclothes. The point here is that the child has told himself previously that he is helpless to do anything about the encopresis, but he can begin to fight against Mr. Mischief. Separating themselves from the problem can be a useful first step in helping people notice other possible choices for their own behavior or in their expectations of others (Zimmerman & Dickerson, 1996).

White employs directed questions (unlike Goolishian's more unstructured, conversational tone) in order to encourage families to view the problem as some entity or thing that is outside the family, separate from their sense of identity. Stated another way, his intent is to counter the family's previously unworkable and self-defeating assumptions that the person who has the problem is the problem. Parents with a symptomatic adolescent (say, refusing to attend school) might be asked: How has the problem affected Johnny's life? Your life? Your relationships? How has the problem affected you as parents? Affected your view of yourselves? How does your view of yourself as a failure affect your behavior with Johnny? Your behavior with one another? With your friends? The technique, based on a social constructionist rationale, allows the family to gain distance from the problem, detach from the story line that has shaped their self-view and dominated their lives, and begin to create an alternative account of themselves.

Externalizing is apt to hold great appeal for families who see their inability to rid the symptomatic person of the problem as a reflection of themselves as failures. Or perhaps they have blamed the symptomatic person ("It's Harry's nature to be depressed" or "His constant depression is destroying the family"). Now they are presented with a nonpathological, externalized view of the problem ("Sadness sometimes overtakes Harry"), one in which no one is to blame. Perhaps they begin to realize that the symptomatic person doesn't like the effects of his feelings any more than any other family member does. Next, they are offered an empowering opportunity to co-construct with the therapist a new narrative that provides an alternate account of their lives.

Two processes are operating here: deconstructing or unraveling the history of the problem that has shaped their lives, and reconstructing or reauthoring an alternate (but previously subjugated) story that has been obscured by the dominant story. Holding externalizing conversations with all family members enables them to separate from the stories they have told themselves about themselves, and begin working as a team on the now-externalized problem they work together to defeat (White, 1991).

As is also the case for most social constructionist therapists, White (1989) is less interested in the cause of a problem than in how the problem impacts negatively on family life over time, sometimes to the point of dominating all aspects of family relationships. He suggests that families with problems typically offer *problem-saturated stories,* pessimistic and self-defeating narratives about themselves, likely to reflect their sense of frustration, despair, and powerlessness ("We never know from day to day what mood Harry will be in"). Narrative therapists attempt to identify previously obscured *subjugated stories* involving success or alternative views by locating "facts" about themselves (times when Harry overcame his sadness and was fun to be around) that they were not able to perceive when they held problem-saturated accounts of their family life. Seen in a new light, these "facts" commonly contradict earlier self-descriptions of their failures or feelings of impotence in dealing with the problem.

Following externalization of the problem, the narrative therapist asks the family to search for **unique outcomes**—perhaps exceptional events, actions, or thoughts that contradict their dominant problem-saturated story,[8] where the problem did not defeat them. ("Can you think of a time when you refused to go along with Sadness's commands? How were you able to trust your own thoughts or desires? What did this

---

[8]The reader will detect a resemblance between this deconstruction tactic and that employed by solution-focused therapists such as Steve deShazer, described earlier in this chapter. Both direct clients to move away from talk about those problems that have a central place in their thinking, and to search for exceptions—experiences that contradict a problem-dominated story. Both also attempt to help clients restory their lives and find more empowering alternative stories.

Michael White, B.A.S.W.

tell you about yourself?") Unique outcomes serve as an entry point to exploring alternative narratives—the beginning of a new family story line. For example, examining the experience further, the narrative therapist might ask:

"When was the last time you were able to turn Sadness away?"
"How did you get to that point?"
"What did you tell yourself that was different?"
"What exactly did you do?"
"What does it say about you, Harry, that you could do this?"
"What else was Harry able to do in the past that helps explain how he's standing up to Sadness now?"
"What does it show the rest of the family about living with Harry when Sadness no longer runs his life?"

All these interventions are in the service of gaining an alternate view of their life history, rediscovering neglected aspects of themselves, starving the problem rather than feeding it, and reauthoring their stories to now include a new sense of empowerment. In effect, problem-saturated stories start to be replaced by stories emphasizing solutions. Later, families no longer blaming themselves or one another are helped to redescribe themselves in terms of these unique outcomes and encouraged to engage in behavior consistent with these alternative stories.

Epston in particular (White & Epston, 1990) also routinely employs therapeutic letters written to clients, summarizing sessions, inviting reluctant members to attend future sessions, addressing the future, and so on, extending conversations while encouraging family members to record or map out their own individualized view of the sequences of events in their lives over a period of time. Letters, because they can be read and reread days or months or even years later, have great continuity value; to use the language of the narrative therapists, they "thicken" or enrich an alternative story and help clients stay immersed in the reauthoring process. White (1995) estimates the usefulness of a single letter as at least four or five sessions of therapy.

Letters in narrative therapy[9] typically help therapy endure over time and space. Epston (1994) writes a *summary letter* to the client following each session, based on careful note-taking, and attuned to discussion (and in the client's own words) during the session that opened up the possibilities for alternatives to the clients' problem-saturated stories. In other cases, he sends *letters of invitation* to family members reluctant to attend sessions; most are surprised and pleased about his caring about them and their place in the family and may begin to attend. *Redundancy letters* note that certain members have taken on duplicate roles in the family (a father to one's brother) and wish to change them. In a related *discharge letter,* written with a client, another family member is thanked but informed that they are no longer needed to play that role. *Letters of prediction,* written at the conclusion of therapy, generally predict continued success in the search for new possibilities.

For Epston, letters are not separate interventions, but rather organically intertwined with what took place in the consultation room. Whatever their form, letters render lived experiences into narrative form. Consistent with the narrative therapist's egalitarian relationship with clients, the therapist's thoughts are not kept secret but are out in the open, to be confirmed or amended or challenged by the family. Taken together, the letters create an ongoing picture of therapist-clients collaboration as they seek to construct new solutions.

The Reflecting Team

One final postmodern approach, again reflecting the constructivist notion of multiple realities, comes from Tom Andersen (1991; 1993) and also relies heavily on therapy as a conversational and collaborative enterprise. In this simple but highly original technique, first developed by psychiatrist Andersen in Norway but increasingly a part of outpatient family therapy programs worldwide, a "two-way mirror" has replaced the more traditional "one-way mirror," so that in the course of a therapeutic session professionals and families have an opportunity to reverse roles and observe one another openly offering perspectives on the family's issues.

Whereas the earlier Milan interviews called for the therapist to halt a session with a family in order to consult with a team of professionals observing through a one-way mirror, Andersen expands on this tactic, breaking boundaries and opening up family-therapist-consultant team dialogues. He contends that his approach of sharing hypotheses about them directly with the family helps demystify therapy.

Consistent with social constructionist thinking, this approach is more egalitarian, calls for less of a subject-object dichotomy between therapist and family, and thus

---

[9]The reader might be interested in comparing narrative letters with those sent by the Milan systemic therapists. The latter, as we illustrated in Chapter 11, are of a paradoxical nature, intended to provoke a response, and typically are given the client directly or mailed after verbal paradoxical tactics have failed.

is less hierarchical than most therapies, including the Milan team approach. Andersen (1995) makes the following observation from his experiences using **reflecting teams:**

> When we finally began to use this mode we were surprised a how easy it was to talk without using nasty or hurtful words. Later it became evident that how we talk depends on the context in which we talk. If we choose to speak about the family without them present, we easily speak "professionally," in a detached manner. If we choose to speak about them in their presence, we naturally use everyday language and speak in a friendly manner. (p. 16)

In Andersen's original use of reflecting teams, at one or more times during the session, especially during an impasse, the therapist will solicit comments from the professionals behind the mirror, the lights and sound systems are reversed, and the family and therapist become the observers as team members have a conversation about the family conversation they have just observed. Without prior knowledge of the family or preplanning strategies, and unencumbered by hypotheses in order to understand the family's own construction of reality, the team members spontaneously present their views based upon what they observed during that particular session. Typically, these are offered for what they are—tentative, nonpejorative speculations regarding the problematic issues—with the team members careful not to make pronouncements or offer interpretations or instruct family members regarding what they should talk about. After the team has finished its reflections, family members have an opportunity to have a conversation about the reflecting team's conversations about the family's earlier conversations. Shifting between inner and outer dialogue offers two differing perspectives on the same events and stimulates the search for new outlooks and understanding. In the process, the family feels heard, uncriticized, and important to the process.

Language plays a key role in providing a vocabulary that sets our realities and provides stories that we construct to understand our experiences. Andersen (1991) is more interested in listening to what people say than in inferring what they mean. He (Andersen, 1992) has likened the reflecting team approach to a walk into the future. Many roads are possible; some routes lead to dead ends. What did the family expect by taking the road they chose? Might there be other routes to take now? Have you considered those? How can you talk to yourself about which routes were taken and which future routes might be best? Stimulated by reflecting team ideas in an egalitarian and collaborative fashion, and free to select those that are deemed useful, family members are encouraged to develop a new dialogue among themselves from which new perceptions emerge that lead to new meanings and ultimately new solutions.

In true postmodern fashion, therapists practicing differing approaches have offered differing ways of using the reflecting process. Narrative therapists in particular see reflecting teams as offering an opportunity to join with the family, support the development of new narratives, and facilitate the deconstruction of problem-saturated descriptions (Freedman & Combs, 1996). By observing and listening to therapy sessions, and attending to events that do not fit the dominant narrative, team members are in a position to notice unique outcomes. Addressing all family members, without leading or in any way making evaluative statements, the members of the team hold a genuine conversation in which each has an opportunity to personally comment on what he or she observed ("I noticed that Sam said . . ."). Team members speak as individuals, not knowledge experts, so that the "eavesdropping" family can adapt their ideas to fit their own experiences. Later, after the therapy session, Freedman and Combs (1996) gather together everyone involved—therapist, supervisor, team members, family members if they choose—to reflect on the entire process.

SUMMARY

The postmodern revolution in family therapy challenges systems thinking, especially of the first-order cybernetic type. In the postmodern view, there is no objectively knowable universe, but rather what we call "reality" is socially constructed; people, together, construct their realities as they live them. Therapists with a social constructionist view focus on the meaning or shared set of premises a family holds regarding a problem. Advocates of this position argue that multiple, socially constructive views of the same observations coexist depending primarily on the personal experiences of the observers. Reality exists only in the context of each person's set of constructs for thinking about it. The postmodern-influenced therapist is interested in engaging families in collaborative dialogues in which language and meaning given events take precedence over behavioral sequences or family interactive patterns, and where gender, ethnicity, race, sexual orientation, and social class issues are considered. Together, they help clients to find their own new meanings in their lives and to restory their problems and find more workable solutions.

Five examples of social constructionist family therapy are solution-focused brief therapy (deShazer), solution-oriented therapy (O'Hanlon and Weiner-Davis), the collaborative language systems approach (Goolishian and Anderson), narrative therapy (White), and the reflecting team (Andersen). Solution-focused therapy emphasizes aiding clients in seeking solutions rather than searching for explanations about their miseries. Miracle questions, exception-finding questions, and scaling questions are commonly employed techniques. A related set of procedures, solution-oriented therapy, helps clients use their inherent skills to develop solutions without imposing therapist explanations or solutions on the problem.

The collaborative language systems approach pays particular attention to meanings generated between people. Therapists and clients become conversational partners engaged in a shared inquiry aimed at dissolving problems by cocreating stories that open up new possibilities. Narrative therapy centers on the narrative metaphor—that our sense of reality is organized and maintained by stories we tell about ourselves. Cultural narratives provide dominant discourses, masquerading as objective "truths," that are often oppressive and eliminate alternate accounts of the same events, and thus prevent free choice. Narrative therapists together with families, help externalize an oppressive problem, and attend to unique outcomes in order to co-construct new narratives that provide more fulfilling accounts of their lives.

The reflecting team technique employs two-way mirrors, so that professionals and families can reverse roles and observe one another offering differing perspectives on family issues. Narrative therapists use the reflecting team technique to notice new outcomes and help families develop new narratives.

14

Psychoeducational
Family Therapy

Psychoeducation offers an empirically based form of therapy that seeks to impart information to distressed families, educating them so that they might develop skills for understanding and coping with their disturbed family member or troubled family relationships. Whether directed at families with schizophrenic members, or those where alcohol or substance abuse is uncontrolled, or families struggling with chronic illness, or perhaps those simply wishing to improve their relationship skills, the advent of psychoeducational programs represents a significant development in the field over the last two decades.

Reflecting the trend in family therapy toward a therapist-family collaborative partnership, these stress management, skills-building techniques help families harness their strengths and resiliency to deal with problems that affect all family members, not simply the symptomatic person. They typically offer educational/informational programs, supportive in nature and directed at the entire burdened and often despairing family. In other cases, dealing with less severe problems, programs might offer skills training in enhancing family relationships, improving couples communications, or perhaps helping remarried couples become more effective stepparents. Although psychoeducational family therapy does not, strictly speaking, follow customary family therapy procedures, practitioners do utilize many of the techniques of more traditional family therapy (joining the family, establishing an alliance with its members, maintaining neutrality, assessing how best to foster positive outcomes) in their interventions. Interventions tend to be *manually based,* reproducible techniques that follow a how-to-do-it format that can be copied by all mental health workers without necessarily requiring high levels of training.

Psychoeducational family therapy did not derive from any specific theory of family functioning, nor does it adhere to any one set of family therapy techniques. Rather, it is an eclectic approach, empirically derived, typically involving, in some combination depending upon the family or its circumstances, the application of family systems theory, behavior therapy, and educational psychology; in severe cases, such as schizophrenia, these are wedded to a psychopharmacological treatment program. Overall, psychoeducational efforts are directed at educating families in how best to maximize their effectiveness as they attempt to cope with mentally or physically disabled family members or deteriorating family relationships, or perhaps as they simply learn new problem-solving techniques for increasing the likelihood of future successful marital relationships.

FAMILIES AND MENTAL DISORDERS

Interest in schizophrenia among family therapists has waxed and waned over the last 40 years. Heralded in the late 1950s and 1960s as a breakthrough in understanding family factors contributing to the etiology or maintenance of the disorder, such concepts as schizophrenogenic mother, double-binding communications, pseudomutuality, and maritally schismed and maritally skewed families initially were greeted with excitement by many in the professional family therapy community as offering a new paradigm for understanding this complex disorder (see Chapter 5). By the mid-1970s and early 1980s, largely as a result of research (twin and adoption studies) into a possible genetic link in schizophrenia, as well as increased recognition that families were unfairly being blamed for "causing" the disorder in the affected member, family therapists appeared to be making a hasty retreat from working with the major psychoses.

General skepticism followed that concerned itself with whether family-related treatments for schizophrenia alone could be effective. By the 1990s, however, now viewing schizophrenia as a thought disorder in a biologically vulnerable person, many therapists were once again working with previously hospitalized schizophrenics and their families, this time focused on developing methods for preventing acute psychotic episodes in the former patient and the need to return to the hospital. As Steinglass (1996, p. 1) notes,

> psychoeducational family therapy is now seen as a mandatory component (along with psychopharmacology) of the state-of-the-art treatment of the major psychoses.

One example of such educationally based interventions, developed by Carol Anderson and her colleagues at the Western Psychiatric Institute in Pittsburgh (Anderson, Reiss, & Hogarty, 1986), offers a collaborative undertaking between therapist and family directed at reducing some of the anguish associated with living together as a family with a schizophrenic member. Without blaming the family—or in general looking for a culprit somewhere in society who must surely be at fault—these therapists go about the practical business of helping all family members, including the schizophrenic, overcome obstacles to family functioning. Thus, instead of searching for the source of the symptoms and the disability by ferreting out causal transactional patterns within the family, they favor a more matter-of-fact approach, teaching coping skills to families who must attend daily to "the devastating impact of watching one's child deteriorate into someone who is all but a stranger, and a most incapacitated one" (McFarlane, 1991, p. 364).

Programs developed by Anderson and her associates (1986), along with similar efforts by other like-minded clinicians/researchers such as Michael Goldstein (1981) at UCLA, Ian Falloon (Falloon, Boyd, McGill, Williamson, Razani, Moss, Gilderman, & Simpson, 1985) at the University of Southern California, and David Miklowitz (Miklowitz & Goldstein, 1997) at the University of Colorado, are examples of family-focused programs that have emerged as a result of briefer mental hospitalization in recent years for patients experiencing a major psychosis (schizophrenia or **bipolar disorder**). Because patients are often discharged while only in partial remission from their psychotic symptoms, they and their families must cope with problems connected with reentry into the community. Psychoeducational programs were designed to fit the bill—to be a part of community-based care, to educate patients and their families regarding the disorder, to address family concerns, to be coordinated with maintenance medication, all directed at forestalling relapse. One consequence of such community-based treatment was to place partially remitted patients in closer contact with their family members (Goldstein & Miklowitz, 1995).

Mental illness in a family can be a "ravaging, devastating disease" that disrupts a family and permits little opportunity for respite (Marsh & Johnson, 1997). In addition to the social stigma, and the ostracism of people with mental illness, household disarray, financial difficulties, employment problems, strained marital and family relationships, impaired physical health, and a diminished social life are just the most obvious consequences. Grief, chronic sorrow, the loss of dreams and hopes for the affected person, the emotional roller coaster punctuated by periods of relapse and remission, the potentially harmful or self-destructive behavior, the unpreparedness of families to deal with the challenges—these are the common experiences of family members (Marsh & Johnson, 1997). Marsh (1992) offers the following poignant account from the mother of a mentally ill daughter:

> The problems with my daughter were like a black hole inside of me into which everything else had been drawn. My grief and pain were so intense sometimes that I barely got through the day. It felt like a mourning process, as if I were dealing with the loss of the daughter I had loved for 18 years, for whom there was so much potential. (p. 10)

No family with a mentally ill member can avoid the consequences of the disorder without experiencing some family disruption. Teaching anguished family members how and from whom in the community[1] to obtain mental health, welfare, and medical services (or in some cases, legal services) is often of great benefit, especially to those families who feel helpless and confused when such new roles are thrust upon them (Lefley, 1996). Problem-solving training to manage day-to-day stressful events, thus guarding against relapses, and crisis management to handle extreme stress involving one or more family members or when signs of recurrence are evident

---

[1]The National Alliance for the Mentally Ill (NAMI), with over 1000 local affiliates in 50 states is a particularly important source of information, education, and support. Its membership includes professionals, family members of mentally ill persons, and members of the general public interested in problems of the mentally ill. The organization also serves as an advocacy group for expanding research and obtaining improved services.

are often a part of the educational undertaking. Simultaneously, therapeutic efforts are intended to ensure that to the extent possible family members preserve the integrity of their own lives. One major therapeutic task is to bring the family's competencies and resiliency into play, as together the members learn to the extent possible those techniques for prevailing over adversity and changing in constructive ways.

Among the experiences of Anderson, Reiss, and Hogarty (1986), ultimately leading to their adoption of the psychoeducational approach, was the observation that recovering hospitalized schizophrenics frequently relapsed when released to the custody of their families. Existing interventions intended to head off relapse, including traditional forms of family therapy, failed to stave off rehospitalization in most cases. More to the point, they found that the customary therapeutic search for causes within family life only aroused guilt and defensiveness, and sometimes resulted in failure—or worse, relapse—as the therapist tried to change family dynamics. Moreover, they contended that the encouragement of highly charged emotional exchanges sometimes sought by family therapists may actually be antitherapeutic in the case of schizophrenia. Instead of the customary focus on the family's effect on the schizophrenic, they proposed a turnaround—attending to the impact of the schizophrenic on family life.

Family Functioning and Schizophrenia

Family therapists with a psychoeducational orientation believe general family functioning is not causally related to the development of schizophrenia. That is, schizophrenia—which they view as a biological disease whose symptoms are best dealt with by using antipsychotic medication—may arise in well-functioning families as well as those that show a high degree of dysfunction. However, environmental factors within family life do play a role in schizophrenic relapse rates. Advocates of this psychoeducation-oriented set of interventions maintain that helping family members gain knowledge of the disorder and learn specific coping skills is essential in supplementing medication. The combination of antipsychotic drugs and psychoeducational interventions together are intended as a therapeutic package aimed at reducing family stress and preventing symptomatic relapse in the schizophrenic member.

Families, relieved at not being blamed or shamed for the development of the disorder in one of its members, are apt to be receptive to such integrated treatment programs, thus increasing the likelihood of increased treatment compliance.[2] Their willingness to collaborate with supportive therapists is increased if they become persuaded that these efforts will help them reduce the family's level of emotional intensity so that relapse in the schizophrenic might be delayed or reduced in severity.

---

[2]Not all families are so receptive, of course. Some reject these therapeutic efforts out of denial, or because they continue to believe any intervention publicly calls attention to the family as pathological. Some families do not wish to be together with other families with schizophrenic members because they fear the social stigma it might bring to them.

Expressed Emotion and Schizophrenia

While the *causes* of schizophrenia remain incompletely understood, researchers have begun to make headway in linking family interaction to the *course* of the disorder. One promising area of research involves the investigation of stress in the schizophrenic's family environment, particularly the manner in which members express criticism and hostility and become emotionally overinvolved with one another. Studies of schizophrenics following release from the hospital, initially carried out by George Brown and his colleagues (Brown, Monck, Carstairs, & Wing, 1962) at the Institute for Social Psychiatry in London, England, attended especially to the relationship between the degree to which intense emotion was expressed in the family and the degree of relapse. This was in contrast with the then prevalent view that relapse was due specifically to patients, unmonitored, discontinuing their medication once released from the hospital.

The emerging theory of **expressed emotion** (EE) suggested that schizophrenia is a thought disorder in which the individual is especially vulnerable to, as well as highly responsive to, stress caused by the expression of intense, negative emotions. Researchers thus reasoned that perhaps affective factors might account for patient relapse as he or she tried, unsuccessfully, to process incoming communication. That is, when former patients returned to a stressful family environment where EE was high—emotionally intense exchanges, especially expressed in negative and hypercritical comments about the patient's overtly disturbed behavior—arousal in schizophrenics was more likely to occur, and symptoms soon followed as relapse took place. On the other hand, for patients returning to households manifesting low EE, while family members also tended to be concerned about the disturbed (and disturbing) behavior of the schizophrenic, these relatives were not overly anxious in their response to the patient's condition, allowing the individual more psychological space (Leff & Vaughn, 1985).

Expressed emotion is perhaps the most well-validated indicator for relapses of schizophrenia (Miklowitz, 1995). The value of reducing EE in helping families cope with schizophrenia has now been well documented by subsequent research (Atkinson & Coia, 1995). Lowering EE has also been linked to reduced relapse rates for various forms of depression and bipolar disorder (Mueser & Glynn, 1995). As Miklowitz (1995) observes:

> The family, then, is seen as a risk or protective factor that may augment or diminish the likelihood that underlying genetic and/or biological vulnerabilities in a family member will be expressed as symptoms of a mental disorder. (p. 194)

This line of investigation regarding family stress and patient biological vulnerability has stimulated much research aimed at developing operational aftercare programs directed at decreasing relapse rates—Goldstein, Rodnick, Evans, May, and Steinberg (1978) combining a conflict-reducing aftercare home-based program along with patient compliance in continuing medication; Falloon and associates (Falloon, Boyd, McGill, Williamson, Razani, Moss, Gilderman, & Simpson, 1985) devising an aftercare family management plan following behavioral principles, along with medication, and aimed less at cure than decreasing negative affect, and correspondingly decreasing the probability of relapse by increasing patient social functioning; and Anderson, Reiss, and Hogarty (1986) experimenting with a program in which a psychoeducational effort directed at the family supplements (but does not replace) drug therapy for the schizophrenic family member. Unlike earlier family therapy efforts with schizophrenics, Anderson and her colleagues were not so much interested in "fixing" a dysfunctional system, probing ever deeper in family dynamics, as they were in creating a nonjudgmental learning environment in which families can improve their skills in understanding and coping with a disturbed family member.

The Therapeutic Process

Family psychoeducation efforts follow one of two formats—working with individual families (Anderson, Reiss, & Hogarty, 1986), or with multiple families simultaneously (McFarlane, 1991). In the former, Anderson and her colleagues describe a set of phased interventions, beginning with engaging the family, typically when an acute schizophrenic decompensation has occurred. Gaining the family's cooperation, the team sets up psychoeducational programs—typically a day-long Survival Skills Workshop—during which they teach family members about the prevalence and course of mental illness, its biological etiology, current modes of pharmacological and psychosocial treatment, common medications, and prognosis. Patient and family needs are discussed, and family coping skills strategized. EE findings are likely to be aired here, and efforts made to provide basic behavioral guidelines for keeping EE in check, taking pressure off the patient to hurry up and behave in a normal manner. Because schizophrenics are usually sensitive to overstimulation, families are urged to respect boundaries, allowing schizophrenics to withdraw whenever necessary. This respect for individual boundaries is supplemented later by the reinforcing of generational boundaries, as parents are urged to form a stronger bond with one another and together remain in charge lest the patient's needs come to dominate all family decisions.

During the subsequent reentry period into the social environment, regularly scheduled outpatient sessions, which may go on for a year or more, are aimed at achieving stability outside of the hospital. Patients may be assigned small tasks and their progress monitored. The therapy team typically uses this period to shift attention to the family structure, which may have changed as a result of accommodating to the patient's return from the hospital. The team uses the final rehabilitation phase to consolidate gains and raise the patient's level of functioning. Anderson and her associates' emphasis on boundaries, hierarchy, and maintaining the integrity of subsystems reflects the influences of structural family therapy.

McFarlane's (1991) multifamily version owes its heritage to multiple family therapy (MFT) (Laqueur, 1976), an early effort to treat several families of hospitalized schizophrenic patients together. Originally designed to bring families together in order to solve ward-management problems, MFT also provided social support for families with similar problems who otherwise would feel isolated. In its psychoeducational reincarnation, informal lecture-and-discussion educational workshops with relatives, attended together by five or six families, occurs, the families again meeting together with patients and therapist for subsequent sessions for at least 12 months. The multiple families are believed by McFarlane to offer increased social support. Table 14.1 presents a typical set of guidelines offered by psychoeducators for managing rehabilitation following a schizophrenic episode.

Psychoeducational family therapy is less dependent on intervention techniques than traditional family therapy, and sets limited goals; symptoms are reduced rather than cured. Psychoeducation nevertheless provides a quiet, sound, stabilizing milieu in which family members do not feel criticized or blamed, and where they can begin to learn coping techniques for the difficult and probably long-term task of living with a schizophrenic person and preventing (or delaying) his or her relapse and rehospitalization.

Overall, Goldstein and Miklowitz's (1995) careful review of the effectiveness of psychoeducational family therapy with schizophrenics found that family intervention is superior to routine care involving medication and crisis intervention as needed. Such intervention at the family level was more effective, measured by delayed relapses (over two years in some studies cited) and improved social functioning, than individual supportive or skills-oriented therapies.

Table 14.1   Psychoeducational Guidelines for Families and Friends of Schizophrenics

Here is a list of things everyone can do to make things run more smoothly:

1. *Go slow.* Recovery takes time. Rest is important. Things will get better in their own time.
2. *Keep it cool.* Enthusiasm is normal. Tone it down. Disagreement is normal. Tone it down, too.
3. *Give 'em space.* Time out is important for everyone. It's okay to offer. It's okay to refuse.
4. *Set limits.* Everyone needs to know what the rules are. A few good rules keep things calmer.
5. *Ignore what you can't change.* Let some things slide. Don't ignore violence or use of street drugs.
6. *Keep it simple.* Say what you have to say clearly, calmly, and positively.
7. *Follow doctor's orders.* Take medications as they are prescribed. Take *only* medications that are prescribed.
8. *Carry on business as usual.* Reestablish family routines as quickly as possible. Stay in touch with family and friends.
9. *No street drugs or alcohol.* They make symptoms worse.
10. *Pick up on early signs.* Note changes. Consult with you family clinician.
11. *Solve problems step by step.* Make changes gradually. Work on one thing at a time.
12. *Lower expectations, temporarily.* Use a personal yardstick. Compare this month with last month rather than with last year to next year.

Source: McFarlane, 1991, p. 375.

MEDICAL FAMILY THERAPY

The most effective way to prevent relapse in schizophrenics as we have just pointed out, appears to be with a combined regimen of antipsychotic medication and psychoeducational family therapy. If we consider schizophrenia as a chronic disease,
then this medical/psychological set of interventions qualifies as **medical family therapy**, defined as a coordinated effort by an interdisciplinary team to treat a chronic
medical illness, trauma, or disability. In general, the psychoeducational thrust here
is not so much to "cure," but rather to help families to better cope with a chronic illness, engage in less conflict over managing medication, communicate better with
medical providers, accept a medical problem that cannot be cured, or perhaps make
constructive lifestyle changes (McDaniel, Hepworth, & Doherty, 1995).

Pioneered by Don Bloch, former head of the Ackerman Institute, who in 1983 was
one of the founders of the journal *Family Systems Medicine*, medical family therapy tries
to deal with the complex interface between family relationships and family health. In
this model's view, the family serves as the primary social context for health care and,
correspondingly, what goes on within the family inevitably influences a family member's medical condition. (The journal has now been renamed *Families, Systems, and
Health,* to reflect the burgeoning of the field into all aspects of health care, including
health promotion and disease prevention.) Simultaneously, medical family therapy (or
family systems medicine) has begun to be enthusiastically embraced by the broader
field of family therapy. A review of research into the effectiveness of family interventions in the treatment of physical illness offers support for the role of medical family
therapy in today's health care system (Campbell & Patterson, 1995).

Medical family therapy attempts to treat illness by first recognizing that it occurs
at several systemic levels simultaneously—the biological, the psychological, the
social, and the interpersonal—and then planning interventions targeting these levels. George Engel (1977), a psychiatrist, is usually credited with having been the first
to call for an integrated approach to medical problems that he designated the
"biopsychosocial approach." Engel argued that the patient and the disease must be
understood in context, that families must be involved in medical care, and that all
systems must be considered equally. In an effort to promote family-centered medical
care, further linking family therapy and family medicine, Doherty and Baird (1983;
1987), a psychologist and family physician, respectively, delineated five levels of
physician engagement with families, ranging from little if any involvement through
keeping family members informed of patient treatment to offering support to planning interventions and finally to family therapy.

In 1992, Susan McDaniel, Jeri Hepworth, and William Doherty (1992) coined
the term *medical family therapy* to refer to the "biopsychosocial treatment of individuals and families who are dealing with medical problems" (p 2). In particular, these
authors called attention to the inevitable impact of medical illness on the personal
life of the patient, and also on the interpersonal life of the family. Combining the
biopsychosocial and systems perspectives, their book was the first to describe new
roles for family therapists in a variety of medical or other health care settings.

No biomedical event occurs without psychosocial consequences. Endorsing a
psychosocial perspective for understanding a wide array of chronic disorders affect-

ing individuals and families across their life spans, Rolland (1994) offered a useful family-systems-illness model in which family belief systems (including those associated with gender, culture, and ethnicity) about illness were highlighted. A family's belief system that is discrepant with the belief system of the health providers may lead to rejection of the treatment or noncompliance with medical/ psychological recommendations and prescriptions.

Consistent with the work of Rolland and others, such as Cole and Reiss (1993), to understand the impact of illness on a specific family, family therapists, physicians, nurses, and other health care workers joined together in 1994 to discuss the rapidly changing health care delivery system, and together formed the Collaborative Family Healthcare Coalition (Bloch, 1994). Researchers, educators, administrators, health care policymakers, social workers, and consumer group representatives are also represented in this family-oriented effort, which now has regional chapters throughout the United States and Europe. The Coalition serves as a clearinghouse, disseminating information with the purpose of promoting a more coordinated, family-centered model of health care delivery integrating traditional medical/nursing care, psychosocial services, and the services of related health care providers. Patients, family, community, and providers of health care services are seen as parts of one ecosystem and as equal participants in the health care process. In contrast to conventional, compartmentalized, and often wasteful procedures that involve repeated diagnostic procedures and expensive referrals to specialists, the coalition seeks to help establish a collaborative, team-based family health care paradigm aimed at cost-effective, humane, and integrated patient and family services.

Clinical collaboration between medical providers, family therapists, and other related health professionals is the cornerstone of this comprehensive approach for dealing with a variety of medical problems (McDaniel, 1995). Family therapists may serve as consultants, referral resources, or cotherapists with fellow health care professionals. Ideally, when family therapists, primary care physicians, nurses and nurse practitioners, rehabilitation specialists, and related professionals can work as a team, adopting a broad biopsychosocial systems perspective, they can benefit families attempting to cope with the impact of chronic illness (diabetes, leukemia, cardiovascular disease), life threatening conditions (AIDS, anorexia nervosa, infants born prematurely), or impairment and disability (spinal cord injury, blindness or deafness, neurological impairment in the elderly) of one of its members on overall family life. Family-level interventions for lifestyle changes (quitting smoking, losing weight, eating healthier diets) represent a relatively new area for such psychoeducational efforts to improve health and longevity.

Partnerships between therapist and physician, nurse, or rehabilitation specialist to achieve more comprehensive care calls for accepting each other's language, therapeutic assumptions, and working styles,[3] which often are in conflict. Physicians are able to educate the therapist about the causes, likely course, and prognosis of a disease, while the therapist, acting as a consultant or cotherapist, can enlighten the

---

[3]The traditional medical style is to be action-oriented, advice giving, and physician dominant, while mental health care is more process-oriented, facilitative, and patient-centered. Another obvious difference is the amount of time spent with a patient or family: most therapists spend 50–60 minutes, while physicians are likely to spend 10–20 minutes (McDaniel, 1995).

physician and other caregivers about the patient's experience of illness, perhaps how to minimize patient or family anxiety, help them accept the disease, and enable them to participate in their own healing (McDaniel, 1995). Family therapists might also help families examine their belief systems, including possible reasons for noncompliance with a prescribed medical regime. In other cases, overutilization of health care services by a family might be examined. An additional positive outcome from this collaboration is that therapists who are nonphysicians will not overlook some important biological aspect of a complex presenting problem. By the same token, working with therapists or social workers, physicians are less apt to overlook the psychosocial levels of a problem or illness. The task of tending to a family's emotional needs, say after major surgery, often falls on the mental health person, and leaves the surgeon free to care for the patient's biomedical needs.

Medical family therapists need a working knowledge of the major chronic illnesses and disabilities, as well as their emotional sequelae, along with familiarity with the health care system. Physicians need to understand and accept the help offered by the family therapist without feeling a loss of sovereignty over patient care. While battles over turf and professional competition often exist, working partnerships offering a holistic, ecosystemic approach to health care are increasing in frequency.

One goal of a successful therapist-physician collaboration is to strengthen the shaken family system, allowing its members to regain a sense of choice about impending medical decisions. Another is to reduce the emotional consequences to the family of an ongoing medical condition, perhaps reducing the clinical course of the illness in the process.

Some serious disorders, such as AIDS, call for special therapeutic sensitivities. Individuals with this diagnosis may appropriately fear disclosure will stigmatize them and expose them to discrimination in employment, housing, insurance coverage, and even medical care by health workers afraid of close contact with the disease. Working closely with physicians, therapists need to help patients deal with loss of independence, physical incapacity, rejection by a lover, and disclosure to family and others. The medical family therapist can be helpful to all concerned—the patient, the patient's partner, his family of origin—in coming to terms with this devastating disease (Macklin, 1989; Landau-Stanton, 1993).

SHORT-TERM EDUCATIONAL PROGRAMS

The psychoeducational approach has also been extended to couples or families without a symptomatic member who wish to acquire better skills to cope with their everyday relationship problems more effectively. In other cases, some may wish to learn how best to prevent the occurrence of problems before they develop, say before an impending marriage, or perhaps upon remarriage where stepchildren are involved. Here the therapist, taking the contemporary view, is less the expert who diagnoses a problem and offers treatment, and more the facilitator who educates people in the skills they need to manage their current difficulties and head off future distress. Brief, practical, positive in tone and outlook, and cost-effective, this form of intervention, when successful, helps empower people to function more effectively within marriage, family, or work situations.

Programs involving relationship enhancement, preparations for marriage or childbirth, marriage enrichment, and parent effectiveness training are all examples of these psychoeducational efforts, as are the behavioral parent skills training procedures we described in Chapter 12. Their objectives, depending upon the needs of client families, range from ameliorating an identified problem to enhancing existing skills in order to further improve the quality of family life (Levant, 1986). As in most forms of family therapy, here the therapist joins the family and identifies client strengths and growth potential along with potential problem areas. Unlike most other family therapy procedures, however, the therapist's goal in this situation is to deliver educational training and not psychotherapy. Moreover, both the therapist and family share a vision of the educational goals and specific objectives of skills to be acquired in advance of their engagement, and termination usually occurs when the content has been delivered or when a previously agreed-upon time frame has been completed (Fournier & Rae, 1999).

In the following sections, we group and offer a sampling of the many psycho-educational programs of interest to marriage and family therapists.

Relationship Enhancement Programs

Probably the best-known family skills training approach is the highly developed and researched Relationship Enhancement (RE) program created by Bernard Guerney, Jr. (1977), at Pennsylvania State University. Guerney, who had earlier been one of the authors of the breakthrough *Families of the Slums* (Minuchin, Montalvo, Guerney, Rosman, & Schumer, 1967), had also worked with Carl Rogers, and his client-centered orientation to therapy is evident in his interventions with families. Thus, empathy, genuineness, positive regard for clients, and other Rogerian principles are recognizable in his work, as is his interest, seen in his work with Minuchin, in developing techniques for helping troubled family relationships. Barry Ginsberg, a student of both Bernard Guerney and Louise Guerney, husband and wife colleagues, has recently described the contemorary practices of the RE approach (Ginsberg, 1997).

The Guerneys' early psychoeducational endeavors go back to the *filial therapy* program they developed during the 1960s (Guerney, 1964; Guerney, Guerney, & Andronico, 1966) to help parents deal better with their young, emotionally disturbed children. In this therapeutic undertaking, usually conducted in groups of six to eight parents, the Guerneys explained how Rogerian principles applied to parent-child relationships and instructed parents in the use of the technique to develop structuring, acknowledging, and limit-setting skills. Weekly play therapy sessions at home augmented the process. In general, the technique was devised to help children with emotional, behavioral, or developmental problems to better understand and communicate their feelings and gain a sense of mastery over their actions. At the same time, if successful, parents developed more realistic expectations, became more receptive to the children's feelings and experiences, and learned to communicate their new understanding and acceptance. This RE approach later was supplemented by the Parent-Adolescent Relationship Development (PARD) program (Ginsberg, 1977; Guerney, Coufal, & Vogelsang, 1981) to foster trust, empathy, genuineness, intimacy, openness, and satisfaction in parent and adolescent relationships.

From its origins, RE programs have provided couples with training in four sets of skills:

- The *expressive mode* (gaining self-awareness and learning self-expression)
- The *empathic mode* (acquiring listening and reflective responding skills)
- *Mode switching* (in order to facilitate communication)
- The *facilitative mode* (in which participants learn to help one another develop the previous skills)

Later, two skills were added:

- *Problem-solving and conflict-resolution skills*
- *Maintenance and generalization skills* (both to be practiced at home, using the facilitative mode) (Levant, 1986)

RE is an intensive, time-limited program (usually ten sessions), based upon an educational model, in which clients are taught to recognize their problems more clearly and to understand how learning specific skills (how to improve one's self-concept, how to recognize and express what they are feeling, how to work through problems, how to achieve interpersonal satisfaction) helps them deal with their ongoing lives and also with problems they may encounter in the future. Both didactic presentations and skills practice take place in each session. The program requires people dedicated enough to work at mastering these skills during therapy sessions and to continue outside to carry out homework assignments.

The intent, according to Ginsberg (1997), is less to help people change than to help them create a context in which constructive change is more likely to occur. Once the context is established, RE practitioners believe clients become more autonomous and ultimately able to become more intimate with other significant persons in their lives. With greater trust in their own ability to solve problems, they are in a better position to deal with possible future crises should they arise. Table 14.2 demonstrates the major differences between the educational model and that based upon medical practice.

In addition to experiential elements (especially client-centered and emotionally focused therapies), psychodynamic, behavioral, communications, and family systems concepts are utilized. RE offers cognitive instruction—critically examining one's thoughts, attitudes, and values—along with behavioral instruction—building skills for handling emotions or engaging in interpersonal relationships. The practitioner's values are explicitly stated, and the client-therapist relationship is one of shared planning and decision making. Regardless of the specific population RE addresses, its signature techniques involve empathy, nonjudgmental acceptance, fostering genuine conversations between clients, as well as teaching clients to recognize and acknowledge feelings and to express them openly and honestly.

Table 14.2 Educational Model versus Medical Model

Educational Model	Medical Model
Emphasizes developmental processes, psychological needs, and life stresses.	Emphasizes sickness (maladaptation/pathology).
De-emphasizes insight and etiology.	Emphasizes insight and etiology.
Problem lies within individual's control.	Problem lies outside the individual's control.
Client agrees to learn from the practitioner (teacher).	Client depends on the expertise of the practitioner for change.
Best healing and change come from the client's own efforts.	Healing is dependent on the practitioner's skill.
Clients are encouraged to seek the knowledge and resources they need.	Generally, clients under the exclusive care of the provider.
Methods include: setting goal(s), understanding rationale and methods of skill, skill practice and learning, generalizing the problems of everyday life, and maintaining skills.	Methods include: diagnosis, treatment, and cure.
No distinction between prevention and amelioration.	Methods are skewed more toward treatment than prevention.

Source: Ginsberg, 1997, p. 3

Marriage Preparation Programs

In an effort to produce a useful and reliable method for evaluating a couple's preparation for marriage, David Olson and his colleagues (Olson, Fournier, & Druckman, 1986) developed and refined the aptly titled PREPARE (PREmarital Personal and Relationship Evaluation). In its latest revision (Olson, 1996), this well-researched 165-item inventory (including 30 background and demographic questions), filled out separately by each person, is designed to aid premarital couples to better understand and discuss their families of origin with one another, to more easily identify areas where they experience differences in outlook, and to think about what needs attention about such differences if they are to develop a harmonious relationship.

Computer scored and presented in graphic profile form on a Couple and Family Map, information is supplied to the couple regarding their "relationship strengths" and "growth areas" where further work is necessary. Eleven content areas are explored, including *marriage expectations* (what each expects regarding love, commitment, how to deal with conflict), *communication* (the degree of comfort each feels about sharing emotions, listening and being listened to), and the couple's *sexual relationship* (feelings and concerns regarding affection, sexual behavior, family planning). *Personality differences, financial management,* attitudes regarding *conflict resolution,* and *child rearing,* preferences for how to spend *leisure* time, expectations about the amount of time spent with *family and friends,* attitudes regarding *marital roles,* and *spiritual beliefs* are also examined together with the premarital counselor.

PREPARE is especially useful for its early identification of potential conflict areas and for promoting couple dialogue likely to be beneficial ir their future together. Psychoeducational efforts to help premarital couples begin tc work at resolving key differences frequently are carried out using a companion Ten Steps for Conflict Resolution program (Olson, 1987).

Marital Enrichment Programs

The Preventive Intervention and Relationship Enhancement Program (PREP) (Floyd, Markman, Kelly, Blumberg, & Stanley, 1995) represents a carefully designed attempt to help married couples improve their relationship before problems possibly set in and lead to relational deterioration and ultimately heightened conflict and the risk of divorce. Originally developed in the early 1980s to help young couples planning marriage, this *social learning approach,* melding behavior therapy, relationship enhancement, and communication skills instruction (see Chapter 12) is based on the premise that

> marital satisfaction results from the exchange of rewarding behaviors between spouses, paired with the ability to resolve conflicts in a mutually satisfying way, without resorting either to escalation of negative affect and aggression, or withdrawal and avoidance. (p. 213)

Couples are taught constructive communication and conflict resolution skills, along with realistic attitudes and expectations about marriage. In particular, they learn to develop behavioral interactive patterns that satisfy the emotional and psychological needs of each partner. Overall, the thrust is future-oriented; couples learn to resolve disputes effectively and in a timely manner so that avoidant patterns do not build up, making conflict resolution that much more difficult in the future.

PREP sessions come in two formats (Floyd, Markman, Kelly, Blumberg, & Stanley, 1995): (1) an extended version, in which groups of 4 to 10 couples attend a series of weekly lectures on skills or relationship issues, followed by exercises to learn the discussed skills; and (2) a marathon version, in which 20 to 60 couples at a time hear the lectures in a group setting over the course of a weekend. In the former, each couple is assigned a communication consultant, who acts as a coach as the couple practices skills acquisition, providing them with feedback to facilitate the learning process. Homework assignments and readings are part of the therapeutic package. In the latter, often held at a hotel, couples practice skills on their own in their rooms. PREP also supplies videotapes and audiotapes for further study. Positive steps to preserve a marriage, based on ongoing research, have been described by Markman, Stanley, and Blumberg (1994).

Markman, at the Center for Marital and Family Studies at the University of Denver, in particular is a well-known behavioral researcher into marital distress and its prevention (Markman, Renick, Floyd, Stanley, & Clements, 1993). Outcome studies of the PREP program have been encouraging. Not surprisingly, short-term gains (measured immediately after the intervention) involving improved communication are especially promising. Long-term follow-ups, up to 18 months, in general, show sustained benefits as couples undergoing the program continued to rate the impact of their communication behaviors positively.

Less carefully researched, but popular and widespread, is *marriage encounter*—a weekend enrichment program for couples, frequently sponsored by church groups—directed at raising couple awareness of communication, problem-solving, sexual, intimacy, and spiritual issues in an effort to prevent marriage complacency or, worse, deterioration. In some cases, such programs appeal to couples who have a satisfactory relationship but wish to make improvements or those who wish to examine and reaffirm their relationship.

Marriage encounter programs first appeared in Barcelona, Spain, in the early 1960s, developed by a Jesuit priest, Father Gabriel Calvo. He originally conceived of arranging weekend retreats to provide support and enrichment for Catholic married couples (Chartier, 1986). Introduced into the United States in 1966, similar religiously oriented programs have been adopted by Protestant and Jewish groups to meet the needs of their members. In addition to couples in long-standing marriages, premarital and remarried couples have also found the experience enlightening and beneficial (Stahmann & Hiebert, 1997). Some denominations require engaged couples to participate in such a program before they can be married in church.

In addition to these religiously based efforts, certain nonreligious marital enrichment programs, such as the Minnesota Couple Communication Program (MCCP) have become popular. The MCCP program, intended to appeal to married and pre-married couples, is educationally focused rather than remedial, helping participants with satisfactory communication skills enhance these skills still further. As in the case with the PREP program described above, emphasis is on the couple or dyad, although the group context is believed to facilitate learning.

Programs sponsored by the Association for Couples in Marital Enrichment offer marriage encounters generally led by married couples who have successfully been through the program and received some additional training. Didactic material is kept to a minimum, as is group interaction; the major emphasis is on skills building through partner dialogue. Outcome studies, especially of a long-term nature, are inconclusive at this point.

By the end of the 1980s, according to Lasswell and Lasswell (1991), as many as a million people had participated in weekend encounter workshops for married couples and those engaged to be married. These authors suggest that, based on limited studies, marriage encounter can be a valuable experience for couples in good marriages who want to make them better, but not for couples who have serious problems; the latter run the risk of further deterioration.

Stepfamily Preparation Programs

Stepfamilies are an increasingly widespread phenomenon as we enter the twenty-first century; close to half of all new marriages today involve a remarriage of one partner, and one in four a remarriage for both (Saxton, 1996). Of the more than 11 million remarried households in the United States (Bray, 1995), most include minor children living in a stepfamily household (Ganong & Coleman, 1994). Inevitably, living through a series of disruptive transitions—from intact family to single parenthood to remarried family—generates a series of structural and relationship shifts and role changes requiring in some cases major adaptations and reorganizations for parents and children alike (Goldenberg & Goldenberg, 1998).

Successful adaptation to stepfamily life calls for the ability to recognize and cope with a variety of problems: stepparents assuming a parental role, rule changes, jealousy and competition between stepsiblings as well as between birth parents and stepparents, loyalty conflicts in children between the absent parent and the stepparent, financial obligations for child support while entering into a new marriage, to name but a few. Remarriage itself may resurrect old, unresolved feelings, such as anger and hurt, left over from a previous marriage.

Children and adults alike come with expectations from previous families, and a major task for most stepfamilies is coming to terms with these differences. Stepfamilies must deal with losses and changes, must negotiate different developmental needs of its members, must create a parental coalition, and must establish new traditions of their own (Visher & Visher, 1988). Parenting and stepparenting are particularly stressful aspects in most stepfamilies, both during the early years of remarriage and in stepfamilies of longer duration (Bray, 1995).

Despite both the frequency and magnitude of these problems, with few exceptions (Visher & Visher, 1996) there is little guidance typically available from mental health professionals to help families become a more cohesive system and achieve stepfamily integration. For most families, "instant intimacy" is impossible; time is needed for negotiating values and beliefs, for distributing and trying out new roles, and for strengthening the parental bond.

Psychoeducational programs designed to help family members understand common stepfamily relationship patterns are frequently effective ways to cement a compatible and united stepfamily life. Knowing that other families are dealing with the same issues is often comforting. One important resource to whom stepfamilies can turn is the Stepfamily Association of America, founded by stepparents Emily Visher and John Visher, a psychologist and psychiatrist, respectively. The Vishers have been at the forefront of psychoeducational efforts to offer informational programs in stepfamily living. Visher and Visher (1986) developed a stepfamily workbook manual (an excerpt of which appears in Box 14.1) as an aid in group discussions aimed at accomplishing those tasks that lead to restructured stepfamily systems. The Stepfamily Foundation provides a variety of educational programs (training for professionals, referral to therapists who work with families) and offers a network of mutual help services (survival courses in stepfamily living).

SUMMARY

Psychoeducational therapy approaches have directed their efforts primarily at reducing the stress on families by educating them so that they might develop better coping skills for dealing with a disturbed family member or a troubled family relationship. In some cases, information and education are offered to prevent conflict or to

BOX 14.1   Tasks that must be completed to develop a stepfamily identity

1. Dealing with losses and changes
2. Negotiating different developmental needs
3. Establishing new traditions
4. Developing a solid couple bond
5. Forming new relationships
6. Creating a "parenting coalition"
7. Accepting continual shifts in household composition
8. Risking involvement despite little societal support

1. Dealing with losses and changes
   - Identify/recognize losses for all individuals
   - Support expressions of sadness
   - Help children talk and not act out feelings
   - Read stepfamily books
   - Make changes gradually
   - See that everyone gets a turn
   - Inform children of plans involving them
   - Accept the insecurity of change

2. Negotiating different developmental needs
   - Take a child development and/or parenting class
   - Accept validity of the different life-cycle phases
   - Communicate individual needs clearly
   - Negotitate incompatible needs
   - Develop tolerance and flexibility

3. Establishing new traditions
   - Recognize ways are *different,* not right or wrong
   - Concentrate on important situations only
   - Stepparents take on discipline enforcement slowly
   - Use family meetings for problem solving and giving appreciation
   - Shift "givens" slowly whenever possible
   - Retain/combine appropriate rituals
   - Enrich with new creative traditions

4. Developing a solid couple bond
   - Accept couple as primary long-term relationship
   - Nourish couple relationship
   - Plan for couple "alone time"
   - Decide general household rules as a couple
   - Support one another with the children
   - Expect and accept different parent-child and stepparent-stepchild feelings
   - Work out money matters together   *(continued)*

BOX 14.1   *(continued)*

5. Forming new relationships
   - Fill in past histories
   - Make stepparent-stepchild one-to-one time
   - Make parent-child one-to-one time
   - Parents make space for stepparent-stepchild relationship
   - Do not expect instant love and adjustment
   - Be fair to stepchildren even when caring not developed
   - Follow children's lead in what to call stepparent
   - Do fun things together

6. Creating a "parenting coalition"
   - Deal directly with parenting adults in other household
   - Keep children out of the middle of parental disagreements
   - Do not talk negatively about adults in other household
   - Control what you can and accept limitations
   - Avoid power struggles between households
   - Respect parenting skills of former spouse
   - Contribute own "specialness" to children
   - Communicate between households in most effective manner

7. Accepting continual shifts in household composition
   - Allow children to enjoy their households
   - Give children time to adjust to household transitions
   - Avoid asking children to be messengers or spies
   - Consider teenager's serious desire to change residence
   - Respect privacy (boundaries) of all households
   - Set consequences that affect own household only
   - Provide personal place for nonresident children
   - Plan special times for various household constellations

8. Risking involvement despite little societal support
   - Include stepparents in school, religious, sports activities
   - Give legal permission for stepparent to act when necessary
   - Continue stepparent-stepchild relationships after death or divorce of parent when caring has developed
   - Stepparent include self in stepchild's activities
   - Find groups supportive of stepfamilies
   - Remember that all relationships involve risk

Source: Visher & Visher, 1986

teach specific skills for managing everyday, nonclinical situations. Typically, psychoeducational programs involve a combination of systems theory, behavior therapy, and educational psychology.

Psychoeducational efforts are most prominent in working with families where there is a member with a severe mental disorder, such as schizophrenia or bipolar disorder. Viewing such problems as occurring in a biologically vulnerable person, therapists with a psychoeducational viewpoint adopt a nonblaming stance and do not presuppose a dysfunctional family responsible for the disorder. Instead, they direct their therapeutic efforts at teaching coping skills as well as offering guidelines aimed at reducing obstacles to harmonious family living and decreasing the likelihood of patient symptomatic relapse. Schizophrenia is viewed as a biological disease best treated with medication in combination with educational workshops in which families learn to reduce the level of expressed emotion in their households.

Medical family therapy, a form of psychoeducation, utilizes the collaboration of an interdisciplinary team in dealing with patients with various illnesses, traumas, or disabilities. Their biopsychosocial undertakings are designed to help families better cope with problems associated with the illness, have less conflict over managing medication, communicate better with medical providers, and in some cases make constructive lifestyle changes to prevent disease and prolong health. Family therapists may serve in a psychoeducational capacity, as consultants, referral resources, or cotherapists with fellow health care providers.

Short-term educational programs are psychoeducational endeavors designed to help families who wish to acquire better coping skills for managing everyday relationships more effectively, or preventing the occurrence of problems before they develop. Brief, practical, and cost-effective, these programs may involve a wide variety of potential educational areas, including relationship enhancement, marriage preparation, marriage enrichment, parent effectiveness training, and stepparenting preparation.

V

RESEARCH, TRAINING, AND PROFESSIONAL ISSUES

15

Family Therapy Research

Historically speaking, research in family therapy has provided the fertile soil for the blossoming of the field in the last four decades. As we noted in Chapter 5, and as Wynne (1983), himself a pioneer in the field, has observed, working with families in the 1950s was regarded primarily as a research idea; the notion of seeing family members together for therapeutic purposes came later and followed from research discoveries and subsequent theorizing.[1] Wynne recalls that the therapy offered to families in those early years was distinctly intended to facilitate the maintenance of contact with research families. Haley (1978), too, looks back on that decade as a time when it "was taken for granted that a therapist and a researcher were of the same species (although the therapist had a more second-class status)" (p. 73).

REBUILDING BRIDGES BETWEEN
PRACTITIONERS AND RESEARCHERS

Priorities began to change drastically beginning in the 1960s, as clinicians, on the basis of their experiences of working therapeutically with families, generated a multitude of new and exciting clinical techniques, in most cases without benefit of research support. While there was some noteworthy research during the 1960s and 1970s—for example, Minuchin's (Minuchin et al., 1967) work with delinquent adolescents and their families; Langsley, Pittman, Machotka, and Flomenhaft's (1968) demonstration of the superiority of outpatient family crisis therapy to hospitalization; and Masters and Johnson's (1970) behaviorally designed procedures for overcoming sexual inadequacies—family research and family therapy seemed to become different realms, with distinct languages, observational procedures, and philosophical orientations toward

---

[1]There are some notable historical exceptions to this research-to-treatment sequence that deserve mention here. Some pioneers in the field, such as John Bell, came upon family therapy more inadvertently, in a search for a new therapeutic modality to help troubled youngsters (see Chapter 5), and hence did not follow the research route Wynne describes.

Lyman Wynne, M.D., Ph.D.

inquiry. Framo's (1972) call in a well-known conference in 1967 for a "dialogue" between family therapist and family researcher attested to the developing polarization.

The 1980s seemed to bring some renewed connection between researcher and therapist. Behaviorally oriented family therapists in particular led the way in assessing the effectiveness of their efforts. For example, Dangel and Polster (1984) described a number of empirically oriented behavioral parent training research programs, including an examination of their usefulness and appropriateness for serving parents from different cultural, ethnic, and socioeconomic backgrounds. In a similar vein, Falloon, Boyd, McGill, Williamson, Razani, Moss, Gilderman, and Simpson's (1985) behavioral family management program to prevent relapse in schizophrenics, as well as Anderson, Reiss, and Hogarty's (1987) efforts to conceptualize and carry out psychoeducational programs with families of schizophrenics to prevent rehospitalization, represent noteworthy research attempts to develop effective clinical interventions.

Research on family factors in the development and course of alcoholism/drug abuse also gained prominence during this period (Steinglass, Bennett, Wolin, & Reiss, 1987). Stanton, Todd, and Associates (1982) at the Philadelphia Child Guidance Clinic offered a well-designed and carefully controlled research study in which structural-strategic techniques successfully were employed for treating families with an adult member who engages in drug abuse and addiction. These interventions proved to be effective both in eliciting family support and reducing drug use. Working with adolescent substance abusers alone, but with a family therapy orientation (called *one-person family therapy*), Szapocznik, Kurtines and Contributors (1989) utilized similar structural-strategic techniques (the dominant family therapy approach of the 1980s) to reduce drug reliance in this group.

Overall, however, as Barton, Alexander, and Sanders (1985) observe, during the 1980s therapists interested in furthering their clinical skills by and large tended to dismiss most published research papers as irrelevant to their real-world needs and interests, while most researchers believed family therapists too readily adopt newly minted therapeutic techniques despite lack of backup support from randomized, controlled clinical trials testing their effectiveness. These authors did suggest, however, that advances in methodology, statistics, and family theory might lessen the clinician-researcher gap, as research procedures become more relevant to the complex family processes encountered daily by therapists.

One encouraging development of the 1990s[2] was a greater willingness by researchers to engage in *qualitative research* in addition to the more customary *quantitative research* methodology (Piercy & Sprenkle, 1990). Most scientific disciplines rely on the latter—observing phenomena, formulating a theory to account for what is being observed, generating hypotheses or predictions to test that theory experimentally, controlling variables. recording and statistically analyzing resulting data; if the predicted observation is verified, the hypothesis is strengthened because the results were correctly deduced, and support is obtained for the theory from which the hypothesis was derived. However laudable, it may be premature to apply this quantitative method to family therapy, according to Bednar, Burlingame, and Masters (1988), because its concepts and operational procedures are not yet clearly defined or sufficiently differentiated from other forms of psychotherapy.

Quantitative research emphasizes experimentation, large samples whenever feasible, data collection and statistical analysis, objectivity, and verification. Here the researcher is an outside observer who manipulates variables and measures resulting changes. Qualitative research, on the other hand, a frequent tool for educational research, tends to be exploratory, open-ended, directed more at discovery than at evaluating or justifying a set of hypotheses. Its methods are intended to expand and enhance quantitative research techniques, and to provide a context for better understanding the meaning of the quantitative data collected (Moon, Dillon, & Sprenkle, 1990). Qualitative research methodologies are especially well-suited for describing complex phenomena, defining new constructs, discovering new relationships among variables, and trying to answer "why" questions (Sprenkle, 1994).

In the clinical realm, qualitative methods (in-depth interviewing, case studies, observations by teams through one-way mirrors, audio- and videotapes, focus groups, document analysis) usually search for universal principles by examining a small number of cases intensively; the researcher is often a participant who deals with any resulting subjectivity by making the researcher role explicit (Moon, Dillon, & Sprenkle, 1990).

Although such qualitative investigations of complex phenomena may begin modestly, with small samples, their results may lead to the discovery of new relationships among variables, leading further to theory development. As illustration, Alexander and Barton (1995) cite the early field-defining paper by Minuchin, Baker, Rosman, Liebman, Milman, and Todd (1975) on their preliminary work with diabetic children, which ultimately led to the breakthrough treatment of psychosomatic families, including children with anorexia nervosa (Minuchin, Rosman, & Baker, 1978).

While both quantitative and qualitative methods generate knowledge, the latter is apt to have far greater appeal to clinicians, since it is consistent with their everyday

[2]To emphasize the renewed interest in coming to grips with the particular problems of family therapy research in the 1990s, it should be noted that Sprenkle and Moon (1996) published the first book during this period dedicated to the unique methodological issues of family therapy research.

clinical procedures, and thus is more likely to capture the essence and the richness of the therapeutic family-therapist encounter. Moreover it is compatible with systems theory in emphasizing context, multiple perspectives, and client perspectives.

Clinicians are likely to be more interested in data revealing *clinical significance* (say, the extent to which a specific previously dysfunctional family, following treatment, develops sufficient skills to become functional) rather than *statistical significance* (group differences in improvement between families receiving treatment and those who receive no treatment). In some cases, differences between the groups may be significantly different statistically, but those who improved statistically may not have become functional as a result of treatment; clinical significance provides such information (Sprenkle & Bischoff, 1995).

Interestingly, early theory-generating research in the field, such as the work of Bowen or Wynne at NIMH, had a markedly qualitative or discovery-oriented flavor. It was only later, as researchers sought greater scientific control, that more rigorous research designs as well as more formal data collection and more precise statistical analysis occurred. The use of qualitative, quantitative, and mixed research methodologies seems to characterize the field today, as researchers recognize that traditional experimental designs are not readily applicable to family therapy settings in which a multitude of interactions and circular systemic processes are occurring.

At this point we believe it is instructive to note Stanton's (1988) distinction between *exploratory research,* consistent with qualitative clinical research methodology, breaking new ground, discovering relationships, generating hypotheses, and *confirmatory research,* more similar to quantitative methods, directed at verifying the efficacy of a particular intervention technique, such as comparing it with a baseline no-treatment control group or with other treatment methods. Both approaches are important, and although the latter may be more amenable to existing research methods—and thus more commonly carried out today—Stanton argues that it must not obscure the need for the development of new methods, which may necessitate a nontraditional (qualitative) research methodology.

A polarity need not exist between the two research methodologies. Qualitative research methods can expand upon, enrich, and thus complement traditional quantitative methods, providing results usable to researcher and therapist alike (Piercy & Sprenkle, 1990). Similarly, researcher and clinician need not—should not—remain polarized. Despite acknowledged differences in outlooks, priorities, and methods of discovery, both researchers and therapists benefit from the cross-fertilization of ideas, particularly since they share a common goal of ferreting out the underlying issues that determine family functioning. As Wynne (1988) points out, therapists would do well to examine the premises, circumstances, and ingredients of their clinical interventions, and researchers too would profit from moving beyond systematic data collection to becoming more responsive to the more informal conceptual inquiries carried out in the daily practices of their clinical colleagues.

Several notable efforts in the 1990s to rebuild bridges between family therapists and family researchers stand out: (1) an entire 1992 issue of the Newsletter of the American Family Therapy Academy was devoted to qualitative research and its contribution to furthering knowledge about family functioning and improving family therapy interventions; (2) conferences devoted to the topic of Research and Clinical

Practice are becoming regular features of AAMFT and AFTA meetings, and annual awards are made by each of these organizations for outstanding contributions to research as well as awards for outstanding contributions to practice; and (3) a special October 1995 issue of *the Journal of Marital and Family Therapy* contained the most up-to-date information on the efficacy of marriage and family therapy. All attest to current efforts to strengthen the research base of the field, as increasingly, health care professionals are asked to justify the treatment they offer by providing valid and reliable scientific data about its costs and effectiveness. As Pinsof and Wynne (1995) observe:

> Now, for the first time, family clinicians, training directors, clinic administrators, and family organizations have anxiously begun to clamor for "hard evidence" about the effectiveness of marital and family therapy that they can present to students, third-party payers, legislative bodies, and fellow professionals. (p. 341)

We'll return to the subject of available scientific findings regarding outcome studies of family interventions later in this chapter.

RESEARCH ON FAMILY PSYCHOPATHOLOGY

Early family therapy research studies, quantitative in orientation, by and large were carried out with inadequate samples, lacked matching control groups, and in general would be considered primitive by today's standards (Wynne, 1983). With some exceptions (such as Lewis, Beavers, Gossett, & Phillips, 1976, described later in this chapter), relevant rating scales or self-report measures were not yet highly developed for dealing with the special problems involved in family evaluations. A number of studies did attempt to compare family interaction patterns in so-called healthy families and families with at least one disturbed family member (Doane, 1978; Riskin & Faunce, 1972), but generally speaking failed to deal adequately with the complex methodological issues involved (finding comparable samples, defining "healthy" families, combining samples with mixed diagnoses, pinpointing precisely what aspects of complex interactions should be teased out and measured, using independent judges, and so forth). Qualitative research efforts to describe single cases (Rabin, 1981), while often instructive, nevertheless were themselves not always generalizable to larger populations.

Goldstein (1988) goes so far as to describe the period from the late 1960s to the late 1970s as representing a kind of "Dark Age" in research on psychopathological family conditions. Direct observational studies of dysfunctional families such as those containing a schizophrenic member, a major research effort barely a decade earlier, seemed to diminish markedly during this period. A fundamental assumption of the earlier studies—that direct observations contrasting families with and without a mental disorder could provide clues to the psychological precursors of that disorder—began to be reappraised a decade later. Two premises—that disturbances in family relationships were the major cause of mental disorders in general, and that each mental disorder resulted from distinctive patterns of family dynamics—also were reassessed because of the research complications they posed.

One major methodological drawback to testing the assumptions arising from such cross-sectional research was that the families were studied long after the disorder in a member had affected the family system. Thus the family interaction data, while it well might have reflected a complex amalgam of family processes, inevitably included some patterns that anteceded the onset of the disorder as well as some that represented various accommodations by family members to the presence of the disorder. Gradually researchers concluded that cross-sectional studies undertaken only after a mental disorder was present were limited in their ability to reveal significant information regarding family etiological processes. In addition, considerable evidence began to accumulate by the late 1960s that schizophrenia, bipolar and unipolar affective disorders, and alcoholism all had strong genetic predispositions, and that psychopharmacological interventions were often effective in reducing symptomatology. These results also challenged the underlying paradigm of the previous family studies in which family interaction was thought to be the predominant etiological agent and family therapy a potent model of intervention (Goldstein, 1988).

As we noted in the previous chapter in our discussion of psychoeducational efforts, there is currently renewed interest in the relationship between family interaction patterns and the major mental disorders, largely guided by a **vulnerability-stress model** (Nuechterlein & Dawson, 1984). In this model, sometimes also referred to as the diathesis-stress model, the genetic *predisposition* to a psychotic disorder such as schizophrenia is recognized as forming the basis for the disorder; additional *psychobiological* vulnerability may be environmental, due to such factors as exposure to influenza virus during the second trimester of fetal development or perhaps the impact of obstetric complications (Nuechterlein, Dawson, Ventura, Gitlin, Subotnik, Snyder, Mintaz, & Bartzokis, 1994). These nongenetic contributors to vulnerability may operate by affecting the likelihood of the genetic predisposition getting expressed, or by creating brain dysfunctions that parallel those resulting from genetic factors.

The course of schizophrenia, especially the likelihood of psychotic exacerbation or relapse, may also be influenced by psychosocial factors, especially those involving family life. These factors in the schizophrenic's social environment may involve lack of support or acceptance by the family, particularly if members are highly critical, hostile, or emotionally overinvolved.

Family researchers have also turned their attention to the interaction between relationships within the family and indexes of vulnerability to specific mental disorders, such as being the offspring of a parent with the disorder. Longitudinal investigations have by and large replaced cross-sectional studies, and families are selected for study prior to the onset of a disorder. Targeted "high risk" children of disturbed parents are carefully followed and evaluated for several years, especially as they pass through the risk period for that disorder.

An example of such a longitudinal research undertaking comes from the UCLA High Risk Study (Goldstein, 1985) in which 64 intact families with a nonpsychotic but emotionally disturbed teenager referred to a university psychology clinic were followed and periodically assessed for 15 years. The incidence of schizophrenia and related disorders within the family was found to be highest in those families classified as high in *communication deviance* (CD)[3] (Wynne, Singer, Bartko, & Toohey, 1977) during the assessment carried out 15 years previously. No cases of schizophrenia were found in families judged in blind diagnostic appraisals to be low in CD. The combination of a high CD score and a high EE (expressed emotion) score (a measure of negative family affect expressed toward the patient and/or emotional overinvolvement toward that person) enabled judges to increase their ability to predict those families most likely to manifest schizophrenia and related symptoms in the follow-up period.

The results lend support to the idea that certain communication disturbances and disturbances in the expression of affect within the family antecede the onset of schizophrenia, although, as Goldstein (1988) himself acknowledges, "they do not indicate how these patterns arise or interact with the vulnerability of the child at risk" (p. 287). Subsequent research on the behavioral correlates of relatives' expressed emotions (Cook, Strachan, Goldstein, & Miklowitz, 1989) has suggested that high-EE mothers, unlike their low-EE counterparts, evoke reciprocal responses in disturbed adolescents; once set off, they are far more likely to engage together in a negative chain of behaviors.

Following up on the idea that the course of schizophrenia is highly correlated with the family atmosphere, Weisman, Neuchterlein, Goldstein, and Snyder (1998) found that highly critical relatives (high-EE) viewed the schizophrenic's symptoms as being more under his or her control than did less critical relatives (low-EE). Most frequently criticized were symptoms reflecting behavioral deficits or personality characteristics (for example, poor hygiene) than those reflecting behavioral excesses (hallucinations), suggesting that the former were viewed as intentional while the latter were attributed to the mental illness.

DISCOVERING FAMILY PARADIGMS

Research studies of family processes tend to focus on structures and functions within a family, emphasizing patterns, relationships, and reciprocal interactions. Two influential sets of studies, both focused on **family paradigms,** deserve special mention, since they led family therapists to think of a typology of families based on the shared constructs of its members. One group of researchers (Kantor & Lehr, 1975;

[3]Communication deviance refers to a family's fragmented and confusing style of communicating with one another, making it impossible for members to attain a shared focus of attention or meaning from what is being expressed, since they seem to be talking about different topics. One another's meaning may be denied and another meaning substituted, or true meaning may be concealed or distorted. When such deviance occurs regularly, according to Wynne, it becomes a vehicle for developing a thought disorder such as schizophrenia. In risk research that Wynne and his associates (Wynne, 1970; Wynne, Singer, Bartko, & Toohey, 1977) have carried out for over two decades, involving hundreds of families, these researchers found that the cognitive capacities of attending and transactionally focusing are consistently impaired in parents of schizophrenics; they show higher CD scores than do parents of nonpsychotic offspring. "Healthy communication" between parents, according to Wynne, Jones, and Al-Khayyal (1982), promotes adaptive behavior in their children by providing a model for developing the essential cognitive task of attending, focusing, and remaining task-oriented, as well as a model for communicating ideas and feelings clearly and directly. Wynne's research has application in prevention and early intervention with disturbed families (Wynne, 1983).

Constantine, 1986) has been particularly intent on differentiating family systems through an analysis of their structural development and transactional styles. In a related series of research undertaking, Reiss (1981) classifies families according to the way they construct reality and make sense out of their social environment. According to Reiss, each family consensually develops its own shared and distinctive set of explanations about the world and the principles that guide its events.[4] Such a paradigm helps frame how its members organize their lives, react to other people, maintain continuity with the past, and help plan for the future.

Based on the observations of a wide sample of families over a period of nearly a decade, and without attempting to distinguish "normal" from "pathological" families, Kantor and Lehr (1975) provided an early example of exploratory research aimed at developing a system for identifying and classifying types of family structures. In particular, they concerned themselves with how families process information and evolve strategies for regulating distances between one another. How do family subsystems "interface" with one another, they asked, and how does the family unit as a whole communicate with the outside world?

These researchers were able to distinguish three basic family types or family paradigms—open, closed, and random—representing different configurations for structuring the family's internal relationships as well as its access to, and exchange with, the outside world. No one type appeared to be superior or inferior to the others; no type was found to exist in pure form, although Kantor and Lehr discovered that families cluster around the three categories.

Each family paradigm was found to have its own rules, boundary arrangements, and tactics for achieving and maintaining homeostatic balance. Open families, neither too tightly nor too loosely bounded, are essentially democratic. Honest exchange is encouraged both within the family and with outsiders. Although there is a sense of order, flexibility is given high priority; negotiation is encouraged; adaptation through consensus is endorsed; the rights of individuals are taken for granted; and loyalty to oneself and to the family is expected. Open families develop and maintain a lifestyle that emphasizes dialogue, patience, and collaboration, as well as a willingness to hear each other out and to change behavior patterns should that become necessary.

Within closed family structures, rules and a hierarchical power structure make individual members subordinate their needs for the benefit of the group. As White (1978) depicts such families, parents make sure that doors are locked, family reading material and television programs are screened, and children scrupulously report their comings and goings. The quest for privacy may border on suspiciousness, and strangers are given a hard look before being allowed access to the family. Rigid daily schedules (wake-up time, mealtimes, bedtime) are apt to be followed. The "core purpose" of such closed families, as Kantor and Lehr define it, is stability through tradition; security and belongingness for such families come from their emphasis on continuity, predictability, steadiness, and conventional ways of doing things understood and adhered to by all family members.

---

[4]Reiss's formulations foreshadow current social constructionist ideas (Chapter 13).

Videotaping family sessions preserves these events for research study. This psychologist is rating certain family interactive patterns along previously determined empirical categories in an effort to clarify what distinguishes the functioning levels of different families.

Random families were identified in this observational research study as fragmented. Novelty and individuality are emphasized—each person does whatever he or she wishes, which may or may not be related or connected to what others are doing. There are few, if any, family rules. Boundaries are blurred and easily crossed. Traffic in and out of the family is loosely regulated as everyone, strangers included, comes and goes in an irregular pattern. Mealtimes are seldom scheduled for the family as a whole but are left up to the individual. In a random family, the "core purpose" is identified by Kantor and Lehr as exploration through intuition.

As we noted, Kantor and Lehr do not assume that dysfunctional families necessarily stem from one or another of these structural types. Potentially, each type may be flawed, and confronted by problems, each family type exaggerates its own unique characteristics. Constantine (1986), following up on the earlier Kantor and Lehr study,[5] discovered that the more a closed family is confronted with problems, the more insistent become its efforts at family obedience and conformity, and the more isolated becomes its struggle to resist the outside threatening world. If closed family structures become too rigid, family members may rebel or even bolt from the family and run away.

Randomly organized families, under increased pressure, run the risk of uncoordinated action; the family process becomes chaotic and leads to greater separateness.

[5]Constantine actually adds a fourth type of pattern, less common than the others, which he designates as a *synchronous* family paradigm. Family members in such an arrangement tend to "think alike" in order to avoid conflict and regulate their family processes. Harmony, tranquility, and mutual identification are among its prominent charactersitics. Synchronous families, utopian in outlook, believe they will be able to move through life with little conflict or, should dissension occur, that they have the necessary tools for resolving the ensuing conflict.

Even open families may become overwhelmed under stress, inundated with too much information and ultimately questioning their basic rules. Open families may thus be disposed toward schism or divorce if incompatibilities produce excessive strain and create a family impasse.

These research efforts underscore the fact that families differ from one another in how they organize themselves, and in the paradigms by which they define themselves as a family and view the outside world. In assessing families, it is important for the appraiser to understand that different family types have different strengths and weaknesses as families. Should disabling stress occur, each is likely to go in a different, predictable direction of failure (Constantine, 1986).

A laboratory undertaking to study how families solve problems together led prominent family researcher David Reiss (1981), to identify and differentiate the essential elements of a family's problem-solving style. Originally intent on discovering through laboratory research how families with schizophrenic members process information, in the hope of learning more about comparable information-processing deficits in the identified patient, Reiss initially was struck by how the families distorted the instructions he gave them in a series of laboratory puzzles (Reiss, 1991). What has emerged from his research efforts—now extending over 30 years and including nonclinical or normal families—is a differentiation of family perceptual and interactive patterns that goes beyond arbitrary functional/dysfunctional distinctions (Oliveri & Reiss, 1982; Reiss, 1981; Reiss & Oliveri, 1991). The research has led to interest in discovering how families develop paradigms (shared assumptions about the social world), how such family paradigms may be changed, and what happens when a paradigm breaks down.

Reiss actually coined the term *family paradigm* to refer to those implicit, enduring, fundamental, shared assumptions or beliefs that families develop regarding how most effectively to cope with the world. Shared by all members, even if differences exist within the family, Reiss suggests that the very core of individual family membership rests on his or her acceptance of, and belief in, certain abiding assumptions. These assumptions direct members to view the world in specific ways; they determine what aspects of the world they wish to involves themselves in, and what conclusions they are likely to draw from such involvement.

Beginning in the late 1950s, Reiss presented families with a number of problem-solving tasks (puzzles or card-sorting exercises) and observed how they developed strategies, shared information, and traded ideas with one another in pursuit of solutions. Soon it became clear to him that what was most significant was not how they processed information but how they perceived the laboratory setting in which they were being tested. For example, families with schizophrenic adolescents often perceived danger and a threat to family ties; families with delinquent adolescents tended to view the laboratory as a place to demonstrate distance and independence from one another; and families with normal adolescents were apt to perceive the experience as an opportunity to explore and master a challenging situation together.

Thus, the family's reaction to the unfamiliar experimental situation itself was the crucial determinant of their behavior as a family. Reiss then reasoned that perhaps the laboratory response reflected a general construct with which the family tried to make sense of the world. It was this construct or blueprint or set of fantasies or expectations for dealing with new situations that Reiss labeled the "family paradigm." Just as an individual develops ways to comprehend the meaning of events in the environment, so a family unit—integrating the construing styles of all its members—evolves a mode of perceiving, interpreting, and interacting with the social world.

Reiss distinguishes three dimensions (see Table 15.1) along which characteristics of family paradigms vary: (1) *configurations* (the way families differ in their experiences of the world as ordered, and the belief that its mysteries are discoverable through reasoned search); (2) *coordination* (the extent to which they believe the world is equally open to all family members); and (3) *closure* (the extent to which the family perceives events as familiar and thus interpretable on the basis of past experiences, or novel and fresh and requiring some new means of interpretation).

On the basis of his exploratory research, Reiss (1981) differentiated three ways of constructing reality. **Environment-sensitive families** (high in coordination *and* configuration) believe the world is knowable and orderly and expect each member to contribute to its understanding and mastery. **Interpersonal distance–sensitive families** (low on both coordination and configuration) are composed of disengaged members, loners, who strive to demonstrate their autonomy and believe that any attention paid to suggestions of others is a sign of weakness. **Consensus-sensitive families** (high on coordination, low on configuration) are made up of enmeshed members who perceive the world as so chaotic and confusing that they must join together, maintain agreement at all times, and in that way protect themselves from danger.

In Reiss's typology, it is the resilient environment-sensitive family that is apt to be most problem-free. Its members are able to accept aid and advice from others, benefit from cues from the environment, act individually or jointly, and delay closure in order

Table 15.1 Summary of Patterns of Association of Family Problem-Solving Behavior with (a) Perceptions of Social Relationships, and (b) Orientations to Kin

High levels of:	(a) . . . were associated with high levels of:	(b) . . . and with high levels of:
Configuration Belief in a masterable environment	Nonstereotypic view of family Openness to individuals outside the family	Child-parent independence in kin ties
Coordination Sense that the environment functions similarly for all members	Nonstereotypic view of family	Child-parent congruence in kin ties Investment in close-knit networks of kin
Closure (delayed) View of the environment as source of new and changing experience	Openness to inanimate aspects of the environment	Investment in large networks of kin

Source: Oliveri & Reiss, 1982, p. 109

to make an effective response based on consideration of a number of alternative solutions. Should its family paradigm be threatened as a result of a family crisis, this type of family will attempt to maintain family integrity and overcome adversity together. Reiss (1981) cites the example of a family called upon to deal with the birth of a handicapped child, an event that temporarily threatened the family's notion that the world was predictable and thus comprehensible. By learning all they could about the infant's disability and arranging for the best available treatment, family members once again confirmed for themselves that they live in an orderly, manageable world, adding the realization that certain afflictions or adversities are inevitable but that together they will be able to prevail.

Working therapeutically with families, the clinician needs to be aware of the family's key paradigms—those framing assumptions that are not subject to dispute nor verifiable or disproved with experience or analysis. They represent the "central organizers" (Reiss, 1981, p. 2) that do the shaping, fashioning, and guiding of what families do when interacting with their environments.

RESEARCH ON FAMILY MEASUREMENT TECHNIQUES

In practice, many family therapists form impressions of individual family members as well as global impressions of whole families without the aid of formal psychological tests. With the exception of those with a behavioral orientation, who do place importance on administering their own specific standardized tests to family members, family therapists in general make their clinical judgments by observing and interacting with families. Theoretical orientation determines to a large extent what they look for—structuralists at boundaries and overall transactional patterns; strategists observe triads, hierarchies, and patterns that maintain symptoms; Bowenians evaluate levels of differentiation; and so forth. Social constructionists in particular are interested in how clients view their world, rather than attempting to score how well client responses fit a tester's preconceived categories (Neimeyer, 1993).

All therapists carry out some form of ongoing assessments with families, although most do so without following some predetermined evaluation procedure. Striving to keep their inquiries as naturalistic as possible, they utilize the therapist-family interactive process to learn about family behavioral patterns. They are likely to believe that a formal testing setting prior to therapy, especially where the subsequent therapist is also the family evaluator, gets family therapy off on the wrong foot. Moving from this outside, detached, and ascendant testing position to one that calls for democratically interacting with family members is frequently resisted by the family and may make joining the family system that much more difficult. By interacting in a more genuine way with families from the start, they do not need to undo any artificial relationship created as a result of a formal test inquiry.

On the other hand, in recent years some family therapists have argued for family assessment measures they believe facilitate later therapeutic interventions. Bagarozzi (1985) urges the selection of test instruments tailored to the situation under study; the results can be used to form a multidimensional "family profile" and thus act as an aid in outlining treatment goals and evaluating therapeutic efforts. LAbate (1994) challenges current practices, contending that an overall impressionistic view of the family system may obscure differences in individual contributions to the problem, and thus both a systems (family) and psychological (individual) assessment are needed. As he puts it:

> A traditional systems perspective stresses the subjective nature of the therapist's understanding of the family, whereas a psychological perspective finds an additional need for the objective understanding of the family and therefore uses both subjective (interview) and objective observations (questionnaires, rating sheets, tests). (p. 4)

Acknowledging the complexity of measuring systems concepts, some researchers nevertheless have persisted in developing instruments for assessing family functioning. Typically, researchers in the area of family assessment have worked for many years to develop reliable and valid self-report measures and observational measures for appraising overall family functioning as well as how each family member experiences the family system. Before and after therapy testing is sometimes used as a measure of change.

Self-Report Measures

Typically designed in the form of questionnaires, self-report measures attempt to elicit family members' attitudes, values, roles, self-perceptions, and satisfactions with family relationships (Huston & Robins, 1982). Their principal value lies in their ability to expose privately held thoughts and viewpoints ordinarily covered in behavior and thus not directly open to therapist observation. Having each family member provide his or her separate, subjective perspective on family relationships allows the therapist an "inside" picture that then can be related to better comprehending behavioral interactions within the family (Grotevant & Carlson, 1989).

A carefully developed and thus appealing example of such an "insider" or family member's view of two central properties of family life—flexibility and cohesion—may be obtained from the technique developed and refined by Olson and his colleagues (Olson, 1986; Olson, Russell, & Sprenkle, 1989). Their painstaking investigation, which has extended for over two decades and studied over 1000 families (100 or more in each of seven life cycle stages), has been directed at understanding how families cope with various situational stresses and demands throughout the life cycle. Because diagnosis by family pattern, even using newly devised DSM-IV categories,[6] is not very satisfactory, a more applicable classification system for families may emerge from this and related research undertakings. While the assessment instrument originally was developed primarily with intact Caucasian two-parent families, it now has been studied with multiform families (single-parent-led families, stepfamilies, same-sex couples) as well as racially and ethnically diverse groups (Gorall & Olson, 1995).

---

[6]One stumbling block here is that the DSM-IV, as well as its predecessors, are individually focused and do not include family diagnosis except to note briefly in its V-Code that certain relational problems (parent-child; marital partners) may be associated with impaired functioning in one or both participants. Kaslow (1996) has led a Coalition on Family Diagnosis attempting to include "relational diagnoses" in the latest DSM revision, but has not been successful in persuading members of the DSM task force of its utility. More research is needed on relational problems so that degrees of severity—a key parameter for classifications—can be obtained.

Olson and his associates have produced a family typology—what they refer to as the *Circumplex Model*—based on the family's degree of *flexibility* (its ability to permit changes in its role relationships, family leadership, and relationship rules) and *cohesion* (the emotional bonding of the family members to one another). (A third dimension, *communication,* involves the family's skill level in listening to each other, and facilitates or impedes family movement on the two primary dimensions.) These researchers contend that a balance on each of these dimensions is most desirable; extremes represent increasingly dysfunctional family patterns. That is, flexible family functioning calls for a balance between stability (morphostasis) and change (morphogenesis) and cohesion requires a balance between enmeshment and disengagement (to use Minuchin's terminology). As we noted in Chapter 4, family stability is rooted in change—to function smoothly, a family must preserve a familiar sense of order while accommodating to changing circumstances. Similarly, regarding family cohesion, families must try to maintain a balance between the ever-changing demands for both togetherness and separateness. To do so, family boundaries must remain clear and permeable, firm yet flexible, as the family offers support along with the freedom to experiment in becoming independent adults.

As seen in Figure 15.1, a two-dimensional graph, steps along each dimension are divided into four levels resulting in a four-by-four matrix (or relationship map) yielding 16 possible family types. With too much cohesion, the family is enmeshed and its members overly entwined in each other's lives; with too little, the members remain distant, isolated, and disengaged. Excessive flexibility leads to too much change, unpredictability, and possible chaos; too little may cause rigidity and stagnation.

A family's placement on this grid is determined by their responses to a 20-item self-report research instrument called the Family Adaptability and Cohesion Evaluation Scale (FACES III) (Olson, 1986). Each family member completes the test twice; responses indicate how he or she presently views the family and also his or her ideal description of family functioning. The discrepancy provides a measure of satisfaction: the greater the discrepancy, the less satisfaction.

Research results indicate that high-functioning families show moderate scores (within inner circles) on the two dimensions, while low-functioning families reveal extreme scores (outer circles). According to Olson's research, and as indicated in Figure 15.1, balanced family functioning may take one of four forms: *flexibly separated, flexibly connected, structurally separated,* and *structurally connected.* Such families are said to combine stability, the flexibility to change whenever necessary, and sufficiently open boundaries to permit effective communication. Note that the four central types are labeled open family systems, and that the outer rings are characterized as closed or random systems, thus linking this model to the typology of Kantor and Lehr (1975).

Continuing research on the Circumplex Model has been of two types: refining test items and improving test validity of FACES III (Perosa & Perosa, 1990), and applying the model to different types of families (Mathis & Tanner, 1991). Olson and his colleagues (Olson, Fournier, & Druckman, 1986; Fowers & Olson, 1992) also have developed and continue to improve a related assessment device evaluating a couple's preparation for marriage—PREPARE—PREmarital, Personal and Relationship

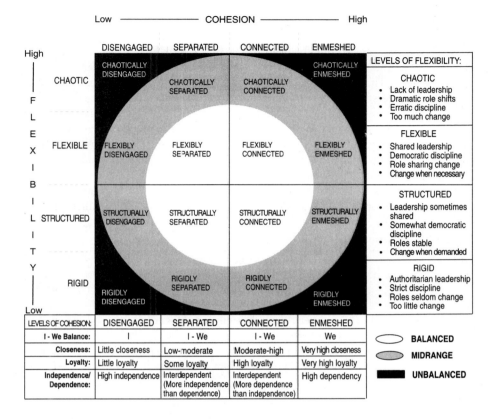

Low ——————— COHESION ——————— High

LEVELS OF COHESION:	DISENGAGED	SEPARATED	CONNECTED	ENMESHED
I - We Balance:	I	I - We	I - We	We
Closeness:	Little closeness	Low-moderate	Moderate-high	Very high closeness
Loyalty:	Little loyalty	Some loyalty	High loyalty	Very high loyalty
Independence/ Dependence:	High independence	Interdependent (More independence than dependence)	Interdependent (More dependence than independence)	High dependency

Figure 15.1   Circumplex model of family systems
Source: Gorall & Olson, 1995

Evaluation, a 165-item inventory intended to identify and measure the future marital partners' relationship strengths and weaknesses (Chapter 14).

A second psychometric evaluative approach, the Family Environment Scale (FES), widely used in family research since its introduction by Rudolph Moos (1974), attempts to assess the impact of the family environment on individual and family functioning. Moos began his research with the assumption that all social climates have characteristics that can be portrayed (and thus measured) accurately. For example, some are more supportive than others, some more rigid, controlling, and autocratic; in others, order, clarity, and structure are given high priority. Moos argues that to a large extent, the family environment regulates and directs the behavior of the people within it.

The Family Environment Scale (Moos & Moos, 1986) now translated into eleven languages, has proven to be a reliable test instrument (Boyd, Gullone, Needleman, & Burt, 1997). The scale contains 90 statements to be labeled "true" or "false" by each family member ("Family members really help and support one another"; "Family members often keep their feelings to themselves"; "We fight a lot in our family"). Respondents are asked to rate their families as they see them and then as how he or she would like them ideally to be. (Once again, the discrepancy provides a measure of satisfaction.) The set of responses measure three key dimensions of family life: relationships, personal growth, and systems maintenance. Taken together, these dimensions are assumed to characterize the family climate and its influence on behavior. That is, scores on the three sets of dimensions provide a framework for understanding the relationships (for example, its cohesiveness) among family members, the kinds of personal growth (for example, intellectual, religious) emphasized in the family, and the family's basic organizational structure.

Ten subscales make up the Family Environment Scale, as indicated in Table 15.2. Three relationship subscales (cohesion, expressiveness, and conflict) charac-

Table 15.2   Description of Subscales of Moos's Family Environment Scale

	Relationship Dimensions
1. Cohesion	The extent to which family members are concerned and committed to the family and the degree to which family members are helpful and supportive of each other.
2. Expressiveness	The extent to which family members are allowed and encouraged to act openly and to express their feelings directly.
3. Conflict	The extent to which the open expression of anger and aggression and generally conflictual interactions are characteristic of the family.
	Personal Growth Dimensions
4. Independence	The extent to which family members are encouraged to be assertive, self-sufficient, to make their own decisions, and to think things out for themselves.
5. Achievement orientation	The extent to which different types of activities (for example, school and work) are cast into an achievement-oriented or competitive framework.
6. Intellectual-cultural orientation	The extent to which the family is concerned about political, social, intellectual, and cultural activities.
7 Active recreational orientation	The extent to which the family participates actively in various kinds of recreational and sports activities.
8. Moral-religious emphasis	The extent to which family actively discusses and emphasizes ethical and religious issues and values.
	System Maintenance Dimensions
9. Organization	How important order and organization are in the family in terms of structuring the family activities, financial planning, and explicitness and clarity in regard to family rules and responsibilities.
10. Control	The extent to which the family is organized in hierarchical manner, the rigidity of family rules and procedures, and the extent to which family members order each other around.

Source: Moos, 1974

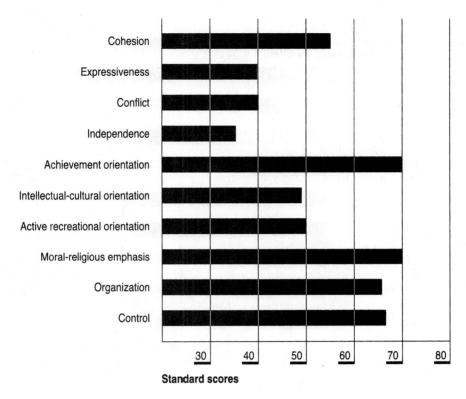

Figure 15.2   Family Environment Scale scores for an achievement-oriented family
Source: Adapted from Moos, 1974

terize the interpersonal transactions that take place within the family. Five subscales (independence, achievement, intellectual-cultural orientation; active recreational orientation; moral-religious emphasis) refer to personal development or growth dimensions. Two subscales (organization, control) refer to system maintenance dimensions, providing information about the family structure and its roles. A score is obtained for each subscale and average scores for the family are placed on a family profile. (If desired, the differing perceptions of various family members—for example, parents and children or husband and wife—can be compared for possibly divergent views of the same family environment.)

The family whose profile is shown in Figure 15.2, made up of parents and two children in their early twenties, is strongly upwardly mobile, emphasizing personal development (especially achievement and moral-religious emphasis) above other aspects of family life. These same two factors are deemphasized by the young couple (no children) whose profile is depicted in Figure 15.3. They agree that, for them, relationships are far more important than achievement, conflict is minimal, and control is low. This couple feels very positive about the social environment they have created.

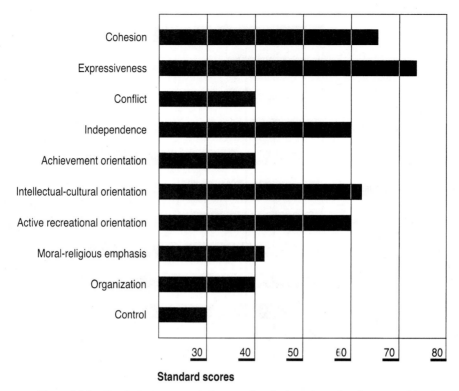

Figure 15.3   Family Environment Scale scores for a higher-relationship, low-control family
Source: Adapted from Moos, 1974

Observational Methods

The techniques we are about to describe are especially appealing to those who prefer objective "outsider" measures of family functioning to what they consider the less reliable self-reports of family members. These observational measures are likely to take the form of *interactive coding schemes* (diagramming family interactive patterns along a series of cognitive, affective, and interpersonal dimensions) or *rating scales* (judging and scoring those overt, observable patterns along previously determined dimensions)(Grotevant & Carlson, 1989). The former are designed to capture the moment-to-moment contingencies of the behavior of family members toward one another,[7] while the latter seek a more global objective summary judgment of family interdependent relationship patterns. Carefully constructed test manuals often help ensure objectivity and enhance reliability and validity of judgments made about the family.

Rather than rely on family members' subjective self-reports, Lewis, Beavers, Gossett, and Phillips (1976) at the Timberlawn Psychiatric Foundation in Dallas,

---

[7]See Minuchin's use of family mapping in Chapter 9 as an example of charting a family's ongoing transactional patterns.

Texas, employed judges to rate the strengths and weaknesses of individual family members and to identify those interactions within a "healthy" family system that make for optimal functioning. Members of intact families (each of which had at least one adolescent but no member identified as a psychiatric patient) were interviewed and their interactions as they carried out a variety of tasks videotaped. While the design of the study had limitations ("healthy" was defined negatively as the absence of psychopathology; subjects were all from white, middle-class, urban homes; videotaped behavior might not have represented their ordinary day-to-day interactions), the findings of this research study, carried out over a seven-year period, do expand our understanding of common relationship patterns in competent families.

The research plan required several judges to observe and rate each family's videotaped behavior along five major dimensions and according to a variety of subtopics and themes:

I. Structure of the family
   A. Overt power (how family dealt with influence and dominance)
   B. Parental coalitions (strength of husband-wife alliance)
   C. Closeness (presence or absence of distinct boundaries and degrees of interpersonal distance)
   D. Power structure (ease in determining family "pecking order")
II. Mythology (degree to which a family's concept of itself was congruent with rater's appraisal of family behavior)
III. Goal-directed negotiation (the effectiveness of family negotiations)
IV. Autonomy
   A. Communication of self-concept (degree to which family nourished or discouraged clear communication of feelings and thoughts)
   B. Responsibility (degree to which the family system reflected members' acceptance of responsibility for their own feelings, thoughts, and actions)
   C. Invasiveness (extent to which the family system tolerated or encouraged family members to speak for one another)
   D. Permeability (degree to which the family system encouraged the acknowledgement of the stated feelings, thoughts, and behavior of its members)
V. Family affect
   A. Expressiveness (extent to which the open communication of affect was encouraged within the family system; see Table 15.3)
   B. Mood and tone (ranging from warm and affectionate to cynical and hopeless; see Table 15.3)
   C. Conflict (degree of family conflict and its effect on family functioning)
   D. Empathy (degree to which the family system encouraged members to be sensitive to each other's feelings and to communicate this awareness)

On the basis of these ratings, each family received a score on a global health-pathology scale. The 33 families labeled as healthy were then compared with 70 families with a hospitalized adolescent; 12 families in the former group were studied intensively.

Table 15.3   Two of 13 Rating Scales Used to Score Family Interaction Patterns

A. *Expressiveness:* Rate the degree to which this family system is characterized by open expression of feelings.

1	1.5	2	2.5	3	3.5	4	4.5	5
Open, direct expression of feelings		Direct expression of feelings despite some discomfort		Obvious restriction in the expression of some feelings		Although some feelings are expressed, there is masking of most feelings		No expression of feelings

B. *Mood and Tone:* Rate the feeling tone of this family's interaction.

1	1.5	2	2.5	3	3.5	4	4.5	5
Unusually warm, affectionate, humorous, and optimistic		Polite, without impressive warmth or affection; or frequently hostile with times of pleasure		Overtly hostile		Depressed		Cynical, hopeless, and pessimistic

Source: Lewis et al., 1976

Research results indicated that no single quality was unique to highly functional or competent families; a number of variables in combination accounted for family members' special styles of relating to one another. Thus, family health was considered not as a single thread but as a tapestry reflecting differences in degree along many dimensions. The capacity of the family to communicate thoughts and feelings and the cardinal role of the parental coalition in establishing the level of functioning of the family stand out as key factors. The parental coalition was found by these researchers to be especially instrumental in providing family leadership and also important in serving as a model for interpersonal relationships. Lewis and his colleagues have continued their long-term research to better understand the development of family competence over the family life span (Lewis, 1988).

Beavers (Beavers, 1981, 1982; Beavers & Voeller, 1983) in follow-up observational research, again over many years, developed and refined a 14-item rating scale for judges, the Beavers-Timberlawn Family Evaluation Scale, for assessing and classifying family functioning. Now referred to simply as the Beavers Interactional Scales, the results offer convincing evidence that families can be ordered along an infinite linear continuum with respect to their competence. At the low end, he describes leaderless, invasive, chaotic families, with diffuse boundaries between members. Closer to the midpoint of competence, families show rigid interpersonal control, with frequent distancing, projection, and little consequent closeness. At the high end of the scale, families were found to be better structured; they are composed of

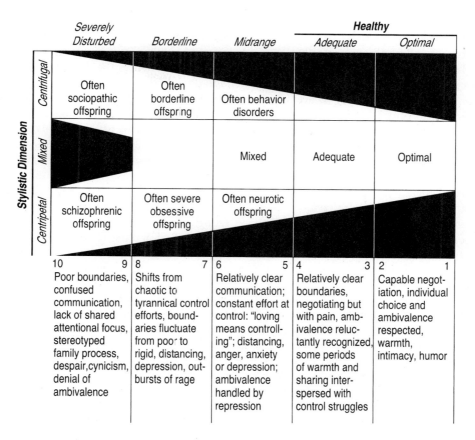

Figure 15.4   The Beavers System Model, in the form of a sideways A, with one leg representing centripetal families and the other leg representing centrifugal families.
Source: Beavers & Voeller, 1983, p. 90

autonomous individuals who share intimacy and closeness but at the same time respect separateness.

The Beavers Systems Model, an attempt to integrate systems theory and developmental theory, rates families on the *stylistic quality of their interactions* and their *degree of competent family functioning* on a five-point scale. As indicated in Figure 15.4, optimal and adequate families are considered competent; midrange, borderline, and severely disturbed families represent progressively poorer functioning levels. In regard to interactive style, members of **centripetal** families tend to be inner-oriented and to view relationship satisfactions as emanating from within the family; those in extreme **centrifugal** families, outwardly directed and more openly expressive of anger, seek satisfaction outside the family (Hampson & Beavers, 1996). The arrow shape of the diagram is intended to convey that extremes in style—whether profoundly centripetal or centrifugal—are associated with poor family functioning. Thus, severely dysfunctional families with a centrifugal style are prone to produce sociopathic children (antisocial, irresponsible, egocentric), while those extreme families with a centripetal style run the risk that one or more of their children will become schizophrenic (socially isolated, progressively withdrawn, disorganized). As families become more competent or more adaptive, as noted in the diagram, their excessive centripetal or centrifugal styles tend to diminish.

The Beavers Model (Beavers & Hampson, 1993) shares with the Circumplex Model the cross-sectional analysis of current family functioning. Both make use of two axes to conceptualize differences between families. In Beavers's more "outside" approach, the structure, flexibility, and competence of a family and its members are scored on one dimension and their interactive style on the other. To bring the two models even further into line with one another, Beavers and his associates have translated their observational rating scales into a complementary 36-item Self-Report Inventory (Beavers, Hampson, & Hulgas, 1985). Filled out by family members about themselves, and used in conjunction with rating scales about the family made by outside judges, the combined results offer a multimethod, multilevel family systems evaluation. Agreement between these self-reports of family functioning and the judgments made by outside observers has been found to be high (Hampson, Beavers, & Hulgas, 1989).

Another long-term systems-based research project, begun in the late 1950s at McGill University in Montreal, and later shifted to McMaster University in Hamilton, Ontario, Canada, in the 1960s and 1970s, attends especially to family structure and organization as well as family transactional patterns. Continued during the 1980s at Brown University in Providence, Rhode Island, this carefully crafted measurement technique pays particular heed to how the family develops and maintains itself through developing coping skills for dealing with certain necessary tasks.

The McMaster Model (Epstein, Bishop, & Baldwin, 1982; Eptsein, Bishop, Ryan, Miller, & Keitner, 1993) focuses on those dimensions of family functioning selected, on the basis of research, as having the most impact on the emotional and physical well-being of family members. In particular, attention is focused on current functioning in three areas:

I. *Basic task area* (how the family deals with problems of providing food, money, transportation, shelter)
II. *Developmental task area* (how they deal with problems arising as a result of changes over time, such as first pregnancies or last child leaving home)
III. *Hazardous task area* (how they handle crises that arise as a result of illness, accident, loss of income, job change, and such)

A family's difficulty in coping with these three task areas is especially indicative of a propensity to develop clinically significant problems.

The McMaster Clinical Rating Scale (Epstein, Baldwin, & Bishop, 1983) probes family functioning in six crucial areas:

A. *Family problem solving* (the ability to resolve problems sufficiently well to maintain effective family functioning)
B. *Family communication* (how, and how well a family exchanges information and affect; also whether communication is clear or masked, direct or indirect)

C. *Family roles* (how clearly and appropriately roles are defined, how responsibilities are allocated and accountability is monitored in order to sustain the family and support the personal development of its members)

D. *Affective responsiveness* (the family's ability to respond to a given situation with the appropriate quality and quantity of feelings)

E. *Affective involvement* (the extent to which the family shows interest in and values the particular activities and interests of its members)

F. *Behavior control* (the pattern the family adopts for handling dangerous situations, situations involving social interactions within and outside the family, and for satisfying members' psychobiological needs such as eating, sleeping, sex, handling of aggression, and so on)

The McMaster Clinical Rating Scale attempts to assess how well the family performs its primary mission of providing an environment in which social and biological development can flourish. Ratings are made on a seven-point scale (from 1, *severely disturbed* to 7, *superior functioning*); a rating of below 4 suggests the need for therapeutic intervention. Based on how each family member responds, the family's collective health-pathology score is obtained. As is the case with the Beavers approach, the McMaster group has constructed a companion Family Assessment Device (FAD), a 60-item self-report questionnaire filled out by family members and covering the six aspects of family functioning described above. Both the Clinical Rating Scale and the Family Assessment Device follow from the same rationale: Family health is related to its ability to carry out certain essential family tasks.

FAMILY THERAPY PROCESS AND OUTCOME RESEARCH

What constitutes therapeutic change? What are the conditions or in-therapy processes that facilitate or impede such changes? How are those changes best measured? How effective is family therapy in general, and are some intervention procedures more efficacious than others? Do certain specific therapist characteristics and family characteristics influence outcomes? Is family therapy the most cost-effective way to proceed in a specific case, say in comparison with alternate interventions such as individual therapy or drug therapy or perhaps a combined set of therapeutic undertaking? These are some of the questions that researchers in family therapy continue to grapple with in an effort to understand and improve the complex psychotherapeutic process.

For the last 40 years, psychotherapy research has concerned itself with investigating the therapeutic process (the mechanisms of client change) to develop more effective methods of psychotherapy. While the earlier years were devoted largely to outcome research studies in order to confirm the overall legitimacy of the therapeutic endeavor, "by about 1980 a consensus of sorts was reached that psychotherapy, as a generic treatment process, was demonstrably more effective than no treatment" (VandenBos, 1986, p. 111). Rather than continue single-focus outcome investigations to justify therapeutic efficacy, researchers have turned their attention to comparative outcome studies in which the relative advantages and disadvantages of alternate treatment strategies for clients with different sets of problems are being probed. Increasingly, explorations of process variables are taking place, so that differential outcomes from various therapeutic techniques can be tentatively linked to the presence or absence of specific therapeutic processes.

Process Research

Process research, still in its infancy, attempts to discover and operationally describe what actually takes place during the course of therapy. What are the day-to-day features of the therapist-client relationship, the actual events that transpire during sessions that together make up the therapeutic experience? Can these be catalogued and measured? What specific clinical interventions lead to therapeutic breakthroughs? How can these best be broken down into smaller units that can be replicated by others, and thus taught to trainees learning to become family therapists? Are there specific ways of intervening with families with specific types of problems that are more effective than other ways?

Greenberg and Pinsof (1986) offer the following definition of process research:

> Process research is the study of the interaction between the patient and therapist systems. The goal of process research is to identify the change processes in the interaction between these systems. Process research covers all the behaviors and experiences of these systems, within and outside the treatment sessions, which pertain to the process of change. (p. 18)

Note that in this definition the terms are used broadly. The patient (or client) system, for example, consists of more than the identified patient; other nuclear and extended family members are included, as well as members of other social systems that interact with the client and the family. Similarly, the therapist system might include other therapeutic team members in addition to the therapist who meets with the family. Data from measuring the therapist-family interaction is also relevant here. Note too that process research does not simply concern itself with what transpires within the session, but also with out-of-session events occurring during the course of family therapy. Finally, the experiences, thoughts, and feelings of the participants are given as much credence as their observable actions. Thus, certain of the self-report methods we described earlier in this chapter may provide valuable input in the process analysis.

Process research attempts to reveal how therapy works, and what factors are associated with improvement or deterioration. For example, a researcher might investigate a specific process variable concerning family interaction—who speaks first, who talks to whom, who interrupts whom, and so forth. Or perhaps, attending to therapist-family interaction, the researcher might ask if joining an anorectic family in an active and directive way results in a stronger therapeutic alliance than joining the family in a different way, such as being more passive or more reflective. Or perhaps the process researcher wants to find out what special ways of treating families with alcoholic members elicit willing family participation as opposed to those that lead to resistance or dropouts from treatment. Are there certain intervention techniques that work best at an early treatment stage and others that are more effective during either the middle stage or terminating stage of family therapy?

Answers to such process research questions have significant clinical relevance to practitioners planning future intervention strategies (Pinsof, 1986). Note here how process and outcome research efforts fit hand in glove. Measuring outcome or therapeutic effectiveness, the resourceful process researcher ideally could break the treatment down and analyze it in a series of episodes or micro-outcomes occurring during the therapy process that together produce the final results. In practice, however, the task is often a painstaking one, involving intricate statistical analyses of events difficult to measure reliably, to say nothing of the complexities involved in linking in-therapy events to ultimate therapeutic outcomes. Not surprisingly, few high-quality process reports exist, although greater attention is currently being paid to overcoming methodological roadblocks.

Process research calls for a detailed description of the intended intervention to be employed, along with an equally detailed description of the family to whom it is being applied and its specific problems. As noted, the implementation is often extremely difficult, however, and some critics (Keeney & Sprenkle, 1982) argue that efforts to make the therapist's task so consciously deliberate in formulating a change-promoting plan may create "packaged cookbook cures" (p. 16) that are inappropriate to the overall purposes of the therapy. On the other hand, without such a plan, interventions by a therapist would be strictly artistic and idiosyncratic, difficult to replicate or teach to others, and we would have no inkling of what procedures carried out by the therapist achieved what therapeutic outcomes.

Unfortunately, there still are few reliable and valid research assessment procedures that would be sensitive enough to adequately ferret out those processes specifically related to successful and unsuccessful outcomes (Piercy & Sprenkle, 1990). Process research, moreover, is time-consuming, expensive to conduct, and tends to be less glamorous than outcome studies demonstrating a new technique's viability. However, one effort to study the verbal behavior of therapists within sessions, and to compare beginning and advanced therapist behavior by means of a Family Therapist Coding System (Pinsof, 1986), appears to be promising. A similar behavioral observation system in which trained observers use some kind of coding system to make notations on therapist and client communication patterns (Hahlweg, 1988) also may be useful in tying specific interventions to specific therapeutic outcomes.

Most researchers would probably agree with Reiss (1988) that family therapy research should be primarily process research. We need to operationally describe what actually transpires in the therapy process before we can make any significant headway in determining what interventions work best for what clients under what circumstances. While the temptation to do outcome research—seeking out answers to the practical issue of what works—is understandable, therapists need first to know how, when, and under what conditions the therapy works (Auerswald, 1988). We need to understand better what processes bring about change, and how to identify and measure those processes during the course of family therapy. While there continues to be a paucity of empirical process studies, family therapy researchers and practitioners alike are beginning to recognize that greater understanding of the therapeutic process will pay big dividends in improving the effectiveness of family therapy. Instead of process *or* outcome research, Piercy and Sprenkle (1990) call for a move toward combining process *and* outcome investigations—attending to significant therapeutic episodes in which a significant change occurred, then examining what preceded or followed that change in order to develop causal or at least correlational hypotheses about events related to outcomes. A combined methodology is called for here, underscoring the desirability for the coexistence of qualitative and quantitative forms of inquiry.

Outcome Research

Ultimately, all forms of psychotherapy must provide some answer to this key question: Is this procedure more efficient, more cost-effective, less dangerous, with more long-lasting results than other therapeutic procedures (or no treatment at all)? Outcome research in family therapy must address the same problems that hinder such research in individual psychotherapy, in addition to the further complications of gauging and measuring the various interactions and changes taking place within a family group and between various family members. To be meaningful, such research must do more than investigate general therapeutic efficacy; it must also determine the conditions under which family therapy is effective—the types of families, their ethnic or social class backgrounds, the category of problems or situations, the level of family functioning, the therapeutic techniques, the treatment objectives or goals, and so on. With such a formidable task, it should come as no surprise that the family therapy outcomes empirical research is relatively meager compared with the abundant research on individual therapies.

Particularly germane to outcome research is Paul's (1967) effort to operationalize therapeutic interventions and make them open to empirical validation: "What therapy is most effective for what problems, treated by what therapists, according to what criteria, in what setting?" (p. 111). While data are now available (see following section) to provide some specific answers in the area of family therapy, the question cannot be fully answered at this time, although there are now encouraging signs of sophisticated research efforts to find those specific answers (Hazelrigg, Cooper, & Borduin, 1987). Despite research advances, however, more than three decades after Paul's challenge, the overriding question in psychotherapy research remains that of *specificity:* "What are the specific effects of specific interventions by specified therapists at specific points in time with particular patients with particular presenting problems?" (Gurman, Kniskern, & Pinsof, 1986, p. 601).

Another outcome issue involves what criteria to use in order to evaluate the results of interventions at the family level. Since most studies ultimately rely on quantification, must we continue to depend on traditional statistical significance as the sole method for determining a treatment's effectiveness, or can we also use the measure of clinical significance in some cases. Customarily, researchers look for statistical significance between groups (say, between those families receiving treatment and those in no-treatment control groups). However, as we indicated earlier, some researchers (Jacobson, Follette, & Revenstorf, 1984; Piercy & Sprenkle, 1990) have concluded that how much someone (a previously dysfunctional person) improves (moves significantly toward greater functional behavior) as a result of therapy should also be a legitimate way of measuring change, although significant statistical change may not have occurred between groups. As an example, Jacobson, Schmaling, and Holtzworth-Munroe (1987), analyzing the results of behavioral marital therapy, designed a set of categories—"Improved," "Happily married," "Unchanged," "Deteriorated," "Separated or divorced," or "Relapsed"—that proved to be more informative regarding outcomes than relying exclusively on statistically significant findings.

Methodological Challenges in Outcome Research   Progress in measuring the outcome of treatment has been slow in developing in the field of family therapy. Several historical factors are involved: (1) family therapy originated in parallel but separate ways within different disciplines, each with its own explanatory framework, language, and type of client population (Olson, 1970); (2) most family therapy was practiced in psychiatric (child guidance) or social work (family service agency) settings where the emphasis was more on providing clinical service than conducting research, while psychology—the discipline most apt to engage in psychotherapy research—had not yet made a significant impact on the field (Gurman, 1971); and (3) during the first half of this century, the general devaluation of direct intervention with a family system and of any kind of clinical practice by nonphysicians had a pronounced negative effect on interprofessional collaboration (Gurman & Kniskern, 1981b).

In addition to these historical factors, as we have suggested, outcome research in family therapy faces some critical methodological problems: the unit of study is large and complex; events that occur during sessions usually result from many factors, making it difficult to identify and control the variables; the family unit is in a state of continuous change; the observer (therapist/researcher) is considered part of the system and may change with it; the researcher must consider intrapsychic, relationship, communication, and ordinary group variables as well as taking into account such contextual variables as the community, cultural backgrounds, and social pressures (Fox, 1976).

Moreover, philosophical differences regarding the appropriateness of conventional research methodologies must be resolved. Critics, especially in the 1980s, argued that most family therapy research designs reflect the assumptions of logical positivism and, correspondingly, attempt to emulate the traditional scientific methods of the natural sciences based on objective observation (Tomm, 1983). The scientific outlook presumes that observing is a passive rather than an active process, and that it is possible to remain detached and unbiased in one's observations. In the traditional scientific method, by differentiating independent from dependent variables, and by varying the former, hypotheses can be tested regarding what factor causes what outcome.

Yet, argued this group calling for a "new epistemology," the assumptions of the scientific method are incompatible with the following underlying assumptions of family therapy: (1) that many viewpoints of what constitutes reality exist (rather than a single objective reality); (2) that multiple causalities account for most events (not simple cause-and-effect sequences); (3) that the wholeness of the system should be the unit of study (rather than smaller and smaller units to ensure "scientific rigor"); and (4) that the therapist must search for systemic connections (and not explanations based on linear causality). Tomm contends that by breaking phenomena down into smaller and smaller segments in order to make their investigations more precise, scientists may inadvertently destroy the possibility of ever really knowing the phenomenon they set out to study. In the view of some family therapists (Colapinto, 1979; Keeney & Sprenkle, 1982; Tomm, 1983), traditional research methodologies are of little use in untangling the complexities of systemic phenomena or in helping establish a causal relationship between a method of treatment and its effect on the family.

Can existing research methods ever capture the richness of family interaction or of the therapeutic experience? Qualitative research methods, discovery-oriented and open to the idea of multiple perspectives, are gaining in popularity; qualitative reviews of outcome results are likely to rely on *narrative reports* in which the researcher makes subjective or "eyeball" judgments regarding the meaning of the collected data. However, outcome research by definition requires verification, and quantitative methods permit such substantiation. Schwartz and Breunlin (1983) question whether it is necessary to throw out the baby (rigor and clear methodology) with the bathwater (outdated assumptions and attitudes about understanding reality). Many family therapists would probably agree with Gurman (1983a) that standard research methods are the only means available for assessing the capability of family therapy in an ethically responsible manner. He maintains that outcome researchers do attend to the context by studying the interactions of client, therapist, treatment, and setting variables and by using multiple levels and vantage points for assessing systemic change. To Gurman, then, the charge that psychotherapy researchers are overly linear is inaccurate.

Put in terms of current research issues, quantitative outcome studies, based on an experimental methodology, may be more appropriate for evaluating pragmatic approaches (concerned with behavior change), such as behavioral, cognitive, structural, and strategic therapies. So-called aesthetic[8] approaches. seeking out those unifying patterns that connect individuals who make up a family, such as contextual, humanistic, and more recently, therapies based on social constructivism, are unlikely to concern themselves with the traditional empirical verification procedures. Those models, rejecting traditional quantitative methodologies, are far more inclined to turn to qualitative research procedures. At least in the past, that has meant being underrepresented in the more scientifically oriented journals in the field. Moon, Dillon, and Sprenkle (1990) contend that a better balance in the outcome research literature will occur as qualitative research methodologies gain greater acceptance.

Efficacy Studies and Effectiveness Studies   Published outcome research studies today appear in one of two forms: *efficacy studies,* conducted under controlled ("laboratory") conditions, and *effectiveness studies,* as in the everyday practice ("in the field") of providing family therapy services (Pinsof & Wynne, 1995). The former seeks to discover whether a particular treatment works under ideal "research thera-

[8]The pragmatic vs. the aesthetic viewpoint is discussed in greater detail in Chapter 5.

py" situations, while the latter wants to determine whether it works under normal real-life ("clinic therapy") circumstances.

Outcome research projects carrying out efficacy studies are able to approximate ideal experimental requirements: patients are randomly assigned to treatment or no-treatment groups, treatment manuals define the main procedures to be followed, therapists receive training and supervision to ensure standardization of interventions, multiple outcome criteria are designed, and independent evaluators (rather than the therapist or clients) measure outcomes. While such a "dream" setup, under such controlled conditions, often lends itself to a clarification of what components of the therapy specifically affect certain outcomes, and as such may be illuminating, the conclusions from such studies, usually carried out in university clinics or hospital settings, are often difficult to translate into specific recommendations for therapy under more real-world, consultation room conditions.

To date, most research is of the efficacy kind, although Pinsof and Wynne (1995) offer this encouraging note: The federally funded National Institute of Mental Health is shifting some of its research grants into service settings, acknowledging the necessity for more real-world clinical effectiveness studies. Such a move provides a better chance for effectiveness (including cost-effectiveness) evaluations—comparing the results of alternate interventions as to their costs as well as their effects—which is especially important in the age of greater scrutiny of health care expenditures (Goldenberg & Goldenberg, 1999).

Measuring the Effectiveness of Family Therapy   Overall, according to the latest **meta-analysis** of the findings of 163 published and unpublished outcome studies on the efficacy and effectiveness of marital and family therapy, Shadish, Ragsdale, Glaser, and Montgomery (1995) conclude that, based mainly on efficacy studies, these modalities work; marital/family therapy clients did significantly better than untreated control group clients. As they put it in more concrete terms:

> It means that if you randomly chose a client who received MFT, the odds are roughly two out of three that the treatment client will be doing better than a randomly chosen control client at posttest. . . . An effect this big is also considerably larger than one typically finds in medical, surgical, and pharmaceutical outcome trials (p. 347).

While different marital and family therapy approaches all were found to be superior to no treatment, these reviewers found no single model's efforts stood out over others. (It should be noted, however, that one approach or another may "fit" certain families better than do others, or work best for certain kinds of presenting problems). In some cases, a combination of therapeutic efforts (psychoeducational, medication, individual therapy, group therapy) may be the treatment of choice (Pinsof, Wynne, & Hambright, 1996).

In another meta-analytic review, looking this time specifically at marital therapy by examining 15 methodologically rigorous, published outcome studies, Dunn and Schwebel (1995) found that behavioral marital therapy, cognitive-behavioral marital therapy, and insight-oriented marital therapy were all more effective than no treatment in bringing about changes in spouses' behavior and in the general assessment of the marriage relationship. Taken together, Shadesh and associates and Dunn and Schwebel reaffirm the conclusions of favorable relationship changes found in earlier empirical reviews (Gurman, Kniskern, & Pinsof, 1986; Hazelrigg, Cooper, & Borduin, 1987) on the effectiveness of family therapy.

As for the often difficult empirical and clinical question of what treatment for what problem, Gurman and Kniskern (1981a, 1981b), Gurman, Kniskern, and Pinsof (1986), and Henggeler, Borduin, and Mann (1993), and Pinsof, Wynne, and Hambright (1996) offer some definite conclusions based on their literature search:

1. Conjoint treatment for marital discord is clearly the method of choice over the individual, collaborative (each spouse sees a separate therapist), or concurrent (one therapist treats marital partners in separate sessions) approaches.
2. The beneficial effects of both nonbehavioral and behavioral marital/family therapy often occur in treatment of fewer than 20 sessions.
3. Compared with no treatment, nonbehavioral marital/family therapies are effective in approximately two-thirds of all cases.
4. Behavioral marital therapy is about as effective for minimally distressed couples as nonbehavioral methods, somewhat less so when severe dysfunction is involved.
5. Increasing a couple's communication skills, however achieved, is the essence of effective marital therapy.
6. Conjoint, behaviorally oriented sex therapy should be considered the treatment of choice for such problems, especially when severe nonsexual problems do not exist.

In their survey of research, these reviewers found family therapy to be more effective than individual therapy, even for problems that seem more intrapsychic in nature than interpersonal. More specifically:

7. Structural family therapy appears to be particularly helpful for certain childhood and adolescent psychosomatic symptoms.
8. As for the relative efficacy of behavioral and nonbehavioral approaches, no conclusions are justifiable on the basis of published research; however, either strategy is clearly preferable to no treatment at all.
9. No empirical evidence yet exists for the superiority of cotherapy over single-therapist interventions with couples or families.
10. Child management training, a behavioral technique, produces more favorable results with children engaged in antisocial behavior than do nonbehavioral techniques.
11. Psychoeducational programs, including the use of medication, directed at aiding families manage members diagnosed with schizophrenia and affective disorders, are more effective than medication alone or individual psychotherapy (Goldstein & Miklowitz, 1995).
12. Conjoint couples therapy is the treatment of choice in marriages where alcohol abuse is a problem, and is superior to individual therapy with the

alcohol-abusing spouse. Family therapy is especially effective in motivating alcoholics to enter treatment (Edwards & Steinglass, 1995).

13. There is evidence for the efficacy of family therapy in treating childhood conduct disorders, phobias, anxieties, and especially autism (Estrada & Pinsof, 1995).

Well-designed research on both the process and outcomes of family therapy have now come to occupy a significant, and also a permanent, place in the field of marital and family therapy. While the need for carefully designed quantitative research continues, there is also a growing recognition that there is a place for complementary qualitative research, especially in its ability to help us better comprehend complex events and interactions in their natural context. Data provided by qualitative research may lay the groundwork for discovering emerging themes, facilitating the development of new successful intervention techniques (Strauss & Corbin, 1990).

Today, there is focused research interest in investigating "specificity questions"—what therapeutic intervention works best with a particular problem or type of client. No longer is it necessary to demonstrate that psychotherapy, as a generic treatment process, is effective. Rather, the current research thrust is to explore "the relative advantages and disadvantages of alternative treatment strategies for patients with different specific psychological or behavioral difficulties (and including in the investigations such factors as cost, length of time necessary to effect change, nature and extent of change, and so forth)" (VandenBos, 1986, p. 111).

Such comparative outcome studies most certainly need to include a simultaneous exploration of related process variables in order to continue current efforts to provide some linkage between outcomes achieved by distinctive therapeutic interventions and the presence or absence of specific therapist-client(s) interactive processes. The synergistic relationship between process and outcome research, as well as between quantitative and qualitative research, should encourage further collaboration between researchers and their clinical colleagues, as the latter group continues to respond to health care demands for providing the briefest, most effective, most cost-contained ways (with or without medication?) for serving troubled families.

SUMMARY

Research in family therapy preceded the development of therapeutic intervention techniques, but beginning in the 1960s priorities changed, and the proliferation of techniques outdistanced research. That situation has now begun to equal out, and a renewed family research-therapy connection is beginning to be reestablished. Some practitioners, likely in the past to dismiss research findings as not relevant to their everyday needs and experiences, have found qualitative research methodologies more appealing than the more formal, traditional experimental methodologies based on quantitative methods. Some controversy remains, however, regarding the applicability of a traditional logical positivistic scientific methodology to evaluating the effects of family therapy on family functioning.

The study of the relationship between family interaction patterns and family psychopathology, previously based on a cross-sectional research approach, has reemerged in recent years with a longitudinal outlook based on a vulnerability-stress model. Researchers have attended particularly to families judged to be high in communication deviance and expressed emotion.

In another set of research endeavors, there is renewed interest in early efforts to discover family paradigms, differentiating family systems according to their structural development and transactional styles.

Various research attempts to classify and assess families exist, employing either a self-report or an observational format. Most noteworthy among the former are the attempts by Olson and his associates to construct their Circumplex Model of family functioning based on the family properties of flexibility and cohesion, and work by Moos to construct his Family Environment Scale. Observational measures, usually in the form of rating scales by outside observers, have been designed by Beavers to depict degrees of family competence, and by Epstein, Bishop, and Baldwin to classify family coping skills according to the McMaster Model.

Both the process and outcome of family therapy interventions have been studied with increased interest in recent years. The former, involved with what mechanisms in the therapist-client(s) encounter produce client changes, requires the higher priority, since the identification of the processes that facilitate change helps ensure greater therapeutic effectiveness. Outcome research, including both efficacy and effectiveness studies, having established that marital and family therapy are beneficial, has turned its attention to what specific interventions work most effectively with what client populations. Of particular interest today is the search for the relative advantages and disadvantages of alternative therapeutic approaches for individuals and families with different sets of relational difficulties. The synergistic efforts of researchers and clinicians today are directed at the most effective and cost-contained ways of intervening with troubled families.

16

Becoming a Family Therapist:
Training and Supervision

How to obtain training, for what purposes, where to get it, and what kind of training to pursue have been the major issues for those wishing to learn more about family therapy. Trainees need to grasp theoretical constructs, expose themselves to systems as well as postmodern thinking, gain personal awareness and relationship skills, remain aware of gender, power, and cultural issues with families, and master specific observational and intervention procedures. They need to make a conceptual shift from methods that rely upon linear thinking to a cybernetic view of family functioning. Finally, they must sort out the various approaches and discover their own therapeutic styles. Learning effective intervention skills from supervisors and more experienced clinicians, the fledgling family therapist must take care not to become overly dependent on the other's directions, losing the invaluable sense of self in the therapeutic transition and simply cloning what she or he has observed in admired mentors.

In short, training requires not merely learning a set of therapeutic tools (paradoxical interventions, reframing, contingency contracting, circular questioning, externalizing problems, and so on), but also the theoretical understanding of how, and under what circumstances, to use them. The alternative, as Minuchin and Fishman (1981, p. 9) picturesquely put it, is a field of family therapy

> full of clinicians who change chairs a la Minuchin, give directions a la Haley, go primary process a la Whitaker, offer paradoxes in Italian, tie people with ropes a la Satir, add a pinch of ethics a la Nagy, encourage cathartic crying a la Paul, review a tape of the session with the family a la Alger, and sometimes manage to combine all of these methods in one session.

The pioneers—Ackerman, Bell, Jackson, Haley, Minuchin, Whitaker, Satir, Framo, Bowen, Wynne—were essentially self-taught, in turn offering their insights and experiences to others wishing to learn not only a new set of intervention techniques but, more important, a change in thinking about how best to understand human behavior. Early efforts to mimic their charismatic therapeutic styles have now been replaced not merely by a technology of therapy but, as Liddle, Breunlin, and Schwartz (1988) point out, by a corresponding technology of training, transmitting the field's values, body of knowledge, professional roles, and skills to new clinicians.

Early training programs, narrow by today's standards, first insisted that clinicians trained in one-to-one psychotherapy make a paradigmatic shift in their thinking. Haley (1970), Ackerman (1973), and others made the then radical proposal that therapists view behavior, including the manifestation of symptoms in an individual, as occurring within a social or familial context. These trailblazers contended that the family system, not the symptomatic person, be the therapeutic unit for achieving change—a tradition-breaking idea in its time.

Haley (1970), early on, was concerned that some therapists would fail to enlarge their perspective but would simply continue to perceive individual psychopathology as their central concern while acknowledging the importance of the family context in which such psychopathology developed (see Table 16.1). Others might find it easier to widen their lenses, viewing the amelioration of individual intrapsychic conflicts as secondary to improving overall family functioning. In either case, he and others maintained that to work in a family systems approach, the therapist must give up the passive, neutral, nonjudgmental stance developed with so much care in conventional individual psychotherapy. Using a dramatically different approach, Haley urged the therapist to become involved in the family's interpersonal processes (without losing balance or independence); support and nurture at some points, challenge and demand at others; attend to (but not overidentify with) members of different ages; and move swiftly in and out of emotional involvements without losing track of family interactions and transaction patterns.

Some clinicians in those early years were concerned that a therapist schooled in individual psychotherapy, asked to adopt such a family systems focus, might be resistant for several reasons: (1) the therapist may see the identified patient as a victim to be supported; (2) he or she may be unwilling to give up exercising control, and may try to maintain a hierarchically superior position as expert, remaining at the hub of all family interactions; and (3) he or she may find it difficult to learn how to be a collaborating participant in the family social system, while avoiding entangling alliances. There was great risk, as Bowen (1966) observed early on, that the individually focused therapist may become caught up in the family members' ongoing relationships and, if not careful, lose the necessary sense of balance between being a part of what transpires and maintaining an individual boundary. He or she may begin to believe family members' myths about themselves (for example, that they are jinxed, exploited, or powerless) and adopt their labels for other family members (such as stupid, selfish, unambitious) (Goldenberg, 1973).

With some of these professional concerns in mind, a number of innovative training devices were proposed for preparing family therapists. Just as individual psychotherapy or psychoanalysis was considered highly desirable or even mandatory for therapists in training at the time, Bowen (1975) suggested family therapy for his students and their spouses in order to differentiate themselves from their families of origin. He reasoned that to be effective, family therapists needed to free themselves of unresolved conflicts with their families, so that such unfinished business from their

Table 16.1 A Comparison Between Individual-Oriented and Family-Oriented Family Therapy

Individual-oriented	Family-oriented
1. Family therapy is one of many methods of treatment.	1. Family therapy is a new orientation to viewing human problems.
2. The individual's psychopathology is the focus of study and treatment; the family is seen as a stress factor.	2. The disordered family system is seen as needing some family member to express its psychopathology.
3. The identified patient is the victim of family strife.	3. The identified patient contributes to and is an essential part of family strife.
4. The family is a collection of individuals behaving on the basis of past experiences with each other.	4. The present situation is the major causal factor, since current problems must be currently reinforced if they are to continue to exist.
5. Diagnosis and evaluation of the family problem should precede intervention.	5. Immediate action-oriented intervention takes place at the first session, which is usually a time of family crisis, when the family is ripe for change.
6. The therapist is an observer evaluating the family's problem.	6. The therapist is a part of the context of treatment; his or her active participation affects the family system.
7. The therapist brings out client's feelings and attitudes toward each other; he or she uses interpretation to show them what they are expressing.	7. The therapist uses fewer interpretations; he or she is interested in enhancing positive aspects of the relationships.
8. The therapist talks to one person at a time; family members talk largely to him or her rather than to each other.	8. Family members talk to each other, not the therapist; all members are urged to participate.
9. The therapist takes sides in family conflict, supporting one member (for example, a child, a schizophrenic).	9. The therapist avoids being caught up in factional struggles in the family.
10. Family therapy is seen as a technique for gathering additional information about individuals in the family.	10. Individual psychological problems are seen as social problems involving the total ecological system, including the social institutions in which the family is embedded.

Source: Based on Haley, 1970.

own past did not intrude on their current dealings with client families. While most trainers still recognize the central importance of ferreting out the person of the therapist as part of his or her training, they no longer *require* family-of-origin work for trainees, considering it unnecessary or impractical in contemporary family therapy supervision and training (Liddle, 1991).

Two other innovative training devices, reflecting the times, were popular for a period but enjoy little general use today. Whitaker's (1967) use of cotherapy followed from his earlier efforts with individual schizophrenics in which he routinely used a cotherapist because of the difficulties in reaching the distancing patient and to allow one therapist to observe and track the interactional processes while his partner actively made therapeutic interventions. Although still practiced by symbolic-experiential therapists (Roberto, 1991), especially with hard-to-reach patients and their families, the technique today is generally considered unrealistic due to cost constraints and inefficient use of professional time (see fuller discussion later in this chapter).

Marathons, extended group experiences popular during the heyday of the human potential movement in the 1960s, were adapted by Goldenberg, Stier, and Preston (1975) as a family therapy group training device. Ten advanced trainees and their client families, along with the three supervisors, together engaged in a six-hour, multiple-family marathon utilizing various role-playing, psychodrama, and encounter-group techniques throughout the session. Results on a postmarathon questionnaire revealed the experience to be a valuable training aid. However, once again this training technique has proven less cost-effective than others and is rarely undertaken today.

By the mid-1970s, the need for establishing standards for setting up formal family therapy training and supervisory programs had become evident. Bodin (1969a) had outlined certain criteria for student selection and proper professional settings, as well as training methods, many of which (use of videotapes, group supervision) continue three decades later. Stier and Goldenberg (1975) had enumerated the merits of group supervision, and Mendelsohn and Ferber (1972) had concluded that their trainees' therapeutic skills were best developed in small groups of 5 to 15 trainees who met regularly with one or two supervisors over a prolonged period of time, such as a year. Cleghorn and Levin (1973), in a landmark paper, had identified those perceptual, cognitive, and executive skills needed by basic-level advanced, and experienced family therapists regardless of theoretical outlook. Different schools of family therapy were emerging, and their advocates, such as Haley (1976b), as an aid to future trainees, were beginning to elucidate training philosophies and their relationship to therapeutic approaches to family therapy.

OBTAINING CLINICAL TRAINING

All family therapy training programs, of whatever theoretical persuasion, recognize that both conceptual knowledge and clinical skills need to be acquired and integrated in the process of becoming a professional. Learning to think of human problems in systems terms remains axiomatic today (Nichols, Nichols, & Hardy, 1990) although not nearly the radical idea it was three decades ago when first proposed by family therapy pioneers. The growing influence of social constructionist thinking has begun to be felt in many contemporary training programs (Anderson & Swim, 1993).

Beyond the acquisition of a knowledge base and learning when and how to make effective interventions with families, trainees today are likely to be exposed to a number of current issues in the field of family therapy: (1) a greater sensitivity to feminist thinking and its relevance for overcoming trainee gender-bias and sex-role stereotyped thinking (Avis, 1996); (2) a raised consciousness regarding the role played by ethnic, social class, and cultural factors in influencing outlooks and behavior in order to better differentiate among universal, transcultural, culture-specific, or idiosyncratic family behaviors (Falicov, 1988b); (3) a knowledge of family law (divorce, custody, child welfare laws, disposition of juvenile offenders) as well as relevant ethical issues (reporting child abuse, maintaining confidentiality) (Welfel, 1998); and (4) a familiarity with both simple cybernetic and second-order cybernetic ideas regarding therapist roles and influences in changing family patterns.

Today's trainee also must be aware that becoming a family therapist calls for becoming a part of an expanded (family-therapist) system, which in turn is influenced by larger social systems (schools, work systems, religious institutions, health care systems, and for some families public welfare, child welfare, foster care, courts, mental health systems, or the justice system) that surround families (Imber-Black, 1991). To be effective, he or she must learn how best to collaborate with representatives of outside agencies, rather than remaining a detached outside healer as in many forms of individual treatment.

On the other hand, new generations of therapists, particularly if educated in marital or family therapy training programs directed specifically at learning relevant intervention techniques, may insist on a family focus to the exclusion of attention to the issues brought to family relationships by individual family members. As we noted in the first chapter, a systems orientation should not preclude an interest in the individual; rather, it broadens that traditional emphasis to attend to the nature of the roles individuals play in their primary relationship networks, such as the family. Increasingly, family therapists are paying attention to the individual family member, that person's relationships within the family, and the family's interactions with persons or institutions within society that might affect the course of therapy. Today's family therapist is as likely as not to apply systems ideas to better understanding the individual family members and their interface with both the family and larger social systems (Schwartz, 1995).[1]

Training Programs

Before 1960, individuals wishing to enter the field of marriage counseling typically secured the appropriate education and clinical experience in one of the established professions (psychiatry, clinical psychology, psychiatric social work, psychiatric nursing) and then added further specialized training at the postdegree level (Nichols, 1979). With the advent of the family therapy movement, marriage counseling came increasingly to be seen as a professional field in its own right. Alternative training opportunities developed, and direct entry into the profession, at the master's or doc-

---

[1]Schwartz (1995) proposes a multiplicity model, *Internal Family Systems Therapy,* in which both individual intrapsychic dynamics and family systems are considered. Embracing aspects of traditional family therapy approaches along with a postmodern emphasis on collaboration and the cocreation of changes in family stories, he utilizes systemic principles and techniques to ferret out the subpersonalities ("parts") or internal, subterranean voices of each client's inner life. As the struggle between an individual's subdivided parts, usually manifested in the form of internal debates within oneself, becomes resolved and the self more unified, Schwartz hypothesizes that the person becomes more problem-free and that parallel changes occur in family funcitoning.

toral level, became possible. Some universities began to offer graduate education in marriage counseling, thus shifting much training away from postgraduate work.

Growth in graduate programs during the last three decades has been primarily at the master's level (Sprenkle & Wilkie, 1996). Considering the master's degree to represent the entry-level education for independent clinical practice for those beginning a practice in the profession, AAMFT's Commission on Accreditation for Marriage and Family Therapy Education (COAMFTE) also accredits doctoral-level programs (for those interested in academic careers, research, advanced clinical practice, and supervision work) and postgraduate programs (for those with master's or doctoral degrees who wish further specialized training in a particular modality or treatment population).

COAMFTE continually develops more stringent standards for accrediting master's, doctoral, and postgraduate clinical training programs in marriage and family therapy throughout the United States and Canada. To help students make informed choices, the commission offers a directory of its currently accredited programs along with application procedures, tuition rates, financial aid, course requirements, types of supervision offered, and faculty profiles. Table 16.2 represents the list of over 80 accredited programs at the master's, doctoral, and postgraduate levels in the United States and Canada at the start of 1999.

At present, training in family therapy occurs in three basic kinds of settings—degree-granting programs in family therapy, freestanding family therapy training institutes, and university-affiliated programs—which differ significantly in the nature, scope, and desired outcome of the training they offer (Liddle, Breunlin, & Schwartz, 1988). To a large extent, the depth and breadth of that training reflects the setting's definition of family therapy.

Degree-granting programs view family therapy as a profession, an orientation for conceptualizing problems people encounter, and a field or body of knowledge in itself; as a consequence, they offer the most in-depth training. Freestanding family therapy institutes (see Table 16.3) similarly by and large define family therapy as a profession, a separate and distinct field of knowledge, and an orientation to human problems. They, too, offer intensive family therapy training, but compared with degree-granting programs the training is less comprehensive, since it tends to be of shorter duration and to be offered to trainees on a part-time basis. Freestanding programs are likely to hold greatest appeal to those professionals who already hold advanced degrees but who seek intensive training in marital/family therapy free of the usual constraints of a formal degree program (Sprenkle & Wilkie, 1996). A U.S. Consortium of non-degree-granting Family Therapy Training Programs now exists, organized by social worker Phoebe Prosky at the Freeport, Maine, Center for the Awareness of Pattern.

With regard to university-affiliated programs, the academic disciplines of psychiatry, psychology, and social work focus on family therapy as one field of study among many, perhaps another therapeutic modality or a field with a body of knowledge and set of clinical skills that are interesting but hardly central to their training mission. Family therapy training in such settings is apt to be less intense and secondary to the overall purposes of the academic program. Thus, as Liddle, Breunlin, and Schwartz (1988) point out, the variety of settings in which training is obtained

Table 16.2   AAMFT-Accredited Graduate and Postgraduate Clinical Training Programs (1999)

State of Province	School	Degree Program
UNITED STATES		
Alabama	Auburn University	M.S.
Arkansas	Harding University	M.S.
California	Fuller Theological Seminary	M.S.
	Loma Linda University	M.S.
	University of San Diego	M.A.
	University of So. California	Ph.D.
	So. California Counseling Center	Postgrad.
	U.S. International University	M.A., PsyD.
Colorado	Colorado State University	M.S.
	Family Therapy Training Center	Postgrad.
Connecticut	Central Conn. State University	M.S.
	University of Connecticut	M.A., Ph.D.
	Fairfield University	M.A.
	Saint Joseph College	M.A.
	Southern Conn. State University	M.S.
Florida	Florida State University	Ph.D.
	Gainsville Family Institute	Postgrad.
	Nova Southeastern University	M.S.
Georgia	University of Georgia	Ph.D.
	Mercer University	M.F.T.
Illinois	Advocate–Family Care Network	Postgrad.
	Family Institute at Northwestern	Postgrad.
	Family Institute–Northwestern Univ.	M.S.
	Northern Illinois University	M.S.
Indiana	Christian Theological Seminary	M.A.
	Indiana State University	M.S.
	Purdue University	Ph.D.
	Purdue University-Calumet	M.S.
Iowa	Iowa State University	Ph.D.
Kansas	Friends University	M.S.
	Kansas State University	M.S., Ph.D.
Kentucky	University of Kentucky	M.S.
	University of Louisville	M.S.S.W.–Postgrad.
	Louisville Presbyterian Theological Seminary	M.A.
Louisiana	Northeast Louisiana University	M.A.
Maryland	University of Maryland	M.S.
Massachusetts	University of Massschusetts (Boston)	M.Ed.
Michigan	Michigan State University	M.A., Ph.D.
Minnesota	University of Minnesota	Ph.D.
Mississippi	Reformed Theological Seminary	M.A.
	University of So. Mississippi	M.S.
Missouri	Provident Counseling	Postgrad.
Nebraska	University of Nebraska (Lincoln)	M.S.

(continued)

Table 16.2   *(continued)*

State or Province	School	Degree Program
New Hampshire	Antioch New England Graduate School	M.A.
	University of New Hampshire	M.S.
New Jersey	Seton Hall University	Ed.S.
New York	Blanton-Peale Graduate Institute	Postgrad.
	University of Rochester Med. Center	Postgrad.
	Syracuse University	M.A., Ph.D.
North Carolina	Appalachian State University	M.A.
	East Carolina University	M.S.
North Dakota	North Dakota State University	M.S.
Ohio	Ohio State University	Ph.D.
Oklahoma	Oklahoma State University	M.S.
Pennsylvania	Allegheny University	M.F.T.
	Family Institute of Philadelphia	Postgrad.
	PENN Council of Relationships	Postgrad.
	Philadelphia Child Guidance Clinic	Postgrad.
Rhode Island	University of Rhode Island	M.S.
South Carolina	WestGate Training & Consulation Network	Postgrad.
South Dakota	North American Baptist Seminary	Postgrad.
Texas	Abilene Christian University	M.F.T.
	University of Houston-Clear Lake	M.A.
	Our Lady of the Lake University	M.S.
	St. Mary's University	M.A., Ph.D.
	Texas Tech University	Ph.D.
Utah	Brigham Young University	M.S., Ph.D.
Utah	Utah State University	M.S.
Virginia	Virginia Polytechnic Institute & State University–Falls Church	M.S.
	Virginia Polytechnic Institute & State University–Blacksburg	Ph.D.
Washington	Pacific Lutheran University	M.A.
	Presbyterian Counseling Service	Postgrad.
	Seattle Pacific University	M.S.
Wisconsin	Family Service of Milwaukee	Postgrad.
	University of Wisconsin-Stout	M.S.
CANADA		
Alberta	Calgary Regional Health Authority	Postgrad.
Manitoba	Interfaith Marriage & Family Institute	Postgrad.
Ontario	University of Guelph	M.S.
	Interfaith Pastoral Counseling Centre	Postgrad.
Quebec	Argyle Institute of Human Relations	Postgrad.
	Sir Mortimer B.Davis–Jewish General Hospital	Postgrad.

Table 16.3   A Sample of Freestanding Family Therapy Training Institutes in the United States

Name	Location
The Family Institute of Cambridge	Watertown, MA
The Kantor Family Institute	Somerville, MA
Ackerman Institute for Family Therapy	New York, NY
Minuchin Center for the Family	New York, NY
The Center for Family Learning	Rye Brook, NY
The Family Institute of Westchester	White Plains, NY
The Family Therapy Training Program at the University of Rochester	Rochester, NY
The Family Institute of New Jersey	Metuchen, NJ
The Georgetown Family Center	Washington, DC
The Institute for Contextual Growth	Ambler, PA
The Family Institute of Washington, DC	Rockville, MD
The Philadelphia Child Guidance Center	Philadelphia, PA
Eastern Virginia Family Therapy Institute	Virginia Beach, VA
The Atlanta Institute for Family Studies	Atlanta, GA
The Family Institute	Chicago, IL
The Chicago Center for Family Health	Chicago, IL
The Brief Family Therapy Center	Milwaukee, WI
Menninger Foundation	Topeka, KS
The Houston Galveston Institute	Houston, TX
Mental Research Institute	Palo Alto, CA

helps explain why there currently exists a heterogeneous pool of professionals who define and practice family therapy in a multitude of ways.

Is family therapy a profession, an orientation to human problems, or simply another modality of psychotherapy? The degree-granting programs in marriage and family therapy insist that it is a distinct profession, with its own professional organization (AAMFT), code of ethics, growing body of theory and research, and proliferating graduate programs in family therapy (Sprenkle, 1988). At the same time, they view family therapy as offering a unique systems view or orientation for conceptualizing problems. Graduates of such programs define their professional affiliation as *family therapist* or perhaps *family psychologist*. In a similar way, trainees who receive a certificate upon completing a program at a freestanding institution are likely to think in systems terms, and to identify themselves as family therapists.

On the other hand, students in university-affiliated programs, while exposed to systems thinking, also learn the discipline's established theoretical traditions as well as its other therapeutic techniques. Graduates of these programs, even if they have a family therapy orientation, are most likely to call themselves by the name of their academic discipline (psychiatrist, clinical psychologist, licensed clinical social worker). In some cases, they may even be opposed to thinking of family therapy as a separate discipline. In other cases, however, by obtaining additional postdegree training, some graduates of university programs might adopt a professional identity that incorporates their training as well as their new affiliation.

Still to be finally determined, and the heart of the issue, is the status of marital/ family therapy as a profession. Is marital/family therapy (1) a separate, independent profession; (2) a professional specialty area or subset within the parent mental health profession; (3) a profession that partially overlaps with other mental health professions; or (4) an area of elective study within another mental health profession? The issue is loaded with vocal advocates on all sides (Fenell & Hovestadt, 1986). Regardless of how one answers this question, it should be noted that family psychology is now a specialty area recognized by the American Board of Professional Psychology, which certifies the competency of practitioners in applied areas of psychology.

The AAMFT, officially designated by the U.S. Department of Health and Human Services to establish certification standards for the **accreditation** of training programs, primarily supports the position that marital/family therapy is a distinct and separate discipline. Promoting the idea that marital/family therapy is an independent profession, AAMFT awards clinical membership only to those persons who meet both the organization's rigorous specialized academic requirements and its supervised professional experience requirements. On the other hand, many practitioners not specifically schooled in marital/family therapy take the position that their professional background plus additional specialized training is sufficient for helping clients experiencing problems in their marriage or family as a whole.

Objectives of Training

Learning family therapy requires theoretical understanding (human development and personality theory; family life cycle concepts, including sensitivity to cross-cultural issues; psychopathology; research methodology; group dynamics; systems theory; and so on); understanding of legal and ethics standards of practice; and perhaps more important, firsthand clinical contact assessing and treating families. Gender awareness is a necessary part of family therapy training programs (Coleman, Avis, & Turin, 1990), as is the general growth in awareness of personal issues that might impact the interpersonal encounter with clients (Aponte, 1994b). Being supervised on a continuous basis while working with families helps improve a student's therapeutic skills as he or she gains invaluable clinical experience (Saba & Liddle, 1986).

There exists no current consensus on how best to achieve clinical competence as a family therapist. Each trainee must find a comfortable style of interacting with families and his or her own orientation to what makes for successful therapy. The opportunity to work therapeutically with a variety of families (with different structures, different age groups, from different ethnic backgrounds and socioeconomic situations, with different presenting problems) within a training program offering comprehensive **didactic** course work and clinical supervision seems to be the ideal learning situation. Liddle (1988) underscores the **isomorphic** nature of therapy and training, maintaining that the supervisor's theoretical outlook on how systems operate and families are helped to change is applicable as a guide for how best to train and supervise.

What are the learning objectives of a family therapy training program? Depending on the supervisor's theoretical and therapeutic outlook, goals range from an emphasis on the trainee's personal growth and development to a focus on the acquisition of skills and competencies. As noted earlier, Cleghorn and Levin (1973), in a seminal paper in family therapy training written more than two decades ago, set goals of training, based on the acquisition of a variety of skills, that remain relevant today. Particularly useful is the distinction between the competency objectives they describe for basic-level, advanced, and experienced family therapists. Specifically, these authors distinguish three sets of skills—perceptual, conceptual, and executive—needed by all family therapists at each level of training. Table 16.4 presents a checklist for the trainee's development of basic observational or *perceptual skills* (recognizing interactions and their meaning to and effect on the family members and the family system), *conceptual skills* (formulating the family's problems in systems terms), and therapeutic or *executive skills* (extracting and altering the family's sequences of transactions); these are the skills necessary to be potentially effective with ordinarily functional families who have had trouble coping with unusual (and presumably temporary) stress. Having developed these basic competencies, the trainee should be able to deal with families exposed to situational problems (for example, shared grief over a death of a family member), helping to mobilize the family's natural restorative devices in working toward a solution. Essentially, the therapist's role is to facilitate constructive problem-solving communication.

Advanced training is required before the therapist can deal successfully with families with chronically fixed, rigid, and unproductive problem-solving transactional patterns. As Table 16.5 suggests, *an agent of change must possess different skills than a helper of distressed families.* The trainee must learn to catalyze interactions, understand and label relationship messages, and confront family members with what they are doing to each other; he or she must challenge the family to find new solutions, to use its strength as a family in order to take the responsibility for change in its members. Finally, the advanced therapist must be able to judge the effectiveness of his or her interventions and to alter the approach whenever necessary to help the family work with greater efficiency and with less distress. Cleghorn and Levin's schema represents a generic set of objectives, not attached to any specific school of

Table 16.4   Checklist of Basic Objectives in Training Family Therapists

Perceptual and conceptual skills	Executive skills
1. Recognize and describe interactions and transactions.	1. Develop collaborative working relationship with family
2. Describe a family systematically; include assessment of current problem.	2. Establish therapeutic contract.
3. Recognize effect of family group on onself.	3. Stimulate transactions.
4. Recognize and describe the experience of being taken into the family system.	4. Clarify communications.
5. Recognize one's idiosyncratic reactions to family members.	5. Help family members label effects of interactions.
	6. Extricate oneself from the family system.
	7. Focus on a problem.

Source: Cleghorn & Levin, 1973

Table 16.5   Checklist of Advanced Objectives in Training Family Therapists

Perceptual and conceptual skills	Executive skills
Regarding the family	1. Redefine the therapeutic contract periodically.
1. Conceive of symptomatic behaviors as a function of the family system.	2. Demonstrate relationship between transactions and the symptomatic problem.
2. Assess family's capacity to change.	
3. Recognize that change in a family is more threatening than recognition of a problem.	3. Be a facilitator of change, not a member of the group.
4. Define key concepts operationally.	4. Develop a style of interviewing consistent with one's personality
Regarding oneself	5. Take control of maladaptive transactions by:
1. Deal with feeling about being a change agent, not just a helper.	a. stopping a sequence and labeling the process
2. Become aware of how one's personal characteristics influence one's becoming a family therapist.	b. making confrontations in the context of support.
3. Assess the effectiveness of one's interventions and explore alternatives.	6. Work out new adaptive behaviors and rewards for them.
4. Articulate rewards to be gained by family members' making specific changes.	7. Relinquish control of the family when adaptive patterns occur.

Source: Cleghorn & Levin, 1973

family therapy. It remains today a training model followed by the various schools of family therapy that have tailored its perceptual, conceptual, and executive skills learning objectives to their specific training goals.

TRAINING AIDS

Family therapy programs use three primary methods for training: (1) didactic presentations, in course work or seminar form, in which trainees learn family therapy's body of knowledge; (2) direct clinical experiences with families; and (3) supervision, on a regular, ongoing basis, by an experienced family supervisor who, together with trainees, may observe ongoing sessions by a fellow trainee through a one-way mirror and/or through videotaped sessions (Liddle, Breunlin, & Schwartz, 1988).

The extent to which each of these training methods is emphasized, however, varies widely in different settings, depending on the skills, experiences, and viewpoints of those offering the training. While these elements of family therapy training are discussed separately in the following pages, the reader should be aware that in practice a mixture of techniques are used simultaneously, different settings offering different emphases. Reading about families and family theory, observing trainers as they demonstrate work with families, seeing videotapes of master family therapists at work, critiquing (and being critiqued by) fellow trainees reviewing taped sessions, even studying examples of family therapy failures (Coleman, 1985), all add to conceptual and clinical knowledge, but in the last analysis the trainee learns experientially—by treating families under supervision.

Didactic Course Work

Entrants into the field of marital/family therapy typically come from diverse academic backgrounds: psychology, psychiatry, social work, nursing, counselor education, pastoral counseling, and others. Correspondingly, their academic preparation may vary considerably. In an effort to provide some uniform structure for evaluating the relevance and completeness of such training, the AAMFT (1994)[2] has established educational and training guidelines involving preparation in theory (systems theory, personality theory, gender and cultural issues), practice (assessment, treatment, and intervention methods), human development (individual and family life cycle changes, human sexuality), research (methodology, quantitative and qualitative approaches), and ethics (legal responsibilities and liabilities).

The didactic component of family therapy training typically includes lectures, group discussion, demonstrations, instructional videotapes, assigned readings, role playing, and observations through the use of one-way mirrors (allowing multiple therapists or therapists-in-training to observe the family in action). The academic courses provide the theoretical underpinnings for the corresponding clinical intervention techniques. Supervisors not only lead discussions but also may comment to the trainees on what is taking place behind the one-way mirror. In some cases the trainees' formal course work follows the actual experience of conducting family therapy sessions, in order to avoid premature conceptualizing by trainees before they have had firsthand contact with families. This sequence, according to Shapiro (1975) puts trainees in a better position to integrate family therapy concepts into their understanding of family process. More often, some introductory lectures, assigned readings, and demonstrations precede the trainees' first clinical experiences; students thus prepared are less likely to be overwhelmed by the abundance of clinical material gathered from the family interview. Following these initial didactic presentations, trainees begin the clinical work of evaluating and treating families while continuing to attend clinical seminars.

Regardless of the sequence in which the trainee attends didactic seminars, or the method of training used, readings in the field constitute a significant part of the learning experience. Gurman and Kniskern's (1991) edited *Handbook of Family Therapy*, Wolman and Stricker's (1983) edited *Handbook of Family and Marital Therapy*, L'Abate's (1985) edited *The Handbook of Family Psychology*, and Falloon's (1988) edited *Handbook of Behavioral Family Therapy* all offer large collections of the-

---

[2]The AAMFT recognizes four sets of members: clinical, associate, student, and affiliate. Clinical members must possess a graduate degree in marriage and family therapy from a regionally accredited institution, have completed 11 courses in theory, practice, human development, and ethics, and have had a minimum of 300 hours of supervision during their graduate training, as well as 1000 hours of direct clinical contact with couples and families and 200 hours of supervision following graduation. Associate membership calls for the completion of a qualifying graduate degree, 8 of the 11 courses in theory, practice, human development, research, and ethics, and a minimum of 300 hours of supervised clinical practicum during their graduate program. To become a student member, the applicant must be currently enrolled in an accredited program leading to a graduate degree or postgraduate certificate in marriage and family therapy. Affiliate membership is for those mental health workers who are not pursuing a marriage and family therapy license, but who want to develop their clinical skills in working with couples and families. All classes of membership must agree to abide by the AAMFT Code of Ethics (see Appendix C at the back of this book).

oretical as well as clinical papers, usually by experts in their respective areas. More recent updates can be found in Mikesell, Lusterman, and McDaniel's (1995) *Integrating Family Therapy* and Piercy, Sprenkle, Wetchler, and Associates' (1996) *Family Therapy Sourcebook*.

A proliferation of journals help keep students and professionals abreast of developments in family therapy. Those addressing a variety of contemporary issues in the field include:

American Journal of Family Therapy
American Journal of Orthopsychiatry
Australian and New Zealand Journal of Family Therapy
Contemporary Family Therapy
Family Coordinator
Familes in Society
Family Process
Family Relations
Family Therapy
Family Therapy Case Studies
Family Therapy Collections
Human Systems
International Journal of Family Therapy
Journal of Family Psychology
Journal of Family Psychotherapy
Journal of Family Therapy
Journal of Marital and Family Therapy
Journal of Marriage and the Family
Journal of Psychotherapy and the Family
Journal of Social Casework
Marriage and Family Review
The Family Journal
Topics in Family Psychology and Counseling

More specialized journals include:

Alternative Lifestyles
Dulwich Centre Review (Australian) (Narrative Therapy)
Family Systems (Bowen)
Families, Systems, and Health (coordinating family medicine and family therapy)
Journal of Couples Therapy
Journal of Divorce and Remarriage
Journal of Feminist Family Therapy
Journal of Sex and Marital Therapy
Journal of Systemic Therapies

In addition, influential periodicals help keep practitioners abreast of developments in the field:

AFTA Newsletter (American Family Therapy Academy)

Brown University Family Therapy Newsletter
Family Therapy News (AAMFT Newsletter)
The Family Psychologist (Newsletter of APA Division of Family Psychology)
The Family Therapy Networker

Most of the field's leaders have published their theoretical and conceptual ideas in book form: Ackerman (Bloch & Simon, 1982), Boscolo and Cecchin (Boscolo, Cecchin, Hoffman, & Penn, 1987), Boszormenyi-Nagy (Boszormenyi-Nagy & Krasner, 1986), Bowen (1978), deShazer (1988; 1991), Framo (1982; 1992), Haley (1976a; 1984; 1996), Kempler (1981), Madanes (1990), Minuchin (1974; 1984), Satir (1967; 1972), Selvini-Palazzoli (Selvini-Palazzoli, Cirillo, Selvini, & Sorrentino, 1989), Watzlawick (1978; 1984), Whitaker (Whitaker & Bumberry, 1988), White (White & Epston, 1990; White, 1995). Finally, it is a worthwhile and at times exciting experience to read verbatim accounts of family therapy sessions (for example, Haley & Hoffman, 1967; Napier & Whitaker, 1978; Satir & Baldwin, 1983) following step-by-step what takes place as a master therapist puts theory into practice. More recently, Dattilio (1998) as well as Lawson and Prevatt (1999) have edited case study books in which contributors expert in various approaches to couple and family therapy describe their theoretical orientation, followed by examples of their interventions with clients.

Videotapes

Videotaping therapeutic sessions has provided an indispensable tool for teaching family therapy. Students early in their training have an opportunity to watch tapes of master therapists at work with real families; they also can record their own sessions with families for later playback during supervisory meetings. The technique came into general use in the 1950s, as taboos in this area of therapy against breaching the privacy of the therapeutic relationship began to diminish. In the years since, a multitude of videotapes demonstrating a variety of techniques with different types of families have been distributed. Together with videotapes of current, ongoing therapy sessions, they now play a significant part in training family therapists because they convey an immediate sense of awareness of the processes by which therapists and families communicate.

Videotapes of master therapists demonstrating their techniques in actual sessions with families are readily available from the following organizations: Boston Family Institute; Philadelphia Child Guidance Center; Ackerman Institute for Family Therapy; Georgetown University Family Center; the Center for Family Learning in New Rochelle, New York; the Institute of Contextual Growth in Ambler, Pennsylvania; the Eastern Pennsylvania Psychiatric Institute; the Family Therapy Institute of Washington, D.C.; the Kempler Institute in Laguna Niguel, California; and the Mental Research Institute in Palo Alto.[3] Beyond these training centers, teach-

---

[3]All of these centers offer descriptive catalogues of their tapes that are generally available for a period of two or three days and are copyrighted so that they may not legally be reproduced. Most insist that videotapes be shown only to audiences of students or professionals in the field of family therapy.

ing tapes are available for purchase from Master's Work Productions in Los Angeles, Golden Triad Films in Kansas City, Missouri, as well as the AAMFT through its "Master Series" of tapes of live demonstrations by noted family therapists carried out at that organization's annual conference. In addition, video training tapes demonstrating specific techniques with volunteer families, or hired actors, sometimes prepared and marketed by professional filmmakers, are advertised in the family therapy newsletters and periodicals described earlier.

Clearly one of the greatest boons to the field of family therapy, videotape has opened new avenues of development in training. For example, supervisors can tape initial sessions with a family for later presentation to students; the tapes give students a basis for noting changes in family interactive patterns as they watch "live" demonstrations of subsequent sessions with the same family (Bodin, 1969b). Tape libraries of family therapy sessions from initial interview to termination and follow-up can be compiled for students to view at their leisure or when confronted with a particular kind of technical problem or therapeutic impasse. Of course, the student can monitor his or her own progressive proficiency by comparing tapes made early and late in training. Away from the emotional intensity of the family session, the trainee and supervisor can see how he or she presents himself or herself to the family, what was missed or overlooked, what characteristic patterns appear and reappear, what facial expressions belied which family member's verbal communication, and so on (Berger, 1978). Similarly, the trainee gains an opportunity to observe his or her own style, mannerisms, and appearance, an invaluable self-teaching tool.

According to Whiffen (1982), videotaping has three unique properties that make it especially valuable in supervision: (1) it freezes time so that every aspect and angle of a crucial sequence is available for posttherapy play and replay by the therapist, impossible to achieve during the session; (2) it enables the therapist to see himself or herself more objectively as a contributor to the whole system, a different perspective from the one available in the midst of the often-bewildering multiple stimuli occurring during the session; and (3) it allows the effect of a therapeutic intervention to be studied and its success evaluated.

A trainee's verbal report of a family therapy session to a supervisor and/or class is subject to the inherent risks of unreliable recall, defensiveness, distortion, and subjective description. The instant replay of the session on tape overcomes many of these obstacles. Subtle idiosyncratic patterns of interviewing style (for example, avoiding certain topics or retreating from certain emotional expressions) may become more obvious to the trainee after supervisor comments or self-observation following the viewing of a taped family session. The interplay of verbal and especially nonverbal messages and interactions may become clearer. Not only does the trainee confront his or her own behavior with a family, but also the other viewers provide additional corrective feedback. Trainees learn from each other's errors as well as successes. The tape can be played and replayed over and over again, preserved, and retrieved for further study and analysis (Berger, 1978).

By observing trainees with families over closed-circuit television, the supervisor and others retain all of the benefits of a one-way mirror along with a permanent videotaped record of precisely what took place. In some cases, the supervisory sessions themselves are videotaped for later playback as the trainee plans further therapeutic strategies with the family.

DEVELOPING THERAPEUTIC SKILLS THROUGH SUPERVISION

Supervision in marital and family therapy refers to an ongoing relationship, in a work setting, in which a trainer helps a less experienced or novice therapist develop specific therapeutic skills as the trainee gains practical experience in treating families (Saba & Liddle, 1986). In recent years, the supervisory process has itself become a subspecialty within the field (Haber, 1996; Todd & Storm, 1997; Watkins, 1997), as greater research attention has begun to be paid to developing the personal and conceptual skills necessary to carry out supervisory functions. What once was considered a skill that came naturally to any experienced family therapist is now viewed increasingly as an area involving more than the general transmission of conceptual and clinical knowledge. The trainer or supervisor must be attuned to his or her transactional patterns with the trainee, their degree of personal interaction, their social and emotional distance, the differences in their power, authority, and status, and so on. At the same time, the supervisor must take care to draw the line, in this personal/professional encounter, between offering training and offering therapy. The boundaries between the two are not always easy to maintain (Aponte, 1994b). That is, while training programs aim at producing personal changes in the trainee in order to improve that person's therapeutic skills, the extent to which the trainee's personal life should be examined remains controversial.

Whereas supervising beginning trainees might call for closely monitoring the therapy session, frequently issuing directives if missteps are occurring, later supervision of more experienced trainees is apt to become increasingly egalitarian and to foster trainee autonomy and creativity. The supervisor-supervisee relationship thus is not static, but one that continuously evolves.

Similarly, supervisors cultivate their skills through stages. Haber (1996) suggests that beginning supervisors are like new parents: they have added responsibility, newfound status, and the chance to pass their knowledge and experience on to another. However, as in the case of first-time parents, they may lack knowledge about how best to go about doing the job. Beginning supervisors may at times become too close when professional distance is called for, or too distant when a more inviting and friendly stance would be preferable while maintaining a hierarchical role. Table 16.6 delineates the polarized characteristics of beginning and more advanced supervisors (whose differences in real life are not apt to be quite so absolute).

Ganahl, Ferguson, and L'Abate (1985) are critical of training and supervision that limits itself to teaching clinical techniques only, ignoring the need to help trainees integrate theory with what they are learning experientially in practice. They insist that training offered by supervisors should be both academic and experiential, and urge supervisors to take the personal style of the trainee into account, not simply attempt to make him or her over in the supervisor's image.

Table 16.6   Characteristics of Beginning and Advanced Supervisors

Beginning Supervisor	Advanced Supervisor
Lacks substantial knowledge of supervision theory and methodology	Well-informed about supervision theory and methodology
Overuses one approach to supervision	Implements diverse approaches suitable to specific instance
Anxious in the role of supervisor; over-identifies with therapist role	Understands role and responsibilities in the supervisory process
Intervenes largely by being the expert clinician	More apt to use the resources of the supervisee
Engages in power struggles with the supervisee over the right way	Able to connect and work with the supervisee's worldview
Underemphasizes or overemphasizes the person of the therapist in supervision	Discriminantly explores the personal/professional interface when it is relevant for clinical issues
Overreacts to the supervisee	More aware of and able to utilize personal reactions in the supervision process
Experiences diffuse boundaries and inability to confront supervisee	Able to use clear boundaries to keep the supervisee appropriately on task
Ignores cultural differences and learning styles of the supervisee	Respects cultural and learning idio-syncrasies
Works with supervisee in isolation ignoring ecological context	Considers all of the floors in the professional and client houses
Content-oriented	Works with process, including the parallel process between the therapeutic and supervisory systems

Source: Haber, 1996, p. 57

Beavers (1985) emphasizes the role of the AAMFT in upgrading supervisory standards. That organization sets high educational, experiential, and supervisory standards by which trainers can qualify as AAMFT Approved Supervisors, and periodically publishes *The Supervision Bulletin* addressing conceptual issues and innovative techniques relevant to improving the supervisory process. Approved supervisors may work from a variety of marital/family therapy theoretical positions, but all must work from a systemic orientation. *The Supervision Bulletin* periodically provides an update of newly published articles and books, acting as a resource for continuing education into family therapy supervision.

An effective teaching program in family therapy must meld relevant theory with profitable practical experience. However, clinical contact with families is of limited value without regularly scheduled, attentive supervision, especially crucial during the early stages of training. Such supervision, when provided by highly competent and experienced family therapists who also have teaching as well as supervisory skills, may take a number of forms:

Reviewing audiotapes of trainee sessions
Reviewing videotapes of trainee sessions
Reviewing trainee's written process notes

Observing ongoing sessions through a one-way mirror

Cotherapy with trainees

Conducting continuous case conferences during which a trainee presents an outline of his or her work with a client family for several class sessions

Live, on-the-spot supervision in which the supervisor stays in direct communication with the trainee during a session

Live Supervision

Live supervision, in which a supervisor or observing team watches an ongoing session through a one-way mirror or on a video monitor, introduces an immediacy to the supervisory process. Introduced by Montalvo (1973) at the Philadelphia Child Guidance Clinic, this procedure has become a major supervisory technique in the family therapy field. Live supervision calls for the supervisor (or more frequently today, an observing or reflecting team) to actively guide the trainee's work by providing feedback on what the trainee is doing while he or she is working with the family. Not surprisingly, its appeal is greatest among advocates of the structural and strategic approaches (hence, Montalvo's initial involvement), since efforts to modify ongoing transactions characterize the thrust of their therapeutic interventions.

As we have noted earlier, the advent of the one-way mirror in the 1950s was a significant breakthrough for clinicians and researchers alike, allowing them to observe live family interviews unobtrusively. By separating the supervisor from the family's ongoing emotional system yet allowing a firsthand look at that system in operation, the one-way mirror added a new dimension to the process of comprehending interaction within the family and between the family and therapist. The live supervisor was now in an ideal position to note developing patterns, able to think about them more objectively than the therapist on the "firing line" (and subject to being caught up in, and becoming part of, the family system). Today's reflecting team members are likely to participate even more directly in the treatment, sending messages into the consultation room that may bypass, support, or oppose the therapist's stance (Liddle, 1991).

The supervisor can intervene in several ways:

1. By calling the therapist out of the room midway through a session for consultation, the therapist then returning with directives to be given to the family (the technique employed by the Milan group, among others, in their systemic family therapy, as described in Chapter 11)

2. By calling the therapist by telephone with suggestions during the treatment process (MRI's Brief Therapy Center approach, discussed in Chapter 10)

3. By entering the consultation room during a session with comments and suggestions (used by Minuchin in structural family therapy as an attempt to reshape or reframe the experience the family is having and thus produce change in their transactional patterns)

4. By using a "bug in the ear" wireless transmitter to communicate directly, and relatively unobtrusively, to the therapist (a technique used primarily with beginning therapists today)

When the earphone is used in supervision (Byng-Hall, 1982), the novice therapist listens through a small "bug" worn in the ear while the supervisor, behind a one-way mirror or at a video monitor, speaks into a microphone. Since the family does not hear the interventions, advocates argue that the technique is superior to the use of the telephone or direct entering of the room by a supervisor. British psychiatrist Byng-Hall (1982) insists that the earphone is the best tool for supervising the therapy process because the flow of interaction is not interrupted and the family responds as if the interventions came from the trainee, not from others. The technique is controversial, however, and runs the risk of overuse by an exuberant supervisor; the trainee may have the feeling of being simply an "echo" of the supervisor or of having his or her concentration interrupted and autonomy invaded. For these reasons, the "bug" has largely been replaced by the more conspicuous telephone in the consultation room. Whether the intervention is by telephone or "bug," however, critics caution against overindulgence in this procedure, contending that the supervisor should adopt a "call with reluctance" philosophy and offer only one or two very specific suggestions during a session.

According to Byng-Hall (1982), live supervisory interventions are likely to take the form of instructions ("Ask . . ." or "Say to the mother . . ."; suggestions for strategies ("Get father and son to negotiate on that"); efforts to direct the therapist's attention ("Notice how . . ." or "See how they repeat . . ."); moves to increase or decrease intensity ("Encourage mother and father to confront . . ." or "Tell them to stop and listen to one another, instead of . . ."); or perhaps encouragement ("That was well done"). As we have noted, trainees nowadays may be observed through one-way mirrors by supervisory teams (including fellow trainees), who offer reflections and suggestions for intervention while therapy is taking place.

As live supervision in any of the forms just described typically is practiced, the person supervising watches the session from behind a one-way mirror (with or without a group of trainees or other colleagues) and enters the session to make suggestions to the therapist at the very moment that the action is taking place; the objective is to help the trainee get disentangled from recurring, nonproductive interactional sequences with the family in order to regain control and direction of the session. Both parties must feel comfortable with the procedure: The trainee must accept the supervisor's right to intervene if the latter believes that a disservice is done to the family by allowing what is occurring to continue; the supervisor must accept the trainee's right to question or challenge the suggestion and ignore it as he or she sees fit. Trainees are often comforted by the idea that they are being backed up and not allowed to sink.

Live team supervision has become increasingly popular in training settings. In one interesting variation, Papp (1980) describes the use of a **Greek chorus** or consultation team (supervisor and trainees) who watch a session from behind a one-way mirror and periodically send messages regarding possible interventions into the therapy room, rather like a Greek chorus.[4] The therapist has the option of accepting or

---

[4]The observer team effort to participate in the treatment by sending back information regarding their perceptions is a forerunner of Tom Andersen's (1991) reflecting team technique (Chapter 13). Both intend to provide information regarding different perspectives about the family's problems and their efforts at solution. One difference is that Papp employs a "one-way mirror" while Andersen, influenced by constructivism, utilizes a "two-way mirror" as family plus therapist reverse roles with the observing team, observing them as they reflect on what they have just witnessed.

opposing the team's suggestions, which are meant, at various times, to challenge or provoke or at other times to support what is transpiring. This team process is particularly appropriate for strategic techniques (Chapter 10), in which reframing and prescriptions are offered families; the team is likely to suggest paradoxical interventions in order to provoke, confuse, or challenge a family that appears to them to be resistant to other directives. The therapist can side with the chorus or oppose them; in the latter case, the split can call attention to the family's ambivalence about change, allowing the therapist to capitalize on the paradoxical offering ("My colleagues seem to think you won't be able to make the change I have suggested, but I think you can"). A basic assumption in live supervision is that any family can direct the therapist away from his or her function as a change agent by maneuvering the therapist into behaving in ways that reinforce the very patterns that brought the members of the family into therapy. The experienced supervisor, not caught up in the action, can help the supervisee correct such missteps at the time they occur. The supervisor—as a coach on the sidelines—introduces feedback into the ongoing system, comprising the student therapist–supervisor–family.

The advantages of live supervision lie in the timeliness and relevance of supervisor questions or suggestions, and the reduction of possible distortions by the trainee who, in the past, reported later to the supervisor what had taken place during the session. Probably the major disadvantage is the added stress felt by the trainee being observed. Schwartz, Liddle, and Breunlin (1988) warn against the tendency toward robotization of the trainee, as he or she becomes little more than a performing automaton, mechanically carrying out the supervisor's every command. More experienced trainees in particular are likely to want more autonomy. According to Loewenstein, Reder, and Clark's (1982) description of themselves as trainees receiving live supervision, the experience can arouse intense emotions: the shame of self-exposure in front of others, the potential loss of self-esteem, loss of a sense of autonomy ("feeling under remote control") and of ego boundaries, problems over compliance, and the issue of authority. (The authors also report that the anticipatory fantasies of live supervision were far more frightening than the actual experience and that these fears were greatly reduced over time.)

In addition, the student therapist may become too dependent on supervisory interventions, and this may interfere with the evolution of his or her own style (Liddle & Halpin, 1978). Some sense of confidentiality may be jeopardized if the family knows (and it must be told) that it is being observed. Whitaker (1976c), consistent with his nonplanning approach, opposed live supervision, contending that the procedure tends to make the supervisee less self-confident, and more reliant on following a prearranged method rather than relying on the ongoing process for direction. Bowenians too make little use of live supervision or one-way mirrors in their training (Papero, 1988), viewing such procedures as distractions. Instead, they insist that any observations of ongoing sessions take place in the therapy room and in full view of the family, who then are in a position to deal with the visitors directly.

Despite these objections, authorities beginning with strategist Haley (1976b) consider this method the most effective form of supervision. In the past, all that was revealed about a session was what the student therapist chose to reveal, relying on notes taken during or immediately afterward. With the introduction of audiotapes some 50 years ago, the supervisor could learn what was actually said; videotapes go even further, revealing both words and actions. But none of these procedures provides guidance at the time the student needs it most—in the act of interviewing. Strategic therapists in particular believe that live supervision not only teaches inexperienced therapists how to do therapy, but also protects client families from incompetent practice.

Practically speaking, however, how often is live supervision or videotaping of sessions used? Video equipment is expensive and takes up room, professional supervisory time is likely to be limited, and private practitioners who use their offices to supervise trainees are not in a position to set up a live supervisory facility employing one-way mirrors. Within university medical center psychiatry departments, service requirements tend to restrict time spent in live supervision, although freestanding institutes training a smaller number of students may find it more feasible. According to McKenzie, Atkinson, Quinn, and Heath's (1986) survey data, despite their preference for the procedure, over one-quarter did not use live supervision because of the lack of proper facilities.

Cotherapy Teams

Cotherapy—the simultaneous involvement of two therapists in the treatment setting—provides a trainee with an opportunity to work hand in glove with a supervisor. Today, the technique is employed largely by symbolic-experiential family therapists (Roberto, 1991) who contend that two-person cotherapy teams provide families with mutual complementarity and support, continuity of care, autonomy, models of intimacy, division of roles during the session, and an opportunity for increased creativity on the part of both therapists. The technique also may be employed in managed care situations in which the payors do not accept trainee billing unless the attending supervisor is available during the entire session.

Cotherapy has some obvious training advantages. The trainee has an opportunity to learn a distinctive approach at close range and to see an expert in action without taking the full or even the major responsibility for treating the family. The trainee has the added benefit of seeing his or her mentor as a real person who makes mistakes at times, doesn't always understand all that is happening, and isn't always positive in outlook—all very reassuring to a beginning family therapist who has felt exactly the same way at times about himself or herself! The supervisor as cotherapist can provide the supervisee with an opportunity to try creative interventions with the family, assured of skillful support and rescue when trouble arises, as it inevitably does.

As a training device, however, cotherapy is not without its disadvantages, real and potential. The trainee may become so identified with the supervisor (especially if the latter's style is colorful and dramatic) that he or she merely mimics the authority figure—the so-called "cloning effect"—instead of developing a style more personally authentic. Overdependency on the supervisor for making intervention moves with the family may also become a problem. The student acting as cotherapist with a more experienced person may simply sit back and not take responsibility for the case, as he or she must ultimately learn to do.

On the other hand, trainees, especially if assigned difficult families, may find themselves, working alone, to be overwhelmed or "swallowed up" by the family system, seduced or otherwise manipulated by family resistance into maintaining the family status quo. A supervisor's presence during the session may help prevent that from occurring. When supervisor and trainee work as cotherapists, additional supervision, perhaps the bulk of supervision, is likely to take place immediately after and between therapy sessions (Whitaker & Keith, 1981).

SUMMARY

Becoming a family therapist calls for training that focuses on learning a set of therapeutic techniques along with an underlying theoretical understanding of how and under what circumstances to use them. Early training programs emphasized the importance of clinicians trained in individual psychotherapy making a paradigmatic shift in order to think in family systems terms.

Formal training in family therapy began over two decades ago, as the necessary perceptual, cognitive, and executive skills were delineated for becoming a competent professional. Currently, training occurs in three kinds of settings: degree-granting programs in family therapy, freestanding family therapy training institutes, and university-affiliated graduate programs. The three differ significantly in the nature, scope, and desired outcome of the training they provide. Degree-granting programs in particular view marital/family therapy as a distinct profession, a position supported by the AAMFT, officially designated by the government to certify standards for accreditation in the United States and Canada. Training aids include (1) didactic course work; (2) the use of master therapist videotapes plus trainee tapes for post-session viewing by the trainee and his or her supervisor and classmates; and (3) supervision through the active guidance by a supervisor who may watch the session behind a one-way mirror.

Supervision has become a subspecialty within the field of family therapy. Audiotapes, videotapes, written process notes, cotherapy, and live supervision are commonly employed supervisory methods. Supervisors using live supervision offer trainees corrective feedback by telephone, earphone, calling the trainee/therapist out of the therapy session for consultation, or physically entering the session with comments and suggestions. Cotherapy teams of supervisor and trainee are sometimes used for training purposes, particularly by advocates of the symbolic-experiential approach.

17

Professional Issues
and Ethical Practices

In this final chapter of the text, we concern ourselves with two continually evolving sets of professional issues—how to ensure the highest quality of professional practice at the least cost to society and how to remain alert to ethical standards, particularly as practice shifts from attention to the individual client to the family system as a whole.

PROFESSIONAL ISSUES

Regulating Professional Practice

Most established professions seek some form of legal statute to gain public acceptance and respectability. Statutes in all of the United States and Canadian provinces control the practice of medicine, law, and psychology, and since 1970 there has been a concerted effort to seek similar legal standards for credentialling marital/family therapists. Marital and family therapists have sought legal recognition primarily because licensure has become synonymous with professionalism (Huber, 1994) and also because reimbursements from health plans for providing clinical services are paid only to licensed providers.

A number of important premises support efforts at licensure (Corey, Corey, & Callanan, 1998; Fretz & Mills, 1980): (1) licensure protects the public by establishing minimum standards of service and holding professionals accountable if they do not measure up; (2) it protects the public from its ignorance or naivite regarding mental health services, helping potential consumers choose practitioners more judiciously; (3) it increases the likelihood that practitioners will be competent, having met the standards to obtain a license; (4) it makes mental health services more affordable, since clients going to licensed practitioners may be partly reimbursed; (5) it upgrades the profession by gathering together practitioners committed to improving and maintaining the highest standards of excellence; and (6) it allows the profession to define itself and its activities more clearly, thus becoming more independent. Licensing assures the public that the practitioner has completed an approved educational program, has had an acceptable number of hours of supervised training, and has successfully gone through some screening or evaluative program. Advocates of licensing thus maintain that the consumer's welfare is better safeguarded when legal regulations exist.

Possessing a license, of course, does not assure competency. Licenses are generic in the sense that they do not specify what client problems the licensee is competent to work with nor what techniques he or she is trained to use (Corey, Corey, & Callanan, 1998). So, for example, a practitioner may be trained to work with individuals but lacks the experience or skills for family interventions. Ethically, that person should seek additional training and supervision before undertaking clinical work in a new modality.

As we indicated in the previous chapter, an individual seeking professional status in marital/family therapy may earn a graduate and/or professional degree from a university or obtain professional preparation at a center offering specialized training in marital/family therapy. A person who follows the academic route and has obtained the requisite training supervision in a program accredited by the appropriate professional association (for example, the American Psychological Association) may seek either **licensing** or **certification** (according to the law governing practice in a particular state or province) in his or her specialty.

A state licensing law, the more restrictive of the two, regulates who may practice (for example, licensed psychologist, licensed clinical social worker) by defining education and experience criteria, administering qualifying examinations, and stating the conditions under which a license may be revoked (thereby terminating the right to practice) for ethical or other reasons. A certification law, a weaker and less comprehensive form of regulation, simply certifies who has the right to use a particular professional title. Such a law does not restrict practice or define permissible activities but simply guarantees that the title (for example, "psychologist") will be used only by people who meet the standards established by the law. Like the licensing laws, certification laws set up criteria for issuing and revoking certificates; in that sense they help to monitor practice, at least in regard to the use of the title. Both kinds of laws are designed to ensure that practitioners have met certain minimal standards of education, training, and supervised experience. Regulatory boards and legislatures in a number of states have mandated the successful completion of specific **continuing education** courses (for example, child abuse, human sexuality, chemical dependency) as a condition of renewal of a license or certificate (Goldenberg, 1983).

After a slow start, licensing of marital/family therapists is now proceeding swiftly in the United States. One reason for the earlier lag in licensure was the fact that it is easier to establish criteria for licensing the graduates of recognized university programs than those from newly established training programs in freestanding family institutes. In addition, some members of the established mental health professions initially opposed an independent profession of marital/family therapy; according to their view, marital/family therapy is but a subspecialty of psychotherapy. However, marital/family therapists argue that they are a separate profession, and that university preparation in the mental health field generally does not provide sufficient emphasis on work with families; graduates of such programs should themselves seek additional training and acquire a license in marital/family therapy if they wish to practice in the field. The subject remains controversial, touching on professional issues such as eligibility for third-party payments from health insurance plans[1] to cover the treatment of marital or family dysfunction as well as the updating of professional skills and conceptual knowledge. Clearly, practitioners accustomed to working with individual clients need further training before working with families. On the other hand, marital/family therapists may lack the requisite grounding to treat individuals.

Efforts to gain recognition for marriage and family therapists in every state and Canadian province have been led by the AAMFT in conjunction with local practitioner groups. In a single decade—1984 to 1994—the number of states regulating such grew from 9 to 34 (Lynch & Hutchins, 1994). By early 1999, 41 states regulated marriage and family therapy practice, and other state legislatures were considering regulatory bills. Marriage and family therapists now are recognized as qualified health care providers in Alabama, Alaska, Arizona, Arkansas, California, Colorado, Connecticut, Florida, Georgia, Hawaii, Illinois, Indiana, Iowa, Kansas, Kentucky, Maine, Maryland, Massachusetts, Michigan, Minnesota, Mississippi, Missouri, Nebraska, Nevada, New Hampshire, New Jersey, New Mexico, North Carolina, Oklahoma, Oregon, Rhode Island, South Carolina, South Dakota, Tennessee, Texas, Utah, Vermont, Virginia, Washington, Wisconsin, and Wyoming.

Requirements may vary between states, although all require that those licensed or certified as marriage and family therapists meet certain educational and clinical experience criteria, usually comparable to the standards for Clinical Membership in AAMFT (see Chapter 16). In California, as an example, the applicant must possess a two-year master's degree in marriage, family, and child counseling from an academic institution accredited by the Western College Association or an equivalent accrediting agency, plus 3000 counseling hours under the supervision of a licensed marriage, family, and child counselor, clinical social worker, licensed psychologist, or licensed physician certified in psychiatry. After completing the required 3000 hours, the candidate must pass both a written and an oral exam prior to licensure as a marriage and family therapist. In addition, in order to renew a license every two years, the counselor must complete 36 hours of continuing education.

Peer Review

Monitoring, examining, or assessing the work of one's colleagues, or having one's own work reviewed by one or more colleagues, is hardly new for anyone who has completed a training program in any of the disciplines involved in marital/family

[1]Freedom-of-choice laws in most states permit consumers to choose among various licensed practitioners, including marital/family therapists, disallowing third-party payors from discriminating against any one discipline. As a consequence, most insurance programs, as well as the government-sponsored CHAMPUS (Civilian Health and Medical Program of the Uniformed Services) program for armed forces retirees and dependents of active military personnel, now recognize marital/family therapists as authorized mental health service providers.

therapy. By the time someone has become a professional, he or she probably has presented work samples in numerous case conferences, to say nothing of having been videotaped or observed through a one-way mirror working with families. No doubt cases have been dissected by supervisors and classmates while in training. Having become a professional, further consultation may be sought when therapeutic impasses arise, in dealing with otherwise difficult or sticky clinical procedures, or whenever upcoming ethical decisions need scrutiny. Therapists in private practice often seek **peer review** and peer support by belonging to peer-consultation groups, where they seek help and support from colleagues in dealing with problematic cases, discuss ethical and legal issues that arise, or simply exchange experiences to counter feelings of loneliness that are an inevitable part of functioning as a sole practitioner (Greenburg, Lewis, & Johnson, 1985). Borders (1991) views such groups as valuable for practitioners, regardless of years of experience, particularly in gaining instructional feedback from others, honing skills, and monitoring the therapist's own outlook and behavior.

Managed Care and Professional Practice

Undoubtedly, the major change in professional practice in recent years has come about as a result of the unprecedented growth of **managed care.** In contrast to practices prior to the 1980s, where independent practitioners billed insurance carriers ("third party payors") on a fee-for-service basis (and health costs soared), today's employers, who pay the bills, are more mindful of controlling the escalating costs (Hersch, 1995). As a result, managed care has become the dominant economic force in health care delivery in the United States, and, as Cummings (1995) observes, has forced mental health workers to reassess cherished attitudes regarding professional practice.

Managed care or health maintenance organizations (HMOs) contract with employers, insurance companies, or union trusts to administer and finance their health benefit program. Increasingly, employers who offer health benefits have opted for managed care programs for their employees—prepaid insurance in which a fixed monthly fee is collected from each member enrolled in the plan who has selected a particular medical (including mental health) group practice.

Such a system for delivering mental health services, sometimes but not always including marital and family therapy, has at its core a contract between a therapist (usually referred to as a *provider*) or a group of therapists and a managed care organization. In exchange for being admitted into the provider network and agreeing to accept referrals by being part of the managed care organization roster, the professional agrees under contract to provide services for a previously negotiated fee (usually significantly lower than the customary rates of fee-for-service providers in the community) and to abide by the managed care organization's explicit provisions. Managed care groups believe that this system helps ensure quality management and increased provider accountability to justify clinical decisions.

Aimed at cost containment, managed care plans typically call for preauthorization before the therapist may begin treatment, and further authorization after a previously approved number of sessions (anywhere from two to six) if the therapist can justify additional treatment to the satisfaction of the managed care group's peer reviewer. Typically, only a limited number of sessions per designated time period are approved (whether or not short-term therapy is the provider's treatment of choice), and the client's choice of therapist is restricted to providers on the managed care roster. To keep costs down, managed care programs may limit services and contract with less qualified providers who often are expected to rely on treatment manuals for short-term interventions. According to critics Seligman and Levant (1998), this determination to favor brief therapy and the use of manuals may benefit some clients, especially in simple cases, but it ignores the needs of others, where cases are complicated and where the therapist judges that longer-term intensive treatment is necessary to achieve therapeutic gains.

Miller (1996) sees an overall decline in the quality of mental health services as a result of managed care's inherent economics. He contends that in the name of efficiency, essential services have been cut and access to treatment denied for a significant portion of the population with moderate to serious problems. In his view, underdiagnosis, undertreatment, and overly restrictive hospital admissions and hospital stays belie the claim of improved quality of care. Indeed, there exists wide differences in the policies of different health maintenance organizations in the variety of services approved, how restrictive they are in the number of sessions okayed, and in the freedom allowed providers. As larger companies swallow up smaller HMOs, changes in service contracts and in providers may change for consumers, sometimes during treatment.

Managed mental health care programs usually include a fixed number of mental health practitioners (individually or as part of a provider network); others are excluded when the panel of providers is full, a particular problem for newly licensed practitioners getting ready to enter the field. Referrals are made to providers within defined geographic areas; in most plans the practitioner must be available for emergencies on a 24-hour basis. Whether a client can be seen, for how many visits, at what fee, covering what services, for what problems or conditions, all are negotiated with the managed care organization. Peer reviewers or case managers (usually but not always professionals) act as "gatekeepers," carrying out *utilization reviews,* the conclusions of which are often in conflict with the practitioner about how best to manage the case.

Cost containment is likely to have a high priority for the managed care group, and since HMOs are competitive for employer contracts, reimbursement rates are likely to continue to decrease and services be further restricted to cut costs. However, either the client or provider who believes the client will experience direct harm from discontinuing treatment can appeal the case manager's decision.

Under managed mental health care contracts, therapists are thrust into carrying out new (and especially for older therapists, unfamiliar) tasks. Typically, the practitioner is required on a regular basis to submit to case managers a written treatment plan for each client or family, establishing therapeutic goals and justifying procedures, before being authorized to begin (or continue a previously submitted treatment plan) for a finite number of sessions. It is the responsibility of the therapist to explain why services are necessary and to account for procedures carried out. As noted, managed care plans support short-term, directive, problem-solving therapy aimed at returning clients to their previous levels of functioning (rather than optimal functioning) (Shueman, Troy, & Mayhugh, 1994). That is, their aim is to limit treatment to whatever it takes to return clients to a functional level as soon as possible, but nothing more. A secondary goal is the prevention of recurrence of the presenting symptoms. Just how much treatment is enough remains a debatable issue.

While the therapist might seek to protect the privacy of clients, he or she is called upon to share information—diagnosis, types of services provided, duration of treatment—that compromises previously determined ideas regarding **confidentiality** (Keith-Spiegel & Koocher, 1985)[2]. Such cost-saving measures are becoming the standard for mental health care in the United States (Vesper & Brock, 1991) as more and more employers replace fee-for-service insurance plans with lower-cost managed care programs.

Remaining a solo private practitioner who wishes to receive payment for services outside of managed care organizations is becoming less and less economically feasible. Cummings (1995) recognized the inevitability of this "rapid industrialization" of health care early, and for a decade has been critical of the American Psychological Association's initial resistance, since in his view such opposition prevented the organization's participation in health economics decisions. He argues for retraining therapists in time-limited therapeutic procedures, urging them to engage in personally conducted outcome research to measure and justify what works in what they do. In his view, the mental health profession is undergoing perhaps its greatest change, as more and more practitioners are forming large group practices in order to provide an integrated system of care, acquire an arsenal of time-effective techniques, and learn which of their interventions are most effective through outcome research in their group practice.

Managed care has challenged therapists to reexamine their professional ethics, rethink how best to allocate professional resources, come to terms with accounting for what they do with clients, and develop more speedy and effective interventions. The situation regarding how best to deliver professional services is likely to remain turbulent for many years to come.

Legal Liability

Every practitioner is exposed to the possibility of financial liability—that the therapist intentionally or unintentionally harmed a client in some specific manner, and as a consequence may be financially accountable. While such suits are still relatively rare,[3] there remains the possibility, especially in an increasingly litigious society, that

[2]In a recent national survey of 718 psychologists, Tucker and Lublin (1994) reported that, partially as a result of concerns over confidentiality, 38% refused to participate in managed care programs.

[3]According to available data from the American Psychological Association Insurance Trust, the probability of a psychologist being sued is extremely small—less than half of 1 percent (Bennett, Bryant, VanderBos, & Greenwood, 1990). Nevertheless, litigation remains an ever present possibility and in certain cases, such as sexual contact with clients or suits over repressed memories presumably induced by a therapist, are increasing. All practitioners maintain professional liability insurance, in varying amounts of coverage, for safety as well as peace of mind.

clients may file a legal action against a therapist for one or more of the following reasons: malpractice, breach of confidentiality, sexual misconduct, negligence, breach of contract (in regard to such items as fees, promised availability), failure to protect them from a dangerous person's conduct, or even for exercising undue influence over a patient. Bringing such charges into civil court, the client or family may sue for compensatory damages (compensating them for their loss) as well as punitive damages (punishing the therapist for reckless, wanton, or heinous behavior) (Vesper & Brock, 1991).

Malpractice, either deliberately or through ineptitude or carelessness, represents the most likely form of alleged wrongful behavior to produce client litigation. Here the therapist is accused of failing to render professional services or exercise the degree of skill ordinarily expected of other professionals in a similar situation (Corey, Corey, & Callanan, 1998). That is, professional negligence is said to have occurred; the claim is that the therapist departed from usual practices or did not exercise sufficient care in carrying out his or her responsibilities. (One important note: Practitioners are not expected always to make correct judgments or predict the future, but they are expected to possess and exercise the knowledge and skills common to members of their profession.) If sued for malpractice, they will be judged in terms of actions appropriate to other therapists with similar qualifications and duties. However, if they acted in good faith but the client failed to make progress, they are not liable, if they made a mistake that knowledgeable and skilled colleagues, similarly trained, could ordinarily make.

Common types of malpractice suits include:

- Failure to obtain or document **informed consent** (including failing to discuss significant risks, benefits, and alternative procedures) prior to commencing treatment
- Misdiagnosis (as in the case where a client attempts suicide)
- Practicing outside of one's area of competence
- Negligent or improper treatment
- Abandonment of a client
- Physical contact or sexual relations with a client
- Failure to prevent clients from harming themselves or others
- Failure to consult another practitioner or refer a client
- Failure to adequately supervise students or assistants

Perhaps the most common grounds for a malpractice suit involve sexual contact (Stromberg & Dellinger, 1993), and some states have now declared such activity to be a felony. The number of sexually based complaints is increasing, although it is unclear whether the incidence of sexual relations with clients is accelerating or whether clients are more likely to come forward today than in the past. In either case, as attorneys Stromberg and Dellinger (p. 8) note, "for therapists who have engaged in sexual intimacies with patients, a *finding of liability against the therapist is highly likely*" (italics theirs). Any initial consent by the patient is not a defense, since it is assumed that the client may be experiencing emotional distress, feel low self-esteem, and thus to be in a position of heightened vulnerability to sexual exploitation than under normal circumstances. A history of emotional or sexual abuse may increase vulnerability and compound the subsequent damage inflicted (Pope, 1994).

Under such circumstances, the courts reason that refusing the overtures of an unscrupulous therapist, whose motives the client wants to trust, may be difficult, especially if the therapist labels such advances as "therapeutic" for relieving the client's problems (Welfel, 1998). Suicide attempts, hospitalizations, and prolonged symptoms of post-traumatic stress may occur; moreover, following the experience, the client may be reluctant to reenter therapy with another therapist precisely at a time when such treatment is most needed (Bates & Brodsky, 1989). If the therapist is found guilty by the court, the likelihood of a suspended or lost license is substantial, as is the probability of losing a malpractice suit amounting to hundreds of thousands of dollars (Reaves & Ogloff, 1996).

In general, for a malpractice suit to succeed, four elements must be present: (1) a professional relationship existed, so that the therapist incurred a legal duty to care; (2) there is a demonstrable standard of care that was breached when the practitioner performed below that standard; (3) the plaintiff suffered harm or injury, physical or psychological; and (4) the professional's breach of duty as a result of negligence or injurious actions was the direct cause of the harm done the plaintiff. The plaintiff must prove all four elements exist in order to win the malpractice litigation (Bennett, Bryant, VandenBos, & Greenwood, 1990). Corey, Corey, and Callanan (1998) offer this example: In the case of suicide, could a practitioner have foreseen (that is, made a comprehensive risk assessment and documented his or her findings) the suicide risk, and did he or she take reasonable care or precautions, again well documented, to prevent the self-destructive act?

Ways of avoiding a malpractice suit include keeping accurate and complete records of treatment plans, following informed consent procedures, protecting confidentiality of client records to the extent possible, consulting with colleagues when in doubt, operating within an area in which one was trained or studied later in order to maintain a level of competency, taking professional responsibilities seriously and not abandoning a difficult or frustrating case, making referrals when appropriate, and making certain that clients will be seen in emergency situations when the therapist is away. Beyond that, as we have noted, individual professional liability insurance is necessary for all marital/family therapists (unless the organization for which they work carries malpractice insurance covering them) if they are to afford the costs of litigation. Most professional organizations, such as the American Psychological Association and the American Association for Marriage and Family Therapy, offer group professional liability (malpractice) insurance for purchase by their members.

MAINTAINING ETHICAL STANDARDS

Beyond legal regulation through licensing or certification, professions rely on self-regulation through a variety of procedures—mandatory continuing education as prerequisite for license renewal, peer review, consultation with colleagues, and so forth—to monitor the professional activities of their members. Codes of ethics, in particular, offer standards whose potential violations may provoke both informal and formal discipline (Huber, 1994). The former involves pressures colleagues may exert upon violators through consultations regarding questionable practices; the latter may involve censure by professional associations, in some cases barring violators from continued membership.

Professional Codes of Ethics

Should an ethics committee, in response to a colleague or client complaint, determine that a practitioner has violated the code of ethics of his or her profession, a range of sanctions may be imposed (see Table 17.1 for the American Psychological Association guidelines). Generally speaking, the degree of seriousness of the violation is the major determinant of what level of sanction an ethics committee might impose (Keith-Spiegel & Koocher, 1985). These code violations range from behavior reflecting poor judgment compared with prevailing standards but without malicious intent (for example, advertising infractions; inappropriate public statements), calling for educative resolutions (Level I), to those cases where substantial harm to others has resulted from the practitioner's behavior and that person is not prone to rehabilitation (defrauding insurance carriers; sexual exploitation), calling for expulsion from the professional organization (Level III). Ethics committees may be lenient

Table 17.1   Levels of Ethical Sanctions and Categories

Level	Sanction	Rationale/Mediating Factors
Level 1A	Educative Advisory	Not clearly unethical, but in poor taste or insufficiently cautious, this offense might fall in "gray areas" or deal with newly emerging issues and problems.
Level 1B	Educative Warning	A "cease and desist" notice from an ethics committee might accompany a finding that a mild or minor infraction had occurred
Level IIA	Reprimand	A finding of clearly ethical misconduct, when the psychologist should have known better, although the consequence of the action or inaction may have been minor.
Level IIB	Censure	Deliberate or persistent behavior that could lead to substantial harm of the client or public, although little harm may actually have accrued.
Level IIIA	Stipulated Resignation or Permitted Resignation	Continuing or dramatic misconduct producing genuine hazard to clients, the public, and the profession; questionable motivation to change or demonstrate concern for the behavior in question. May include "no reapplication" stipulation.
Level IIIB	Expulsion (Voided Membership)	Individual clients or others with whom one worked are substantially injured with serious questions about the potential rehabilitation of the psychologist in question.

Source: Keith-Spiegel & Koocher, 1985, p. 46

toward a nonmalevolent first offender, offering him or her an educative solution; that same offense, committed repeatedly by an experienced but recalcitrant practitioner would be greeted with more severe sanctions.

Ethical codes define standards of conduct subscribed to by the members of the profession, aiding members in their decision making with clients whenever possible areas of conflict arise. As Van Hoose and Kottler (1985) point out, such codes help clarify the member's responsibilities to clients as well as society as a whole. Through membership in a professional organization, the member pledges to abide by a set of ethical standards that helps reassure the public that he or she will demonstrate sensible and responsible behavior. In clinical practice, this means guiding members in identifying situations in which an ethical decision is called for with a client (for example, breaking confidentiality to protect the client or another person), formulating an ethical course of action, and implementing an action plan (Huber & Baruth, 1987). In the case of the AAMFT Code of Ethics (1998) (presented in its entirety in Appendix C of this text), eight areas are highlighted:

Responsibility to clients
Confidentiality
Professional competence and integrity
Responsibility to students, employees, and supervisees
Responsibility to research participants
Responsibility to the profession
Financial arrangements
Advertising

Values, Ethical Dilemmas, and Family Therapy

Some unique ethical issues arise as therapy shifts from an individual focus to one that involves a marital/family system. For example, to whom and for whom does the therapist have primary loyalty and responsibility? The identified patient? The separate family members as individuals? The entire family? Only those members who choose to attend family sessions? To whom does the therapist report when working with children? Is the primary goal one of increasing family harmony or maximizing individual fulfillment? (Patten, Barnett, & Houlihan, 1991).

Wendorf and Wendorf (1985) contend that family therapy, because of its nonlinear, systemic outlook, calls for a rethinking of traditional ethical standards based upon individual treatment. They believe the therapist's task is to help people become more competent in solving their problems both as individuals and as family systems. Consistent with this goal, they urge therapists, in addition to helping with problem solving, to adopt a broader view, focusing on the context of a family's interactive behavior, and to remain mindful of the "short- and long-term needs, growth, and welfare of the other individuals and subsystems that are involved in this mutually recursive system of influence" (p. 447). Boszormenyi-Nagy (1985), on the other hand, offering a therapeutic approach immersed in ethical decision making (see Chapter 6), argues that whether therapy is carried out in an individual or family mode, the individual remains accountable for the consequences of his or her decisions. Moreover, he maintains that the therapist is accountable for therapy's effects on all family members, those present during sessions as well as those who stay away (Boszormenyi-Nagy & Krasner, 1986).

Most family therapists struggle at one time or another with the ethical dilemma of family needs versus individual needs (Green & Hansen, 1989). More than academic hairsplitting is involved here. Early feminist thinking represented by Hare-Mustin (1980) warned that "family therapy may be dangerous to your health"; the changes that most benefited the entire family were not in every case in the best interests of each of its members. Hare-Mustin was especially concerned that female family members not be influenced by therapists to subjugate their individual rights for the sake of family needs, further perpetuating society's gender roles. Margolin (1982) too was concerned that family therapists might endorse—and thus perpetuate—some familiar sexist myths concerning women: that remaining in a marriage is usually best for women, that her career deserves less attention than her husband's, that child rearing is a mother's sole responsibility, and in general that a husband's needs are more significant than a wife's. Now two decades after these warnings, family therapists have generally become more gender-sensitive and informed, beginning in their training, in addressing gender issues.

Family therapists inevitably engage in an active valuing process with families, whether intentionally or not. As Doherty and Boss (1991) point out, the notion of value neutrality by the therapist is naive and no longer even debatable. They maintain that family therapists take value positions continually in their thinking as well as their interventions with families. As they put it, values and ethics are closely related; values are the beliefs and preferences that undergird the ethical decisions made by individuals and groups. For therapists, as for everyone else, values are the cherished beliefs and preferences that guide human decisions.

No therapy is value-free, whether it be Minuchin's notion of how best to achieve optimum family structure or Haley's view of the proper hierarchy within the family or Bowen's emphasis on the importance of separating intellectual processes from more emotional ones or the feminist insistence that outmoded sexual stereotyping into gender-determined roles is oppressive and ultimately destructive to both men and women. Family therapists should and do have value systems; rather than pretend they don't, they need to search out what their personal values are, and be aware of their effect on the family they are treating. Should a conflict in values between therapist and clients occur (for example, regarding child-rearing techniques, such as spanking, or the role of grandparents in the family), the therapist would do well to state explicitly what his or her values are without insisting that they also become the values clients must live by.

Because specific therapist values (attitudes toward divorce, extramarital affairs, gender-defined roles in the family or society at large) may be enormously influential in the process of marital or family therapy, guiding decision making, therapists must examine their own attitudes closely. The danger here is that the therapist might be biased against families whose attitudes differ radically from his or her own, or might side with one family member (say, a father) against the behavior and stated attitudes of other members (an adolescent). In another scenario, a family therapist—deliberately or unwittingly, consciously or unconsciously—may proselytize for maintaining a current marriage, when one or both partners wish to divorce.

Whether the family therapist's values are such that he or she chooses to be responsible to the individual as opposed to, say, the marriage, may have significant consequences. To cite a common problem described by Bodin (1983), suppose a husband is contemplating divorcing his wife, an action his wife opposes. The husband may feel his individual happiness is so compromised by remaining in the marriage that he hopes the therapist attaches greater importance to individual well-being than to maintaining some abstraction called the "family system." The wife, on the other hand, hopes the therapist gives higher priority to collective well-being, helping individuals adjust their expectations for the sake of remaining together. Many therapists caught in such a situation take the position that a strife-torn marriage all but guarantees unhappiness for everyone, including the children. Others argue that the stress and uncertainty of separation and divorce may do irreparable damage to the children and thus the maintenance of family life, imperfect as it is, is preferable to the breakup of the family. As Bodin observes, the therapist's position may have a profound impact not only in terms of the rapport established with the various family members but also on the therapist's formulation of the problems, the goals, and the plans for treatment.

Morrison, Layton, and Newman (1982) identify four sets of ethical conflicts in the therapist's decision-making process. We have touched on the first: Whose interest should the therapist serve? When working with an individual client, the therapist must decide whether, and to what extent, to involve family members. On the other hand, when working with a family, should the therapist see certain individuals or combinations of family members separately? How should confidentiality be handled under such circumstances?

The second set of ethical dilemmas, according to Morrison, Layton, and Newman, involves the handling of secrets. Should parental secrets (for example, sexual problems) be aired before the family or be brought up in a separate couple's session? How should an extramarital affair—hidden from the spouse but revealed to the therapist in an individual session—be handled? What about family secrets—incest between the father and teenage daughter, or inferred physical abuse of the wife or young children, or child neglect? Here the therapist has legal responsibilities that supersede confidentiality; he or she must report the possibility of abuse or neglect to the police or child welfare authorities, even in the absence of proof. In such a situation, the therapist must make careful observations of family interactions, formulate an ethical course of action, and take steps to ensure the safety and well-being of family members.

A third set of ethical considerations concerns the use of diagnostic labeling of individuals, since such labels may ultimately be used by others in litigation (such as child custody disputes) or other forms of intrafamilial power struggles. Fourth, Morrison, Layton, and Newman point to the need for therapists to be aware of their power to increase or decrease marital or family conflict. They must be careful not to impose traditional male/female role expectations that may be disadvantageous to a particular family. They also run the risk of unconsciously being agents of the parents against the children, the children against the parents, or of one parent against the other. More than most therapists, family therapists must continue to wrestle with the question of whose agent they are.

Undertaking therapeutic work with a family, then, poses a variety of complications with respect to the therapist's professional responsibilities. The help offered to one family member may be temporarily depriving or disturbing to another, especially in a rigid family system. A preference for one or the other spouse implies favoritism and, potentially, the loss of necessary impartiality. As Margolin (1982) observes:

> Attempting to balance one's therapeutic responsibilities toward individual family members and toward the family as a whole involves intricate judgments. Since neither of these responsibilities cancels out the importance of the other, the family therapist cannot afford blind pursuit of either extreme, that is, always doing what is in each individual's best interests or always maintaining the stance as family advocate. (p. 790)

Confidentiality

When a client enters a professional relationship with a therapist, the latter takes on the ethical responsibility of safeguarding the former from revealing what was discussed during the therapeutic relationship. Confidentiality, protecting the client from unauthorized disclosures of personal information by the therapist without prior client consent, has long been a hallmark of individual psychotherapy. Its rationale is based on encouraging clients to develop the trust necessary for them to make full disclosures without fear of exposure outside the consultation room.

In marital/family therapy, some therapists take the position that they must ensure that information given to them in confidence by a family member will be treated as it would be in individual therapy, and thus not be divulged to a spouse or other family member (although they may encourage the individual to share his or her secret in a subsequent conjoint session). Other therapists, in an effort to avoid an alliance with a family member, refuse to see any member separately, in effect insisting that secrets be brought out into the open to the marital partner or family in sessions together. Still other therapists, if they see individually, or talk to by telephone, or receive a written message from a family member, tell the informant beforehand that whatever is divulged may be communicated to the others, if in the judgment of the therapist it would benefit the couple or family. Whatever the procedure, it is essential to ethical practice that the therapist makes his or her stand on confidentiality clear to each family member from the outset of therapy.

Confidentiality between clinician and patient had its origin as far back as the sixteenth century, and was intended originally to protect patients with contagious diseases from community discovery and certain social ostracism (Huber, 1994). Confidentiality is still intended to assure the right to privacy, and a therapist is ethically obligated to refrain from revealing private client information obtained in therapy unless given client authorization to do so. However, there are exceptions where confidentiality can be breached. Corey, Corey, and Callanan (1998) list the following exceptions:

- When necessary to protect clients from harming themselves or when they pose a danger to others

- When mandated by law, as in reporting child abuse, incest, child neglect, or elder abuse
- When the therapist is a defendant in a civil, criminal, or disciplinary action arising from the therapy
- When a waiver has been obtained in writing

As we observed earlier in this chapter, the increased use of "third party payors" for therapeutic services often calls for disclosure of personal information to an insurance company or managed care organization. This loss of privacy may become a therapeutic issue—clients holding back information—when peer reviews or utilization reviews of therapeutic procedures require therapists to inform clients that some information may be revealed (Miller, 1996).

The duty to protect clients from harming themselves, and protecting others from potentially dangerous clients are especially important professional responsibilities (Swenson, 1997). In the former, therapists may intervene—call in family members, the police, get the client to a hospital emergency room—if they believe a client is seriously considering suicide. Indeed, the failure to prevent suicide has become a leading reason for successful malpractice suits against therapists (Szasz, 1986).

A therapist who determines that there is clear and imminent danger to someone the client vows to harm must take personal action and inform the responsible authorities; the therapist also has a duty to warn and protect the intended victim because the courts have ruled (Tarasoff decision) that "the rights of clients to privacy ends where the public peril begins" (Fulero, 1988). It often poses a serious dilemma for therapists—deciding the client is sufficiently dangerous to an identifiable victim (not just letting off steam about someone) that reasonable steps to warn that person must be taken, thus breaching confidentiality (Ahia & Martin, 1993). While no therapist is expected to make perfect predictions of calculable danger, care is necessary in making the assessment of risk to a potential victim; good written records should be kept, and discussions with supervisors, consultants, or even attorneys are advisable (Monahan, 1993). Some states protect therapists from malpractice lawsuits for breaching confidentiality if they can establish having acted in good faith to protect third parties (Stromberg, Schneider, & Joondeph, 1993).

Similarly, mandatory reporting laws, while they differ from state to state, all require therapists to disclose suspicions of incest or child abuse to the proper child protective agency. If a therapist has reason to suspect (or a child discloses) abuse or neglect, therapists are held liable if they fail to do so. Once again, states provide immunity from civil lawsuit for reporting suspected abusers. Sometimes problems arise because the therapist has previously failed to inform clients of this limitation on confidentiality (Nicolai & Scott, 1994) and sometimes therapists, in violation of the law, choose not to report suspected abusers for what they consider to be therapeutic reasons (Kalichman, & Craig, 1991).

The limits of confidentiality should be spelled out by the therapist at the start of therapy, lest family members agree to proceed while operating under wrong assumptions (Doherty & Boss, 1991). The issue is linked to informed consent, which we consider next.

Informed Consent

The matters of informed consent and the right to refuse treatment have become critical ethical issues in the practice of marital and family therapy. Gill (1982) argues that before families enter therapy they must be adequately informed concerning the nature of the process they are about to undertake. The purposes of the sessions, typical procedures, risks of possible negative outcomes (divorce, job changes), possible benefits, costs, what behavior to expect from the therapist, the limits of confidentiality, information provided third-party payors, the conditions that might precipitate a referral to another therapist or agency, available alternative treatments—these issues all require explanation at the outset, before each client agrees to participate. Two issues are operating here—full disclosure by the therapist so the client can decide whether to proceed, and free consent (deciding to engage in an activity without coercion or pressure) (Welfel, 1998). In some cases, therapists provide written documents ("Patient's Rights and Responsibilities") to accompany their oral presentations, to be read, signed, and kept at home for future reference.

Bray, Shepherd, and Hays (1985) go further, insisting the systems-oriented therapist tell the family that the therapeutic focus will be the family system rather than the specific set of symptoms of the identified patient. Failure to adequately inform clients of possible risks runs the risk of malpractice suits for negligence. Some therapists deal with this issue by handing clients a brochure describing issues around informed consent, or in some cases have the information posted in their waiting areas.

How should a therapist deal with family members who refuse treatment? Doherty and Boss (1991) focus on the issue of *coercion* regarding reluctant adults or children, as in the case where therapists insist that all members attend before family therapy can get under way. Willing members are thus in a position of being coerced by denying them access to treatment unless they successfully persuade the others to participate. Both these authors as well as Margolin (1982) agree that a therapist with such a policy would do well to have a list of competent referral sources where the family members willing to take part might go for help.

Children present another thorny issue. Here, therapists need to inform children at their level of understanding of what is likely to transpire in family therapy and then ask for their consent to participate. Consent should also be obtained before videotaping, audiotaping, or observing families behind a one-way mirror. The entire issue of informed consent is gaining prominence, fitting in as it does with current concerns over patient and consumer rights.

Privileged Communication

Client privilege, particularly **privileged communication,** is closely linked to confidentiality (Arthur & Swanson, 1993). Privileged communication is a legal right, protecting a client from having his or her confidences revealed by a therapist from the witness stand during court proceedings without his or her prior consent. Since the privilege belongs to the client, the client's waiving that privilege leaves the therapist with no legal grounds for withholding the information. The issue, however, in family therapy, is who is the client: the individual, the couple, the family? In the case of a divorcing pair, suppose one spouse seeks testimony from the therapist while the other does not wish the information revealed?

State statutes vary widely in regard to who "owns" the right to waive privilege regarding information revealed in conjoint therapy sessions (Gumper & Sprenkle, 1981). Because this is often an awkward problem for marital/family therapists, these authors suggest therapists not only acquaint themselves with the laws of their state, but also try to get the couple to agree in writing that in the event of any court action neither will seek disclosures of what transpired in joint sessions with the therapist. Even so, courts may differ in the way they honor such agreements. Generally speaking, the therapist should always demand a written release from a client before revealing any information to others.

Therapeutic Power and Responsibility

Because the therapist is in a position of power, there is the possibility of imposing control over client families or assuming responsibility for defining how change should occur.[4] For example, criticism of structural therapies, such as practiced by Minuchin, has focused on the danger that the role of the therapist as an active agent of change may shift responsibility for change from the family to the therapist (Fieldsteel, 1982). Corey, Corey, and Callanan (1998) question whether new sets of (therapist) values may be imposed on the family as family members defer their own judgment to the views of the structural therapist, who has joined the family system in order to help families transform themselves.

Similarly, in strategic or systemic therapies, especially when paradoxical techniques are employed, care must be exercised when offering an intervention intended to escalate the symptoms ("Practice being depressed") by steering the family into a course of action based on the therapist's counterintuitive directive (Doherty & Boss, 1991). Here the therapist can never be certain how the family will interpret and respond to a particular intervention, particularly when offered as a prescriptive directive given without explicit explanation or rationale. Although the therapist's intention is to provoke defiance in the symptomatic client (who presumably stops being depressed), that outcome is by no means certain. As Huber and Baruth (1987, p. 54) point out, "paradoxical procedures are clearly unethical if they are used as a spur-of-the-moment ploy based on limited data." On the other hand, they are quick to add that when carried out in a careful, planned fashion, by competent and experienced therapists who understand the role of the symptom within the family relationship system, such procedures can be both ethical and therapeutic. Doherty and Boss (1991) agree that paradoxical interventions are not inherently manipulative to clients, although they can be used in a manipulative fashion by some therapists.

The use of power, and what some critics label as deceptive practice, is at the basis of the controversy over these strategic maneuvers. Doherty and Boss (1991)

---

[4]Social constructionist therapists (Chapter 13) attempt to circumvent this problem by deliberately avoiding the role of expert intending to change family behavior and interactive patterns.

contend that in the absence of harmful consequences, paradoxical interventions can be ethically justified. They view the use of prescribing a symptom in an effort to eliminate it as ethically equivalent to other advice on how best to avoid a symptom. In their view, paradoxical procedures are not in and of themselves necessarily deceptive. They maintain that the key to employing both straightforward and paradoxical methods is to pass this simple test: Do no harm. The ethical issue concerns whether the therapist assumes inappropriate power over the clients through deceptive means that violate client autonomy.

Although intriguing, paradoxical procedures may be powerful and do pose an ethical problem if they are used in ways that invade client autonomy or undermine therapist trustworthiness (Brown & Slee, 1986). As Weeks and L'Abate (1982) put it: "Paradoxical interventions must be carefully formulated, appropriately timed, convincingly delivered, and followed up. In order to make paradoxical interventions, the therapist must first have skills necessary to make active and direct interventions" (p. 249).

Training and Supervision

Adequate preparation for doing marital/family therapy is still more the exception than the rule for most mental health professionals (Margolin, 1982). Therapists need periodic upgrading of their clinical skills as new developments in the field (for example, gender-sensitive therapy, postmodern therapeutic approaches, psychoeducation, multicultural considerations) and new populations served (AIDS patients and their families; substance abusers) require continuing education.

Exceeding the bounds of one's competence and experience in assessing and treating marital or family problems is considered unethical. Therefore, therapists must know the boundaries of their own competence and refer to fellow professionals those clients who require services beyond the therapist's professional training or experience. Reaching a prolonged therapeutic impasse with a family should also alert a therapist that a reassessment is in order and that a consultation with a peer who has expertise in the particular troublesome area might help resolve the problem and move the therapeutic process forward.

Clients with whom therapists experience serious and unresolvable conflicts in values should also be directed to other therapists competent to deal with their problems. Even highly experienced family therapists seek the input of a consultant for purposes of verifying diagnostic impressions or confirming therapeutic strategies. In addition, psychiatric consultants may be called upon to administer medication (for example, antidepression drugs) or hospitalize a client if the family therapist lacks hospital privileges or has not dealt with hospitalization in his or her training.

Supervision presents its own set of ethical issues. As we indicated in the previous chapter, effective supervision calls for more than the accumulation of clinical experience or even the achievement of clinical skills. Someone who takes on the responsibility for supervising others on specific cases should acquire training in the supervisory process (Liddle, 1991). Supervising trainees or fellow professionals calls for attending regularly (weekly or biweekly) to the supervisee's treatment plan and record keeping, as well as keeping track of family problems and the ongoing therapeutic process. Supervisors may sit in on a family session, or more likely observe the treatment through a one-way mirror or listen to audiotapes of the session. The more client families the trainee undertakes, the closer the supervision needed.

Supervisors are ultimately responsible, both ethically and legally, for the actions of their trainees; thus, they must see to it that their trainees comply with all relevant legal and ethical standards of the profession. Sherry (1991) contends that supervisors bear the responsibility for protecting the welfare of the client, the supervisee, the public, and the profession as a whole. Of these, client welfare takes first priority.

To maintain ethical standards, supervisees must inform clients that they are trainees, that they are being supervised (thus complete confidentiality cannot be assured although it will be protected by the supervisor), and that their session may be video- or audiotaped or observed behind a one-way mirror. As Harrar, VandeCreek, and Knapp (1990) observe, supervisors in effect have both the final ethical and legal responsibility—including professional liability—for decisions regarding clients made by their supervisees.

SUMMARY

Professional practice in marital/family therapy is regulated by legal statutes and self-regulated by ethical codes, peer review, continuing education, and consultation. Forty-one states currently license marriage and family therapists as qualified health care providers. Managed care organizations, dedicated to containing costs and insisting on therapist accountability, increasingly are administering and financing the delivery of mental health services in the United States.

The ethical code of professional organizations, defining standards of conduct for members of the profession, offers guidance in identifying clinical situations in which the therapist must make ethical decisions, and offers principles on which those decisions can best be based. Family therapists frequently must deal with the dilemma involved in concerning themselves with individual needs versus family needs.

Confidentiality of a client's disclosures, providing clients with informed consent before commencing treatment, and assuring clients of their legal protection through privileged communication are common ethical concerns. Therapists must take care in how they use their power and influence with families. Ethically, trainees should not exceed the boundaries of their competence and experience but instead should seek consultation and supervision. Supervisors are ultimately responsible, ethically and legally, for the actions of their supervisees

Appendixes

Appendix A A Comparison of Theoretical Viewpoints in Family Therapy

Model	Primary Theme	Unit of Study	Time Frame	Title or Derivation	Leading Figures	Major Concepts
Psychodynamic	Unresolved conflicts from past continue to attach themselves to current situations	Monadic; individual intrapsychic conflict brought to current family	Past; early internalized family conflicts lead to interpersonal conflicts	Psychoanalytic	Ackerman Scharff & Scharff	Interlocking pathology; scapegoating; role complementarity; projective identification
Experiential	Free choice; self-determination; growth of the self; maturity achieved by overcoming impasses in process of gaining personal fulfillment	Dyadic; problems arise from flawed interactions and communication lapses between family members (e.g., husband and wife)	Present; here-and-now data from immediate, ongoing interactions	Symbolic-Experiential Gestalt Human Validation Emotionally Focused	Whitaker Kempler Satir Greenberg; Johnson	Symbolic factors represent family's internal world and determine meaning given external reality Self-awareness of the moment Self-esteem; clarity of communication Explore inner experiences and relationships
Transgenerational	Emotional attachments to one's family of origin need to be resolved	Triadic; problems arise and are maintained by relational binds with others	Past and present; current marital relations assumed to result from partner's fusions to their families of origin	Family Systems Theory Contextual	Bowen; Kerr; Friedman Boszormenyi-Nagy	Differentiation of self vs. fusion; triangles; multigenerational transmission process Family ledger; ethics; family legacies, entitlements
Structural	Symptoms in an individual are rooted in the context of family transaction patterns, and family restructuring must occur before symptoms are relieved	Triadic; family enmeshment and disengagement involve family subsystems and family system as a whole	Present; ongoing interactions maintained by unadaptive family organization, typically unable to deal with transitions in the family life cycle	Structural Family Theory	Minuchin; Montalvo, Aponte; Fishman	Boundaries; subsystems; coalitions; enmeshment and disengagement

Model	Primary Theme	Unit of Study	Time Frame	Title or Derivation	Leading Figures	Major Concepts
Strategic	Reluctant communication patterns offer clues to family rules and possible dysfunction; a symptom represents a strategy for controlling a relationship while claiming it to be involuntary	Dyadic and Triadic; symptoms are interpersonal communications between at least two, and probably three participants in reciprocal relationships	Present; current problems or symptoms are maintained by ongoing, repetitive sequences between family members	Communication Theory; Strategic Family Theory	Haley; Madanes; Weakland; Watzlawick; Jackson	Symmetrical and complementary communication patterns; paradox; family hierarchy
Milan	Dysfunctional families are caught up in destructive "games" and are guided by belief systems that do not fit the realities of their lives	Triadic; problems express connecting relationship patterns between family members	Present; recognition of circular nature of current problems helps family abandon previous limited linear perspectives	Systemic Family Theory	Selvini-Palazzoli; Boscolo; Cecchin; Prata	Paradox and counter-paradox; invariant prescriptions; circular questioning; second-order cybernetics
Cognitive-Behavioral	Personal functioning is determined by the reciprocal interaction of behavior and its controlling social conditions	Monadic; symptomatic person is the problem; linear view of causality	Present; maladaptive behavior in an individual is maintained by current reinforcements from others	Learning Theory; Social Learning Theory	Paterson; Stuart; Liberman; Alexander; Falloon; Ellis; Beck	Conditioning; reinforcement; shaping; modeling; schemas
Social Constructionist	People use language to subjectively construct their views of reality and provide the basis for how they create "stories" about themselves	Triadic; family problems are stories its members have agreed to tell about themselves	Past and present; current problems based on past "stories" that influence current choices and behavior	Social Construction Theory	deShazer; White; O'Hanlon; Goolishian; Hoffman; Andersen	No fixed truths, only multiple perspectives of reality; constructions of meaning

Appendix B A Comparison of Therapeutic Techniques and Goals in Family Therapy

Model	Role of Therapist	Assessment Procedures	Key Methods of Intervention	Insight vs. Action	Title or Derivation	Goals of Treatment
Psychodynamic	Neutral, blank screen upon whom each family member projects fantasies	Unstructured; ongoing effort to uncover hidden conflict within and between family members	Interpretations regarding the unconscious meaning of individual verbalizations and behavior and their impact on family functioning	Insight leads to understanding, conflict reduction, and ultimately individual intrapsychic and system change	Psychoanalytic Object Relations	Individual intrapsychic change; resolution of family pathogenic conflict Detriangulation; removal of projections; individuation
Experiential	Egalitarian; active facilitator providing family with new experiences through the therapeutic encounter	Unstructured; search for suppressed feelings and impulses that block growth and fulfillment	Confrontation to provoke self-discovery; self-disclosure by therapist; exercises (e.g., sculpting, family reconstruction) to uncover previously unexpressed inner conflicts	Self-awareness of one's immediate existence leads to choice, responsibility, and change	Symbolic-Experiential Gestalt Human Validation Emotionally Focused	Simultaneous sense of togetherness and healthy separation and autonomy Genuineness; learning to express one's sense of being Building self-esteem; relieving family pain; overcoming blockages to personal growth Overcoming negative interactive patterns
Transgenerational	Coach; direct but non-confrontational; detriangulated from family fusion Aids family in developing relational fairness	Family evaluation interviews with any combination of family members; genograms Attention to intergenerational indebtedness	Teaching differentiation; individuation; taking "I"-stands; reopening cut-off relations with extended family Balancing family ledgers	Rational processes used to gain insight into current relationships and intergenerational experiences; leads to action with family of origin	Family Systems Theory Contextual	Anxiety reduction, symptom relief, and increased self differentiation of individuals leads to family system change Restoration of trust, fairness, ethical responsibility

Model	Role of Therapist	Assessment Procedures	Key Methods of Intervention	Insight vs. Action	Title or Derivation	Goals of Treatment
Structural	Active; stage director manipulates family structure to change dysfunctional sets	Observation of family transactional patterns for clues to family structure; family mapping; enactments; tracking	Joining; accommodating; reframing; helping families create flexible boundaries and integrated subsystems	Action precedes understanding; change in transactional patterns leads to new experiences and corresponding insights	Structural Family Theory	Restructured family organization; change in dysfunctional transactional patterns; symptom reduction in individual members
Strategic	Active; manipulative problem-focused; prescriptive; paradoxical	Unstructured; search for family's repetitive, destructive behavior patterns and flawed solutions that perpetuate the presenting problem	Paradoxical interventions; prescribing the symptom; therapeutic double binds; directives; pretend techniques; relabeling	Action-oriented; symptom reduction and behavior change brought about through directives rather than insight and understanding	Communication Theory; Strategic Family Theory	Symptom relief; resolution of presenting problem
Milan	Neutral; active therapeutic partner; offers hypotheses as new information for family belief system; use of reflecting team behind one-way mirror	Unstructured; nonmanipulative; collaborates with family in developing systemic hypotheses regarding their problems	Positive connotations; circular questioning; reframing; paradox; invariant prescription; rituals	Emphasis on family gaining new meaning rather than insight or action based on therapist choice of therapeutic outcome	Systemic Family Theory	System change chosen by family as a result of new meaning given to their life patterns; interruption of destructive family "games"
Cognitive-Behavioral	Teacher; trainer; model of desired behavior; contract negotiator	Structured; reliance on formal standardized tests and questionnaires; behavioral analysis before commencing treatment	Reinforcement of desired behaviors; skills training; contingency contracting; positive reciprocity between marital partners as well as parents and children	Actions taught to reward desired outcomes and ignore or punish undesired behavior; unconcerned with insight	Learning Theory; Social Learning Theory	Modification of behavioral consequences between persons in order to eliminate maladaptive behavior and/or alleviate presenting symptoms

continued

Appendix B *(continued)*

Model	Role of Therapist	Procedures	Key Methods of Intervention	Insight vs. Action	Title or Derivation	Goals of Treatment
Social Constructionist	Collaborative; engages in therapeutic conversation; non-expert co-constructing meaning and understanding	Unstructured; examination of explanations and interpretations families have used to account for their views of "truth"	Solution-focus rather than focus on problems; miracle questions; exception-finding questions; externalization of oppressive problems; use of reflecting teams and two-way mirrors	Emphasis on gaining new meaning through narrative reconstructions of stories families have told about themselves	Social Construction Theory	Learning and creating new viewpoints by giving new meanings or constructions to old sets of problems

C

AAMFT Code of Ethics

The Board of Directors of the American Association for Marriage and Family Therapy (AAMFT) hereby promulgates, pursuant to Article 2, Section 2.013 of the Association's Bylaws, the Revised AAMFT Code of Ethics, effective July 1, 1998. The AAMFT Code of Ethics is binding on Members of AAMFT in all membership categories, AAMFT Approved Supervisors, and applicants for membership and the Approved Supervisor designation (hereafter, AAMFT Member). If an AAMFT Member resigns in anticipation of, or during the course of an ethics investigation, the Ethics Committee will complete its investigation. Any publication of action taken by the Association will include the fact that the Member attempted to resign during the investigation. Marriage and family therapists are strongly encouraged to report alleged unethical behavior of colleagues to appropriate professional associations and state regulatory bodies.

1. RESPONSIBILITY TO CLIENTS

Marriage and family therapists advance the welfare of families and individuals. They respect the rights of those persons seeking their assistance, and make reasonable efforts to ensure that their services are used appropriately.

1.1 Marriage and family therapists do not discriminate against or refuse professional service to anyone on the basis of race, gender, religion, national origin, or sexual orientation.

1.2 Marriage and family therapists are aware of their influential position with respect to clients, and they avoid exploiting the trust and dependency of such persons. Therapists, therefore, make every effort to avoid dual relationships with clients that could impair professional judgment or increase the risk of exploitation. When a dual relationship cannot be avoided, therapists take appropriate professional precautions to ensure judgment is not impaired and no exploitation occurs. Examples of such dual relationships include, but are not limited to, business or close personal relationships with clients. Sexual intimacy with clients is prohibited. Sexual intimacy with former clients for two years following the termination of therapy is prohibited.

1.3   Marriage and family therapists do not use their professional relationships with clients to further their own interests.

1.4   Marriage and family therapists respect the right of clients to make decisions and to help them to understand the consequences of these decisions. Therapists clearly advise a client that a decision on marital status is the responsibility of the client.

1.5   Marriage and family therapists continue therapeutic relationships only so long as it is reasonably clear that clients are benefiting from the relationship.

1.6   Marriage and family therapists assist persons in obtaining other therapeutic services if the therapist is unable or unwilling, for appropriate reasons, to provide professional help.

1.7   Marriage and family therapists do not abandon or neglect clients in treatment without making reasonable arrangements for the continuation of such treatment.

1.8   Marriage and family therapists obtain written informed consent from clients before videotaping, audiorecording, or permitting third party observation.

2. CONFIDENTIALITY

Marriage and family therapists have unique confidentiality concerns because the client in a therapeutic relationship may be more than one person. Therapists respect and guard confidences of each individual client.

2.1   Marriage and family therapists may not disclose client confidences except: (a) as mandated by law; (b) to prevent a clear and immediate danger to a person or persons; (c) where the therapist is a defendant in a civil, criminal, or disciplinary action arising from the therapy (in which case client confidences may be disclosed only in the course of that action); or (d) if there is a waiver previously obtained in writing, and then such information may be revealed only in accordance with the terms of the waiver. In circumstances where more than one person in a family receives therapy, each such family member who is legally competent to execute a waiver must agree to the waiver required by subparagraph (d). Without such a waiver from each family member legally competent to execute a waiver, a therapist cannot disclose information received from any family member.

2.2   Marriage and family therapists use client and/or clinical materials in teaching, writing, and public presentations only if a written waiver has been obtained in accordance with Subprinciple 2.1(d), or when appropriate steps have been taken to protect client identity and confidentiality.

2.3   Marriage and family therapists store or dispose of client records in ways that maintain confidentiality.

3. PROFESSIONAL COMPETENCE AND INTEGRITY

Marriage and family therapists maintain high standards of professional competence and integrity.

3.1 Marriage and family therapists are in violation of this Code and subject to termination of membership or other appropriate action if they: (a) are convicted of any felony; (b) are convicted of a misdemeanor related to their qualifications or functions; (c) engage in conduct which could lead to conviction of a felony, or a misdemeanor related to their qualifications or functions; (d) are expelled from or disciplined by other professional organizations; (e) have their licenses or certificates suspended or revoked or are otherwise disciplined by regulatory bodies; (f) are no longer competent to practice marriage and family therapy because they are impaired due to physical or mental cues or the abuse of alcohol or other substances, or (g) fail to cooperate with the Association at any point from the inception of an ethical complaint through the completion of all proceedings regarding that complaint.

3.2 Marriage and family therapists seek appropriate professional assistance for their personal problems or conflicts that may impair work performance or clinical judgment.

3.3 Marriage and family therapists, as teachers, supervisors, and researchers, are dedicated to high standards of scholarship and present accurate information.

3.4 Marriage and family therapists remain abreast of new developments in family therapy knowledge and practice through educational activities.

3.5 Marriage and family therapists do not engage in sexual or other harassment or exploitation of clients, students, trainees, supervisees, employees, colleagues, research subjects, or actual or potential witnesses or complainants in investigations and ethical proceedings.

3.6 Marriage and family therapists do not diagnose, treat, or advise on problems outside the recognized boundaries of their competence.

3.7 Marriage and family therapists make efforts to prevent the distortion or misuse of their clinical and research findings.

3.8 Marriage and family therapists, because of their ability to influence and alter the lives of others, exercise special care when making public their professional recommendations and opinions through testimony or other public statements.

4. RESPONSIBILITY TO STUDENTS, EMPLOYEES, AND SUPERVISEES

Marriage and family therapists do not exploit the trust and dependency of students, employees, and supervisees.

4.1 Marriage and family therapists are aware of their influential positions with respect to students, employees, and supervisees, and they avoid exploiting the trust and dependency of such persons. Therapists, therefore, make every effort to avoid dual relationships that could impair professional judgment or increase the risk of exploitation. When a dual relationship cannot be avoided, therapists take appropriate professional precautions to ensure judgment is not impaired and no exploitation occurs. Examples of such dual relationships include, but are not limited to, business or close personal relationships with students, employees, or supervisees. Provision of therapy to students, employees, or supervisees is prohibited. Sexual intimacy with students or supervisees is prohibited.

4.2 Marriage and family therapists do not permit students, employees, or supervisees to perform or to hold themselves out as competent to perform professional services beyond their training, level of experience, and competence.

4.3 Marriage and family therapists do not disclose supervisee confidences except: (a) as mandated by law; (b) to prevent a clear and immediate danger to a person or persons; (c) where the therapist is a defendant in a civil, criminal, or disciplinary action arising from the supervision (in which case supervisee confidences may be disclosed only in the course of that action); (d) in educational or training settings where there are multiple supervisors, and then only to other professional colleagues who share responsibility for the training of the supervisee; or (e) if there is a waiver previously obtained in writing, and then such information may be revealed only in accordance with the terms of the waiver.

5. RESPONSIBILITY TO RESEARCH PARTICIPANTS

Investigators respect the dignity and protect the welfare of participants in research and are aware of federal and state laws and regulations and professional standards governing the conduct of research.

5.1 Investigators are responsible for making careful examinations of ethical acceptability in planning studies. To the extent that services to research participants may be compromised by participation in research, investigators seek the ethical advice of qualified professionals not directly involved in the investigation and observe safeguards to protect the rights of research participants.

5.2 Investigators requesting participants' involvement in research inform them of all aspects of the research that might reasonably be expected to influence willingness to participate. Investigators are especially sensitive to the possibility of diminished consent when participants are also receiving clinical services, have impairments which limit understanding and/or communication, or when participants are children.

5.3 Investigators respect participants' freedom to decline participation in or to withdraw from a research study at any time. This obligation requires special thought and consideration when investigators or other members of the research team are in positions of authority or influence over participants. Marriage and family therapists, therefore, make every effort to avoid dual relationships with research participants that could impair professional judgment or increase the risk of exploitation.

5.4 Information obtained about a research participant during the course of an investigation is confidential unless there is a waiver previously obtained in writing. When the possibility exists that others, including family members, may obtain access to such information, this possibility, together with the plan for protecting confidentiality, is explained as part of the procedure for obtaining informed consent.

6. RESPONSIBILITY TO THE PROFESSION

Marriage and family therapists respect the rights and responsibilities of professional colleagues and participate in activities which advance the goals of the profession.

6.1 Marriage and family therapists remain accountable to the standards of the profession when acting as members or employees of organizations.

6.2 Marriage and family therapists assign publication credit to those who have contributed to a publication in proportion to their contributions and in accordance with customary professional publication practices.

6.3 Marriage and family therapists who are the authors of books or other materials that are published or distributed cite persons to whom credit for original ideas is due.

6.4 Marriage and family therapists who are the authors of books or other materials published or distributed by an organization take reasonable precautions to ensure that the organization promotes and advertises the materials accurately and factually.

6.5 Marriage and family therapists participate in activities that contribute to a better community and society, including devoting a portion of their professional activity to services for which there is little or no financial return.

6.6 Marriage and family therapists are concerned with developing laws and regulations pertaining to marriage and family therapy that serve the public interest, and with altering such laws and regulations that are not in the public interest.

6.7 Marriage and family therapists encourage public participation in the design and delivery of professional services and in the regulation of practitioners.

7. FINANCIAL ARRANGEMENTS

Marriage and family therapists make financial arrangements with clients, third party payors, and supervisees that are reasonably understandable and conform to accepted professional practices.

7.1 Marriage and family therapists do not offer or accept payment for referrals.

7.2 Marriage and family therapists do not charge excessive fees for services.

7.3 Marriage and family therapists disclose their fees to clients and supervisees at the beginning of services.

7.4 Marriage and family therapists represent facts truthfully to clients, third party payors, and supervisees regarding services rendered.

8. ADVERTISING

Marriage and family therapists engage in appropriate informational activities, including those that enable laypersons to choose professional services on an informed basis.

General Advertising

8.1   Marriage and family therapists accurately represent their competence, education, training, and experience relevant to their practice of marriage and family therapy.

8.2   Marriage and family therapists assure that advertisements and publications in any media (such as directories, announcements, business cards, newspapers, radio, television, facsimiles) convey information that is necessary for the public to make an appropriate selection of professional services. Information could include: (a) office information, such as name, address, telephone number, credit card acceptability, fees, languages spoken, and office hours; (b) appropriate degrees, state licensure and/or certification, and AAMFT Clinical Member status; and (c) description of practice. (For requirements for advertising under the AAMFT name, logo, and/or the abbreviated initials AAMFT, see Subprinciple 8.15 below).

8.3   Marriage and family therapists do not use a name which could mislead the public concerning the identity, responsibility, source, and status of those practicing under that name and do not hold themselves out as being partners or associates of a firm if they are not.

8.4   Marriage and family therapists do not use any professional identification (such as a business card, office sign, letterhead, or telephone or association directory listing) if it includes a statement or claim that is false, fraudulent, misleading, or deceptive. A statement is false, fraudulent, misleading, or deceptive if it (a) contains a material misrepresentation of fact; (b) fails to state any material fact necessary to make the statement, in light of all circumstances, not misleading; or (c) is intended to or is likely to create an unjustified expectation.

8.5   Marriage and family therapists correct, wherever possible, false, misleading, or inaccurate information and representations made by others concerning the therapist's qualifications, services, or products.

8.6   Marriage and family therapists make certain that the qualifications of persons in their employ are represented in a manner that is not false, misleading, or deceptive.

8.7   Marriage and family therapists may represent themselves as specializing within a limited area of marriage and family therapy, but only if they have the education and supervised experience in settings which meet recognized professional standards to practice in that specialty area.

Advertising Using AAMFT Designations

8.8 The AAMFT designations of Clinical Member, Approved Supervisor, and Fellow may be used in public information or advertising materials only by persons holding such designaticns. Persons holding such designations may, for example, advertise in the following manner:

- *Jane Doe, Ph.D., a Clinical Member of the American Association for Marriage and Family Therapy.* Alternately, the advertisement could read, *Jane Doe, Ph.D., AAMFT Clinical Member.*
- *John Doe, Ph.D., an Approved Supervisor of the American Association for Marriage and Family Therapy.* Alternately, the advertisement could read, *John Doe, Ph.D., AAMFT Approved Supervisor.*
- *Jane Doe, Ph.D., a Fellow of the American Association for Marriage and Family Therapy.* Alternately, the advertisement could read, *Jane Doe, Ph.D., AAMFT Fellow.*

More than one designation may be used if held by the AAMFT Member.

8.9 Marriage and family therapists who hold the AAMFT Approved Supervisor or the Fellow designation may not represent the designation as an advanced clinical status.

8.10 Student, Associate, and Affiliate Members may not use their AAMFT membership status in public information or advertising materials. Such listings on professional resumes are nct considered advertisements.

8.11 Persons applying for AAMFT membership may not list their application status on any resume or advertisement.

8.12 In conjunction with their AAMFT membership, marriage and family therapists claim as evidence of educational qualifications only those degrees (a) from regionally accredited institutions or (b) from institutions recognized by states which license or certify marriage and family therapists, but only if such state regulation is recognized by AAMFT.

8.13 Marriage and family therapists may not use the initials AAMFT following their name in the manner of an academic degree.

8.14 Marriage and family therapists may not use the AAMFT name, logo, and/or the abbreviated initials AAMFT or make any other such represen-

tation which would imply that they speak for or represent the Association. The Association is the sole owner of its name, corporate logo, and the abbreviated initials AAMFT. Its committees and divisions, operating as such, may use the name, corporate logo, and/or the abbreviated initials, AAMFT, in accordance with AAMFT policies.

8.15 Advertisements of Clinical Members may include the following: AAMFT

Clinical Member Logo, Clinical Member's name, degree, license or certificate held when required by state law, name of business, address, and telephone number. If a business is listed, it must follow, not precede the Clinical Member's name. Such listings may not include AAMFT offices held by the Clinical Member, nor any specializations, since such a listing under the AAMFT name, Clinical Member logo, and/or the abbreviated initials AAMFT would imply that this specialization has been credentialed by AAMFT. The logo shall be used in accordance with stated guidelines.

8.16 Marriage and family therapists use their membership in AAMFT only, in connection with their clinical and professional activities.

8.17 Only AAMFT divisions and programs accredited by the AAMFT Commission on Accreditation for Marriage and Family Therapy Education, not businesses nor organizations, may use any AAMFT-related designation or affiliation in public information or advertising materials, and then only in accordance with AAMFT policies.

8.18 Programs accredited by the AAMFT Commission on Accreditation for Marriage and Family Therapy Education may not use the AAMFT name, corporate logo, and/or the abbreviated initials, AAMFT. Instead, they may have printed on their stationery and other appropriate materials a statement such as:

The (name of program) of the (name of institution) is accredited by the AAMFT Commission on Accreditation for Marriage and Family Therapy Education.

8.19 Programs not accredited by the AAMFT Commission on Accreditation for Marriage and Family Therapy Education may not use the AAMFT name, corporate logo, and/or the abbreviated initials, AAMFT. They may not state in printed program materials, program advertisements, and student advisement that their courses and training opportunities are accepted by AAMFT to meet AAMFT membership requirements.

This Code is published by:
American Association for Marriage and Family Therapy
1133 15th Street, NW Suite 300
Washington, DC 20005-2710
(202) 452-0109
(202) 223-2329 FAX
www.aamft.org

Glossary

accommodating A therapeutic tactic, used primarily by structural family therapists, whereby the therapist attempts to make personal adjustments in order to adapt to the family style, in an effort to build a therapeutic alliance with the family.

accreditation The granting of status to an academic institution or training program, certifying that its offerings are in accord with the standards established by the accrediting body.

alignments Clusters of alliances between family members within the overall family group; affiliations and splits from one another, temporary or permanent, occur in pursuit of homeostasis.

anorexia nervosa Prolonged, severe diminution of appetite, particularly although not exclusively in adolescent females, to the point of becoming life-threatening.

baseline A stable, reliable performance level, against which changes, particularly of a behavioral nature, can be compared.

behavioral The viewpoint that objective and experimentally verified procedures should be the basis for modifying maladaptive, undesired, or problematic behaviors.

behavioral analysis An assessment procedure in which a therapist identifies the targeted behavior to be changed, determines the factors currently maintaining the behavior, and formulates a treatment plan that includes specific criteria for measuring the success of the change effort.

behavioral couple therapy Training couples in communication skills, the exchange of positive reinforcements, cognitive restructuring, and problem-solving skills in order to facilitate marital satisfaction.

behavioral parent training Training parents in behavioral principles and the use of contingency management procedures in altering or modifying undesirable behavior in their children.

binuclear family A postdivorced family structure in which the former spouses reside in separate households and function as two separate units; although living separately, their nuclear family is thus restructured but remains intact.

434

bipolar disorder   An affective disorder in which the patient experiences alternating periods of depression and mania.

blank screen   In psychoanalytic therapy, the passive, neutral, unrevealing behavior of the analyst, onto which the patient may project his or her fantasies.

boundary   An abstract delineation between parts of a system or between systems, typically defined by implicit or explicit rules regarding who may participate and in what manner.

boundary making   A technique of structural family therapists aimed at realigning boundaries within a family by changing the psychological proximity (closer or further apart) between family subsystems.

calibration   Setting of a limit in a system, determining the range in which it may operate and how much deviation will be tolerated.

centrifugal   Tending to move outward or away from the center; within a family, forces that push the members apart, especially when the family organization lacks cohesiveness, so that they seek gratification outside of, rather than within, the family.

centripetal   Tending to move toward the center; within a family, forces that bind or otherwise keep the members together so that they seek fulfillment from intrafamilial rather than outside relationships.

certification   A statutory process established by a government agency, usually a state or province, granting permission to persons, having met predetermined qualifications, to call themselves by a particular title, and prohibiting the use of that title without a certificate.

circular causality   The view that causality is nonlinear, occurring instead within a relationship context and by means of a network of interacting loops; any cause is thus seen as an effect of a prior cause, as in the interactions within families.

circular questioning   An interviewing technique, first formulated by Milan systemic therapists, aimed at eliciting differences in perception about events or relationships from different family members, particularly regarding points in the family life cycle when significant coalition shifts and adaptations occurred.

classical conditioning   A form of learning in which a previously neutral stimulus, through repeated pairing with a stimulus that ordinarily elicits a response, eventually elicits the response by itself.

closed system   A self-contained system with impermeable boundaries, operating without interactions outside the system, resistant to change and thus prone to increasing disorder.

coalitions   Covert alliances or affiliations, temporary or long-term, between certain family members against others in the family.

cognitive   Pertaining to mental processes, such as thinking, remembering, perceiving, expecting, and planning.

cognitive behavior therapy   A set of therapeutic procedures, derived from behavior therapy, that attempts to change behavior by modifying or altering faulty thought patterns or destructive self-verbalizations.

cognitive restructuring   An intervention procedure whereby the therapist attempts to modify client thoughts. perceptions, and attributions about an event.

communication theory   As developed at the Palo Alto Mental Research Institute, the study of interpersonal sequences between people in terms of the verbal and non-verbal messages they exchange.

complementarity   The degree of harmony in the meshing of family roles, as between husband and wife; to the extent that the roles dovetail satisfactorily, the partners both are able, together, to provide and receive satisfaction from the relationship.

complementary   A type of dyadic transaction or communication pattern in which inequality and the maximization of differences exist (for example, dominant/submissive) and in which each participant's response provokes or enhances a counter-response in the other in a continuing loop.

conductor   A type of family therapist who is active, aggressive, charismatic, and who openly and directly confronts the family's dysfunctional interactive patterns.

confidentiality   An ethical standard aimed at protecting client privacy by ensuring that information received in a therapeutic relationship will not be disclosed without prior client consent.

conjoint   Involving two or more family members seen together in a therapy session.

conjoint sex therapy   Therapeutic intervention with a couple in an effort to treat their sexual dysfunction.

consensus-sensitive families   Enmeshed families who view the world as unpredictable and therefore dangerous unless they maintain agreement at all times and on all issues.

constructivism   The belief that an individual's knowledge of reality results from his or her subjective perceiving and subsequent constructing or inventing of the world rather than the result of how the world objectively exists.

contextual   Pertaining to circumstances or situations in which an event took place; as a therapeutic approach, an emphasis on relational determinants, entitlements, and indebtedness across generations that bind families together.

contingency contract   An agreement, usually in written form, made by two or more family members specifying the circumstances under which each is to do something for the other, so that they may exchange rewarding behavior.

continuing education   Voluntary or, increasingly, mandated postgraduate training, typically in the form of workshops and in-service training programs.

cotherapy   The simultaneous involvement of two therapists often for training purposes, in working with an individual, couple, or family.

counterparadox   In systemic family therapy, placing the family in a therapeutic double bind in order to counter the members' paradoxical interactions.

countertransference   According to psychoanalytic theory, the analyst's unconscious emotional responses to a patient that are reminiscent of feelings he or she experienced with a person in the past.

culture   Shared behaviors, meanings, symbols, and values transmitted from one generation to the next.

cybernetics   The study of methods of feedback control within a system, especially the flow of information through feedback loops.

deconstruction   A postmodern procedure for gaining meaning by reexamining assumptions previously taken for granted, in the service of constructing new and unencumbered meanings.

defense mechanism   According to psychoanalytic theory, the process, usually unconscious, whereby the ego protects the individual from conscious awareness of threatening and therefore anxiety-producing thoughts, feelings, and impulses.

detriangulate   The process of withdrawing from a family role of buffer or go-between with one's parents, so as to not be drawn into alliances with one against the other.

developmental tasks   Problems to be overcome and conflicts to be mastered at various stages of the life cycle, enabling movement to the next developmental stage.

didactic   Used for teaching purposes.

differentiation of self   According to Bowen, the separation of one's intellectual and emotional functioning; the greater the distinction, the better one is able to resist being overwhelmed by the emotional reactivity of his or her family, thus making one less prone to dysfunction.

directive   A technique instructing a family to carry out a therapeutic command.

disengagement   A family organization with overly rigid boundaries, in which members are isolated and feel unconnected to each other, each functioning separately and autonomously and without involvement in the day-to-day transactions within the family.

double-bind concept   The view that an individual who receives important contradictory injunctions at different levels of abstraction and about which he or she is unable to comment is in a no-win, conflict-producing situation.

dyad   A liaison, temporary or permanent, between two persons.

dysfunctional   Abnormal or impaired in the ability to accommodate to or cope with stress.

ecosystemic approach   A perspective that goes beyond intrafamilial relationships to attend to the family's relationships with larger systems (schools, courts, health care).

ego   According to psychoanalytic theory, the mediator between the demands of the instinctual drives (id) and the social prohibitions (superego); thus, the rational, problem-solving aspect of personality.

emotional cutoff   The flight from unresolved emotional ties to one's family of origin, typically manifested by withdrawing or running away from the parental family, or denying its current importance in one's life.

emotionally focused couple therapy   An experiential approach, based upon humanistic and systemic foundations, that attempts to change a couple's negative interactions while helping them to cement their emotional bond.

enactment   In structural family therapy, a facilitating intervention in which the family is induced to enact or play out its relationship patterns spontaneously during a therapeutic session, allowing the therapist to observe and ultimately to develop a plan or new set of rules for restructuring future transactions.

encounter group   A kind of therapeutic group in which intense interpersonal experiences are promoted in order to produce insight, personal growth, and sensitivity to the feelings and experiences of others.

enmeshment   A family organization in which boundaries between members are blurred and members are overconcerned and overinvolved in each other's lives, limiting individual autonomy.

entropy   The tendency of a system to go into disorder, and if unimpeded, to reach a disorganized and undifferentiated state.

environment-sensitive families   Families in which the members share the belief that they can cope with the world because it is knowable, orderly, and predictable.

epistemology   The study of the origin, nature, and methods, as well as the limits, of knowledge; thus, a framework for describing and conceptualizing what is being observed and experienced.

ethnicity   The defining characteristics of a social grouping sharing cultural traditions, transmitted over generations and reinforced by the expectations of the subgroup in which the individual or family maintains membership.

exceptions   In solution-focused therapy, attention to the times when the problem did not occur, intended to help build problem-solving skills.

experiential   The therapeutic approach in which the therapist reveals himself or herself as a real person and uses that self in interacting with a family.

expressed emotion   The degree of affect expressed within a family, especially noteworthy in families with schizophrenic members, where emotionally intense and negative interactions are considered a factor in the schizophrenic's relapse.

extended family   An enlarged and interpersonally complex family unit made up of a nuclear family (a married couple and their children) plus relatives (grandparents, aunts and uncles, cousins) with consanguine ties.

externalization   In the narrative approach, helping families view the problem or symptom as occurring outside of themselves, in an effort to mobilize them to fight to overcome it.

family crisis therapy   A crisis-oriented therapeutic approach in which the family as a system is helped to restore its previous level of functioning; in some cases, as with schizophrenia, rehospitalization can be avoided.

family group therapy   The intervention technique developed by Bell based on social-psychological principles of small-group behavior

family life cycle   The series of longitudinal stages or events that mark a family's life, offering an organizing schema for viewing the family as a system proceeding through time.

family life fact chronology   An experiential technique of Satir's in which clients retrace their family history, particularly the family's relationship patterns, to better understand current family functioning.

family mapping   An assessment technique used by structural family therapists to graphically describe a family's overall organizational structure and determine which subsystem is involved in dysfunctional transactions.

family of origin   The family into which one is born or adopted.

family paradigm   A family's shared assumptions about the social environment, determining its priorities, self-image, and strategies for dealing with the outside world.

family projection process   The mechanism by which parental conflicts and immaturities are transmitted, through the process of projection, to one or more of the children.

family reconstruction   An auxiliary therapeutic approach developed by Satir, whereby family members are guided back through stages of their lives in order to discover and unlock dysfunctional patterns from the past.

family sculpting   A physical arrangement of the members of a family in space, with the placement of each person determined by an individual family member acting as "director"; the resulting tableau represents that person's symbolic view of family relationships.

family systems theory   The theory advanced by Bowen that emphasizes the family as an emotional unit or network of interlocking relationships best understood from a historical or transgenerational perspective.

feedback   The reinsertion into a system of the results of its past performance, as a method of controlling the system.

feedback loops   Those circular mechanisms by which information about a system's output is continuously reintroduced back into the system, initiating a chain of subsequent events.

feminist family therapy   A form of collaborative, egalitarian, nonsexist intervention, applicable to both men and women, addressing family gender roles, patriarchal attitudes, and social and economic inequalities in male-female relationships.

first-order changes   Temporary or superficial changes within a system that do not alter the basic organization of the system itself.

first-order cybernetics   A view from outside of the system of the feedback loops and homeostatic mechanisms that transpire within a system.

functional analysis   A behavioral assessment of a problem in order to determine what interpersonal or environmental contingencies elicit the problematic behavior and how to extinguish or reduce its occurrence.

functional family therapy   A therapeutic approach based on systems theory, cognitive theory, and behavioral principles in which clients are helped to understand the function or interpersonal payoff of certain of their behaviors as a prelude to substituting more effective ways to achieve the same results.

fusion   The merging of the intellectual and emotional aspects of a family member, paralleling the degree to which that person is caught up in, and loses a separate sense of self in, family relationships.

gender   A learned set of culturally prescribed attitudes and behaviors as masculine or feminine, associated with but distinct from the biological status of being male or female.

gender-sensitive family therapy   A therapeutic perspective, regardless of theoretical persuasion, that examines the impact of gender socialization on the outlooks, attitudes, behaviors and interpersonal relationships of men and women; its aim is to empower clients to make sexist-free role choices rather than be limited by roles determined by their biological status as male or female.

general systems theory   As proposed by Bertalanffy in regard to living systems, the study of the relationship of interactional parts in context, emphasizing their unity and organizational hierarchy.

genogram   A schematic diagram of a family's relationship system, in the form of a genetic tree, usually including at least three generations, used in particular by Bowen and his followers to trace recurring behavior patterns within the family.

Gestalt family therapy   A form of experiential family therapy, loosely based on the principles of Gestalt psychology, that focuses on here-and-now experiences in an effort to heighten self-awareness and increase self-direction.

Greek chorus   A live form of supervision in which a consultation group observes a family session from behind a one-way mirror, and from time to time sends messages back to the therapy room.

group therapy   A form of psychotherapy in which several people are treated simultaneously by a therapist, and in addition are helped therapeutically through their interactions with one another.

homeostasis   A dynamic state of balance or equilibrium in a system, or a tendency toward achieving and maintaining such a state in an effort to ensure a stable environment.

humanistic   The life-affirming view that emphasizes each person's uniqueness and worth, as well as potential for continued personal growth and fulfillment.

hypothesizing   As used by systemic therapists, the process by which a team of therapists forms suppositions, open to revision, regarding how and why a family's problems have developed and persisted; in advance of meeting the family, in order to facilitate asking relevant questions and organizing incoming information.

identified patient   The family member with the presenting symptom; thus, the person who initially seeks treatment or for whom treatment is sought.

information processing   The gathering, distilling, organizing, storing, and retrieving of information through a system or between that system and larger systems.

informed consent   The legal rights of patients or research subjects to be told of the purposes and risks involved before agreeing to participate.

integrative couples therapy   A behaviorally based technique emphasizing the emotional acceptance of behavior in a partner not open to change.

interactional approach   As practiced by communication theorists, an effort to change ongoing family transactional patterns without searching for their origins; verbal and nonverbal behaviors, as well as their congruence, are examined.

interlocking pathology   Multiple forms of disability or dysfunction within and between family members that are interdependent in the ways in which they are expressed, maintained, and controlled.

interpersonal   Interactional, as between persons.

interpersonal distance-sensitive families   Disengaged families whose members refuse to depend on each other, out of fear that dependence reflects personal weakness and insecurity.

intrapsychic   Within the mind or psyche; used especially in regard to conflicting forces.

introjects   Imprints or memories from the past, usually based on unresolved relationships with one's parents, that continue to impose themselves on current relationships, particularly with a spouse or one's children.

invariant prescription   As developed by Selvini-Palazzoli, a single, unchanging verbal directive issued to all parents with symptomatic children, intended to help the parents and children break out of collusive and destructive "games" and establish clearer and more stable intergenerational boundaries.

isomorphic   Exhibiting a similar form or parallel process, as in conducting therapy and providing supervision.

joining   The therapeutic tactic of entering a family system by engaging its separate members and subsystems, gaining access in order to explore and ultimately to help modify dysfunctional aspects of that system.

licensing   A statutory process established by a government agency, usually a state or province, granting permission to persons having met predetermined qualifications to practice a specific profession.

linear causality   The view that a nonreciprocal relationship exists between events in a sequence, so that one event causes the next event, but not vice versa.

live supervision   The active guidance of a therapist while at work by an observer or team of observers who offer suggestions by telephone, earphone, or after calling the therapist out of the consultation room.

malpractice   A legal concept addressing the failure to provide a level of professional skill or render a level of professional services ordinarily expected of professionals in a similar situation.

managed care   A system in which third-party payors regulate and control the cost, quality, and terms of treatment of medical (including mental health) services.

marathons   Intensive, uninterrupted group experiences generally extending over considerable lengths of time.

marital quid pro quo   An initial rule arrangement or bargain between husband and wife regarding the ways in which they intend to define themselves vis-à-vis one another in the marital relationship.

marital schism   A disturbed marital situation characterized by family disharmony, self-preoccupation, the undermining of the spouse, and frequent threats of divorce by one or both partners.

marital skew   A disturbed marital situation in which one partner dominates the family to an extreme degree, and in which the marriage is maintained at the expense of the distortion of reality.

medical family therapy   A form of psychoeducational family therapy involving collaboration with physicians and other health care professionals in the treatment of persons or families with health problems.

meta-analysis   A statistical technique for reviewing, analyzing, and summarizing the results of a discrete group of studies, as in investigating the differences between treatment and no-treatment groups in outcome research.

metacommunication   A message about a message, typically nonverbal (a smile, a shrug, a nod, a wink), offered simultaneously with a verbal message, structuring, qualifying, or adding meaning to that message.

metarules   A family's unstated rules regarding how to interpret or, if necessary, to change its rules.

mimesis   A tactic used particularly by structural family therapists, who attempt to copy or mimic a family's communication and behavioral patterns in order to gain acceptance by the family members.

monad   Properties or characteristics of a single individual.

multigenerational transmission process   The process, occurring over several generations, in which poorly differentiated persons marry similarly differentiated mates, ultimately resulting in offspring suffering from schizophrenia or other severe mental disorders.

multiple family therapy   A form of therapy in which members of several families meet together as a group to work on individual as well as family problems.

multiple impact therapy   A crisis-focused form of intervention in which members of a single family are seen all together or in various combinations for intensive interaction with a team of professionals over a two-day period.

negative feedback   The flow of corrective information from the output of a system back into the system in order to attenuate deviation and keep the system functioning within prescribed limits.

negentropy   The tendency of a system to remain flexible and open to new input, necessary for change and survival of the system.

network therapy   A form of therapy, typically carried out in the home of a patient (for example, a schizophrenic recently discharged from a hospital), in which family members, friends, neighbors, and other involved persons participate in treatment and rehabilitation.

neutrality   As used by systemic family therapists, a nonjudgmental and non side-taking position, eliciting all viewpoints, intended to enable the therapist to avoid being caught up in family "games" through coalitions or alliances.

nuclear family   A family composed of a husband, wife, and their offspring, living together as a family unit.

nuclear family emotional system   An unstable, fused family's way of coping with stress, typically resulting in marital conflict, dysfunction in a spouse, or psychological impairment of a child; their pattern is likely to mimic the patterns of past generations and to be repeated in future generations.

object relations theory   The theory that the basic human motive is the search for satisfying object (human) relationships, and that parent-child patterns, especially if frustrating or unfulfilling, are internalized as introjects and unconsciously imposed on current family relationships.

open system   A system with more or less permeable boundaries that permits interaction between the system's component parts or subsystems.

operant conditioning   A form of learning in which correct or desired responses are rewarded or reinforced, thus increasing the probability that these responses will recur.

operant interpersonal therapy   A marital therapy approach based on operant conditioning theory, particularly the exchange between partners of positive rewards.

organization   The notion that the components of a system relate to each other in some consistent fashion, and that the system is structured by those relationships.

paradigm   A set of assumptions, delimiting an area to be investigated scientifically and specifying the methods to be used to collect and interpret the forthcoming data.

paradoxical injunction   A communication to obey a command that is internally inconsistent and contradictory, as in a double-bind message, forcing the receiver to disobey in order to obey.

paradoxical intervention   A therapeutic technique whereby a therapist gives a client or family a directive he or she wants resisted; a change takes place as a result of defying the directive.

pathogenic   Pathology-producing.

peer review   A process for obtaining an independent evaluation of a therapist's professional procedures or intended procedures in a particular case by a colleague or case management coordinator representing a "third-party payor."

permeability   The ease or flexibility with which members can cross subsystem boundaries within the family.

phenomenological   The view that to fully understand the causes of another person's behavior requires an understanding of how he or she subjectively experiences the world, rather than of the physical or objective reality of that world.

phobia   An intense, irrational fear of a harmless object or situation that the individual seeks to avoid.

positive connotation   A reframing technique used primarily by systemic family therapists whereby positive motives are ascribed to family behavior patterns because these patterns help maintain family balance and cohesion; as a result, the family is helped to view each other's motives more positively.

positive feedback   The flow of information from the output of a system back into the system in order to amplify deviation from the state of equilibrium, thus leading to instability and change.

postmodern   A philosophical outlook that rejects the notion that there exists an objectively knowable universe discoverable by impartial science, and instead argues that there are multiple views of reality ungoverned by universal laws.

power   Influence, authority, and control over an outcome.

prescribing the symptom   A paradoxical technique in which the client is directed to voluntarily engage in the symptomatic behavior; as a result, the client is put in the position of rebelling and abandoning the symptom or obeying, thereby admitting it is under voluntary control.

pretend techniques   Paradoxical interventions based on play and fantasy, in which clients are directed to "pretend" to have a symptom; the paradox is that if they are pretending, the symptom may be reclassified as voluntary and unreal, and thus able to be altered.

privileged communication   A legal concept protecting a client's disclosure to a therapist from being revealed in court; if the client waives the right, the therapist has no legal grounds for withholding the information.

problem analysis   An investigation of a presenting problem, typically carried out by behaviorists, in order to determine as precisely as possible what behavioral deficiencies require targeting.

projective identification   An unconscious defense mechanism whereby certain unwanted aspects of oneself are attributed to another person (e.g., a spouse), who is then induced or incited to behave according to the first person's projected but split-off feelings.

projective systems   The unrealistic expectations, carried over from childhood, of people with relationship difficulties.

pseudomutuality   A homeostasis-seeking relationship between and among family members that gives the surface appearance of being open, mutually understanding, and satisfying, when in fact it is not.

psychoanalysis   A comprehensive theory of personality development and set of therapeutic techniques developed by Sigmund Freud in the early 1900s.

psychodrama   A form of group therapy in which participants role-play themselves or significant others in their lives to achieve catharsis or to resolve conflicts and gain greater spontaneity.

psychodynamics   The interplay of opposing forces within an individual as the basis for understanding that person's motivation.

psychoeducational   A therapeutic effort offering educational programs directed at helping families better understand and learn skills for dealing with a seriously disturbed family member, such as a schizophrenic recently released from a psychiatric hospital.

psychopathology   A disease concept derived from medicine referring to the origins of abnormal behavior.

punctuation   The communication concept that each participant in a transaction believes whatever he or she says is caused by what the other says, in effect holding the other responsible for his or her reactions.

radical behaviorism   The outlook offered by B. F. Skinner that overt or observable behavior is the only acceptable subject of scientific investigation.

reactor   Therapist whose style is subtle and indirect, and who prefers to observe and clarify the family process rather than serve as an active, aggressive, or colorful group leader.

redundancy principle   Repetitive behavioral sequences within a family.

reflecting teams   A process involving two-way mirrors in which team members observe a family and then discuss their thoughts and observations in front of the family and therapist. Later, the therapist and family discuss the team's conversations about them.

reframing   Relabeling behavior by putting it into a new, more positive perspective ("Mother is trying to help" rather than "She's intrusive"), thus altering the context in which it is perceived and inviting new responses to the same behavior.

reinforcement   A response, in the form of a reward or punishment, intended to change the probability of the occurrence of another person's previous response.

relabeling   Verbal redefinition of an event in order to make dysfunctional behavior seem more reasonable and understandable, intended to provoke in others a more positive reaction to that behavior.

relational ethics   In contextual family therapy, the overall, long-term preservation of fairness within a family, ensuring that each member's basic interests are taken into account by other family members.

rituals   Symbolic ceremonial prescriptions offered by a therapist, intended to address family conflict over its covert rules, to be enacted by the family in order to provide clarity or insight into their roles and relationships.

rubber fence   As proposed by Wynne, a shifting boundary around a family, intended to protect them from outside contact, arbitrarily permitting certain acceptable bits of information to penetrate but not others.

rules   Within a family, organized, repetitive patterns of interaction helping regulate and stabilize family functioning.

schemas   Relatively stable cognitive structures involving underlying core beliefs a person develops about the world.

schizophrenia   A group of severe mental disorders characterized by withdrawal from reality, blunted or inappropriate emotion, delusions, hallucinations, incoherent thought and speech, and an overall breakdown in personal and social functioning.

schizophrenogenic mother   According to Fromm-Reichmann, a cold, domineering, possessive but rejecting mother (usually married to an inadequate, passive husband) whose behavior toward her son is thought to be a determining factor in his schizophrenic behavior.

second-order changes   Fundamental changes in a system's organization, function, and frame of reference, leading to permanent change in its interactive patterns.

second-order cybernetics   A view of an observing system in which the therapist, rather than attempting to describe the system by being an outside observer, is part of what is being observed and treated.

shaping   A form of behavioral therapy, based on operant conditioning principles, in which successive approximations of desired behavior are reinforced until the desired behavior is achieved.

sibling position   The birth order of children in a family, which influences their personalities as well as their interactions with future spouses.

single-parent-led family   A family led by a single custodial parent, most often a woman, as a result of divorce, death of a spouse, desertion, or never having married.

social construction theory   The postmodern theory that there is no objective "truth," only versions of "reality" constructed from social interaction, including conversation, with others.

social learning theory   The theory that a person's behavior is best understood when the conditions under which the behavior is learned are taken into account.

societal regression   The notion that society responds emotionally in periods of stress and anxiety, offering short-term "Band-Aid" solutions, rather than seeking more rational solutions that lead to greater individuation.

splitting   According to object relations theory, a primitive process by which an infant makes contradictory aspects of a mother or other nurturing figure less threatening by dividing the external person into a good object and a bad object and internalizing the split perception.

stepfamily   A linked family system created by the marriage of two persons, one or both of whom has been previously married, in which one or more children from the earlier marriage(s) live with the remarried couple.

strategic   A therapeutic approach in which the therapist develops a specific plan or strategy and designs interventions aimed at solving the presenting problem.

structural   A therapeutic approach directed at changing or realigning the family organization or structure in order to alter dysfunctional transactions and clarify subsystem boundaries.

subsystem   An organized, coexisting component within an overall system, having its own autonomous functions as well as a specified role in the operation of the larger system; within families, a member can belong to a number of such units.

suprasystem   A higher-level system in which other systems represent component parts and play subsystem roles.

symbiosis   An intense attachment between two or more individuals, such as a mother and child, to the extent that the boundaries between them become blurred, and they respond as one.

symmetrical   A type of dyadic transaction or communication pattern characterized by equality and the minimization of differences; each participant's response provokes a similar response in the other, sometimes in a competitive fashion.

symmetrical escalation   A spiraling competitive effect in the communication between two people whose relationship is based on equality, so that vindictiveness leads to greater vindictiveness in return, viciousness to greater viciousness, and so forth.

system   A set of interacting units or component parts that together make up a whole arrangement or organization.

systemic family therapy   A Milan model therapeutic approach in which the family, as an evolving system, is viewed as continuing to use an old epistemology that no longer fits its current behavior patterns; the therapist indirectly introduces new information into the family system and encourages alternative epistemologies to develop.

systems theory   A generic term in common use, encompassing general systems theory and cybernetics, referring to the view of interacting units or elements making up the organized whole.

therapeutic contracts   As used by behavioral family therapists, written negotiated agreements between family members to make specific behavior changes in the future.

therapeutic double bind   A general term for a variety of paradoxical techniques in which clients are directed to continue to manifest their presenting symptoms; caught in a bind, they must give up the symptom or acknowledge control over it.

time out   A behavioral technique for extinguishing undesirable or inappropriate behavior by removing the reinforcing consequences of that behavior; the procedure is used primarily with children.

token economy   A program in which tokens (points, gold stars) are dispensed contingent upon the successful completion of previously designated desired behaviors; the accumulated tokens can be redeemed later for money or special privileges.

tracking   A therapeutic tactic associated with structural family therapy, in which the therapist deliberately attends to the symbols, style, language, and values of the family, using them to influence the family's transactional patterns.

transference   In psychoanalytic treatment, the unconscious shifting onto the analyst of a patient's feelings, drives, attitudes, and fantasies, displaced from unresolved reactions to significant persons in the patient's past.

transference neurosis   That point in classical psychoanalysis in which the patient's fantasies about the analyst are at their peak, during which their relationship becomes the focus of treatment.

transgenerational   Involving patterns and influences occurring over two or more generations.

triad   A three-person set of relationships.

triangle   A three-person system, the smallest stable emotional system; according to Bowen, a two-person emotional system, under stress, will recruit a third person into the system to lower the intensity and anxiety and gain stability.

triangulation   A process in which each parent demands that a child ally with him or her against the other parent during parental conflict.

unbalancing   In structural family therapy, a technique for altering the hierarchical relationship between members of a system or subsystem by supporting one member and thus upsetting family homeostasis.

undifferentiated family ego mass   Bowen's term for an intense, symbiotic nuclear family relationship; an individual sense of self fails to develop in members because of the existing fusion or emotional "stuck-togetherness."

unique outcomes   In narrative therapy, those instances when the client did not experience the problem, intended to help contradict a problem-saturated outlook.

vulnerability-stress model   The viewpoint that a predisposition or vulnerability to a severe mental disorder, such as schizophrenia, is inherited; its ultimate manifestation is determined by how that vulnerability is later modified by life events, especially those involving the family.

wholeness   The systems view that combining units, components, or elements produces an entity greater than the sum of its parts.

REFERENCES

Ackerman, N. J. (1984). *A theory of family systems.* New York: Gardner Press.

Ackerman, N. W. (1937). The family as a social and emotional unit. *Bulletin of the Kansas Mental Hygiene Society, 12*(2).

Ackerman, N. W. (1956). Interlocking pathology in family relationships. In S. Rado & G. Daniels (Eds.), *Changing conceptions of psychoanalytic medicine.* New York: Grune & Stratton.

Ackerman, N. W. (1958). *The psychodynamics of family life.* New York: Basic Books.

Ackerman, N. W. (1966). *Treating the troubled family.* New York: Basic Books.

Ackerman, N. W. (1970). *Family therapy in transition.* Boston: Little, Brown.

Ackerman, N. W. (1972). The growing edge of family therapy. In C. Sager & H. Kaplan (Eds.), *Progress in group and family therapy.* New York: Brunner/Mazel

Ackerman, N. W. (1973). Some considerations for training in family therapy. In Sandoz Pharmaceuticals (Eds.), *Career developments* (Vol. II). East Hanover, NJ: Sandoz.

Ahia, C. E., & Martin, D. (1993). *The danger-to-self-or-others exception to confidentiality.* Alexandria, VA: American Counseling Association.

Ahrons, C. R., & Rodgers, R. H. (1987). *Divorced families: A multidisciplinary approach.* New York: Norton.

Alexander, J. F., & Barton, C. (1995). Family therapy research. In R. H. Mikesell, D-D. Lusterman, & S. H. McDaniel (Eds.), *Integrating family therapy: Handbook of family psychology and systems theory.* Washington, DC: American Psychological Association.

Alexander, J. F., Holtzworth-Munroe, A., & Jameson, P. (1994). The process and outcome of marital and family therapy: Research review and evaluation. In A. Bergin & S. Garfield (Eds.), *Handbook of psychotherapy and behavior change* (4th ed.). New York: Wiley.

Alexander, J. F., & Parsons, B. V. (1982). *Functional family therapy.* Pacific Grove, CA: Brooks/Cole.

Alger, I. (1976). Integrating immediate video playback in family therapy. In P. J. Guerin, Jr. (Ed.), *Family therapy: Theory and practice.* New York: Gardner Press.

Allman, L. R. (1982). The aesthetic preference: Overcoming the pragmatic error. *Family Process, 21,* 43–56.

American Association for Marriage and Family Therapy. (1994). *Membership requirements and applications.* Washington, DC: AAMFT.

American Association for Marriage and Family Therapy. (1998). *Code of ethics.* Washington, DC: AAMFT.

Andersen, T. (1987). The reflecting team: Dialogue and metadialogue in clinical work. *Family Process, 26*, 415–426.

Andersen, T. (1991). *The reflecting team: Dialogues and dialogues about dialogues.* New York: Norton.

Andersen, T. (1992). Personal communication.

Andersen, T. (1993). See and hear, and be seen and heard. In S. Friedman (Ed.), *The new language of change: Constructive collaboration in psychotherapy.* New York: Guilford Press.

Andersen, T. (1995). Reflecting processes: Acts of informing and forming: You can borrow my eyes, but you must not take them away from me! In S. Friedman (Ed.), *The reflecting team in action: Collaborative practices in psychotherapy.* New York: Guilford Press.

Anderson, C. M., Reiss, D., & Hogarty, B. (1986). *Schizophrenia and the family.* New York: Guilford Press.

Anderson, H. D. (1993). On a roller coaster: A collaborative language systems approach to therapy. In S. Friedman (Ed.), *The new language of change: Constructive collaboration in psychotherapy.* New York: Guilford Press.

Anderson, H. D. (1995). Collaborative language systems: Toward postmodern therapy. In R. H. Mikesell, D-D. Lusterman, & S. H. McDaniel (Eds.), *Integrating family therapy: Handbook of family psychology and systems theory.* Washington, DC: American Psychological Association.

Anderson, H. D. (1997). *Conversation, language, and possibilities: A postmodern approach to therapy.* New York: HarperCollins.

Anderson, H. D., Burney, J. P., & Levin, S. B. (1999). A postmodern collaborative approach to therapy. In D. M. Lawson & F. F. Prevatt (Eds.), *Case book in family therapy.* Pacific Grove, CA: Brooks/Cole.

Anderson, H. D., & Goolishian, H. A. (1988). Human systems as linguistic systems: Preliminary and evolving ideas about the implications for clinical theory. *Family Process, 27*, 371–393.

Anderson, H. D., & Goolishian, H. A. (1990). Beyond cybernetics: Comments on Atkinson and Heath's "Further thoughts on second-order family therapy." *Family Process, 29*, 157–163.

Anderson, H. D., & Swim, S. (1993). Learning as collaborative conversations: Combining the student's and teacher's expertise. *Human Systems, 4*, 145–160.

Andolfi, M. (1979). *Family therapy: An interactional approach.* New York: Plenum.

Andrews, J., Clark, D., & Baird, F. (1998). Therapeutic letter-writing: Creating relational case notes. *The Family Journal: Counseling and Therapy for Couples and Families, 5*, 149–158.

Aponte, H. J. (1987). The treatment of society's poor: An ecological perspective on the underorganized family. *Family Therapy Today, 2*, 1–7.

Aponte, H. J. (1994a). *Bread and spirit: Therapy with the new poor.* New York: Norton.

Aponte, H. J. (1994b). How personal can training get? *Journal of Marital and Family Therapy, 20*, 3–15.

Aponte, H. J., & Van Deusin, J. M. (1981). Structural family therapy. In A. S. Gurman & D. P. Kniskern (Eds.), *Handbook of family therapy.* New York: Brunner/Mazel.

Arrington, A., Sullaway, M., & Christensen, A. (1988). Behavioral family assessment. In I. R. H. Falloon (Ed.), *Handbook of behavioral family therapy.* New York: Guilford Press.

Arthur, G. L., & Swanson, C. D. (1993). *Confidentiality and privileged communication.* Alexandria, VA: American Counseling Association.

Atkinson, B. J., & Heath, A. W. (1990). Further thoughts on second-order family therapy—this time it's personal. *Family Process, 29*, 164–167.

Atkinson, J. M., & Coia, D. A. (1995). *Families coping with schizophrenia: A practitioner's guide to family groups.* New York: Wiley.

Atwood, J. D.(1997). *Challenging family therapy situations: Perspectives in social constructions.* New York: Springer.

Auerswald, E. H. (1988). Epistemological confusion and outcome research. In L. C. Wynne (Ed.), *The state of the art in family therapy research: Controversies and recommendations.* New York: Family Process Press.

Avis, J. M. (1985). The politics of functional family therapy: A feminist critique. *Journal of Marital and Family Therapy, 11,* 127–138.

Avis, J. M. (1996). Deconstructing gender in family therapy. In F. P. Piercy, D. H. Sprenkle, J. Wetchler & Associates (Eds.), *Family therapy sourcebook* (2nd ed.). New York: Guilford Press.

Aylmer, R. C. (1986). Bowen family systems marital therapy. In N. S. Jacobson & A. S. Gurman (Eds.), *Clinical handbook of marital therapy.* New York: Guilford Press.

Aylmer, R. C. (1988). The launching of the single young adult. In B. Carter & M. McGoldrick (Eds.), *The changing family life cycle: A framework for family therapy* (2nd ed.). New York: Gardner Press.

Back, K. W. (1974). Intervention techniques: Small groups. In M. R. Rosenzweig & L. W. Porter (Eds.), *Annual Review of Psychology, 39,* 367–387.

Bagarozzi, D. A. (1985). Dimensions of family evaluation. In L. L'Abate (Ed.), *The handbook of family psychology and therapy* (Vol. II). Homewood, IL: Dorsey Press.

Bandler, R., Grinder, J., & Satir, V. M. (1976). *Changing with families.* Palo Alto, CA: Science and Behavior Books.

Bandura, A. (1978). The self system in reciprocal determinism. *American Psychologist, 33,* 344–358.

Barnhill, L. H., & Longo, D. (1978). Fixation and regression in the family life cycle. *Family Process, 17,* 469–478.

Barton, C., & Alexander, J. F. (1981). Functional family therapy. In A. S. Gurman & D. P. Kniskern (Eds.), *Handbook of family therapy.* New York: Brunner/Mazel.

Barton, C., Alexander, J. F., & Sanders, J. D. (1985). Research in family therapy. In L. L'Abate (Ed.), *The handbook of family psychology and therapy* (Vol. II). Homewood, IL: Dorsey Press.

Bates, C. M., & Brodsky, A. M. (1989). *Sex in the therapy hour: A case of professional incest.* New York: Guilford Press.

Bateson, G. (1972). *Steps to an ecology of mind.* New York: Dutton.

Bateson, G. (1979). *Mind and nature: A necessary unity.* New York: Dutton.

Bateson, G., Jackson, D. D., Haley, J., & Weakland, J. (1956). Towards a theory of schizophrenia. *Behavioral Science, 1,* 251–264.

Beavers, W. R. (1981). A systems model of family for family therapists. *Journal of Marital and Family Therapy, 7,* 229–307.

Beavers, W. R. (1982). Healthy, midrange, and severely dysfunctional families. In F. Walsh (Ed.), *Normal family processes.* New York: Guilford Press.

Beavers, W. R. (1985). Family therapy supervision: An introduction and consumer's guide. *Journal of Psychotherapy and the Family, 1*(4), 15–24.

Beavers, W. R., & Hampson, R. B. (1993). Measuring family competence: The Beavers Systems Model. In F. Walsh (Ed.), *Normal family processes* (2nd ed.). New York: Guilford Press.

Beavers, W. R., Hampson, R. B., & Hulgas, Y. F. (1985). Commentary: The Beavers System approach to family assessment. *Family Process, 24,* 398–405.

Beavers, W. R., & Voeller, M. N. (1983). Family models: Comparing and contrasting the Olson circumplex with the Beavers model. *Family Process, 22,* 85–98.

Beck, A. T. (1976). *Cognitive therapy and emotional disorders.* New York: International Universities Press.

Beck, A. T. (1995). Cognitive therapy. In R. J. Corsini & D. Wedding (Eds.), *Current psy-chotherapies* (5th ed). Itasca, IL: Peacock.

Bednar, R. L., Burlingame, G. M., & Masters, K. S. (1988). Systems of family treatment: Substance or semantics? In M. R. Rosenzweig & L. W. Porter (Eds.), *Annual Review of Psychology, 39*, 401–434.

Beels, C., & Ferber, A. (1969). Family therapy: A view. *Family Process, 8*, 280–332.

Bell, J. E. (1961). *Family group therapy* (Public Health Monograph No. 64). Washington, DC: U.S. Government Printing Office.

Bell, J. E. (1975). *Family therapy*. New York: Aronson.

Bennett, B. E., Bryant, B. K., VandenBos, G. R., & Greenwood, A. (1990). *Professional liability and risk management*. Washington, DC: American Psychological Association.

Bentovim, A., & Kinston, W. (1991). Focal family therapy: Joining systems theory with psychodynamic understanding. In A. S. Gurman & D.P. Kniskern (Eds.), *Handbook of family therapy* (Vol. 2). New York: Brunner/Mazel.

Berg, I. K., & deShazer, S. (1993). Making numbers talk: Language in therapy. In S. Friedman (Ed.), *The new language of change: Constructive collaboration in psychotherapy*. New York: Guilford Press.

Berg, I. K., & Miller, S. D. (1992). *Working with the problem drinker: A solution-focused approach*. New York: Norton.

Berger, M. M. (Ed.). (1978). Videotape technique in psychiatric training and treatment (rev. ed.). New York: Brunner/Mazel.

Bergman, J. (1985). *Fishing for barracuda: Pragmatics of brief therapy*. New York: Norton.

Bernard, J. (1974). *The future of marriage*. New York: World.

Bion, W. R. (1961). *Experiences in groups*. New York: Basic Books.

Bloch, D. A. (1985). The family as a psychosocial system. In S. Henao & N. P. Grose (Eds.), *Principles of family systems in family medicine*. New York: Brunner/Mazel.

Bloch, D. A. (1994). Staying alive while staying alive. *Family Systems Medicine, 12*, 103–105.

Bloch, D. A., & LaPerriere, K. (1973). Techniques of family therapy: A conceptual frame. In D. A. Bloch (Ed.), *Techniques of family psychotherapy: A primer*. New York: Grune & Stratton.

Bloch, D. A., & Simon, R. (Eds.). (1982). *The strength of family therapy: Selected papers of Nathan W. Ackerman*. New York: Brunner/Mazel.

Bodin, A. M. (1969a). Family therapy training literature: A brief guide. *Family Process, 8*, 729–779.

Bodin, A. M. (1969b). Videotape in training family therapists. *The Journal of Nervous and Mental Disease, 148*, 251–261.

Bodin, A. M. (1981). The interactional view: Family therapy approaches of the Mental Research Institute. In A. S. Gurman & D. P. Kniskern (Eds.), *Handbook of family therapy*. New York: Brunner/Mazel.

Bodin, A. M. (1983). *Family therapy*. Unpublished manuscript.

Bohannan, P. (1970). *Divorce and after*. Garden City, NY: Doubleday.

Borders, L. D. (1991). A systematic approach to peer group supervision. *Journal of Counseling and Development, 69*(3), 248–252.

Boscolo, L., Cecchin, G., Hoffman, L., & Penn, P. (1987). *Milan systemic family therapy: Conversations in theory and practice*. New York: Basic Books.

Boszormenyi-Nagy, I. (1985). Commentary: Transgenerational solidarity—therapy's mandate and ethics. *Family Process, 24*, 454–456.

Boszormenyi-Nagy, I. (1987). *Foundations of contextual therapy: Collected papers of Ivan Boszormenyi-Nagy*. New York: Brunner/Mazel.

Boszormenyi-Nagy, I., & Framo, J. L. (Eds.). (1965). *Intensive family therapy: Theoretical and practical aspects.* New York: Harper & Row.

Boszormenyi-Nagy, I., Grunebaum, J., & Ulrich, D. (1991). Contextual therapy. In A. S. Gurman & D. P. Kniskern (Eds.), *Handbook of family therapy* (Vol. II). New York: Brunner/Mazel.

Boszormenyi-Nagy, I., & Krasner, B. R. (1986). *Between give and take: A clinical guide to contextual therapy.* New York: Brunner/Mazel.

Boszormenyi-Nagy, I., & Spark, G. M. (1973). *Invisible loyalties: Reciprocity in intergenerational family therapy.* New York: Harper & Row.

Boszormenyi-Nagy, I., & Ulrich, D. (1981). Contextual family therapy. In A. S. Gurman & D. P. Kniskern (Eds.), *Handbook of family therapy.* New York: Brunner/Mazel.

Bowen, M. (1960). A family concept of schizophrenia. In D. D. Jackson (Ed.), *The etiology of schizophrenia.* New York: Basic Books.

Bowen, M. (1966). The use of family theory in clinical practice. *Comprehensive Psychiatry, 7,* 345–374.

Bowen, M. (1975). Family therapy after twenty years. In S. Arieti, D. X. Freedman, & J. E. Dyrud (Eds.), *American handbook of psychiatry V: Treatment* (2nd ed.). New York: Basic Books.

Bowen, M. (1976). Theory in the practice of psychotherapy. In P. J. Guerin, Jr. (Ed.), *Family therapy: Theory and practice.* New York: Gardner Press.

Bowen, M. (1978). *Family therapy in clinical practice.* New York: Aronson.

Bowlby, J. (1969). *Attachment and loss* (Vol. 1). *Attachment.* New York: Basic Books.

Boyd, C. P., Gullone, E., Needleman, G. L., & Burt, T. (1997). The Family Environment Scale: Reliability and normative data for an adolescent sample. *Family Process, 36,* 369–373.

Bradt, J. O. (1988). Becoming parents: Families with young children. In B. Carter & M. McGoldrick (Eds.), *The changing life cycle: A framework for family therapy* (2nd ed.). New York: Gardner Press.

Braverman, S. (1986). Heinz Kohut and Virginia Satir: Strange bedfellows. *Contemporary Family Therapy, 8*(2), 101–110.

Bray, J. H. (1995). Systems-oriented therapy with stepfamilies. In R. H. Mikesell, D-D. Lusterman, & S. H. McDaniel (Eds.), *Integrating family therapy: Handbook of family psychology and systems theory.* Washington, DC: American Psychological Association.

Bray, J. H., Shepherd, J. N., & Hays, J. R. (1985). Legal and ethical issues in informed consent to psychotherapy. *American Journal of Family Therapy, 13,* 50–50.

Breunlin, D. C. (1988). Oscillation theory and family development. In C. J. Falicov (Ed.), *Family transitions: Continuity and change over the life cycle.* New York: Guilford Press.

Brod, H. (1987). A case for men's studies. In M. Kimmel (Ed.), *Changing men: New directions in research on men and masculinity.* Newbury Park, CA: Sage.

Broderick, C. B., & Schrader, S. S. (1991). The history of professional marriage and family counseling. In A. S. Gurman & D. P. Kniskern (Eds.), *Handbook of family therapy* (Vol. II). New York: Brunner/Mazel.

Broderick, C. B., & Smith, J. (1979). The general systems approach to the family. In W. R. Burr, R. Hill, F. I. Nye, & I. L. Reiss (Eds.), *Contemporary theories about the family* (Vol. 2). New York: Free Press.

Brody, E. M. (1974). Aging and family personality: A developmental view. *Family Process, 13,* 23–38.

Brooks, G. R. (1992). Gender-sensitive family therapy in a violent culture. *Topics in Family Psychology and Counseling, 1*(4), 24–36.

Bross, A., & Benjamin, M. (1982). Family therapy: A recursive model of strategic practice. In A. Bross (Ed.), *Family therapy: Principles of strategic practice.* New York: Guilford Press.

Brothers, B. J. (Ed.) (1991). *Virginia Satir: Foundational ideas*. Binghampton, NY: Haworth Press.

Brown, G. W., Monck, E. M., Carstairs, G. M., & Wing, J. K. (1962). Influence on family life in the course of schizophrenic illness. *British Journal of Psychiatry, 16*, 55–68.

Brown, J. E., & Slee, P. T. (1986). Paradoxical strategies: The ethics of intervention. *Professional Psychology: Research and Practice, 17*, 487–491.

Burbatti, G. L., & Formenti, L. (1988). *The Milan approach to family therapy*. Northvale, NJ: Aronson.

Burg, J. E., & Sprenkle, D. H. (1996). Sex therapy. In F. P. Piercy, D.H. Sprenkle, J. Wetchler, & Associates (Eds.), *Family therapy sourcebook* (2nd ed). New York: Guilford Press.

Byng-Hall, J. (1982). The use of the earphone in supervision. In R. Whiffen & J. Byng-Hall (Eds.), *Family therapy supervision: Recent developments in practice*. London: Academic Press.

Cade, B., & O'Hanlon, W. (1993). *A brief guide to brief therapy*. New York: Norton.

Campbell, D. & Draper, R. (Eds.) (1985). *Applications of systemic family therapy: The Milan approach*. London: Grune & Stratton.

Campbell, D., Draper, R., & Crutchley, E. (1991). The Milan systemic approach to family therapy. In A. S. Gurman & D. P. Kniskern (Eds.), *Handbook of family therapy* (Vol. II). New York: Brunner/Mazel.

Campbell, T. L., & Patterson, J. M. (1995). The effectiveness of family interventions in the treatment of physical illness. *Journal of Marital and Family Therapy, 21*, 545–583.

Cannon, W. B. (1932). *The wisdom of the body*. New York: Norton.

Carlson, J., Sperry, L., & Lewis, J. A. (1997). *Family therapy: Ensuring treatment efficacy*. Pacific Grove, CA: Brooks/Cole.

Carlson, K. (1996). Gay and lesbian families. In M. Harway (Ed.), *Treating the changing family: Handling normative and unusual events*. New York: Wiley.

Carter, E. A., & McGoldrick, M. (1980). *The family life cycle: A framework for family therapy*. New York: Gardner Press.

Carter, E. A., & McGoldrick, M. (1988). Overview: The changing family life cycle: A framework for family therapy. In B. Carter & M. McGoldrick (Eds.), *The changing family life cycle: A framework for family therapy* (2nd ed.). Boston: Allyn & Bacon.

Cecchin, G. (1987). Hypothesizing, circularity, and neutrality revisited: An invitation to curiosity. *Family Process, 26*, 405–413.

Chartier, M. R. (1986). Marriage enrichment. In R. F. Levant (Ed.), *Psychoeducational approaches to family therapy and counseling*. New York: Springer.

Cheung, M. (1997). Social construction theory and the Satir model: Toward a synthesis. *American Journal of Family Therapy, 25*, 331–343.

Christensen, A., Jacobson, N. S., & Babcock, J. C. (1995). Integrative behavioral couples therapy. In N.S. Jacobson & A. S. Gurman (Eds.), *Clinical handbook of couple therapy*. New York: Guilford Press.

Cleghorn, J. M., & Levin, S. (1973). Training family therapists by setting learning objectives. *American Journal of Orthopsychiatry, 43*, 439–446.

Colapinto, J. (1979). The relative value of empirical evidence. *Family Process, 18*, 427–441.

Colapinto, J. (1982). Structural family therapy. In A. M. Horne & M. M. Ohlsen (Eds.), *Family counseling and therapy*. Itasca, IL: Peacock.

Colapinto, J. (1991). Structural family therapy. In A. S. Gurman & D. P. Kniskern (Eds.), *Handbook of family therapy* (Vol. II). New York: Brunner/Mazel.

Cole, R. E., & Reiss, D. (1993). *How do families cope with chronic illness?* Hillsdale, NJ: Erlbaum.

Coleman, S. (Ed.). (1985). *Failures in family therapy*. New York: Guilford Press.

Coleman, S., Avis, J., & Turin, M. (1990). A study of the role of gender in family therapy training. *Family Process, 29*, 365–374.

Combrinck-Graham, L. (1988). Adolescent sexuality in the family life cycle. In C. Falicov (Ed.), *Family transitions*. New York: Guilford Press.

Constantine, L. L. (1986). *Family paradigms: The practice of theory in family therapy*. New York: Guilford Press.

Cook, W. L., Strachan, A. M., Goldstein, M. J., & Miklowitz, D. J. (1989). Expressed emotion and reciprocal affective relationships in families of disturbed adolescents. *Family Process, 28*, 337–348.

Corey, G., Corey, M. S., & Callanan, P. (1998). *Issues and ethics in the helping professions* (5th ed.). Pacific Grove, CA: Brooks/Cole.

Cox, F. D. (1996). *Human intimacy: Marriage, the family, and its meaning*. Minneapolis: West.

Cuellar, I., & Glazer, M. (1996). The impact of culture on the family. In M. Harway (Ed.), *Treating the changing family: Handling normative and unusual events*. New York: Wiley.

Cummings, N. A. (1995). Impact of managed care on employment and training: A primer for survival. *Professional Psychology: Research and Practice, 26*, 10–15.

Dangel, R. F., & Polster, R. A. (Eds.). (1984). *Parent training: Foundations of research and practice*. New York: Guilford Press.

Dangel, R. F., Yu, M., Slot, N. W., & Fashimpar, G. (1994). Behavioral parent training. In D. K. Granvold (Ed.), *Cognitive and behavioral treatment: Methods and applications*. Pacific Grove, CA: Brooks/Cole.

Dattilio, F. M. (Ed.). (1998). *Case studies in couple and family therapy: Systemic and cognitive perspectives*. New York: Guilford Press.

Dattilio, F. M., Epstein, N. B., & Baucom, D. H. (1998). An introduction to cognitive-behavioral therapy with couples and families. In F. M. Dattilio (Ed.), *Case studies in couple and family therapy: Systemic & cognitive perspectives*. New York: Guilford Press.

Dattilio, F. M., & Padesky, C. A. (1990). *Cognitive therapy with couples*. Sarasota, FL: Professional Resource Exchange.

del Carmen, R. (1990). Assessment of Asian-American families for family therapy. In F. C. Serafica, A. I. Schwebel, R. K. Russell, P. D. Isaac, & L. B. Myers (Eds.), *Mental health of ethnic minorities*. New York: Praeger.

Dell, P. F. (1982). Beyond homeostasis: Toward a concept of coherence. *Family Process, 21*, 21–42.

deShazer, S. (1985). *Keys to solution in brief therapy*. New York: Norton.

deShazer, S. (1988). *Clues: Investigating solutions in brief therapy*. New York: Norton.

deShazer, S. (1991). *Putting differences to work*. New York: Norton.

deShazer, S. (1994). *Words were originally magic*. New York: Norton.

Dicks, H. V. (1967). *Marital tensions*. New York: Basic Books.

Dinkmeyer, D., & Carlson, J. (1984). *Training in marriage enrichment*. Circle Pines, MN: American Guidance Service.

Dinkmeyer, D., & McKay, G. D. (1976). *Systematic training for effective parenting*. Circle Pines, MN: American Guidance Service.

Doane, J. (1978). Family interaction and communication deviance in disturbed and normal families: A review of research. *Family Process, 17*, 357–376.

Doherty, W. J. (1991). Family therapy goes postmodern. *Family Networker, 15*(5), 36–42.

Doherty, W. J., & Baird, M. A. (1983). *Family therapy and family medicine: Toward the primary care of patients*. New York: Guilford Press.

Doherty, W. J., & Baird, M. A. (Eds.). (1987). *Family-centered medical care: A clinical casebook*. New York: Guilford Press.

Doherty, W. J., & Boss, P. G. (1991). Values and ethics in family therapy. In A. S. Gurman & D. P. Kniskern (Eds.), *Handbook of family therapy* (Vol. II). New York: Brunner/Mazel.

Doyle, J. A. (1994). *The male experience* (3rd ed.). Dubuque, IA: W. C. Brown.

Ducommun-Nagy, C. (1999). Contextual therapy. In D. M. Lawson & F. F. Prevatt (Eds.), *Casebook in family therapy*. Pacific Grove, CA: Brooks/Cole.

Duhl, B. S., & Duhl, F. J. (1981). Integrative family therapy. In A. S. Gurman & D. P. Kniskern (Eds.), *Handbook of family therapy*. New York: Brunner/Mazel.

Duhl, F. J., Kantor, D., & Duhl, B. S. (1973). Learning, space, and action in family therapy: A primer of sculpture. In D. A. Bloch (Ed.), *Techniques of family psychotherapy: A primer*. New York: Grune & Stratton.

Dunn, R. L., & Schwebel, A. I. (1995). Meta-analysis of marital therapy outcome research. *Journal of Family Psychology, 9*, 58–68.

Durrant, M., & Kowalski, K. (1993). Enhancing views of competence. In S. Friedman (Ed.), *The new language of change: Constructive collaboration in psychotherapy*. New York: Guilford Press.

Duvall, E. M. (1977). *Marriage and family development* (5th ed.) New York: Lippincott.

Duvall, E. M., & Hill, R. (1948). *Report to the committee on the dynamics of family interaction*. Washington, DC: National Conference on Family Life.

Duvall, E. M., & Miller, B. C. (1985). *Marriage and family development* (6th ed.). New York: Harper & Row.

Edelman, M. W. (1987). *Families in peril: An agenda for social change*. Cambridge, MA: Harvard University Press.

Edwards, M. E., & Steinglass, P. (1995). Family therapy outcomes for alcoholism. *Journal of Marital and Family Therapy, 21*, 475–510.

Efran, J., & Schenker, M. (1993). A potpourri of solutions: How new and different is solution-focused therapy? *The Family Therapy Networker, 17*(3), 71–74.

Eidelson, R. J., & Epstein, N. (1982). Cognitive and relationship maladjustment: Development of a measure of dysfunctional relationship beliefs. *Journal of Consulting and Clinical Psychology, 50*, 715–720.

Eldridge, K., Christensen, A., & Jacobson, N. S. (1999). Integrative couple therapy. In D. M. Lawson & F. F. Prevatt (Eds.), *Casebook in family therapy*. Pacific Grove, CA: Brooks/Cole.

Elizur, J., & Minuchin, S. (1989). *Institutionalizing madness: Families, therapy, and society*. New York: Basic Books.

Ellis, A. (1979). Rational-emotive therapy. In R. J. Corsini (Ed.), *Current psychotherapies* (2nd ed.). Itaska, IL: Peacock.

Ellis, A. (1995). Rational emotive behavior therapy. In R. J. Corsini & D. Wedding (Eds.), *Current psychotherapies* (5th ed.). Itasca, IL: Peacock.

Engel. G. L. (1977). The need for a new medical model: A challenge for biomedicine. *Science, 196*, 129–136.

Epstein, N. B. (1992). Marital therapy. In A. Freeman & F. M. Dattilio (Eds.), *Comprehensive casebook of cognitive therapy*. New York: Plenum.

Epstein, N. B., Baldwin, L. M., & Bishop, D. S. (1983). The McMaster family assessment device. *Journal of Marital and Family Therapy, 9*, 171–186.

Epstein, N. B., & Baucom, D. H. (1989). Cognitive-behavioral marital therapy. In A. Freeman, K. M. Simon, L. E. Butler, & H. Arkowitz (Eds.), *Comprehensive handbook of cognitive therapy*. New York: Plenum.

Epstein, N. B., Bishop, D. S., & Baldwin, L. M. (1982). McMaster Model of family functioning: A view of the normal family. In F. Walsh (Ed.), *Normal family processes*. New York: Guilford Press.

Epstein, N. B., Bishop, D. S., Ryan, C., Miller, I., & Keitner, G. (1993). The McMaster Model: View of healthy family functioning. In F. Walsh (Ed.), *Normal family processes* (2nd ed.). New York: Guilford Press.

Epstein, N. B., Schlesinger, S. E., & Dryden, W. (Eds.). (1988). Concepts and methods of cognitive-behavioral family treatment. In N. Epstein, S. E. Schlesinger, & W. Dryden (Eds.), *Cognitive-behavioral therapy with families*. New York: Brunner/Mazel.

Epston, D. (1994). Extending the conversation. *The Family Networker, 18* (6), 30–37, 62–63.

Epston, D., & White, M. (1992). *Experience, contradiction, narrative and imagination: Selected papers of David Epston and Michael White.* Adelaide, Australia: Dulwich Centre Publications.

Erikson, E. (1963). *Childhood and society.* New York: Norton.

Eron, J. & Lund, T. (1996). *Narrative solutions in brief therapy.* New York: Guilford Press.

Estrada, A.U., & Pinsof, W. M. (1995). The effectiveness of family therapies by selected behavioral disorders of childhood. *Journal of Marital and Family Therapy, 21,* 403–440.

Fairbairn, W. R. (1952). *An object-relations theory of personality.* New York: Basic Books.

Falicov, C. J. (1986). Cross-cultural marriages. In N. Jacobson & A. S. Gurman (Eds.), *Clinical handbook of marital therapy.* New York: Guilford Press.

Falicov, C. J. (Ed.). (1988a). *Family transitions: Continuity and change over the life cycle.* New York: Guilford Press.

Falicov, C. J. (1988b). Learning to think culturally. In H. A. Liddle D. C. Breunlin, & R. C. Schwartz (Eds.), *Handbook of family therapy training and supervision.* New York: Guilford Press.

Falloon, I. R. H. (Ed.). (1988). *Handbook of behavioral family therapy.* New York: Guilford Press.

Falloon, I. R. H. (1991). Behavioral family therapy. In A. S. Gurman & D. P. Kniskern (Eds.), *Handbook of family therapy* (Vol. II). New York: Brunner/Mazel.

Falloon, I. R. H., Boyd, J. L., McGill, C. W., Williamson, M., Razani, J., Moss, H. B., Gilderman, A. M., & Simpson, G. M. (1985). Family management in the prevention of morbidity of schizophrenia: Clinical outcome of a two-year longitudinal study. *Archives of General Psychiatry, 42,* 887–896.

Falloon, I. R. H., & Lieberman, R. P. (1983). Behavior therapy for families with child management problems. In M. R. Textor (Ed.), *Helping families with special problems.* New York: Aronson.

Falloon, I. R. H., & Lillie, F. J. (1988). Behavioral family therapy: An overview. In I. R. H. Falloon (Ed.), *Handbook of behavioral family therapy.* New York: Guilford Press.

Feldman, L. (1992). *Integrating individual and family therapy.* New York: Brunner/Mazel.

Fenell, L., & Hovestadt, A. J. (1986). Family therapy as a profession or professional specialty: Implications for training. *Journal of Psychotherapy and the Family, 1*(4), 25–40.

Fieldsteel, N. D. (1982). Ethical issues in family therapy. In M. Rosenbaum (Ed.), *Ethics and values in psychotherapy: A guidebook.* New York: Free Press.

Fincham, F. D., & Bradbury, T. N. (1992). Assessing attributions in marriage: The Relationship Attribution Measure. *Journal of Personality and Social Psychology, 62,* 457–468.

Fine, M. J. (1995). Family-school intervention. In R. H. Mikesell, D-D. Lusterman, & S. H. McDaniel (Eds.), *Integrating family therapy: Handbook of family psychology and systems theory.* Washington, DC: American Psychological Association.

Fisch, R., Weakland, J., & Segal, L. (1982). *The tactics of change: Doing therapy briefly.* San Francisco: Jossey-Bass.

Fish, J. M. (1995). Solution focused therapy in global perspective. *World Psychology, 1,* 43–67.

Fishman, H. C. (1988). Structural family therapy and the family life cycle: A four-dimensional model for family assessment. In C. J. Falicov (Ed.), *Family transitions: Continuity and change over the life cycle.* New York: Guilford Press.

Floyd, F. J., Markman, H. J., Kelly, S., Blumberg, S. L., & Stanley, S. M. (1995). Preventive intervention and relationship enhancement. In N. S. Jacobson & A. S. Gurman (Eds.), *Clinical handbook of couple therapy.* New York: Guilford Press.

Fontes, L. A., & Thomas, V. (1996). Cultural issues in family therapy. In F. P. Piercy, D. H. Sprenkle, J. L. Wetchler, & Associates (Eds.), *Family therapy sourcebook* (2nd ed.). New York: Guilford Press.

Forgatch, M. S. & Patterson, G. R. (1998). Behavioral family therapy. In F. M. Dattilio (Ed.), *Case studies in couple and family therapy: Systemic and cognitive perspectives*. New York: Guilford Press.

Foucault, M. (1965). *Madness and civilization: A history of insanity in the age of reason*. New York: Random House.

Foucault, M. (1980). *Power/knowledge: Selected interviews and other writings, 1972–1977*. New York: Pantheon Books.

Fournier, C. J., & Rae, W. A. (1999). Psychoeducational family therapy. In D. M. Lawson & F. F. Prevatt (Eds.). *Casebook in family therapy*. Pacific Grove, CA: Brooks/Cole.

Fowers, B. J., & Olson, D. H. (1992). Four types of premarital couples: An empirical typology based on PREPARE. *Journal of Family Psychology, 6*(1), 10–21.

Fox, R. E. (1976). Family therapy. In I. B. Weiner (Ed.), *Clinical methods in psychology*. New York: Wiley.

Framo, J. L. (1972). *Family interaction: A dialogue between family researchers and family therapists*. New York: Springer.

Framo, J. L. (1976). Family of origin as a therapeutic resource for adults in marital and family therapy: You can and should go home again. *Family Process, 15*, 193–210.

Framo, J. L. (1981). The integration of marital therapy with sessions with family of origin. In A. S. Gurman & D. P. Kniskern (Eds.), *Handbook of family therapy*. New York: Brunner/Mazel.

Framo, J. L. (1982). *Explorations in marital and family therapy: Selected papers of James L. Framo*. New York: Springer.

Framo, J. L. (1992). *Family-of-origin therapy: An intergenerational approach*. New York: Brunner/Mazel.

Freedman, J., & Combs, G. (1996). *Narrative therapy: The social construction of preferred realities*. New York: Norton.

Fretz, B. R., & Mills, D. H. (1980). *Licensing and certification of psychologists and counselors*. San Francisco: Jossey-Bass.

Freud, S. (1955). Analysis of a phobia in a five-year-old boy (1909). *The standard edition of the complete psychological works of Sigmund Freud* (Vol. 10). London: Hogarth.

Freud, S. (1959). Fragments of an analysis of a case of hysteria (1905). *Collected papers* (Vol. 3). New York: Basic Books.

Friedman, E. (1991). Bowen theory and therapy. In A. S. Gurman & D. P. Kniskern (Eds.), *Handbook of family therapy* (Vol. II). New York: Brunner/Mazel.

Friedman, S. (Ed.). (1993). *The new language of change: Constructive collaboration in psychotherapy*. New York: Guilford Press.

Fromm-Reichmann, F. (1948). Notes on the development of treatment of schizophrenics by psychoanalytic psychotherapy. *Psychiatry, 11*, 253–273.

Fulero, S. M. (1988). Tarasoff: Ten years later. *Professional Psychology: Research and Practice, 19*(2), 184–190.

Fulmer, R. (1988). Lower-income and professional families: A comparison of structure and life cycle process. In B. Carter & M. McGoldrick (Eds.), *The changing family life cycle: A framework for family therapy* (2nd ed.). New York: Gardner Press.

Gambrill, E. D. (1994). Concepts and methods of behavioral treatment. In D. K. Granvold (Ed.), *Cognitive and behavioral treatment: Methods and applications*. Pacific Grove, CA: Brooks/ Cole.

Ganahl, G., Ferguson, L. R., & L'Abate, L. (1985). Training in family therapy. In L. L'Abate (Ed.), *The handbook of family psychology*. Homewood, IL: Dorsey Press.

Ganong, L. & Coleman, M. (1994). *Remarried family relationships*. Thousand Oaks, CA: Sage.

Gelcer, E., McCabe, A. E., & Smith-Resnick, C. (1990). *Milan family therapy: Variant and invariant methods*. Northvale, NJ: Aronson.

Gergen, K. J. (1985). The social construction movement in modern psychology. *American Psychologist, 40*, 266–275.

Gergen, K. J. (1993). Foreword. In S. Friedman (Ed.), *The new language of change: Constructive collaboration in psychotherapy.* New York: Guilford Press.

Gerson, R. (1995). The family life cycle: Phases, stages, and crises. In R. H. Mikesell, D-D. Lusterman, & S. H. McDaniel (Eds.), *Integrating family therapy: Handbook of family psychology and systems theory.* Washington, DC: American Psychological Association.

Gill, S. J. (1982). Professional disclosure and consumer protection in counseling. *Personnel and Guidance Journal, 60*, 443–446.

Gilligan, C. (1982). *In a different voice: Psychological theory and women's development.* Cambridge, MA: Harvard University Press.

Ginsberg, B. G. (1977). Parent-adolescent relationship development program. In B. G. Guerney, Jr. (Ed.), *Relationship enhancement: Skills training for herapy problem prevention and enrichment.* San Francisco: Jossey-Bass.

Ginsberg, B. G. (1997). *Relationship enhancement family therapy.* New York: Wiley.

Giordano, J., & Carini-Giordano, M. A. (1995). Ethnic dimensions in family treatment. In R. H. Mikesell, D-D. Lusterman, & S. H. McDaniel (Eds.), *Integrating family therapy: Handbook of family psychology and systems theory.* Washington, DC: American Psychological Association.

Glick, P. C. (1989). Remarried families, stepfamilies, and stepchildren: A brief demographic analysis. *Family Relations, 38,* 24–27.

Goldenberg, H. (1973). *Is training family therapists different from clinical training in general?* Paper presented at the American Psychological Association annual meeting, Montreal, Canada, 1973.

Goldenberg, H. (1983). *Contemporary clinical psychology* (2nd ed.). Pacific Grove, CA: Brooks/Cole.

Goldenberg, H., & Goldenberg, I. (1993). Multiculturalism and family systems. *Progress: Family Systems Research and Therapy, 2,* 7–12.

Goldenberg, H., & Goldenberg, I. (1998). *Counseling today's families* (3rd ed.). Pacific Grove, CA: Brooks/Cole..

Goldenberg, H., & Goldenberg, I. (1999). Current issues and trends in family therapy. In D. M. Lawson & F. F. Prevatt (Eds.), *Casebook in family therapy.* Pacific Grove, CA: Brooks/Cole.

Goldenberg, I., & Goldenberg, H. (1983). Historical roots of contemporary family therapy. In B. B. Wolman & G. Stricker (Eds.), *Handbook of family and marital therapy.* New York: Plenum.

Goldenberg, I., & Goldenberg, H. (1995). Family therapy. In R. J. Corsini & D. Wedding (Eds.), *Current psychotherapies* (5th ed.). Itasca, IL: Peacock.

Goldenberg, I., Stier, S., & Preston, T. (1975). The use of multiple family marathon as a teaching device. *Journal of Marriage and the Family, 1,* 343–349.

Goldner, V. (1985). Feminism and family therapy. *Family Process, 24,* 13–47.

Goldner, V., Penn, P., Sheinberg, M, & Walker, G. (1990). Love and violence: Gender paradoxes in volatile attachments. *Family Process, 29,* 343–364.

Goldstein, M. J. (Ed.). (1981). *New developments in interventions with families of schizophrenics.* San Francisco: Jossey-Bass.

Goldstein, M. J. (1985). Family factors that antedate the onset of schizophrenia and related disorders: The results of a fifteen-year prospective longitudinal study. *Acta Psychiatrica Scandinavia, 71,* 7–18.

Goldstein, M. J. (1988). The family and psychopathology. In M. R. Rosenzweig & L. W. Porter (Eds.), *Annual Review of Psychology, 39,* 283–299.

Goldstein, M. J., & Miklowitz, D. J. (1995). The effectiveness of psychoeducational family therapy in the treatment of schizophrenic disorders. *Journal of Marital and Family Therapy, 21,* 361–376.

Goldstein, M. J., Rodnick, E. H., Evans, J. R., May, P. R., & Steinberg, M. (1978). Drug and family therapy in the aftercare treatment of acute schizophrenia. *Archives of General Psychiatry, 35,* 1169–1177.

Good, G., Gilbert, L., & Scher, M. (1990). Gender aware therapy: A synthesis of feminist therapy and knowledge about gender. *Journal of Counseling and Development, 68,* 376–380.

Gordon, S. B., & Davidson, N. (1981). Behavioral parent training. In A. S. Gurman & D. P. Kniskern (Eds.), *Handbook of family therapy.* New York: Brunner/Mazel.

Gorall, D. M., & Olson, D. H. (1995). Circumplex model of family systems: Integrating ethnic diversity and other social systems. In R. H. Mikesell, D-D. Lusterman, & S. H. McDaniel (Eds.), *Integrating family therapy: Handbook of family psychology and systems theory.* Washington, DC: American Psychological Association.

Gottman, J. M. (1979). *Marital interaction: Experimental investigations.* New York: Academic Press.

Gottman, J. M. (1993). A theory of marital dissolution and stability. *Journal of Family Psychology, 7,* 57–75.

Gottman, J. M. (1994). *What predicts divorce?* Hillsdale, NJ: Erlbaum.

Gottman, J. M., Coan, J., Carrere, S., & Swanson, C. (1998). Predicting marital happiness and stability from newlywed interactions. *Journal of Marriage and the Family, 60,* 5–22.

Gottman, J., & Krokoff, I. (1989). Marital interaction and satisfaction: A longitudinal view. *Journal of Consulting and Clinical Psychology, 57,* 47–52.

Granvold, D. K. (1994). Concepts and methods of cognitive therapy. In D. K. Granvold (Ed.), *Cognitive and behavioral treatment: Methods and applications.* Pacific Grove, CA: Brooks/Cole.

Green, R. J., & Framo, J. L. (Eds.). (1981). *Family therapy: Major contributions.* New York: International Universities Press.

Green, S. L., & Hansen, J. C. (1989). Ethical dilemmas faced by family therapists. *Journal of Marital and Family Therapy, 15,* 149–158.

Greenberg, G. S. (1977). The family interactive perspective: A study and examination of the work of Don D. Jackson. *Family Process, 16,* 385–412.

Greenberg, L. S., & Johnson, S. M. (1986). Emotionally focused couples therapy. In N. S. Jacobson & A. S. Gurman (Eds.), *Clinical handbook of marital therapy.* New York: Guilford Press.

Greenberg, L. S. & Johnson, S. M. (1988). *Emotionally-focused therapy for couples.* New York: Guilford Press.

Greenberg, L. S., & Pinsof, W. M. (Eds.). (1986). *The psychotherapeutic process: A research handbook.* New York: Guilford Press.

Greenberg, L. S., Rice, L. N., & Elliott, R. *Facilitating emotional change: The moment-by-moment process.* New York: Guilford Press.

Greenburg, S. L., Lewis, G. J., & Johnson, J. (1985). Peer consultation groups for private practitioners. *Professional Psychology: Research and Practice, 16*(3), 437–447.

Grotevant, H. D., & Carlson, C. I. (1989). *Family assessment: A guide to methods and measurements.* New York: Guilford Press.

Group for the Advancement of Psychiatry. (1970). *The field of family therapy* (Report No. 78). New York: Group for the Advancement of Psychiatry.

Grove, D., & Haley, J. (1993). *Conversations on therapy.* New York: Norton.

Grunebaum, H. (1997). Commentary: Why integration may be a misguided goal for family therapy. *Family Process, 36,* 19–21.

Guba, E. (Ed.). (1990). *The paradigm dialogue.* Newbury Park, CA: Sage.

Guerin, P. J., Jr. (1976). Family therapy: The first twenty-five years. In P. J. Guerin, Jr. (Ed.), *Family therapy: Theory and practice.* New York: Gardner Press.

Guerney, B. G., Jr. (1964). Filial therapy: Description and rationale. *Journal of Consulting Psychology, 28,* 304–310.

Guerney, B. G., Jr. (Ed.). (1977). *Relationship enhancement: Skills training for therapy problem prevention and enrichment.* San Francisco: Jossey-Bass.

Guerney, B. G., Jr., Coufal, J., & Vogelsang, E. (1981). Relationship enhancement versus a traditional approach to therapeutic/preventive/enrichment parent-adolescent program. *Journal of Consulting and Clinical Psychology, 49,* 927–939.

Guerney, B. G., Jr., Guerney, L., & Andronico, M. (1966). Filial therapy: Description and rationale. *Yale Scientific Magazine, 40,* 6–14.

Gumper, L. L., & Sprenkle, D. H. (1981). Privileged communication in therapy: Special problems for the family and couples therapist. *Family Process, 20,* 11–23.

Gurman, A. S. (1971). Group family therapy: Clinical and empirical implications for outcome research. *International Journal of Group Psychotherapy, 21,* 174-189.

Gurman, A. S. (1983). Family therapy and the new epistemology. *Journal of Marital and Family Therapy, 9,* 227–234.

Gurman, A. S., & Kniskern, D. P. (1981a). Family therapy outcome research: Knowns and unknowns. In A. S. Gurman & D. P. Kniskern (Eds.), *Handbook of family therapy.* New York: Brunner/Mazel.

Gurman, A. S., & Kniskern, D. P. (1981b). The outcome of family therapy: Implications for practice and training. In G. Berenson & H. White (Eds.), *Annual review of family therapy* (Vol. 1.). New York: Human Sciences Press.

Gurman, A. S., Kniskern, D. P., & Pinsof, W. M. (1986). Research on the process and outcome of marital and family therapy. In S. Garfield & A. Bergin (Eds.), *Handbook of psychotherapy and behavior change* (3rd ed.). New York: Wiley.

Gurman, A. S., & Kniskern, D. P., (Eds.) (1991). *Handbook of family therapy* (Vol. II). New York: Brunner/Mazel.

Gurman, A. S., & Knudson, R. M. (1978). Behavior marriage therapy: I. A psychodynamic-systems analysis and critique. *Family Process, 17,* 121–138.

Guttman, H. A. (1991). Systems theory, cybernetics, and epistemology. In A. S. Gurman & D. P. Kniskern (Eds.), *Handbook of family therapy* (Vol. II). New York: Brunner/Mazel.

Haber, R. (1996). *Dimensions of psychotherapy supervision: Maps and means.* New York: Norton.

Hahlweg, K. (1988). Statistical methods for studying family therapy process. In L. C. Wynne (Ed.), *The state of the art in family therapy research: Controversies and recommendations.* New York: Family Process Press.

Hahlweg, K., Baucom, D. H., & Markman, H. (1988). Recent advances in therapy and prevention. In I. R. H. Falloon (Ed.), *Handbook of behavioral family therapy.* New York: Guilford Press.

Haley, J. (1963). *Strategies of psychotherapy.* New York: Grune & Stratton.

Haley, J. (1970). Family therapy. *International Journal of Psychiatry, 9,* 233–242.

Haley, J. (1971). Family therapy: A radical change. In J. Haley (Ed.), *Changing families: A family therapy reader.* New York: Grune & Stratton.

Haley, J. (1973). *Uncommon therapy: The psychiatric techniques of Milton H. Erickson, M.D.* New York: Norton.

Haley, J. (Ed.). (1976a). *Problem-solving therapy.* San Francisco: Jossey-Bass.

Haley, J. (1976b). Problems of training therapists. In J. Haley (Ed.), *Problem-solving therapy.* San Francisco: Jossey-Bass.

Haley, J. (1978). Ideas which handicap therapists. In M. M. Berger (Ed.), *Beyond the double-bind: Communication and family systems, theories, and techniques with schizophrenics*. New York: Brunner/Mazel.

Haley, J. (1979). *Leaving home: Therapy with disturbed young people*. New York: McGraw-Hill.

Haley, J. (1984). *Ordeal therapy: Unusual ways to change behavior*. San Francisco: Jossey-Bass.

Haley, J. (1988). Personal communication.

Haley, J. (1996). *Learning and teaching therapy*. New York: Guilford Press.

Haley, J., & Hoffman, L. (1967). *Techniques of family therapy*. New York: Basic Books.

Hampson, R. B., & Beavers, W. R. (1996). Measuring family therapy outcomes in a clinical setting: Families that do better or do worse in therapy. *Family Process, 35,* 347–361.

Hare-Mustin, R. T. (1978). A feminist approach to family therapy. *Family Process, 17,* 181–194.

Hare-Mustin, R. T. (1980). Family therapy may be dangerous to your health. *Professional Psychology, 11,* 935–938.

Hare-Mustin, R. T. (1987). The problem of gender in family therapy theory. *Family Process, 26,* 15–27.

Harrar, W. R., VandeCreek, L., & Knapp, S. (1990). Ethical and legal aspects of clinical supervision. *Professional Psychology: Research and Practice, 21* (1), 37–41.

Harway, M., & Wexler, K. (1996). Setting the stage for understanding and treating the changing family. In M. Harway (Ed.), *Treating the changing family: Handling normative and unusual events*. New York: Wiley.

Hawley, D. R., & DeHaan, L. (1996). Toward a definition of family resilence: Integrating life-span and family perspectives. *Family Process, 35,* 283–298.

Hazelrigg, M. D., Cooper, H. M., & Borduin, C. M. (1987). Evaluating the effectiveness of family therapies: An integrative review and analysis. *Psychological Bulletin, 101,* 428–442.

Healy, M. (1998). Study says poverty persists for kids of working poor. *Los Angeles Times,* March 13, 1998.

Heiman, J. R., Epps, P. H., & Ellis, B. (1995). Treating sexual desire disorders in couples. In N. S. Jacobson & A. S. Gurman (Eds.), *Clinical handbook of couple therapy*. New York: Guilford Press.

Heiman, J. R., LoPiccolo, L., & LoPiccolo, J. (1981). The treatment of sexual dysfunction. In A. S. Gurman & D. P. Kniskern (Eds.), *Handbook of family therapy*. New York: Brunner/Mazel.

Heiman, J. R., & Verhulst, J. (1990). Sexual dysfunction and marriage. In F. D. Fincham & T. N. Bradbury (Eds.), *The psychology of marriage: Basic issues and applications*. New York: Guilford Press.

Held, B. S. (1998). The antisystematic impact of postmodern philosophy. *Clinical Psychology, 5,* 264–273.

Henggeler, S. W., Borduin, C. M., & Mann, B. J. (1993). Advances in family therapy: Empirical foundations. *Advances in Clinical Child Psychology, 15,* 207–241.

Hersch, L. (1995). Adapting to health care reform and managed care: Three strategies for survival and growth. *Professional Psychology: Research and Practice, 26,* 16–26.

Hines, P. M. (1988). The family life cycle of poor black families. In B. Carter & M. McGoldrick (Eds.), *The changing family life cycle: A framework for family therapy* (2nd ed.). New York: Gardner Press.

Ho, M. K. (1987). *Family therapy with ethnic minorities*. Newbury Park, CA: Sage.

Hoffman, L. (1981). *Foundations of family therapy*. New York: Basic Books.

Hoffman, L. (1985). Beyond power and control: Toward a second-order family systems therapy. *Family Systems Medicine, 3,* 381–396.

Hoffman, L. (1988). The family life cycle and discontinuous change. In B. Carter & M. McGoldrick (Eds.), *The changing family life cycle* (2nd ed.). New York: Gardner Press.

Hoffman, L. (1990). Constructing realities: An art of lenses. *Family Process, 29,* 1–12.

Holtzworth-Munroe, A., & Jacobson, N. S. (1991). Behavioral marital therapy. In A. S. Gurman & D. P. Kniskern (Eds.), *Handbook of family therapy* (Vol. II). New York: Brunner/Mazel.

Homma-True, R., Greene, B., Lopez, S. R., & Trimble, J. E. (1993) Ethnocultural diversity in clinical psychology. *Clinical Psychologist, 46,* 50–63.

Howells, J. G. (1975). *Principles of family psychiatry.* New York: Brunner/Mazel.

Huber, C. H. (1994). *Ethical, legal, and professional issues in the practice of marriage and family therapy* (2nd ed.). New York: Macmillan.

Huber, C. H., & Baruth, L. G. (1987). *Ethical, legal, and professional issues in the practice of marriage and family therapy. Columbus,* OH: Merrill.

Hudson, P., & O'Hanlon, W. H. (1992). *Rewriting love stories: Brief marital therapy.* New York: Norton.

Huston, T. L., & Robins, E. (1982). Conceptual and methodological issues in studying close relationships. In L. H. Brown & J. S. Kidwell (Eds.), Methodology: The other side of caring. *Journal of Marriage and the Family, 44* (4), 901–925.

Imber-Black, E. (1988). *Families and larger systems: A family therapist's guide through the labyrinth.* New York: Guilford Press.

Imber-Black, E. (1991). A family–larger system perspective. In A. S Gurman & D. P. Kniskern (Eds.), *Handbook of family therapy* (Vol. II). New York: Brunner/Mazel.

Incan, J., & Ferran, E. (1990). Poverty, politics, and family therapy: A role for systems theory. In M. P. Mirkin (Ed.), *The social and political contexts of family therapy.* Boston: Allyn & Bacon.

Jackson, D. D. (1957). The question of family homeostasis. *Psychiatric Quarterly Supplement, 31,* 79–90.

Jackson, D. D. (1959). Family interaction, family homeostasis, and some implications for conjoint family therapy. In J. Masserman (Ed.), *Individual and family dynamics.* New York: Grune & Stratton.

Jackson, D. D. (1965a). Family rules: Marital quid pro quo. *Archives of General Psychiatry, 12,* 589–594.

Jackson, D. D. (1965b). The study of the family. *Family Process, 4*(1), 1–20.

Jacobson, N. S. (1991). To be or not to be behavioral when working with couples. *Journal of Family Psychology, 4,* 436–445.

Jacobson, N. S., & Christensen, A. (1996). *Integrative couple therapy: Promoting acceptance.* New York: Norton.

Jacobson, N. S., & Margolin, G. (1979). *Marital therapy: Strategies based on social learning and behavior exchange principles.* New York: Brunner/Mazel.

Jacobson, N. S., Follette, W. C., & Revenstorf, D. (1984). Psychotherapy outcome research: Methods for reporting variability and evaluating clinical significance. *Behavior Therapy, 15,* 336–352.

Jacobson, N. S., & Martin, B. (1976). Behavioral marital therapy. *Psychological Bulletin, 83,* 540–556.

Jacobson, N. S., Schmaling, K. B., & Holtzworth-Munroe, A. (1987). Component analysis of behavioral marital therapy: Two-year follow-up and prediction of relapse. *Journal of Marital and Family Therapy, 13,* 187–195.

Johnson, S. M. (1998). Emotionally focused couples therapy. In F. M. Dattilio (Ed.), *Case studies in couple and family therapy.* New York: Guilford Press.

Johnson, S. M., & Greenberg, L. S. (1995). The emotionally-focused approach to problems in adult attachment. In N. S. Jacobson & A. S. Gurman (Eds.), *Clinical handbook of couple therapy.* New York: Guilford Press.

Jones, E. (1993). *Family systems therapy: Developments in the Milan-Systemic therapies*. New York: Wiley.

Jones, J. M. (1991). Psychological models of race: What have they been and what should they be? In J. D. Goodchilds (Ed.), *Psychological perspectives on human diversity in America*. Washington, DC: American Psychological Association.

Kalichman, S. C., & Craig, M. E. (1991). Professional psychologists; decisions to report suspected child abuse: Clinical and situational influences. *Professional Psychology: Research and Practice, 26*, 5–9.

Kantor D., & Lehr, W. (1975). *Inside the family*. San Francisco: Jossey-Bass.

Kaplan, H. S. (1974). *The new sex therapy: Active treatment of sexual dysfunction*. New York: Brunner/Mazel.

Kaplan, H. S. (1979). *Disorders of sexual desire and other new concepts and techniques in sex therapy*. New York: Brunner/Mazel.

Kaplan, H. S. (1983). *The evaluation of sexual disorders: Psychological and medical aspects*. New York: Brunner/Mazel.

Kaplan, H. S. (1995). *The sexual desire disorders: Dysfunctional regulation of sexual motivation*. New York: Brunner/Mazel.

Kaplan, M. L., & Kaplan, N. R. (1978). Individual and family growth: A Gestalt approach. *Family Process, 17*, 195–206.

Karpel, M. A. (Ed.). (1986). *Family resources: The hidden partner in family therapy*. New York: Guilford Press.

Karpel, M. A., & Strauss, E. S. (1983). *Family evaluation*. New York: Gardner Press.

Kaslow, F. W. (1996). (Ed.). *Handbook of relational diagnosis and dysfunctional family patterns*. New York: Wiley.

Kaye, K. (1985). Toward a developmental psychology of the family. In L. L'Abate (Ed.), *The handbook of family psychology and therapy* (Vol. 1). Homewood, IL: Dorsey Press.

Kazdin, A. E. (1984). *Behavior modification in applied settings* (3rd ed.). Homewood, IL: Dorsey Press.

Keeney, B. P. (1983). *Aesthetics of change*. New York: Guilford Press.

Keeney, B. P., & Sprenkle, D. H. (1982). Ecosystemic epistemology: Critical implications for the aesthetics and pragmatics of family therapy. *Family Process, 21*, 1–19.

Keeney, B. P., & Thomas, F. N. (1986). Cybernetic foundations of family therapy. In F. P. Piercy, D. H. Sprenkle, & Associates (Eds.), *Family therapy sourcebook*. New York: Guilford Press.

Keim, J. (1998). Strategic family therapy. In F. M. Dattilio (Ed.), *Case studies in couple and family therapy: Systemic and cognitive perspectives*. New York: Guilford Press.

Keith, D. V. (1989). The family's own system: The symbolic content of health. In L. Combrinck-Graham (Ed.), *Children in family context: Perspectives on treatment*. New York: Guilford Press.

Keith, D. V. (1998). Symbolic-experiential family therapy for chemical imbalance. In F. M. Dattilio (Ed.), *Case studies in couple and family therapy: Systemic and cognitive perspectives*. New York: Guilford Press.

Keith, D. V., & Whitaker, C. A. (1982). Experiential-symbolic family therapy. In A. M. Horne & M. M. Ohlsen (Eds.), *Family counseling and therapy*. Itasca, IL: Peacock.

Keith-Spiegel, P., & Koocher, G. P. (1985). *Ethics in psychology: Professional standards and cases*. New York: Random House.

Kempler, W. (1974). *Principles of Gestalt family therapy*. Costa Mesa, CA: The Kempler Institute.

Kempler, W. (1981). *Experiential psychotherapy with families*. New York: Brunner/Mazel.

Kempler, W. (1982). Gestalt family therapy. In A. M. Horne & M. M. Ohlsen (Eds.), *Family counseling and therapy*. Itasca, IL: Peacock.

Kendall, P. C. (1981). Assessment and cognitive-behavioral interventions: Purposes, proposals, and problems. In P. C. Kendall & S. D. Hollon (Eds.), *Assessment strategies for cognitive-behavioral interventions*. New York: Academic Press.

Kerr, M. E. (1981). Family systems theory and therapy. In A. S. Gurman & D. P. Kniskern (Eds.), *Handbook of family therapy*. New York: Brunner/Mazel.

Kerr, M. E., & Bowen, M. (1988). *Family evaluation: An approach based on Bowen theory*. New York: Norton.

Kimmel, M. (1987). Rethinking masculinity: New directions in research. In M. Kimmel (Ed.), *Changing men: New directions in research on men and masculinity*. Newbury Park, CA: Sage.

Kliman, J. (1994). The interweaving of gender, class, and race in family therapy. In M. P. Mirkin (Ed.), *Women in context: Toward a feminist reconstruction of psychotherapy*. New York: Guilford Press.

Korzybski, A. (1942). *Science and sanity: An introduction to non-Aristotelian systems and general semantics* (2nd ed.). Lancaster, PA: Science Books.

Kressel, K. (1985). *The process of divorce: How professionals and couples negotiate settlements*. New York: Basic Books.

Kuhn, T. (1970). *The structure of scientific revolutions*. Chicago: University of Chicago Press.

L'Abate, L. (Ed.). (1985). *The handbook of family psychology and therapy* (Vols. I & II). Homewood, IL: Dorsey Press.

L'Abate, L. (1994). *Family evaluation: A psychological approach*. Thousand Oaks, CA: Sage.

Landau-Stanton, J. (1993). *AIDS, health, and mental health: A primary sourcebook*. New York: Brunner/Mazel.

Langsley, D. G., Pittman, F. S., Machotka, P., & Flomenhaft, K. (1968). Family crisis therapy: Results and implications. *Family Process, 7*, 145–158.

Laqueur, H. P. (1976). Multiple family therapy. In P. J. Guerin, Jr. (Ed.), *Family therapy: Theory and practice*. New York: Gardner Press.

Lasswell, M., & Lasswell, T. (1991). *Marriage and the family* (3rd ed.). Belmont, CA: Wadsworth.

Lawrence, E. C. (1999). The humanistic approach of Virginia Satir. In D. M. Lawson & F. F. Prevatt (Eds.), *Casebook in family therapy*. Pacific Grove, CA: Brooks/Cole.

Lawson, D. M., & Prevatt, F. F. (Eds.). (1999). *Casebook in family therapy*. Pacific Grove, CA: Brooks/Cole.

Lazarus, A. A. (1977). Has behavior therapy outlived its usefulness? *American Psychologist, 32*, 550–554.

Lebow, J. (1997). The integrative revolution in couple and family therapy. *Family Process, 36*, 1–17.

Leff, J., & Vaughn, C. (1985). *Expressed emotions in families*. New York: Guilford Press.

Lefley, H. P. (1996). *Family caregiving in mental illness*. Thousand Oaks, CA: Sage.

Lerner, G. (1986). *The creation of patriarchy*. New York: Oxford University Press.

Leslie, L. A. (1988). Cognitive-behavioral and systems models of family therapy: How compatible are they? In N. Epstein, S. E. Schlesinger, & W. Dryden (Eds.), *Cognitive-behavioral therapy with families*. New York: Brunner/Mazel.

Levant, R. F. (Ed.). (1986). *Psychoeducational approaches to family therapy and counseling*. New York: Springer.

Lewis, J. A. (1992). Gender sensitivity and family empowerment. *Topics in Family Psychology and Counseling, 1*(4), 1–7.

Lewis, J. M. (1988). The transition to parenthood: I. The rating of prenatal marital competence. *Family Process, 27*, 149–165.

Lewis, J. M., Beavers, W. R., Gossett, J. T., & Phillips, V. A. 1976). *No single thread: Psychological health in family systems*. New York: Brunner/Mazel.

Liberman, R. P. (1970). Behavioral approaches to family and couple therapy. *American Journal of Orthopsychiatry, 40*, 106–118.

Liddle, H. A. (1982). On the problem of eclecticism: A call for epistemological clarification and human-scale theories. *Family Process, 21*, 243–250.

Liddle, H. A. (1987). Family psychology: The journal, the field. *Journal of Family Psychology, 1*, 5–22.

Liddle, H. A. (1988). Systemic supervision: Conceptual overlays and pragmatic guidelines. In H. A. Liddle, D. C. Breunlin, & R. C. Schwartz (Eds.), *Handbook of family therapy training and supervision*. New York: Guilford Press.

Liddle, H. A. (1991). Training and supervision in family therapy: A comprehensive and critical analysis. In A. S. Gurman & D. P. Kniskern (Eds.), *Handbook of Family Therapy* (Vol. II). New York: Brunner/Mazel.

Liddle, H. A., Breunlin, D. C., & Schwartz, R. C. (Eds.). (1988). *Handbook of family therapy training and supervision*. New York: Guilford Press.

Liddle, H. A., & Halpin, R. J. (1978). Family therapy training and supervision: A comparative review. *Journal of Marriage and Family Counseling, 4*, 77–98.

Lidz, R., & Lidz, T. (1949). The family environment of schizophrenic patients. *American Journal of Psychiatry, 106*, 332–345.

Lidz, T., Cornelison, A., Fleck, S., & Terry, D. (1957a). The intrafamilial environment of schizophrenic patients: I. The father. *Psychiatry, 20*, 329–342.

Lidz, T., Cornelison, A., Fleck, S., & Terry, D. (1957b). The intrafamilial environment of schizophrenic patients: II. Marital schism and marital skew. *American Journal of Psychiatry, 114*, 241–248.

Lindahl, K. M., Clements, M., & Markman, H. (1997). Predicting marital and parent functioning in dyads and triads: A longitudinal investigation of marital processes. *Journal of Family Psychology, 11*, 139–151.

Lipchik, E. (1993). "Both/and" solutions. In S. Friedman (Ed.), *The new language of change: Constructive collaboration in psychotherapy*. New York: Guilford Press.

Loewenstein, S. F., Reder, P., & Clark, A. (1982). The consumers' report: Trainees' discussion of the experience of live supervision. In R. Whiffen & J. Byng-Hall (Eds.), *Family therapy supervision: Recent developments in practice*. London: Academic Press.

Lowe, R. N. (1982). Adlerian/Dreikursian family counseling. In A. M. Horne & M. M. Ohlsen (Eds.), *Family counseling and therapy*. Itasca, IL: Peacock.

Luepnitz, D. A. (1988). *The family interpreted: Feminist theory in clinical practice*. New York: Basic Books.

Lusterman, D-D. (1988). Family therapy and schools: An ecosystemic approach. *Family Therapy Today, 3*(7), 1–3.

Lynch, K., & Hutchins, J. (1994). Three more states lead MFT legislative victories. *Family Therapy News, 25*(4), 1–8.

MacGregor, R., Ritchie, A. N., Serrano, A. C., & Schuster, F. P. (1964). *Multiple impact therapy with families*. New York: McGraw-Hill.

MacKinnon, L. K. (1983). Contrasting strategic and Milan therapies. *Family Process, 22*, 425–440.

Macklin, E. (Ed.). (1989). *AIDS and the family*. New York: Haworth.

Madanes, C. (1981). *Strategic family therapy*. San Francisco: Jossey-Bass.

Madanes, C. (1984). *Behind the one-way mirror: Advances in the practice of strategic therapy*. San Francisco: Jossey-Bass.

Madanes, C. (1990). *Sex, love, and violence*. New York: Norton.

Madanes, C. (1991). Strategic family therapy. In A. S. Gurman & D. P. Kniskern (Eds.), *Handbook of family therapy* (Vol. II). New York: Brunner/Mazel.

Madanes, C., & Haley, J. (1977). Dimensions of family therapy. The Journal of Nervous and Mental Disease, 165, 88–98.

Madigan, S. (1994). Body politics. The Family Therapy Networker, 18(6), 18.

Malcolm, J. (1978). A reporter at large: The one-way mirror. New Yorker, May 15, 39–114.

Manns, W. (1988). Supportive roles of significant others in Black families. In H. P. McAdoo (Ed.), Black families (2nd ed.). Newbury Park, CA: Sage.

Manus, G. (1966). Marriage counseling: A technique in search of a theory. Journal of Marriage and the Family, 28, 449–453.

Margolin, G. (1982). Ethical and legal considerations in marital and family therapy. American Psychologist, 37, 788–801.

Markman, H. J. (1992). Marital and family psychology: Burning issues. Journal of Family Psychology, 5, 264–275.

Markman, H. J., Renick, M. J., Floyd, F. J., Stanley, S. M., & Clemerts, M. (1993). Preventing marital distress through communication and conflict management training: A 4 & 5 year follow-up. Journal of Consulting and Clinical Psychology, 61, 70–77.

Markman, H. J., Stanley, S. M., & Blumberg, S. L. (1994). Fighting for your marriage: Positive steps for preventing divorce and preserving a lasting love. San Francisco: Jossey-Bass.

Marsh, D. T. (1992). Families and mental illness: New directions in professional practice. New York: Praeger.

Marsh, D. T. & Johnson, D. L. (1997). The family experience of mental illness: Implications for intervention. Professional Psychology: Research and Practice, 28, 229–237.

Martin, P. A., & Bird, W. H. (1963). An approach to the psychotherapy of marriage partners: The stereoscopic technique. Psychiatry, 16, 123–127.

Mason, M. J. (1991). Family therapy as the emerging context for sex therapy. In A. S. Gurman & D. P. Kniskern (Eds.), Handbook of family therapy (Vol. II). New York: Brunner/Mazel.

Masters, W. H., & Johnson, V. E. (1970). Human sexual inadequacy. Boston: Little, Brown.

Mathis, R. D., & Tanner, Z. (1991). Cohesion, adaptability, and satisfaction in later life. Family Therapy, 18(1), 47–60.

Maturana, H. R. (1978). Biology of language: The epistemology of reality. In G. A. Miller & E. Lennenberg (Eds.), Psychology and biology of language and thought. New York: Academic Press.

McDaniel, S. H. (1992). Harold A. Goolishian, Ph.D. (1924–1991): In memoriam. Family Process, 31, 101–102.

McDaniel, S. H. (1995). Collaboration between psychologists and family physicians: Implementing the biopsychosocial model. Professional Psychology, 26, 117–122.

McDaniel, S. H., Hepworth, J., & Doherty, W. J. (1992). Medical family therapy: A biopsychosocial approach to families with health problems. New York: Basic Books.

McDaniel, S. H., Hepworth, J., & Doherty, W. J. (1995). Medical family therapy with somatizing patients: The co-creation of therapeutic stories. In R. H. Mikesell, D-D. Lusterman, & S. H. McDaniel (Eds.), Integrating family therapy: Handbook of family psychology and systems theory. Washington, DC: American Psychological Association.

McFarlane, W. R. (1991). Family psychoeducational treatment. In A. S. Gurman & D. P. Kniskern (Eds.), Handbook of family therapy (Vol. II). New York: Brunner/Mazel.

McGoldrick, M. (1988a). Ethnicity and the family life cycle. In B. Carter & M. McGoldrick (Eds.), The changing family life cycle: A framework for family therapy (2nd ed.). New York: Gardner Press.

McGoldrick, M. (1988b). Women and the life cycle. In B. Carter & M. McGoldrick (Eds.), The changing family life cycle: A framework for family therapy (2nd ed.). New York: Gardner Press.

McGoldrick, M., Anderson, C. M., & Walsh, F. (1989). Women in families and in family therapy. In M. McGoldrick, C. M. Anderson, & F. Walsh (Eds.), Women in families: A framework for family therapy. New York: Norton.

McGoldrick, M., & Carter, B. (1988). Forming a remarried family. In B. Carter & M. McGoldrick (Eds.), *The changing family life cycle: A framework for family therapy* (2nd ed.). Boston: Allyn & Bacon.

McGoldrick, M., Garcia Preto, N., Hines, P. M., & Lee, E. (1991). Ethnicity and family therapy. In A. S. Gurman & D. P. Kniskern (Eds.), *Handbook of family therapy* (2nd ed.). New York: Brunner/Mazel.

McGoldrick, M., & Gerson, R. (1985). *Genograms in family assessment.* New York: Norton.

McGoldrick, M., Giordano, J., & Pearce, J. K. (1996). *Ethnicity and family therapy* (2nd ed.). New York: Guilford Press.

McGoldrick, M., Pearce, J. K., & Giordano, J. (1982). *Ethnicity and family therapy.* New York: Guilford Press.

McKenzie, P. N., Atkinson, B. J., Quinn, W. H., & Heath, A. W. (1986). Training and supervision in marriage and family therapy: A national survey. *American Journal of Family Therapy, 14,* 293–303.

McLanahan, S., & Booth, K. (1989). Mother-only families: Problems, prospects, and politics. *Journal of Marriage and the Family, 51,* 557–588.

Meichenbaum, D. (1977). *Cognitive behavior therapy.* New York: Plenum.

Meissner, W. W. (1978). The conceptualization of marriage and family dynamics from a psychoanalytic perspective. In T. J. Paolino & B. S. McCrady (Eds.), *Marriage and marital therapy: Psychoanalytic, behavioral, and systems perspectives.* New York: Brunner/Mazel.

Mendelsohn, M., & Ferber, A. (1972). A training program. In A. Ferber, M. Mendelsohn, & A. Napier (Eds.), *The book of family therapy.* New York: Science House.

Midelfort, C. F. (1957). *The family in psychotherapy.* New York: Viking Press.

Mikesell, R. H., Lusterman, D-D., & McDaniel, S. H.(Eds.). (1995). *Integrating family therapy: Handbook of family psychology and systems theory.* Washington, DC: American Psychological Association.

Miklowitz, D. J. (1995). The evolution of family-based psychopathology. In R. H. Mikesell, D-D. Lusterman, & S. H. McDaniel (Eds.), *Integrating family therapy: Handbook of family psychology and systems theory.* Washington, DC: American Psychological Association.

Miklowitz, D. J., & Goldstein, M. J. (1997). *Bipolar disorder: A family-focused treatment approach.* New York: Guilford Press.

Miller, I. J. (1996). Managed care is harmful to outpatient mental health services: A call for accountability. *Professional Psychology: Research and Practice, 27,* 349–363.

Miller, J. G. (1978). *Living systems.* New York: McGraw-Hill.

Miller, N. (1992). *Single parents by choice: A growing trend in family life.* New York: Insight Books.

Minuchin, P., Colapinto, J., & Minuchin, S. (1998). *Working with families of the poor.* New York: Guilford press.

Minuchin, S. (1974). *Families and family therapy.* Cambridge, MA: Harvard University Press.

Minuchin, S. (1984). *Family kaleidoscope.* Cambridge, MA: Harvard University Press.

Minuchin, S. (1991). The seductions of constructivism. *The Family Networker, 15*(5), 47–50.

Minuchin, S., Baker, L., Rosman, B., Liebman, R., Milman, L., & Todd, T. (1975). A conceptual model of psychosomatic illness in children: Family organization and family therapy. *Archives of General Psychiatry, 32,* 1031–1038.

Minuchin, S., & Fishman, H. C. (1981). *Family therapy techniques.* Cambridge, MA: Harvard University Press.

Minuchin, S., Lee, W-Y., & Simon, G. M. (1996). *Mastering family therapy: Journeys of growth and transformation.* New York: Wiley.

Minuchin, S., Montalvo, B., Guerney, B. G., Jr., Rosman, B. L., & Schumer, F. (1967). *Families of the slums: An exploration of their structure and treatment.* New York: Basic Books.

Minuchin S., & Nichols, M. P. (1993). *Family healing: Tales of hope and renewal from family therapy*. New York: Free Press.

Minuchin, S., & Nichols, M. P. (1998). Structural family therapy. In F. M. Dattilio (Ed.), *Case studies in couple and family therapy: Systemic and cognitive perspectives*. New York: Guilford Press.

Minuchin, S., Rosman, B. L., & Baker, L. (1978). *Psychosomatic families: Anorexia nervosa in context*. Cambridge, MA: Harvard University Press.

Monahan, J. (1993). Limiting therapist exposure to *Tarasoff* liability Guidelines for risk containment. *American Psychologist, 48*, 242–250.

Montalvo, B. (1973). Aspects of live supervision. *Family Process, 12*, 343–359.

Moon, S. M., Dillon, D. R., & Sprenkle, D. H. (1990). Family therapy and qualitative research. *Journal of Marital and Family Therapy, 16*, 357–373.

Moos, R. H. (1974). *Combined preliminary manual: Family, work, and group environment scales*. Palo Alto, CA: Consulting Psychologists Press.

Moos, R. H., & Moos, B. (1986). *Family Environmental Scale manual. Second edition*. Palo Alto, CA: Consulting Psychologists Press.

Morris, S. B., Alexander, J. F., & Waldron, H. (1988). Functional family therapy. In I. R. H. Falloon (Ed.), *Handbook of behavioral family therapy*. New York: Guilford Press.

Morrison, J. K., Layton, D., & Newman, J. (1982). Ethical conflict in decision making. In J. C. Hansen & L. L'Abate (Eds.), *Values, ethics, legalities, and the family therapist*. Rockville, MD: Aspen.

Moultrop, D. J. (1986). Integration: A coming of age. *Contemporary Family Therapy, 8*, 157–167, 189.

Mudd, E. H. (1951). *The practice of marriage counseling*. New York: Association Press.

Mueser, K. T., & Glynn, S. M. (1995). *Behavioral family therapy for psychiatric disorders*. Boston: Allyn & Bacon.

Munson, C. E. (1994). Cognitive family therapy. In D. K. Granvold (Ed.), *Cognitive and behavioral treatment: Methods and applications*. Pacific Grove, CA: Brooks/Cole.

Napier, A. Y. (1987a). Early stages in experiential marital therapy. *Contemporary Family Therapy, 9*, 23–41.

Napier, A. Y. (1987b). Later stages in experiential marital therapy. *Contemporary Family Therapy, 9*, 42–57.

Napier, A. Y., & Whitaker, C. A. (1978). *The family crucible*. New York: Harper & Row.

Neill, J. R., & Kniskern, D. P. (Eds.). (1982). *From psyche to system: The evolving therapy of Carl Whitaker*. New York: Guilford Press.

Neimeyer, G. J. (Ed.). (1993). *Constructivist assessment: A casebook*. Thousand Oaks, CA: Sage.

Nerin, W. F. (1986). *Family reconstruction: Long day's journey into light*. New York: Norton.

Nerin, W. F. (1989). You can go home again. *The Family Networker, 13*(1), 54–55.

Neugarten, B. (1976). Adaptation and the life cycle. *Counseling Psychologist, 6*, 16–20.

Nichols, M. P. (1987). *The self in the system: Expanding the limits of family therapy*. New York: Brunner/Mazel.

Nichols, W. C. (1979). Introduction to Part I. Education and training in marital and family therapy. *Journal of Marital and Family Therapy, 5* (3), 3–5.

Nichols, W. C. (1988). *Marital therapy: An integrative approach*. New York: Guilford Press.

Nichols, W. C., & Everett, C. A. (1986). *Systemic family therapy: An integrative approach*. New York: Guilford Press.

Nichols, W. C., Nichols, D. P., & Hardy, K. V. (1990). Doctoral programs in marital and family therapy. *Journal of Marital and Family Therapy, 16*, 275–285

Nicolai, K. M., & Scott, N. A. (1994). Provisions of confidentiality information and its relation to child abuse reporting. *Professional Psychology, Research and Practice, 25*, 154–160.

Norton, A. J., & Glick, P. C. (1986). One-parent families: A social and economic profile. *Family Relations, 35,* 9–17.

Nuechterlein, K. H., & Dawson, M. E. (1984). A heuristic vulnerability/stress model of schizophrenic episodes. *Schizophrenia Bulletin, 10,* 300–312.

Nuechterlein, K. H., Dawson, M. E., Ventura, J., Gitlin, M., Subotnik, K. L., Snyder, K. S., Mintz, J., & Bartzokis, G. (1994). The vulnerability-stress model of schizophrenic relapse: A longitudinal study. *Acta Psychiatrica Scandinavica 89,* 58–64.

O'Hanlon, W. H. (1993). Take two people and call them in the morning: Brief solution-oriented therapy with depression. In S. Friedman (Ed.), *The new language of change: Constructive collaboration in psychotherapy.* New York: Guilford Press.

O'Hanlon, W. H. & Martin, M. (1992). *Solution-oriented hypnosis: An Ericksonian approach.* New York: Norton.

O'Hanlon, W. H., & Weiner-Davis, M. (1989). *In search of solutions: A new direction in psychotherapy.* New York: Norton.

Oliveri, M. E., & Reiss, D. (1982). Family styles of construing the social environment: A perspective on variation among nonclinical families. In F. Walsh (Ed.), *Normal family processes.* New York: Guilford Press.

Olson, D. H. (1970). Marital and family therapy: Integrative reviews and critique. *Journal of Marriage and Family Counseling, 4,* 77–98.

Olson, D. H. (1986). Circumplex model VII: Validation studies and FACES III. *Family Process, 26,* 337–351.

Olson, D. H. (1987). *Building a strong marriage.* Minneapolis, MN: Prepare-Enrich.

Olson, D. H. (1996). *PREPARE-ENRICH counselor's manual.* Minneapolis, MN: Life Innovations.

Olson, D. H., Fournier, D. G., & Druckman, J. M. (1986). *Prepare/Enrich counselor's manual.* Minneapolis, MN: Prepare/Enrich, Inc.

Olson, D. H., Russell, C. S., & Sprenkle, D. H. (Eds.). (1989). *Circumplex model: Systemic assessment and treatment of families.* New York: Haworth Press.

O'Neil, J. M. (1982). Gender-role conflict and strains in men's lives. In K. Solomon & N. Levy (Eds.), *Men in transition: Theory and therapy.* New York: Plenum.

Papero, D. V. (1983). Family systems theory and therapy. In B. B. Wolman & G. Stricker (Eds.), *Handbook of family and marital therapy.* New York: Plenum.

Papero, D. V. (1988). Training in Bowen theory. In H. A. Liddle, D. C. Breunlin, & R. C. Schwartz (Eds.), *Handbook of family therapy training and supervision.* New York: Guilford Press.

Papero, D. V. (1990). *Bowen family system theory.* Boston: Allyn & Bacon.

Papero, D. V. (1995). Bowen's family systems and marriage. In N. S. Jacobson & A. S. Gurman (Eds.), *Clinical handbook of couple therapy.* New York: Guilford Press.

Papp, P. (1980). The Greek chorus and other techniques of paradoxical therapy. *Family Process, 19,* 45–57.

Papp, P. (1983). *The process of change.* New York: Guilford Press.

Parry, A., & Doan, R. E. (1994). *Story re-visions: Narrative therapy in the postmodern world.* New York: Guilford Press.

Parry, T. A. (1993). Without a net: Preparations for postmodern living. In S. Friedman (Ed.), *The new language of change: Constructive collaboration in psychotherapy.* New York: Guilford Press.

Parsons, T,. & Bales, R. F. (1955). *Family, socialization, and interaction process.* Glencoe, IL: Free Press.

Patten, C., Barnett, T., & Houlihan, D. (1991). Ethics in marital and family therapy: A review of the literature. *Professional Psychology: Research and Practice, 22*(2), 171–175.

Patterson, C. J. (1995). *Lesbian and gay parenting: A resource for psychologists.* Washington, DC: American Psychological Association.

Patterson, G. R. (1971). *Families: Application of social learning to family life.* Champaign, IL: Research Press.

Patterson, G. R. (1985). Beyond technology: The next stage in developing an empirical base for parent training. In L. L'Abate (Ed.), *Handbook of family psychology and therapy* (Vol. II). Homewood, IL: Dorsey Press.

Patterson, G. R., & Brodsky, M. (1966). Behavior modification for a child with multiple problem behaviors. *Journal of Child Psychology and Psychiatry, 7,* 277–295.

Patterson, G. R., & Forgatch, M. S. (1995). Predicting future clinical adjustment from treatment outcome and process variables. *Psychological Assessment, 7,* 275–285.

Patterson, G. R., & Reid, J. (1970). Reciprocity and coercion: Two facets of social systems. In C. Neuringer & J. Michael (Eds.), *Behavior modification in clinical psychology.* New York: Appleton-Century-Crofts.

Patterson, G. R., Reid, R. B., Jones, R. R., & Conger, R. E. (1975). *A social learning approach to family intervention, Vol. I: Families with aggressive children.* Eugene, OR: Castalia.

Patterson, T. (1997). Theoretical unity and technical eclecticism: Pathways to coherence in family therapy. *American Journal of Family Therapy, 25,* 97–109

Paul, G. L. (1967). Outcome research in psychotherapy. *Journal of Consulting Psychology, 31,* 109–188.

Paul, N. L. (1974). The use of empathy in the resolution of grief. In J. Ellard, V. Volkan, & N. L. Paul (Eds.), *Normal and pathological responses to berecvement.* New York: MSS Information Corporation.

Peake, T. H., Borduin, C. M., & Archer, R. P. (1988). *Brief psychotherapies: Changing frames of mind.* Newbury Park: Sage.

Peck, J. S., & Manocherian, J. (1988). Divorce in the changing family life cycle. In B. Carter & M. McGoldrick (Eds.), *The changing family life cycle: A framework for family therapy* (2nd ed.). New York: Gardner Press.

Penn, P. (1982). Circular questioning. *Family Process, 21,* 267–280.

Penn, P. (1985). Feed-forward: Future questions, future maps. *Family Process, 24,* 299–310.

Perls, F. S. (1969). *Gestalt therapy verbatim.* Lafayette, CA: Free People Press.

Perosa, L. M., & Perosa, S. L. (1990). The use of bipolar item format for FACES III: A reconsideration. *Journal of Marital and Family Therapy, 16,* 187–199.

Perry, H. S. (1982). *Psychiatrist of America: The life of Harry Stack Sullivan.* Cambridge, MA: Harvard University Press.

Philpot, C. L., & Brooks, G. R. (1995). Intergender communication and gender-sensitive family therapy. In R. H. Mikesell, D-D. Lusterman, & S. H. McDaniel (Eds.), *Integrating family therapy: Handbook of family psychology and systems theory.* Washington, DC: American Psychological Association.

Philpot, C. L. ,Brooks, G. R., Lusterman, D-D., & Nutt, R. L. (1997). *Bridging separate gender worlds: Why men and women clash and how therapists can bring them together.* Washington, DC: American Psychological Assocoation.

Piercy, F. P., & Sprenkle, D. H. (1990). Marriage and family therapy: A decade review. *Journal of Marriage and the Family, 52,* 1116–1126.

Piercy, F. P., Sprenkle, D. H., Wetchler, J. L., & Associates. *Family therapy sourcebook* (2nd ed.). New York: Guilford Press.

Pinsof, W. M. (1986). The process of family therapy: The development of the Family Therapist Coding System. In L. Greenberg & W. M. Pinsof (Eds.), *The psychotherapeutic process: A research handbook.* New York: Guilford Press.

Pinsof, W. M. (1995). *Integrative problem-centered therapy: A synthesis of family, individual, and biological therapies.* New York: Basic Books.

Pinsof, W. M., & Wynne, L. C. (1995). The effectiveness and efficacy of marital and family therapy: Introduction to the special issue. *Journal of Marital and Family Therapy, 21,* 341–343.

Pinsof, W. M., Wynne, L. C., & Hambright, A. B. (1996). The outcomes of couple and family therapy: Findings, conclusions, and recommendations. *Psychotherapy, 33,* 321–331.

Pirrotta, S. (1984). Milan revisited: A comparison of the two Milan schools. *Journal of Strategic and Systemic Therapies, 3,* 3–15.

Pittman, F. (1987). *Turning points: Treating families in transition and crisis.* New York: Norton.

Pittman, F. (1989). Remembering Virginia. *The Family Therapy Networker, 13*(1), 34–35.

Pope, K. S. (1994). *Sexual involvement with therapists: Patient assessment, subsequent therapy, forensics.* Washington, DC: American Psychological Association.

Prata, G. (1990). *A systemic harpoon into family games: Preventive interventions in therapy.* New York: Brunner/Mazel.

Preto, N. G. (1988). Transformation of the family system in adolescence. In B. Carter & M. McGoldrick (Eds.), *The changing family life cycle: A framework for family therapy* (2nd ed.). New York: Gardner Press.

Prevatt, F. F. (1999). Milan systemic therapy. In D. M. Lawson & F. F. Prevatt (Eds.), *Casebook in family therapy.* Pacific Grove, CA: Brooks/Cole.

Price, J. (1996). *Power and compassion: Working with difficult adolescents and abused parents.* New York: Guilford Press.

Prochaska, J. O., & Norcross, J. C. (1994). *Systems of psychotherapy: A transtheoretical analysis* (3rd ed.). Pacific Grove, CA: Brooks/Cole.

Rabin, C. (1981). The single-case design in family therapy evaluation research. *Family Process, 20,* 351–366.

Real, T. (1990). The therapeutic use of self in constructionist systematic therapy. *Family Process, 29,* 255–272.

Reaves, R. P., & Ogloff, J. R. P. (1996). Liability for professional misconduct. In L. J. Bass, S. T. DeMers. J. R. P. Ogloff, C. Peterson, J. L. Pettifor, R. P. Reaves, N. P. Simon, C. Sinclair, & R. M. Tipton (Eds.). *Professional conduct and discipline in psychology.* Washington, DC: American Psychological Association.

Reiss, D. (1981). *The family's construction of reality.* Cambridge, MA: Harvard University Press.

Reiss, D. (1988). Theoretical versus tactical inferences: Or, how to do family psychotherapy research without dying of boredom. In L. C. Wynne (Ed.), *The state of the art in family therapy research: Controversies and recommendations.* New York: Family Process Press.

Reiss, D. (1991). Voyeurism: The link between good family therapy and good family research. *Newsletter of the American Family Therapy Association, 43,* 34–37.

Reiss, D., & Oliveri, M. E. (1991). The family's conception of accountability and competence: A new approach to the conceptualization and assessment of family stress. *Family Process, 30,* 193–214.

Rice, E. P. (1993). *Intimate relationships, marriages, and families.* Mountain View, CA: Mayfield.

Riskin, J., & Faunce, E. (1972). An evaluative review of family interaction research. *Family Process, 11,* 365–456.

Roberto, L. G. (1991). Symbolic-experiential family therapy. In A. S. Gurman & D. P. Kniskern (Eds.), *Handbook of family therapy* (Vol. II). New York: Brunner/Mazel.

Roberto, L. G. (1992). *Transgenerational family therapies.* New York: Guilford Press.

Roberto, L. G. (1998). Transgenerational family therapy. In F. M. Dattilio (Ed.), *Case studies in couple and family therapy: Systemic and cognitive perspectives.* New York: Guilford Press.

Rolland, J. S. (1994). *Families, illness, and disability: An integrative treatment model.* New York: Basic Books.

Rosen, R. C., & Leiblum, S. R. (Eds.). (1995). *Case studies in sex therapy.* New York: Guilford Press.

Rosenberg, J. B. (1983). Structural family therapy. In B. B. Wolman & G. Stricker (Eds.), *Handbook of family and marital therapy.* New York: Plenum.

Rotheram, M. J. (1989). The family and the school. In L. Combrinck-Graham (Ed.), *Children in family context: Perspectives on treatment.* New York: Guilford Press.

Rutledge, A. L. (1966). *Premarital counseling.* Cambridge, MA: Schenkman.

Saba, G. W., & Liddle, H. A. (1986). Perceptions of professional needs, practice patterns and initial issues facing family therapy trainees and supervisors. *Journal of Family Therapy, 14,* 109–122.

Sager, C. J. (1966). The treatment of married couples. In S. Arieti (Ed.), *American handbook of psychiatry* (Vol. III). New York: Basic Books.

Sager, C. J., Brown, H. S., Crohn, H., Engel, T., Rodstein, E., & Walker, L. (1983). *Treating the remarried family.* New York: Brunner/Mazel.

Sander, F. M. (1979). *Individual and family therapy: Toward an integration.* New York: Aronson.

Sander, F. M. (1998). Psychoanalytic couple therapy. In F. M. Dattilic (Ed.), *Case studies in couple and family therapy: Systemic and cognitive perspectives.* New York: Guilford Press.

Sanders, M. R., & Dadds, M. R. (1993). *Behavioral family intervention.* Needham Heights, MA: Allyn & Bacon.

Satir, V. M. (1964). *Conjoint family therapy.* Palo Alto, CA: Science and Behavior Books.

Satir, V. M. (1972). *Peoplemaking.* Palo Alto, CA: Science and Behavior Books.

Satir, V. M. (1967). *Conjoint family therapy* (rev. ed.). Palo Alto, CA: Science and Behavior Books.

Satir, V. M. (1982). The therapist and family therapy: Process model. In A. M. Horne & M. M. Ohlsen (Eds.), *Family counseling and therapy.* Itasca, IL: Peacock.

Satir, V. M. (1986). A partial portrait of a family therapist in process. In H. C. Fishman & B. L. Rosman (Eds.), *Evolving models for family change: A volume in honor of Salvador Minuchin.* New York: Guilford Press.

Satir, V. M., & Baldwin, M. (1983). *Satir step by step: A guide to creating change in families.* Palo Alto, CA: Science and Behavior Books.

Satir, V. M., & Bitter, J. R. (1991). The therapist and family therapy: Satir's human validation process model. In A. M. Horne & J. L. Passmore (Eds.), *Family counseling and therapy* (2nd ed.) Itasca, IL: Peacock.

Satir, V., Banmen, J., Gerber, J., & Gomori M. (1991). *The Satir model: Family therapy and beyond.* Palo Alto, CA: Science and Behavior Books.

Saxton, L. (1996). *The individual, marriage, and the family* (9th ed.). Belmont, CA: Wadsworth.

Scharff, D. E. (1989). An object relations approach to sexuality in family life. In J. S. Scharff (Ed.), *Foundations of object relations family therapy.* Northvale, NJ: Aronson.

Scharff, D. E., & Scharff, J. S. (1987). *Object relations family therapy.* Northvale, NJ: Aronson.

Scharff, J. S. (1989). The development of object relations family therapy. In J. S. Scharff (Ed.), *Foundations of object relations family therapy.* Northvale, NJ: Aronson.

Scharff, J. S. (1995). Psychoanalytic marital therapy. In N. S. Jacobson & A. S. Gurman (Eds.), *Clinical handbook of couple therapy.* New York: Guilford Press.

Scharff, J. S., & Scharff, D. E. (1992). *Scharff notes: A primer of object relations therapy.* Northvale, NJ: Aronson.

Schnarch, D. M. (1991). *Constructing the sexual crucible: An integration of sexual and marital therapy.* New York: Norton.

Schnarch, D. M. (1995). A family systems approach to sex therapy and intimacy. In R. H. Mikesell, D-D. Lusterman, & S. H. McDaniel (Eds.), *Integrating family therapy: Handbook of family psychology and systems theory.* Washington, DC American Psychological Association.

Schwartz, R. C. (1995). *Internal family systems therapy.* New York: Guilford Press.

Schwartz, R.C., & Breunlin, D. (1983). Why clinicians should bother with research. *The Family Therapy Networker,* 7(4), 22–27.

Schwartz, R. C., Liddle, H. A., & Breunlin, D. C. (1988). Muddles in live supervision. In H. A. Liddle, D. C. Breunlin, & R. C. Schwartz (Eds.), *Handbook of family therapy training and supervision.* New York: Guilford Press.

Segal, L. (1982). Brief family therapy. In A. M. Horne & M. M. Ohlsen (Eds.), *Family counseling and therapy.* Itasca, IL: Peacock.

Segal, L. (1987). What is a problem? A brief family therapist's view. *Family Therapy Today,* 2(7), 1–7.

Segal, L. (1991). Brief therapy: The MRI approach. In A. S. Gurman & D. P. Kniskern (Eds.), *Handbook of family therapy* (Vol. II). New York: Brunner/Mazel.

Segal, L., & Bavelas, J. B. (1983). Human systems and communication theory. In B. B. Wolman & G. Stricker (Eds.), *Handbook of family and marital therapy.* New York: Plenum.

Seibt, T. H. (1996). Nontraditional families. In M. Harway (Ed.), *Treating the changing family: Handling normative and unusual events.* New York: Wiley.

Selekman, M. D. (1993). Solution-oriented brief therapy with difficult adolescents. In S. Friedman (Ed.), *The new language of change: Constructive collaboration in psychotherapy.* New York: Guilford Press.

Seligman, M. E. P. & Levant, R. F. (1998). Managed care policies rely on inadequate research. *Professional Psychology: Research and Practice, 29,* 211–212.

Seltzer, L. F. (1986). *Paradoxical strategies in psychotherapy: A comprehensive overview and guidebook.* New York: Wiley.

Selvini-Palazzoli, M. (1978). *Self-starvation.* New York: Aronson.

Selvini-Palazzoli, M. (1980). Why a long interval between sessions? The therapeutic control of the family-therapist suprasystem. In M. Andolfi & I. Zwerling (Eds.), *Dimensions of family therapy.* New York: Guilford Press.

Selvini-Palazzoli, M. (1986). Towards a general model of psychotic family games. *Journal of Marital and Family Therapy, 12,* 339–349.

Selvini-Palazzoli, M., Boscolo, L., Cecchin, G., & Prata, G. (1974). The treatment of children through brief therapy of their parents. *Family Process, 13,* 429–442.

Selvini-Palazzoli, M., Boscolo, L., Cecchin, G. F., & Prata, G. (1978). *Paradox and counterparadox: A new model in the therapy of the family in schizophrenic transaction.* New York: Aronson.

Selvini-Palazzoli, M., Boscolo, L., Cecchin, G. F., & Prata, G. (1980). Hypothesizing-circularity-neutrality: Three guidelines for the conductor of the session. *Family Process, 19,* 3–12.

Selvini-Palazzoli, M., Cirillo, S., Selvini, M., & Sorrentino, A. M. (1989). *Family games: General models of psychotic processes in the family.* New York: Norton.

Shadish, W. R., Ragsdale, K., Glaser, R. R., & Montgomery, L. M. (1995). The efficacy and effectiveness of marital and family therapy: A perspective from meta-analysis. *Journal of Marital and Family Therapy, 21,* 345–360.

Shapiro, R. J. (1975). Problems in teaching family therapy. *Professional Psychology, 6,* 41–44.

Sherman, J. R., & Dinkmeyer, D. (1987). *Systems of family therapy: An Adlerian integration.* New York: Brunner/Mazel.

Sherry, P. (1991). Ethical issues in the conduct of supervision. *The Counseling Psychologist, 19* (4), 566–584.

Shoham, V., Rohrbaugh, M., & Patterson, J. (1995). Problem- and solution-focused couples therapies: The MRI and Milwaukee models. In N. S. Jacobson & A. S. Gurman (Eds.), *Clinical handbook of couple therapy.* New York: Guilford Press.

Shueman, S. A., Troy, W. G., & Mayhugh, S. L. (1994). Principles and issues in managed behavioral health care. In S. A. Shueman, W. G. Troy, & S. L. Mayhugh (Eds.), *Managed behavioral health care: An industry perspective.* Springfield, IL: Thomas.

Silberstein, L. R. (1992). *Dual-career marriage: A system in transition.* Hillsdale, NJ: Erlbaum.

Simon, R. (1984). Stranger in a strange land: An interview with Salvador Minuchin. *The Family Therapy Networker, 6*(6), 22–31.

Simon, R. (1987). Goodbye paradox, hello invariant prescription: An interview with Mara Selvini-Palazzoli. *Family Therapy Networker, 11*(5), 16–33.

Simon, R. (1997). Fearsome foursome: An interview with the Women's Project. *Family Therapy Networker, 21*(6), 58–68.

Singleton, G. (1982). Bowen family systems theory. In A. M. Horne & M. M. Ohlsen (Eds.), *Family counseling and therapy.* Itasca, IL: Peacock.

Skynner, A. C. R. (1976). *Systems of family and marital psychotherapy.* New York: Brunner/Mazel.

Skynner, A. C. R. (1981). An open-systems, group analytic approach to family therapy. In A. S. Gurman & D. P. Kniskern (Eds.), *Handbook of family therapy.* New York: Brunner/Mazel.

Slavson, S. R. (1964). *A textbook in analytic group psychotherapy.* New York: International Universities Press.

Slipp, S. (1988). *The technique and practice of object relations family therapy.* Northvale, NJ: Aronson.

Slipp, S. (1991). *Object relations: A dynamic bridge between individual and family treatment.* Northvale, NJ: Aronson.

Slovik, L. S., & Griffith, J. L. (1992). The current face of family therapy. In J. S. Rutan (Ed.), *Psychotherapy for the 1990s.* New York: Guilford Press.

Sluzki, C. E. (1978). Marital therapy from a systems theory perspective. In T. J. Paolino & B. S. McCrady (Eds.), *Marriage and marital therapy: Psychoanalytic, behavioral, and systems theory perspectives.* New York: Brunner/Mazel.

Speck, R. V., & Attneave, C. L. (1973). *Family networks.* New York: Pantheon Books.

Sprenkle, D. H. (1988). Training and supervision in degree-granting graduate programs in family therapy. In H. A. Liddle, D. C. Breunlin, & R. C. Schwartz (Eds.), *Handbook of family therapy training and supervision.* New York: Guilford Press.

Sprenkle, D. H. (1994). Editorial: The role of qualitative research and a few suggestions for aspiring authors. *Journal of Marital and Family Therapy, 20,* 227–229.

Sprenkle, D. H., & Bischoff, R. (1995). Research in family therapy: Trends, issues, and recommendations. In M. Nichols & R. Schwartz (Eds.), *Family therapy: Concepts and methods* (3rd ed.). Needham Heights, MA: Allyn & Bacon.

Sprenkle, D. H., & Moon, S. (Eds.). (1996). *Research methods in family therapy.* New York: Guilford Press.

Sprenkle, D. H., & Wilkie, S. G. (1996). Supervision and training. In F. P. Piercy, D. H. Sprenkle, J. L. Wetchtler, & Associates (Eds.), *Family therapy sourcebook* (2nd ed.). New York: Guilford Press.

Stahmann, R. F., & Hiebert, W. J. (1997). *Premarital and remarital counseling: The professional's handbook.* San Francisco: Jossey-Bass.

Stanton, M. D. (1988). The lobster quadrille: Issues and dilemmas for family therapy research. In L. C. Wynne (Ed.), *The state of the art in family therapy research: Controversies and recommendations.* New York: Family Process Press.

Stanton, M. D., Todd, T., & Associates. (1982). *The family therapy of drug abuse and addiction.* New York: Guilford Press.

Steinglass, P. (1996). Editorial: Family Process at 35. *Family Process, 35,* 1–2.

Steinglass, P., Bennett, L., Wolin, S., & Reiss, D. (1987). *The alcoholic family.* New York: Basic Books.

Stier, S., & Goldenberg, I. (1975). Training issues in family therapy *Journal of Marriage and Family Therapy, 1,* 63–68.

Stierlin, H. (1972). *Separating parents and adolescents.* New York: Quadrangle.

Stierlin, H. (1977). *Psychoanalysis and family therapy.* New York: Aronson.

Stierlin, H., Simon, F. B., Schmidt, G. (Eds.). (1987). *Family realities: The Heidelberg Conference.* New York: Brunner/Mazel.

Stierlin, H., & Weber, G. (1989). *Unlocking the family door: A systemic approach to the understanding and treatment of anorexia nervosa.* New York: Brunner/Mazel.

Strauss, A. L., & Corbin, J. (1990). *Basics of qualitative research: Grounded theory procedures and techniques.* Newbury Park, CA: Sage.

Stromberg, C., & Dellinger, A. (1993). *Malpractice and other professional liability.* Washington, DC: National Register of Health Service Providers in Psychology.

Stromberg, C., Schneider, J., & Joondeph, B. (1993). Dealing with potentially dangerous patients. *The Psychologist's Legal Update.* Washington, DC: National Register of Health Service Providers in Psychology.

Stuart, R. B. (1969). Operant-interpersonal treatment of marital discord. *Journal of Consulting and Clinical Psychology, 33,* 675–682.

Stuart, R. B. (1976). An operant-interpersonal program for couples. In D. H. L. Olson (Ed.), *Treating relationships.* Lake Mills, IA: Graphic.

Stuart, R. B. (1980). *Helping couples change: A social learning approach to marital therapy.* Champaign, IL: Research Press.

Sullivan, H. S. (1953). *The interpersonal theory of psychiatry.* New York: Norton.

Sutherland, J. (1980). The British object relations theorists: Balint, Winnicott, Fairbairn, Guntrip. *British Journal of Medical Psychology, 28,* 829–860.

Swenson, L. C. (1997). *Psychology and law for the helping professions.* Pacific Grove, CA: Brooks/Cole.

Szapocznik, J., Kurtines, W., & Contributors. (1989). *Breakthroughs in family therapy with drug-abusing and problem youth.* New York: Springer.

Szasz, T. (1986). The case against suicide prevention. *American Psychologist, 41,* 806–812.

Terkelson, K. G. (1980). Toward a theory of the family life cycle. In E. A. Carter & M. McGoldrick (Eds.), *The family life cycle: A framework for family therapy.* New York: Gardner Press.

Thibaut, J. W., & Kelley, H. H. (1959). *The social psychology of groups.* New York: Wiley.

Thomas, A., & Sillen, S. (1974). *Racism and psychiatry.* Secaucas, NJ: Citadel.

Todd, T. C. (1988). Behavioral and systemic family therapy. In I. R. H. Falloon (Ed.), *Handbook of behavioral family therapy.* New York: Guilford Press.

Todd, T. C., & Storm, C. L. (Eds.). (1997). *The complete systemic supervisor: Context, philosophy and pragmatics.* Needham Heights, MA: Allyn & Bacon.

Toman, W. (1961). *Family constellation: Its effects on personality and social behavior.* New York: Springer.

Tomm, K. M. (1983). The old hat doesn't fit. *Family Therapy Networker, 7*(4), 39–41.

Tomm, K. M. (1984a). One perspective on the Milan approach: Part I. Overview of development, theory, and practice. *Journal of Marital and Family Therapy, 10,* 113–125.

Tomm, K. M. (1984b). One perspective on the Milan approach: Part II. Description of session format, interviewing style, and interventions. *Journal of Marital and Family Therapy, 10,* 253–271.

Tomm, K. (1987a). Interventive interviewing: Part I. Strategizing as a fourth guideline for the therapist. *Family Process, 26,* 3–13.

Tomm, K. (1987b). Interventive interviewing: Part II. Reflexive questioning as a means to enable self-healing. *Family Process, 26,* 167–183.

Tomm, K. (1988). Interventive interviewing: Part III. Intending to ask lineal, circular, strategic, or reflexive questions? *Family Process, 27,* 1–15.

Towards a differentiation of self in one's family. (1972). In J. L. Framo (Ed.), *Family interaction: A dialogue between family researchers and family therapists*. New York: Springer.

Tucker, L., & Lubin, W. (1994). *National survey of psychologists. Report from Division 39, American Psychological Association*. Washington, DC: American Psychological Association.

Ulrich, D. N. (1983). Contextual and marital therapy. In B. B. Wolman & G. Stricker (Eds.), *Handbook of family and marital therapy*. New York: Plenum.

Ulrich, D. N. (1998). Contextual family therapy. In F. M. Dattilio (Ed.), *Case studies in couple and family therapy: Systemic and cognitive perspectives*. New York: Guilford Press.

Umbarger, C. C. (1983). *Structural family therapy*. New York: Grune & Stratton.

VandenBos, G. R. (1986). Psychotherapy research: A special issue. *American Psychologist, 41*, 111–112.

Van Hoose, W. H., & Kottler, J. A. (1985). *Ethical and legal issues in counseling and psychotherapy* (2nd ed.). San Francisco: Jossey-Bass.

Varela, F. J. (1979). *Principles of biological autonomy*. New York: Elsevier North Holland.

Vesper, J. H., & Brock, G. W. (1991). *Ethics, legalities, and professional practice issues in marriage and family therapy*. Boston: Allyn & Bacon.

Visher, E. B., & Visher, J. S. (1986). *Stepfamily workbook manual*. Baltimore, MD: Stepfamily Association of America.

Visher, E. B., & Visher, J. S. (1988). *Old loyalties, new ties: Therapeutic strategies with stepfamilies*. New York: Brunner/Mazel.

Visher, E. B., & Visher, J. S. (1993). Remarriage families and stepparenting. In F. Walsh (Ed.), *Normal family processes* 2nd ed.). New York: Guilford Press.

Visher, E. B., & Visher, J. S. (1996). *Therapy with stepfamilies*. New York: Brunner/Mazel.

von Foerster, H. (1981). *Observing systems*. Seaside, CA: Intersystems.

von Glaserfeld, E. (1987). *The construction of knowledge*. Salinas, CA. Intersystems.

Wachtel, E. F., & Wachtel, P. L. (1986). *Family dynamics in individual psychotherapy: A guide to clinical strategies*. New York: Guilford Press.

Wachtel, P. L. (1997). *Psychoanalysis, behavior therapy, and the relational world*. Washington, DC: American Psychological Association.

Walen, S. R., & Perlmutter, R. (1988). Cognitive-behavioral treatment of adult sexual dysfunctions from a family perspective. In N. Epstein, S. E. Schlesinger, & W. Dryden (Eds.), *Cognitive-behavioral therapy with families*. New York: Brunner/Mazel.

Walrond-Skinner, S. (1976). *Family therapy: The treatment of natural systems*. London: Routledge.

Walsh, F. (1988). The family in later life. In B. Carter & M. McGoldrick (Eds.), *The changing family life cycle: A framework for family therapy* (2nd ed.). New York: Gardner Press.

Walsh, F. (1996). The concept of family resilence: Crisis and challenge. *Family Process, 35*, 261–281.

Walters, M., Carter, B., Papp, P., & Silverstein, O. (1989). *The invisible web: Gender patterns in family relationships*. New York: Guilford Press.

Waters, D., & Lawrence, E. C. (1993). *Competence, courage and change: An approach to family therapy*. New York: Norton.

Watkins, C. E., Jr. (Ed.). (1997). *Handbook of psychotherapy supervision*. New York: Wiley.

Watzlawick, P. (1978). *The language of change*. New York: Basic Books.

Watzlawick, P. (Ed.) (1984). *The invented reality: How do we know what we believe we know?* New York: Norton.

Watzlawick, P., Beavin, J. H., & Jackson, D. D. (1967). *Pragmatics of human communication*. New York: Norton.

Watzlawick, P., Weakland, J. H., & Fisch, R. (1974). *Change: Principles of problem formation and problem resolution*. New York: Norton.

Waxler, N. (1975). The normality of deviance: An alternative explanation of schizophrenia in the family. *Schizophrenia Bulletin, 14*, 38–47.

Weakland, J. H. (1976). Communication theory and clinical change. In P. J. Guerin, Jr. (Ed.), *Family therapy: Theory and practice*. New York: Gardner Press.

Weakland, J. H., & Fisch, R. (1992). Brief therapy—MRI style. In S. H. Budman, M. F. Hoyt, & S. Friedman (Eds.), *The first session in brief therapy*. New York: Guilford Press.

Weathers, L., & Lieberman, R. P. (1975). The family contracting exercise. *Journal of Behavior Therapy and Experimental Psychiatry, 6*, 208–214.

Weeks, G. R., & L'Abate, L. (1982). *Paradoxical psychotherapy: Theory and technique*. New York: Brunner/Mazel.

Weiner-Davis, M. (1992). *Divorce-busting*. New York: Summit Books.

Weisman, A., Nuechterlein, K. H., Goldstein, M. J., & Snyder, K. (1998). Expressed emotion, attributions, and schizophrenia symptom dimensions. *Journal of Abnormal Psychology, 107*, 355—359.

Weiss, R. S. (1985). Men and the family. *Family Process, 24*, 49–58.

Welfel, E. R. (1998). *Ethics in counseling and psychotherapy: Standards, research, and emerging issues*. Pacific Grove, CA: Brooks/Cole.

Wells, R. A., & Dezen, A. E. (1978). The results of family therapy revisited: The nonbehavioral methods. *Family Process, 17*, 251–274.

Wendorf, D. J., & Wendorf, R. J. (1985). A systemic view of family therapy ethics. *Family Process, 24*, 443–460.

Wetchler, J. L., & Piercy, F. P. (1996). Experiential family therapies. In F. P. Piercy, D. H. Sprenkle, J. L. Wetchler, & Associates. (Eds.), *Family therapy sourcebook* (2nd ed.). New York: Guilford Press.

Whiffen, R. (1982). The use of videotape in supervision. In R. Whiffen & J. Byng-Hall (Eds.), *Family therapy supervision: Recent developments in practice*. London: Academic Press.

Whitaker, C. A. (Ed.). (1958). *Psychotherapy of chronic schizophrenic patients*. Boston: Little, Brown.

Whitaker, C. A. (1967). The growing edge. In J. Haley & L. Hoffman (Eds.). *Techniques of family therapy*. New York: Basic Books.

Whitaker, C. A. (1976a). The hindrance of theory in clinical work. In P. J. Guerin, Jr. (Ed.), *Family therapy: Theory and practice*. New York: Gardner Press.

Whitaker, C. A. (1976b). Comment: Live supervision in psychotherapy. *Voices, 12*, 24–25.

Whitaker, C. A. (1977). Process techniques of family therapy. *Interaction, 1*, 4–19.

Whitaker, C. A., & Bumberry, W. M. (1988). *Dancing with the family: A symbolic-experiential approach*. New York: Brunner/Mazel.

Whitaker, C. A., & Keith, D. V. (1981). Symbolic-experiential family therapy. In A. S. Gurman & D. P. Kniskern (Eds.), *Handbook of family therapy*. New York: Brunner/Mazel.

Whitaker, C. A., & Malone, T. P. (1953). *The roots of psychotherapy*. New York: Blakiston.

Whitaker, C. A,. & Ryan, M. O. (1989). *Midnight musings of a family therapist*. New York: Brunner/Mazel.

White, C., & Hales, J. (Eds.). (1997). *The personal is the professional: Therapists reflect on their families, life, and work*. Adelaide, Australia: Dulwich Centre Publications.

White. M. (1989). *Selected papers*. Adelaide, Australia: Dulwich Centre Publications.

White, M. (1991). Deconstruction and therapy. *Dulwich Centre Newsletter, 3*, 21–40.

White, M. (1995). *Re-authoring lives: Interviews and essays*. Adelaide, South Australia: Dulwich Cewntre Publications.

White, M. (1997). *Narratives of therapist's lives*. Adelaide, Australia: Dulwich Centre Publications.

White, M., & Epston, D. (1990). *Narrative means to therapeutic ends* New York: Norton.

White, S. L. (1978). Family theory according to the Cambridge Model. *Journal of Marriage and Family Counseling, 4,* 91–100.

Wiener, N. (1948). *Cybernetics. Scientific American, 179*(5), 14–18.

Williamson, D. (1991). *The intimate paradox: Personal authority in the family system.* New York: Guilford Press.

Wittgenstein, L. (1968). *Philosophical investigations* (3rd ed.). New York: Macmillan.

Wolin, S., & Wolin, S. (1993). *The resilent self: How survivors of troubled families rise above adversity.* New York: Villard.

Wolman, B. B., & Stricker, G. (Eds.). (1983). *Handbook of family and marital therapy.* New York: Plenum.

Wolpe, J. (1958). *Psychotherapy by reciprocal inhibition.* Stanford, CA: Stanford University Press.

Woods, M. D., & Martin, D. (1984). The work of Virginia Satir: Understanding her theory and technique. *American Journal of Family Therapy 11*(1), 35–46.

Wylie, M. S. (1990a). Brief therapy on the couch. *Family Therapy Networker, 14,* 26–34, 66.

Wylie, M. S. (1990b). Family therapy's neglected prophet. *Family Networker, 15*(2), 25–37.

Wynne, L. C. (1970). Communication disorders and the quest for relatedness in families of schizophrenics. *American Journal of Psychoanalysis, 30,* 100–114.

Wynne, L. C. (1983). Family research and family therapy: A reunion? *Journal of Marital and Family Therapy, 9,* 113–117.

Wynne, L. C. (Ed.). (1988). *The state of the art in family therapy research: Controversies and recommendations.* New York: Family Process Press.

Wynne, L. C., Jones, J. E., & Al-Khayyal, M. (1982). Healthy family communication patterns: Observations in families "at risk" for psychopathology. In F. Walsh (Ed.), *Normal family processes: Implications for clinical practice.* New York: Guilford Press.

Wynne, L. C., McDaniel, S. H., & Weber, T. T. (1986). *Systems consultation: A new perspective for family therapy.* New York: Guilford Press.

Wynne, L. C., Ryckoff, I. M., Day, J., & Hirsch, S. I. (1958). Pseudomutuality in the family relationships of schizophrenics. *Psychiatry, 21,* 205–220.

Wynne, L. C., & Singer, M. T. (1963). Thought disorder and family relations of schizophrenics, I and II. *Archives of General Psychiatry, 9,* 191–206.

Wynne, L. C., Singer, M. T., Bartko, J. J., & Toohey, M. L. (1977). Schizophrenics and their families: Research on parental communication. In J. M. Tanner (Ed.), *Developments in psychiatric research.* London: Hodden & Stoughton.

Yalom, I. D. (1995). *The theory and practice of group psychotherapy* (4th ed.). New York: Basic Books.

Zeig, J. K. (Ed.). (1980). *A teaching seminar with Milton H. Erickson.* New York: Brunner/Mazel.

Zilbach, J. J. (1989). The family life cycle: A framework for understanding children in family therapy. In L. Combrinck-Graham (Ed.), *Children in family contexts: Perspectives on treatment.* New York: Guilford Press.

Zimmerman, J., & Dickerson, V. (1996). *If problems talked: Adventures in narrative therapy.* New York: Guilford Press.

Zuk, G. H., & Boszormenyi-Nagy, I. (Eds.). (1967). *Family therapy and disturbed families.* Palo Alto, CA: Science and Behavior Books.

Name Index

479

Subject Index

CREDITS

This page constitutes an extension of the copyright page. We have made every effort to trace the ownership of all copyrighted material and to secure permission from copyright holders. In the event of any question arising as to the use of any material, we will be pleased to make the necessary corrections in future printings. Thanks are due to the following authors, publishers, and agents for permission to use the material indicated.

Chapter 2: 24: Table 2.1 from "The Family Life Cycle: A Framework for Understanding Children in Family Therapy, by J. J. Zilbach. In L. Combrinck-Graham (Ed.), *Children in Family Contexts: Perspectives on Treatment*, p. 65. Copyright © 1989 Guilford Press. Reprinted by permission. **26:** Excerpt from *Marriage and Family Development*, Fifth Edition, by E. M. Duvall. Copyright © 1957, 1962, 1971, 1977 by J. B. Lippincott Company. Reprinted by permission of Harper & Row, Publishers, Inc. **39:** Table 2.3 from Betty Carter and Monica McGoldrick, *The Changing Family Life Cycle: A Framework for Family Therapy*, Second Edition, p. 22. Copyright © 1988 by Allyn and Bacon. Reprinted by permission. **40:** Table 2.4 from Betty Carter and Monica McGoldrick, *The Changing Family Life Cycle: A Framework for Family Therapy*, Second Edition, p. 24. Copyright © 1988 by Allyn and Bacon. Reprinted by permission. **Chapter 3: 50:** Table 3.1 from "Gender Sensitivity and Family Empowerment, by J. A. Lewis, 1992, *Topics in Family Psychology and Counseling*, 1(4), pp. 1–7. Copyright © 1992 Aspen Publishers Inc. Reprinted by permission. **Chapter 4: 67:** Figure 4.1 from "The Study of Family, by D. D. Jackson, 1965, *Family Process*, 4, pp. 1–20. Reprinted by permission. **70:** Figure 4.2 from *Living Systems*, by J. G. Miller, p. 36. Copyright © 1978 McGraw-Hill, Inc. Reprinted by permission. **79:** Figure 4.3 from *Families and Larger Systems: A Family Therapist's Guide Through the Labyrinth*, by E. Imber-Black, p. 117. Copyright © 1988 Guilford Press. Reprinted by permission. **Chapter 5: 96:** Table 5.1 from *Contemporary Clinical Psychology*, Second Edition, by H. Goldenberg. Copyright © 1983 Brooks/Cole Publishing Company. Used by permission of Wadsworth Publishing Co. **Chapter 6: 121:** Excerpt from *Treating the Troubled Family*, by N. W. Ackerman, pp. 3-4. Copyright © 1966 by Nathan W. Ackerman, Basic Books, Inc., Publishers, New York. Reprinted by permission. **Chapter 7: 143:** Excerpt from *Dancing with the Family: A Symbolic-Experiential Approach*, by C. A. Whitaker, and W. M. Bumberry, pp. 62-64. Copyright © 1988 Brunner/ Mazel. Reprinted with permission from Brunner/Mazel, Inc. **147:** Excerpts from *Principles of Gestalt Family Therapy*, by W. Kempler, pp. 27–28. Copyright © 1974 by the Kempler Institute, P. O. Box 1692, Costa Mesa, CA 92626. Reprinted by permission. **149:** Excerpts from *Experiential Psychotherapy within Families* by W. Kempler, pp. 11–13. Copyright © 1981 by Brunner/Mazel, Inc. Reprinted by permission. **157:** Excerpt from *Conjoint Family Therapy*, Revised Edition, by V. M. Satir, p. 143-145 Copyright © 1967 Science and Behavior Books. **Chapter 8: 173:** Figure 8.2 reprinted from *Family Evaluation: An Approach Based on Bowen Theory*, by Michael E. Kerr and Murray Bowen, p. 71, with the permission of W. W. Norton & Company, Inc. Copyright © 1988 by Michael E. Kerr and Murray Bowen. **184:** Figure 8.4 from *Counseling Today's Families*, Third Edition, by H. Goldenberg, and I. Goldenberg, p. 53. Copyright © 1998 Brooks/Cole Publishing Company. Reprinted with permission of Wadsworth Publishing Co. **191:** Excerpts from *Between Give and Take: A Clinical Guide to Contextual Therapy* by I. Boszormenyi-Nagy, and B. R. Krasner, pp. 9, 45–46. Copyright © 1986 Brunner/Mazel, Inc. Reprinted with permission from Brunner/Mazel, Inc. **Chapter 9: 209:** Figure 9.1 reprinted by permission of the publishers from *Families and Family Therapy* by Salvador Minuchin, p. 53, Cambridge, Mass.: Harvard University Press, Copyright © 1974 by the President and Fellows of Harvard College. **210:** Figure 9.2 reprinted by permission of the publishers from *Families and Family Therapy*, by Salvador Minuchin, p. 61, Cambridge, Mass.: Harvard University Press, Copyright © 1974 by the President and Fellows of Harvard College. **210:** Figure 9.3 from *Structural Family Therapy*, by C. C. Umbarger, p. 36. Copyright © 1983 Grune & Stratton. **Chapter 11: 251:** Box 11.1 "Paradoxical Letter," from *Paradoxical Psychotherapy: Theory and Technique*, by G. R. Weeks and L. L'Abate. Copyright © 1982 by Brunner/Mazel, Inc. Used by permission. **257:** Table 11.1 from *Casebook in Family Therapy*, by David M. Lawson and Frances F. Prevatt, p. 191. Copyright © 1999 by Wadsworth Publishing Co. Reprinted by permission. **Chapter 12: 267:** Table 12.1 from *Contemporary Clinical Psychology*, Second Edition, by H. Goldenberg, p. 221. Copyright © 1983 Brooks/Cole Publishing Company. Reprinted by permission of Wadsworth Publishing Co. **275:** Table 12.2 from "An Operant-Interpersonal Program for Couples, by R. B. Stuart. In D. H. L. Olson (Ed.), *Treating Relationships*. Copyright © 1976 Graphic Publishing Company. Reprinted by permission. **275:** Table 12.3 from *Helping Couples Change: A Social Learning Approach to Marital Therapy*, by R. B. Stuart, p. 248. Copyright © 1980 Research Press. **283:** Table 12.4 from "Behavioral Therapy for Families with Child Management Problems, by I. R. H. Falloon and R. P. Liberman. In M. Textor (Ed.), *Helping Families with Special Problems*, p. 123. Copyright © 1983 by Jason Aronson, Inc. Reprinted by permission. **284:** Figure 12.1 from *Families: Application of Social Learning to*

Family Life, by G. R. Patterson. Copyright © 1971 by Research Press Company. Reprinted by permission. **286:** Figure 12.2 reprinted with permission from *Journal of Behavior Therapy and Experimental Psychiatry, 6*, L. Weathers and R. P. Liberman. "The Family Contracting Exercise," copyright 1975, Pergamon Press, Ltd. **289:** Table 12.5 from *Functional Family Therapy*, by J. Alexander and B. V. Parsons, p. 28. Copyright © 1982 Brooks/Cole Publishing Company. **Chapter 14: 329:** Table 14.1 from "Family Psychoeducational Treatment, by W. R. MacFarlane. In A. S. Gurman, and D. P. Kniskern (Eds.), *Handbook of Family Therapy, Vol. III*, p. 375. Copyright © 1991 Brunner/Mazel, Inc. Reprinted with permission from Brunner/Mazel, Inc. **339:** Box 14.1 from *Stepfamily Workshop Manual*, by E. B. Visher and J. S. Visher. Copyright © 1986 Stepfamily Association of America, Lincoln, NE. Used by permission. **Chapter 15: 355:** Table 15.1 from "Family Styles of Construing the Social Environment A Perspective on Variation among Nonclinical Families, by M. E. Oliveri and D. Reiss. In F. Walsh (Ed.) *Normal Family Processes*, p. 109. Copyright © 1982 Guilford Press. Reprinted by permission. **359:** Figure 15.1 from "Circumplex Model VII: Validation Studies and FACES III, by D. H. Olson. In *Family Process*, 1986, 26, pp. 337-351. Copyright © 1995 by *Family Process*. **360:** Table 15.2 from *Combined Preliminary Manual: Family, Work, and Group Environment Scales*, by R. H. Moos. Copyright © 1974 Consulting Psychologists Press. Reprinted by permission. **361:** Figure 15.2 adapted from *Combined Preliminary Manual: Family, Work, and Group Environment Scales*, by R. H. Moos. Copyright © 1974 Consulting Psychologists Press. Reprinted by permission. **362:** Figure 15.3 adapted from *Combined Preliminary Manual: Family, Work, and Group Environment Scales*, by R. H. Moos. Copyright © 1974 Consulting Psychologists Press. Reprinted by permission. **364:** Table 15.3 from *No Single Thread: Psychological Health in Family Systems*, by J. M. Lewis, W. R. Beavers, J. T. Gossett, and V. A. Phillips. Copyright © 1976 by Brunner/Mazel, Inc. Reprinted by permission. **365:** Figure 15.4 from "Family Models: Comparing and Contrasting the Olson Circumplex with the Beavers Model, by W. R. Beavers and M. N. Voeller, p. 90. In *Family Process*, 1983, 22, pp. 85-98. Copyright © 1983 by *Family Process*. **Chapter 16: 387:** Table 16.4 from "Training Family Therapists by Setting Learning Objectives, by J. M. Cleghorn and S. Levin, 1973, *American Journal of Orthopsychiatry, 43*(3), pp. 439-446. Copyright © 1973 by the American Orthopsychiatric Association, Inc. Reproduced by permission. **388:** Table 16.5 from "Training Family Therapists by Setting Learning Objectives, by J. M. Cleghorn and S. Levin, 1973, *American Journal of Orthopsychiatry, 43*(3), pp. 439-446. Copyright © 1973 by the American Orthopsychiatric Association, Inc. Reproduced by permission. **394:** Table 16.6 from *Dimensions of Psychotherapy Supervision: Maps and Means,* by Russell Haber. Copyright © 1996 by Russell Haber. Reprinted by permission of W. W. Norton Co., Inc. **Chapter 17: 408:** Table 17.1 from *Ethics in Psychology: Professional Standards and Cases*, by P. Keith-Spiegel, and G. P. Koocher, p. 46. Copyright © 1985 Lawrence Erlbaum Associates. Reprinted by permission. **Appendix C: 425:** Reprinted from the *AAMFT Code of Ethics.* Copyright © 1998 American Association for Marriage and Family Therapy. NO ADDITIONAL COPIES MAY BE MADE WITHOUT OBTAINING PERMISSION FROM AAMFT.

TO THE OWNER OF THIS BOOK:

We hope that you have enjoyed *Family Therapy*, Fifth Edition, as much as we have enjoyed writing it. We'd like to know as much about your experiences with the book as you care to offer. Only through your comments and the comments of others can we learn how to make *Family Therapy*, Fifth Edition a better book for future readers.

School: _____

Instructor's name: _____

1. What I like most about this book is: _____

_____

_____

2. What I like least about this book is: _____

_____

_____

3. The name of the course in which I used this book is: _____

_____

4. If you used the Glossary, how helpful was it as an aid in understanding psychological concepts and terms? _____

_____

5. Were all of the chapters of the book assigned for you to read? _____

   If not, which ones weren't? _____

6. In the space below, or on a separate sheet of paper, please write specific suggestions for improving this book and anything else you'd care to share about your experience using the book.

_____

_____

_____

_____

Optional:

Your name: _____   Date: _____

May Brooks/Cole quote you, either in promotion for *Family Therapy*, Fifth Edition or in future publishing ventures?

Yes: _____   No: _____

Sincerely,

Irene Goldenberg
Herbert Goldenberg

FOLD HERE

- -

BUSINESS REPLY MAIL
FIRST CLASS   PERMIT NO. 358   PACIFIC GROVE, CA

POSTAGE WILL BE PAID BY ADDRESSEE

ATT: *Irene Goldenberg and Herbert Goldenberg*

Brooks/Cole Publishing Company
511 Forest Lodge Road
Pacific Grove, CA 93950-9968

IIııI.ıIIıIιIιıIıIιIIııIIuIIıIılııIIıIı IıııIıII

- -

FOLD HERE